Not Just Green,
Not Just White

Not Just Green, Not Just White

Race, Justice, and Environmental History

EDITED BY MARY E. MENDOZA
AND TRACI BRYNNE VOYLES

FOREWORD BY PATTY LIMERICK

University of Nebraska Press

LINCOLN

Publication of this volume was assisted by
the Department of History at Penn State University.

The University of Nebraska Press is part of a land-grant institution with campuses
and programs on the past, present, and future homelands of the Pawnee, Ponca,
Otoe-Missouria, Omaha, Dakota, Lakota, Kaw, Cheyenne, and Arapaho Peoples,
as well as those of the relocated Ho-Chunk, Sac and Fox, and Iowa Peoples.

∞

Library of Congress Cataloging-in-Publication Data

Names: Mendoza, Mary E., editor. | Voyles, Traci Brynne, editor.
Title: Not just green, not just white: race, justice, and environmental history /
edited by Mary E. Mendoza and Traci Brynne Voyles ; foreword by Patty Limerick.
Description: Lincoln: University of Nebraska Press, [2025] |
Includes bibliographic references and index.
Identifiers: LCCN 2024024803
ISBN 9781496204202 (hardcover; acid-free paper)
ISBN 9781496241733 (paperback; acid-free paper)
ISBN 9781496241849 (epub)
ISBN 9781496241856 (pdf)
Subjects: LCSH: Human ecology—United States—History. | Environmental policy—
United States—History. | Green movement—United States. | Environmental
justice—United States. | Social justice—United States. | Race discrimination—
United States. | United States—Race relations. | BISAC: HISTORY / Social History
| SOCIAL SCIENCE / Ethnic Studies / American / Native American Studies
Classification: LCC GF503 .N68 2025 | DDC 304.20973—dc23/eng/20241118
LC record available at https://lccn.loc.gov/2024024803

Set in Minion Pro by Scribe Inc.

CONTENTS

ILLUSTRATIONS

ACKNOWLEDGMENTS

We have wanted to put a book like this together for a long time, and we are so grateful that it is finally out. We began talking about this book more than a decade ago, when Mary was still in graduate school, as we thought more and more about how a book that integrates race and environment could be especially useful. After years of just talking and dreaming, we finally got to work, and we have been so fortunate to have found such a wonderful group of colleagues who opted to join us in this endeavor. As a result, we want to thank all the contributors to this volume: Kent Blansett, Elizabeth Grennan Browning, Erika Bsumek, Carolyn Finney, Colin Fisher, Katherine Johnston, Ari Kelman, Kathy Morse, David Naguib Pellow, Miles Powell, Cecilia Tsu, Bryon Williams, Teona Williams, and Carl Zimring. We'd especially like to thank Patty Limerick for agreeing to write the foreword for the book.

Other people were critical to helping make this book happen as well. Our editor, Bridget Barry, has been more amazing than we could have ever hoped. Her patience, kindness, and skill have undoubtedly helped make this book better. Thank you, Bridget. Joshua Reid and Finis Dunaway read this volume as a manuscript in its entirety and provided extensive comments. Their time and care most certainly elevated the quality of the scholarship in this volume. Any remaining errors are ours. Ann Piersall Logan created the art that is featured on the cover of this book and allowed us to use it. We are grateful for her creativity and the care she took in making sure we had what we needed to have the best-quality image possible. Connie Chiang and Kathy Morse, too, were both critical in our journey to finding this cover, and Lacey Greene also proved invaluable to the process. The History Department at Penn State University provided critical funding to help produce this book, which will undoubtedly make it more accessible to students, faculty, and the broader public. Thank you to the History Department head, Michael Kulikowski, for helping us secure those funds.

Many others provided friendship, guidance, and help along the way. Mary would like to thank the many mentors, colleagues, students, and friends whose words of wisdom shaped many of the ideas in this book. There are too many people to list them all, but she would like to especially thank Ari Kelman for all his care and guidance over the years—he is the true example of a magnificent scholar, advisor, and friend. Kathy Brosnan, Kathy Morse, Sara Gregg, Christina Snyder, Cathleen Cahill, Susan Johnson, Elaine Nelson, Erika Perez, Susan Burch, Jacob Lee, Vicki Ruiz, Erika Bsumek, Paul Conrad, Virginia Scharff, Patty Limerick, and Marisela Ramos are a truncated list of some of the incredible historians I have leaned on for support, looked to when I needed examples of strength, and learned from as I have found my way in this profession and through this project. Thanks as well to Traci Brynne Voyles for co-editing this book. Chosen family—you know who you are—I am so grateful to you for your unwavering love and encouragement. Finally, everything I do is possible because of the unyielding support and sacrifice of my parents and my grandparents, who worked diligently and doggedly every day to ensure that I could pursue my dreams. Thank you for your work and your love.

Traci Brynne would like to thank all the people whose insights, over years of conversation and study, shaped many of the analyses that formed the inspiration for this work. Ross Frank will see his influence here in his role as her teacher in graduate school many, many years ago. So will her grad school colleagues, especially Maile Arvin, Angie Morrill, Rebecca Kinney, and José Fuste. For years now, Traci has been working and thinking with Teresa Montoya, Andrew Curley, and Erika Bsumek—a research team that helps her continue to see the immense promise in and power of environmental history. Susan Burch and Sarah Whitt have been enormously generative colleagues and friends to think and write with. Additional thanks go to the good folks at the Malki Museum and, with fond memories, to Natale (Nat) Zappia. To Coco and Beni—the ones who say, "Write another book, Mama!"—and to Juan, who sets the world upright so that she can: it's always all for you.

- - - - - - - - - - - - - - - -

Field Trip: A Tour through New Scholarly Terrain

PATTY LIMERICK

Definition: *Field*. 1. An area of open land, typically bounded by hedges or fences. 2. A particular branch of study or sphere of activity or interest.

—Oxford dictionaries

We believe that the *field* of environmental history, with its core questions and critical engagement with the nonhuman world, provides a *fertile* context for understanding racism and ongoing colonialism as power structures in the United States. So how can we begin to reconceptualize our approaches to the *field* while simultaneously building on the important work of our predecessors? . . . Rather than simply asking the central question of the *field* that many have rearticulated over time—how has the environment both shaped and been shaped by human behavior?—we build on the work of the founders of the *field* in search of a more inclusive, dynamic approach to our work. (italics added).

—Mary E. Mendoza, *Not Just Green, Not Just White*

In the early 2020s, forty additional sports received the designation "Olympic level." Surprisingly, even though it is as strenuous and adrenaline saturated as gymnastics, ski jumping, or wrestling, the interpretation of history was not listed among the forty. If it did make the list as the forty-first sport, *Not Just Green, Not Just White* should receive consideration for a gold medal. This is a collection of articles written by scholars who are determined to raise and answer questions that their elders rarely, if ever, asked. As a scholarly work that squares off against a heritage of inattention, this book makes it clear that generational change in the history profession is an invigorating and consequential sport.

But here is a twist, peculiar to the scholarly world: contestants who line up for what seems certain to be a hard-fought match over the interpretation of history always retain the option of approaching one another at midcourt, shaking hands, departing to a locale set up to supply congenial beverages, and replacing the pitched battle with an invigorating conversation that will launch a series of similar exchanges.

So readers, welcome to this foreword, an alternative to energy-draining contestation brought together by the kindness and grace of coeditors Mary E. Mendoza and Tracy Brynne Voyles, who invited a venerable colleague to write the welcoming remarks for this volume. My positionality rests on a solid evidentiary base. In the same year that the founders of the American Society for Environmental History recruited inaugural members and drafted bylaws, I was preparing for PhD qualifying exams, feverishly reviewing an array of books and articles in which the word *nature* made frequent appearances. Preoccupied with that rite of passage, I did not realize that I was missing the chance to sign up as one of the earliest members of the American Society for Environmental History. In fact, the phrase *environmental history* did not appear in the paperwork for my exams, and some cobbled-together wording like "Nature in American History" had to fill in.

Now, a half-century later, I have been given an enviable opportunity to demonstrate the satisfaction—and even exhilaration—of intergenerational transition in the interpretation of history.

At its foundation, *Not Just Green, Not Just White* rests on an appraisal of the performance of environmental historians over the decades since my examiners assembled to ask me "some historical, literary, and architectural topics connected in some way to nature." The authors and editors of this volume focus their attention on the power dynamics at work at the crossroads where race and environment intersect, and they present their conviction that their elders paid insufficient attention to this juncture.

Capitalizing on my venerability, I can offer my own intellectual history as a data point in support of that appraisal. Writing my dissertation on attitudes toward deserts, I was responding to what I saw as an overobsession with green places in early studies about American attitudes toward nature. And yet, over several years of working on *Desert Passages*, I never once said to myself, "This is curious: the only holders of 'attitudes toward deserts' that I have included in my study are hyperliterate white men. Might there be something wrong with my sampling strategy?" Moreover, in volunteering myself as a specimen who has arrived in the twenty-first century from a distant point of origin, I can cite one of the first opportunities I had to create a course: just before I finished my notably uninclusive dissertation in 1980, I taught a seminar on nature writing. And yes, all the authors whose works appeared on that syllabus were white men.

So how much has the field of environmental history changed from those distant times? "More robust engagement with histories of marginalized communities," the editors of this volume acknowledge, "has emerged since the 1990s." But they then note that "opinions" of the scale and intensity of this change "differ," and some commentators have characterized these "shifts" as "paltry." And now I will declare the one opinion I hold with complete certainty: If I were to choose to spend a day milling around the hallways at the annual conference of the American Society for Environmental History, and if I were to ask each passerby to help me calibrate the degree to which the practitioners in this field have increased the attention they pay to the experiences of marginalized people, I would not end the day lamenting the absence of spirited and thought-provoking conversations. While I do not have the data to offer a credible estimate of the degree of change in the field, various statements that I made on public record make it much easier to answer the question, "How much did my own assumptions and convictions change over time?"

The introduction to *Not Just Green, Not Just White* ends with a quotation expressing concern over "the unfortunate distance separating environmental history from ethnic history." Those words appear in an article I wrote for the *Journal of American History* in 1992, just five years after the publication of my book on "white men trying to figure out the desert." That same article offered this observation: "Until quite recently, environmental historians paid little attention to ethnic history; they focused their inquiries on the attitudes and behavior of white men."[1] The phrase "Physician, heal thyself" may have just appeared in the minds of readers of this foreword.

The story behind the writing of that article is something of a parable of the capacity of midcareer scholars to change course. In 1987, I published a book called *The Legacy of Conquest: The Unbroken Past of the American West*. In that book, I pushed as hard as I could to move the center of gravity, in the interpretation of the history of the West, toward a full recognition of people of color. And yet when I was asked to write an article for the *Journal of American History*'s special issue in response to the Columbian Quincentenary, I dashed off a draft that tracked the usual cast of characters—Lewis and Clark, Zebulon Pike, John C. Fremont, and so on—on their westward journeys of "discovery." And then, at a gathering to discuss the drafts for this special issue, the noted historian Ron Takaki gave robust expression to the surprise and dismay that my first draft had evoked in him. So that draft took a long walk, from which it never returned. In the second draft, I reversed the conventional directionality of Western American history, and I shifted the framework of the article to the west-to-east trajectory of the Asian American "discovery" of the Western landscape—a feat I could not have taken on without the help of fluent translators.

To sum this up: Ron Takaki had pushed *me* to live with some consistency and to apply to the field of environmental history some semblance of the same expectations I had imposed on the field of Western American history with *The Legacy of Conquest*. In a pattern that I bet journal editors have seen plenty of times, the second draft was much better than the first, primarily because it bore no resemblance to my first try. Risking the self-indulgence of the venerable, I am going to claim that in 1992, I declared—on public record—the hope that somewhere on the planet, there was a scattered cohort of infants, toddlers, or perhaps teenagers who would in some distant future pool their efforts and create a book in the spirit of *Not Just Green, Not Just White*. And here is where self-indulgence comes to a blessed halt: even as I look back at my on-record hope for a uniting of ethnic history and environmental history, that is a world apart from any claim that "I knew just what these younger people were going to write!" On the contrary, the introduction and the conclusion, as well as every article in this book, gave me multiple opportunities to say to myself, "I did not see this coming."

Here is my best effort to provide an overview of the intentions, visions, purposes, and goals of the contributors to this book.

1. Every imaginable topic in environmental history comes with a multiplicity of reasons to look for and appraise power dynamics that reconfigured the lives of people and the conditions of the nonhuman environment.

2. The correction of the omissions that figured in earlier versions of environmental history has required much more than simple gestures of addition and inclusion. That is truly good news, since it effectively winnows and sifts the stockpile of propositions and generalizations that had once taken up residence in the dreary land of the taken-for-granted while also opening up vast territories for researchers in environmental history.

3. While environmental historians must look thoroughly and honestly at the injuries and injustices that are omnipresent in the historical record, they must also look—with equal thoroughness and honesty—at the resistance, resilience, creativity, and ingenuity with which less empowered populations have set their own terms in their relationships with the nonhuman world.

4. This book unites the histories of material action with studies of ideas. In an earlier era in the writing of environmental history, some studies discussed what people thought and other studies explored what people did, and it often seemed that the authors of those different studies had not sought out opportunities to meet one another. In this collection, attention often goes to the quest for *meanings* conducted by historical figures, with the meanings so identified serving as the bridge between thoughts and actions, followed by reverse traffic on that bridge, as actions produce results that provoke further thought.

5. To understand a movement, trend, idea, or phenomenon, it is crucial to challenge conventional thinking about the origins of that movement, trend, idea, or phenomenon. This quest for a more energetic and accurate identification of origins provides a doubled service when it comes to applying history to present dilemmas: first, a knowledge of the *roots* of beneficial ideas and practices from

the past is essential if you want to cultivate them in the present, and second, a knowledge of the *roots* of perilous ideas and practices from the past is essential if you want to *uproot* them in the present.

6. Noting the relationships between race and environment reveals a breathtaking range of relationships between the nonhuman world and human communities, and many of these relationships remain understudied. While it is sometimes the case that customs of archival acquisition have produced a shortage of sources for the study of these relationships, it is often the case that conventional thinking—about what sources exist and what they can reveal—needs to be shaken up. Unexpected treasures await in a variety of forms of storage and preservation.

7. In the profession of history, specialized inquiries have produced many findings of value. And yet specialization awaits a searching cost/benefit analysis as well as a major overhaul. Specialized inquiry has produced an arrangement of dispersed and scattered findings, and this book celebrates the promise of bringing those findings together to enrich and support one another.

At this point, I will hazard a guess: Even though people reading this foreword probably found those seven points to be worth contemplating, they would be eager to have at least a hint of the stories, told in the chapters, that bring these seven points to life.

And so, readers, responding to that yearning for specificity, I have prepared a chapter-by-chapter preview of what is in store for you. Of course, you are licensed to skip around as you read this preview, just as you are licensed to skip around as you read these chapters. Most importantly, you should be fully aware of the fact that the short summaries I offer here are far from comprehensive; rather, they highlight the reasons for my gratitude for having had the chance to read these articles. And if this is the first time you have ever encountered a feature like this inventory in a foreword to a collection of articles, then imagine that you are in an old-fashioned movie theater where the projectionist has queued a lineup of movie trailers and then headed off on a lunch break that lasts longer than she had planned.

Chapter 1, by Katherine Johnson, "Naturalizing Difference: Labor and Slavery in Colonial Georgia"

Soon after the arrival of Europeans in North America, a sector of the settler population, trying to figure out where they were and how they were to live there, cooked up an abundance of improbable ideas about the varying capacity of human populations to work in different settings and climates, and some of those improbable ideas, arising from settler determination to avoid hard work, have persisted for centuries.

Chapter 2, by Carl A Zimring, "Dirty Work Reconsidered: On the Historical Dynamics of Labor, Waste, and Race in Industrial Society"

The generation of waste is a reliable source of trouble in the human relationship to nature. Certain sectors of society, despite generating a good share of that waste, exercise their power to offload the bulk of the labor of dealing with it onto the sectors of society that have not (yet!) had the power to insist that everyone who generates waste should play a direct role in dealing with it.

Chapter 3, by Elizabeth Grennan Browning, "City of Destruction: The Chicago School of Sociology's Ecological Interpretation of Race, Migration, and Inequality"

The northward migration of African Americans led scholars affiliated with the University of Chicago to ask consequential questions about the impact and influence of the urban environment on populations originating in rural areas. Not surprisingly, white scholars and Black scholars (including the novelist Richard Wright) found different meanings in the supposed biological ties that shaped the adaptations of newcomers to urban life.

Chapter 4, by Colin Fisher, "Collective Memory for the African Motherland in Interwar Black Chicago and the Limits of the Environmental Justice Model"

With timing that challenges conventional assumptions about the chronology of African American activism, in 1934 a forceful group of folks in Chicago organized a pageant, "O, Sing a New Song," that put forward connections to a homeland in West Africa, thereby steering clear of nostalgia for plantations in the South. The recognition of the effectiveness with which the pageant planners brought visions of nature into relationship with visions of community drains the force from a multitude of stereotypes.

Chapter 5, by David Naguib Pellow, "States of Confinement and Ecological Violence: Incarceration and the Struggle for Environmental Justice"

The disproportionate incarceration of African Americans has involved an equally disproportionate proximity to sites of environmental pollution in spaces that are both confined and perilous. Sticking with my practice of the self-disclosure of the venerable, this is the essay that most unsettled me; whatever I thought I might learn from the merging of ethnic history and environmental history, I did not anticipate this revelation of the central place of incarceration in an irresistibly persuasive argument for rectifying environmental injustice and social injustice at the same time. It is an argument that cannot be dismissed.

Chapter 6, by Teona Wiliams, "Islands of Freedom: The Struggle to Desegregate Shenandoah and Great Smoky Mountains National Parks, 1936–41"

National parks got started in the American West in locales lightly populated by African Americans. The creation of parks in the American South put a spotlight on the regional differences of the populations in proximity to these federal lands. The upshot: African American activists put sufficient pressure on federal officials to generate an order desegregating the national parks—in 1941, well before the usual chronological configurations of the civil rights movement.

Chapter 7, by Kathryn Morse, "Conserving Whiteness: The Crisis of Tenancy and New Deal Rural Rehabilitation in the Cotton South"

The desperately impoverished state of Southern tenant farmers in the 1930s received a great deal of national attention and a strong response from the federal government. But officials in the Farm Security Administration focused their remedial actions on white tenant farmers, with only a few officials noting the even more disturbing circumstances of Black tenant farmers. The history of this exclusiveness of compassion is a high-powered cautionary tale.

Chapter 8, by Cecilia Tsu, "Harvest of Self-Help: The Problems and Paradoxes of Southeast Asian Refugee Community Gardens"

When American involvement in the wars of Southeast Asia displaced thousands of Hmong people, cities in the United States sometimes worked with refugees to create urban gardens that provided nutrition and—to a degree—a sense of healing. There are heartening features in these stories, but there are also cautionary tales about the risks of white folks who assume they have a deep knowledge of the people they set out to help.

Chapter 9, by Bryon Williams, "Amputated from the Land: Black Refugees from America and the Racialized Roots of the Environmentalism–Environmental Justice Divide"

> As my own syllabus from the 1970s demonstrated, written records of thoughts and feelings about nature seemed, for a long time, to be stuck in the status of a segregated literary territory. But unexpected sources await discovery, and a treasure trove of stories told by mid-nineteenth-century African Americans who found freedom and dignity in rural Canada has provided an extraordinary opportunity to explore the idea of nature as a refuge rather than the conventional mythic construction of nature as a retreat.

Chapter 10, by Erika Marie Bsumek, "Glen Canyon Dam, Rainbow Bridge, and Hole-in-the-Rock: Diversifying Environmentalisms and the Struggle over 'Sacred' Landmarks in the American West"

> The struggle over the construction of the Glen Canyon Dam figures in every retelling of the American environmental movement. But paying attention to the role played by the Navajo Nation—especially in the effort to recognize Rainbow Bridge as a sacred site—reveals previously unrecognized dimensions of the story, including the complicated relationships between stakeholders ranging from Navajo leaders to Mormon river rafters, with non-Indian environmentalists struggling to get their bearings on the range of meanings carried by the word *sacred*.

Chapter 11, by Miles A. Powell, "'How Would You Feel If Someone Were Allowed to Kill One of Your Grandparents?': Native Hawaiian Opposition to the Shark Fin Trade"

> Anyone who has come to think that histories of the passage of federal laws are a dreary trudge through arcane congressional deliberations can recover from that misapprehension with this story. The aspiration to understand the law to restrict the killing of sharks (in order to harvest the delicacy of their fins) requires an immersion in the intense relationship between sharks and Native Hawaiians as well as a recognition of the impact that Indigenous groups have had in shaping "mainstream" environmental causes and effects.

Chapter 12, by Carolyn Finney, "Radical Presence—the Shadows Take Shape: African Americans (Re)making a Green World"

Creativity, originality, and humor are powerful components of radical resistance and presence. When you learn that definitions of the word *radical* "speak to new origins or roots," you will be fully readied to receive the stories of African Americans who lived every minute in full engagement with nature and with their fellow human beings. Treated with three perfectly told stories of people who have transformed the margin into the place to be, the idea of separating the history of the environment from the history of marginalized peoples pleads for an irreversible retirement.

Chapter 13, by Mary E. Mendoza, "¡Turnerian, Si! ¡Americano, No! Disentangling Wilderness, Whiteness, and the American Immigration Story"

Pairing the stories of two lives—a westward-moving Euro-American settler and a northward-moving Mexican immigrant—works well to point out that an old narrative, structured by east-to-west movements across the continent, really must yield to new narratives, with attention reallocated to a south-to-north axis. Executing this change requires a visit to the chest where old narratives are stored, pulling out the "frontier" articles of national faith and asking, "Do we really want to hold on to that?"

Chapter 14, by Traci Brynne Voyles, "Pushed into the Margins: New Approaches to Environmental History in Settler California"

Evidence-based generalizations—about the disruption of Indigenous people's lives by the invasion of their homelands by Euro-Americans—are important contributions to national self-understanding. But this intense, respectful, and empathetic reading of the autobiography of Delfina Cuero, a Kumeyaay woman born at the beginning of the twentieth century, can deliver more impact than a multiplicity of those generalizations. Separation from a homeland is a misfortune beyond estimation, and the record of a mother's desperation to find food for her children conveys that misfortune with a clarity that no one can dismiss.

Chapter 15, by Kent Blansett, "From Idle No More to Standing Rock: The Fight for Indigenous Environmental Justice"

International borders have disrupted communities and alliances that would otherwise have held together, but those boundaries do not necessarily sever the ties that would permit Indigenous communities to join together to resist threats to their well-being. Exploring "the juncture" of Native nationalism and Red Power, Blansett illuminates the origins of the binational activism that brought international attention to the environmental peril posed by the Keystone Pipeline.

Chapter 16, by Ari Kelman, "Seeing the Trees: The Fight for Cultural Sovereignty along the Banks of Sand Creek"

The Sand Creek massacre site obscures any distinction between the visible and the invisible in the contemplation of a landscape. The memories of the dead, held by the living, are as actual and immediate as the trees that may have been witnesses to the brutality manifested on November 29, 1864. As "the first unit within the national parks system to question the logic and rectitude of settler colonialism," the Sand Creek Massacre National Historic Site reminds environmental historians that they are participants in intensely meaningful reckonings with the memories layered into the landscapes of North America.

Thinking about Fields and Fences

One of the most thought-provoking features of this book is the attention that the contributors pay to the widespread custom of drawing on nature to find words that have captured and conveyed—in positive ways and pernicious ways—people's assumptions about human conduct. I reflected on that line of interpretation and commentary until it took hold in my own cognitive operating system.

And that's how I started noticing the constant use of the word *field* in this book.

While the evocation of *fields* might seem to be exactly what one would expect from environmental historians, the figure of speech gets equal use in every *field* of history. Why on earth (so to speak) am I calling attention to this omnipresent verbal habit?

Let's return to the definition I used as an epigraph at the start of a foreword entitled "Field Trip": "Definition: *Field*: 1. An area of open land, typically bounded by hedges or fences; 2. A particular branch of study or sphere of activity or interest." Readers may well have leaped ahead of me on the sequence of thought this definition inspired, but I will retrace my steps anyway.

It is very appealing to think of the terrain and turf of academic inquiry as "an area of open land." But in the Oxford dictionaries, the enchantment of that vision quickly collides with the phrase "typically bounded by hedges or fences."

And now the punchline: the instant interruption of open space by infrastructure of confinement makes a far-too-direct fit with the word's second definition: "a particular branch of study or sphere of activity and interest." That's where this book offers a spirit-lifting alternative vision. Over the last century and a half, practitioners in the *field* of history have devoted a good share of their time and effort to the planting of hedges and the building of fences—otherwise known as the lines that divide up departments, disciplines, specialties, and areas of expertise.

Exercising the license of the venerable, I am now going to say what I see as the most important message of this book: the time has come for the history profession to break from the intense labor required to maintain those fences and let them collapse under their own weight. With this book in hand, we can now see the *field* of environmental history without limits.

Note

1. Patricia Nelson Limerick, "Disorientation and Reorientation: The American Landscape Discovered from the West," Journal of American History 79, no. 3 (December 1992): 1031.

Not Just Green,
Not Just White

Introduction

The Ownership of the Earth

MARY E. MENDOZA

> Always, somehow, some way, silently but clearly, I
> am given to understand that whiteness is the own-
> ership of the earth forever and ever, Amen!
> —W. E. B. Du Bois, "The Souls of White Folk," 1920

The world's oldest living organism sits deep within the Inyo National Forest on the east side of California's Sierra Nevada. At nearly five thousand years old, Methuselah, a mighty bristlecone pine tree, rests in a grove about an hour's drive from the town of Bishop. This community of trees has survived storms, droughts, and fires. Their dense wood has shielded them from bug and fungal infestations. Their genomes, which are nine times longer than the human genome, have allowed them to adapt to climate changes. These trees can "deal with crisis by sectioning off parts of their structures, enabling the rest of the tree to keep living" while an injured limb dies.[1] They thrive in Death Valley despite severe weather and poor soil. Each ancient tree, from seedling to sapling, to mighty, gnarly, twisted, colorful elder, tells a story of survival, resistance, and knowing when to let go.

People of color and Indigenous peoples in the United States tell similar stories of environmental endurance. The goal of *Not Just Green, Not Just White* is to push historians not only to think more judiciously about race as a power structure that shapes and informs U.S. environmental history but also to consider the ways that marginalized communities resist those very power structures. The white settler project is just that—a project—and it is long-standing and ongoing.[2] That project is complex, contingent, contested, and fraught, and at its heart are stories of human relationships to nonhuman nature. Our purpose as scholars and in this volume is to move the field of U.S. environmental history in a direction that exposes the problems of white settler supremacy in the past and present by looking at the entanglements of racial and colonial relations of power with the nonhuman world. Through critical analysis of white settler supremacy, we offer un- or underexplored histories of injustice (environmental and social), but also uncover stories of resistance to injustice and of diverse human relationships to myriad environments. By expanding what environmental historians have traditionally analyzed about people, power, and the natural world, we begin to reimagine and redefine the relationship between race and environment.

The field of U.S. environmental history has long suffered from a dearth of scholarship that meaningfully engages with race or the formation of racial hierarchies and their relationship to the environment. Several scholars note that although the field's early work was notoriously white, more robust engagement with histories of marginalized communities has emerged since the 1990s. Others argue that even these shifts have been paltry.[3] Adequate or inadequate, there is still much to be done. So far, this kind of work in environmental history has focused on relatively narrow questions of environmental inequalities and the disproportionate exposure of communities of color to industrial pollution in urban areas. Although the body of scholarship on race and environment has increased, environmental history narratives continue to be troublingly uncritical of racial power structures and couched wholly within what we call a white settler supremacist framework—a framework that combines histories of settler colonialism and white supremacy. By deconstructing and looking critically at white settler supremacy in U.S. environmental history, the essays in this book highlight a range of nuanced and diverse histories across space and time. To peel back stories centering on whiteness is to reveal a world of overlooked understandings of and experiences with a multitude of environments.

More often than not, existing histories of race and environment articulate how racial difference works to the detriment of nonwhite actors. In these histories, communities of color and Indigenous peoples might be dispossessed in the name of conservation, their bodies may suffer as they toil in plantations in the South or the orchards of the hot and arid West, or they may find themselves exposed to toxins at the hands of powerful corporations. These are familiar stories about race, environment, and (in)justice, and they are important. But there are other stories to tell: stories of strength, of finding freedom in the clouds as they float over a prison or detention camp, of finding one's ancestors, oneself, or one's future in nature.[4]

Stories about race and nature need not just be stories of environmental injustice and degradation—they can also be stories of liberation, grit, and resistance. They can, in fact, be stories of different kinds of environmentalism, of underrepresented politics of advocacy or understudied relationships with the nonhuman world. The challenge for scholars of environmental history is to analyze and interpret our diverse histories and myriad relationships with the natural world while understanding the racial hierarchies that undergird this nation's settler colonial past and present.

This debate, then, over whether U.S. environmental history has done a good job with race, should not merely address the number of books published "about" nonwhite and Indigenous people and communities—our evaluation of the field must be more robust than that. We must ask how our accounting of these histories addresses power structures such as white settler supremacy, settler colonialism, racism, and patriarchy and how these power structures intersect to mediate historical relationships among different kinds of humans and their environments. We must ask how nonwhite and Indigenous peoples are represented in our studies and what kinds of archives we turn to when we write about communities whose worldviews have too often been excised from official or colonial documentation. Finally, and crucially, we must ask who is doing the representing, how to diversify the academy itself to include more scholars of color, how to mentor and support students and faculty who are systematically deterred from doing scholarly work, and how to push our institutions to be robustly diverse intellectual spaces. This means that the work falls on white and nonwhite scholars alike.

We use the term *white settler supremacy* to broaden understandings of the United States' troubled settler colonial history (and present) from one that is often mostly associated with Native dispossession to one that encapsulates the experiences of many peoples across many environments and historical moments, caught up in what historian Alaina Roberts calls the "dual nature of settler colonialism"—"spatial occupation and white supremacy."[5] In short, we use *white settler supremacy* as a term that combines both settler colonialism and white supremacy into a single holistic frame—one that explicitly calls out whiteness, places emphasis on structural supremacy, and points to not only the eliminatory logic of settler colonialism but also the ways in which acts of expulsion, enslavement, exclusion, and exploitation have served as critical avenues for racial and colonial domination.[6] These acts—expulsion, enslavement, exclusion, exploitation, and elimination—are central tools of white settler supremacy. Each of these terms carries with it significant environmental components.

The effects of white settler supremacy involve racial domination and environmental exploitation of multiple diverse groups, landscapes, and resources, but this approach also makes room, in historically contingent ways, for many distinct relationships between people and nature. Contrary to the assertions of some environmental historians that the frame of settler colonialism renders nature and Natives as passive actors or that environmental history and settler colonialism are at odds, we contend that settler colonialism is actually organized and enriched by the combination of environment, resources, and territory.[7] In fact, we concur with major works in Indigenous studies that see these things as foundational to settler colonialism.[8] Because much of the earliest processes of settler colonialism involved massive dispossession of land, access to natural resources for Native peoples became severely limited, forming a lopsided power system in an emerging capitalist society.[9] That uneven power system produced a structure in which white people controlled land and wealth, rendering them more powerful than other populations. Put succinctly, settler colonialism created a context for white supremacy. Together, they built a system of structural racism that was generally governed by white domination. Building on settler colonial frames, then, white settler supremacy does not preclude Native agency, nor does it omit environmental intervention from the historical record, just as structural racism today does not mean that marginalized communities cannot or do not resist those structures. Similarly, it does not homogenize white settlers; rather, it holds all white actors accountable to a power structure that accrues wealth and privileges to them at the expense of other people and the environment.[10] Although not all white settlers actively sought (or seek) to destroy or dispossess marginalized peoples, they did (and do) all benefit from systemic remunerations—this is critical because when we ignore this truth, we cannot take environmental or social justice seriously.

The State of the Field
In 1728, William Byrd II, a wealthy Virginian from a slave-owning plantation family, trekked west in the company of a surveying party toward the Appalachian Mountains, arriving at the base of the range in early October.

Byrd delighted in the mountains and all the adventure that they invited: sleeping outside under the stars, breathing in the cold and crisp morning air, and gazing up at views of "blue clouds" as he lyrically described the Appalachians. Inspired by these experiences, Byrd's account of his trip, *History of the Dividing Line*, featured passages describing the beauty, wildness, and adventure of life in the mountains. His account later became a key text in U.S. environmental history. In fact, Byrd is broadly recognized as providing "the first extensive American commentary on wilderness" that reflected feelings other than contempt and revulsion—attitudes toward nature more common among his contemporaries.[11]

Byrd's writings reveal where the limits of hostility to wilderness as a dangerous and unknown threat to human life could be drawn: namely, around one's social location. Whereas "in the backwoods" through which he passed, "he saw and deplored people who had absorbed the wildness of their surroundings." Byrd himself had no trouble experiencing wildness without reverting to "feeling himself a barbarian or in danger of reverting to one"—he had the prophylaxis of privilege.[12] Byrd "carefully distinguished his own relation to wilderness from theirs," those "wretches liv[ing] in a dirty state of nature," creating a rationale by which the more civilized the man, the more he could enjoy nature without "feeling himself a barbarian."[13]

Byrd's descriptions reveal how the binary distinctions between civilization and wilderness in the United States became conceived of as deeply racialized and classed: the civilized man—say, a wealthy, London-educated enslaver—could enjoy and appreciate nature, but "barbarians" could only be a part of it. Byrd's writings thus serve as a starting point for U.S. environmental history in two crucial ways. First, his *History of the Dividing Line* foreshadowed the American wilderness ethic and the major themes of white Americans' love of wilderness—its beauty, adventure, and salubriousness—that would come to define seminal texts like those of Henry David Thoreau, Theodore Roosevelt, John Muir, Edward Abbey, and others.[14] Second, and more importantly for our purposes, Byrd laid out unapologetically (if parenthetically) the racial and class rubrics by which this wilderness experience could be enjoyed.

This example helps explain how environmental history has been organized around white settler frameworks and power structures. The wilderness lens that has captivated environmental historians, whether they are celebrating it or ripping it "deservedly in tatters," shows how foundational a white point of view has been to the field.[15] In her 1992 article "Disorientation and Reorientation: The American Landscape Discovered from the West," Patricia Limerick points out that this kind of ideological limitation has also been tied to a methodological one; the very archives that environmental history draws from—detailed accounts of landscapes, careful inventories of resources, painstakingly drawn maps—were created by and for "a 'landowning-literati class'" that became "the source of much of the Anglo-American literature of discovery of landscape" on which environmental historians rely.[16] The white settler point of view, in other words, is built into the very framework of the field, creating a kind of center of gravity for our stories about people and the environment.

This center of gravity frames the major narratives and themes that have organized the field and the activism associated with it. For example, environmental historian Paul Sutter notes that in the United States, unlike in many other parts of the world, the political project of environmentalism has been "a movement dominated by the colonizers, not the colonized."[17] This is in large part because of the deeply rooted entanglements of whiteness and the wilderness ethic with environmental advocacy—the idealized form of non-human nature that Byrd found so captivating has been a privileged motivator of environmental advocacy.[18] Yet in much of U.S. history, the whiteness of wilderness has been overdetermined—wilderness is not the green and brown of trees and soil; it is the white of those who have recreated in it, painted it, lovingly described it, and excluded nonwhites from it.[19]

Our focus on environmentalism associated with the wilderness ethic is not intended to exclude other forms of mainstream environmental politics but rather to point out strikingly similar patterns in white environmental politics in different contexts. Environmentalism, whether we connect that to conservation movements to protect "wilderness" in the late nineteenth century or to make polluters pariahs a hundred years later, has had the effect of universalizing white peoples' ideas and experiences of the human and nonhuman world. With the so-called birth of the environmental movement instigated by Rachel Carson's publication of *Silent Spring* in 1962, white people's concerns have dominated the conversations about environmental politics despite the fact that people of color had long been articulating the kinds of environmental concerns that made Carson's work so popular. If we wonder now why "nature" seems to exist for some people and not for others, the answer lies in how nature has, over and over again, been understood, bounded, represented, and peopled in ways that have produced exclusionary outcomes.[20] The fact that this has been true whether or not historical actors had discriminatory (versus democratic) intent points to the structural and systematic nature of the problem. The whiteness of wilderness has been a powerful and obstinate structure that has seemed to drive our interactions with and our understandings of the nonhuman world. It is the purpose of this volume to identify and critique that white settler center of gravity and uncover how we can pull ourselves away from it.

Scholars point to two exceptions regarding the whiteness of environmental history: first, the inclusion of Indigenous peoples in a range of U.S. environmental histories, and second, the burgeoning consideration by historians of environmental injustices against marginalized communities, particularly in cities.[21] U.S. environmental historians have discussed Native peoples in greater detail and with greater rigor than non-Native people and communities of color. This is no accident, nor is it necessarily unproblematic; it is the outcome of two troubling frameworks in U.S. environmental history. The first of these frameworks is the "ecological Indian" stereotype, which collapses all things environmental and Indigenous and makes it seem self-evident that environmentally inclined scholars would turn more toward Native (versus white or non-Native people of color) relationships to nature.[22] The trope of Indigenous peoples as romantic environmental stewards is tempting for non-Native scholars of all stripes—and perhaps more so for those of us who yearn for counterpoints and counterexamples to rampant, industrialized environmental ruination. The second framework that produces more environmental histories of Indigenous communities than non-Native communities of color is the close affinity between U.S. environmental history and U.S. Western history.[23] This relationship weds environmental historians to the legacy of Frederick Jackson Turner's ideas, centering on Indian-white conflict on the "frontier," often with an insufficient accounting of the power imbalance and historical contingency of these relationships.[24] In some ways, westward expansion into the "frontier" was the Turnerian narrative framework into which U.S. environmental history was "shoehorned."[25]

Environmental histories of environmental justice have likewise been problematic and to address those problems, interventions must be made in the standard chronologies of both the environmental movement and the environmental justice movement. When environmental historians turn to the environmental justice movement, they often view it as a latter-day incarnation of a primarily white history of environmental activism against industrial pollution. Commonly taught examples of this history cover Rachel Carson's seminal *Silent Spring* (1962), antinuclear activism during the Cold War and particularly the work of organizations like Women Strike for Peace (1961). Others include reactions to the meltdown of the Three Mile Island nuclear reactor in Pennsylvania (1979) and the protests against groundwater pollution in the suburban New York community of Love Canal (late 1970s).[26] While the "beginning" of the environmental justice movement in this country is generally recognized as occurring in Warren County, North Carolina, in 1982 when an African American community mobilized against the siting of a PCB landfill near their homes, it is often seen as part of a genealogy of white environmental activism rather than an extension of much longer racial justice and civil rights movements.[27]

The tendency in environmental history to link environmental justice to antitoxics movements undercuts the environmental justice movement's larger significance, abbreviates its long history, and elides the transformative framework of race, class, and indigeneity for the movement.[28] As historian Dolores Greenberg has argued, the contemporary environmental justice movement has its roots not in *Silent Spring* and Love Canal but in nonwhite agitation for racial justice going as far back as W. E. B. Du Bois's claim that racial power was experienced by Black Americans primarily through environmental "conditions of life." Others have seen similar connecting histories of environmental thought in antiracist and anticolonial movements by Indigenous peoples and people of color, arguing that the Indigenous environmental justice movement began in 1492.[29] Still others, such as environmental historian Connie Chiang, argue that environmental justice politics can and should be understood in environmental histories in which "one group used the natural world to assert authority over another group" or when "those with less power . . . used the environment to amplify their strength and fight back."[30] Certainly, the protests in Warren County in 1982 shared more in common—from tactics and rhetoric to individual activists (such as Charles Cobb of the Student Nonviolent Coordinating Committee)—with the civil rights movement than Love Canal.[31] This contrast of competing points of origin became very clear during the 1991 First National POC Environmental Leadership Summit, when activists of color from across the country clearly outlined their connections to racial and class justice campaigns rather than white environmental movements. This history exposes how the environmental justice movement is not merely antipollution environmentalism but with Indigenous nations and communities of color at the helm; it is a natural articulation of how nonwhite environmental politics and practices are central to struggles for racial liberation.

People of color and Indigenous peoples have long had a rich relationship with nature and have thus had many reasons to fight for environmental causes and justice. Although disproportionate exposure to industrial pollution has been an important concern of the environmental justice movement, even a cursory look at its founding documents points to a much richer framing of its politics than that.[32] The implication of this limited view of environmental justice concerns is that people of color and Indigenous nations in these stories seem to only engage with environmental concerns to save their lives, whereas for whites, environmentalism—from John Muir to *Silent Spring*—has a spiritual praxis of interspecies altruism. While people of color in these histories experience environmental problems in terms of pesticide exposure in the farms of Central Valley, California, and lead in the tap water of Flint, Michigan, white people fret about threats to wolves, whales, and other megafauna or worry about access to recreation opportunities in the open-air cathedrals of Yosemite Valley National Park—or so the standard stories go. The problematic implications of this cut both ways: not only does it box in the parameters by which Indigenous peoples and people of color are expected to care about the environment, but it also makes environmentalism seem to be a sentimental hobby for wealthy white folks, not a life-and-death politics of real urgency for all humans and nonhumans alike.

One of the greatest challenges in the field is that we lack truly nuanced representation across the board in much of our scholarship. Like Joan Wallach Scott's call to explore gender as a power structure that organizes all social life rather than simply adding on stories about women's lives, environmental historians must unpack the role of the environment in shaping racialized power relations and vice versa.[33] We can no longer simply explore stories about "people" and "nature." For example, although environmental historians have produced an impressive array of studies that explore Indigenous nations and their roles in U.S. environmental history, "only recently have environmental historians of the United States started looking at *state conservation as a colonizing force*."[34] In other words, having Natives represented as subjects of study is not the same as exploring the settler colonial and white supremacist power systems that have sought to shape and control human relationships to the environment. By the same token, stories of communities of color exposed to industrial toxins are crucial, but so are analyses of how those cases of environmental injustice flow from nature and help shore up racist hierarchies. Nature and ideas about it shape how people understand and treat one another. When people treat each other badly, the result can be harmful to one group, making them seem inferior to another, which only reinforces racist ideas.[35] Environmental history has the potential to explain exactly how these complex processes have unfolded in a way that no other subfield can.

This is not to say that environmental history as a field has not done wonders for the discipline of history to date—in fact, it has been nothing short of transformative. Nor are we saying that the field has ignored entirely the myriad groups of people affected by settler colonialism and white supremacy. Numerous works have helped us understand the history of the American West, histories of extraction, and the ways that nature has shaped and been shaped by human action. We are not suggesting that the fundamental questions of the subfield should change. As always, we should be asking three fundamental questions, which historian Ellen Stroud has outlined: How did nature change? How did ideas about nature change? And how did interactions between people and their dynamics change in any given historical moment? In short, the three main branches of the field—the study of the material, the intellectual, and the political—remain at the core of our work.[36] But as Stroud also points out, what is and is not environmental history is up for debate.[37] Below, we suggest that new approaches to these core questions might offer a more inclusive and critically analytical way forward.

The Future of the Field

Given this background, we believe that the field of environmental history, with its core questions and critical engagement with the nonhuman world, provides a fertile context for understanding racism and ongoing colonialism as power structures in the United States. So how can we begin to reconceptualize our approaches to the field while simultaneously building on the important work of our predecessors? How can we use environmental history to expose racist power relations while also uncovering and celebrating moments in which historically marginalized communities push against those structures? And how can the field both acknowledge and explain inequality without consistently placing historically marginalized communities in static roles as victims, perpetual losers in ongoing competitions for more and more exploitation of more and more resources? That is, how can we acknowledge lopsided systems of power while also recognizing human agency, grit, and resistance among people of color and Indigenous peoples?

This book demonstrates the ways in which environments, in their various forms, mediate and shape human relationships and social hierarchies. Rather than simply asking the central question of the field that many have rearticulated over time—how has the environment both shaped and been shaped by human behavior?—we build on the work of the founders of the field in search of a more inclusive, dynamic approach to our work. We contend that neither humans nor the environment are monolithic, and when we treat them as such, we diminish vibrant histories with multiple actors and forces converging in the stories we tell. When we write environmental histories we must acknowledge and account for the pervasiveness of white settler supremacy as a system of power and how the various tools of that system have enabled white settlers to create and justify uneven power dynamics that have shaped access to resources and land that have affected relationships between and among humans and nonhumans. We must simultaneously keep an eye out for the myriad ways that people have resisted those power dynamics. And finally, as all historians do, we should consider how all of this has played out across space and time. We see a critical approach to white settler supremacy in environmental history that, if built into the core questions of the field, offers a fundamental mechanism for reconceptualizing the field going forward.

This begs the question, Why *white settler supremacy*? The answer is that this framing combines the forces of settler colonialism and white supremacy and their intersections with racism, all of which cannot be divorced from one another in U.S. environmental history. Settler colonialism refers to a colonial practice of land dispossession and the genocidal elimination of Native people for the purpose of white settlement. Once settled, colonists exploit nonwhite labor to cultivate stolen land to "produce excessively."[38] In other words, settler colonialism is inextricably linked to environment and racialized labor on stolen property. Without a critical analysis of the functions of white supremacy, however, it does not always fully account for racialized domination across the board.[39] White supremacy, meanwhile, refers to a set of structural conditions that accrue race-based cultural, economic, and political power to people marked as "white," a shifting assemblage of mostly European-descended people.[40] Settler colonialism provides the context and conditions for the racial authority that establishes white supremacy as well as other forms of power.[41]

Scholars of settler colonialism explicitly engage with its implications for the natural world precisely because "'civilization' is defined as production in excess of the 'natural' world."[42] Making the natural world produce "in excess" requires, in turn, excess labor. In the United States, that has almost always meant racialized labor—enslaved, or cheapened, alienated from the product of their work and ultimately excludable from the category and privileges of whiteness or even from the nation itself.[43] The natural world—often reinterpreted within white settler supremacy as territory or property and resources—is inherent to this system of colonization.

White supremacy has been less directly understood in terms of its implications for the environment, despite the fact that there are many. White supremacy, too, plays a vital role in exploiting racialized labor for excess resource production.[44] Moreover, white supremacy relies on ideas of racial purity and pollution, drawing lines around racial categories and making violations of those borders taboo—in the process, making violations of other kinds of borders taboo as well, from borders around segregated city neighborhoods to borders between nations. All these projects of border enforcement are designed to protect the purity and privilege of whiteness. They also all entail very real implications for the environment as well as the organization and distribution of property and resources.

As such, the frame of white settler supremacy encompasses the process of dispossession and domination that undergirds our past as well as much of our historiography. Indigenous studies scholar Patrick Wolfe famously argued that "the primary motive for [settler colonial] elimination is not race (or religion, ethnicity, grade of civilization, etc.), but access to territory."[45] The frame of white settler supremacy implies otherwise, requiring that environmental historians contend with racial domination that accrues unearned privileges to whites through excess exploitation of natural resources, even as they address the environmental implications of the territorial dispossession inherent to settler colonialism. In other words, the primary motivation for settler colonialism might be territory, but that motivation has always been mobilized through race and racial power. As W. E. B. Du Bois noted in his 1920 essay "The Souls of White Folk," "whiteness is the ownership of the earth forever and ever, Amen!"; if white supremacy is the function of maintaining white ownership, settler colonialism is the function by which that land is first emptied and then worked.[46] White settler supremacy is about race *and* territory.

Expulsion, enslavement, exclusion, exploitation, and elimination in various environments are the underlying acts and tools of white settler supremacy. By breaking down this process into these five critical terms, we hope to enable scholars to consider how some or all of these have been at play in environmental history at any historical moment. All of these terms are distinct practices within white settler supremacy, but they should not be understood as operating in vacuums or existing in siloes; they, like racial hierarchies, are relational and function in conjunction with one another to produce larger structures of power that ultimately shape and inform our environmental histories.[47] The unique contribution that environmental historians can offer to the understanding of these processes is not just how they impact the nonhuman world (which is, of course, vital) but also how the nonhuman world in turn shapes how they function, how they interrelate, and perhaps most enticingly, how they fail and might best be resisted.

Of course, underpinning all these acts is racism, defined here as a system of power and deep-seated ideology that people marked as nonwhite are inferior to whites, making them vulnerable to cruelty and mistreatment.[48] People of color and Indigenous peoples are often relegated to positions in U.S. society that correlate with the nonhuman world, making them both subjects of and subject to the natural world: as people whose bodies are built for hard labor and often people who are seen as nothing more than animals.[49] Thus, racism is a central function of white settler supremacy, one that ultimately enables the acts of expulsion, enslavement, exclusion, exploitation, and elimination, all of which not only reinforce systems of power but also render marginalized bodies—human and nonhuman—more vulnerable to injury, disability, or death.

The environment has figured prominently in racial and settler politics and processes of expulsion. From the Latin root meaning "to drive out," expulsion has animated some of the earliest moments of territorial encroachment in North America. It can likewise be seen in the mid-twentieth-century removal and incarceration of Japanese and Japanese Americans during World War II, among other examples. The expulsion of marginalized peoples has supported white settler supremacist goals of land dispossession or racial and ethnic cleansing to "protect" the purity of the United States and its white settler "imagined community."[50] In some of the earliest instances of European contact, Europeans viewed much of the land they saw as empty—land up for grabs. Seeing no fences to mark territory or show what they thought of as good stewardship over nature, Europeans brought animals and built structures to claim the land as their own, which quickly complicated the human-nature dynamics in the region.[51] As settlers sought to enclose Native homelands, Indigenous peoples found themselves fenced out of lands they had been using for their own means, without restriction. Settlers' fences functioned most immediately for the containment of livestock, which complicated relations with Natives as these cattle, pigs, and other creatures trod and defecated over Indigenous-stewarded ecosystems.[52] As settlers pushed westward, they continued to displace Native peoples, although not without resistance from those they sought to expel. Native peoples often formed alliances with other Native groups or with Europeans, playing one European empire, vying for power and land, off another.[53]

Expulsion and dispossession continued well beyond the colonial era. Well into the twentieth century, white U.S. officials removed Indigenous peoples from their homes and forced their children into boarding schools or stole Native people away to more carceral institutions, particularly insane asylums and prisons.[54] Scholars have shown that these twentieth-century acts of expulsion continued to be tied, often explicitly, to settlers' desires for Native land—or to resources that could be extracted from beneath its surface.[55]

Expulsion has not been limited to the experiences of Native peoples. In 1942, in response to the bombing of Pearl Harbor and the onset of the U.S. entry into World War II, Franklin D. Roosevelt signed Executive Order 9066, which called for the removal of Japanese and Japanese Americans from their homes across the United States so that they could be placed in incarceration camps, most of which were located in the U.S. West on lands removed from Native peoples. The environment played a crucial role in this process of expulsion in at least three ways. First, the physical environments where government officials chose to place the camps were selected because they were deemed remote, inaccessible, and difficult to escape. People incarcerated described their confinement in ways that focused on natural conditions—wind, dust, blazing heat, frigid snowstorms—in shaping their experiences in the camps.[56]

Second, nature served as a powerful metaphor that justified both this racist expulsion of Japanese and Japanese American people away from their homes and the killing of the Japanese abroad in World War II's Pacific Front. As historian Edmund Russell has made clear, the racist vitriol of white settlers during the war relied on propaganda campaigns that drew comparisons between Japanese and Japanese American people and insects, which posed a threat and could thus be removed or terminated. Russell argues, "The science and technology of pest control sometimes became the science and technology of warfare."[57] New chemical warfare weapons of the time, he notes, involved chemicals also used across the American West to exterminate pests in American fields. In this case, relegating the Japanese abroad to nothing more than pests justified their killing; at home, they needed to be removed to a place of containment.

Finally, after fighting for years for their release, many Japanese and Japanese Americans returned home to find that many of them either had lost their property or felt that they needed to relocate because people in their neighborhood abhorred them. Families came home to hostile signs telling them to leave; others found property destroyed. Some estimates show that those incarcerated at the camps lost at least $400 million in property.

Although white Americans targeted Japanese and Japanese Americans at home and abroad, many of those incarcerated in the camps found refuge in nature. Historian Connie Chiang has argued that the very act of engaging with nature provided incarcerated Japanese and Japanese Americans with a sense of human dignity and autonomy, even as they found themselves confined by barbed wire, poorly protected against weather and extreme temperatures by government-built housing.[58] Although environmental conditions shaped the literal ground of their expulsion from their homes into dry and dusty locales, nature also provided creative opportunities for resistance. In the case of Japanese and Japanese American incarceration, Chiang has adeptly highlighted how human engagement with the natural world provided an outlet for dealing with the experience of being expelled from one's home.[59]

Despite moments of resistance, expulsion has figured prominently as a foundational tool of white settler supremacy. Seizing and exploiting territory and subjugating and excluding those who inhabited it have provided access to resources that have solidified the wealth, power, and privilege that whites have enjoyed for centuries. The environment has been a critical part of these stories.

ELIMINATION

Elimination is a central function of settler colonialism and, as such, applies most directly to the historical and current experiences of Indigenous nations; however, it is also crucial to our understandings of the range of non-Native (white and nonwhite) experiences of the environment.[60] Elimination, or the ongoing removal or attempted removal of Indigenous peoples of the North American continent, involves a desire for control over land and its resources. Settlers seek to own the land, to reap its bounty, to define its worth, and to decide which landscapes are protectable and which are pollutable. Attempted elimination of its original inhabitants is crucial to this process, as is "racial disappearance" and the protection of whiteness as a hermetically sealed category of human life.[61] This process was well underway as early as the sixteenth century in what is currently the United States, with European diseases spreading well in advance of their human corollaries with massive implications for Indigenous human populations and the environment.[62]

By the nineteenth century, settlers targeted Indigenous nations for more deliberate and focused forms of elimination.[63] California provides an apt example of this history; while California Native peoples experienced centuries of disease outbreaks, the most rapid (and rabid) elimination occurred after 1848, when mostly white U.S. settlers reduced the population by strategic and bloody genocide—from more than 150,000 in 1845 to fewer than 16,000 by 1900.[64] In the example of California, as elsewhere in U.S. history, the principal motive for elimination was land, and the primary form of white settler racialization of Native people was to animalize them—not only were the people of these nations compared, over and over again, to animals; they were described consistently as a *lower* form of animals according to everyone from Mark Twain to the environmentalist forebearer John Muir.[65]

In the United States as a whole, white settlers engaged in eliminatory violence against people, animals, and natural resources alike: massacres by settlers, for example, targeted women, children, and animals in a way that "was not merely incidental or spur of the moment but rather intrinsic to" the larger process of elimination.[66] The slaughter of bison herds in the 1850s and 1860s can be described as elimination by environmental means, as can the targeting of Diné (Navajo) crops in the attempt to force a removal in what the Diné called the "Long Walk" to Bosque Redondo in the 1860s.[67] Elimination "also unfolded across Indigenous marine spaces" when settlers assumed rights to a marine commons, eliminating Makah marine property.[68] These forms of settler violence deliberately attacked Indigenous peoples' nonhuman relations—the floral and faunal kin with which Native peoples lived in familial relations—as a means to the end.[69] Native peoples live in intimate connection to homelands, meaning that Native history, geography, politics, economics, culture, and linguistics are tied to stewardship and relationships with a particular landscape or waterscape, its ecosystem, and its unique set of resources. As a result, targeting those land bases and the resources within them—plants, soil, water, and animals—functions as an eliminatory form of settler violence.[70]

Elimination of Indigenous peoples and other targets of white settler violence results in "ownership" of territory for settlers in ways that sometimes dovetail with white ideas of environmental protection. For example, historian Mark David Spence explores how the creation of national parks involved direct dispossession of Native communities. Glacier National Park went from being part of the Blackfeet Reservation to a white American place through environmentalist politics. In these instances, Native elimination took the form of perhaps the most well-known project of white settler conservation—the creation of national parks, a project the United States touts as its "best idea."[71]

Elimination is most frequently understood as a project that targets Indigenous peoples, but history reveals the ways in which it reaches non-Native people of color. In this vein, scholars have examined the relationships between unhealthy environmental conditions and the eliminatory function of white settler racism. For example, if anti-Black racism means that Black life is a "lived impossibility" in the context of white settler supremacy, systematic environmental racism that shortens the life expectancy for people of color can be seen alongside various histories of state-sanctioned violence, enslavement, incarceration, and health care disparities as eliminatory for the purpose of paving the way for white settlement.[72] Prisons have also been seen by scholars as eliminatory. Kelly Lytle Hernández, for example, explores the history of incarceration as a settler means of racial domination and clearing access to territory and resources.[73]

Finally, and crucially, elimination, like settler colonialism, is both aspirational and ongoing. One argument against seeing elimination as the primary function of settler colonialism is that it erases the existence of contemporary Native people and their rich and diverse Native nations.[74] This argument assumes that settler colonialism, and its drive toward Indigenous elimination, is in the past rather than a clear and present danger to Indigenous peoples and other nonwhite people targeted by eliminatory logic at the heart of white settler supremacy at the moment and into its foreseeable future.

ENSLAVEMENT

In her book on the Atlantic slave trade, historian Stephanie Smallwood follows the capture and sale of roughly three hundred thousand people from the Gold Coast of Africa to the American Colonies from 1625 to 1725.[75] *Saltwater Slavery* recounts the soul-crushing journey across the middle passage, detailing the complete bewilderment and sense of loss and displacement that many Africans packed into slave ships felt. Jammed into dark spaces below deck, those stolen from their homes struggled to sustain their humanity. Environmental conditions exacerbated their experiences of abduction: unable to see the sky, they lost their sense of time. Cast into a vast ocean, they lost all sense of connection to their homelands, which had informed their very existence.[76] That spiritual loss rendered them what Smallwood refers to as "the living dead."[77]

Some people forced into these vessels also experienced physical death. The ways in which Europeans shoved Africans into crowded spaces created dangerous environments for any human to withstand for extended periods. Motion sickness combined with exposure to unfamiliar diseases and unsanitary living conditions created toxic environments where illness could spread rapidly. If they died onboard the ship, traders would cast them into the sea. If they survived, they went on to perform forced labor in the Americas, transforming the landscape into productive, crop-yielding fields that built an economic foundation for what would become the United States.

Enslavement has been a foundational tool of white settler supremacy, providing the labor that created U.S. (settler) wealth and institutionalizing anti-Black racism for the material and cultural benefit of whiteness. The environmental conditions of enslavement offer critical insights into the larger environmental implications of white settler supremacy and, in turn, how it is formed and how it has functioned in the United States. The history of the material conditions of slave ships provides a window for environmental historians to consider how various and perhaps less traditional environments intersect with racial slavery. Of course, Europeans leaned on enslavement to transform traditional environments, exploiting both people as commodities as well as "natural" environments for profit (as described in the section on exploitation). But that is not the only way to consider how the enslavement of human beings has been and remains deeply relevant to our nation's environmental past and present. Nature, climate, and animals, for example, were weaponized in the system of enslavement to strengthen systems of domination over enslaved Black laborers.[78] As such, the association between enslaved Black people and animals, coupled with climactic theories of racial difference (which falsely claimed Africans were physically better suited to labor in brutal weather and climate conditions than whites), underscored the role of the environment in enslavement.[79]

The environment here was not limited to terrestrial spaces. Africans and African Americans often labored near and along waterways where they would navigate the transportation of goods and sometimes themselves, leaning on skills inherited from their homelands on the African continent.[80] Chattel labor practices that marked enslaved Black people as somehow less than human functioned by considering Africans closer to animals and nature as well as by legally classifying Black people as possessions—property and, in the eyes of the law, not fully human at all. On the other hand, the skills carried by enslaved people from Africa, particularly their aquatic knowledge, sometimes provided great refuge and moments of privacy in a system of profound exploitation.[81]

Although this system of *chattel* enslavement was almost exclusively endured by enslaved Black people—and, in fact, Blackness eventually became legally codified as a precondition of chattel enslavement—Africans and African Americans have not been the only historically marginalized community to have endured unfree labor conditions that can be described as enslavement. Scholars have argued that indentured servitude, debt peonage, and other forms of unfree labor constitute pre- and postabolition forms of slavery because, in many instances, those who toiled in toxic, unhealthy environments for long hours with little sleep, crowded living conditions, and subpar nutrition were more often coerced, forced, or fleeing something else that pushed them into those conditions. Historian Christina Snyder argues that American slavery has had "a much longer scale and broader scope" than many think and, even postemancipation, the institution of slavery has had "many afterlives."[82]

Indigenous people, for example, have been subject to enslavement in a wide range of U.S. geographies and historical contexts, from the earliest colonial periods to the development of strong agricultural economies in post–Treaty of Guadalupe Hidalgo California.[83] In a wide range of time periods and geographies, the entrapment of Indigenous laborers created de facto and de jure systems of enslavement, coercing people into bondage that was, at times, "ambivalently codified" but clearly unfree.[84]

Asian immigrant laborers and Asian American citizens have likewise experienced coercive labor conditions that rise to the level of enslavement at key points in U.S. history. Lucie Cheng Hirata traces how Chinese women and girls were systematically kidnapped, transported to the United States, and held in bondage as sex workers in nineteenth-century California for laborers in cities and in mining camps, white and Chinese alike. Methods of control of these women included imprisonment and confinement, "whipping, torture by fire, banishment to brothels in the mining districts," and the ever-present threat of death.[85] This systematic enslavement of Chinese women and girls, a product of the combination of "white racism and Chinese patriarchy," served as a sexual resource for Chinese and white laborers and an economic resource for the larger California economy. In California and elsewhere throughout the West, white settlers treated Chinese laborers as virtual slaves—a system of bondage and forced labor that characterized mines and railroad construction.[86] As historian Moon-Ho Jung has demonstrated, this system of virtual slavery extended beyond just mines and railroads and persisted past the nineteenth century, a time in which it is generally considered to have ended.[87]

Mexican and other Latin American immigrants have also endured inhumane working conditions that have made them ill or disabled, in systems of labor that approximate deep systems of coercion.[88] During the Bracero Program, a guest worker program between Mexico and the United States (1942–64), railroad companies and agribusinesses employed millions of men whom they saw and treated as disposable. As such, when a worker became unable to perform because of injury or illness, the United States would simply deport them and replace them with others, treating them as nothing more than material commodities. These laborers, we acknowledge, did enter that labor system willingly and for wages but argue that the system was designed to employ some of Mexico's most impoverished citizens. As a result, desperation to join the program was rampant. Men starved to death, waiting in line penniless just for a chance to enlist, only to face harsh working environs once they reached U.S. soil.[89]

Ultimately, the enduring extent of unfree or coerced labor in the United States, among Africans and African Americans in addition to other nonwhite and Indigenous populations, indicates that racial enslavement has not been geographically limited to the slave states of the United States *or* temporally limited to the period before emancipation.[90] Furthermore, the legacy of the Thirteenth Amendment to the Constitution, which declared slavery unconstitutional "except as a punishment for crime whereof the party shall have been duly convicted," calls into question the success of abolition and draws a line from the history of slavery to the contemporary problem of mass incarceration of disproportionately Black and Brown people. That link offers important insights into connecting the environments of slavery's fields to those of prisons and jails, including the environmental conditions and health of enslaved and incarcerated bodies.[91] Certainly, the environmental implications of these contiguous histories—of slave ships and plantations, sharecroppers' fields and prisons—resonate today and offer powerful new ways of understanding the *nature* of enslavement and its "many afterlives."

EXCLUSION

Exclusion—or the act of denying access to a place or privilege—in the United States has always been deeply intertwined with ideas about nature. In various moments in U.S. history and at various scales, nonwhite people have been perceived as "naturally different" and have thus been excluded from citizenship, from the rights associated with being fully human, or from the territory of the United States altogether. At the same time that white settlers moved to North America and associated Native peoples with nature rather than civilization, and while white Southern planters used climatic arguments that Black peoples' bodies were better suited to work in particular climates to justify racial slavery, Europeans and Americans alike began using science to shore up their belief that racial difference was biological.[92] In short, medical doctors and scientists considered racial difference "natural." Although ideas about biological racial difference were not entirely solidified until the late eighteenth and early nineteenth centuries, scientists, doctors, and others understood nature to be fundamental to human ranking, and many believed that they could prove it.[93] This process of associating people of color and Indigenous peoples with nature and animals has been essential to their systematic exclusion from the places and privileges reserved for whiteness and white people.

By the early nineteenth century, after centuries of racialized exclusion of Indigenous peoples and the enslavement of Africans, a physician named Samuel Morton tried to demonstrate how marginalized peoples were inherently inferior—Morton was one example of many practitioners across the world who set out to prove such theories through "scientific means." From the early 1820s until his death in 1851, Morton, a doctor with two medical degrees, collected more than one thousand human skulls, which he claimed could demonstrate a biological (natural) basis for racial difference and white privilege. He authored influential texts in which he used skull size to argue that human craniums could provide seemingly empirical evidence about the worth and mental capacity of different races of human beings. His findings placed whites at the top of five racial categories and Natives and Black people at the bottom of his biological racial hierarchy.[94] Morton, who had one of the largest collections of human skulls in the world and whose theories inspired generations of eugenicist thinkers, found a way to rationalize racial difference by turning to "nature." His findings, which professed to prove that Natives and Africans were "naturally" inferior, provided a seemingly scientific rationale for the continuation of racial exclusion in the United States.[95]

By the late nineteenth century, scientific racism had strong roots in American society.[96] With the rise of germ theory in the 1880s, nature and biology gave new power to national and local politicians hoping to reshape and reform American society—to improve it. Ideas about racial inferiority, disease, and infection provided additional means to target nonwhite racial and ethnic groups as threats to the (white) American populace. In the case of the Chinese, for instance, "health experts played an important role in the eventual ban on Chinese immigration" because they pointed to health risks that the Chinese were thought to pose to the (white) American populace in urban centers like Los Angeles.[97] In the 1870s San Francisco and Los Angeles drafted stipulations referred to as the "Cubic Air Acts" to target Chinese neighborhoods where living quarters were tight and waste disposal was complex. The laws required new means for sewage disposal because health officials claimed that air contaminated with human waste was poisonous.[98] As historian Natalia Molina pointedly explains, "these new theories and the laws that they helped to generate should have applied to everyone. Officials targeted only the Chinese."[99]

As concern about Chinese health ballooned into panic about disease spreading to white Americans, Congress acted to stem the influx of Chinese laborers, passing the first comprehensive immigration law in the nation's history—the 1882 Chinese Exclusion Act.[100] "Whereas in the opinion of the Government of the United States," the act opened, "the coming of Chinese laborers to this country endangers the good order of certain localities within the territory thereof." In the following decades, immigration law became increasingly stringent; by 1917, a series of immigration laws created an Asiatic "barred zone," denying entry to the United States to any person from Japan, much of eastern Asia, and the Pacific Islands. It was not only the first series of immigration laws but also the first time any group of people was barred from entering U.S. territory. The basis for exclusion was largely racial, although the laws also barred people with disabilities, queer people (sexual deviates), and any person that an immigration official thought might become a public charge (mostly women).[101] In short, the laws ensured that entry to U.S. territory was contingent on perceived difference, rooted in notions of race, nature, and biology. To keep "good order"—or rather, to protect whiteness—Congress set a precedent for increasingly rigid immigration laws that would limit or deny access to the United States altogether for many foreigners whose "endanger[ments]" to the nation were rooted in ideas about the nature of their bodies. By 1920, a nation that claimed it had been made by immigrants solidified an anti-immigrant and exclusionary foundation for its future.

Ideas about nature informed ideas about race, which justified the exclusion of people of color from the privileges of whiteness.[102] Views about racial inferiority, masked in the pretense of scientific objectivity, not only kept entire groups of people from entering U.S. territory but also controlled social mobility. As the twentieth century progressed, policies large and small—from those governing single farms or ranches to municipal, state, and national levels—kept African Americans from buying homes in white neighborhoods or placed migrant workers in subpar living conditions.[103] This poor treatment placed impoverished racialized groups in close living quarters or unsanitary places, which actually produced the very conditions that the Chinese had been targeted for in the 1870s.[104] In other words, ideas about the nature of racial difference ultimately produced conditions that fueled a cycle of associations between race, social status, and health. Perceived "natural" or biological difference justified policies that relegated particular bodies to unsanitary environments, which then produced difference by rendering those bodies unhealthy. And if those bodies posed a threat, they could be targeted for exclusion not only from prosperity but from the nation itself.[105]

In 1916, a typhus outbreak in South Texas caused U.S. Public Health Service (USPHS) officials to target and potentially bar any Mexican person crossing into the United States. Because health officials believed that Mexicans were unclean and diseased, they forced any Mexican person who crossed into the United States to undergo a health inspection where public health inspectors not only examined Mexican migrants but also stripped and deloused them with kerosene and vinegar.[106] White Americans who had gone into Mexico did not have to withstand the same treatment because, as one USPHS official noted, they would surely return home and bathe. This treatment lasted for decades, long after the threat of typhus subsided. From 1942 to 1964, Mexican migrants entering the United States as a part of the aforementioned Bracero Program endured the same treatment but with new technologies—health inspectors sprayed them with DDT instead of kerosene. By the end of that program, long-standing ideas about Mexican immigrants as a threat led to the passing of yet another exclusionary immigration law that, for the first time ever, placed a cap on the number of people from Latin America who could enter the country. In the decades that followed, immigrants continued to cross the border in large numbers, leading to a massive militarization of the U.S.-Mexico border. Since then, growing border fences have funneled immigrants to dangerous landscapes where they risk death, and an increasing number of border patrol agents have tried to apprehend and then cage unsanctioned migrants. Today, the U.S.-Mexico border is a patchwork of built and natural environments meant to deter or halt the migration of Latin Americans, grounded in the rationale that these immigrants pose a biological threat—infectious, racial, or reproductive—to the United States. Here, exclusion and environment are inextricably bound.

EXPLOITATION

In his 1690 *Second Treatise of Civil Government*, philosopher John Locke proposed a formula for the process of privatizing property. Locke believed that property could be privatized from its God-given state of being commonly held among all men through *labor*: according to Locke, mixing labor with the land made it private property. That labor, however, could function through proxy. Locke wrote that "the grass my horse has bit; the turfs my servant has cut; and the ore I have digged in any place . . . become my property."[107] Even though Thomas Jefferson, in the Declaration of Independence, took some poetic license with Locke's summary of the three crucial rights that accrue to citizens of liberal democracies—Locke's *life, liberty, and property* became Jefferson's *life, liberty, and pursuit of happiness*—the Lockean formula of privatizing land through labor became an undeniably central feature of white settler supremacy in the United States. The push of settlers into recently dispossessed Native land west of the Mississippi River, for example, was orchestrated through the Homestead Acts (a series of land laws passed from 1862 to 1916 and beyond). The Acts required that settlers make "improvements" on the land in order to withdraw it from the public domain—effectively mixing their labor, or their proxies' labor, with the land to privatize it. The General Mining Act (1872) similarly required only that a mining claim be worked in order for it to be removed from the public domain.

The labor of privatizing property has functioned in the United States in inherently exploitative ways. In the example Locke provides, the wealth produced by the proxy labor of horse and servant accrue to the landlord, and their labor is exploited to his benefit. This is key to how labor—of humans and nonhumans alike—developed in the United States as a primarily exploitative system. The privatization of property (and the accruement of wealth to the owners of that private property) has fundamentally shaped U.S. history and has consistently entailed the exploitation of natural resources and land and the exploitation of labor to work that land.

The relationships between the exploitation of labor, race, and environment in U.S. history can be understood in three moves: First, Karl Marx famously theorized that exploited workers in capitalism are alienated from the products of their labor. Second, critical race theorists have built on this to show how in what they call "racial capitalism," race becomes one of the primary ways in which labor is exploited. Labor is undervalued because racialized *laborers* are undervalued.[108] Moreover, when employers have the option of employing undercompensated laborers of color (often migrants or other workers of color excluded from the privileges of citizenship and/or whiteness) or entirely uncompensated enslaved workers, this keeps wages low for everyone, white workers included.[109] In this way, race is central to capitalist exploitation.[110] Third, studies of environmental racism show how the exploitation of racialized environments fuels industrial capitalism.[111] For example, in her formulation of *wastelanding*, historian Traci Brynne Voyles traces how Navajo workers in Navajo Country mined uranium for low wages for the benefit of the U.S. energy program. That work ultimately destroyed both the workers' bodies and the region, resulting in a sea of abandoned mines. Here, Voyles contends that systems of exploitation that drain land and marginalized people's bodies of their resources by making them "produce and produce excessively" involved a process of racializing an entire landscape.

Exploited laborers in industrial and agricultural schemes have participated in refashioning entire landscapes and ecosystems, fundamentally reconfiguring the natural world to the benefit of those with wealth and to the benefit of the larger system as a whole. While settlers and industrialists exploited the West in often inherently unsustainable ways—digging and blasting ore from mine sites, redirecting rivers, draining wetlands and underground aquifers, displacing indigenous plants and animals with crops and livestock, and so on—the laborers engaged in the real work of this exploitation were often nonwhite. For example, in the early twentieth century, large-scale agriculture in the Southwest exploited the labor of undercompensated migrant workers whose exploitation rendered them, as Mae Ngai puts it, "impossible subjects," necessary for the wealth they produced but excluded from the privileges of citizenship.[112] In fact, their noncitizen status functioned as a primary mechanism for their exploitation. Their (exploited) labor enabled the exploitation of environmental resources, from water to animal and plant habitats to soil quality and air quality.[113]

At the same time, labor in cities, in factories, or in rural or so-called wilderness areas has shaped the ways in which laborers experience their exploitation—sometimes to their own detriment, and that of their bodily health, and sometimes to their benefit as they develop their own relationships to the natural world.[114] Historian Mary E. Mendoza has tracked the ways in which Bracero Program laborers often experienced the natural environment as part of their experiences of exploitation; their bodies suffered debilitating consequences of their labor in the form of injury, sickness, and even death.[115] Environmental histories of labor in factories reveal related experiences of bodily harm as inherent and often unavoidable consequences of exploitation; particularly in the postwar period, as industrialism has grown increasingly reliant on chemicals, the exploitation of labor in factories is increasingly tied in ecological ways to the exploitation of the nonhuman world. Factory laborers' bodies and the larger environment alike are exploited as repositories—dumping grounds—for chemical pollution.[116] As Richard White points out, however, in the midst of exploitative working conditions or in the midst of participating in the exploitation of the natural world (or both), laborers have also come to appreciate the environment through their work, understanding it in new ways through their lived experience of cutting, harvesting, digging, and planting.[117]

EXTRICATION

Before we conclude, we want to offer a sixth *E* term for environmental historians to use in wrestling with race and nature: extrication—to get out of what is hindering you. Extrication, we argue, is always present, and it constantly pushes against the aforementioned tools of white settler supremacy, which, admittedly, emphasize the ways in which people of color face systems of domination and oppression. But it is clear and extremely important to recognize that domination and oppression are not the whole story. Extrication points us to the ways in which communities of color have consistently engaged with nature to elide the structural barriers of white settler supremacy that seek to control and govern their relationships to nature and to other humans. Extrication is the story of resistance in the face of constant systemic and structural challenges.

Some scholars have argued that critical scholarship that uses the lens of settler colonialism renders Indigenous peoples and nature as passive, but that is not true of settler colonialism, nor is it true of scholarship that uses the lens of white settler supremacy. That scholarship does not cast people of color as passive either. None of these groups have ever simply sat down and taken what has come at them. They have always fought for their rights and their resources. Extrication provides a path toward acknowledging both that white settler supremacy is not some all-encompassing, unidirectional process that has resulted in the total domination of marginalized communities and that those peoples have had their own ways of engaging with nature.

Looking for moments of extrication—when those fighting white settler supremacy resist it or when they escape it altogether—then ensures that when we write environmental histories of race, we tell the whole story and acknowledge ways of being in nature that do not center on whiteness. This could mean considering the ways that nature provides refuge for people of all kinds. It could mean examining diverse environmental relationships—or diverse environmentalisms. It could mean taking seriously Indigenous relations with the nonhuman world. It could mean recognizing that there is more than one way to live sustainably and that Indigenous people and people of color in the United States and around the world have been doing it in myriad ways for decades, if not centuries—not by putting their plastics in blue bins or buying electric cars but by using and reusing what is around them, being resourceful, and taking only what they need. It could mean realizing that some environmentalists don't hike, but they do lay brick or harvest food all day and just want to sit inside after work. These approaches would result in histories that shift our center of gravity, insisting that environmental historians pivot from thinking about white relationships with nature to respecting and learning from other ways of experiencing and valuing the earth.[118]

Recognizing moments of extrication speaks to the consistency with which people of color have engaged with nature outside of the hindrances of white settler supremacy, cultivating different relationships with the environment that produce—and emerge from—nonwhite worldviews, cultures, and politics. Here we offer a suggestion for environmental history as the field moves forward: being open to new possibilities and perspectives will only enliven our field. Placing nonwhite relationships to the natural world at the center of our analyses will not just diversify our studies and "close the unfortunate distance separating environmental history from ethnic history"—it promises, instead, to produce new understandings that give us powerful new insights into our collective past.[119]

Notes

The author would like to thank Traci Brynne Voyles for her generous contributions that helped shape this essay.

1. Susan Kaplan, "Scientists Rush to Save 1,000 Year Old Trees on the Brink of Death," *Washington Post*, July 15, 2022.
2. We draw our understanding of "project" in this context from Omi and Winant, whose classic work on racial formation highlighted the role of "racial projects," which "connect what race means in a particular discursive practice and the ways in which both social structures and everyday experiences are racially organized." Omi and Winant, *Racial Formation in the United States*, 56.
3. Some, like Patricia Limerick, Carolyn Merchant, and Dolores Greenberg, take a dim view of the field's work on race and argue that environmental historians have been preoccupied with white individuals and communities, to the exclusion of people of color and Indigenous nations. Limerick, "Disorientation"; Merchant, "Shades of Darkness"; Greenberg, "Reconstructing Race." William Cronon has called race "one of the least studied aspects of environmental history," and Martin Melosi made this a focus of his 1995 presidential address to the ASEH (Cronon, "Kennecott Journey"; Melosi, "Equity, Eco-racism and Environmental History"). Others, like Kathleen Brosnan, make the point that when environmental historians engage with nonwhite communities, they concentrate largely on environmental justice issues, focusing on white-Brown/Black/Native inequities and ignoring the many diverse relationships that various populations have with the natural world. See Brosnan, "Lifting Fog." Still others take the view that in recent decades, quite an impressive number of studies have addressed, if not rectified, this problem, particularly with regard to Native American environmental history. Sackman, introduction to *Companion to American Environmental History*, xv; Fisher, "Race and US Environmental History," 99–115; Sutter, "What Can US Environmental Historians Learn," 109–29. Thus while the former opinion is popular, it is not uncontroversial.
4. Chiang, "Imprisoned Nature"; Todd, "Fish, Kin and Hope"; Yazzie and Baldy, "Introduction."
5. Tuck and Yang, "Decolonization," Arvin, Tuck, and Morrill, "Decolonizing Feminism"; Hernández, *City of Inmates*; King, *Black Shoals*; Bruyneel, *Settler Memory*; Roberts, *I've Been Here All the While*, 3.

6. Implicit in our framing of white settler supremacy is the recognition that not all settlers are white and not all of them benefit from white supremacy. We find these works particularly helpful in problematizing the category of "settler": Byrd, *Transit of Empire*; Roberts, *I've Been Here All the While*; King, *Black Shoals*; and Gómez, *Manifest Destinies*.

7. Andrew Isenberg and Lawrence H. Kessler assert that "because environments are inherently dynamic and unpredictable, the perspective of environmental history complicates settler colonialism, restoring many of the contingencies and complexities that the metanarrative elides." Isenberg and Kessler, "Settler Colonialism," 57–66.

8. See especially Whyte, "Settler Colonialism"; Liboiron, *Pollution Is Colonialism*; Estes, *Our History Is the Future*.

9. William Cronon discusses the development of this emerging capitalist society in *Changes in the Land*.

10. For more on the ways in which settling the West has been costly for one group while it has benefited another, see Limerick, *Legacy of Conquest*. For more on the dangers of homogenizing white settlers, see Limerick, "Comments," 90–96. Margaret Jacobs points to the crucial role of land and resources in settler colonialism in her differentiation between it and *extractive* colonialism: "In contrast to . . . 'extractive colonies,' which have focused on mobilizing a native labor force to enable colonizers to extract natural resources or to farm cash crops for export, settler colonies sought to appropriate land through a dual process of dispossessing indigenous people while replacing them with a settler population and importing labor." Jacobs, "Parallel or Intersecting Tracks?," 156.

11. Nash, *Wilderness and the American Mind*, 51.

12. Quoted in Nash, *Wilderness and the American Mind*, 52

13. Byrd, "History of the Dividing Line," 14.

14. Thoreau, *Walden*; Theodore Roosevelt, "The Strenuous Life," speech before the Hamilton Club (Chicago, April 10, 1899); Muir, *Our National Parks* and *Mountains of California*; Abbey, *Journey Home* and *Desert Solitaire*.

15. Limerick, "Disorientation," 1029.

16. Limerick, "Disorientation," 1029.

17. Sutter, "What Can US Environmental Historians Learn," 114.

18. Here, we mean wilderness as not an objective set of "natural" material conditions—woods and mountains, untouched landscapes, and so on—but, following Cronon, "quite profoundly a human creation—indeed, the creation of very particular human cultures at very particular moments in human history." Cronon, "Trouble," 7.

19. We draw here from comments offered by an anonymous reviewer of an early draft of this chapter as well as from comments offered in Morse and Sturgeon, *Environmentalism in Popular Culture*; and Dunaway, *Seeing Green*.

20. Finney, *Black Faces, White Spaces*.

21. Bullard, *Dumping in Dixie*; Pellow and Park, *Silicon Valley of Dreams*; Pellow, *Garbage Wars*; Pellow and Brulle, *Power, Justice, and the Environment*; Washington, *Packing Them In*; Sze, *Noxious New York*; Voyles, *Wastelanding*; Zimring, *Clean and White*; Gilio-Whitaker, *As Long as Grass Grows*.

22. Krech III, *Ecological Indian*, 20–21. For an excellent critique of this, see Ray, *Ecological Other*; Harkin and Lewis, *Native Americans and the Environment* (see in particular the chapter by Darren J. Ranko, 32–51).

23. Johnston, "Beyond 'The West,'" 239.

24. Turner, *Significance of the Frontier*.

25. Hixson, *American Settler Colonialism*, 14–15, 16. Borderlands studies has sought to interrupt this Turnerian inclination in both Western history and environmental history by bringing in multiple peoples and multidirectional power structures—more work in this vein can only benefit the field as a whole, although some argue that borderlands studies has thus far insufficiently accounted for larger power structures such as settler colonialism. As Sutter helpfully points out, U.S. environmental historians would do well to follow the lead of non-U.S. environmental historians—the primary difference between these fields lies in non-U.S. environmental historians' "focus on colonialism and imperialism as environmental processes," which is either "absent" or "understated" among U.S.-based scholars. Sutter, "Reflections," 110. See also Mendoza's chapter in this volume.

26. Greenberg, "Reconstructing Race," 227.

27. This movement inspired the coining of the term *environmental racism* and the landmark study *Toxic Wastes and Race*, which showed a definitive correlation between toxic and hazardous waste siting and race over other socioeconomic indicators. Sandler and Pezzullo, eds. *Environmental Justice and Environmentalism*, 5.

28. They also contradict the claims of environmental justice leaders themselves, who "openly disclaimed connection to the traditional, or mainstream, American environmental movement" (Glave and Stoll, *To Love the Wind*, 123). Scholars have explored how environmentalisms themselves are as diverse as the people who espouse them; Barbara Deutsche Lynch, for example, shows how Latino environmentalisms eschew "the frontier, wild rivers, and forests" of white environmental ideals; "the ideal or utopian natural landscapes of Latino writers," in contrast, "are peopled and productive." Lynch, "Garden and the Sea," 111.

29. Voyles, *Wastelanding*, 7; Zoltan Grossman, quoted by Robin Lanette Turner and Diana Pei Wu, "Environmental Justice and Environmental Racism: An Annotated Bibliography with General Overview, Focusing on the US Literature, 1996–2002," Institute of International Studies, University of California, Berkeley, August 2002, 2.

30. Chiang, "Imprisoned Nature," 239.

31. Bryant and Mohai argue that the environmental justice movement is a resurgence of the civil rights movement.

32. See, for one prime example, the 17 Principles of Environmental Justice, produced at the Proceedings to the First National People of Color Environmental Leadership Summit in 1991 (found at https://www.ejnet.org/ej/principles.pdf). For another, consult the 1990 "SWOP letters" (nicknamed for the main organization that authored them, the Southwest Organizing Project) sent by environmental justice activists to the leadership of the Audubon Society, Sierra Club, Natural Resources Defense Council (NRDC), and Friends of the Earth. Both documents speak to the broad and nuanced critiques that the environmental justice movement brought to mainstream environmentalism as well as the fruitful ways these activists framed and understood environmental politics. More details about these documents can be found in Jedediah Purdy, "Environmentalism's Racist History," *New Yorker*, August 13, 2015, http://www.newyorker.com/news/news-desk/environmentalisms-racist-history; Marty Durlin, "The Shot Heard Round the West," *High Country News*, February 1, 2010, https://www.hcn.org/issues/42.2/the-shot-heard-round-the-west; and Sandler and Pezzullo, *Environmental Justice and Environmentalism*, 3–4.

33. Scott, *Gender and the Politics of History*.

34. Emphasis added. Sutter, "Reflections," 111–12.

35. Mendoza, "La Tierra Pica," 474.

36. Stroud, "From Six Feet Under," 618–27.

37. For an extended discussion of what is and is not environmental history and its intersections with material history, see also LeCain, *Matter of History*.

38. Tuck and Yang, "Decolonization," 6.

39. Isenberg and Kessler, "Settler Colonialism"; McNeill, "State of the Field"; Limerick, "Comments."

40. Whiteness is a social construct, which changes over time, place, and culture. It is precisely the instability of whiteness as a category rather than an essential or stable identity based in phenotype that lends it its exclusionary power. Jacobson, *Whiteness*.

41. Glen Coulthard calls this an "inherited background field within which market, racist, patriarchal, and state relations *converge* to facilitate certain power effects." Coulthard, *Red Skin, White Masks*, 14.

42. Tuck and Yang, "Decolonization," 6.

43. Hernández, *City of Inmates*, 7–8.
44. This is a manifestation of what Black Marxist Cedric Robinson called racial capitalism. Robinson, *Black Marxism*; Melamed, "Racial Capitalism"; Koshy et al., *Colonial Racial Capitalism*.
45. Wolfe, "Settler Colonialism." For more on this debate, see Day, "Being or Nothingness," 107–8.
46. Du Bois, "Souls of White Folk," 30. Kelly Lytle Hernández concurs, arguing that the idealized settler community relies on extinguishing Native sovereignty to take the land and the exploitation of "coerced, unfree, and racialized labor to build and sustain that community." Hernández, *City of Inmates*, 8.
47. For more on race as relational, see Molina, *How Race Is Made*, 6.
48. Gilmore, *Golden Gulag*, 27.
49. On May 16, 2018, U.S. president Donald Trump described immigrants coming into the country by saying, "These aren't people; these are animals," which shows the ways in which pervasive dehumanization of marginalized communities persists today. See "Trump Compares MS-13 Gang Members to 'Animals,'" *Washington Post*, May 16, 2018, https://www.washingtonpost.com/video/politics/trump-compares-illegal-immigrants-to-animals/2018/05/16/3442ddf2-5948-11e8-9889-07bcc1327f4b_video.html?utm_term=.6e28428ae560.
50. "Imagined community" is a term used by political scientist Benedict Anderson to describe the ideological work of nationalism and the groups of people who are generally considered as constituting a nation's body politic; the work of historian Matthew Frye Jacobson (and others) has shown how the whiteness of the U.S. "imagined community" was, in Jacobson's terms, overdetermined. B. Anderson, *Imagined Communities*; Jacobson, *Whiteness*, 23.
51. Cronon, *Changes in the Land*; Brooks, *Our Beloved Kin*; Seed, *Ceremonies of Possession*.
52. For examples of the tensions created by settlers' livestock, see Brooks, *Our Beloved Kin*. According to historian Virginia DeJohn Anderson, settlers' "livestock caused major problems with subsistence practices, land use, property rights, and ultimately, political authority." V. Anderson, *Creatures of Empire*.
53. White, *Middle Ground*; Taylor, *Divided Ground*; DuVal, *Native Ground*.
54. Haig-Brown, *Resistance and Renewal*; Lomawaima, *They Called It Prairie Light*; Burch, *Committed*.
55. Gilio-Whitaker, *As Long as Grass Grows*, 60–72.
56. Houston and Houston, *Farewell to Manzanar*.
57. Russell, "'Speaking of Annihilation,'" 1505–29.
58. Chiang, *Nature behind Barbed Wire*.
59. Chiang, "Imprisoned Nature."

60. Veracini, *Settler Colonialism*; Wolfe, "Settler Colonialism"; Tuck and Yang, "Decolonization." Elimination has also been among the most hotly contested contributions of settler-colonial studies, as non-Native U.S. historians have been reluctant to recognize the relationship between settlers and Natives in the United States as explicitly eliminatory or rising to the threshold of genocide. Margaret Jacobs points out that the reluctance to consider settler colonialism as eliminatory and/or genocidal runs counter to current trends in U.S. Western history that seek to understand Natives as actors with considerable agency— not as passive victims (Jacobs, "Parallel or Intersecting Tracks?," 158). Limerick seconds these concerns (Limerick, "Comments").

61. Voyles, *Wastelanding*; Hernández, *City of Inmates*.

62. Crosby, "Virgin Soil Epidemics," 289; Kelton, *Cherokee Medicine*; Trafzer, *Fighting Invisible Enemies*. This is not to say that disease was not deployed as a weapon of settler elimination projects. A range of historians have debated whether smallpox epidemics were the result of biological nature, absent human agency, or settler malice. The answer is probably both, but the archive provides evidence to support the latter in ways that are crucial to understand—and often not taken into account. Kelton, *Cherokee Medicine*; Trafzer, *Fighting Invisible Enemies*.

63. Ostler, *Surviving Genocide*. See in particular part 1: "Disease, War, and Dispossession."

64. Norton, *When Our Worlds Cried*; Heizer, *Destruction of California Indians*; Risling Baldy, *We Are Dancing*; Lindsay, *Murder State*; Madley, *American Genocide*.

65. Twain, *Roughing It*; Fleck, "John Muir's Evolving Attitudes."

66. Hixson, *American Settler Colonialism*, 20; Sleeper-Smith, *Indigenous Prosperity and American Conquest*.

67. Isenberg, *Destruction of the Bison*; Weisiger, *Dreaming of Sheep*.

68. Reid, "From 'Fishing Together,'" 49.

69. Whyte, "Settler Colonialism, Ecology, and Environmental Injustice"; Todd, "Fish, Kin and Hope"; Gilio-Whitaker, *As Long as Grass Grows*.

70. Reid points out, "Genocidal at times, settler violence against Indigenous peoples sought to exterminate Natives bodily, while assimilation policies such as boarding schools, child removal, allotment, missionary efforts, blood quantum definitions, and destruction of resources sought to eradicate Indigenous identities, cultures, and autonomy." Reid, "From 'Fishing Together,'" 48.

71. Spence, *Dispossessing the Wilderness*.

72. Dillon and Sze, "Police Power and Particulate Matters." Pellow, "Toward a Critical Environmental Justice Studies." We are drawing directly, here, from Ruth Wilson Gilmore's definition of racism. Gilmore, "Fatal Couplings."

73. Hernández, *City of Inmates*.

74. Limerick, "Comments."

75. Smallwood, *Saltwater Slavery*, 3.

76. Haymes, "Africana Studies Critique," 34–49.

77. Smallwood, *Saltwater Slavery*, 121.

78. Andrews, "Beasts of the Southern Wild"; Parry and Yingling, "Slave Hounds and Abolition."

79. See Katherine Johnston's chapter in this volume.

80. Dawson, *Undercurrents of Power*.

81. Dawson, *Undercurrents of Power*.

82. Christina Snyder's forthcoming book, a project for which she won a Guggenheim Award, makes this argument. The project is called *American Abolitions: The Slow Death and Many Afterlives of Slavery*. Information and quotes about the project can be found here: https://www.psu.edu/news/liberal-arts/story/history-faculty-member-christina-snyder-named-guggenheim-fellow.

83. Gallay, *Indian Slavery in Colonial America*; Snyder, *Slavery in Indian Country*; Madley, "'Unholy Traffic.'"

84. Brooks, *Captives and Cousins*; Barr, "From Captives to Slaves"; Blackhawk, *Violence over the Land*; Madley, "'Unholy Traffic'"; Reséndez, *Other Slavery*; Newell, *Brethren by Nature*.

85. Hirata, "Free, Indentured, Enslaved." See also Shah, *Contagious Divides*, 79; Yung, *Unbound Feet*, 35.

86. Jung, *Coolies and Cane*; White, *Railroaded*.

87. Jung, *Coolies and Cane*.

88. Mendoza, "La Tierra Pica."

89. Mendoza, "La Tierra Pica."

90. As Saidiya Hartman puts it, "racial slavery was transformed rather than annulled." Hartman, *Scenes of Subjection*, 10.

91. See Pellow's chapter in this volume. Hall, *Prison in the Woods*; Chiang, *Nature behind Barbed Wire*; Voyles, *Settler Sea*.

92. Gossett, *Race*; Bancel, David, and Thomas, *Invention of Race*.

93. As historian Christina Snyder points out, for example, biological racism became more prominent in the 1820s than climactic/environmental theories of race, in part due to being elevated by President Andrew Jackson and his contemporaries to serve their political purposes in pursuit of a policy of "Indian removal." Christina Snyder, *Great Crossings*.

94. He broke these categories down further to include Jews and Mongols, but we have opted to summarize this for brevity.

95. Gossett, *Race*, 58–63.

96. Kline, *Building a Better Race*; Graves, *Emperor's New Clothes*.

97. Molina, *Fit to Be Citizens?*, 26–27.
98. Zimring, *Clean and White*.
99. Molina, *Fit to Be Citizens?*, 27.
100. Historian Beth Lew-Williams points out that exclusion was aspirational at best and functioned more as a form of restriction in lived reality. Lew-Williams, *Chinese Must Go*.
101. Scholars in a range of disciplines have demonstrated the complexity of these processes, and particular intersections with the exclusion of people with disabilities, queer people, and women/public charges. All of these intersectional exclusions, however, intersected with ideas about racial inferiority. Luibhéid, *Entry Denied*; Park, *Entitled to Nothing*; Baynton, *Defectives in the Land*; Dolmage, *Disabled upon Arrival*.
102. Lipsitz, *Possessive Investment in Whiteness*.
103. Mckiernan-González, *Fevered Measures*; Sugrue, *Origins of the Urban Crisis*.
104. Zimring, *Clean and White*.
105. Mendoza, "Treacherous Terrain."
106. Stern, "Buildings, Boundaries, and Blood"; Molina, *Fit to Be Citizens?*; Mckiernan-González, *Fevered Measures*; Mendoza, "Unnatural Border."
107. Locke, "Chapter V: Of Property," *Second Treatise of Civil Government*.
108. Melamed, "Racial Capitalism."
109. Roediger, *Wages of Whiteness*.
110. Cedric Robinson writes, "There has never been a moment in modern European history (if before) that migratory and/or immigrant labor was not a significant aspect of European economies." *Black Marxism*, 23.
111. Voyles, *Wastelanding*; Tuck and Yang, "Decolonization."
112. Ngai, *Impossible Subjects*.
113. Pulido, *Environmentalism and Economic Justice*; Nash, *Inescapable Ecologies*.
114. White, "'Are You an Environmentalist?'"; Jimenez Sifuentez, *Of Forests and Fields*.
115. Mendoza, "La Tierra Pica."
116. Pellow and Park, *Silicon Valley of Dreams*.
117. White, "'Are You an Environmentalist?'"
118. Langston, *Climate Ghosts*.
119. Limerick, "Disorientation," 1031.

Bibliography

Abbey, Edward. *Desert Solitaire*. Ballantine Books, 1971.
———. *The Journey Home: Some Words in the Defense of the American West*. Dutton, 1977.
Anderson, Benedict. *Imagined Communities: Reflections of the Origin and the Spread of Nationalism*. Verso, 1998.

Anderson, Virginia DeJohn. *Creatures of Empire: How Domestic Animals Transformed Early America*. Oxford University Press, 2006.

Andrews, Thomas G. "Beasts of the Southern Wild: Slaveholders, Slaves, and Other Animals in Charles Ball's Slavery in the United States." In *Rendering Nature: Animals, Bodies, Places, Politics*, edited by Marguerite S. Shaffer and Phoebe S. K. Young, 21–47. Philadelphia: University of Pennsylvania Press, 2015.

Arvin, Maile, Eve Tuck, and Angie Morrill. "Decolonizing Feminism: Challenging Connections between Settler Colonialism and Heteropatriarchy." In *Feminist Theory Reader*, edited by Carole McCann, Seung-kyung Kim, Emek Ergun, 169–80. Routledge, 2020.

Bancel, Nicolas, Thomas David, and Dominic Thomas, eds. *The Invention of Race: Scientific and Popular Representations*. Routledge, 2014.

Barr, Juliana. "From Captives to Slaves: Commodifying Indian Women in the Borderlands." *Journal of American History* 92, no. 1 (2005): 19–46.

———. *Peace Came in the Form of a Woman: Indians and Spaniards in the Texas Borderlands*. Chapel Hill: University of North Carolina Press, 2009.

Baynton, Douglas C. "Defectives in the Land: Disability and American Immigration Policy, 1882–1924." In *Beginning with Disability*, edited by Lennard J. Davis, 85–98. Routledge, 2017.

Berkhofer, Robert F. *The White Man's Indian: Images of the American Indian from Columbus to the Present*. Vintage, 1979.

Blackhawk, Ned. *Violence over the Land: Indians and Empires in the Early American West*. Cambridge MA: Harvard University Press, 2008.

Bonds, Anne, and Joshua Inwood. "Beyond White Privilege: Geographies of White Supremacy and Settler Colonialism." *Progress in Human Geography* 40, no. 6 (2016): 715–33.

Brosnan, Kathleen A. "The Lifting Fog: Race, Work, and the Environment." *Environmental History* 24, no. 1 (2019): 9–24.

Brooks, James F. *Captives and Cousins: Slavery, Kinship, and Community in the Southwest Borderlands*. Chapel Hill: University of North Carolina Press, 2011.

Brooks, Lisa Tanya. *Our Beloved Kin: A New History of King Philip's War*. New Haven CT: Yale University Press, 2018.

Bruyneel, Kevin. *Settler Memory: The Disavowal of Indigeneity and the Politics of Race in the United States*. Chapel Hill: University of North Carolina Press, 2021.

Bullard, Robert D. *Dumping in Dixie: Race, Class, and Environmental Quality*. Routledge, 2018.

Burch, Susan. *Committed: Remembering Native Kinship in and beyond Institutions*. Chapel Hill: University of North Carolina Press, 2021.

Byrd, Jodi A. *The Transit of Empire: Indigenous Critiques of Colonialism*. Minneapolis: University of Minnesota Press, 2011.

Byrd, William, II. "The History of the Dividing Line betwixt Virginia and North Carolina." Documenting the American South, 1841. http://docsouth.unc.edu/nc/byrd/byrd.html.

Chiang, Connie Y. "Imprisoned Nature: Toward an Environmental History of the World War II Japanese American Incarceration." *Environmental History* 15, no. 2 (April 1, 2010): 236–67.

———. *Nature behind Barbed Wire: An Environmental History of the Japanese American Incarceration*. Oxford University Press, 2018.

Cohn, Julie, and Sara Pritchard. "Report on Gender and the American Society for Environmental History." American Society for Environmental History. Accessed April 2, 2020. https://aseh.net/resources/report-on-gender.

Coulthard, Glen Sean. *Red Skin, White Masks: Rejecting the Colonial Politics of Recognition*. Minneapolis: University of Minnesota Press, 2014.

Cronon, William. *Changes in the Land: Indians, Colonists, and the Ecology of New England*. Hill and Wang, 2011.

———. "Kennecott Journey: The Path out of Town." In *Under an Open Sky: Rethinking America's Western Past*, 28–51. New York: W. W. Norton, 1993.

———. "The Trouble with Wilderness: Or, Getting Back to the Wrong Nature." *Environmental History* 1, no. 1 (1996): 7–28.

Crosby, Alfred W. "Virgin Soil Epidemics as a Factor in the Aboriginal Depopulation in America." *William and Mary Quarterly: A Magazine of Early American History* (1976): 289–99.

Dawson, Kevin. *Undercurrents of Power: Aquatic Culture in the African Diaspora*. Philadelphia: University of Pennsylvania Press, 2018.

Day, Iyko. "Being or Nothingness: Indigeneity, Antiblackness, and Settler Colonial Critique." *Critical Ethnic Studies* 1, no. 2 (2015): 102–21.

Deloria, Philip J. *Playing Indian*. New Haven: Yale University Press, 2022.

DeLuca, Kevin, and Anne Demo. "Imagining Nature and Erasing Class and Race: Carleton Watkins, John Muir, and the Construction of Wilderness." *Environmental History* (2001): 541–60.

Denevan, William M. "The Pristine Myth: The Landscape of the Americas in 1492." *Annals of the Association of American Geographers* 82, no. 3 (1992): 369–85.

———. "The 'Pristine Myth' Revisited." *Geographical Review* 101, no. 4 (October 1, 2011): 576–91.

Dillon, Lindsey, and Julie Sze. "Police Power and Particulate Matters: Environmental Justice and the Spatialities of In/securities in US Cities." *English Language Notes* 54, no. 2 (2016): 13–23.

Dolmage, Jay Timothy. *Disabled upon Arrival: Eugenics, Immigration, and the Construction of Race and Disability*. Columbus: Ohio State University Press, 2018.

Du Bois, W. E. B. "The Souls of White Folk." In *Darkwater: Voices from Within the Veil*, 29–52. New York: Harcourt, Brace and Howe, 1920.

Dunaway, Finis. *Seeing Green: The Use and Abuse of American Environmental Images.* Chicago: University of Chicago Press, 2019.

DuVal, Kathleen. *The Native Ground: Indians and Colonists in the Heart of the Continent.* Philadelphia: University of Pennsylvania Press, 2011.

Estes, Nick. *Our History Is the Future: Standing Rock versus the Dakota Access Pipeline, and the Long Tradition of Indigenous Resistance.* Verso, 2019.

Finney, Carolyn. *Black Faces, White Spaces: Reimagining the Relationship of African Americans to the Great Outdoors.* Chapel Hill: University of North Carolina Press, 2014.

Fisher, Colin. "Race and US Environmental History." In Sackman, *A Companion to American Environmental History*, 99–115.

Fleck, Richard F. "John Muir's Evolving Attitudes toward Native American Cultures." *American Indian Quarterly* (1978): 19–31.

Gallay, Alan, ed. *Indian Slavery in Colonial America.* Lincoln: University of Nebraska Press, 2009.

Gilio-Whitaker, Dina. *As Long as Grass Grows: The Indigenous Fight for Environmental Justice, from Colonization to Standing Rock.* New York: Beacon, 2019.

Gilmore, Ruth Wilson. "Fatal Couplings of Power and Difference: Notes on Racism and Geography." *Professional Geographer* 54, no. 1 (2002): 15–24.

———. *Golden Gulag: Prisons, Surplus, Crisis, and Opposition in Globalizing California.* Berkeley: University of California Press, 2007.

Glave, Dianne D., and Mark Stoll, eds. *To Love the Wind and the Rain: African Americans and Environmental History.* Philadelphia: University of Pittsburgh Press, 2005.

Glenn, Evelyn Nakano, Grace Chang, and Linda Rennie Forcey, eds. *Mothering: Ideology, Experience, and Agency.* Routledge, 2016.

Graves, Joseph L. *The Emperor's New Clothes: Biological Theories of Race at the Millennium.* Rutgers University Press, 2001.

Greenberg, Dolores. "Reconstructing Race and Protest: Environmental Justice in New York City." *Environmental History* 5, no. 2 (2000): 223–50.

Gómez, Laura E. *Manifest Destinies: The Making of the Mexican American Race.* 2nd ed. New York: New York University Press. 2018.

Gossett, Thomas F. *Race: The History of an Idea in America.* Oxford University Press, 1997.

Haig-Brown, Celia. *Resistance and Renewal: Surviving the Indian Residential School.* Vancouver: Arsenal Pulp, 1988.

Hall, Clarence Jefferson. *A Prison in the Woods: Environment and Incarceration in New York's North Country.* University of Massachusetts Press, 2020.

Haller, Kaycie. "A Prison in the Woods: Environment and Incarceration in New York's North Country by Clarence Jefferson Hall Jr." *New York History* 104, no. 1 (2023): 210–12.

Harkin, Michael Eugene, and David Rich Lewis, eds. *Native Americans and the Environment: Perspectives on the Ecological Indian.* Lincoln: University of Nebraska Press, 2007.

Hartman, Saidiya. *Scenes of Subjection: Terror, Slavery, and Self-Making in Nineteenth-Century America.* New York: W. W. Norton, 2022.

Haymes, Stephen Nathan. "An Africana Studies Critique of Environmental Ethics." *Racial Ecologies* (2018): 34–49.

Heizer, Robert Fleming, ed. *The Destruction of California Indians.* Lincoln: University of Nebraska Press, 1993.

Hernández, Kelly Lytle. *City of Inmates: Conquest, Rebellion, and the Rise of Human Caging in Los Angeles, 1771–1965.* Chapel Hill: University of North Carolina Press, 2017.

Hirata, Lucie Cheng. "Free, Indentured, Enslaved: Chinese Prostitutes in Nineteenth-Century America." *Signs: Journal of Women in Culture and Society* 5, no. 1 (1979): 3–29.

Hixson, Walter. *American Settler Colonialism: A History.* Springer, 2013.

Houston, Jeanne Wakatsuki, and James D. Houston. *Farewell to Manzanar: A True Story of Japanese American Experience during and after the World War II Internment.* Houghton Mifflin Harcourt, 2002.

Isenberg, Andrew C. *The Destruction of the Bison: An Environmental History, 1750–1920.* Cambridge University Press, 2020.

Isenberg, Andrew C., and Lawrence H. Kessler. "Settler Colonialism and the Environmental History of the North American West." *Journal of the West* 56, no. 4 (2017): 57–66.

Jacobs, Margaret D. "Parallel or Intersecting Tracks? The History of the US West and Comparative Settler Colonialism." *Settler Colonial Studies* 4, no. 2 (2014): 155–61.

Jacobson, Matthew Frye. *Whiteness of a Different Color.* Cambridge MA: Harvard University Press, 1999.

Jimenez Sifuentez, Mario. *Of Forests and Fields: Mexican Labor in the Pacific Northwest.* Rutgers University Press, 2016.

Johnston, Robert D. "Beyond 'The West': Regionalism, Liberalism and the Evasion of Politics in the New Western History." *Rethinking History* 2, no. 2 (1998): 239–77.

Jung, Moon-Ho. *Coolies and Cane: Race, Labor, and Sugar in the Age of Emancipation.* Baltimore: Johns Hopkins University Press, 2006.

Kelton, Paul. *Cherokee Medicine, Colonial Germs: An Indigenous Nation's Fight against Smallpox, 1518–1824.* Norman: University of Oklahoma Press, 2015.

King, Tiffany Lethabo. *The Black Shoals: Offshore Formations of Black and Native Studies.* Durham NC: Duke University Press, 2019.

Kline, Wendy. *Building a Better Race: Gender, Sexuality, and Eugenics from the Turn of the Century to the Baby Boom.* Berkeley: University of California Press, 2001.

Koshy, Susan, Lisa Marie Cacho, and Jody A. Byrd, eds. *Colonial Racial Capitalism*. Durham NC: Duke University Press, 2022.

Krech, Shepard, III. *Ecological Indian: Myth and History*. W. W. Norton, 1999.

LaDuke, Winona. "White Earth: Recovering a Homeland." In *Natural Assets: Democratizing Environmental Ownership*, edited by James Boyce and Barry Shelley, 153–68. Washington DC: Island, 2003.

Langston, Nancy. *Climate Ghosts: Migratory Species in the Anthropocene*. Waltham MA: Brandeis University Press, 2021.

LeCain, Timothy J. *The Matter of History: How Things Create the Past*. Cambridge University Press, 2017.

Lew-Williams, Beth. *The Chinese Must Go: Violence, Exclusion, and the Making of the Alien in America*. Cambridge MA: Harvard University Press, 2018.

Liboiron, Max. *Pollution Is Colonialism*. Durham NC: Duke University Press, 2021.

Lindsay, Brendan C. *Murder State: California's Native American Genocide, 1846–1873*. Lincoln: University of Nebraska Press, 2012.

Limerick, Patricia Nelson. "Comments on Settler Colonialism and the American West." *Journal of the West* 56, no. 4 (2017): 90–96.

———. "Disorientation and Reorientation: The American Landscape Discovered from the West." *Journal of American History* 79, no. 3 (1992): 1021–49.

———. *Legacy of Conquest: The Unbroken Past of the American West*. New York: W. W. Norton, 1987.

Lipsitz, George. *The Possessive Investment in Whiteness: How White People Profit from Identity Politics*. Philadelphia: Temple University Press, 2006.

Locke, John. *The Second Treatise of Civil Government*. Broadview, 2015.

Lomawaima, K. Tsianina. *They Called It Prairie Light: The Story of Chilocco Indian School*. Lincoln: University of Nebraska Press, 1995.

Luibhéid, Eithne. *Entry Denied: Controlling Sexuality at the Border*. Minneapolis: University of Minnesota Press, 2002.

Lynch, Barbara Deutsch. "The Garden and the Sea: U.S. Latino Environmental Discourses and Mainstream Environmentalism." *Social Problems* 40, no. 1 (1993): 108–24.

Madley, Benjamin. *An American Genocide: The United States and the California Indian Catastrophe, 1846–1873*. New Haven CT: Yale University Press, 2016.

———. "'Unholy Traffic in Human Blood and Souls': Systems of California Indian Servitude under U.S. Rule." *Pacific Historical Review* 83, no. 4 (2014): 626–67.

Mckiernan-González, John. *Fevered Measures: Public Health and Race at the Texas-Mexico Border, 1848–1942*. Durham NC: Duke University Press, 2012.

McNeill, John R. "The State of the Field of Environmental History." *Annual Review of Environment and Resources* 35 (2010): 345–74.

Melamed, Jodi. "Racial Capitalism." *Critical Ethnic Studies* 1, no. 1 (2015): 76–85.

Melosi, Martin V. "Equity, Eco-racism and Environmental History." *Environmental History Review* 19, no. 3 (1995): 1–16.

Mendoza, Mary E. "La Tierra Pica / The Soil Bites." In *Disability Studies and the Environmental Humanities: Toward an Eco-Crip Theory*, edited by Sarah Jaquette Ray and Jay Sibara, 474. Lincoln: University of Nebraska Press, 2017.

——. "Treacherous Terrain: Racial Exclusion and Environmental Control at the U.S.-Mexico Border." *Environmental History* 23, no 1 (2018): 117–27.

——. "Unnatural Border: Race and Environment at the U.S.-Mexico Divide." PhD diss., University of California, Davis, 2015.

Merchant, Carolyn. "Shades of Darkness: Race and Environmental History." *Environmental History* 8, no. 3 (2003): 380–94.

Molina, Natalia. *Fit to Be Citizens? Public Health and Race in Los Angeles, 1879–1939*. Berkeley: University of California Press, 2006.

——. *How Race Is Made in America: Immigration, Citizenship, and the Historical Power of Racial Scripts*. Berkeley: University of California Press, 2014.

Morse, Kathryn T., and Noël Sturgeon. *Environmentalism in Popular Culture: Gender, Race, Sexuality, and the Politics of the Natural*. Tucson: University of Arizona Press, 2009.

Muir, John. *The Mountains of California*. Penguin, 2008.

——. *Our National Parks*. New York: Houghton Mifflin, 1909.

Nash, Linda Lorraine. *Inescapable Ecologies: A History of Environment, Disease, and Knowledge*. Berkeley: University of California Press, 2006.

Nash, Roderick Frazier. *Wilderness and the American Mind*. 1967. Reprint, New Haven CT: Yale University Press, 2014.

Newell, Margaret Ellen. *Brethren by Nature: New England Indians, Colonists, and the Origins of American Slavery*. Ithaca NY: Cornell University Press, 2015.

Ngai, Mae M. *Impossible Subjects: Illegal Aliens and the Making of Modern America*. Princeton University Press, 2014.

Norton, Jack. *When Our Worlds Cried: Genocide in Northwestern California*. Indian Historian Press, 1979.

Omi, Michael, and Howard Winant. *Racial Formation in the United States*. 1994. Reprint, Routledge, 2014.

Ostler, Jeffrey. *Surviving Genocide: Native Nations and the United States from the American Revolution to Bleeding Kansas*. New Haven CT: Yale University Press, 2019.

Park, Lisa Sun-Hee. *Entitled to Nothing: The Struggle for Immigrant Health Care in the Age of Welfare Reform*. New York: New York University Press, 2011.

Parry, Tyler D., and Charlton W. Yingling. "Slave Hounds and Abolition in the Americas." *Past & Present* 246, no. 1 (2020): 69–108.

Pellow, David, and Lisa Sun-Hee Park. *The Silicon Valley of Dreams: Environmental Injustice, Immigrant Workers, and the High-Tech Global Economy*. New York: New York University Press, 2002.

Pellow David N., and Robert J. Brulle, eds., *Power, Justice, and the Environment: A Critical Appraisal of the Environmental Justice Movement*. Cambridge MA: MIT Press, 2005.

Pellow, David Naguib. *Garbage Wars: The Struggle for Environmental Justice in Chicago*. Cambridge MA: MIT Press, 2004.

———. "Toward a Critical Environmental Justice Studies: Black Lives Matter as an Environmental Justice Challenge." *Du Bois Review* (2016): 1–16.

Pulido, Laura. *Environmentalism and Economic Justice: Two Chicano Struggles in the Southwest*. University of Arizona Press, 1996.

Ray, Sarah Jaquette. *The Ecological Other: Environmental Exclusion in American Culture*. Tucson: University of Arizona Press, 2013.

Reid, Joshua L. "From 'Fishing Together' to 'To Fish in Common With': Makah Marine Waters and the Making of the Settler Commons in Washington Territory." *Journal of the West* 56, no. 4 (Fall 2017): 48–56.

Reséndez, Andrés. *The Other Slavery: The Uncovered Story of Indian Enslavement in America*. New York: Houghton Mifflin, 2016.

Risling Baldy, Cutcha. *We Are Dancing for You: Native Feminisms and the Revitalization of Women's Coming-of-Age Ceremonies*. 1st ed. Seattle: University of Washington Press, 2018.

Roberts, Alaina E. *I've Been Here All the While: Black Freedom on Native Land*. Philadelphia: University of Pennsylvania Press, 2021.

Robinson, Cedric. "Black Marxism." In *Social Theory Re-Wired*, edited by Wesley Longhofer and Daniel Winchester, 156–64. Routledge, 2023.

Roediger, David R. *The Wages of Whiteness: Race and the Making of the American Working Class*. Verso, 1999.

Russell, Edmund P., III. "'Speaking of Annihilation': Mobilizing for War against Human and Insect Enemies, 1914–1945." *Journal of American History* 82, no. 4 (1996): 1505–29.

Sackman, Douglas Cazaux. *A Companion to American Environmental History*. Wiley-Blackwell: 2014.

———. *Orange Empire: California and the Fruits of Eden*. Berkeley: University of California Press, 2005.

Sandler, Ronald D., and Phaedra C. Pezzullo, eds. *Environmental Justice and Environmentalism: The Social Justice Challenge to the Environmental Movement*. Cambridge MA: MIT Press, 2007.

Scott, Joan Wallach. *Gender and the Politics of History*. New York: Columbia University Press, 1988.

Seed, Patricia. *Ceremonies of Possession in Europe's Conquest of the New World, 1492–1640*. Cambridge University Press, 1995.

Shah, Nayan. *Contagious Divides: Epidemics and Race in San Francisco's Chinatown*. Berkeley: University of California Press, 2011.

Sleeper-Smith, Susan. *Indigenous Prosperity and American Conquest: Indian Women of the Ohio River Valley, 1690–1792*. Chapel Hill: University of North Carolina Press, 2018.

Smallwood, Stephanie E. *Saltwater Slavery: A Middle Passage from Africa to American Diaspora*. Cambridge MA: Harvard University Press, 2007.

Snyder, Christina. *Great Crossings: Indians, Settlers, and Slaves in the Age of Jackson*. Oxford University Press, 2017.

———. *Slavery in Indian Country: The Changing Face of Captivity in Early America*. Cambridge: Harvard University Press, 2010.

Spence, Mark David. *Dispossessing the Wilderness: Indian Removal and the Making of the National Parks*. Oxford University Press, 1999.

Stern, Alexandra Minna. "Buildings, Boundaries, and Blood: Medicalization and Nation-Building on the US-Mexico Border, 1910–1930." *Hispanic American Historical Review* 79, no. 1 (1999): 41–81.

Stroud, Ellen. "From Six Feet under the Field: Dead Bodies in the Classroom." *Environmental History* 8, no. 4 (2003): 618–27.

Sturgeon, No'L. *Environmentalism in Popular Culture: Gender, Race, Sexuality, and the Politics of the Natural*. Tucson: University of Arizona Press, 2009.

Sugrue, Thomas J. *The Origins of the Urban Crisis: Race and Inequality in Postwar Detroit*. Updated ed. Princeton University Press, 2014.

Sutter, Paul S. "What Can US Environmental Historians Learn from Non-US Environmental Historiography?" *Environmental History* 8, no. 1 (2003): 109–29.

Sze, Julie. *Noxious New York: The Racial Politics of Urban Health and Environmental Justice*. Cambridge MA: MIT Press, 2006.

Taylor, Alan. *The Divided Ground: Indians, Settlers, and the Northern Borderland of the American Revolution*. New York: Vintage, 2007.

Thoreau, Henry David. *Walden*. New Haven CT: Yale University Press, 2006.

Todd, Zoe. "Fish, Kin and Hope: Tending to Water Violations in Amiskwaciwâskahikan and Treaty Six Territory." *Afterall: A Journal of Art, Context and Enquiry* 43, no. 1 (2017): 102–7.

Trafzer, Clifford E. *Fighting Invisible Enemies: Health and Medical Transitions among Southern California Indians*. Norman: University of Oklahoma Press, 2019.

Tuck, Eve, and K. Wayne Yang. "Decolonization Is Not a Metaphor." *Tabula Rasa* 38 (2021): 61–111.

Turner, Frederick Jackson. *The Significance of the Frontier in American History*. State Historical Society of Wisconsin, 1894.

Twain, Mark. *Roughing It.* 1872. Reprint, New York: Penguin, 2008.

Veracini, Lorenzo. *Settler Colonialism: A Theoretical Overview.* Houndmills, UK: Palgrave Macmillan, 2010.

Voyles, Traci Brynne. *The Settler Sea: California's Salton Sea and the Consequences of Colonialism.* Lincoln: University of Nebraska Press, 2021.

———. *Wastelanding: Legacies of Uranium Mining in Navajo Country.* Minneapolis: University of Minnesota Press, 2015.

Washington, Sylvia Hood. *Packing Them In: An Archaeology of Environmental Racism in Chicago, 1865–1954.* Lexington Books, 2004.

Weisiger, Marsha. *Dreaming of Sheep in Navajo Country.* Seattle: University of Washington Press, 2011.

White, Richard. "'Are You an Environmentalist or Do You Work for a Living?': Work and Nature." In *Uncommon Ground: Rethinking the Human Place in Nature,* edited by William Cronon, 172. New York: W. W. Norton, 1996.

———. *"It's Your Misfortune and None of My Own": A New History of the American West.* Oxford University Press, 1991.

———. *The Middle Ground: Indians, Empires, and Republics in the Great Lakes Region, 1650–1815.* Cambridge University Press, 1991.

———. *Railroaded: The Transcontinentals and the Making of Modern America.* First published as a Norton paperback. New York: W. W. Norton, 2012.

———. *The Roots of Dependency: Subsistence, Environment, and Social Change among the Choctaws, Pawnees, and Navajos.* Lincoln: University of Nebraska Press, 1988.

Whyte, Kyle. "Settler Colonialism, Ecology, and Environmental Injustice." *Environment and Society* 9, no. 1 (2018): 125–44.

Wolfe, Patrick. "Settler Colonialism and the Elimination of the Native." *Journal of Genocide Research* 8, no. 4 (2006): 387–409.

Yazzie, Melanie, and Cutcha Risling Baldy. "Introduction: Indigenous Peoples and the Politics of Water." *Decolonization: Indigeneity, Education & Society* 7, no. 1 (2018): 1–18.

Yung, Judy. *Unbound Feet: A Social History of Chinese Women in San Francisco.* Berkeley: University of California Press, 2023.

Zimring, C. A. *Clean and White: A History of Environmental Racism in the United States.* New York: New York University Press, 2016.

PART 1

Not Just Green

ENVIRONMENTAL HISTORIES OF BODIES,
TRASH, PRISONS, AND CITIES

A key difference—even tension—between environmental history and environmental justice studies has to do with place. Whereas environmental historians have tended to focus on particular kinds of "natural" places (national parks, gardens, the rural West), scholars of environmental justice have tended toward more urban environments and human communities. Environmental historians' tendency toward places like parks predisposes them to telling stories about the mostly white and privileged, who had the resources to access and recreate in the "wilderness." In this section, authors explore the environmental history of unexpected places and sites, from bodies and trash to cities and prisons.

These approaches function to both break the connections between environmental history and whiteness and build an environmental history of race and racial formation in the United States. Katherine Johnston turns to the ways in which understandings of the body, emerging from climatic theories about determining racial difference, have been utilized to support colonial and white supremacist understandings of race and racial differences in colonial Georgia. Carl Zimring explores the ways in which the avoidance of handling garbage became an important part of white identity, helping shape evolving constructions of whiteness. Elizabeth Grennan Browning gives a powerful account of the ways in which African Americans transitioned from a rural to urban environment on arrival in segregated Chicago in the 1930s; rather than viewing the segregated city as a space of constriction, these communities developed a flourishing urban culture. Turning from the *construction* of urban spaces to *recreation* in them, Colin Fischer argues that urban African American history belies the commonplace assumption that only privileged people have histories of turning to nature for leisure. David Pellow turns to places that would seem the polar opposite of those explored in traditional environmental histories: prisons—places of extreme nature deprivation. Pellow looks to histories of incarceration to understand how social movements for prison abolition can and should be seen as connected to the framework of environmental justice. Together, these chapters invite environmental historians to turn to diverse sites of investigation and analysis, looking to the historical interplay of nature and culture in places that are "not just green."

Naturalizing Difference

Labor and Slavery in Colonial Georgia

KATHERINE JOHNSTON

Less than a year into his term as a member of the first U.S. Congress, South Carolina representative William Loughton Smith delivered an impassioned address defending his state's reliance on slavery. In March 1790 the House of Representatives opened a discussion on the question of abolishing the transatlantic slave trade. Fearing that eliminating the trade would threaten the institution of slavery itself, Smith argued in a lengthy speech that ending slavery would ruin the nascent United States. According to Smith, the nation depended on products grown in the plantation South, and South Carolina could "only be cultivated by slaves." Its climate and soil "forbid the whites from performing the labor" necessary to grow crops, he insisted. To convince skeptics, Smith offered proof. "Experience convinces us of the truth of this. Great Britain made every attempt to settle Georgia by whites alone and failed, and was compelled at length to introduce slaves," he announced. Smith's account of colonial Georgia would have been familiar to any of his listeners acquainted with the region's history. In the colonial South, Georgia was an anomaly for its late introduction of slavery. Nevertheless, the colony appeared to serve as an object lesson. Popular portrayals of Georgia's history—particularly the failed effort to cultivate land without enslaved Africans—left white Americans decades later with the conviction that the lowcountry climate required Black laborers.[1]

Smith well understood the stakes of the matter at hand. Abolition was a serious issue; over the preceding two years, from 1788 to 1790, a British Parliamentary committee had conducted an extensive investigation into the proposed abolition of the transatlantic slave trade, and by the time Congress met, the committee had not yet reached a decision. In the States, abolitionist campaigns were growing in strength and number, and abolition of the slave trade—perhaps even the end of slavery itself—seemed a potentially imminent possibility. In Smith's view, enslaved Black labor was essential to the economy of South Carolina as well as to the new United States, and abolitionist sentiment presented a serious threat to both the state and the country. As members of Congress considered slavery's future, Smith found it imperative to present convincing evidence to ensure that his fellow representatives would dismiss any and all petitions for the abolition of slavery and the slave trade.[2]

Invoking the history of Georgia gave Smith a strong case. Referencing the state's colonial past appeared to offer compelling evidence as to why enslaved Africans and their descendants were necessary for the cultivation of the Carolina and Georgia lowcountry. After all, Georgia's history had been told and retold, a familiar narrative entrenched in the history books. One of the more succinct versions had been published only two years before, in a book by Jacques Pierre Brissot, a visitor to the United States with firm abolitionist leanings. When the colony of Georgia was founded in the early 1730s, Brissot wrote, enslaved Africans were "forever forbidden." Yet this prohibition was "soon violated," he explained, because "it was believed that whites could not work in the hot climate and that to till the soil it was necessary to import workers and that this justified slavery." While Brissot himself opposed slavery, he did not question Georgia's history. It was a well-known and oft-repeated history: the colony began without enslaved Black laborers and failed. Eighteenth-century historians explained that only Black people could cultivate crops in the climate, so to save the colony, its founders grudgingly allowed the introduction of Black slavery, and eventually the colony flourished. All these published histories—and there were many of them in the 1760s, 70s, and 80s—either implied or stated outright that white bodies were physically incapable of labor that Black bodies could easily perform. Georgia's experiment with free white laborers lasted less than two decades and, according to the consensus, spectacularly failed because the colonists were unable to work in the lowcountry environment. The result of the experiment—a capitulation to slaveholding interests and the colony's turn to slavery—justified enslaved Black labor across Southern plantations for over a century.[3]

Histories far beyond the eighteenth century continued to repeat Georgia's story, recounting the colony's years without slaves as a curious aberration in the history of the slaveholding South. But any suggestions that white colonists could not work in Georgia's climate, while Black people could, were part of a deceptive narrative rooted in racism. Colonists' experiences in Georgia gave them no reason to believe that skin color determined physical capability. Instead, Georgia's history was a case of environmental racism on two fronts. First, the colony showcased an instance of white colonists forcing Black people to perform difficult and dangerous labor. Colonists regarded the Georgia lowcountry environment as an unhealthy place, and the climatic argument justified placing Black bodies instead of white bodies in hazardous spaces. Second, the climatic language colonists used to justify Black labor in such spaces, and the subsequent repetition of this language, attempted to naturalize differences between Black and white bodies. By insisting that Black bodies could withstand environmental conditions that white bodies could not, white colonists associated ingrained and inheritable bodily differences with particular environments. Each retelling of the story further solidified this association, so that by the end of the eighteenth century, white theorists' emerging conceptions of biological race began to appear almost natural. White colonists, in other words, read race into the environment. Claiming that Black bodies fit certain spaces while white bodies fit others shifted a social and economic issue to one of biological bodily difference and environmental racism.[4]

The story of Georgia was fundamental to the transformation of race as a colonial social structure to an Early Republican biological certainty, a difference rooted in the body and naturalized by the environment. Georgia's history reveals the importance of a prevailing rhetoric about manual labor, particularly in Southern climates, to the emergence of categorical racial difference in early America. The persistent erroneous history had significant consequences, including justifications for racial slavery that lasted for generations. In the late eighteenth century, as Smith stood before Congress, scientists formulating concepts of biological race already had a foundation of environmental racism upon which to construct their theories. Georgia's story, which reverberated for decades, influenced long-standing notions of race and continued practices of environmental racism in the United States.[5]

A Malcontent History: The Georgia Experiment, 1732–50

In the summer of 1732, an advertisement began making the rounds of philanthropically inclined Britons. Printed on large sheets of thick paper and dominated by an image, a few lines of text urged potential donors to contribute to the new American colony of Georgia (see fig. 1.1). Supporters could be assured their money was going to a good cause because a significant part of the colony's mission was to provide a place where unemployed Britons could find work, cultivating crops for subsistence and for export. The image depicted European and Indigenous men laboring side by side, dutifully transforming forests into fields and buildings. Two Europeans wielded axes above their shoulders, poised to strike at a large tree, while an Indigenous man sunk another axe into a fallen trunk, preparing it for sawyers who would turn the trees into lumber. In the background of the image, forested land had been cleared and divided into neat plots ready for planting. The message was clear: this would be a colony dependent on European labor, with Indigenous help. With diligent work, laborers could cut trees, clear land, and use the lumber, and the colony would flourish.[6]

Enslaved Africans were notably absent from the picture. This was neither an oversight nor a purposeful erasure; concurrent images advertising tobacco, for example, readily displayed Black laborers cultivating and harvesting the crop. But Georgia would not be like other Southern British colonies, particularly South Carolina, which by the 1730s relied almost entirely on enslaved Black labor. Instead, Georgia's founders, known as the Trustees, wanted to instill a strong work ethic in the colony's future inhabitants. Other colonies from Virginia to the Caribbean had initially been cleared and cultivated by white people.[7] It was only as enslaved Africans began to replace indentured European servants that white people gradually stopped doing much of the manual labor of previous generations. The Trustees wanted to ensure that their colony, specifically designed to encourage Britons to labor and to produce desirable exports such as silk and wine, did not undergo the same process. Convinced that the presence of enslaved Africans would dissuade colonists from laboring themselves, the Trustees prohibited Black slavery—and anyone of African descent—from the colony altogether. The British government agreed to let the Trustees manage the colony in this way because they thought the absence of enslaved Africans in Georgia would help protect colonists against slave rebellions and because they thought a colony without Black people would dissuade enslaved Black South Carolinians from self-emancipating and heading south to Spanish-held Florida.[8]

FIG. 1.1. Engraving by John Pine. Courtesy of the John Carter Brown Library.

There was one early exception to this rule. Because the land in Georgia was thickly forested and the colonists few in number, the Trustees permitted James Oglethorpe, a Trustee who went with the settlers, to temporarily borrow enslaved people from South Carolina to help clear the woods. These laborers, the Trustees assumed, could help the settlers in the first few months, showing them the best way to cut down trees and slice them into even boards. For in spite of the urgings of South Carolina's governor, who wrote to the Trustees advising them to "send none but People used to Labour," the vast majority of Georgia's early settlers had no experience with manual labor whatsoever.[9]

That exception turned out to be a mistake. Barely six months after breaking ground in Savannah, which was to be Georgia's principal town, Oglethorpe wrote to the Trustees. He explained that he had "sent away" the enslaved Carolinians because "so long as they continued here our men were encouraged in Idleness by their working for them." Discouraged, he wrote that he "could not revive the Spirit of Labour" among the settlers. Despite the Trustees' high hopes, Indigenous people did not prove especially eager to work alongside Georgia's colonists. Oglethorpe formed a relatively good relationship with Tomochichi, the leader of the local Yamacraws, but that relationship was grounded in trade and diplomacy. Some colonists held enslaved Indigenous laborers because the slavery ban did not apply to them. But for the most part, the migrants themselves were left to clear land and plant crops, and many of them had little incentive to do this work.[10]

Naturalizing Difference   53

The settlers' reluctance to work stemmed from a number of issues, including insufficient organization and oversight, near total inexperience with clearing or cultivating land, and especially, prevailing social perceptions of who was fit to perform which types of labor. Across the Savannah River in South Carolina, British colonists used enslaved Black laborers for most manual labor—and certainly for the most difficult jobs. Georgia's settlers understood the hierarchy of this local labor system and absorbed it as part of colonial culture. British settlers who saw Black people performing hard labor across the river were disinclined to do the same work themselves.

South Carolinians, too, made Georgians and the Trustees aware of the situation. Charleston merchant Samuel Eveleigh expressed his skepticism about the Trustees' prohibition early on, particularly for certain tasks like procuring lumber. Georgia had some excellent land, he informed the Trustees in April 1733, "plentifully stored with large trees which I can't think can be felled by persons that are not used to work." Most of South Carolina's lumber was cut by enslaved laborers, and Eveleigh saw significant potential in heavily forested Georgia. But the unskilled, inexperienced settlers who populated the colony seemed unlikely to be able to saw through an abundance of solid tree trunks. Because it made more sense to use workers accustomed to manual labor, Eveleigh urged the Trustees to reconsider their ban on Black slavery. "Besides," Eveleigh added, "it will be very difficult for white people to hoe and tend their corn in the Hot wether [sic]." Eveleigh presented no evidence for his misgivings about the ability of white people to cultivate land in Georgia. Instead, his comment reflected the social milieu of South Carolina. There, white people, especially those of means with whom Eveleigh interacted, left manual labor to Black and Indigenous bondspeople. The settler colonists who populated South Carolina beginning in the 1670s had largely arrived from Barbados, and many of them brought enslaved Black laborers with them. South Carolina's planters, then, had only ever relied on forced labor.[11]

Life in the nascent colony proved more difficult than Georgia's settlers had expected. Some had arrived as indentured servants, committed to work for four or five years to pay off their passage. Other settler colonists acquired land grants on the condition that they clear and plant their plots. Either way, Georgia settlers were expected to work hard: that was the purpose of the colony. Although the colonists left Britain aware of these conditions, they were unprepared for the physical and social realities of life in the lowcountry.

First, many of the plots of land settlers received were far from the main settlement, and the colony had insufficient roads to access the land. Second, most of the land was entirely covered in lush growth, which was, as Eveleigh predicted, difficult to clear for people unused to manual labor. Burning, a method some settlers and Indigenous people used to clear forested land, was dangerous in vast woodlands, and girdling, a technique that involved stripping the bark around a tree's trunk and waiting until the tree died, took too long. Moreover, neither of these methods made use of the valuable lumber. The woods had to be cleared by hand, using axes and saws. In fact, upon seeing the work expected of them, significant numbers of white servants promptly ran away to South Carolina. Finally, Georgia's settlers were not wealthy, but they savored their new place in the colonial social hierarchy. In Britain, many of them had occupied the bottom rungs of the social ladder; lack of opportunity was often the main reason they went to Georgia in the first place. But in the colonies, these settlers found themselves automatically in a higher social position than in Britain. They may have been poor, but they were white. And in the Southern plantation system of the 1730s, the settlers' whiteness ensured that they were not enslaved. They did not, then, particularly relish the idea of doing the work that enslaved people did.[12]

Letters from colonial residents clarified the social situation preventing settlers and servants from laboring in the woods and fields. Explaining white peoples' reluctance to work, Virginia planter William Byrd informed the Trustees that the proximity of enslaved laborers to servants tended to "blow up the pride, and ruin the Industry of our White People, who seing [sic] a Rank of poor Creatures below them, detest work for fear it shoud [sic] make them look like Slaves." In a place with deeply ingrained social conditions where work was divided along racial lines, settlers equated Blackness with the most difficult labor and whiteness with immunity from such work.[13]

The labor white colonists rejected involved exposure to the most hazardous environments. Eighteenth-century colonists considered both forested areas and marshland to be unhealthy; Euro-American medical thought held that forests and swamps bred miasmas, or dangerous air that could sicken people. According to these beliefs, newly cleared land exhaled sickly vapors and only became healthy after the sun had dried it, usually over a period of years. Damp, swampy areas were notoriously unhealthy, and rice—a lucrative lowcountry crop—grew in these conditions. Because of these perceived dangers, lowcountry residents believed that *all* people had an increased risk of developing fevers of various sorts in particular environments. Herein lay the first form of environmental racism in early Georgia. It was for the most perilous tasks—namely, clearing woodland and cultivating rice—that colonists began to petition the Trustees to allow Black slavery in Georgia.[14]

In the summer of 1735 a group of disgruntled settlers known to historians as the Malcontents wrote to the Trustees urging them to permit slavery in the colony. The colonists would not, the Malcontents assured the Trustees, rely entirely on enslaved laborers—they would just prefer that enslaved Africans perform the more difficult labor. "We do not propose to employ Negroes in any Mechanick Business," they wrote, "but only in cutting down Trees and Stumps, howing, trenching and fencing the Ground and all other ways of clearing the Land, making Turpentine and Tar, beating of Rice &c. so that we should still use our white Servants in all Handicraft Trades," including the Trustees' anticipated wine and silk industries. Enslaved Africans, in other words, would not do *all* the labor in the colony—just most of it, and just the difficult tasks that colonists did not want to perform themselves. In a subsequent petition, the Malcontents informed the Trustees that if Black slavery was sanctioned in Georgia, "the Negroes should not be allow'd to work at any thing but producing Rice, (a labour too hard for white men) and in felling timber." In their fervor to convince the Trustees of the need for enslaved workers, the Malcontents even admitted the universal danger of this labor. Rice swamps were such deadly places that enslaved laborers suffered significant rates of illness and death. "Many *Hundreds* of them . . . yearly lose their Lives" from such work, they wrote. White colonists sought to avoid this risk.[15]

As they attempted to convince the Trustees to allow slavery in Georgia, the Malcontents added economic arguments to their cause. Anyone hoping to hire laborers for various tasks—clearing land, constructing buildings, farming, or anything else—could employ servants or free white laborers, often from South Carolina, or else pay a slaveholder for the temporary use of bondspersons. Using enslaved workers was the cheapest of these options, but bonded labor was not always available. The downside of using white workers was, as some Georgia settlers complained, that white people demanded payment for their labor. The Malcontents pleaded with the Trustees to consider their predicament. Because wine and silk would take several years to produce, timber, they wrote, was "the only thing we have here which we might Export." Yet Georgia's timber industry would never take off because it was "at double the Expence of other Colonies." At a nearby river in South Carolina where the wood was cut by enslaved laborers, timber cost half of what it did in Georgia—"and what should induce persons to bring Ships here when they can be loaded with one half of the Expence so near us[?]" the Malcontents complained. Merchant Samuel Eveleigh had similar concerns about the lumber industry. In spite of his earlier reservations about the capability of white people to labor, in the summer of 1735 Eveleigh sent seventy tons of live oak timber to London for sale. But because it "was cut by white people," he grumbled, it cost him "a great deal of money." A few months later he again complained that the wood "(being cutt [sic] by white People) [cost] four times as much" as it would have if he had been able to use enslaved laborers.[16]

An inability of white people to labor, then, was not the issue. As these comments demonstrate, some white settlers did undertake hard labor. While some worked for merchants like Eveleigh, felling trees and sawing lumber, others worked on their own plots of land, clearing and planting them with corn, potatoes, and other crops, including rice. Yet for all of those who were willing to labor, there remained a steadfast—and increasingly vocal—group determined not to do so. Although the colonists were clearly capable of manual labor, to regularly do the work indicative of slavery and Blackness would diminish their social standing.[17]

In the late 1730s a group of Malcontents, including former servants, wrote that if they could not hold bondspeople in Georgia, they would leave the fledgling colony for South Carolina, where their skin color would exempt them from hard work. In 1740 these Malcontents followed through on their threat and decamped to Charleston, but they continued to write to the Trustees encouraging them to allow slavery in Georgia. In one letter, the Malcontents invited the Trustees to imagine themselves in the colony. Think "how Shocking" it would be, they urged, "even to a person of the least humanity to See his own Countryman, perhaps his own Townsman Labouring in the Corn or Rice Field, Broiling in the Sun." This sort of labor, according to the Malcontents, was not fit for Britons. Yet "a white Serv[an]t in the Southern parts of America is as much a Slave during the Term of his Indenture as 'ere a Negroe," they insisted. White and Black alike had to perform "the

Same hard work"—a circumstance which "must" ignite "Compassion" for any person witnessing "the misery of his fellow Creatures."[18]

In this assessment, the colonists drew a clear divide between Black and white bodies. "Fellow Creatures" referred only to the white laborers—to a British person's "own Townsman"—while Black laborers inspired no such "Compassion." Instead, the Malcontents insisted that enslaved Black laborers easily and happily worked in the "Broiling" sun. If the Trustees could imagine themselves witnessing their "own Countryman" fainting in the heat, the Malcontents wrote, then "Let [an imagined witness] turn his Eyes round to the Negroes in the same fields. There he will See the reverse, he will see the utmost Vigours Exerted in every Act, they go through the Work with pleasure." This letter encapsulated the Malcontents' perspective. Labor in Georgia's climate—toiling under the hot sun for long days tending fields—was difficult and dangerous. Workers could suffer from any number of environmental hazards, including heatstroke, snakebites, and illness resulting from miasmas. Regardless of the reality that both Black and white workers suffered from the same environmental conditions and consequent dangers, the Malcontents argued for a difference along the lines of skin color. The Trustees should—as the Malcontents did—feel compassion for white people laboring in the hot, humid fields and swamps but not for Black people doing the same work.[19]

Writing from Savannah, Trustee James Oglethorpe was unable to mask his frustration with the wayward colonists and servants. He believed their complaints arose not from experience but from sheer laziness and an unjustified sense of social superiority. In one letter to his fellow Trustees, he pointed out that although some settlers had diligently worked the land to produce crops, others arrived in Georgia "hoping to Live in Idleness and avoid Labour." They had "fled from Labour in Europe, and when they Saw it Stare them in the Face in Georgia, they fled from it into Carolina, where they hoped to Live by Whipping of Negroes instead of Working." Starting a colony with unemployed Britons was a risk; while some would work hard, Oglethorpe believed that others would shirk labor as much as possible. Some other Savannah settlers agreed with Oglethorpe's assessment and sent letters to the Trustees explaining that many of their servants, "being picked up in the Streets of London, or Some such manner," had deserted the colony to avoid labor. These letters assured the Trustees that white settlers were physically capable of labor in Georgia's climate, but a contingent of settlers disinclined to work sought to avoid it. Buoyed by these reports, the Trustees made no move to allow slavery in Georgia.[20]

Frustrated by the Trustees' resolve, the Malcontents went public. In Charleston, they published a history of Georgia relating the hardships they had undergone and protesting the limitations of the Trustees' regulations, particularly the ban on slavery. The inability to own enslaved Black laborers meant that they would never be able to afford to compete in the export market, the Malcontents wrote. But their laments also drew a stark picture of Georgia's climate and its effects on white bodies. Drawing on Samuel Eveleigh's early warnings to the Trustees, the Malcontents complained that felling trees "was a Task very unequal to the Strength and Constitution of white Servants, and the *Hoeing the Ground*, they being exposed to the sultry Heat of the Sun, insupportable." According to the Malcontents, when white workers in Georgia were exposed to the heat, they fell sick and died.[21]

By complaining about the climate, the Malcontents made a calculated decision. Colonial promotional literature almost always emphasized the benevolent nature of any new colony's climate in order to attract settlers. These concerns were particularly acute in warm places; in Britain, hot climates held a reputation for being unhealthy, and grim reports about death tolls in the Caribbean appeared to confirm these fears. Pamphlets advertising Carolina from the 1660s through the early eighteenth century noted "the Healthfulness of the Place," with environmental conditions that made its inhabitants "exceedingly healthy." Although neither the Caribbean colonies nor South Carolina appeared to be especially healthy places by the time the Trustees founded Georgia, both were home to wealthy planters who made their fortunes with enslaved labor. If slaveholding and large cash crop plantations were not options in Georgia, the colony needed a way to attract migrants. A place's reputation for health played a part in determining whether or not settlers would arrive, and it was unclear how Georgia would fare. The colony's healthiness remained an unknown but important factor for the Trustees and could determine the fate of the colony. The Malcontents' climatic complaints, then, held the power to dissuade potential settlers and ruin the colony.[22]

Nevertheless, the Trustees remained unmoved by the Malcontents' arguments for slavery. On the economic front, all the regulations the Trustees had imposed were intended to curtail the possibility of colonists amassing large amounts of wealth, so financial pleas were unlikely to appeal to the Trustees. They also had good reason to be skeptical of the climatic argument, as other settlers in Georgia reported clearing land and planting and harvesting crops. Many of these settlers pleaded with the Trustees to keep the ban on slavery, agreeing with the conviction that the presence of enslaved laborers would prevent free laborers from working.[23] In addition, the Trustees had information that some of the Malcontents had personal stakes in the slavery issue. The two main leaders of the faction, who were related by marriage, had relatives involved in the slave trade. Patrick Tailfer was one of these two Malcontent leaders, a "proud Sawcy fellow" who ignored his land grant of five hundred acres to practice as a physician in town (in the process indebting many Savannah settlers to himself), along with his brother-in-law Robert Williams. Williams had a younger brother, James, who "was a trader to the West Indies" and in the late 1730s lived in Bristol, England, a major slave port. Tailfer and Williams saw Georgia as a place full of potential to become a second South Carolina, with themselves at the helm of the colony as its wealthiest and most prosperous inhabitants. The Trustees had no intention of enabling this scheme, though, and reaffirmed the ban on slavery.[24]

But to their dismay, the Trustees witnessed a gradual depopulation of Georgia during the 1740s. Some colonists who had labored on their land but whose neighbors had deserted theirs eventually became discouraged and left, and Savannah was not a popular destination for new arrivals. Despite their best efforts, the Trustees found themselves unable to recruit colonists to settle in a place without enslaved Black laborers. For the Trustees, allowing slavery would give individual colonists too much control over the colony's prospects and would open the door to potentially enormous personal wealth. As indignant philanthropists, the Trustees saw the colony as their project to manage. But Georgia was faltering—it had no stable economy, and strong factions on the ground hamstrung its prospects. Finally, in 1750, as the colony threatened to sink into oblivion, the Trustees permitted slavery in Georgia and turned control over to the crown. In the following decades Georgia became exactly like other colonial American plantation societies: a place where white slaveholders forced Black bondspeople to perform difficult manual labor.[25]

A Legacy Solidified, 1768–90

When the Malcontents published their climatic complaint, they could not have known its lasting impact. In their pamphlet, they claimed that "from *March* to *October*, hardly one half of the Servants and working People" (i.e., white people) were unable to work because of Georgia's heat. The Trustees received numerous letters refuting this claim, and some of the evidence— settlers' bountiful crops of potatoes, corn, and rice—belied the Malcontents' assertion. But in their efforts to demonstrate to "the World" the various "Hardships and Oppressions" they had faced as Georgia colonists, the Malcontents went to extremes. As one of the "Causes of the Ruin and Desolation" of Georgia, they listed "*the Impossibility of making Improvements to any Advantage with white Servants.*" Although in the short term this claim did not influence the Trustees' decision on slavery, it did cause potential colonists to think twice about relocating to the colony. If Georgia's climate made it "impossible" for them to cultivate the land, they might be better off staying where they were.[26]

In the longer term, the legacy of the Malcontents' claims reverberated for decades and influenced debates over slavery as well as perceptions of race and labor in colonial America and the United States. Starting in the late 1760s, historians began publishing accounts of the colonies and included sections on Georgia. Many of these histories relied directly on one another—the authors would occasionally cite other works but more often than not silently copy passages word for word. One such text, published in 1768, briefly recounted Georgia's history. The colony had begun without enslaved Black laborers, wrote the author, but Georgia's climate was "excessively hot, and field work very laborious . . . as the ground must be cleared, tilled, and sowed, all with great and incessant toil," so that "the load was too heavy for the White men, especially men who had not been seasoned to the country." Immediately following this passage, the author admitted that it was not, in fact, the climate but rather social conditions that determined who would labor in Georgia. All the other colonies, he wrote, "even Virginia and Carolina, were originally settled without the help of Negroes. The White men were obliged to labour, and they underwent it," he added. But he explained it was not in "the nature of man" to willingly labor if others could do the work. As Georgia's settlers felt themselves to be at an unfair disadvantage and the colony began to flounder, the Trustees eventually corrected "the error" of prohibiting slavery so that Georgia could be "upon a par" with the other colonies. The author acknowledged that white men *could* labor but that they were not inclined to do so if enslaved Black people could do the work instead.[27]

Other histories quickly followed. A book published in 1770 and again in 1776 reproduced these passages almost exactly. Others appearing in 1778 and 1779 followed as well—and as these authors copied from one another, subtle changes began appearing in their texts. John Huddlestone Wynne, for example, added a section on the slave trade at the end of his two-volume history. After offering various defenses of the trade, Wynne drew on the history of Georgia to prove his case. "It is certain," he wrote, that the colony's past clearly demonstrated that "Africans, or their descendants, are better able to support severe labour in hot countries than any of European blood."[28]

The history of Georgia, then, underwent a shift in its retelling. Just as the Malcontents themselves had at first complained of the price difference between Black and white labor and of the "disadvantage" they felt compared to Carolina, only later insisting that white people could not work in Georgia's climate, published histories followed a similar trajectory. Earlier historians admitted that social and financial conditions made the Georgia settlers yearn for slavery and that "the nature of man" pushed the colonists to laziness, but later narratives began to claim that the story was a matter of environmental determinism—that Black people could work where white people could not.

These historians turned a social condition into an environmental one and in the process appeared to legitimize the Malcontents' complaints. One after another, the history books repeated Georgia's story in progressively simpler and starker terms. Thus when the issue appeared before the U.S. House of Representatives in 1790, South Carolina representative William Loughton Smith merely repeated a familiar narrative. Georgia's official history was all the proof he needed. Because white men supposedly could not labor in the lowcountry climate, he announced that ending slavery would cause "all the fertile rice and indigo swamps [to] be deserted, and become a wilderness." For Smith, a lack of bonded labor would devastate the South.[29]

A few white people—most often not in print—expressed some doubts as to the humanity of forcing enslaved Black laborers to perform difficult work. Labor in such a climate, they reasoned, was not just difficult for white people. One man, interviewed in 1791 as part of Britain's hearings on the slave trade, announced that South Carolina's climate was "hostile to the human constitution." In other words, all people suffered from the heat, but white people saw themselves as worth preserving, while they treated Black people as expendable. Similarly, a traveler in the 1760s noted that the rice plantations of South Carolina were "often fatal to the lower set of people, as well white as black." Those who could not afford to avoid the swampy lands suffered health consequences regardless of skin color. Even the Malcontents had noted that rice planting was dangerous for enslaved Black laborers. And the abolitionist Brissot, whose 1788 history gave a perfunctory account of Georgia turning to slavery because "it was believed that whites could not work in the hot climate," added a hopeful footnote to his text. "This idea is beginning to disappear, even in Georgia," he wrote. According to Brissot, a Georgia planter had recently expressed his hopes for productive free workers in the state. "*If we can get the sort of white men who are not too proud to till the soil instead of slaves,*" Brissot quoted, "the country will grow rich." Inklings of racial divisions based on social conditions, and not on bodily ability, appear in these writings.[30]

But racist beliefs—or what Brissot's planter termed pride—were too entrenched in society to allow any significant changes to the labor force. Instead, as a former governor of South Carolina put it in 1788, "to imagine that white people are to be found to supply the place of those slaves . . . or willing to degrade themselves so far as to work in the field with Negroes, is being very ignorant of men and things." By the end of the eighteenth century, and by the time Congress met to discuss the future of slavery, few thought it possible to convince white people to do the work they associated with Blackness.[31]

Framing these social circumstances as environmental issues masked slave-holding interests by making it seem as though Black and white bodies fit different environments. In reality, working in the lowcountry was a health hazard for all bodies, and when pressed, even slavery's defenders did not deny these dangers. But as Georgia's story slowly changed from one of economic woes to a lesson in the impossibility of white labor in Southern climates, white slaveholders were able to use environmental excuses to justify racial slavery. And by portraying the differences between Black and white bodily labor as entirely due to environmental factors, defenders of slavery contributed to the naturalization of emerging notions of race. The following century, when Mississippi followed South Carolina's secession from the Union, its leaders issued a statement declaring that a "law of nature" had ensured that "none but the black race" could cultivate cotton on Southern plantations. Regardless of Georgia's actual history, ultimately the colony's narrative had become an axiom of environmental racism with a long legacy in American history.[32]

Notes

The author wishes to thank Ann Davies, Mary E. Mendoza, and Traci Voyles for their valuable comments and suggestions.

1. *Annals of Congress*, House of Representatives, 1st Congress, 2nd Session, March 17, 1790.

2. In 1785, when South Carolina's legislature considered suspending the state's participation in the slave trade, Charles Cotesworth Pinckney successfully used Georgia's history as evidence to argue that Carolina "was not capable of being cultivated by white men." Donnan, *Documents*, 480–84. On abolitionist movements, see Brown, *Moral Capital*; Davis, *Problem of Slavery*; and Sinha, *Slave's Cause*.

3. Brissot de Warville, *New Travels*, 223. For examples of eighteenth-century histories, see Russell, *History of America*, vol. 2, 305; Carver, *New Universal Traveller*, 607; and Hewatt, *Historical Account*, vol. 1, 120.

4. Works published in the early twentieth century that repeat this history of Georgia include Brooks, *History of Georgia*, 65–67; Flanders, "Free Negro in Ante-Bellum Georgia," 250–72; and Potter, "Rise of the Plantation System," 124.

5. On the development of conceptions of biological race in the late eighteenth and early to mid-nineteenth centuries, see Stepan, *Idea of Race in Science*; Schiebinger, "Medical Experimentation and Race"; Hannaford, *Race*; and Curran, *Anatomy of Blackness*.

6. GB233/CH2634, National Library of Scotland, Edinburgh. The image was later reproduced in Benjamin Martyn's promotional pamphlet, *Some Account of the Designs of the Trustees for Establishing the Colony of Georgia in America* (London, 1732).

7. Although by the 1730s enslaved Black people comprised the dominant—and in some cases exclusive—labor force in these colonies, in the early decades of the seventeenth century, indentured European servants performed this work. On the labor transition in the Caribbean, see Beckles, *White Servitude and Black Slavery*, especially chaps. 3 and 5; Newman, *New World of Labor*, especially chap. 4; and Dunn, *Sugar and Slaves*, 67–73.

8. The ban on slavery was specific to Black people and did not apply to Indigenous people, some of whom were enslaved in Georgia. See Baine, "Indian Slavery in Colonial Georgia," 418–24. For more on the Trustees' reasons for prohibiting

Black slavery, see Martyn, *Reasons for Establishing the Colony*, 30. See also Reese, *Colonial Georgia*, 47; Miller, "Failure of the Colony of Georgia," 7; Ready, "Philanthropy," 51; Spalding, "James Edward Oglethorpe's Quest," 69; and Wood, "Earl of Egmont," 85–86.

9. Governor Robert Johnson to Trustees, September 28, 1732, Egmont Papers 14200. Although the Trustees assured Johnson that they had indeed sent only people "inured to labor," this was not actually the case. See Benjamin Martyn to Robert Johnson, January 24, 1733, CO 5/666, f. 2, National Archives, Kew (hereafter TNA). On the composition of the Georgia settlers, see Wood, *Slavery in Colonial Georgia*.

10. James Oglethorpe to Trustees, August 12, 1733, Egmont Papers 14200. As Christina Snyder notes, Indigenous slavery in Georgia "persisted in the colony even after the African ban was reversed." See Snyder's chapter in Harris and Berry, *Slavery and Freedom in Savannah*, 26. On Oglethorpe, see Sweet, "Thirteenth Colony in Perspective," 455; and Sweet, "'These Difficulties.'"

11. Samuel Eveleigh to Trustees, April 6, 1733, Egmont Papers 14200. On early English settler colonists arriving in Carolina from Barbados, see Greene, "Colonial South Carolina," 192–210; McCandless, *Slavery, Disease, and Suffering*; Edelson, *Plantation Enterprise*, especially 43–44; and Roberts and Beamish, "Venturing Out."

12. Letters to Trustees complaining about land and servants can be found in CO 5/636 and CO 5/637, TNA.

13. William Byrd to Earl of Egmont, July 12, 1736, in Donnan, *Documents*, vol. 4, 131.

14. On perceptions of the unhealthiness of uncleared land (and its improved health once cleared), see Golinski, "American Climate," 162; McCandless, *Slavery, Disease, and Suffering*, 33. In his 1785 argument in favor of the slave trade, Charles Cotesworth Pinckney of South Carolina noted of Georgia's history, "Such part of this country was unhealthy as had not yet been cleared, so that the useful labours of negroes contributed to promote salubrity in the air." See Donnan, *Documents*, 482.

15. Patrick Tailfer et al. to Trustees, n.d., received August 27, 1735, Egmont Papers 14201; entry for June 6, 1739, in Candler, *Journal of the Earl*, 178; Tailfer, Anderson, and Douglas, *True and Historical Narrative*, 104 (emphasis in original). The Malcontents almost certainly sent their letter to the Trustees in direct response to the official ban on slavery, which took effect in June 1735.

16. Henry Parker et al. to Trustees, December 9, 1738, Egmont Papers 14203; Samuel Eveleigh to William Jeffreys, July 4, 1735, Egmont Papers 14201; Eveleigh to Benjamin Martyn, September 10, 1735, CO 5/637, f. 224, TNA.

17. Some Georgia settlers who grew rice were discouraged from doing so by Carolina planters who saw them as competitors. Entry for August 7, 1740, in Candler,

William Stephens's Journal, 636. Examples of Savannah settler colonists successfully producing these crops can be found in the Egmont Papers and the Colonial Records. In addition, the Trustees received large amounts of evidence from the Salzburgers, a group of German Protestants living about twenty-five miles from Savannah, regarding their abundant harvests. The Salzburger community wrote in opposition to slavery and pointed out their ability to grow large amounts of rice, corn, and other crops with their own labor. Some of these letters can be found in Reese, *Clamorous Malcontents*, and many more are in the National Archives at Kew; see especially the co 5/640 series, though letters are scattered from co 5/636–co 5/642. For more on the Salzburgers, see Jones, *Georgia Dutch*; Auman, "'English Liberties'"; and Melton, *Religion, Community, and Slavery*.

18. "Petition of the Malcontents," December 29, 1740, Egmont Papers 14205.

19. "Petition of the Malcontents," December 29, 1740, Egmont Papers 14205.

20. Oglethorpe to Trustees, October 11, 1739, Egmont Papers 14204; Patrick Graham et al. to Trustees, November 10, 1740, Egmont Papers 14205.

21. Tailfer, Anderson, and Douglas, *True and Historical Narrative*, 31 (emphasis in original). For more on settlers' frustration with the Trustees' policies, see Stewart, "'Policies of Nature and Vegetables.'"

22. On South Carolina promotional pamphlets, see Horne, *Brief Description*, 14; and Wilson, *Account of the Province of Carolina*, 26. See also Blome, *Present State*, 154. For a discussion of this promotional literature for Georgia, see Stewart, "*What Nature Suffers to Groe*," 35–36; and Sweet, "'Natural Advantages.'" On English attitudes toward hot climates, see Kupperman, "Fear of Hot Climates." On climatic thinking in early colonial endeavors, see White, "Unpuzzling American Climate."

23. Some of those writing against slavery were other Savannah settlers, but the two main groups who appeared united on the issue were the Salzburgers and a group of Scottish Highlanders at Darien, recruited to protect and defend the colony against Spanish Florida. A petition by the Darien settlers, "The Petition of the Inhabitants of *New Inverness*" (January 3, 1739), can be found in Reese, *Clamorous Malcontents*, 169–70. For more on the Darien settlers, see Parker, *Scottish Highlanders in Colonial Georgia*; and Jackson, "Darien Antislavery Petition."

24. Egmont Papers 14203, f. 137. For more on Tailfer's and Williams's roles in the Malcontent plea for slavery, see letter from Oglethorpe to Trustees, March 12, 1739, co 5/640, f. 297, TNA; Egmont's diary entry for July 16, 1739, in Candler, *Journal of the Earl*, 209; and William Stephens to Trustees, January 2, 1739, co 5/640, f. 247, TNA.

25. On the first several decades of slavery in Georgia, see James A. McMillin, "The Transatlantic Slave Trade Comes to Georgia," in Harris and Berry, *Slavery and Freedom in Savannah*, 1–25.

26. Tailfer, Anderson, and Douglas, *True and Historical Narrative*, 31, 116–17 (emphasis in original).

27. Goldsmith, *Present State*, 333–35.

28. Wynne, *General History*, vol. 2, 310–11, 541. For some other examples, see Russell, *History of America*, vol. 2, 305; Carver, *New Universal Traveller*, 607; Hewatt, *Historical Account*, vol. 1, 120.

29. *Annals of Congress*, House of Representatives, 1st Congress, 2nd Session, March 17, 1790.

30. Testimony of Thomas Irving, Esq., from *Abridgement of the Minutes of the Evidence, Taken before a Committee of the Whole House, to Whom It Was Referred to Consider of the Slave-Trade*, no. 4, 1791, 157; *Journal of an Officer, Who Travelled over a Part of the West Indies, and of North America, in the Course of 1764 & 1765*, Kings MS 213, f. 27, British Library, London; Brissot de Warville, *New Travels*, 223n (emphasis in original).

31. Henry Ellis to Lord Hawkesbury, March 27, 1788, included as part of British committee of hearings on African slave trade, BT 6/10, f. 218–19, TNA.

32. See "A Declaration of the Immediate Causes Which Induce and Justify the Secession of the State of Mississippi from the Federal Union," accessed through the Avalon Project: Documents in Law, History and Diplomacy, Lillian Goldman Law Library, Yale Law School, 2008, http://avalon.law.yale.edu/19th_century/csa_missec.asp.

Bibliography

ARCHIVES

Egmont Papers. Hargrett Library. University of Georgia, Athens. https://sclfind.libs .uga.edu/sclfind/view?docId=ead/ms1786.xml;query=;brand=default.
The National Archives (TNA). Kew, UK.
The National Library of Scotland, Edinburgh.

PUBLISHED WORKS

Annals of Congress. House of Representatives, 1st Congress, 2nd Session.
Auman, Karen. "'English Liberties' and German Settlers in Colonial America: The Georgia Salzburgers' Conceptions of Community, 1730–1750." *Early American Studies* 11, no. 1 (2013): 37–54.
Baine, Rodney M. "Indian Slavery in Colonial Georgia." *Georgia Historical Quarterly* 79, no. 2 (1995): 418–24.

Beckles, Hilary McD. *White Servitude and Black Slavery in Barbados, 1627–1715*. Knoxville: University of Tennessee Press, 1989.

Blome, Richard. *The Present State of His Majesties Isles and Territories in America*. London: H. Clark, 1687.

Brissot de Warville, Jacques-Pierre. *New Travels in the United States of America*. 1788. Translated by Mara Soceanu Vamos and Durand Echeverria. Cambridge MA: Harvard University Press, 1964.

Brooks, Robert Preston. *History of Georgia*. Boston: Atkinson, Mentzer, 1913.

Brown, Christopher Leslie. *Moral Capital: Foundations of British Abolitionism*. Chapel Hill: University of North Carolina Press, 2006.

Candler, Allen D., ed. *Journal of the Earl of Egmont*. Vol. 5 of *Colonial Records of the State of Georgia*. Atlanta: Franklin-Turner, 1908.

———. *William Stephens's Journal*. Vol. 4 of *Colonial Records of the State of Georgia*. Atlanta: Franklin, 1906.

Carver, Jonathan. *The New Universal Traveller*. London: G. Robinson, 1779.

Curran, Andrew S. *The Anatomy of Blackness: Science and Slavery in an Age of Enlightenment*. Baltimore: Johns Hopkins University Press, 2011.

Davis, David Brion. *The Problem of Slavery in the Age of Revolution, 1770–1823*. Ithaca NY: Cornell University Press, 1975.

Donnan, Elizabeth, ed. *Documents Illustrative of the History of the Slave Trade to America*. 4 vols. New York: Octagon, 1965.

Dunn, Richard S. *Sugar and Slaves: The Rise of the Planter Class in the English West Indies, 1624–1713*. New York: W. W. Norton, 1973.

Edelson, S. Max. *Plantation Enterprise in Colonial South Carolina*. Cambridge MA: Harvard University Press, 2006.

Flanders, Ralph B. "The Free Negro in Ante-Bellum Georgia." *North Carolina Historical Review* 9, no. 3 (1932): 250–72.

Goldsmith, Oliver. *The Present State of the British Empire in Europe, America, Africa and Asia*. London: W. Griffin, 1768.

Golinski, Jan. "American Climate and the Civilization of Nature." In *Science and Empire in the Atlantic World*, edited by James Delbourgo and Nicholas Dew, 153–74. New York: Routledge, 2008.

Greene, Jack P. "Colonial South Carolina and the Caribbean Connection." *South Carolina Historical Magazine* 88, no. 4 (1987): 192–210.

Hannaford, Ivan. *Race: The History of an Idea in the West*. Washington DC: Woodrow Wilson Center, 1996.

Harris, Leslie M., and Daina Ramey Berry, eds. *Slavery and Freedom in Savannah*. Athens: University of Georgia Press, 2014.

Hewatt, Alexander. *An Historical Account of the Rise and Progress of the Colonies of South Carolina and Georgia*. 2 vols. London: Alexander Donaldson, 1779.

Horne, Robert. *A Brief Description of the Province of Carolina*. London: Robert Horne, 1666.

Jackson, Harvey H. "The Darien Antislavery Petition of 1739 and the Georgia Plan." *William and Mary Quarterly* 34, no. 4 (1977): 618–31.

Jackson, Harvey H., and Phinizy Spalding, eds. *Forty Years of Diversity: Essays on Colonial Georgia*. Athens: University of Georgia Press, 1984.

Jones, George Fenwick. *The Georgia Dutch: From the Rhine and Danube to the Savannah, 1733–1783*. Athens: University of Georgia Press, 1992.

Kupperman, Karen Ordahl. "Fear of Hot Climates in the Anglo-American Colonial Experience." *William and Mary Quarterly* 41, no. 2 (1984): 213–40.

Martyn, Benjamin. *Reasons for Establishing the Colony of Georgia*. London: W. Meadows, 1733.

McCandless, Peter. *Slavery, Disease, and Suffering in the Southern Lowcountry*. New York: Cambridge University Press, 2011.

McMillin, James A. "The Transatlantic Slave Trade Comes to Georgia." In Harris and Berry, *Slavery and Freedom in Savannah*, 1–25.

Melton, James Van Horn. *Religion, Community, and Slavery on the Colonial Southern Frontier*. New York: Cambridge University Press, 2015.

Miller, Randall L. "The Failure of the Colony of Georgia under the Trustees." *Georgia Historical Quarterly* 53, no. 1 (1969): 1–17.

Newman, Simon P. *A New World of Labor: The Development of Plantation Slavery in the British Atlantic*. Philadelphia: University of Pennsylvania Press, 2013.

Parker, Anthony W. *Scottish Highlanders in Colonial Georgia: The Recruitment, Emigration, and Settlement at Darien, 1735–1748*. Athens: University of Georgia Press, 1997.

Potter, David. "The Rise of the Plantation System in Georgia." *Georgia Historical Quarterly* 16, no. 2 (1932): 114–35.

Ready, Milton L. "Philanthropy and the Origins of Georgia." In Jackson and Spalding, *Forty Years of Diversity*, 46–59.

Reese, Trevor R., ed. *The Clamorous Malcontents: Criticisms and Defenses of the Colony of Georgia, 1741–1743*. Savannah GA: Beehive, 1973.

———. *Colonial Georgia: A Study in British Imperial Policy in the Eighteenth Century*. Athens: University of Georgia Press, 1963.

Roberts, Justin, and Ian Beamish. "Venturing Out: The Barbadian Diaspora and the Carolina Colony, 1650–1685." In *Creating and Contesting Carolina: Proprietary Era Histories*, edited by Michelle LeMaster and Bradford J. Wood, 49–72. Columbia: University of South Carolina Press, 2013.

Russell, William. *The History of America, from Its Discovery by Columbus to the Conclusion of the Late War.* 2 vols. London: Fielding & Walker, 1778.

Schiebinger, Londa. "Medical Experimentation and Race in the Eighteenth-Century Atlantic World." *Social History of Medicine* 26, no. 3 (2013): 364–82.

Sinha, Manisha. *The Slave's Cause: A History of Abolition.* New Haven CT: Yale University Press, 2016.

Spalding, Phinizy. "James Edward Oglethorpe's Quest for an American Zion." In Jackson and Spalding, *Forty Years of Diversity*, 60–79.

Stepan, Nancy. *The Idea of Race in Science: Great Britain, 1800–1960.* London: Macmillan, 1982.

Stewart, Mart A. "'Policies of Nature and Vegetables': Hugh Anderson, the Georgia Experiment, and the Political Use of Natural Philosophy." *Georgia Historical Quarterly* 77, no. 3 (1993): 473–96.

———. *"What Nature Suffers to Groe": Life, Labor, and Landscape on the Georgia Coast, 1680–1920.* Athens: University of Georgia Press, 1996.

Sweet, Julie Anne. "'The Natural Advantages of This Happy Climate': An Analysis of Georgia's Promotional Literature." *Georgia Historical Quarterly* 98, no. 1–2 (2014): 1–25.

———. "The Thirteenth Colony in Perspective: Historians' Views on Early Georgia." *Georgia Historical Quarterly* 85, no. 3 (2001): 435–60.

———. "'These Difficulties . . . Rather Animate Than Daunt Me': James Oglethorpe as a Leader." *Georgia Historical Quarterly* 99 no. 3 (2015): 131–55.

Tailfer, Patrick, Hugh Anderson, and David Douglas. *A True and Historical Narrative of the Colony of Georgia in America, from the First Settlement Thereof until This Present Period.* Charleston SC: P. Timothy, 1741.

White, Sam. "Unpuzzling American Climate: New World Experience and the Foundations of a New Science." *Isis* 106, no. 3 (2015): 544–66.

Wilson, Samuel. *An Account of the Province of Carolina, in America.* London: G. Larkin, 1682.

Wood, Betty. *Slavery in Colonial Georgia, 1730–1775.* Athens: University of Georgia Press, 1984.

———. "The Earl of Egmont and the Georgia Colony." In Jackson and Spalding, *Forty Years of Diversity*, 80–96.

Wynne, John Huddlestone. *A General History of the British Empire in America.* 2 vols. London: W. Richardson and L. Urquhart, 1770.

2

Dirty Work Reconsidered

On the Historical Dynamics of Labor, Waste, and Race in Industrial Society

CARL A. ZIMRING

Work matters. This is the central tenet of labor history, as the conditions and cultural associations of particular forms of work shape wealth, family, community, and society in what E. P. Thompson called the historical phenomenon of class. The history of work provides perspective on how humans have interacted with their environments past and present, a perspective that illuminates the complex ways in which labor provides opportunities and dangers to the people who perform it. This is not a novel revelation in the field of environmental history; readers of this chapter may have already read (to name just two examples) Arthur F. McEvoy's studies of the experiences of California fishermen or Thomas Andrews's work on the struggles of coal miners in Colorado as studies that center work in understanding environmental history.[1]

Labor history also provides an understanding of environmental inequalities. In her 2017 presidential address to the American Society for Environmental History (ASEH), Kathleen A. Brosnan argued that environmental historians should contemplate how people historically have experienced nature through racially segregated workscapes. Brosnan's address in turn referenced Martin V. Melosi's 1995 presidential address to the ASEH calling on environmental historians to center issues of race and racism. The need to better understand the historical dynamics of racism in shaping past and present experiences of environments is well documented in our field.[2]

How then to proceed? One of the inspiring aspects of environmental history as a field is the extent to which it welcomes methodologies and questions from other history fields as well as from other disciplines in the social sciences and humanities. This chapter examines some of the ways environmental historians can address issues of work, race, and waste that emanate from questions posed by urban historians, labor historians, and scholars of critical discard studies.

Brosnan and Melosi both worked in urban environmental history for years before making their presidential addresses, and that attention informed how the racial segregation of urban and suburban spaces has shaped their awareness of experiences of different environments in the United States. Their work has influenced my thinking, as has reading the work of labor historians—especially those such as Joe William Trotter Jr. and Tera Hunter who center Black experiences in U.S. labor history—as well as reading beyond history to relevant new work in other fields of the social sciences and humanities.[3]

The emergence of critical discard studies in recent years invites us to think about how practices of waste and wasting are formed by systems of production, consumption, and disposal. The Discard Studies Collaborative—catalyzed by Robin Nagle's ethnographic inquiry into the experiences of sanitation workers in New York City, Samantha MacBride's arguments about how waste-management systems such as municipal recycling collection function, Josh Lepawsky's interrogation of international flows of electronic waste, and Max Liboiron's arguments about how actions of discarding reveal power relations—provides a powerful approach for thinking about how environmental history may be told. While discard studies illuminates how systems of disposal and waste management operate, the field provides opportunities to interrogate larger systems within industrial society. As Liboiron and Lepawsky argue in their 2022 book *Discard Studies: Wasting, Systems, and Power*, a "broad and systematic approach to how some materials, practices, regions, and people are valued and devalued, become disposable or dominant, is at the heart of discard studies."[4]

Discard studies notes the establishment of centers and peripheries and how people and places on peripheries of systems are discarded within sacrifice zones. Labor history provides an important dimension to this exploration of systemic injustices, as the work of upholding sanitary norms, processing discarded commodities, and otherwise engaging with waste may shunt workers into sacrifice zones and may also involve complex dynamics in which such works play vital roles in maintaining systems. Integrating this systems-based approach to discards into historical inquiries of workers and their environments offers opportunities to expand the role of labor history within environmental history.

This approach can offer better understandings of how conditions of environmental racism developed and how those conditions have been maintained over time. *Environmental racism*, a term that came into use to describe unequal proximity to polluted environments based on race and has since inspired activism resisting a wide range of inequities, is a set of power relations privileging people on the basis of racial identity. Within the United States, this set of power relations shapes the privileges of white people at the expense of nonwhite people, and this chapter builds on work I have published since 2004 in trying to understand the history of these power relations.[5]

The context for this work is geographic and temporal. White identity is not static but historically situated. In 1991's *The Wages of Whiteness*, labor historian David R. Roediger argued that the social construction of whiteness in the United States shaped the ways that working-class Americans viewed their jobs, their communities, and one another. In his subsequent *Working towards Whiteness*, Roediger argued that Henry James's "new immigrants" from eastern and southern Europe achieved white identities through a long and contested process between the end of the U.S. Civil War and the end of World War II. Roediger, bell hooks, Nell Irvin Painter, Robin D. G. Kelley, and Matthew Fry Jacobson tell histories that reveal a complex process of constructing and redefining white identity that ties closely to the labor people perform as well as the status, hazards, and opportunities of that labor.[6]

A discard studies approach that accounts for ways in which peoples and places are marginalized within systems leads to several ways to consider how systems inform the experiences of people working within particular environments. Such an approach can sharpen our understanding of the systems that the fishermen in McEvoy's history experienced and the systems that the coal miners in Andrews's history experienced. A discard studies approach that discusses the lands of Indigenous peoples as sacrifice zones where extractive industries affect the land and people has vast implications for telling environmental history.[7]

More modestly, a discard studies approach can illuminate one specific way in which environmental historians can grapple with the dynamics of environmental racism in the particular historical experiences of peoples in the United States: waste matters. Status is, as the anthropologist Mary

Douglas argued in 1966's *Purity and Danger*, closely tied to conceptions of dirt and hygiene, reflecting upon the people who handle the materials that are classified as waste. The Dalit waste workers in Indian caste society constitute one example, but marginalization of waste workers may be found in different times and places throughout human history. Despite the importance of handling discards in industrial society, it was work identified in the 1960s by Douglas and her fellow anthropologists Erving Goffman and Everett Hughes as stigmatized activity. Handling waste, Douglas argued, transgressed taboos, upsetting established orders and increasing danger.[8]

How historians can draw on this observation without advancing simplistic or deterministic models of waste work can lead to valuable insights into how the systems of waste making, handling, and processing shape the experiences of the people performing these jobs. As the United States industrialized, more people became involved in what sociologist Stuart E. Perry identifies as the dangerous "dirty work" of handling the variety of discard materials that were classified as waste. Unpleasant tasks that improve the living environments of residents of industrial societies by making them cleaner and safer have complex roles in human history, and they deserve consideration by historians seeking to understand environmental inequalities in these societies. This chapter examines the ways in which waste work reveals changing structures of racial inequality, how waste work presents aspects of hazard and opportunity to the people who perform it, and how the historical constructions of waste work provide new avenues of inquiry for environmental historians.[9]

Environmental history has benefited from attention to work and workers, including their perspectives on the air, land, and water they interact with and their understandings of the hazards of the work they perform.[10] Deepening the relationship between environmental history and labor history is an opportunity to engage with intersectional constructions of race and gender and constructions of waste and hygiene as they have evolved in industrial society. The work of Christopher C. Sellers (among others) on the relationships of workers to their environments provides context for the environmental inequalities historians Sylvia Hood Washington, Andrew Hurley, and Eileen McGurty (among others) have examined, and many of the topics labor historians have studied reflect environmental justice concerns about safety in residential communities and workplaces.[11]

Looking at waste work provides an opportunity to understand the lived experience of historical actors in industrial environments. Doing so builds on the approaches to urban environmental history laid out by Samuel P. Hays, Joel A. Tarr, and Melosi. It also provides opportunities to examine the racial dimensions of environmental history, including but not limited to the ways in which anti-Black animus has informed the establishment and policing of environments ranging from densely populated cities to wilderness. Where attention to spatial location risks producing a binary Black-white axis of power, looking at occupational structures can reveal complex interactions with and resistance to white power by a wide variety of men and women in American history. The history of dirty work in the United States reveals the labor force evolved as definitions of whiteness evolved. The work was—and is—seen as unfit for white people to perform. As a result, labor inequities for nonwhite men and women emerged.[12]

In particular, the history of waste handling provides perspective into the historical construction of the inequalities that sparked the modern environmental justice movement. One of the defining characteristics of environmental racism is the spatial relationship of people to hazardous waste. This is true of the resistance movements in Houston and Warren County, North Carolina, where Black community members identified the siting of toxic waste facilities as racially discriminatory, resulting in protests that reflected the rhetoric and strategies of the civil rights movement. This definition of environmental racism was the focus of the 1987 *Toxic Wastes and Race in the United States* report and Robert Bullard's *Dumping in Dixie*. From these origins, the accumulation of body burdens resulting from exposure to pollution on a racially discriminatory basis (including but not exclusively anti-Black discrimination) is an environmental justice concern. While these issues resonate worldwide, focusing on their historical development within the United States allows us to understand how inequalities and responses to inequalities are constructed. As geographer Laura Pulido argued in 2016, the environmental justice movement originated in the United States, and it is in that country that the movement "has most fully articulated a racial framework."[13]

The historical dynamics of waste work in the United States can illuminate aspects of the history of environmental racism. Tensions and labor structures associated with waste work may highlight issues Douglas raised in 1966, and while (as Liboiron and Lepawsky caution) scholars cannot conflate the work of classifying and handling waste with genocidal zeal to suppress or eliminate undesirable peoples, what historians can do is examine how waste work shapes particular opportunities, restrictions, hazards, and sacrifice zones within the society where the work takes place.[14]

In the United States, several waste-handling occupations have histories in which the workforce since the mid-nineteenth century has consisted of people who were not perceived at the time as native-born white Americans. The historical processes that produced those occupational structures reveal ways in which white identity in the United States evolved during a period when the racial order shaped by colonialism and enslavement was challenged by the upheavals of abolition, mass migration to and within the United States, and new dynamics of industrialization and urbanization.

Among those new dynamics was a quest by producing industries to secure affordable inputs to their systems of production. Reclamation of rags in the paper industry and scrap iron in the steel industry formed the basis of a growing set of businesses identifying and securing materials that had been discarded by industries or consumers and returning them to industrial production. The scrap recycling industry's development during this period found a conflation between waste work and attacks on the ethics and racial identities of the workers. Those who handled waste in the United States before the Civil War were usually described in economic terms—indigent, orphaned, widowed. After the war, several developments altered the work from being simply subsistence scavenging to being potentially lucrative. The economic dimensions changed, and with them, waste handling was no longer seen as exclusively work for poor people.[15]

What replaced it was a new, racialized definition of waste handling as work done by mysterious foreigners. Waste work could provide the people who performed it upward economic mobility even as it exposed their bodies to poisons, punctures, and other hazards and stigmatized the workers as just as morally hazardous as the materials they handled. Waste was an unwanted hazard, and waste workers were also perceived as hazards, even accused of being physical and moral dangers to children by progressive reformers such as Jane Addams. The skills waste workers developed to succeed provided resilience even as they coped with the hazards of the job. Crucially, the stigma these workers faced was due not simply to the conditions of their work but also to the deep discomfort of those Americans who were able to identify with the dominant (white, native-born) social group as they attempted to keep their status and safety separate from the peoples they viewed as threats to that status and safety.[16]

The Integrated Public Use Microdata Series (IPUMS) samples of the United States Census of Population reveal a strong correlation between foreign place of birth and occupation in the scrap and rag trades in the United States between the years 1870 and 1930. The 1880 IPUMS sample indicates that over 70 percent of the workers in the waste trades that year were born in Europe.[17]

By 1920, so many Jews—many fleeing repression in Russia and Ukraine—had started businesses trading in scrap iron, rags, and other secondary materials that the public face of the American scrap dealer was that of an immigrant Jew. Sixty-eight percent of the junk workers in the 1920 IPUMS sample were from countries in eastern and central Europe from which Jews had emigrated in large numbers over the previous four decades. A majority of the junk workers from eastern Europe spoke a native tongue of Yiddish, Hebrew, or "Jewish." Even leaving aside the caveat that this technique may omit Jewish individuals whose mother tongue may have been recorded as Russian, German, or another language, defining workers' ethnicity by native tongue indicates that first-generation Jewish immigrants were by far the most represented group in America's junk trade in the early twentieth century. These workers faced stigma combining their immigrant status with the hazards of waste handling, leaving them subject to police harassment and xenophobic caricature. The work was dirty, and the workers were considered dirty and thus inferior.

Why did so few native-born white Americans enter the scrap trade? The work was unpleasant compared to other occupations open to those with options. In the late nineteenth century, opportunities to profit rather than simply subsist were new. Handling waste was not seen as a path to upward economic mobility. The work required uncomfortable physical labor in city dumps and other settings considered unhealthful and unsanitary. Even though demand for removing and processing waste materials increased so much that a few businesses could become wealthy performing these tasks, the work was of low status.

Though the economics of scrap recycling changed in the late nineteenth century so that it was not associated with impoverished people, stigma persisted. The onus had shifted from class to race; dirty work was work unfit for native-born whites, regardless of how much money it earned. By 1930, scrap recycling was considered "dirty" for its associations with discarded materials and with disreputable foreign workers. It was also an activity sufficiently unpleasant so as to be zoned out of residential neighborhoods or, at least, out of white residential neighborhoods. Some scrap dealers grew their operations, amassing enough profits to hire others to do the dirty work or even using the money to purchase more respected businesses or educate the next generation in white-collar professions. The dynamics of this marginalization shifted over time; scrap recycling in the twenty-first century tends to be handled by Black Americans and recent immigrants, providing a continuity in native-born whites avoiding the burdens of the work. The history of scrap recycling workers in the United States anticipates modern environmental inequalities.

Reconsidering Dirty Work

Several studies have examined dirty work in the past two decades, with social science analyses including comparisons with waste work and other occupations involving "visceral repugnance."[18] Stigmatized occupations include work as correctional facility guards, nurses, truckers, secretaries, prostitutes, and police, as the 2007 edited volume *Dirty Work: The Social Construction of Taint* and 2012 edited volume *Dirty Work: Concepts and Identities* illustrate. In the latter volume, editors Ruth Simpson, Natasha Slutskaya, Patricia Lewis, and Heather Höpfl characterize dirty work as largely invisible and defined by "poor pay, limited opportunities for advancement, and unsavory working conditions."[19]

Their operating definition relates to Allan Schnaiberg's "treadmill of production" thesis that Schnaiberg, Kenneth Gould, and David Pellow have used to describe waste work. The perilous low-opportunity model reflects some of the history of waste trade work yet also obscures opportunities for resistance and even advancement within waste-handling jobs. The presence of economic opportunity was an important dimension of the history of the scrap recycling trade as well as the histories of several other sanitary occupations. IPUMS samples of the United States Census of Population reveal the demographic history of street cleaners, laundry workers, garbage haulers, domestic cleaners, janitors, and several related occupations, and analyses of these occupations between 1850 and 1970 indicate that although each of these occupations has its own history, one consistent pattern emerged: since the end of the Civil War, Americans identified as white have been underrepresented in waste-handling occupations, and waste-handling occupations have been disproportionately held by individuals who do not identify as native-born white Americans. Those identities are historically situated, with the shifting boundaries of whiteness Roediger identified shaping the demographics of waste work.[20]

Dirty work in the United States involves distinct eras before and after World War II. Between 1850 and 1940, "dirty" workers and business owners were overrepresented by first- and second-generation immigrant groups from southern and eastern Europe and, in the case of laundry work, China. These workers also included some Black Americans. IPUMS samples indicate increased representation of Black, Latinx, and Asian American and Pacific Islander (AAPI) workers in many waste-handling occupations between 1950 and 1980. The demographic structure of sanitation work has historical contexts in specific occupations, but the underrepresentation of native-born people who identify as white handling waste persists across occupations and throughout the period. The workers may be native-born or foreign-born, of Black, Latino/a, Indigenous, AAPI, southern European, or eastern European heritage, but a consistent theme for janitors, housekeepers, laundry workers, garbage haulers, and scrap dealers is that native-born white Americans were less likely to perform the dirty work society demanded.

The need for these workers increased as the nation industrialized and, as a result, generated more waste. Between 1850 and 1930, the variety of sanitary occupations performed in the United States led the Bureau of the Census to develop new classifications to enumerate the people working to collect garbage, trade junk, wash clothing, sweep streets, and clean homes and businesses. One imprecise occupational category gives an idea of the expansion. In 1860, 1,080,000 people worked in domestic service in the United States. By 1930, 2,550,000 people worked in domestic service in the United States, more than doubling that workforce in seventy years. The number of people hauling garbage, cleaning streets, washing clothes, performing janitorial tasks, and processing and selling secondary materials grew as the United States developed higher standards of hygiene to combat heightened fears of infectious disease and perceived pollution resulting from urban crowding and industrial emissions. In a modernizing environment, norms about how often bodies, clothing, floors, and streets should be cleaned changed rapidly. Increasing demand for cleaner environments employed millions.[21]

Much of the sanitation workforce between 1850 and 1930 was composed of foreign-born individuals or their children. Gender representation varied; janitors and scrap and rag dealers were overwhelmingly male, domestic workers were overwhelmingly female, and laundry workers broke down in intersectional patterns (Black women, Chinese-born men). For all sanitary occupations except laundry (in part due to laundry's large percentage of Black workers), the participation of native-born individuals from native-born parents was significantly smaller than their representation in the general population. In most occupations, the broadest overrepresentation was from foreign-born individuals.

The patterns reflect observations made both by historians of sanitation and labor and by contemporary observers. Solid waste disposal included private businesses and public departments of streets and sanitation that depended on immigrant labor. Colonel George E. Waring transformed New York City's Department of Streets and Sanitation into a giant workforce by 1895 as part of a drive to uplift local sanitary standards that included juvenile street-cleaning groups and White Wings (street sweepers dressed in white uniforms and caps) marching down clean streets. To perform these tasks, Waring specifically hired Italians. In 1881, the *New York Times* reported that the people who "separate from valueless material the atoms that can be put to use again are almost entirely Italians" who are "as industrious as ants, and, apparently, have eyes for nothing but the bits and particles that go to fill their bags."[22]

Waring reasoned that Italians were "a race with a genius for rag-and-bone picking and for subsisting on rejected trifles of food."[23] His stereotyping reflected the tendency of immigrants to handle garbage. In 1910, the proportion of garbage men and scavengers who were foreign-born was 47 percent, more than two standard deviations larger than expected in their proportion to the general population. In 1920, Black Americans made up 27 percent of garbage men and scavengers, again more than two standard deviations larger than expected, as Black Americans were 9.9 percent of the general population in 1920.

The work these people performed was hazardous; a 1917 survey of New York City White Wings by the Department of Sanitation's chief physician,

Dr. S. I. Rainforth, revealed 5,484 workers (comprising 80 percent of the department) were disabled as a result of doing their work. Keeping in mind that New York City's Department of Sanitation was unusual in even having a chief physician who provided the workers medical care at a cost to the department, the workers had endemic issues with injuries and exposure to the elements. Other municipal departments and private waste-handling businesses did not have physicians assessing the workers' health.[24] Physical dangers in garbage hauling mirrored those in the scrap industry, where death and injury on the job were so common that scrapyards seeking workers' compensation insurance as early as World War I paid among the highest premiums of any industry, including mining.[25]

That waste work is dangerous is consistent with a discard studies approach in which people and places where waste is handled become sacrifices upholding systems of industrial production. Discarded materials are unwanted for many reasons—breakage, contamination, and obsolescence being three—and those tasked with waste work must produce order from chaos. Exposure to infectious materials, sharp or rusty edges, chemicals, fumes, excrement, and many other unwanted hazards are realities of the job. Bodily harm goes hand in hand with hazards, so that marginalized peoples often occupy the lowest-paying and highest-hazard positions. Performing these jobs transforms the body, regularly disabling workers through exposure to waste and technologies to remove waste. Within the United States, the marginalized peoples performing this work have been those not considered native-born white Americans at the time and place when the work was performed. The racial dimensions of the work mean these injuries are not simply expressions of working-class life but racialized transformations of the body. The history of the hazardous experience of waste work precedes and informs the rise of chemically toxic industries (such as PCBs, pesticides, and other compounds associated with environmental justice issues), offering a context for studies of more recent environmental inequalities.

The experience of waste trade workers also reflects the spatial inequalities identified in late twentieth-century environmental justice literature. Geographer Gerald Gutenschwager's 1957 analysis of Chicago's junk and rag businesses revealed they clustered in neighborhoods with large concentrations of Black residents between 1917 and 1956. The racialized pattern in where waste was processed was evident in Chicago a quarter century before the Warren County, North Carolina, PCB protests. David Pellow's depiction of racialized waste labor work in Chicago reflects the segregation Gutenschwager observed; focusing on not only who performed waste work but also where waste work was performed may provide a better understanding of the spatial dimensions of environmental racism.[26]

Work removing dirt from homes, businesses, and clothing also expanded, with the racial and nativity dimensions of these occupation patterns similar to those found in garbage hauling. Domestic work in 1900 was a major occupation for women. One-third of all employed women in the United States worked in some sort of service capacity (about two million workers in homes, restaurants, and hotels), with more charwomen and maids employed as middle-class families looked for someone else to do the cooking and more rigorous cleaning. Domestic service had been an entry point for women from northern and western Europe, including Irish women in large numbers starting with the mass migration at midcentury. By the end of the century, women from Germany and the Slavic nations cleaned houses in Northern homes without a lack of English-language fluency hindering them. In the South, Black women performed most domestic cleaning. Overall, the majority of domestic workers were either first- or second-generation immigrants in the first third of the twentieth century.[27]

Janitorial work involved similar patterns for men. In 1910, Americans born to native-born parents (regardless of race) composed less than half the occupation, and while that number grew to 52 percent by 1920, the majority of native-born individuals in this occupation category were Black men. The number of foreign-born individuals each year was more than two standard deviations above their numbers in the general population.[28]

Within this system lay opportunities for the workers to establish better conditions for themselves. Janitorial work offered an economic strategy for the men who performed it. A group of janitors organized the Building Services Employees International Union in 1921, which was renamed the Service Employees International Union (SEIU) in 1968 and has grown to represent more than two million North American workers in the twenty-first century. A majority of the janitors in Kansas City in 1920 were Black men, and historian Charles Edward Coulten noted that the janitors not only received regular wages, but the job might also come with living quarters for the janitor and his family. As residential segregation practices became more stringent in Kansas City during the 1920s, the possibility of adequate living space was a significant benefit of the job. Janitorial work among African Americans was so widespread in Kansas City that the local Urban League office instituted a janitorial training school in the 1930s to best place community members in the wake of massive unemployment and few opportunities in other occupations.[29]

Between the fall of 1949 and winter of 1950, sociologist Ray Gold interviewed thirty-seven Chicago-area janitors. Their responses helped him characterize how janitorial work could, even if the janitors were making good money, be stigmatized as "dirty work." The bodies relegated to work were seen as disposable. Even in those circumstances, however, marginalized people found ways to work their way into whiteness—or improved class standing even if they did not achieve whiteness. This speaks to human resilience while critiquing the structural inequalities of the U.S. labor system. Scrap peddlers could accumulate enough wealth to purchase scrapyards, laundry workers could organize together or individually open businesses, and janitors could organize to ensure their compensation rose well above subsistence level. Gold quoted janitors who observed community members becoming jealous of their income, considering the dirty aspects of their work stigmatizing even when the janitors made more money than the people judging them. Dirty work was not necessarily a treadmill of production but an avenue toward advancement—albeit one risking social stigma.[30]

Although Chicago-area janitors received good wages in the years after the SEIU formed in 1921, the position itself was low status, owing, according to Gold, to the following factors: "(1) Many janitors are foreign-born and therefore strange and suspicious; (2) the janitor is always seen to be wearing dirty clothes, so the tenants seem to feel that he habitually disregards cleanliness; (3) the janitor lives in the basement, which symbolizes his low status; and (4) the janitor removes the tenants' garbage, which subserves him to them."[31]

Gold also noted class and racial jealousy among tenants. One Black janitor expressed the resentment he received after purchasing a new car: "They say 'How is the n-- with the big car?' meaning I am a 'n--' because I got a Buick and my car is bigger than theirs."[32] Even in the period after janitors were able to organize for better wages and working conditions, their work remained dirty and demeaning. Work that could pay well was scorned by white society even as it meant advancement within communities of color.

The evolution of waste work involved mediation between people and technology within industrial systems. Technological change created new forms of waste in industrialized society; it also produced new ways to handle and remove waste. Technology such as the creation of shears, balers, and automobile shredders shaped scrap recycling work. As processing changed, so too did hazards. Scrapyard workers were less likely to suffer lead poisoning in 1980 than their counterparts from the early twentieth century, but they were now exposed to a new set of toxins such as the mix of PCBs, asbestos, and solvents found in automobile shredder residue. Similar effects shaped laundry work during the Gilded Age. Once work done largely by hand in homes, it evolved to work produced within mechanized systems that could be run by one person or staffed by dozens under complex managerial structures. The hazards of the job evolved; if laundry workers became less prone to sores from lye soap, they worked in hotter conditions and faced greater danger of inhaling fumes and particulate matter. (Exposure to contagions in dirty laundry was a continuity.) Varying approaches to laundry during the period produced an expansion of clothes cleaning, and by 1920, affluent and middle-class Americans could contract out the cleaning of their clothes on a regular basis.

The 1860 Census lists a majority of laundry workers in the United States as Chinese. Asian American men were limited in available occupations and restricted from professional occupations such as medicine and teaching. Laundry work, however, was an option, both as an employee and as a business owner. Not only could marginalized immigrants find work in these fields, but enterprising men could start businesses of their own. The initial niche became self-perpetuating and endured for more than a century, with contemporary journalists and sociologists documenting the "Chinese laundryman."

In the 1980s, historians Paul Siu, Ronald Takai, and Henry Yu discussed the experiences and caricatures of the men whose job prospects were limited but who also found opportunity in starting their own businesses. Unlike the retail or restaurant businesses, a small capital outlay of seventy-five to two hundred dollars could open a laundry. The opportunity structure for recent immigrants to open these businesses during this period was very high—there being a strong demand for their services yet few established firms from native-born entrepreneurs as competition. Further, each business could be started with minimal capital costs: a stove, a trough, a dry room, a sleeping apartment, a sign, and the willingness to spend almost every waking hour of one's day washing other people's clothes. Siu noted that a Chinese laundryman did not need to speak much English to operate his business. "In this sort of menial labor," said one laundryman, "I can get along speaking only 'yes' and 'no.'"[33]

Narratives from the Gilded Age indicate this was not a simple transfer of experiences immigrant men brought from China but an adaptation to U.S. society that inverted their traditional gender roles due to restricted opportunities. In 1906, Lee Chew observed, "The Chinese laundryman does not learn his trade in China; there are no laundries in China. The women there do the washing in tubs and have no washboards or flat irons. All the Chinese laundrymen here were taught in the first place by American women just as I was taught." Chin Foo Wong of New York City wrote in 1888 that laundry work in China was a "woman's occupation," and men did not "step into it for fear of losing their social standing."[34]

The "Chinese laundry" represented a retreat into self-employment from a narrowly restricted labor market. "You couldn't work in the cigar factories or the jute or woolen mills any more—all the Chinese had been driven out," elderly Chinese men later recalled. "About all they could be was laundrymen or vegetable peddlers then." At once limitation and opportunity, laundries in the 1900 Census of Population were the workplaces of about one-quarter of all employed men of Chinese ancestry living in the United States.[35]

The laundry trade had evolved by 1900 so that Chinese representation declined—not because of alternative labor options for Chinese men so much as the expansion of laundry work throughout the United States. Between 1850 and 1920, the representation of native-born Black and white workers increased and that of individuals of Chinese origin shrank until the vast majority of people employed in laundry services were native-born to native-born parents. Most of the people working in laundry services in the 1920 Census were white; however, all laundry work was not equal. By 1920, when the census broke laundry work into different occupations, management and ownership were significantly more represented by whites and laborers by African Americans.

In Chicago, as sociologists St. Clair Drake and Horace Cayton observed in *Black Metropolis*, about three thousand women earned their living in 1930 by washing clothes in the homes of their employers or by taking laundry to their own homes, and of these, over half were Black women. Drake and Cayton observed the toils of one such woman: "She is expected to do all the washing, including the linen and towels as well as all the clothes for the five members of the family. She is supposed to finish the work—that is iron the entire wash—and then clean the house thoroughly—all for $2 a day."[36]

The burdens of laundry work observed in Chicago extended to the South. Successful laundries could make their owners wealthy; Henry Loeb Sr., a man of German Jewish ancestry, founded Loeb's Laundries in Memphis in 1887. Employing hundreds of Black women to wash the clothes, Loeb generated enough revenue to purchase competing laundries, consolidating them into the largest laundry business in the city. The resulting wealth afforded his family many privileges, including a political career for grandson Henry Loeb III.[37]

In her 1997 book *To 'Joy My Freedom*, historian Tera Hunter observed that as discretionary income among nineteenth-century women increased, they contracted out laundry services. Even poor urban women might send out at least some of their wash. Large commercial laundries operated in Northern cities by 1900. The South did not adopt mechanized laundry technology as quickly, and instead laundry continued to be largely manual labor, with both affluent and poor whites sending out laundry to Black women.[38]

This work might be completed in the homes of upper- or middle-class employers, but most laundresses worked in their own homes and neighborhoods, where segregation in housing and segregation in work endured, with whites concerned about contagions sending dirty work to Black neighborhoods where "stinkin' n-- wimmin" (in the words of one customer) performed the necessary work to rid the clothes of filth. When washerwomen fell ill with tuberculosis or other infectious diseases, they were blamed by progressive reformers such as the Atlanta Anti-Tuberculosis Association with spreading disease rather than being crucial sanitary agents. As with scrap and garbage, where "dirty" Jews and Italians performed sanitary duties and were scorned by progressive reformers, laundry in the late nineteenth century was a site of racially hypocritical purification in which people seen as unclean were required to keep the clothing of white Americans clean.[39]

Hunter observed that Atlanta's trade in laundry grew significantly after the Civil War. By the end of the 1870s, demand for laundry services in the city had not led to higher wages, and laundry workers organized to strike for better pay. In 1879 and 1880 Atlanta's washerwomen had already engaged in one major strike and had formed a short-lived protective association. In the summer of 1881, concerned over inadequate pay, they formed a new organization—the Washing Society—and called a strike. The resulting protest was the largest in Atlanta's Black community during the late nineteenth century.[40]

Most of Chicago's laundry in 1930 was done in large commercial enterprises employing about fifteen thousand workers. Drake and Cayton calculated that in 1930, 55.4 percent of all the women working in Chicago's laundries were Black, as were 26.3 percent of the men working as semiskilled operatives in the industry. The scale of Chicago laundries was amenable to labor organizing, with local workers affiliating with the American Federation of Labor by the end of the 1930s (including about two thousand white members and eight thousand Black members).[41]

By 1930, these sanitary occupations employed many more people than they had in 1865, cleaning homes, clothes, and streets. These skills were vital to public health and useful to industry, yet they were not valued as skills by most white Americans. Popular stereotypes of these workers presented them as dirty people of low morals and intelligence and unworthy of public respect. Dirty work was of both low status and high importance and unfit for those who identified themselves as white Americans.

Post–World War II Environmental Inequalities in Waste Work

Consistent with Roediger's chronology of definitions of whiteness evolving after World War II, demographic patterns in waste-handling occupations underwent a shift between 1950 and 1970. Americans of southern and eastern European heritage assimilated into white society, leaving waste behind. If the Jewish junk peddler was an iconic figure in the late nineteenth-century U.S. city, the image was a historical artifact at the end of the twentieth century. Jews still participated in the scrap metal industry in large numbers, yet the terms of this participation had changed. Rare in 1980 was the scrap firm employing Jews as yard labor; Jews remained prevalent as owners and in managerial roles in scrap businesses but were less common among the people who regularly handled the materials.

An analysis of occupational category by racial category in the IPUMS samples of the United States population for 1950, 1960, and 1970 indicates the labor force in most waste-handling occupations became progressively more represented by Black and Latino/a workers. This was true of the primarily female workforce serving as private domestic housekeepers, and roughly one-third of American laundry workers in the United States were Black between 1950 and 1970. That share remained static from the mid-twentieth century, while the percentage of Latino/a laundry workers progressively grew. Janitorial work was an outlier, as non-Latino/a whites actually grew as a percentage of the workforce between 1950 and 1970. Janitorial work is an example of the representation of Black workers shrinking over time, from almost three times their representation in the general population to slightly over double their representation between 1950 and 1970.

Opportunities to examine the racial dimensions of each of these trades exist, as do opportunities to see how affected workers demonstrated resistance to environmental inequalities. Michael K. Honey's 2007 book *Going down Jericho Road* documents Memphis's employment of over one thousand Black men to collect garbage in the 1960s, the workers' struggle with Mayor Henry Loeb III, and their influence on labor organizing for sanitation workers in other cities. The dehumanizing aspects of waste handling in Memphis meant the city could not successfully attract white working-class men as replacement labor. Black Memphians would not cross the picket line because they viewed the workers' plight as a civil rights issue, a framework that was quickly adopted as national civil rights organizations and the American Federation of State, County, and Municipal Employees (AFSCME) united around the workers. The slogan "I *Am* a Man!" reflected defiance of the existing waste-management regime. Honey's book offers a framework for exploring the nexus of race, class, and waste work in U.S. history, with one opportunity for study being the founding of the SEIU as a reaction to the burdens of racialized dirty work.[42]

The 1968 strike's emphasis on the workers' plight being a civil rights issue represents the kind of activism and rhetoric recognizable in the environmental justice actions of the 1980s. The strike also illuminates the intensification of environmental inequalities in waste work over more than a century of U.S. history.

The Future of Dirty Work

Industrial society, of course, is not limited to the borders of the United States. Dirty work's nexus of critical discard studies, labor history, and the environment has rich possibilities for further exploration in the United States, in other nations, and in comparative frameworks worldwide. Several studies of waste work in the United States, Europe, Mexico, Central America, Brazil, South Asia, East Asia, Egypt, and sub-Saharan Africa have proliferated over the past two decades, giving historians a better idea of specific experiences in different societies. Most of these studies cover the present day and recent past, reflecting the growth of megacities (and concomitant growth of urban waste-management regimes) since 1990. Many studies reflect intersectional dynamics of race, gender, class, and religion, with several ethnographic profiles of urban scavenging operations in the recent literature.[43] Most involve waste work within individual nations or even cities (with Cairo and São Paulo being prominent sites of study), although recent comparative studies of waste-management practices include Sarah Hill's attention to the border waste trade between the United States and Mexico, Joshua O. Reno's work on waste management at the United States' northern border with Canada, separate studies by Nicky Gregson and Mike Crang and David N. Pellow on global patterns of toxic waste dumping and trading, and Raymond Stokes, Roman Köster, and Stephen Sambrook's comparative study of West German and British waste-management practices after World War II. These studies provide ways to think about comparative historical approaches to the social dimensions of waste work.[44]

All this work must account for the particular times, places, and peoples involved; systems have histories contingent on those factors rather than a deterministic model. The particular constructions of dirty work in the United States have influenced dirty work in other countries. Explicitly comparative publications include Warwick Anderson's approach to colonial public health sanitation efforts as reproducing American cultural constructions of waste and hygiene beyond the nation's borders. One recent model that echoes Anderson's approach involves food systems: Susanna Rankin Bohme's transnational study on the use and regulation of agricultural pesticides in Hawaii (both in the final decade that it was a U.S. territory and after statehood in 1959) and Central America highlights how relations between consumptive wealthy nations and producer nations evolve over time and how large industrial interests such as those of Dow, Shell, and Dole establish systems that reproduce body burdens among workers in different societies. These models may provide ways of viewing existing case studies of waste work as historically situated transnational processes, deepening the work Pellow, Gregson, and Crang are doing with attention to change over time.[45]

Since this chapter has focused on experiences in the United States since the mid-nineteenth century, I emphasize the important caveat that understanding the particular historical constructions of race and waste within each society is vital to understanding that society's labor systems. Racial constructions of waste work in Brazil relate to how race has been constructed in Brazil rather than being simple reproductions or exports of the United States' racial inequities. The same is true of waste work in India, in China, in Ghana, and in all places where scholars cannot assume simple reproductions of inequalities transplanted from other places. A transnational analysis of environmental racism cannot inadvertently colonize constructions of waste, and historians must recognize the geographic, cultural, and temporal contexts in which waste work is done.

That observation is consistent with practicing good history, period, as is a related point. If waste work is part of a system, historians cannot assume the lives of people working within the system are tragically determined to lack agency. Much of the recent literature on dirty work in general focuses on the disposability of workers in unpleasant occupations, such as sex workers and prison guards. While this strain of vulnerability is present in the history of waste trade work, widespread evidence of resilience is also visible in resistance efforts as well as conscious adaptations and accommodations within the system. As the U.S. scrap industry evolved in the early twentieth century, immigrant scrap dealers harassed by the police, sued by clients, and zoned out of urban spaces responded by forming trade associations. Some of the businesses that they formed grew in size and profitability, producing multigenerational economic advancement.

A triumphant narrative of this history involves succession and assimilation. A trope in the memoirs of many successful Jewish Americans is the Walter Mitty–like ascent from humble origins. Kirk Douglas, for example, titled his autobiography *The Ragman's Son*, and similar tales are told by other actors (Mandy Patinkin), steel executives (Aaron Levinson), and academics. My great-grandfather, Abraham Zimring, collected discarded metal from Iowa farmers. My engagement with the themes in this volume stems from a family history that involves this trope of advancing out of waste work either within or across generations.[46]

Even for those who remain in the waste trades, progress is a part of the narrative. Organizing and advancing are themes in the literature. Within garbage hauling, an atypical but famous example involves the business Dutch immigrant Harm Huizenga founded in Chicago. From a one-man ash-hauling business grew a garbage-collection company that Harm's grandchildren built into Waste Management, Inc. In the twenty-first century, this company generates more than $15 billion in revenue through activities in over a dozen countries, and Harm's grandson Wayne grew sufficiently wealthy to own Blockbuster Video, the Florida Marlins baseball team, the Florida Panthers hockey team, and the Miami Dolphins football team.[47]

Amassing wealth on that scale is rare, but advancement was and is possible in the U.S. waste trades. Labor organization among janitors and laundry workers produced safer workplace environments, higher wages, and benefits for members. Their history reminds us that the history of dirty work is contingent on the experiences and opportunities of people in particular times and places. Opportunities as well as hazards exist.[48]

The waste-management systems produced in the nineteenth and twentieth centuries benefit millions of Americans who are relieved of the burdens of waste management due to racial constructions. Injuries and deaths on the job are common in waste work, which annually ranks with fishing and mining among the most dangerous occupations in industrial society. The organization of this system reinforces unjust labor structures through the practices of waste and wasting Americans consider normal.

I do not make this point as a detached observer but as a white American man who is a part of these processes in the early twenty-first century. My position within the system is different from the position that my great-grandfather held. The historical dynamics that brought Abraham Zimring to the United States in 1904 to do the dangerous work of handling scrap materials led our family to a set of accommodations over the next century that placed me in a position of privilege. The social barriers that a Jewish immigrant from Austria faced at the turn of the twentieth century were gone by the time my father was a young law student in the 1960s; my great-grandfather's experience was a distant aspect of my family's history by the time I was a graduate student in the 1990s. My work as a history professor does not expose me to the hazards of handling discards that imperiled workers like my great-grandfather as part of the everyday experiences of that work.

My work as a history professor now exposes workers to the hazards of handling my discards. When I place used paper in my office's recycling bin, I produce a flow of discards that workers ranging from the custodial staff of my office building to the workers on trucks and in materials recovery facilities (MRFS) must handle. A few blocks from my Brooklyn office, the hydraulic press of a paper-recycling truck crushed Dominican American worker Luis Camarillo to death in 2013. For all that I know, that eighteen-year-old person—the same age as the students in my undergraduate classes—was handling some of my paper when he was killed. The system in which I work shifts the burden of handling waste I generate to workers who face risks I do not experience.[49]

This set of inequalities is not invisible; it is articulated in recent U.S. political culture. During one of the 2016 presidential debates, Hillary Clinton raised Donald Trump's insult of beauty pageant winner Alicia Machado as "Miss Housekeeping" as an example of his intersectional bigotry toward women in general and Latinas in particular. That Trump demeaned Machado by associating her identity with domestic cleaning work reveals one of Trump's several conscious invocations of how work, whiteness, and waste have intertwined in U.S. society. During his presidency, Trump equated the majority-Black city of Baltimore with rats and referred to immigrants from Haiti, El Salvador, and African nations as coming from "shithole countries." President Trump's words are stark expressions of how white identities in twenty-first-century America result from how white Americans normalized waste work as nonwhite work over the past two centuries. Confronting this history is an important step in dismantling the enduring structures of environmental racism.[50]

Recognizing how systems of producing, consuming, and discarding have shaped the past and present inequalities of waste work in the United States is the start of telling histories that center the experiences, accomplishments, and sacrifices of workers who are too often belittled or erased from the narratives that historians write. A focus on the ways dirty work has been defined and how it has been done by particular peoples at particular times is crucial in revealing the importance of those systems and the peoples within those systems. Environmental historians engaging in this approach might heed Kathleen A. Brosnan's call to "create pathways for others to find our scholarship and rethink our large concerns about nature and the human place in it."[51]

Notes

1. Thompson, *Making of the English Working Class*, 9; McEvoy, *Fisherman's Problem*; Andrews, *Killing for Coal*.
2. Brosnan, "Lifting Fog"; Melosi, "Equity, Eco-racism and Environmental History."
3. Tera Hunter's work features later in this chapter. Here I will note that Joe William Trotter Jr.'s work at Carnegie Mellon University has included not only the many books he has written or edited but also establishing the Center for Africanamerican Urban Studies and the Economy (CAUSE) and working to have Professor Hunter join Carnegie Mellon's faculty early in her career. Trotter's work is an example of how historians can build structures and opportunities for telling representative histories, and I thank him for his influence on my thinking since my time as a student in his American history graduate seminar in 1994. Two of his many relevant books to this discussion are *Coal, Class, and Color* and *Workers on Arrival*.
4. Liboiron and Lepawsky, *Discard Studies*, 3. This book builds on work developed at discardstudies.com since 2010. Publications by its editors and contributors that shaped my thinking about how scholars can and should engage with these ideas include MacBride, *Recycling Reconsidered*; Nagle, *Picking Up*; Lepawsky, *Reassembling Rubbish*; and Liboiron, *Pollution Is Colonialism*.
5. Zimring, "Dirty Work"; Zimring, *Cash for Your Trash*; Zimring, *Clean and White*.
6. Roediger, *Wages of Whiteness*; Roediger, *Working towards Whiteness*; hooks, "Representing Whiteness"; Jacobson, *Whiteness*; Kelley, "Building Bridges"; Painter, *History of White People*. Benjamin Chavis described environmental racism in 1992 as "racial discrimination in environmental policy-making and the enforcement of regulations and laws, the deliberate targeting of people of color communities for toxic waste facilities, the official sanctioning of the life-threatening presence of poisons and pollutants in our communities, and history of excluding people of color from leadership in the environmental movement." Quoted in Di Charo, "Nature as Community," 304.
7. Recent examples of how American environmental historians may address settler colonialism include works by both editors of this book, including Mendoza, "Treacherous Terrain," and Voyles, *Settler Sea*. Valenčius's *"Health of the Country"* is an earlier environmental history approach to contested racial identities in frontier colonialism.
8. Goffman, *Stigma*; Hughes, "Good People and Dirty Work"; M. Douglas, *Purity and Danger*. For a careful historicizing of the "matter out of place" statement associated with Douglas and how it may be used to understand power relations within systems, see Liboiron, "Matter Out of Place."

9. Perry, *Collecting Garbage*.

10. White, "'Are You an Environmentalist?'" See also Montrie, *Making a Living*; Andrews, *Killing for Coal*; and McEvoy, *Fisherman's Problem*.

11. Hurley, *Environmental Inequalities*; Sellers, *Hazards of the Job*; Washington, *Packing Them In*; McGurty, *Transforming Environmentalism*.

12. Tarr, *Search for the Ultimate Sink*; Hays, *Explorations in Environmental History*; Melosi, *Sanitary City*. Washington's *Packing Them In* is an example of careful historical analysis of environmental racism that encompasses a variety of peoples classified as nonwhite in the nineteenth century.

13. Commission for Racial Justice, *Toxic Wastes and Race in the United States*; Bullard, *Dumping in Dixie*; Pulido, "Geographies of Race and Ethnicity II," 2.

14. Liboiron and Lepawsky's discussion of difference and sorting in chapter 4 of their book *Discard Studies* is especially good for thinking about how to avoid conflating people and experiences within waste systems.

15. Zimring, "Dirty Work," 90–112.

16. Zimring, "Dirty Work," 106.

17. Ruggles et al., *Integrated Public Use Microdata Series*.

18. Ashforth and Kreiner, "Contextualizing Dirty Work."

19. Drew, Mills, and Gassaway, *Dirty Work*; Simpson et al., *Dirty Work*, 2.

20. Pellow, *Garbage Wars*; Gould, Pellow, and Schnaiberg, *Treadmill of Production*. I elaborate on this chapter's summary of census data in *Clean and White*.

21. United States Bureau of the Census, *Historical Statistics of the United States: Colonial Times to 1957 (U.S. G.P.O, 1960)*, Series D 152–166, "Industrial Distribution of Gainful Workers: 1820 to 1940," 138.

22. "The Refuse of the City," *New York Times*, December 4, 1881, 2.

23. Waring, *Street-Cleaning*, 74.

24. "Some Hazards of City Housecleaning," *Survey*, April 14, 1917, 42.

25. Institute of Scrap Iron and Steel, *Addresses*, 41–59.

26. Gutenschwager, "Scrap Iron and Steel Industry," 47–64; Pellow, *Garbage Wars*.

27. Smith, "New Paths to Power"; Van Raaphorst, *Union Maids Not Wanted*; May, *Unprotected Labor*.

28. For more on the history of janitors (as well as the laundry discussion later in this chapter), see "Dirty Work, Dirty Workers" in Zimring, *Clean and White*, 109–36.

29. Coulter, *Take Up*, 74–75.

30. Gold, "Janitors versus Tenants."

31. Gold, "Janitors versus Tenants," 487.

32. Gold, "Janitors versus Tenants," 488.

33. Siu, *Chinese Laundryman*, 52, 119–23. See also Takai, *Different Mirror*; Yu, *Thinking Orientals*.

34. Primary sources discussing the experiences of Chinese immigrants in laundry work include Chew, "Life Story of a Chinaman"; Foo, "Chinese in New York."

35. N. P. Chew, "Chinaman in America," 802. Quoted in Takai, *Different Mirror*, 185.

36. Drake and Cayton, *Black Metropolis*, 249–50.

37. "A Resistant Mayor: Henry Loeb," *New York Times*, April 17, 1968, 24.

38. Hunter, *To 'Joy My Freedom*, 56.

39. Hunter, *To 'Joy My Freedom*, 105, 120, 200.

40. Hunter, *To 'Joy My Freedom*, 85–89.

41. Drake and Cayton, *Black Metropolis*, 250.

42. Organizing waste workers is a largely uncharted topic by historians, a few references (including Hunter and Kelley) excepted. Examples include articles by Stephen Lerner and Jennifer Luff, Don Stillman's organizational history of the SEIU (*Stronger Together*), and two histories on the 1968 Memphis Public Works strike: Joan Turner Beifuss's *At the River I Stand* and Michael K. Honey's *Going down Jericho Road*.

43. Examples include Gutberlet et al., "Participatory Research"; Nunn and Gutberlet, "Cooperative Recycling in São Paulo"; Baabereyir, Jewitt, and O'Hara, "Dumping on the Poor"; Nzeadibe, "Informal Waste Management in Africa"; Zapata Campos and Zapata, "Travel of Global Ideas"; Gidwani, "Work of Waste"; Kirby and Lora-Wainwright, "Exporting Harm, Scavenging Value"; Nguyen, "Trading in Broken Things"; and Spellman, *Trash Talks*.

44. Pellow, *Resisting Global Toxics*; Stokes, Köster, and Sambrook, *Business of Waste*; Gregson and Crang, "From Waste to Resource"; Reno, *Waste Away*.

45. Anderson, "'Where Every Prospect Pleases'"; Bohme, *Toxic Injustice*.

46. K. Douglas, *Ragman's Son*; Mandy Patinkin, "My Story as an American Jew," *Shofar Magazine*, 1998, site discontinued; Levinson, *If Only Right Now*; Zimring, *Cash for Your Trash*.

47. Swierenga, *Dutch Chicago*, 586–88.

48. Lerner, "Black and Brown"; Luff, "Justice for Janitors"; Stillman, *Stronger Together*.

49. Colin Moynihan, "Worker Is Crushed by Garbage Truck Compactor in Brooklyn," *New York Times*, March 16, 2013.

50. Barbaro and Twohey, "For Ex-Miss Universe, a New, Harsh Spotlight," *New York Times*, September 28, 2016, A16; Gay, "No One Is Coming to Save Us from Trump's Racism," *New York Times*, January 13, 2018, A19; Baker, "Trump Calls a House Critic's Baltimore District a 'Rat and Rodent Infested Mess,'" *New York Times*, July 28, 2019, A20. Racialized language surrounding hygiene is not exclusive to the right wing in contemporary American political discourse. As I recounted in *Clean and White*, Joe Biden referred to Barack Obama as "clean"

early in the 2008 presidential campaign, raising questions about why he would use that word to describe a sitting U.S. senator.

51. Brosnan, "Lifting Fog," 18.

Bibliography

Anderson, Warwick. "'Where Every Prospect Pleases and Only Man Is Vile': Laboratory Medicine as Colonial Discourse." *Critical Inquiry* 18, no. 3 (1992): 506–29.

Andrews, Thomas G. *Killing for Coal: America's Deadliest Labor War*. Cambridge MA: Harvard University Press, 2008.

Ashforth, Blake E., and Glen E. Kreiner. "Contextualizing Dirty Work: The Neglected Role of Cultural, Historical, and Demographic Context." *Journal of Management & Organisation* 20, no. 4 (2014): 423–40.

Baabereyir, Anthony, Sarah Jewitt, and Sarah O'Hara. "Dumping on the Poor: The Ecological Distribution of Accra's Solid-Waste Burden." *Environment and Planning A* 44, no. 2 (2013): 297–314.

Beifuss, Joan Turner. *At the River I Stand: Memphis, the 1968 Strike, and Martin Luther King*. Brooklyn NY: Carlson, 1990.

Bohme, Susanna Rankin. *Toxic Injustice: A Transnational History of Exposure and Struggle*. Berkeley: University of California Press, 2014.

Brosnan, Kathleen A. "The Lifting Fog: Race, Work, and the Environment." *Environmental History* 24, no. 1 (January 2019): 9–24.

Bullard, Robert D. *Dumping in Dixie: Race, Class, and Environmental Quality*. 3rd ed. Boulder CO: Routledge, 1990.

Chew, Lee. "Life Story of a Chinaman." In *The Life Stories of Undistinguished Americans as Told by Themselves*, edited by Hamilton Holt, 289–90. New York: J. Pott, 1906.

Chew, Ng Poon. "The Chinaman in America." *Chautauquan* 9, no. 4 (January 1888): 802.

Commission for Racial Justice. *Toxic Wastes and Race in the United States: A National Report on the Racial and Socio-economic Characteristics of Communities with Hazardous Waste Sites*. New York: United Church of Christ, 1987.

Coulter, Charles Edward. *Take Up the Black Man's Burden: Kansas City's African American Communities, 1865–1939*. Columbia: University of Missouri Press, 2006.

Di Charo, Giovanna. "Nature as Community: The Convergence of Environmental and Social Justice." In *Uncommon Ground: Rethinking the Human Place in Nature*, edited by William Cronon, 298–320. New York: W. W. Norton, 1995.

Douglas, Kirk. *The Ragman's Son: An Autobiography*. New York: Simon & Schuster, 1998.

Douglas, Mary. *Purity and Danger: An Analysis of Concepts of Purity and Taboo*. New York: Praeger, 1966.

Drake, St. Clair, and Horace Cayton. *Black Metropolis: A Study of Negro Life in a Northern City*. New York: Harcourt, Brace, 1945.

Drew, Shirley K., Melanie Mills, and Bob M. Gassaway, eds. *Dirty Work: The Social Construction of Taint*. Waco TX: Baylor University Press, 2007.

Foo, Wong Chin. "The Chinese in New York." *Cosmopolitan* 5, no. 4 (1888): 297–311.

Gidwani, Vinery. "The Work of Waste: Inside India's Infra-economy." *Transactions of the Institute of British Geographers* 40, no. 4 (2015): 575–95.

Goffman, Erving. *Stigma: Notes on the Management of Spoiled Identity*. Englewood Cliffs NJ: Prentice-Hall, 1963.

Gold, Ray. "Janitors versus Tenants: A Status-Income Dilemma." *American Journal of Sociology* 57, no. 5 (1952): 486–93.

Gould, Kenneth A., David N. Pellow, and Allan Schnaiberg. *The Treadmill of Production: Injustice and Unsustainability in the Global Economy*. Boulder CO: Paradigm, 2008.

Gregson, Nicky, and Mike Crang. "From Waste to Resource: The Trade in Wastes and Global Recycling Economies." *Annual Review of Environment and Resources* 40, no. 1 (2015): 151–76.

Gutberlet, Jutta, Angela Baeder, Nídia Pontuschka, Sonia Felipone, and Tereza dos Santos. "Participatory Research Revealing the Work and Occupational Health Hazards of Cooperative Recyclers in Brazil." *International Journal of Environmental Research and Public Health* 10, no. 10 (2013): 4607–27.

Gutenschwager, Gerald A. "The Scrap Iron and Steel Industry in Metropolitan Chicago." Master's thesis, University of Chicago, 1957.

Hays, Samuel P. *Explorations in Environmental History*. Pittsburgh: University of Pittsburgh Press, 1998.

Honey, Michael K. *Going down Jericho Road: The Memphis Strike, Martin Luther King's Last Campaign*. New York: W. W. Norton, 2007.

hooks, bell. "Representing Whiteness in the Black Imagination." In *Displacing Whiteness: Essays in Social and Cultural Criticism*, edited by Ruth Frankenberg, 165–79. Durham NC: Duke University Press, 1997.

Hughes, Everett. "Good People and Dirty Work." In *The Other Side: Perspectives on Deviance*, edited by Howard Becker, 23–26. New York: Free Press of Glencoe, 1964.

Hunter, Tera. *To 'Joy My Freedom: Southern Black Women's Lives and Labors after the Civil War*. Cambridge MA: Harvard University Press, 1997.

Hurley, Andrew. *Environmental Inequalities: Class, Race, and Industrial Pollution in Gary, Indiana, 1945–1980*. Chapel Hill: University of North Carolina Press, 1995.

Institute of Scrap Iron and Steel. *Addresses at the 36th Annual Convention*. Washington DC: ISIS, 1964.

Jacobson, Matthew Fry. *Whiteness of a Different Color: European Immigrants and the Alchemy of Race*. Cambridge MA: Harvard University Press, 1999.

Kelley, Robin D. G. "Building Bridges: The Challenge of Organized Labor in Communities of Color." *New Labor Forum* no. 5 (Fall–Winter 1999): 42–58.

Kirby, Peter Wynn, and Anna Lora-Wainwright. "Exporting Harm, Scavenging Value: Transnational Circuits of E-waste Between Japan, China and Beyond." *Area* 47, no. 1 (2015): 40–47.

Lepawsky, Josh. *Reassembling Rubbish: Worlding Electronic Waste.* Cambridge MA: MIT Press, 2018.

Lerner, Stephen. "Black and Brown: The United Colors of Low-Wage Workers." *Race, Poverty, & the Environment* 14, no. 1 (2007): 33–34.

Levinson, Aaron P. *If Only Right Now Could Be Forever.* Hillsboro OR: Blue Heron, 1987.

Liboiron, Max. "Matter Out of Place." In *The Routledge Handbook of Waste Studies,* edited by Zsuzsa Gille and Josh Lepawsky, 31–40. New York: Routledge, 2022.

———. *Pollution Is Colonialism.* Durham NC: Duke University Press, 2021.

Liboiron, Max, and Josh Lepawsky. *Discard Studies: Wasting, Systems, and Power.* Cambridge MA: MIT Press, 2022.

Luff, Jennifer. "Justice for Janitors." In *Encyclopedia of U.S. Labor and Working Class History,* edited by Eric Arensen, 729–31. New York: Routledge, 2007.

MacBride, Samantha. *Recycling Reconsidered: The Present Failure and Future Promise of Environmental Action in the United States.* Cambridge MA: MIT Press, 2011.

May, Vanessa H. *Unprotected Labor: Household Workers, Politics, and Middle-Class Reform in New York, 1870–1940.* Chapel Hill: University of North Carolina Press, 2011.

McEvoy, Arthur F. *The Fisherman's Problem: Ecology and Law in the California Fisheries, 1850–1980.* Cambridge: Cambridge University Press, 1986.

McGurty, Eileen. *Transforming Environmentalism: Warren County, PCBs, and the Origins of Environmental Justice.* New Brunswick NJ: Rutgers University Press, 2007.

Melosi, Martin V. "Equity, Eco-racism and Environmental History." *Environmental History Review* 19, no. 3 (Autumn 1995): 1–16.

———. *The Sanitary City: Urban Infrastructure in America from Colonial Times to the Present.* Baltimore: Johns Hopkins University Press, 2000.

Mendoza, Mary E. "Treacherous Terrain: Environmental Control at the U.S.-Mexico Border." *Environmental History* 23, no. 1 (January 2018): 117–27.

Montrie, Chad. *Making a Living: Work and Environment in the United States.* Chapel Hill: University of North Carolina Press, 2009.

Nagle, Robin. *Picking Up: On the Streets and Behind the Trucks with the Sanitation Workers of New York City.* New York: Farrar, Straus and Giroux, 2013.

Nguyen, Minh T. N. "Trading in Broken Things: Gendered Performances and Spatial Practices in a Northern Vietnamese Rural-Urban Waste Economy." *American Ethnologist* 43, no. 1 (2016): 116–29.

Nunn, Neil, and Jutta Gutberlet. "Cooperative Recycling in São Paulo, Brazil: Towards an Emotional Consideration of Empowerment." *Area* 45, no. 4 (2013): 452–58.

Nzeadibe, Thaddeus Chidi. "Informal Waste Management in Africa: Perspectives and Lessons from Nigerian Garbage Geographies." *Geography Compass* 7, no. 10 (2013): 729–44.

Painter, Nell Irvin. *The History of White People.* New York: W. W. Norton, 2010.

Pellow, David Naguib. *Garbage Wars: The Struggle for Environmental Justice in Chicago.* Cambridge MA: MIT Press, 2002.

———. *Resisting Global Toxics: Transnational Movements for Environmental Justice.* Cambridge MA: MIT Press, 2007.

Perry, Stuart E. *Collecting Garbage: Dirty Work, Clean Jobs, Proud People.* Piscataway NJ: Transaction, 1998.

Pulido, Laura. "Geographies of Race and Ethnicity II: Environmental Racism, Racial Capitalism and State-Sanctioned Violence." *Progress in Human Geography* 41, no. 4 (August 2017): 524–33.

Reno, Joshua O. *Waste Away: Working and Living with a North American Landfill.* Berkeley: University of California Press, 2015.

Roediger, David R. *The Wages of Whiteness: Race and the Making of the American Working Class.* New York: Verso Books, 1991.

———. *Working towards Whiteness: How America's Immigrants Became White; The Strange Journey from Ellis Island to the Suburbs.* New York: Basic Books, 2005.

Ruggles, Steven, J. Trent Alexander, Katie Genadek, Ronald Goeken, Matthew B. Schroeder, and Matthew Sobek. *Integrated Public Use Microdata Series: Version 5.0.* Machine-readable database. Minneapolis: University of Minnesota, 2010.

Sellers, Christopher C. *Hazards of the Job: From Industrial Disease to Environmental Health Science.* Chapel Hill: University of North Carolina Press, 1997.

Simpson, Ruth, Natasha Slutskaya, Patricia Lewis, and Heather Höpfl, eds. *Dirty Work: Concepts and Identities.* New York: Palgrave MacMillan, 2012.

Siu, Paul. *The Chinese Laundryman: A Study of Social Isolation.* New York: NYU Press, 1987.

Smith, Karen Manners. "New Paths to Power: 1890–1920." In *No Small Courage: A History of Women in the United States*, edited by Nancy F. Cott, 375–78. New York: Oxford University Press, 2004.

Spellman, Elizabeth V. *Trash Talks: Revelations in the Rubbish.* New York: Oxford University Press, 2016.

Stillman, Don. *Stronger Together: The Story of SEIU.* Washington DC: SEIU, 2010.

Stokes, Raymond, Roman Köster, and Stephen Sambrook. *The Business of Waste: Great Britain and Germany, 1945 to the Present.* New York: Cambridge University Press, 2013.

Swierenga, Robert P. *Dutch Chicago: A History of the Hollanders in the Windy City*. Grand Rapids MI: Wm. B. Eerdmans, 2002.

Takai, Ronald. *A Different Mirror: A History of Multicultural America*. New York: Little, Brown, 1993.

Tarr, Joel A. *The Search for the Ultimate Sink: Urban Pollution in Historical Perspective*. Akron OH: University of Akron Press, 1996.

Thompson, E. P. *The Making of the English Working Class*. New York: Vintage, 1966.

Trotter, Joe William, Jr. *Coal, Class, and Color: Blacks in Southern West Virginia*. Urbana: University of Illinois Press, 1990.

———. *Workers on Arrival: Black Labor in the Making of America*. Berkeley: University of California Press, 2019.

United States Bureau of the Census, *Historical Statistics of the United States: Colonial Times to 1957*. Washington DC: U.S. Dept. of Commerce, Bureau of the Census, 1960.

Valenčius, Conevery Bolton. *"The Health of the Country": How American Settlers Understood Themselves and Their Land*. New York: Basic Books, 2002.

Van Raaphorst, Donna L. *Union Maids Not Wanted: Organizing Domestic Workers, 1870–1940*. New York: Praeger, 1988.

Voyles, Traci Brynne. *The Settler Sea: California's Salton Sea and the Consequences of Colonialism*. Lincoln: University of Nebraska Press, 2021.

Waring, George E. *Street-Cleaning and the Disposal of a City's Wastes: Methods and Results and the Effect upon Public Health, Public Morals and Municipal Prosperity*. New York: Doubleday & McClure, 1897.

Washington, Sylvia Hood. *Packing Them In: An Archaeology of Environmental Racism in Chicago, 1865–1954*. Lanham MD: Lexington Books, 2005.

White, Richard. "'Are You an Environmentalist or Do You Work for a Living?': Work and Nature." In *Uncommon Ground: Rethinking the Human Place in Nature*, edited by William Cronon, 171–185. New York: W. W. Norton, 1995.

Yu, Henry. *Thinking Orientals: Migration, Contact, and Exoticism in Modern America*. New York: Oxford University Press, 2001.

Zapata Campos, María José, and Patrik Zapata. "The Travel of Global Ideas of Waste Management: The Case of Managua and Its Informal Settlements." *Habitat International* 41, no. 1 (2014): 41–49.

Zimring, Carl A. *Cash for Your Trash: Scrap Recycling in America*. New Brunswick NJ: Rutgers University Press, 2005.

———. *Clean and White: A History of Environmental Racism in the United States*. New York: NYU Press, 2015.

———. "Dirty Work: How Hygiene and Xenophobia Marginalized the American Waste Trades, 1870–1930." *Environmental History* 9, no. 1 (January 2004): 90–112.

3

City of Destruction

The Chicago School of Sociology's Ecological Interpretation of Race, Migration, and Inequality

ELIZABETH GRENNAN BROWNING

In his introduction to African American social scientists Horace R. Cayton and St. Clair Drake's groundbreaking study *Black Metropolis: A Study of Negro Life in a Northern City*, published in 1945, Black novelist Richard Wright described Chicago as the *"known* city," where sociologists had scrutinized social dynamics to the point that more was understood about Chicago—"how it is run, how it kills, how it loves, steals, helps, gives, cheats, and crushes"— than any other city.[1] Founded in 1892, the University of Chicago's sociology department—the first of its kind in the nation—had long studied its neighboring environs to understand the processes of urbanization. By the 1920 Census, more Americans lived in cities than in the countryside. Many of the sociologists were migrants to the city themselves and were curious about how this transition from rural to urban shaped communities and individuals' identities. Under the leadership of white elite academics Robert E. Park and Ernest W. Burgess, the first Chicago school dominated the discipline in the 1920s and 1930s by focusing on qualitative methodology (later embracing quantitative methods) in order to push the discipline to infuse its abstract theory with empiricism. Alongside the study of urban sociology, immigration, and crime, race relations became a central focus of the Chicago school, and numerous African American scholars—including Cayton and Drake—were drawn to the university by its reputation for race studies. The Chicago school established the Windy City as the model city for understanding how the urban environment shaped African Americans' social and economic opportunities.[2]

In the 1910s and 1920s, Park and his colleagues also developed the sociological subdiscipline of human ecology, centered in a naturalistic methodology that viewed urban populations in Darwinian and ecological terms and identified the city as "a laboratory or clinic" conducive to the study of social processes.[3] The development of the discipline of sociology occurred in tandem with both the acceleration of modern industrial capitalism and the growth of the modern conservation movement. Anxiety over the preservation of American wilderness and conservation of natural resources tied into a deep uneasiness about the nation's rapid urbanization. Chicago sociologists believed that conflict was a natural feature of the city. As sociologists considered Americans' shift away from the countryside to urban centers and analyzed the conflict between capital and labor, they encountered a multitude of social problems that they deemed endemic to city life, including labor radicalism, juvenile delinquency, suicide, and family strife. Cities remained in "unstable equilibrium," Park cautioned, and "our urban populations are in a state of perpetual agitation, swept by every new wind of doctrine, subject to constant alarms, and . . . in a chronic condition of crisis."[4] Human ecologists' task was clear: to understand the underlying "natural" processes behind the growth of the city in order to better predict social change and effect social control. Since the city was a product of nature, the Chicago school rationalized, it could be controlled just as Americans had tamed wild nature through technological ingenuity.

The Chicago school's development of human ecology occurred in the context of a contentious transition underway in the American social sciences in the 1920s and 1930s: a movement away from citing racial and biological theories of human behavior and toward explaining the cause of human actions by accounting for environmental, cultural, and historical factors. Park and his students showed the influence of anthropologist Franz Boas's attack on scientific racism and recognition of cultural pluralism against the dominant theory of social evolution. Yet even as Park's writings on race relations abandoned a biologically based notion of a racial hierarchy, he did not go so far as to cite W. E. B. Du Bois's pioneering work *The Philadelphia Negro* (1899), where Du Bois revolutionized the use of empirical sociological research to show race as a social construct and highlight the impact of structural inequalities.[5] By defining the boundaries of the city and modeling patterns of urban growth through ecological metaphors, Chicago sociologists reflected their questioning of eugenicist arguments that attributed urban decay to an individual's inherent character or genetic factors.[6] Instead, Park and his colleagues believed that the urban environment was crucial in influencing personal character and thus contributing to "pathological" problems of poverty, crime, and disease. However, the Chicago sociologists' designation of universal laws to explain social processes revealed that human ecology constituted a transitional approach in the shift toward a hybridized set of cultural and environmental explanations regarding differences in human behavior. At the same time that the Chicago model challenged racialized conceptions of social disorder, it also naturalized socioeconomic inequality and made such injustices appear inevitable.[7]

In the broader national context of racial discourse, Park's shift from biological to cultural theories of racial difference was part of the same intellectual trajectory reflected in the transition from biological racism to cultural racism. Biological racism undergirded works promoting social Darwinism, eugenics, and scientific racism, with Madison Grant's *The Passing of the Great Race* (1916) serving as the most notable example. Yet with the influence of Boas and Park, the social sciences began redefining race as a cultural construct, and thus racism took a cultural turn as well. Theories like the "culture of poverty," established by anthropologist Oscar Lewis in 1959, and the "tangle of pathology," popularized by Daniel Patrick Moynihan in 1965, advanced a cultural interpretation of race but tied this race-as-culture paradigm to patterns of psychological damage and pathological value systems. Ideas about race as a cultural construct continued to underlie racism's fluid forms until they became accompanied by the return of biological theories of race in the 1990s. Biological interpretations of race reappeared through a heightened medicalization of race in explaining the etiology of disease and with works like Richard Herrnstein and Charles Murray's *The Bell Curve: Intelligence and Class Structure in American Life* (1994), which made connections between intelligence and race-based genetic factors, a revival of scientific racism discredited by mainstream science.[8]

Keeping in mind this broader historical and theoretical context of defining both race and racism, this chapter examines how Chicago school African American intellectuals used human ecology both in conceptualizing the shift toward cultural interpretations of race and in liberating African Americans from scientific racism. In uncovering the connections between Wright's *12 Million Black Voices: A Folk History of the Negro in the United States* (1941) and Cayton and Drake's *Black Metropolis: A Study of Negro Life in a Northern*

City (1945), this chapter highlights how environmental thought shaped their understandings of the links between race and culture. These Black intellectuals challenged a racist trope that dated back to the origins of American slavery: that slaves' descendants were incapable of surviving outside of their subordinated existence in the agricultural South—what many white Americans had deemed the "natural home" of African Americans. This myth was perpetuated by both the environmental imaginaries of Southern whites, who associated African Americans with plantation labor, and by the environmentally determinist notion that African Americans were better suited for life in the South because of its climatological similarities to Africa. Much as they resisted this racist and deterministic stereotype because it denied the humanity of African Americans, Wright, Cayton, and Drake agreed that most migrants were ill-prepared for urban life, as the transition from rural to urban required adjusting to a faster-paced environment within a larger community that many found isolating and disorienting. Even as staunch a critic of structural racism as Wright speculated that "perhaps never in history has a more utterly unprepared folk wanted to go to the city."[9]

Yet in investigating the poverty and environmental inequalities experienced by Black city dwellers, Wright, Drake, and Cayton upended the pervading racist myth of African descendants as irredeemably primitive and close to nature. These African American scholars challenged the eugenic argument that Blacks were inherently unfit to integrate with white American society by drawing on an urban ecological view that emphasized environment as a key shaper of identity and behavior. Instead of defining race by biological difference, Chicago sociologists pioneered a modern understanding of race grounded in cultural consciousness and identity.[10] However, to liberate African Americans from the racist notion of their inherent inferiority, sociologists created a new problem— they advanced the idea that it was inevitable that Black culture would fade away and be subsumed by the dominant Anglo-American culture. Although Chicago sociologists moved away from scientific racism in asserting that there was no biological difference between races, they still clung to a cultural hierarchy where African American culture was deemed inferior.

Environment and Race in the Great Migration

Throughout the Great Migration, Chicago's segregated infrastructure shaped arriving African American migrants' perceptions and valuation of the urban environment.[11] The city's Black population grew from 44,000 in 1910 to more than 230,000 by 1930, with most migrants settling in the so-called Black Belt, which later became known as a segregated "Black Metropolis" and then "Bronzeville"—a thin enclave, seven miles long and one and a half miles wide, bordered to the north by Twenty-Second Street and the downtown Loop's skyscrapers, to the south by Sixty-Third Street, to the west by working-class white neighborhoods and the Rock Island railroad tracks west of State Street, and to the east by Cottage Grove Avenue and Hyde Park's affluent white neighborhood along the lakefront. Discrimination restricted African Americans' access to environmental goods—like clean air and water and public parks and beaches—and constrained their mobility to the South Side's limited economic and housing markets and neglected municipal services.[12] However, viewing the city as a space of creativity rather than constriction, these South Side communities developed a flourishing urban culture and aesthetic movement in the Chicago Black Renaissance.[13] From literature, poetry, journalism, and the visual arts to dance, jazz, gospel, and blues, Chicago was the epicenter of Black cultural production in the United States from the early 1930s through the 1950s.

Once Southern whites realized Black migration meant the loss of the exploited labor that the South's agricultural economy relied on, they invoked arguments of environmental determinism and scientific racism to claim that African Americans were unfit for Northern states' climes. This narrative dates back to the antebellum era and was a recurring strategy of racist Southern boosters and proslavery ideologues, including George Fitzhugh, J. D. B. DeBow, Josiah Clark Nott, and Samuel Cartwright. A typical editorial written in 1916 in the Macon *Telegraph* cautioned Blacks that they would die in the North's harsh winters. "The Black man is fitted by nature," the *Telegraph* argued, "by centuries of living in it, to work contentedly, effectively and healthily during the long summers of semi-tropical and tropical countries."[14]

The *Chicago Defender*—the nation's preeminent African American newspaper—repeatedly dismantled these deterministic claims about Blacks' unsuitability for environments north of the Mason-Dixon Line. A columnist consulted the newspaper's department of statistics to find no recorded deaths of African Americans attributed to weather conditions. Noting the great demand for labor in the North, the columnist asserted, "Better a thousand times, even if it was true, to run chances of being nipped by the fingers of

Jack Frost than to shake off this mortal coil at the end of the lynchers' rope, or to the crackling of the lynchers' fire brand."[15] Furthermore, Northern cities' built environments offered greater protection from the cold than the South's "rotten living facilities." Yet even when Black migrants successfully secured employment in the North, they were relegated to the most dangerous jobs on account of environmentally deterministic arguments about race. Black workers in the steel industry, for example, typically had the unpleasant job of managing the hazardous coke ovens because managers claimed that they could endure hot conditions.[16]

Some Southern African American leaders also expressed skepticism about mass migration to Northern cities, as it threatened to destabilize their communities' businesses and schools. Countering the lure of the North's industrial prospects, they touted the South's agricultural fields as fertile ground for Blacks' social and economic progress. Influenced by Booker T. Washington's gradualist approach to assimilation, these leaders prioritized maintaining Black clientele and white patronage. The Tuskegee Institute's publication *The Negro Farmer and Messenger* instructed Southern Blacks, "You are farmers; stick to your job."[17] Washington himself had claimed before the start of the Great Migration that he had "never seen any part of the world where it seemed to me the masses of the Negro people would be better off than right here in these southern states."[18] Establishing an independent yeomanry that was free of white manipulation was central to Washington's vision of a liberated Black society.

If journalists and sociologists (white and Black alike) often viewed African American migrants as predisposed toward agricultural peasantry, these social commentators also viewed city environments as naturally destructive of social ties. Like other social scientists concerned about urbanization, race relations, and criminology, sociologist Clifford Shaw equated the city with an inherent disorganization and lack of shared social values. "Dominantly rural in background," Shaw wrote, "the Negro migrant moved from communities which, despite the handicaps connected with inferiority of status, provided the person with a more or less consistent set of values." By Shaw's account, urban problems like juvenile delinquency were the natural result of Black people's shift from the clear norms of rural communities to the more ambiguous cultural expectations of the metropolis. In the city, African Americans lived in "a cultural atmosphere filled with the heady ozone of individualism," and yet structural inequalities restricted Blacks' opportunities to fulfill the creed of individual achievement that dominated American culture.[19]

This tension between Chicago's promises for equality and the reality of racism came to a head in what was a formative moment for Chicago—the 1919 race riot, which surged from July 27 through August 3. Chicago's conflict was part of a nationwide uptick in racial violence after World War I ended, during the "red summer" of 1919. The flash point for Chicago's violence occurred when a twenty-four-year-old white man named George Stauber murdered a seventeen-year-old African American teenager named Eugene Williams along the shores of Lake Michigan, near the Twenty-Ninth Street breakwater. Stauber hurled a fatal volley of rocks at Williams and his friends when their raft crossed an invisible line separating the segregated areas of the beach. One of Stauber's rocks struck Williams, causing him to drown. Chicago police refused to arrest Stauber. The tragedy launched seven days of beatings, shootings, and arson on the South Side, especially around the stockyards. Fueled by whites' anger over the influx of Black migrants in industrial work and Blacks' strikebreaking activity, the racial violence left 23 African Americans and 15 whites dead and resulted in the injury of 342 Blacks and 195 whites.[20]

Although white gangs known as "athletic clubs" were largely responsible for perpetrating the bloodshed, the Chicago Commission on Race Relations, convened by Illinois governor Frank O. Lowden to study the origins of the riot, naturalized violent crime in the Black Metropolis by attributing it to the instability inherent in the migrants' communities. The investigation was directed by executive secretary Graham Taylor, famed leader of the Chicago Commons settlement house and co-founder of the influential Chicago School of Civics and Philanthropy, which became the city's main institution for training social workers when it joined the University of Chicago as the School of Social Service Administration in 1920. Taylor implied that in order to avoid future racial violence, the South Side needed significant reform measures. In notes for an introductory social work class in 1905, Taylor wrote that poverty and "dependency" were formerly attributed to hereditary factors, but experts now believed that "Good Environment Overcomes Heredity."[21]

The commission's report described Bronzeville as a "vicious environment" plagued by vice districts, poor housing, gambling, and a dearth of wholesome sites of recreation like playgrounds and parks. "That many Negroes live near vice districts is not due to their choice nor to low moral standards," the report clarified, but rather on account of three factors: African Americans were "unwelcome" in more desirable white neighborhoods, limited income forced them to live in the cheapest neighborhoods, and they lacked sufficient political and economic power to challenge the encroachment of vice upon their communities. By emphasizing the structural inequalities and the unsavory urban environments faced by African Americans, the commission challenged the notion that high rates of crime in Bronzeville were on account of Blacks' inherent character. Despite the report's efforts to draw attention to the poor conditions of Bronzeville neighborhoods, it failed to spur political action to provide adequate social services for them.

Chicago school sociologists echoed this emphasis on the importance of the environment in shaping human behavior and social relations.[22] Interweaving human ecology and race relations studies, Robert E. Park created a long-lasting framework for sociologists' analysis of African American urban communities. The same cycle took on different names, depending on the study—the interaction cycle, race relations cycle, or assimilation cycle.[23] The roots of Park's race relations cycle date to his time at the Tuskegee Institute, where he served as public relations director and Booker T. Washington's ghostwriter. Adopting Washington's perspective of gradualist racial accommodation, Park outlined a teleological cycle: competition, conflict, accommodation, and assimilation.[24] Park believed that racial conflict was inevitable, and assimilation was the natural culmination of this process: just as urban space would follow natural laws of social organization, so too would African Americans adapt to fit their urban environment, with Anglo-American culture as the endpoint of social evolution.[25] Following dominant theories of social evolution that underlay the social sciences, Park outlined African Americans' cultural transition away from primitivism and toward civilization.

Park's African American graduate student E. Franklin Frazier, the first Black president of the American Sociological Society, was especially influential in shaping national policy discussions about race relations through the lens of human ecology. In *The Negro Family in Chicago* (1932), Frazier applied Park's notions of human ecology to analyze how migration from Southern plantations to Northern cities affected family organization. Frazier traced shifts in the "natural history" of family organization from the beginnings of slavery to the modern industrial cityscape that greeted African Americans during the Great Migration. Frazier employed white Chicago sociologist Ernest W. Burgess's concentric zone model to analyze the "process of selection and segregation" that determined where Black families lived. Burgess's model was the most prolific visual representation of human ecology and showed competing urban groups divided into ecological niches that occupied distinct concentric zones, with the poor and working classes living closer to the city center and the more affluent at the city's perimeters. Burgess borrowed the concept of succession from plant ecologists to explain this geographic segregation of socioeconomic classes. With the concentric zones, Frazier argued that poverty and disorganization were not the result of African Americans' inherent nature but rather unavoidable symptoms of the "disintegrating forces of the city," which had led to a loss of cultural cohesion within Black communities.[26]

Frazier's and Park's theories came under direct attack by white anthropologist Melville J. Herskovits in his book *The Myth of the Negro Past* (1941). Herskovits adopted his mentor Franz Boas's perspective of cultural relativism and worked to dismantle scientific racism in the social sciences. In 1927 Herskovits began teaching anthropology at Northwestern University, where he founded the nation's first interdisciplinary African Studies program several decades later in 1948. Whereas Park and Frazier thought that African Americans retained little, if any, African cultural traditions after their oppression as enslaved people and in facing the disorienting urban environment, Herskovits argued that descendants of the African diaspora in the United States preserved a rich heritage of African cultural identity. Herskovits quoted Frazier as representative of the scholarly community: "Probably never before in history has a people been so nearly completely stripped of its social heritage as the Negroes who were brought to America. . . . Their children, who knew only the American environment, soon forgot the few memories that had been passed on to them."[27] In this Parkian approach, culture was entirely linked to environment, and migrant peoples inevitably assimilated to hegemonic social norms. However, Herskovits argued that African slaves who were forcibly moved to the New World were not blank slates but rather complex people who carried a diversity of Africanisms to the New World.[28] Denouncing Herskovits, Frazier responded that "if whites came to believe that the Negro's social behavior was rooted in African culture, they would lose whatever sense of guilt they had for keeping the Negro down. Negro crime, for example, could be explained away as an 'Africanism' rather than as due to inadequate police and court protection." Frazier worried that Herskovits's stance might bolster segregationists who could point to Africanisms as evidence of racial inferiority.[29] Assimilating to "Western culture," the Chicago school argued, would uplift African Americans and eliminate discrimination.[30]

12 Million Black Voices

Published in 1941, Richard Wright's *12 Million Black Voices*—accompanied by Farm Security Administration (FSA) photographs selected by FSA editor Edwin Rosskam—offers a sweeping historical account of African American experiences during the Great Migration. Horace R. Cayton praised the book as revealing a complex community that he and his fellow sociologists had tried to capture in maps, graphs, and charts—Wright told its history in an unprecedentedly clear way. The book, Cayton thought, was a complement to Wright's *Native Son*, published just a year prior. *Native Son*'s protagonist, Bigger Thomas, is a twenty-year-old African American living in an impoverished area on Chicago's South Side during the 1930s. In a violent scene, Thomas accidentally murders the daughter of his white employer.[31] Wright portrays Thomas's behavior as inevitably arising from the suffocating forces of his urban environment. In his review of *12 Million Black Voices*, Cayton asserted that the book illustrated the "habitat, the social matrix from which warped social personalities such as Bigger Thomas arise."[32]

This leitmotif of the urban environment molding the individual was woven throughout Wright's work. Wright explained that he escaped the Jim Crow South for Chicago in 1927 at age twenty with the desire to tell his story, which he would eventually pen in his memoir *Black Boy* (1945). He described Chicago as "that great iron city, that impersonal, mechanical city, amid the steam, the smoke, the snowy winds, the blistering suns" where African Americans "were pushed and pounded by facts much too big for us."[33] Wright compared Black Chicagoans to characters in a Greek play, lacking control over their own destinies. The urban environment had agency in Wright's thinking. Its impersonality was coupled with a callousness toward human fate.

Seeking greater understanding of the larger-than-life city that he now called home, Wright journeyed to the ivy-covered walls of the University

FIG. 3.1. Horace R. Cayton (*left*) and Richard Wright examine a WPA map of Bronzeville. Horace R. Cayton Papers, box 42, photo 036, Vivian G. Harsh Research Collection of Afro-American History and Literature, Chicago Public Library.

of Chicago, where a social worker assisting him had suggested that he seek out her husband, sociologist Louis Wirth, to help with Wright's research. Wirth was in a meeting with Cayton when Wright knocked on the door. Wright's collaboration with Chicago sociologists transformed his writing by introducing him to ethnographic methods and helping him discern the underlying processes of urban growth.[34] It was not until he encountered social science, Wright claimed, that he began to discover "some of the meanings of the environment that battered and taunted" him. Marshaling the sociologists' facts as evidence in his own writing, Wright credited sociology with giving him his "first concrete vision of the forces that molded the urban Negro's body and soul."[35]

Throughout *12 Million Black Voices*, the contrasts and yet undeniable connections between American rural landscapes and urban environments loomed large. The "dusty land" of Southern farms and the "hard pavement of city streets" simultaneously offered moments of optimism and oppression. Disillusioned with the South's beautiful and yet harsh land—land controlled by hostile white landowners—Blacks migrated north to escape the crushing racism of their daily lives. Even in this move to a place of greater opportunity, a parallel strain of exploitation extended from the Southern "Lords of the Land" to the Northern "Bosses of the Buildings." Powerful whites in both regions wielded paternalist and unjust practices to subjugate the descendants of Black slaves and ensure that Blacks and poor whites would not collaborate to usurp their control.[36] Southern whites condemned Blacks to the least fertile land and trapped them in sharecropping arrangements. In the North, discrimination became legible in the cityscape through segregated neighborhoods, where Blacks suffered poor sanitation, dilapidated housing, and dangerous working conditions.

Wright portrayed Black sharecroppers as focusing on the agricultural landscape's deceptively idyllic qualities. "The land we till is beautiful," he wrote, "with red and black and brown clay, with fresh and hungry smells, with pine trees and palm trees, with rolling hills and swampy delta—an unbelievably fertile land." Yet Wright also showed that this romantic picture of the rural South remained concealed from Black Southerners who lived "full of fear . . . , bowing and grinning when we meet white faces, toiling from sun to sun, living in unpainted wooden shacks that sit . . . insecurely upon the red clay."[37]

This insecurity was bound up in sharecroppers' subordination to the laws of cotton. Ceaseless production of the crop rendered the land infertile, draining it to "a hard, yellow mat, a mockery to the sky and a curse to us." Black sharecroppers were subject to not only the demands of the Lords of the Land but also the unpredictable hazards of nature, from infectious microbes to floods, droughts, and infestations of pests such as boll weevils. Whites benefited from Black labor, while African Americans struggled to secure subsistence from the soil and ultimately lived "just as man lived when he first struggled against this earth."[38] The land's deception lay in its seeming promise of opportunity and yet incessant reinforcement of Blacks' oppression.

With the onset of World War I, the North's "Bosses of the Buildings" promised Southern Blacks financial opportunities through manual labor in the mines, steel plants, and slaughterhouses. However, Black migrants were entirely unprepared for city life, Wright contended. The process of leaving the South was filled with nostalgia and a sense of loss. Migrants were torn between remembering the Southern sky and imagining a richer life in Northern cities' industrial landscapes. But this faith in Northern opportunity obscured the reality of the challenges facing the Black Metropolis's dense population: "How were we to know that the moment we landless millions of the land—we men who were struggling to be born—set our awkward feet upon the pavements of the city, life would begin to exact of us a heavy toll in death?" Claiming that Blacks continued to live with the social, economic, and psychological legacies of two hundred years of slavery, Wright argued that African Americans were unfit for the city's materialism, competition, and impersonality. Amid the Northern city's impersonal swarms of people and the disorienting sense of alienation from the land, it seemed as if Black migrants began "living inside of a machine; days and events move with a hard reasoning of their own." Wright identified the key transition experienced by migrants: "No longer do our lives depend upon the soil, the sun, the rain, or the wind"; rather it was the "brutal logic" of industrial and domestic labor that defined existence.[39]

As white hostility forced Blacks to remain in a polluted environment with overcrowded housing and exorbitant rents, the Black Belt's core suffered slum-like conditions with dilapidated one- and two-story frame houses.[40] Adopting Burgess's concentric zone theory to convey the urban migration patterns identified by human ecologists, Wright explained that the "Bosses of the Buildings" imposed discriminatory employment and housing policies that kept Blacks from moving beyond factory areas to more desirable residential zones at the city's perimeters. At the same time that Wright addressed the systemic discrimination that limited Blacks' social mobility, his invocation of the concentric zone theory implied an inevitable naturalization of the position of African American marginalized Black communities within the larger city.[41]

Turning from the macroenvironment of the city to the intimate confines of the home, Wright portrayed Bronzeville's kitchenettes as havens from the South's plantations and yet environments that still presented significant dangers to African American families. As a gendered space, kitchenettes also hinted at the racialized gendering of sociological data—particularly sociologists' emphasis on birth rates and infant and maternal mortality. As a focal environment in both Wright's and Horace R. Cayton and St. Clair Drake's works, the kitchenette continued as a key site of analysis in later studies like Daniel Patrick Moynihan's controversial Department of Labor report *The Negro Family: The Case for National Action* (1965). For Wright, kitchenettes were "our prison, our death sentence without a trial." While many white urbanites had the luxury of securing a domestic space that separated them from the hazards of the polluted city and preserved the purity of white womanhood, Black residents' kitchenettes could not protect them from the urban environment's impurities or the city's disorganizing forces. Within academic and policy circles, kitchenette communities came to signify matriarchal structures and disorganized families, which many sociological experts deemed responsible for undermining the development of Black youth. However, unlike the Moynihan Report in 1965, which drew on E. Franklin Frazier's work for inspiration, Frazier did not directly attribute matriarchy to social pathologies or warped personalities. To Frazier, Black families were not damaged but resilient. Frazier, like other Chicago sociologists, argued that African American families and communities were not inherently flawed but rather the victims of urban ecology.[42] The kitchenette's "filth and foul air, with its one toilet for thirty or more tenants, kills our black babies so fast that in many cities twice as many of them die as white babies." The kitchenette was the "seed bed" for malnutrition, typhoid, scarlet fever, tuberculosis, dysentery, gonorrhea, syphilis, and pneumonia. African Americans' death rate so exceeded their birth rate, Wright asserted, that if it were not for the constant stream of Southern migrants, Northern cities' Black populations would vanish within a few years.[43]

FIG. 3.2. Russell Lee, *Negro Children Asleep. Southside of Chicago, Illinois.* Library of Congress, LC-USF34-038820-D (P&P) LOT 1081. From *12 Million Black Voices*, 107.

FIG. 3.3. Russell Lee, *Toilet in the Basement of an Apartment House Rented to Negroes. Chicago, Illinois.* Library of Congress, LC-USF34-038617-D (P&P). From *12 Million Black Voices*, 106. Interwoven throughout Richard Wright's *12 Million Black Voices* are photographs by Farm Security Administration photographers, documenting the hazardous living environments of the South Side, on multiple scales—across both the broader level of the city streets and, as pictured here, the more intimate environs of the home, especially in African American neighborhood kitchenettes, which gained notoriety in part from Wright's novels.

Drawing on the Chicago school of sociology's race relations theories, Wright condemned white elites who "say we speak treasonably when we declare that human life is plastic, that human nature is malleable, that men possess the dignity and meaning of the environmental and institutional forms through which they are lucky or unlucky enough to express themselves." As the Chicago school had argued, Wright viewed African American migrants as not inherently corrupt or incapable of adapting to urban conditions. Therefore, as Wright asserted in his final section "Men in the Making," a more equitable urban environment promised to boost African Americans' socioeconomic mobility in the city. Despite the systemic inequalities of the Northern metropolis, Wright claimed, the ties that connected white and Black Americans were stronger than those that separated them. "What we want, what we represent, what we endure is what America *is*," Wright proclaimed.[44]

Black Metropolis

With funding from the New Deal's Works Progress Administration and research support from the University of Chicago, Horace R. Cayton and St. Clair Drake documented the rise and development of Chicago's African American communities in *Black Metropolis: A Study of Negro Life in a Northern City*. As Park's graduate student at the University of Chicago, Cayton was appointed by W. Lloyd Warner, a white professor of anthropology and sociology, to head a series of studies on African Americans' urban experiences with employment, housing, newspapers, churches, and crime, among other topics. Cayton directed a team of two hundred researchers and staff to organize the Cayton-Warner Project, which would become the main source of data for *Black Metropolis*.[45] Drake joined the team in 1937, upon entering the University of Chicago's graduate program in anthropology. Late in his career, he recalled that he had chosen to study anthropology because he "believed the discipline had relevance to the liberation of black people from the devastating consequences of over four centuries of white racism."[46] For the *Black Metropolis* project, Drake researched the South Side's economically disadvantaged population, voluntary associations, and churches. He also spearheaded the synthesis of the project's diverse studies into the book publication, writing two-thirds of the manuscript.[47]

Both Cayton and Drake embraced the Chicago school's legacy of human ecology to interpret urban relations along the color line. They argued that Chicago's Blacks and whites knowingly competed for space, jobs, social status, and political power. "Underlying this conscious competition," they wrote, "is the struggle for existence, a basic and unconscious biological process" that was modified by economic and demographic factors. Adopting the ideas of spatial segregation behind Burgess's concentric zones, they modified Burgess's focus on socioeconomic differences to account for ethnic and racial divides. Competition among ethnic and racial groups for space in the city, Cayton and Drake asserted, was a "basic ecological process" that created segregated patterns. In Black metropolises across the United States, they saw a mutual sense of fear and uneasiness between the larger city and the "Negro city" that grew up within its borders.[48]

Penning the introduction to *Black Metropolis*, Richard Wright argued that the "labor problem" was more significant than the "Negro problem" in American society. Continuing his treatment of industrial relations from *12 Million Black Voices*, Wright suggested that possibly more corrosive for African Americans than the effects of slavery was the rise of machine production, which forever transformed humankind's relationship to the land. Wright linked African Americans' socioeconomic well-being to their ties to the land, claiming that Black people could overcome slavery's political legacies but could not escape the material consequences of modern industrial capitalism. "Their kinship with the soil altered," Wright explained, "men became atoms crowding great industrial cities, bewildered as to their duties and meaning." The dehumanizing forces of industrialization had made workers mere appendages to machines. Alienating workers from the earth, industrial labor created a cognitive dissonance where both Black and white Americans nostalgically continued to seek the moral order of close-knit country villages within cities that starved them of the emotional basis of such communities.[49]

Claiming that humans were the product of their environments, Wright thought that the stakes for urban reform were high. Cayton and Drake's anthropological and sociological approach showed how African Americans' poor living conditions structured their lives just "like an engineer outlining the blue-prints for the production of machines."[50] African Americans' segregated urban environment and their lack of access to environmental goods were inexorable forces shaping their everyday lives.[51] Breaking down the color line so that each side could see the other was an essential goal of Cayton and Drake's research. Part of this objective relied on showing that despite their resentment at being confined to the least desirable areas of the city, African Americans took great pride in their community, and they thought of the Black Metropolis as "something '*of our own*.'"[52]

Despite recognizing this embrace of shared African roots, Cayton and Drake argued that geographic origins were essential to African American social identity in the Black Metropolis, with the "new settler" migrants from the South considered less sophisticated and more likely to occupy the lower class than earlier generations of migrants. Black elites attributed delinquency in lower-class areas to residents' limited education and their prior environments on Southern farms.[53] Just as whites had prejudiced views of African Americans as tied to agricultural peasantry, "old settler" African Americans were critical of what they deemed as the new arrivals' relatively unsophisticated backgrounds. Yet hope for the next generation's social mobility—that children might "make something out of themselves"—heartened Bronzeville parents, old and new settlers alike, who asserted that they were enduring sacrifices for the sake of their children.[54] Old settlers and new migrants shared the belief that the North's urban environment would always offer more opportunities for social uplift, education, and cultural refinement than life in the rural South, where the landscape was blemished by the legacies of slavery and racial violence.

In Bronzeville's lower-class neighborhoods, an informal economy of bartering defined social relations. An apartment building that formerly housed sixty families became the residence of three hundred families.[55] Not only were African Americans relegated to the least desirable areas of the city; they were also expected to perform the most unpleasant and difficult jobs in industry and sanitary services. The notion that Blacks were "unclean" was a long-standing myth used by whites to maintain racist social hierarchies. To preserve their socioeconomic privileges, whites linked hygiene and public health to race. As a result, African Americans were disproportionately represented among garbage collectors, scavengers, street sweepers, domestic workers, and launderers.[56]

The environmental hazards encountered by Bronzeville's lower-class African American population in the late nineteenth and early twentieth centuries were not entirely exceptional—much of their neighborhood's environmental harms were shared by ethnic whites living in the nearby Back of the Yards neighborhood. Like their white counterparts, poor African Americans suffered polluted air and water, neglected municipal services, noise, noxious fumes, flooding outdoor latrines, overloaded garbage piles, and pests like roaches and flies. However, racial prejudice increasingly confined African

THIS IS THE STORY OF NEGROES IN CHICAGO:

We are becoming city dwellers.

FIGS. 3.4 AND 3.5. Mayor's Committee on Race Relations, *Negroes in Chicago*
(October 1944). Chicago Woman's Aid Papers, box 16, folder 151, Chicago Woman's
Aid Society Records, Special Collections and University Archives, University
of Illinois at Chicago. Concern about migrants' "fitness" for transitioning from
rural to urban settings pervaded municipal reform committees' and nonprofit
organizations' advocacy rhetoric. In the early 1940s the Chicago Mayor's
Committee on Race Relations explained the story of African Americans as one
of becoming urban yet always remaining tied to the Southern plantation's soil.
African American and white reformers believed the biggest challenge facing the
Black Metropolis was rural migrants' inexperience in navigating the modern city.

Out of every ten citizens of Chicago, one is an American Negro.

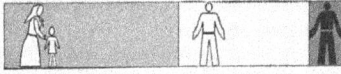

1,775,500 or 53% FOREIGN BORN OR CHILDREN OF FOREIGN BORN	1,239,500 or 37% SECOND GENERATION (or more) NATIVE WHITE STOCK	335,000 or 10% NEGRO

1940 POPULATION ESTIMATES

But our lives were molded in the plantations of the South.

Four-fifths of us came to the city from places outside the state of Illinois. Some of us came from other cities, but most of us were born and brought up in the shadow of the cotton plantations of the Mississippi Valley.

Americans to such hazardous environments, while Chicagoans of European descent could more easily escape to the suburbs.[57] Published in the *Defender* in 1912, a Department of Health bulletin on the "menaces" of smoke and dust in the city endorsed the germ theory, linking the grime of the city to disease-causing microbes. Dust, the bulletin announced, was composed of the mingling of humans and nonhuman nature: "excreta of horses and dogs on the streets, human excreta in tenement districts, human sputum, garbage, . . . dust from buildings being constructed or torn down." The germs within this filth spread countless communicable diseases, including tuberculosis, scarlet fever, influenza, and whooping cough.[58] To prevent these diseases, *Defender* health editor Dr. Wilberforce Williams recommended spending time in the "fresh air and sunlight" of nature. "Go outdoors awhile every day," he instructed, and "especially let the children play awhile outdoors every day," as nature was "the greatest of all teachers."[59]

Whenever possible, leading African American health experts like Williams argued, overcoming the challenges of the polluted urban environment required reconnecting with "pure" nature—something more akin to the South's agricultural landscape than the North's industrial cityscape. This encouragement to get outdoors was also part of an effort to convert Bronzeville's lower classes to the respectable "middle-class way of life." Bronzeville's "New Negro" practiced disciplined behavior in public, pursued a stable marriage and home life, and strove above all for "racial advancement." Cleaning city streets and recreating the wholesomeness of uncorrupted nature within the city through more green space, Black public leaders hoped, would help foster decent and industrious individuals with a race consciousness that was not combative or submissive but rooted in a commitment to self-improvement. Even so, Cayton and Drake stressed the power of the urban environment over Blacks' destiny, claiming that the future of "New Negroes" was determined "by the iron bands of the Black Ghetto and the pressure of the Job Ceiling. Their future and the future of their children is largely beyond their control."[60]

Housed in the Chicago Coliseum in 1940, the American Negro Exposition marked the seventy-fifth anniversary of the abolition of slavery and was a celebratory retrospective of Black visual arts and a high point of the Chicago Black Renaissance. The exposition's social science booth featured dioramas by E. Franklin Frazier, depicting the phases of Black family organization that he had outlined in his study *The Negro Family in Chicago*. In the "City of Destruction," Frazier illustrated the flight of African Americans from a feudal Southern agricultural landscape to the North's modern cities. Frazier's account of the "City of Destruction" resonated in Wright's, Cayton's, and Drake's later works. Although the Northern city was a universal symbol of liberation and hope for a better life for African Americans, so too was it often perceived as a foreboding and disorientating place.[61] The city was initially a disorganizing factor during the dislocation of the Great Migration but then offered new opportunities and stability through improved working conditions. The caption for Frazier's diorama "In the City of Rebirth" explained that Black workers were "helping to build a new America" and witnessing the dissolution of the nation's "color caste."[62]

Frazier's optimistic view of the "City of Rebirth" was ultimately tempered by the legacy of *The Negro Family* in The Moynihan Report.[63] In an effort to spur government intervention, Daniel Patrick Moynihan cited Frazier's work to argue that Blacks were unfit for life in the city.[64] Yet scholars have criticized Moynihan's anachronistic and selective use of Frazier's words as an inaccurate representation of Frazier's thinking. Frazier's concerns about the "disorganization" of family life created by slavery and industrial urbanization were equaled by his belief in Black families' resilience.[65] The "greatest crime of the age," Frazier thought, was "the denial of personality to the Negro" and racism's tendency to reduce African Americans to simply "saints or stones."[66] Despite Moynihan's best intentions in advocating federal action to secure African Americans' social and economic equality, his flawed report produced a mixed legacy. Especially problematic was its emphasis on racial self-help at the expense of highlighting how government programs reproduced structural inequalities.[67]

Another important legacy derived from Park's and Frazier's Chicago school scholarship was Gunnar Myrdal's *An American Dilemma* (1944). A sweeping study of U.S. race relations funded by the Carnegie Corporation, Myrdal's work was cited in the landmark case *Brown v. Board of Education*.[68] Frazier served as an advisor to Myrdal and was a key influence in Myrdal's rejection of Boasian cultural relativity. Myrdal argued that "American Negro culture" was "a distorted development, or a pathological condition, of the general American Culture. . . . This can be said positively: *we assume that it is to the advantage of American Negroes as individuals and as a group to become assimilated into American culture, to acquire the traits held in esteem by the dominant white Americans.*"[69]

To provide a better understanding of the origins of urban inequalities, Cayton, Drake, and Wright worked to reveal the complex interplay of environment, human nature, and structural racism. Urban sociologists and reformers often portrayed the alienating and impersonal city as being at odds with humans' "natural" tendencies. This was doubly the case for African American migrants. From social service agencies to federal and municipal government researchers and newspaper reporters nationwide, many observers expressed skepticism about the capacity of African Americans to make the transition from rural to urban and survive what was a seemingly inhospitable metropolitan environment. The Chicago school insisted that Black migrants were indeed capable of adapting to the modern industrial city. However, the environmental determinism latent in their human ecology approach eclipsed Bronzeville's rich cultural life. Chicago's African American migrants never passively accepted white prescriptions of what kind of environment Blacks were deserving of but rather carved out their own opportunities and forged their own views of the good life in the Black Metropolis.

Notes

Portions of this chapter appeared as *Nature's Laboratory: Environmental Thought and Labor Radicalism in Chicago, 1886–1937* by Elizabeth Grennan Browning, © 2022 Johns Hopkins University Press, reprinted with permission of Johns Hopkins University Press.

1. Wright, introduction to *Black Metropolis*, lx.
2. For the Chicago school's history, see Abbott, *Department & Discipline*; Bulmer, *Chicago School of Sociology*; Kurtz, *Evaluating Chicago Sociology*; and Matthews, *Quest for an American Sociology*.
3. For Chicago school writings on human ecology, see Park, "City," 612. Park later reflected on the novelty of the human ecology approach: "There was, to be sure, an extensive literature on the subject of the city in existence, but no one up to that time had regarded the city as a natural phenomenon." Park, "Notes on the Origin," 3. See also Park, "Human Ecology," 15; McKenzie, "Ecological Approach," 288; Park, "Succession, an Ecological Concept," 176; Park, "Symbiosis and Social-ization," 14; Anderson and Lindeman, *Urban Sociology*, 86. See also Park and Burgess's reference to ecologists in one of the earliest sociology textbooks—*Introduction to the Science of Sociology*—including William Wheeler's *Ants, Their Structure, Development, and Behavior* (167–70, 180–82), Eugenius Warming's *Oecology of Plants* (173–80), Frederick Clements's *Plant Succession* (526–28), and Ernst Haeckel (912).
4. Park, "City," 22.
5. Morris, *Scholar Denied*.
6. Light, *Nature of Cities*, 8n9; Wald, *Contagious*, chap. 3.
7. Boyer, *Urban Masses and Moral Order*, 292.
8. Herrnstein and Murray, *Bell Curve*; Panofsky, Dasgupta, and Iturriaga, "How White Nationalists Mobilize Genetics," 387–98. For the medicalization of race, see Molina, *Fit to Be Citizens?*; Bivins, *Contagious Communities*; and Witzig, "Medicalization of Race," 675–79.

9. Wright, *12 Million Black Voices*, 93.

10. Yu, *Thinking Orientals*, 45–46. See also Park, "Human Migration," 881, 893.

11. For Chicago's history of environmental justice, see S. H. Washington, *Packing Them In*; Pellow, *Garbage Wars*; H. L. Platt, *Shock Cities*, chap. 10; McCammack, *Landscapes of Hope*; Brosnan, Durkin Keating, and Barnett, *City of Lake and Prairie*. For context on the Great Migration, urban segregation, and environmental inequalities beyond Chicago, see Du Bois, *Philadelphia Negro*; Sugrue, *Origins of the Urban Crisis*; Massey and Denton, *American Apartheid*; Hurley, *Environmental Inequalities*; and Taylor, *Toxic Communities*.

12. S. H. Washington, *Packing Them In*, 18, 21.

13. Baldwin, *Chicago's New Negroes*; Bone and Courage, *Muse in Bronzeville*; Green, *Selling the Race*; Hine and McCluskey, *Black Chicago Renaissance*; Reed and Courage, *Roots*; Olson, *Chicago Renaissance*; Reed, *Rise of Chicago's Black Metropolis*; Tracy, *Writers of the Black Chicago*.

14. The *Telegraph*, qtd. in "Farewell, Dixie Land," *Chicago Defender*, October 7, 1916, 12.

15. "Somebody Lied," *Chicago Defender*, October 7, 1916, 3. See also *Chicago Defender* editorial, qtd. in Chicago Commission on Race Relations, *Negro in Chicago*, 88.

16. Grossman, *Land of Hope*, 198; Pellow, *Garbage Wars*, 33.

17. *Negro Farmer and Messenger*, August 12, 1916, qtd. in Grossman, *Land of Hope*, 57.

18. B. T. Washington, "Rural Negro and the South," 127. See also Grossman, *Land of Hope*, 59.

19. Southside Community Committee, *Bright Shadows in Bronzetown*, 7–9.

20. Tuttle, *Race Riot*; Halpern, *Down on the Killing Floor*.

21. Graham Taylor, lecture notes, Introduction to the Study of Social Work and Philanthropic Work, fall 1905, Graham Taylor Papers, box 62, folder 2532, Newberry Library, Chicago.

22. For historical analysis of the Chicago school's human ecology approach, see Light, *Nature of Cities*, chap. 1; Mitman, *State of Nature*, 3, 91–94; Kurtz, *Evaluating Chicago Sociology*, 56–57; Matthews, *Quest for an American Sociology*, 141; Gaziano, "Ecological Metaphors"; Zimring, *Clean and White*, 149–50; Li, *Ethnoburb*, 19; Sampson, *Great American City*, 383; and Browning, *Nature's Laboratory*, chap. 5.

23. Yu, *Thinking Orientals*, 38–42.

24. Park and Burgess, *Introduction*, 506, 508, 735. See also Morris, *Scholar Denied*, chap. 4; Baker, *Anthropology*, 22; McKee, *Sociology and the Race Problem*, 92–93, 109–11; Teele, *E. Franklin Frazier*, 57.

25. Park, "Education in Its Relation," 280. See also P. H. Smith, "Chicago School of Human Ecology," 126–57.

26. Frazier, "Negro Harlem," 73; Frazier, *Negro Family*, 324, 325, 341. See also O'Connor, *Poverty Knowledge*, 82–84; Holloway, *Confronting the Veil*, chap. 3. For Burgess's concentric zone theory, see Burgess, "Growth of the City," 51.

27. Frazier, *Negro Family*, 21; Herskovits, *Myth of the Negro Past*, 3–4.

28. See especially Locke, *New Negro*; K. K. Smith, *African American Environmental Thought*, 128.

29. Gershenhorn, *Melville J. Herskovits*, 114–16; Baker, *From Savage to Negro*, 177; Baker, *Anthropology*, 24–30.

30. Frazier, "Traditions and Patterns," 191–207; Frazier, *Negro Family*, 479; Baker, *From Savage to Negro*, 180; Jackson, "Between Socialism and Nationalism," 128, 133; A. M. Platt, *E. Franklin Frazier Reconsidered*.

31. Wright, *Native Son*, 87–93.

32. Horace R. Cayton, "Black Voices," *Pittsburgh Courier*, November 15, 1941, 13.

33. Wright, introduction to *Black Metropolis*, lix.

34. Dolinar, *Negro in Illinois*, xiv; Cappetti, *Writing Chicago*.

35. Wright, introduction to *Black Metropolis*, lix–lx.

36. Wright, *12 Million Black Voices*, 17, 24.

37. Wright, *12 Million Black Voices*, 35.

38. Wright, *12 Million Black Voices*, 78, 58–60.

39. Wright, *12 Million Black Voices*, 87, 93, 100.

40. Hunter, *Tenement Conditions in Chicago*; Comstock, "Chicago Housing Conditions," 241–57; Hunt, *Blueprint for Disaster*, 10.

41. Wright, *12 Million Black Voices*, x. For a genealogy of the term *ghetto*, see Duneier, *Ghetto*; and Schwartz, *Ghetto*.

42. Scott, *Contempt and Pity*, 49–50.

43. Wright, *12 Million Black Voices*, 101, 105–7.

44. Wright, *12 Million Black Voices*, 130, 146.

45. R. Washington, "Horace Cayton," 55–74.

46. Drake, "Reflections on Anthropology," 86. See also Jordan, "On Being a Committed Intellectual," 15–18.

47. Pattillo, foreword to *Black Metropolis*, xv; Peretz, "Making of *Black Metropolis*," 173.

48. Drake and Cayton, *Black Metropolis*, 12; Cayton, *Long Old Road*, 176.

49. Wright, introduction to *Black Metropolis*, lxiv.

50. Wright, introduction to *Black Metropolis*, lxii.

51. For segregation in Chicago, see Massey and Denton, *American Apartheid*, 72; Pattillo, *Black on the Block*; and Pattillo, *Black Picket Fences*.

52. Drake and Cayton, *Black Metropolis*, 115. Although Bronzeville had far fewer public parks than other areas of Chicago, Black neighborhoods were not entirely

devoid of green space. For African American Chicagoans' recreation in parks, see Fisher, *Urban Green*, chap. 4; and McCammack, *Landscapes of Hope*.

53. Drake and Cayton, *Black Metropolis*, 562.
54. Drake and Cayton, *Black Metropolis*, 666–67.
55. Drake and Cayton, *Black Metropolis*, 572, 577.
56. Zimring, *Clean and White*, 114–35; Hoy, *Chasing Dirt*, 117–21.
57. Fisher, *Urban Green*, 91.
58. "Dust and Smoke a Menace," *Chicago Defender*, December 7, 1912, 6.
59. Dr. A. Wilberforce Williams, "Dr. A. Wilberforce Williams Talks on Preventative Measures, First Aid Remedies, Hygienics and Sanitation," *Chicago Defender*, May 2, 1914, 8; Dr. A. Wilberforce Williams, "Keep Healthy, Health Notes," *Chicago Defender*, August 2, 1913, 7.
60. Drake and Cayton, *Black Metropolis*, 715.
61. Reed, *Knock at the Door*, 97.
62. American Negro Exposition, "Diamond Jubilee of Negro Progress," 12.
63. Green, *Selling the Race*, 33.
64. U.S. Department of Labor, *Negro Family*. See also Wilson, *Truly Disadvantaged*, 21.
65. A. M. Platt, "E. Franklin Frazier Reconsidered," 186–95; Geary, *Beyond Civil Rights*; Scott, *Contempt and Pity*, 42–47.
66. E. Franklin Frazier, "Southern Scenes," qtd. in A. M. Platt, "E. Franklin Frazier Reconsidered," 186; Frazier, "Negro and Non-resistance," 213–14.
67. Geary, *Beyond Civil Rights*, 223.
68. Baker, *Anthropology*, 178–92.
69. Myrdal, *American Dilemma*, 928–29; Baker, *From Savage to Negro*, 180–81.

Bibliography

Abbott, Andrew. *Department & Discipline: Chicago Sociology at One Hundred*. Chicago: University of Chicago Press, 1999.

American Negro Exposition. "Diamond Jubilee of Negro Progress: 75 Years of Negro Achievement." Official Program and Guidebook. Chicago: American Negro Exposition Authority, 1940.

Anderson, Nels, and Eduard Lindeman. *Urban Sociology: An Introduction to the Study of Urban Communities*. New York: Knopf, 1928.

Baker, Lee D. *Anthropology and the Racial Politics of Culture*. Durham NC: Duke University Press, 2010.

———. *From Savage to Negro: Anthropology and the Construction of Race, 1896–1954*. Berkeley: University of California Press, 1998.

Baldwin, Davarian L. *Chicago's New Negroes: Modernity, The Great Migration, and Black Urban Life*. Chapel Hill: University of North Carolina Press, 2007.

Bivins, Roberta. *Contagious Communities: Medicine, Migration, and the NHS in Post War Britain*. New York: Oxford University Press, 2015.

Bone, Robert, and Richard A. Courage. *The Muse in Bronzeville: African American Creative Expression in Chicago, 1932–1950*. New Brunswick NJ: Rutgers University Press, 2011.

Boyer, Paul S. *Urban Masses and Moral Order in America, 1820–1920*. 1978. Reprint, Cambridge MA: Harvard University Press, 1992.

Brosnan, Kathleen A., Ann Durkin Keating, and William C. Barnett, eds. *City of Lake and Prairie: Chicago's Environmental History*. Pittsburgh: University of Pittsburgh Press, 2020.

Browning, Elizabeth Grennan. *Nature's Laboratory: Environmental Thought and Labor Radicalism in Chicago, 1886–1937*. Baltimore: Johns Hopkins University Press, 2022.

Bulmer, Martin. *The Chicago School of Sociology: Institutionalization, Diversity, and the Rise of Sociological Research*. Chicago: University of Chicago Press, 1984.

Burgess, Ernest W. "The Growth of the City." In *The City*, edited by Robert E. Park, Ernest W. Burgess, and Roderick D. McKenzie, 47–62. Chicago: University of Chicago Press, 1925.

Cappetti, Carla. *Writing Chicago: Modernism, Ethnography, and the Novel*. New York: Columbia University Press, 1993.

Cayton, Horace R. *Long Old Road*. New York: Trident, 1964.

Chicago Commission on Race Relations. *The Negro in Chicago: A Study of Race Relations and a Race Riot*. Chicago: University of Chicago Press, 1922.

Comstock, Alzada P. "Chicago Housing Conditions, VI: The Problem of the Negro." *American Journal of Sociology* 18, no. 2 (September 1912): 241–57.

Dolinar, Brian, ed. *The Negro in Illinois: The WPA Papers*. Urbana: University of Illinois Press, 2013.

Drake, St. Clair. "Reflections on Anthropology and the Black Experience." *Anthropology & Education Quarterly* 9, no. 2 (1978): 90–91.

Drake, St. Clair, and Horace R. Cayton. *Black Metropolis: A Study of Negro Life in a Northern City*. 1945. Reprint, Chicago: University of Chicago Press, 2015.

Du Bois, W. E. B. *The Philadelphia Negro: A Social Study*. 1899. Reprint, Philadelphia: University of Pennsylvania Press, 1996.

Duneier, Mitchell. *Ghetto: The Invention of a Place, the History of an Idea*. New York: Farrar, Straus and Giroux, 2015.

Fisher, Colin. *Urban Green: Nature, Recreation, and the Working Class in Industrial Chicago*. Chapel Hill: University of North Carolina Press, 2015.

Frazier, E. Franklin. *The Negro Family in the United States*. Chicago: University of Chicago Press, 1939.

———. "Negro Harlem: An Ecological Study." *American Journal of Sociology* 43, no. 1 (July 1937): 72–88.

———. "The Negro and Non-resistance." *Crisis* 27, no. 5 (March 1924): 213–14.

———. "Traditions and Patterns of Negro Family Life in the United States." In *Race and Culture Contacts*, edited by E. B. Reuter, 191–207. New York: McGraw Hill, 1934.

Gaziano, Emanuel. "Ecological Metaphors as Scientific Boundary Work: Innovation and Authority in Interwar Sociology and Biology." *American Journal of Sociology* 101, no. 4 (1996): 874–907.

Geary, Daniel. *Beyond Civil Rights: The Moynihan Report and Its Legacy*. Philadelphia: University of Pennsylvania Press, 2015.

Gershenhorn, Jerry. *Melville J. Herskovits and the Racial Politics of Knowledge*. Lincoln: University of Nebraska Press, 2004.

Green, Adam. *Selling the Race: Culture, Community, and Black Chicago, 1940–1955*. Chicago: University of Chicago Press, 2007.

Grossman, James R. *Land of Hope: Chicago, Black Southerners, and the Great Migration*. Chicago: University of Chicago Press, 1989.

Halpern, Rick. *Down on the Killing Floor: Black and White Workers in Chicago's Packinghouses, 1904–54*. Urbana: University of Illinois Press, 1997.

Herrnstein, Richard J., and Charles Murray, *The Bell Curve: Intelligence and Class Structure in American Life*. New York: Free Press, 1994.

Herskovits, Melville J. *The Myth of the Negro Past*. 1941. Reprint, Boston: Beacon, 1958.

Hine, Darlene Clark, and John McCluskey Jr., eds. *The Black Chicago Renaissance*. Urbana: University of Illinois Press, 2012.

Holloway, Jonathan Scott. *Confronting the Veil: Abram Harris Jr., E. Franklin Frazier, and Ralph Bunche, 1919–1941*. Chapel Hill: University of North Carolina Press, 2002.

Hoy, Suellen. *Chasing Dirt: The American Pursuit of Cleanliness*. New York: Oxford University Press, 1996.

Hunt, D. Bradford. *Blueprint for Disaster: The Unraveling of Chicago Public Housing*. Chicago: University of Chicago Press, 2009.

Hunter, Robert. *Tenement Conditions in Chicago*. Chicago: City Homes Association, 1901.

Hurley, Andrew. *Environmental Inequalities: Class, Race, and Industrial Pollution in Gary, Indiana, 1945–1980*. Chapel Hill: University of North Carolina Press, 1995.

Jackson, Walter. "Between Socialism and Nationalism: The Young E. Franklin Frazier." *Reconstruction* 1 (1991): 124–34.

Jordan, Glenn. "On Being a Committed Intellectual: St. Clair Drake and the Politics of Anthropology." *Transforming Anthropology* 1, no. 2 (July 1990): 15–18.

Kurtz, Lester. *Evaluating Chicago Sociology: A Guide to the Literature, with an Annotated Bibliography*. Chicago: University of Chicago Press, 1984.

Li, Wei. *Ethnoburb: The New Ethnic Community in Urban America*. Honolulu: University of Hawaii Press, 2009.

Light, Jennifer S. *The Nature of Cities: Ecological Visions and the American Urban Professions, 1920–1960*. Baltimore: Johns Hopkins University Press, 2009.

Locke, Alain, ed. *The New Negro: An Interpretation*. New York: Albert and Charles Boni, 1925.

Massey, Douglas S., and Nancy A. Denton. *American Apartheid: Segregation and the Making of the Underclass*. Cambridge MA: Harvard University Press, 1993.

Matthews, Fred. *Quest for an American Sociology: Robert E. Park and the Chicago School*. Montreal: McGill-Queen's University Press, 1977.

McCammack, Brian. *Landscapes of Hope: Nature and the Great Migration in Chicago*. Cambridge MA: Harvard University Press, 2017.

McKee, James B. *Sociology and the Race Problem: The Failure of a Perspective*. Urbana: University of Illinois Press, 1993.

McKenzie, Roderick D. "The Ecological Approach to the Study of the Human Community." *American Journal of Sociology* 30 (1924): 287–301.

Mitman, Gregg. *The State of Nature: Ecology, Community, and American Social Thought, 1900–1950*. Chicago: University of Chicago Press, 1992.

Molina, Natalia. *Fit to Be Citizens? Public Health and Race in Los Angeles, 1879–1939*. Berkeley: University of California Press, 2006.

Morris, Aldon D. *The Scholar Denied: W. E. B. Du Bois and the Birth of Modern Sociology*. Oakland: University of California Press, 2015.

Myrdal, Gunnar. *An American Dilemma: The Negro Problem and American Democracy*. Vol. 2. New York: Harper & Brothers, 1944.

O'Connor, Alice. *Poverty Knowledge: Social Science, Social Policy, and the Poor in Twentieth-Century U.S. History*. Princeton NJ: Princeton University Press, 2002.

Olson, Liesl. *Chicago Renaissance: Literature and Art in the Midwest Metropolis*. New Haven CT: Yale University Press, 2017.

Panofsky, Aaron, Kushan Dasgupta, and Nicole Iturriaga. "How White Nationalists Mobilize Genetics: From Genetic Ancestry and Human Biodiversity to Counterscience and Metapolitics." *American Journal of Physical Anthropology* 175, no. 2 (June 2021): 387–98.

Park, Robert E. "The City: Suggestions for the Investigation of Human Behavior in the City Environment." *American Journal of Sociology* 20, no. 5 (March 1915): 577–612.

———. "Education in Its Relation to the Conflict and Fusion of Cultures." In *Race and Culture*, 261–83. Glencoe IL: Free Press, 1950.

———. "Human Ecology." *American Journal of Sociology* 42, no. 1 (July 1936): 1–15.

———. "Human Migration and the Marginal Man." *American Journal of Sociology* 33, no. 6 (May 1928): 881–93.

———. "Notes on the Origin of the Society for Social Research." *Bulletin of the Society for Social Research* (August 1939). Reprinted in Kurtz, *Evaluating Chicago Sociology*.

———. "Succession, an Ecological Concept." *American Sociological Review* 1, no. 2 (April 1936): 171–79.

———. "Symbiosis and Socialization: A Frame of Reference for the Study of Society." *American Journal of Sociology* 45, no. 1 (1939): 1–25.

Park, Robert E., and Ernest W. Burgess, eds. *Introduction to the Science of Sociology.* Chicago: University of Chicago Press, 1921.

Pattillo, Mary. *Black on the Block: The Politics of Race and Class in the City.* Chicago: University of Chicago Press, 2007.

———. *Black Picket Fences: Privilege and Peril among the Black Middle Class.* 2nd ed. Chicago: University of Chicago Press, 2013.

———. Foreword to *Black Metropolis: A Study of Negro Life in a Northern City,* by St. Clair Drake and Horace R. Cayton, xiii–liii. 1945. Reprint, Chicago: University of Chicago Press, 2015.

Pellow, David Naguib. *Garbage Wars: The Struggle for Environmental Justice in Chicago.* Cambridge MA: MIT Press, 2002.

Peretz, Henri. "The Making of *Black Metropolis.*" *Annals of the American Academy of Political and Social Science* 595 (2004): 168–75.

Platt, Anthony M. *E. Franklin Frazier Reconsidered.* New Brunswick NJ: Rutgers University Press, 1991.

———. "E. Franklin Frazier Reconsidered." *Social Justice* 16, no. 4 (1989): 186–95.

Platt, Harold L. *Shock Cities: The Environmental Transformation and Reform of Manchester and Chicago.* Chicago: University of Chicago Press, 2005.

Reed, Christopher Robert. *Knock at the Door of Opportunity: Black Migration to Chicago, 1900–1919.* Carbondale: Southern Illinois University Press, 2014.

———. *The Rise of Chicago's Black Metropolis, 1920–1929.* Urbana: University of Illinois Press, 2011.

Reed, Christopher Robert, and Richard A. Courage, eds. *Roots of the Black Chicago Renaissance: New Negro Writers, Artists, and Intellectuals, 1893–1930.* Urbana: University of Illinois Press, 2020.

Sampson, Robert J. *Great American City: Chicago and the Enduring Neighborhood Effect.* Chicago: University of Chicago Press, 2012.

Schwartz, Daniel B. *Ghetto: The History of a Word.* Cambridge MA: Harvard University Press, 2019.

Scott, Daryl Michael. *Contempt and Pity: Social Policy and the Image of the Damaged Black Psyche, 1860–1966.* Durham: University of North Carolina Press, 1997.

Smith, Kimberly K. *African American Environmental Thought: Foundations.* Lawrence: University Press of Kansas, 2007.

Smith, Preston H, II. "The Chicago School of Human Ecology and the Ideology of Black Civic Elites." In *Renewing Black Intellectual History: The Ideological and*

Material Foundations of African American Thought, edited by Adolph Reed Jr. and Kenneth W. Warren, 126–57. New York: Routledge, 2015.

Southside Community Committee. *Bright Shadows in Bronzetown: The Story of the Southside Community Committee*. Chicago: Southside Community Committee, 1949.

Sugrue, Thomas J. *The Origins of the Urban Crisis: Race and Inequality in Postwar Detroit*. Princeton NJ: Princeton University Press, 1996.

Taylor, Dorceta E. *Toxic Communities: Environmental Racism, Industrial Pollution, and Residential Mobility*. New York: New York University Press, 2014.

Teele, James E. *E. Franklin Frazier and Black Bourgeoisie*. Columbia: University of Missouri Press, 2002.

Tracy, Steven C., ed. *Writers of the Black Chicago Renaissance*. Urbana: University of Illinois Press, 2011.

Tuttle, William M., Jr. *Race Riot: Chicago in the Red Summer of 1919*. Urbana: University of Illinois Press, 1996. First published 1970 by Atheneum.

U.S. Department of Labor, Office of Policy Planning and Research. *The Negro Family: The Case for National Action*. Washington DC: GPO, March 1965.

Wald, Priscilla. *Contagious: Cultures, Carriers, and the Outbreak Narrative*. Durham NC: Duke University Press, 2007.

Washington, Booker T. "The Rural Negro and the South." *Proceedings of the National Conference of Charities and Corrections* 41 (1914): 121–27.

Washington, Robert. "Horace Cayton: Reflections on an Unfulfilled Sociological Career." *American Sociologist* 28 (1997): 55–74.

Washington, Sylvia Hood. *Packing Them In: An Archaeology of Environmental Racism in Chicago, 1865–1954*. Lanham MD: Lexington Books, 2005.

Wilson, William Julius. *The Truly Disadvantaged: The Inner City, the Underclass, and Public Policy*. 2nd ed. Chicago: University of Chicago Press, 2012.

Witzig, Ritchie. "The Medicalization of Race: Scientific Legitimization of a Flawed Social Construct." *Annals of Internal Medicine* 125, no. 8 (1996): 675–79.

Wright, Richard. Introduction to *Black Metropolis: A Study of Negro Life in a Northern City*, by St. Clair Drake and Horace R. Cayton, lix–lxxvi. 1945. Reprint, Chicago: University of Chicago Press, 2015.

———. *Native Son*. New York: Harper Perennial, 2005. First published 1941 by Harper & Brothers.

———. *12 Million Black Voices: A Folk History of the Negro in the United States*. New York: Basic Books, 2008. First published 1941 by Viking.

Yu, Henry. *Thinking Orientals: Migration, Contact, and Exoticism in Modern America*. New York: Oxford University Press, 2001.

Zimring, Carl A. *Clean and White: A History of Environmental Racism in the United States*. New York: New York University Press, 2015.

Collective Memory for the African Motherland in Interwar Black Chicago and the Limits of the Environmental Justice Model

COLIN FISHER

Environmental politics have always strongly shaped the field of environmental history. The U.S. wilderness movement of the 1960s and 70s, for instance, prompted dozens of scholars to document the clear-cutting of forests and the disappearance of wildlife, tell the story of early wilderness romantics and activists such as Henry David Thoreau and John Muir, and chronicle early efforts to protect nature in parks. In a similar fashion, 1982 protests over a toxic waste landfill in Warren County, North Carolina, and the subsequent expansion of the environmental justice (EJ) movement during the 1990s inspired a new generation of environmental historians to search for precedents. Starting with Robert Gottlieb and Andrew Hurley, historians showed that environmental disparities were hardly new. Scholars revealed how settler colonists, the state, and industry unjustly stripped marginalized communities of access to private land, natural resources, and public green space. They also documented disproportionate community exposure to environmental hazards, such as pesticides, coal smoke, flooding, fire, or pathogens. Lastly, historians identified proto environmental justice activists such as W. E. B. Du Bois, Jane Addams, and Cesar Chavez and showed that environmentalism had always been far less white, male, and affluent than commonly assumed.[1]

From the outset, historical data complicated the effort to simply project the environmental justice movement backward in time. Like earlier historians of wilderness, historians of environmental inequality, confronted with the strangeness of the past, came to question some of the assumptions of the political movement that inspired them. Scholars employed not only race but also class and gender as important categories of analysis; borrowed new tools from the fields of ethnic, migration, labor, African American, social, and gender/women's history as well as Native American and Indigenous studies; and developed nuanced analyses of the forces that created environmental injustices. Historians also introduced unpredictable nonhuman actants—the San Andreas Fault, the Mississippi River, sardines, bedbugs, bubonic plague—into historical accounts of environmental inequality.[2]

The search for environmental inequalities and resistance reveals the past in striking new ways, but even with adaptation, the EJ model obscures as much as it reveals. If we begin our historical narrative with environmental inequality, we have little concrete sense of marginalized people's complicated relationships with nature prior to an initial act of environmental victimization that presumably sets history in motion. In the absence of rigorous historical research, it is all too easy to fall prey to romanticism and assume the existence of a harmonious community living in balance with nature before the fall. An additional problem is that the EJ model affords marginalized people only limited agency. This is especially true in accounts that only document environmental injustice. But agency remains an issue in histories that go beyond environmental victimization and address resistance. If agency is reduced to a mere response to environmental inequality, our understanding of subaltern agency is necessarily and significantly blinkered. This includes environmental agency, which always *exceeds* the response to environmental inequality.

To explore the trouble with the EJ framework, this article turns to interwar Black Chicago as a case study. It is true, the article argues, that the EJ model illuminates important dimensions of the African American experience in the Windy City. But by positing community as a preexisting and unquestioned fact and limiting agency to such a narrow band, the EJ paradigm obscures the Black environmental imagination—specifically how African Americans in Chicago built community by invoking the landscape of Africa as a common yet distant motherland. The article illuminates what we can learn by taking Black nature romanticism seriously and ends with a call for environmental historians to augment the EJ model with approaches that begin not with environmental victimization but with marginalized people themselves.

Environmental Inequalities on the South Side

When applied to interwar Black Chicago, the EJ conceptual framework brings into focus a community that faced profound environmental inequalities at home, on the factory floor, and in public parks. It also illuminates the varied ways the community responded.

The history of Black Chicago extends back to the eighteenth century and the arrival of Chicago's first non-Indian permanent resident, Jean Baptiste Point du Sable. During the first half of the nineteenth century, few African Americans followed the Haitian fur trader, largely because racist Illinois Black Codes prohibited settlement. Following the liberalization of Illinois state law in 1865 and the collapse of Reconstruction in 1877, Black Chicago grew rapidly, and by 1890, the city was home to a population of 14,271. While the community's center of gravity was just south of the downtown Loop, African Americans were dispersed and often lived near the homes of their white employers. They also used parks throughout the city, seemingly with little trouble, especially compared to later years. While there were Black professionals, businessmen, and pastors, most found no options other than working poorly paid jobs in the domestic service industry as cooks, porters, washerwomen, servants, and waiters. Higher-paying factory jobs were only available to strikebreakers.[3]

Black migration to Chicago increased dramatically with the outbreak of World War I. An increase in war orders and the drying up of European immigration prompted industrial employers to turn to populations they had previously spurned: women, Mexican Americans, and African Americans. Throughout the rural South, stories of high-paying jobs and new lives in the "promised land" lured tens of thousands of African Americans northward. They were also pushed out of the South by acts of racist violence, a crushing cycle of debt and poverty, poor schools, inequality in courts, disenfranchisement, falling cotton prices, and the arrival of the cotton-hungry boll weevil. While the Great Black Migration exceeds any environmental explanation, environmental inequalities in the form of restricted access to Southern land and exploitation on dangerous plantation "workscapes" played significant roles. Regardless of the cause, Chicago's Black population in 1920 had ballooned to 109,458, and African Americans comprised more than 4 percent of Chicago's total population.[4]

As Southern migration increased, whites drew the color line, and African Americans found themselves increasingly concentrated in ghettos. By far the largest was the so-called Black Belt, originally a narrow strip just a few blocks wide that ran along State Street from Twelfth to Fifty-Seventh Streets. Black professionals lived in the Black Belt (or Bronzeville, as it would later be named) in well-appointed middle-class homes, but the area also contained some of the worst slums in the city. Like their immigrant neighbors in Back of the Yards (the setting for Upton Sinclair's famous 1906 novel *The Jungle*), African Americans contended with dangerous and unpleasant environmental conditions (piles of rotting garbage, coal smoke, noise, rats, roaches, overfull backyard latrines) and substandard city services. But unlike their European neighbors who could conceivably decamp to bucolic suburbs, African Americans were a captive population, trapped in an increasingly dense South Side ghetto. Fully aware of these spatial restrictions, landlords charged disproportionately high rent and refused to make needed repairs to substandard, fire-prone, rickety, and drafty apartments. Partially because of poor housing, African Americans by 1925 had the worst health outcomes in the city.[5]

African Americans also encountered environmental inequalities where they worked. While World War I opened positions in meatpacking, steel, and manufacturing, working conditions were hardly equal. Companies frequently hired African Americans last and fired them first or used them as strikebreakers. Employers also typically relegated Black workers to the most dangerous, onerous, and unpleasant jobs. Because of racism in the labor movement, African Americans had less latitude than their European American coworkers to address exploitative conditions, including environmental inequalities on the factory floor.[6]

Black Chicagoans also encountered segregation where they played— notably in public parks. Especially during and after World War I, white city officials, lifeguards, and street gangs drew the color line across Lake Michigan beaches, city parks, and outlying forest preserves. Nonprofit groups also discriminated. For instance, the Prairie Club, the Midwest's answer to the Sierra Club, announced baldly that its wilderness activities were "open to white people of any nationality or creed."[7] Tension over access to urban parks and Lake Michigan beaches would ultimately explode in the 1919 race riot, which was sparked when a white bather drowned Eugene Williams, a Black boy who accidentally floated across the color line dividing segregated beaches.[8]

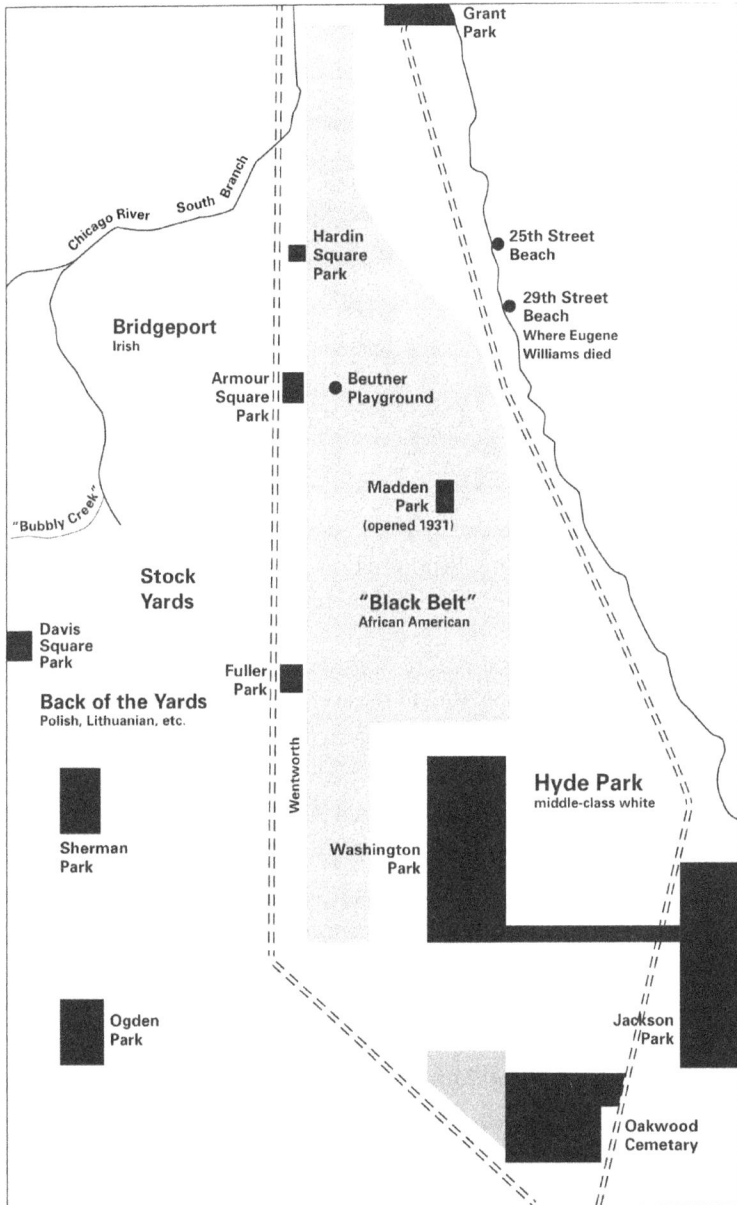

FIG. 4.1. The extent of Chicago's South Side "Black Belt" in the mid-1920s (in gray), with nearby parks and beaches noted. Map based on Chicago Commission on Race Relations, "Distribution of Negro Population in 1920" and "Recreation Facilities," in *The Negro in Chicago* (University of Chicago Press, 1922), 110, 272.

FIG. 4.2. The scene at the Twenty-Ninth Street Beach just after a white bather drowned Eugene Williams. Reprinted from Chicago Commission on Race Relations, *The Negro in Chicago* (University of Chicago Press, 1922), iii.

African Americans responded to these environmental inequalities where they worked, lived, and played in a variety of ways. Civil rights leaders, politicians, journalists, health experts, club women, and others blasted the spatialized "Jim Crowism" that confined African Americans to unhealthy ghettos. At the same time, middle-class Black women spearheaded campaigns to plant trees, build parks, and clean alleys on the South Side. Working-class people, meanwhile, addressed environmental inequalities by laying claim to "white" parks and beaches, engaging in mass action against landlords, and joining unions.[9]

Remembering the African Motherland in Chicago

The EJ model reveals how racism, industrial capitalism, and city government significantly exacerbated Bronzeville's many environmental problems. The model also shows how Black Chicagoans responded to environmental victimization with community action. But by starting with inequality and then limiting agency to the community response, we paint African Americans as narrowly reactive and assume the preexistence of a largely homogenous community. What is obscured are the ways Black Chicagoans built, imagined, and performed community, in part by retroactively positing origins in the soil. To explore this blind spot, this article turns to the 1934 pageant "O, Sing a New Song" and the invocation of tropical West Africa as the common motherland for Black Chicago.

It is difficult to overestimate the importance of this outdoor pageant, which was held in conjunction with the 1934 Century of Progress Exposition. The *Chicago Defender* (the most influential Black newspaper of the era), Republican congressman Oscar DePriest (the first African American elected to Congress since Reconstruction), Mayor Edward Joseph Kelly, the Cook County Democratic Party, the Julius Rosenwald Fund, local businesses, and over a hundred African American preachers eagerly supported the project.[10]

Jazz musician and Broadway composer Noble Sissle created the pageant with the help of other Black composers, choreographers, and experts in West African music and dance. It starred luminaries from the world of entertainment, including actor Richard B. Harrison (who had starred in "De Lawd" and "Green Pastures"), the famous tap dancer Bill "Bojangles" Robinson, and the opera singer and actress Abbie Mitchell. The pageant featured a cast of approximately five thousand (including twenty-one Sotho actors from present-day Lesotho) and attracted an audience of perhaps over sixty thousand. "O, Sing a New Song" was the biggest African American theatrical production in history, and it probably still holds that record today. The National Broadcasting Company and the Columbia Broadcasting System carried the event live, chartered trains brought audience members from St. Louis and Memphis, and President Roosevelt signaled the start of the production by pressing a button in the White House.[11]

The pageant tells the story of the race, through music and song, in three acts. The play's opening scene takes place in West Africa. The "chronicler" (Harrison) explains that each race had its homeland, and Africa was the homeland of Black people. Each homeland "marked the races," but humans also struggled to "take the earth and its fullness" for their own and become "lord" over the "realm of nature." The African, says the chronicler, built his villages, tilled fields, smelt iron, and protected his family from nature. He also "imprisoned the thunder in his drums . . . the patter of rain in a shaken gourd . . . the song of the birds in his wooden flutes."[12]

Following this opening narration, the rising sun reveals a West African village at dawn. People sleep in huts around the dying embers of campfires.

FIG. 4.3. Painter and graphic designer Charles Clarence Dawson's poster art (ca. 1933) for "O, Sing a New Song." Courtesy of Metropolitan Museum of Art, New York.

The rising sun and the sound of birdsong rouse the villagers, some of whom accompany the melody of birds with their drums. A "witch doctor" chants the morning prayer, and the villagers stretch out their arms and sing an "Ode to the Rising Sun." After eating from a common bowl, the men and women pursue different tasks: farming, weaving, basketmaking, carving gourds, tending children, and smelting iron. The scene is interrupted when angry gods send a clap of thunder, which prompts the villagers to cower and offer sacrifices. There are additional dance numbers around the fire, and children bring fruit from the jungle and play West African games. After the men successfully hunt a lion that is threatening the village, King Mumbra, the villagers' sovereign, arrives with his entourage. The village priests are preparing to sacrifice a young maiden to prevent the arrival of dangerous strangers, but the king releases the girl, and the villagers erupt in celebration and dance. But the premonition is correct. The harmony of the African village is violently broken with the arrival of Portuguese slavers, who fire on the Africans and capture the villagers and their king. Foreshadowing the middle passage and slavery in the United States, the captives sing despondently as they are led to a "ghost ship." Spotlights show the shackled group in single file, "exiled to a life of slavery" in "a foreign strange . . . land."[13]

Act two portrays "plantation life." Slave cabins replace the African huts, and in the background looms the portico of a large Southern mansion. When the shackled villagers and their king enter the plantation, African Americans enthusiastically greet the newcomers and integrate the Africans into the community as they sing "Bye and Bye." On the portico, King Mumbra, now a house servant, learns the story of Moses and sings "Go Down Moses" to the other slaves. As a white overseer walks by, the slaves transition to the subversive spiritual "Steal Away to Jesus." There is a voodoo scene in the forest, the chorus sings additional spirituals, and the children play African folk games. In one sequence, five thousand dancers depict a vast field of cotton. The arrival of President Lincoln ends the long-suffering of the slaves, and as Lincoln reads the Emancipation Proclamation, sweeping floodlights fill Soldier Field with light and the freed slaves sing, "Rise! Shine! Give God the Glory." Formerly shacked feet are now free to dance, and jubilant music replaces earlier songs of sadness. From the cotton plantations, tobacco farms, cane brakes, and the banks of the Mississippi, African Americans return to the jubilant music of their African past, and America now begins to pay attention to their voices.

The last act brings the story of the race up to the jazz age. Musicians play ragtime, blues, and jazz numbers. Booker T. Washington makes an appearance, Bill "Bojangles" Robinson tap dances, and actors portray doughboys fighting for their country in Europe. Echoing Busby Berkeley's massive geometric dance numbers of the same period, the pageant concludes with a "Mechanistic Ballet" representing modern urban industrial life. A thousand dancers wearing metallic hats become a giant living machine of rotating wheels. The entire cast, singing in unison, then closes with a rendition of "The Star Spangled Banner" and Sissle's "O, Sing a New Song," a song whose lyrics encouraged the audience to carry the African American story into the future.

Nature Romanticism and Black Identity

How might we interpret "O, Sing a New Song" and its depiction of African American origins in tropical West Africa? According to cultural theorist Stuart Hall, similar invocations of Africa as a motherland have played a critical role in the Black freedom struggle. Against a history of slavery, displacement, and fragmentation, Africa, Hall writes, was figured as a mother, the site where "an imaginary fullness and plentitude" can be restored. The play seemingly confirms that "beneath the shifting divisions and vicissitudes of our actual history," there is a "one-true collective self" that provides "stable, unchanging, and continuous frames of reference and meaning."[14]

Despite the political utility of essentializing Black identity, Hall warns against seeing cultural identity as unchanging, as the natural expression of a folk rooted in soil. A romanticized understanding of identity and community, he argues, denies Black difference and the discontinuities of history. It also denies the creative ways people in the African diaspora continually produced and reproduced cultural identities in response to changing circumstances. Far better, Hall writes, to think about cultural identity not in terms of essence but rather in terms of positionality: "Far from being grounded in mere 'recovery' of the past, which is waiting to be found, and which, when found, will secure our sense of ourselves into eternity, identities are the names we give to the different ways we are positioned by, and position ourselves within, the narratives of the past."[15]

Given Hall's argument that Black cultural identity did not spring organically from the soil of Mother Africa but rather is articulated in the present in part by retroactively positing a homeland, we should not ask whether "O, Sing a New Song" accurately represented the past. Nor should we investigate whether the pageant represents an authentic (or inauthentic) example of traditional Black cultural expression. Rather, we should ask, What prompted the leadership of Black Chicago in 1934 to root African American identity in the African landscape in the way they did? What drove Chicago's Black elite and the multiple authors of the play to take this particular position and imagine community in this particular way?

Black Chicagoans had not always seen Africa as a motherland. During the late nineteenth and early twentieth centuries, novels, scientific tracts, natural history museums, and zoological parks routinely portrayed Africa as the dark continent, an unexplored and unhealthy jungle environment where plants rioted on the earth and savage people lived frozen in time. Partially in response, Black leaders in Chicago emphasized racial uplift and the distance the race had traveled from supposedly benighted African origins. For them, publicly celebrating African roots not only invited racist ridicule but jeopardized the project of assimilating into Anglo-American culture and finally securing full American citizenship.[16]

Increasing racism, ghettoization, and finally World War I—in which Chicago doughboys fought and died to make the world safe for democracy only to return home to white riots and second-class citizenship—made the old integrationist position entirely untenable. It was painfully clear that attempted assimilation would never result in equality, so a new generation of community leaders stressed economic independence, the development of Black institutions, and the building of a Black Metropolis: a city within a city. At the same time, they championed "race pride" and celebrated a distinctive history and common origins.[17]

In articulating a common identity for a heterogeneous, divided urban population, African American cultural leaders did not posit origins in the rural South. While some migrants expressed nostalgia for Southern nature, the vast majority of Black Chicagoans associated the South with slavery, sharecropping, racism, alienation, and violence. The Southern landscape (chillingly depicted in Billie Holiday's song "Strange Fruit" [1939]) was simply an unfit object for collective nostalgia or pastoralism. As can be seen in the pageant, the solution was not to turn away from nature but rather to look farther back in time. Before the rural South, there was Africa, the motherland.[18]

The invocation of a common African homeland during the 1920s is most associated with the Black nationalist Marcus Garvey, founder of the Universal Negro Improvement Association (UNIA). With the intention of fighting racism in the Americas and liberating the African motherland from European colonialism, Garvey and the UNIA organized special units such as the paramilitary Universal African Legions, the Universal African Motor Corps, the Black Cross Nurses, and the Juvenile Divisions as well as numerous businesses, including the *Negro World* newspaper and the Black Star Lines steamship company. Although better-off Black Chicagoans largely rejected Garvey and Garveyism, large numbers of working-class African Americans, the vast majority of whom were new arrivals from the South, joined the movement. As historian Erik S. McDuffie shows, Division 23 on the South Side attracted twenty thousand members, and Garveyism strongly influenced religious and political life in the city.[19]

To convince hundreds of thousands of people on three continents divided by nationality, language, politics, color/race, and generation that they were in fact members of one nation, Garvey and the UNIA pointed to the shared experience of racism but also reminded followers of common origins in Africa, which Garvey described as the Black motherland. The centrality of landscape in Garvey's vision can be seen in his Pan-African flag, composed of three colors: red (signifying the blood that must be shed to liberate the motherland from European colonizers), black (representing the race), and green (symbolic of the "luxuriant vegetation of our motherland").[20]

Despite the popularity of Garveyism in the Windy City, most African Americans during the interwar period rejected Black nationalism and envisioned an American future. But this does not mean they denied Africa. As historian Clare Corbould demonstrates, large numbers of politically moderate African Americans who embraced American citizenship and had no intention of ever leaving the United States also discovered their African roots during the 1920s. Unlike nineteenth-century assimilationists, they took pride in the "ancestral arts" and the glory of ancient Egypt, Ethiopia, and Timbuktu. Africa, Corbould argues, "was no longer simply a place in the past, from which black Americans had come and developed. Africa was now something living and breathing within black identity and at the fore of a newly expanded and dynamic public life."[21] Pride in African origins, she contends, became central to the creation of a distinct African American self, a hyphenated identity not unlike those of European immigrants who honored their Irish, Norwegian, or Greek homelands while simultaneously insisting on full U.S. citizenship. "O, Sing a New Song" is a testament to the degree to which Black Chicago's economic, political, and cultural elite had adopted this new hyphenated African American position.[22]

"O, Sing a New Song" and its romanticization of Mother Africa reveal other aspects of the Black Metropolis in 1934. The pageant illuminates how African American leadership navigated the fraught racial politics of the 1933–34 Century of Progress Exposition and, more broadly, ongoing racist portrayals of Africans as savages and African Americans as people racially incapable of modernity. The extravaganza shows the growing reach of Black political power at the municipal, state, and even federal level. The play also points obliquely to contradictions within Black Chicago. The sexual division of labor in Act 1 of the pageant and the naturalization of Black gender are symptomatic of deep anxiety over female agency (especially during a period of soaring Black male unemployment) and the fate of the Black family. The depiction of African aristocracy and the absence of class antagonism in the pageant (notably in the "Mechanistic Ballet") offer a telling vantage point on a Black social order profoundly destabilized by the economic ravages of the Great Depression and mounting African American labor militancy. One could say much more about the play, but the point here is that the pageant and its portrayal of nature played an important ideological function for a deeply divided Black Metropolis. Facing serious challenges to their authority in the early 1930s, Chicago's Black political, business, and cultural elite looked backward and created a seamless, unbroken, usable past, grounded in the natural environment of tropical West Africa. In so doing, they imagined community for an audience of sixty thousand.[23]

Cultures of Nature and Organic Machines

Some might argue that the invocation of tropical West Africa in "O, Sing a New Song" is beyond the scope of environmental history, a field attentive to ecosystems and bodies and committed to the proposition that nonhuman agents (plants, animals, ecosystems, infectious organisms, and more) shape history. The way marginalized people used landscape to imagine identity, they might respond, is the proper domain of cultural history.

Besides drawing a problematic distinction between nature and culture, such an argument flies in the face of long-standing practice. The significance of nature for identity was in fact the exact subject of U.S. environmental history's first big book, Roderick Nash's *Wilderness and the American Mind* (1967). By the 1990s, environmental historians had rejected the idea that the garden, the middle landscape, the sublime, the frontier, or the wilderness were key to unlocking a singular and supposedly exceptional American character or identity. Even so, environmental historians continued to use the American Natural History Museum, zoological parks, *National Geographic*, national park campgrounds, Sierra Club photography, nature documentaries, SeaWorld, and beaches as optical instruments for observing powerful Americans. Cultural representations of nature, such as the idea of wilderness, no longer revealed the American mind but rather showed the racial, gender, and class anxieties of privileged Americans and the ecologically problematic lines they drew between nature and culture, country and city.[24]

As "O, Sing a New Song" demonstrates, nature romanticism was not a cultural practice unique to privileged European Americans. The United States was in fact home to not one but multiple, overlapping, and unequally privileged *cultures* of nature. In the late nineteenth and early twentieth centuries, European, Mexican, and Asian immigrants remembered the preindustrial villages, regions, and nations left behind. They recalled, often with a surprising degree of nostalgia, the Curonian Spit, the Black Forest, the Tatra Mountains, the Aegean coast, the smell of spring earth in Småland, the bird song of Michoacán. The social movements of the 1960s and 1970s also invoked landscape: Aztlán, Africa, and Turtle Island, among others. If we ignore these subaltern cultures of nature, environmental historians risk leaving readers with the mistaken impression that only one small group of powerful Americans possessed expansive and romantic environmental imaginations, while everyone else only suffered environmental injustice.[25]

While elite Anglo-Americans were hardly the only nature lovers in "nature's nation," this powerful group's romanticism was exceptional in one important regard. This privileged group could use tax funds to stage their idiosyncratic ethnic culture of nature in public parks—more-than-human landscapes long of special interest to environmental historians. The Marxist theorist Antonio Gramsci would argue that U.S. public parks operated as hegemonic institutions. Once open, parks maintained the status quo not through repressive power (state violence, social control, policing, incarceration, and—we might add—the removal of populations, land seizure, or the unequal distribution of environmental risks) but by universalizing and disseminating the dominant culture in a way that inspired at least partial consent from a broad array of constituents.[26]

In the mid-nineteenth century, elite Anglo-Americans typically traced their roots back to the soil of medieval or Elizabethan England. They then built out this fantasy by enrolling a large number of actors (landscape architects, politicians, taxpayers, teams of manual laborers, draft horses, trees, grass, gunpowder, an artificial drainage system, and much more) in an unruly network or assemblage with the objective of creating large pastoral English deer parks, idealized versions of medieval English countryside prior to the Enclosure Act. Central Park in Manhattan is only the most famous example. After park managers opened aristocratic English parks to the American people, they black boxed the material-semiotic assemblage or organic machine that produced and reproduced a romanticized pastoral English landscape. German and Irish immigrants were then encouraged to leave their beer gardens and other places of commercialized working-class leisure and enjoy the dominant culture's ancestral landscape.[27]

Partially in response to mounting European immigration and the necessity of expanding a white historical bloc, Anglo-Americans in the late nineteenth century began to posit the frontier wilderness as the American origin. The notion that a disappearing wilderness had created distinct American characteristics, eliminated aristocratic class distinctions, forged American democracy, and fused European immigrants "into a mixed race, English in neither nationality or characteristics" is most associated with historian Frederick Jackson Turner's 1893 Frontier Thesis.[28] But Turner shaped and gave intellectual gravitas to a position already adopted by many elite Americans. By the opening night of "O, Sing a New Song" in 1934, this ethnic frontier story of blood and soil was endlessly reproduced in novels, Hollywood films, history museums, and history textbooks. It also profoundly shaped public park building. Stephen Mather, the first director of the National Park Service, enrolled members of Congress, railroad companies, taxpayers, rangers, tens of thousands of laborers, state-of-the-art technology (tractors, dynamite, saws and other forestry tools, nurseries, fire suppression equipment, animal traps, and fish hatcheries), and an ever-shifting, unpredictable, and vast array of plants, nonhuman animals, geologic forces, bacteria, fungi, fire, and more into a stable organic machine that produced a certain kind of ethnic nature: a disappearing frontier wilderness that excited desire among a large heterogeneous group of European Americans. As the head of the National Parks Educational Committee put it in 1927, the national parks were the "National Museum of Original America, depository of unique unmodified irreplaceable examples of the vast wilderness which our forefathers conquered."[29]

Progressive Era reformers also brought frontier wilderness parks to Chicago, a rapidly expanding, industrial "shock city" beset by social divisions. Progressives spearheaded the construction of the Cook County Forest Preserves (a vast crescent of popular wilderness parks on Chicago's fringe) and lobbied for the creation of a midwestern national park at the nearby Indiana Dunes. At the same time, they built dozens of block-sized athletic parks whose function was to create "natural" frontier bodies in dense immigrant neighborhoods where space was highly limited. As with the national parks, the purpose of this integrated urban/peri-urban organic machine was to stage a certain version of nature. Reformers argued that outdoor recreation in athletic and wilderness parks would conserve the labor power of industrial workers, defuse class tension, serve as a healthy alternative to "passive" commercialized leisure, assimilate or naturalize the children of European immigrants to their new nation by bringing them into contact with American soil, introduce Chicagoans to American history, and unite the city around the flag.[30]

Just because privileged Anglo-Americans and their allies were the only group that could officially materialize their distinct ethnic culture of nature on public land does not mean that African Americans turned away from public parks. It is true that Black Chicagoans found a hegemonic frontier origin story that celebrated white ethnogenesis almost as alienating as plantation pastoralism. And it is also true that while elite Anglo-Americans and their allies staged ethnic nature in a vast archipelago of public wilderness parks, African Americans could only officially remember their origins in West Africa in an open-air Greco-Roman coliseum in Chicago's Grant Park on one night. But despite these limitations, African Americans appropriated Grant Park on August 25, 1934, and made it their own. Under the stars and along the shore of Lake Michigan, sixty thousand spectators gathered outdoors to remember their distant African motherland, their own distinctive sublime object of ideology. The audience witnessed a largely harmonious West African village situated in a beautiful tropical environment. They learned that this African environment had marked their race but also that their African ancestors had learned to control nature and, in the process, created a vibrant culture that now flourished within the United States. In particular, they witnessed how their music—which originated when their African ancestors captured the sound of thunder, rain, and birds with their musical instruments—profoundly enriched a nation that had stolen their labor and often disowned them. To those lucky enough to attend, the play was a smashing success. According to the *Chicago Defender*, the story of the Black race "from the jungle to Harlem" was nothing less than "the sensational epoch-making spectacle of the century."[31]

The appropriation of Soldier Field in Grant Park was only one example of a much larger phenomenon. Despite considerable limits, Black Chicagoans made public landscapes (English pastoral landscapes, such as Washington and Jackson Parks; working-class athletic parks; Lake Michigan beaches, outlying forest preserves; the Indiana Dunes) into the "natural" antipode of the seemingly artificial Black Metropolis. Black Chicagoans turned these parks into retreats from long hours of mechanized labor, dense apartments, and racism. They were places to swim, fish, play baseball, and enjoy sunshine, fresh air, trees, and sunsets. In these parks, African Americans picnicked with family, church, neighbors, and at the Bud Billiken parade and picnic held annually in Washington Park, seemingly all Black Chicago. Like immigrants from Europe, Asia, and Mexico, industrial workers, interethnic groups of young people, and other Chicagoans, early twentieth-century African Americans used Chicago parks and the nonhuman actants they contained to build communities entirely unimaginable to park creators. The organic machine could be repurposed.[32]

Arguing that the EJ model is limited as a tool for historical research is not a call to abandon it. A large and extraordinarily rich historiography is ample evidence of the value of this conceptual framework. Rather, the argument here is that environmental historians should not let environmental justice become a conceptual straitjacket. The value of looking beyond the frame is demonstrated by a growing number of innovative environmental histories "from the bottom up" that rework or abandon the EJ model and start their narratives not with environmental inequalities but with marginalized people in all their ecological and social complexity.[33]

Some areas outside the frame that deserve more research are the creative ways migrants, racialized people, workers, and others used nature to imagine community. If environmental historians give subaltern cultures of nature the same attention they afford Anglo-American nature romanticism, they are poised to make even greater contributions to Indigenous, labor, migrant, social, ethnic, gender, and queer history, all fields keenly interested in the complicated politics of identity formation but largely inattentive to the importance of nonhuman nature. At the same time, attention to minority cultures of nature can inform environmental history, in particular our understanding of public parks. We can see that one powerful group employed the vast resources of the state to materialize and make hegemonic their own ethnic culture of nature. They were the ones that enrolled labor, technology, and nonhuman biological and geological actants to socially construct wilderness in parks. They were the ones who hoped that outdoor recreation in these parks would temporarily undo the effects of urban modernity and create a homogenous, healthy, and seemingly white nation free of class antagonism, immigrant nationalism, or gender ambiguity. We can see, too, that these public landscapes—these sites not of state repression or social control but of productive power, of nature education—were never totally or completely stable. Marginalized people eagerly entered these landscapes and worked with human and nonhuman actors to socially construct unofficial versions of nature and alternative and even subversive forms of community.

Notes

The author thanks Gary Castañeda, Jonathan Fisher, Bob Johnson, the editors, and the anonymous reviewers for reading and commenting on earlier drafts.

1. For work inspired by the wilderness movement, see, for instance, Nash, *Wilderness and the American Mind*; Baldwin, *Quiet Revolution*; Flader, *Thinking like a Mountain*; Turner, *Beyond Geography*; Fox, *John Muir and His Legacy*; M. P. Cohen, *Pathless Way*; Turner, *Rediscovering America*; Gottlieb, *Forcing the Spring*; and Hurley, *Environmental Inequalities*.
2. The literature on rural and urban inequalities is vast, so I call attention to four historiographic essays: Merchant, "Shades of Darkness"; Fisher, "Race and U.S. Environmental History"; Andrews, "'Single Question'"; and Chiang, "Race and Ethnicity."

3. On nineteenth-century Black life, see Spear, *Black Chicago*, 5–7; Philpott, *Slum and the Ghetto*, 116; Tuttle, *Race Riot*, 160–61; Reed, *Black Chicago's First Century*, 241–66; and Fisher, *Urban Green*, 90–91.

4. See Grossman, *Land of Hope*. On population, see Philpott, *Slum and the Ghetto*, 116, fig. 3. On the Great Black Migration and environmental injustice, see Washington, "'My Soul Looked Back.'" On the notion of a workscape, see Andrews, *Killing for Coal*, 125.

5. On the emergence of the color line, see Spear, *Black Chicago*, 11–27; Philpott, *Slum and the Ghetto*, 113–45; and Grossman, *Land of Hope*, 123–27. On housing conditions and environmental hazards, see "Filthy Chicago," *Illinois Record*, September 3, 1898; Chicago Commission on Race Relations, *Negro in Chicago*, 152–230; Tuttle, *Race Riot*, 157–83; Philpott, *Slum and the Ghetto*, 156–60, 180, 248–52; Grossman, *Land of Hope*, 127, 133–39, 145, 166; Washington, *Packing Them In*, 129–52; and Zimring, *Clean and White*, 145–62. On health, see Washington, *Packing Them In*, 35.

6. See Grossman, *Land of Hope*, 181–207; Pellow, *Garbage Wars*, 33–34.

7. Council of Social Agencies, *Social Service Directory*, 126.

8. Fisher, "African Americans"; Fisher, *Urban Green*, 89–113; McCammack, *Landscapes of Hope*, 31–32, 38–44, 51, 56, 112–16.

9. Washington, *Packing Them In*, 158–92; Fisher, "African Americans"; Zimring, *Clean and White*, 151.

10. On the pageant, see Ohman, "African and African-American Musicians," 387–91; Ganz, *1933 Chicago World's Fair*, 347–68; L. T. A. Ford, *Soldier Field*, 159–64; National Auditions, *National Auditions Annual*.

11. Ohman, "African and African-American Musicians," 387–91. On African American theater in the early twentieth century, see Krasner, *Beautiful Pageant*.

12. National Auditions, *National Auditions Annual*, 15. The pageant plot is reconstructed from the following sources: National Auditions, *National Auditions Annual*; "Greatest Pageant in the History of the Race Was Staged Saturday," *Chicago Defender*, September 1, 1934; "Expect 75,000 to See Negro Pageant Tonight," *Chicago Tribune*, August 25, 1934; "Auditions Pageant Thrills Crowd of 60,000," *Chicago Defender*, September 1, 1934.

13. National Auditions, *National Auditions Annual*, 19.

14. Hall, "Cultural Identity and Diaspora," 223.

15. Hall, "Cultural Identity and Diaspora," 224, 225.

16. On depictions of Africa, see Sears, "Africa in the American Mind"; and Corbould, *Becoming African Americans*, 3–4, 14–15. On assimilation and racial uplift, see Gaines, *Uplifting the Race*; and Spear, *Black Chicago*, 51–89.

17. Spear, *Black Chicago*, 51–89.

18. On the problems of southern pastoralism, see, for instance, Dixon, *Ride Out the Wilderness*, 2; Bennett, "Anti-pastoralism"; Outka, *Race and Nature*, 171–200; Smith, *African American Environmental Thought*, 149–54; and Holiday, "Strange Fruit."

19. On Garveyism, see, for instance, Ewing, *Age of Garvey*. On Garveyism in Chicago, see McDuffie, "Chicago, Garveyism."

20. Universal Negro Improvement Association, *Universal Black Men Catechism*, 37. On Garvey and the imagination of community, see Lemelle and Kelly, "Imagining Home," 7–9.

21. Corbould, *Becoming African Americans*, 214.

22. Corbould, *Becoming African Americans*.

23. On the racial politics of the exposition, see Meier and Rudwick, "Negro Protest"; Reed, "Reinterpretation of Black Strategies"; and Rydell, *World of Fairs*, 82–84, 165–71. On Black politics, see Gosnell, *Negro Politicians*; and Garb, *Freedom's Ballot*. On women and gender, see Hine, "Black Migration"; Hendricks, *Gender, Race, and Politics*; and M. Ford, *Brick and a Bible*. On the impact of the Great Depression on Black Chicago, see L. Cohen, *Making a New Deal*, 215, 226–27, 242, 270–71, 331–32, 363; and Reed, *Depression Comes*.

24. Nash, *Wilderness and the American Mind*. See, for instance, Haraway, *Primate Visions*, 26–58; R. White, "'Are You an Environmentalist?'"; Price, *Flight Maps*, 167–206; Mitman, *Reel Nature*; Davis, *Spectacular Nature*; Shaffer, *See America First*; Dunaway, *Natural Visions*; Cocks, "Children of Light"; Cronon, "Trouble with Wilderness."

25. On migrant memories of homeland nature, see Fisher, *Urban Green*. On new social movements and land, see, for instance, Rickford, "'We Can't Grow Food'"; Fernández, "Abriendo Caminos in the Brotherland"; and Thrush, *Native Seattle*, 162–83.

26. Gramsci, *Selections*.

27. On Anglo-American nostalgia for the English past, see, for instance, Olmsted, *Walks and Talks*; Pomeroy, *In Search*, 31–72; Lears, *No Place of Grace*, 97–140; and Glassberg, *American Historical Pageantry*, 288. On park building, see, for instance, Fisher, "Nature in the City." The term "organic machine" is borrowed from R. White, *Organic Machine*. White argues that the Columbia River was neither wholly natural nor artificial but an organic machine that produced salmon, water for irrigation, electricity, and much more. Public parks are also organic machines, but their primary work is to stage nature for visitors. As a necessary result, these organic machines also produce culture.

28. Turner, "Significance of the Frontier," 216.

29. Yard, *Our Federal Lands*, 231. On the ideology of the frontier, see Slotkin, *Gunfighter Nation*; Wrobel, *End of American Exceptionalism*; R. White, "Frederick Jackson

Turner"; and Bold, *Frontier Club*. On early twentieth-century park building, see, for instance, Runte, *National Parks*; Sellars, *Preserving Nature*; McClelland, *Building the National Parks*; Spence, *Dispossessing the Wilderness*; Sutter, *Driven Wild*, 3–53; Louter, *Windshield Wilderness*; and O'Brien, *Landscapes of Exclusion*.

30. Bachin, *Building the South Side*, 127–204; Fisher, *Urban Green*, 7–37; Fisher, "Multicultural Wilderness."

31. See Žižek, *Sublime Object of Ideology*. "Auditions Pageant Thrills Crowd of 60,000," *Chicago Defender*, September 1, 1934.

32. On African American park usage in Chicago, see Fisher, "African Americans"; Fisher, *Urban Green*, 89–113; and McCammack, *Landscapes of Hope*.

33. For U.S. work on marginalized groups that pushes against the model or abandons it entirely, see, for instance, Stewart, *"What Nature Suffers to Groe"*; Montrie, "'I Think Less'"; Sze, *Noxious New York*; Thrush, *Native Seattle*; Smith, *African American Environmental Thought*; Perales, *Smeltertown*; Weisiger, *Dreaming of Sheep*; Finney, *Black Faces, White Spaces*; Fisher, *Urban Green*; McCammack, *Landscapes of Hope*; M. M. White, *Freedom Farmers*; and Chiang, *Nature behind Barbed Wire*.

Bibliography

Andrews, Thomas G. *Killing for Coal: America's Deadliest Labor War*. Cambridge MA: Harvard University Press, 2008.

———. "'A Single Question That Once Moved like Light': Work, Nature, and History." In *The Oxford Handbook of Environmental History*, edited by Andrew Isenberg, 425–66. New York: Oxford University Press, 2014.

Bachin, Robin Faith. *Building the South Side: Urban Space and Civic Culture in Chicago, 1890–1919*. Historical Studies of Urban America. Chicago: University of Chicago Press, 2004.

Baldwin, Donald N. *The Quiet Revolution: Grass Roots of Today's Wilderness Preservation Movement*. Boulder CO: Pruett, 1972.

Bennett, Michael. "Anti-pastoralism, Frederick Douglass, and the Nature of Slavery." In *Beyond Nature Writing: Expanding the Boundaries of Ecocriticism*, edited by Karla Armbruster and Kathleen R. Wallace, 195–209. Charlottesville: University of Virginia Press, 2001.

Bold, Christine. *The Frontier Club: Popular Westerns and Cultural Power, 1880–1924*. New York: Oxford University Press, 2013.

Chiang, Connie Y. *Nature behind Barbed Wire: An Environmental History of the Japanese American Incarceration*. New York: Oxford University Press, 2018.

———. "Race and Ethnicity in Environmental History." In *The Oxford Handbook of Environmental History*, edited by Andrew C. Isenberg, 573–99. New York: Oxford University Press, 2014.

Chicago Commission on Race Relations. *The Negro in Chicago*. Chicago: The University of Chicago Press, 1922.

Cocks, Catherine. "Children of Light: The Nature and Culture of Suntanning." In *Rendering Nature: Animals, Bodies, Places, Politics*, edited by Marguerite S. Shaffer and Phoebe S. K. Young, 122–37. Philadelphia: University of Pennsylvania Press, 2015.

Cohen, Michael P. *The Pathless Way: John Muir and American Wilderness*. Madison: University of Wisconsin Press, 1984.

Cohen, Lizabeth. *Making a New Deal: Industrial Workers in Chicago, 1919–1939*. New York: Cambridge University Press, 1990.

Corbould, Clare. *Becoming African Americans: Black Public Life in Harlem, 1919–1939*. Cambridge MA: Harvard University Press, 2009.

Council of Social Agencies. *Social Service Directory*. Chicago: Council of Social Agencies, 1939.

Cronon, William. "The Trouble with Wilderness: Or, Getting Back to the Wrong Nature." In *Uncommon Ground: Rethinking the Human Place in Nature*, edited by William Cronon, 69–90. New York: W. W. Norton, 1995.

Davis, Susan G. *Spectacular Nature: Corporate Culture and the Sea World Experience*. Berkeley: University of California Press, 1997.

Dixon, Melvin. *Ride Out the Wilderness: Geography and Identity in Afro-American Literature*. Urbana: University of Illinois Press, 1987.

Dunaway, Finis. *Natural Visions: The Power of Images in American Environmental Reform*. Chicago: University of Chicago Press, 2005.

Ewing, Adam. *The Age of Garvey: How a Jamaican Activist Created a Mass Movement and Changed Global Black Politics*. Princeton NJ: Princeton University Press, 2014.

Fernández, Roberta. "Abriendo Caminos in the Brotherland: Chicana Writers Respond to the Ideology of Literary Nationalism." *Frontiers: A Journal of Women Studies* 14, no. 2 (1994): 23–50.

Finney, Carolyn. *Black Faces, White Spaces: Reimagining the Relationship of African Americans to the Great Outdoors*. Chapel Hill: University of North Carolina Press, 2014.

Fisher, Colin. "African Americans, Outdoor Recreation, and the 1919 Chicago Race Riot." In *"To Love the Wind and Rain": African Americans and Environmental History*, edited by Dianne Glave and Mark Stoll, 63–76. Pittsburgh: University of Pittsburgh Press, 2006.

———. "Multicultural Wilderness: Immigrants, African Americans, and Industrial Workers in the Forest Preserves and Dunes of Jazz-Age Chicago." *Environmental Humanities* 12, no. 1 (2020): 51–87.

———. "Nature in the City: Urban Environmental History and Central Park," *OAH Magazine of History* 25, no. 4 (2011): 27–31.

———. "Race and U.S. Environmental History." In *A Companion to American Environmental History*, edited by Douglas Cazaux Sackman, 97–115. Malden MA: Blackwell, 2010.

———. *Urban Green: Nature, Recreation, and the Working Class in Industrial Chicago*. Chapel Hill: University of North Carolina Press, 2015.

Flader, Susan L. *Thinking like a Mountain: Aldo Leopold and the Evolution of an Ecological Attitude toward Deer, Wolves, and Forests*. Columbia: University of Missouri Press, 1974.

Ford, Liam T. A. *Soldier Field: A Stadium and Its City*. Chicago: University of Chicago Press, 2009.

Ford, Melissa. *A Brick and a Bible: Black Women's Radical Activism in the Midwest during the Great Depression*. Carbondale: Southern Illinois University Press, 2022.

Fox, Stephen. *John Muir and His Legacy: The American Conservation Movement*. Boston: Little, Brown, 1981.

Gaines, Kevin Kelly. *Uplifting the Race: Black Leadership Politics and Culture in the Twentieth Century*. Chapel Hill: University of North Carolina Press, 1995.

Ganz, Cheryl. *The 1933 Chicago World's Fair: Century of Progress*. Urbana: University of Illinois Press, 2008.

Garb, Margaret. *Freedom's Ballot: African American Political Struggles in Chicago from Abolition to the Great Migration*. Chicago: University of Chicago Press, 2014.

Glassberg, David. *American Historical Pageantry: The Uses of Tradition in the Early Twentieth Century*. Chapel Hill: University of North Carolina Press, 1990.

Gosnell, Harold S. *Negro Politicians: The Rise of Negro Politics in Chicago*. Chicago: University of Chicago Press, 1935.

Gottlieb, Robert. *Forcing the Spring: The Transformation of the American Environmental Movement*. Washington DC: Island, 1993.

Gramsci, Antonio. *Selections from the Prison Notebooks of Antonio Gramsci*. Edited by Quintin Hoare and Geoffrey Nowell-Smith. New York: International, 1972.

Grossman, James R. *Land of Hope: Chicago, Black Southerners, and the Great Migration*. Chicago: University of Chicago Press, 1989.

Hall, Stuart. "Cultural Identity and Diaspora." In *Identity: Community, Culture, Difference*, edited by Jonathan Rutherford, 222–37. London: Lawrence & Wishart, 1998.

Haraway, Donna. *Primate Visions: Gender, Race, and Nature in the World of Modern Science*. New York: Routledge, 1989.

Hendricks, Wanda A. *Gender, Race, and Politics in the Midwest: Black Club Women in Illinois*. Bloomington: Indiana University Press, 1998.

Hine, Darlene Clark. "Black Migration to the Urban Midwest: The Gender Dimension, 1915–1945." In *Historical Perspective: New Dimensions of Race, Class, and Gender*, edited by Joe William Trotter Jr., 127–46. Bloomington: Indiana University Press, 1991.

Holiday, Billie. "Strange Fruit." Commodore Records, 1939.

Hurley, Andrew. *Environmental Inequalities: Class, Race, and Industrial Pollution in Gary, Indiana, 1945–1980*. Chapel Hill: University of North Carolina Press, 1995.

Krasner, David. *A Beautiful Pageant: African American Theatre, Drama, and Performance in the Harlem Renaissance, 1910–1927*. New York: Palgrave Macmillan, 2002.

Lears, T. J. Jackson. *No Place of Grace: Antimodernism and the Transformation of American Culture, 1880–1920*. Chicago: University of Chicago Press, 1994.

Lemelle, Sidney, and Robin D. G. Kelly. "Imagining Home: Pan-Africanism Revisited." In *Imagining Home: Class, Culture, and Nationalism in the African Diaspora*, edited by Sidney Lemelle and Robin D. G. Kelly, 7–9. New York: Verso, 1994.

Louter, David. *Windshield Wilderness: Cars, Roads, and Nature in Washington's National Parks*. Seattle: University of Washington Press, 2009.

McCammack, Brian. *Landscapes of Hope: Nature and the Great Migration in Chicago*. Cambridge: Harvard University Press, 2017.

McClelland, Linda Flint. *Building the National Parks: Historic Landscape Design and Construction*. Baltimore: Johns Hopkins University Press, 1997.

McDuffie, Erik S. "Chicago, Garveyism, and the History of the Diasporic Midwest." *African and Black Diaspora: An International Journal* 8, no. 2 (2015): 129–45.

Meier, August, and Elliott M. Rudwick. "Negro Protest at the Chicago World's Fair, 1933–1934." *Journal of the Illinois State Historical Society* 59, no. 2 (1966): 161–71.

Merchant, Carolyn. "Shades of Darkness: Race and Environmental History." *Environmental History* 8, no. 3 (2003): 380–94.

Mitman, Gregg. *Reel Nature: America's Romance with Wildlife on Films*. Cambridge MA: Harvard University Press, 1999.

Montrie, Chad. "'I Think Less of the Factory Than of My Native Dell': Labor, Nature, and the Lowell 'Mill Girls.'" *Environmental History* 9, no. 2 (2004): 275–95.

Nash, Roderick. *Wilderness and the American Mind*. New Haven CT: Yale University Press, 1967.

National Auditions. *National Auditions Annual: A Century of Progress Souvenir Edition of Afro-American Pageant, Inc.* Soldier Field, August 25, 1934.

O'Brien, William E. *Landscapes of Exclusion: State Parks and Jim Crow in the American South*. Amherst: University of Massachusetts Press, 2015.

Ohman, Mariam M. "African and African-American Musicians Seeking Progress at a Century of Progress." *Journal of the Illinois State Historical Society* 102, no. 314 (2009): 387–91.

Olmsted, Frederick Law. *Walks and Talks of an American Farmer in England*. London: D. Bogue, 1852.

Outka, Paul. *Race and Nature from Transcendentalism to the Harlem Renaissance*. New York: Palgrave Macmillan, 2008.

Pellow, David N. *Garbage Wars: The Struggle for Environmental Justice in Chicago*. Cambridge MA: MIT Press, 2002.

Perales, Monica. *Smeltertown: Making and Remembering a Southwest Border Community*. Chapel Hill: University of North Carolina Press, 2010.

Philpott, Thomas Lee. *The Slum and the Ghetto: Neighborhood Deterioration and Middle-Class Reform, Chicago, 1880–1930*. New York: Oxford University Press, 1978.

Pomeroy, Earl. *In Search of the Golden West: The Tourist in Western America*. New York: Knopf, 1957.

Price, Jennifer. *Flight Maps: Adventures with Nature in Modern America*. New York: Basic, 1999.

Reed, Christopher Robert. *Black Chicago's First Century*. Columbia: University of Missouri Press, 2005.

———. *The Depression Comes to the South Side: Protest and Politics in the Black Metropolis 1930–1933*. Bloomington: Indiana University Press, 2011.

———. "A Reinterpretation of Black Strategies for Change at the Chicago World's Fair, 1933–1934." *Illinois Historical Journal* 81, no. 1 (1988): 2–12.

Rickford, Russell. "'We Can't Grow Food on All This Concrete': The Land Question, Agrarianism, and Black Nationalist Thought in the Late 1960s and 1970s." *Journal of American History* 103, no. 4 (2017): 956–80.

Runte, Alfred. *National Parks: The American Experience*. Lincoln: University of Nebraska Press, 1984.

Rydell, Robert. *World of Fairs: The Century-of-Progress Expositions*. Chicago: University of Chicago Press, 1993.

Sears, Cornelia. "Africa in the American Mind, 1870–1955: A Study in Mythology Ideology and the Reconstruction of Race." PhD diss., University of California, Berkeley, 1997.

Sellars, Richard West. *Preserving Nature in the National Parks: A History*. New Haven CT: Yale University Press, 1997.

Shaffer, Marguerite S. *See America First: Tourism and National Identity, 1880–1940*. Washington DC: Smithsonian Institution Press, 2001.

Slotkin, Richard. *Gunfighter Nation: The Myth of the Frontier in Twentieth-Century America*. Norman: University of Oklahoma Press, 1992.

Smith, Kimberly K. *African American Environmental Thought: Foundations*. Lawrence: University Press of Kansas, 2007.

Spear, Allan H. *Black Chicago: The Making of a Negro Ghetto, 1890–1920*. Chicago: University of Chicago Press, 1967.

Spence, Mark David. *Dispossessing the Wilderness: Indian Removal and the Making of the National Parks*. New York: Oxford University Press, 1999.

Stewart, Mart A. *"What Nature Suffers to Groe": Life, Labor, and Landscape on the Georgia Coast, 1680–1920*. Athens: University of Georgia Press, 1996.

Sutter, Paul. *Driven Wild: How the Fight against Automobiles Launched the Modern Wilderness Movement*. Seattle: University of Washington Press, 2002.

Sze, Julie. *Noxious New York: The Racial Politics of Urban Health and Environmental Justice*. Cambridge MA: MIT Press, 2006.

Thrush, Coll-Peter. *Native Seattle: Histories from the Crossing-Over Place*. Seattle: University of Washington Press, 2007.

Turner, Frederick Jackson. "Significance of the Frontier in American History." In *Annual Report of the American Historical Association for the Year 1893*, 197–227. Washington DC: GPO, 1894.

Turner, Frederick. *Beyond Geography: The Western Spirit against the Wilderness*. New York: Viking, 1980.

———. *Rediscovering America: John Muir in His Time and Ours*. New York: Viking, 1985.

Tuttle, William M. *Race Riot: Chicago in the Red Summer of 1919*. New York: Atheneum, 1984.

Universal Negro Improvement Association and George Alexander McGuire. *Universal Black Men Catechism*. New York: Universal Negro Improvement Association, 1921.

Washington, Sylvia Hood. "'My Soul Looked Back': Environmental Memories of the African in America, 1600–2000." In *Echoes from the Poisoned Well: Global Memories of Environmental Injustice*, edited by Sylvia Hood Washington, Paul C. Rosier, and Heather Goodall, 55–72. Lanham MD: Lexington, 2006.

———. *Packing Them In: An Archaeology of Environmental Racism in Chicago, 1865–1954*. Lanham MD: Lexington, 2005.

Weisiger, Marsha. *Dreaming of Sheep in Navajo Country*. Seattle: University of Washington Press, 2011.

White, Monica M. *Freedom Farmers: Agricultural Resistance and the Black Freedom Movement*. Chapel Hill: University of North Carolina Press, 2018.

White, Richard. "'Are You an Environmentalist or Do You Work for a Living?': Work and Nature." In *Uncommon Ground: Toward Reinventing Nature*, edited by William Cronon, 171–85. New York: W. W. Norton, 1995.

———. "Frederick Jackson Turner and Buffalo Bill." In *The Frontier in American Culture: Essays by Richard White and Patricia Nelson Limerick*, edited by James Grossman, 7–65. Berkeley: University of California Press, 1994.

———. *The Organic Machine: The Remaking of the Columbia River*. New York: Hill and Wang, 1995.

Williams, Raymond. *Keywords: A Vocabulary of Culture and Society*. New York: Oxford University Press, 1976.

Wrobel, David M. *The End of American Exceptionalism: Frontier Anxiety from the Old West to the New Deal*. Lawrence: University Press of Kansas, 1993.

Yard, Robert Sterling. *Our Federal Lands: A Romance of American Development.* New York: Charles Scribner's Sons, 1928.

Zimring, Carl A. *Clean and White: A History of Environmental Racism in the United States.* New York: New York University Press, 2015.

Žižek, Slavoj. *The Sublime Object of Ideology.* London: Verso, 1989.

States of Confinement and Ecological Violence

Incarceration and the Struggle for Environmental Justice

DAVID NAGUIB PELLOW

The United States is the world's leader in the business of mass incarceration, with more than two million persons held captive in prisons, jails, immigrant and juvenile "detention centers," and other "correctional" institutions. The vast majority of those incarcerated are people of color and low-wealth individuals—along with a growing number of immigrants, women, and LGBTQIA people—whose incarceration negatively impacts both their health and the well-being and life chances of their nonincarcerated family members.[1] How might mass incarceration relate to concerns about environmental justice? While a growing number of scholars are exploring this question, activist groups like Critical Resistance, the Prison Moratorium Project, Mothers of East LA, the Silicon Valley Toxics Coalition, the Prison Ecology Project, and the Campaign to Fight Toxic Prisons have worked to investigate and highlight the links between the U.S. prison system and environmental threats, uncovering numerous cases across the nation where incarcerated persons, corrections officers, and nearby ecosystems and communities were placed at risk due to prison proposals, construction, and daily operations. For example, there are confirmed reports of water contaminated with arsenic, lead, and other pollutants at prisons in at least twenty states, including the now infamous case of Flint, Michigan, where the Genesee County jail's inmates—including pregnant women—were forced to drink toxic water while prison guards drank filtered water out of bottles. In another case, the Northwest Detention Center in the Seattle-Tacoma area is a privately operated prison designed to house more than 1,500 immigrant prisoners and is built adjacent to a federally designated toxic Superfund site, reflecting the ways in which white supremacy, racial capitalism, and settler colonialism intersect to produce built environments in which undocumented persons are devalued and treated as "pollution sinks."[2] Finally, a number of prisons built in the Adirondack Mountains of upstate New York have contributed to the further incapacitation of marginalized populations that are caged as well as the decline of local natural habitats, increased pollution, and deforestation— all in a region that many people associate with outdoor recreation and the enjoyment of wilderness.[3]

In this chapter I ask, How might environmental justice histories and futures be transformed if we examined them through the lens of the prison industrial complex in particular and the challenge of enslavement and incarceration more generally? I argue that prison studies and prison abolition are critical components of environmental justice studies and politics because (1) there is a wealth of evidence that reveals myriad intersections between spaces of incarceration and environmental threats, (2) there is a strong link between ecological unsustainability and threats to social justice and democracy, and (3) enslavement and incarceration are incompatible with democracy and environmental sustainability.

In the next sections, I consider the intersections of enslavement, incarceration, and environmental justice struggles from a perspective that views forced labor and violent captivity as prime examples of practices that are antidemocratic, deeply hierarchical, and also contribute to environmental injustice and threats to ecological sustainability.

Histories of Incarceration and Environmental Injustice

During the latter half of the nineteenth century, the U.S. federal government led campaigns of extermination and conquest against Indigenous peoples, particularly those viewed as "hostiles," and placed many members of tribes in concentration camps where mass starvation, illness, and death were the norm.[4] This included, among many others, the camps at Fort Snelling, Minnesota, where hundreds of Dakota nation members were imprisoned (1862); Fort Marion, Florida, where Indigenous prisoners of war were incarcerated (1875–78); and Bosque Redondo, New Mexico, where members of the Diné/Navajo nation were imprisoned (1864–68). The conditions of confinement were not only a component of the war on Native peoples; they were a clear case of genocide, as they reflected an intent to destroy, in whole or in part, a national group by killing members of that group, causing serious mental or bodily harm, and imposing measures intended to prevent births within the group (in many cases such as the Fort Snelling camp, this included gender-segregated living quarters, which contributed to the prevention of reproduction).[5] Indigenous prisoners resisted their incarceration by revolting, escaping, and gathering food off-site, actions that were punished mercilessly by government forces.

African Americans were subjected to chattel enslavement for generations and were officially granted freedom via the Emancipation Proclamation. Soon afterward, however, convict leasing practices and Black Codes swept up many Black folks into the carceral system—a different form of enslavement. This system involved states leasing incarcerated persons to corporations and other businesses that often worked them to death, since there was little incentive to keep these laborers healthy and alive, as they were no longer considered private property.[6] Moreover, most of the forced labor in this system involved extractive and violent practices such as cotton and turpentine production, coal mining, deforestation, and building railroads—all of which place considerable stress on ecosystems and human health.[7] Thus the intersections between unfreedom and environmental justice struggles have long roots. And as many scholars argue, confronting and abolishing the prison industrial complex today is an important effort to complete the work of slavery abolition begun centuries ago, in order to create a future where freedom is enjoyed by all.[8] The environmental injustices that are evident today in what we call the United States are a continuation of practices and policies that began during the onset of settler colonialism. As Nick Estes writes, "US history is all about land and the transformation of space, fundamentally driven by territorial expansion, the elimination of Indigenous peoples, and white settlement."[9] The theft of land and dispossession of Indigenous peoples contributed to the massive ecological harms visited upon the soil, waterways, air, and climate across the United States and beyond, and it is that land on which today's prison system sits.

After Japan's military bombed Pearl Harbor in World War II, President Franklin D. Roosevelt signed Executive Order 9066 in February 1942, directing the U.S. Army to remove people of Japanese ancestry from the West Coast and place them into concentration camps. While in these camps, Japanese Americans suffered many health problems due to hazardous environmental and living conditions and neglect by the state. For example, many concentration camps were located in arid valleys, southwestern deserts, high plains, and swamps. Before the War Department built the structures, they would strip the land of the native vegetation, which led to dust control problems that affected the prisoners. As a result, many camps had severe dust storms that caused prisoners to suffer respiratory problems, including asthma and valley fever.[10] Compounding that problem, extreme weather conditions also negatively impacted prisoners' health because of harsh climates and poor-quality building materials that failed to provide adequate shelter. The southern camps suffered from intense heat, while the northern camps suffered from the bitter cold, including winter temperatures that sometimes reached thirty below zero degrees Fahrenheit. In camps that experienced intense heat, some children died from fevers and dehydration.[11] Finally, the lack of infrastructure and supplies during an era of wartime scarcities led the U.S. Army to utilize pipes formerly used for oil wells and gas line supplies for the concentration camps' water supplies.[12] These pipes produced drinking water that reeked of hydrocarbons and had a rusty, oily residue, thus posing serious health hazards for prisoners.[13]

Japanese American prisoners continually resisted their conditions of confinement. One such effort involved cultivating large gardens and building ponds in order to provide the basic necessities of food and water, which were in short supply.[14] As one historian notes, "this endeavor helped to ameliorate the hardships of incarceration while allowing Japanese Americans to resist state power."[15] More broadly, engaging with the local ecosystems in ways that produced food and lessened the stressors associated with incarceration was important to the survival of those imprisoned.

A related but lesser-known story is that of the more than eight hundred Indigenous Unangan persons who were also incarcerated by the United States during World War II because their homes on the Aleutian and Pribilof islands were allegedly located in a war zone. Many of their villages were burned, and they were incarcerated for years in buildings that had previously served as fish canneries. The physical and emotional toll of their confinement was particularly harsh, according to a Commission on Wartime Relocation and Internment of Civilians report that condemned the U.S. government for "indifference" to the "deplorable conditions," which included a lack of clean or running water, electricity, medical care, or furniture inside dilapidated buildings where prisoners were overcrowded. Approximately 10 percent of these prisoners died as a result of these conditions—which also included influenza and measles outbreaks—and many more were scarred for life.[16] After years of community mobilizing around key demands, the U.S. government paid financial "compensation" to both Japanese Americans and Unangan peoples for these atrocities in the late 1980s.

Contemporary Riskscapes of Incarceration

In this section I draw on ecofeminist and feminist environmental justice scholarship that views human bodies—particularly those of people of color, Indigenous peoples, LGBTQIA folks, women, immigrants, and working-class peoples—and bodies of land, water, and other animals as sites of environmental justice struggles.[17] These dynamics play out in the context of prisons in the way that toxic chemicals contaminate the bodies of prisoners and ecosystems simultaneously and through the sexual abuse of prisoners.

Geography, climate change, and reactionary politics can result in major risks to incarcerated persons. In one case, prisoners at Texas's Wallace Pack Unit brought a class action lawsuit against the state because the combination of extreme heat and arsenic-laced water produced a lethal threat that authorities willfully ignored in a conservative political context where an ideology of punishment was the order of the day. Ultimately a judge ordered new safety measures as a result of that lawsuit.[18] In another example, the federal prison complex in Beaumont, Texas, flooded during the Hurricane Harvey storm in August 2017. The incarcerated population was placed on lockdown, and no evacuation was ordered despite the fact that water levels rose considerably inside the prison and were mixed with a toxic cocktail of petrochemicals originating from a nearby ExxonMobil refinery.[19] The water supply was shut off, and many prisoners experienced dehydration while their families and friends called the Texas Department of Criminal Justice to demand that their loved ones be protected from the ravages of the storm. This was one of many recent climate disruption–driven extreme weather events in a region with an economy that is deeply committed to fossil fuel extraction.

Furthermore, carceral facilities frequently produce hazards from within that can result in increased harm to ecosystems and public health on either side of the walls of confinement. Many prisons are sites of water contamination that stems from overflowing sewage systems or the importation of contaminated water from a nearby government facility, which also often affects residents of those areas. For example, in California's state prison system over the last two decades, there have been numerous such incidents, including a 700,000-gallon sewage spill from Folsom State Prison into the nearby American River and a 220,000-gallon sewage spill from the California Men's Colony into the Chorro Creek, placing both human and nonhuman (aquatic and plant) populations at risk.[20]

The connections between prisons and environmental injustice are no less disturbing and direct when we consider the deliberate use of toxins on prisoners' bodies. University of Pennsylvania professor and dermatologist Dr. Albert Kligman conducted experiments during the 1950s and 1960s at Holmesburg Prison in Pennsylvania, subjecting primarily African American incarcerated persons to large doses of dioxin, the most toxic substance known to science and the main poisonous ingredient in Agent Orange.[21] Agent Orange is the infamous chemical compound and herbicide the U.S. military used during the war in Vietnam to destroy forest cover and crops throughout that nation, resulting in massive harm to human and environmental health. The Dow Chemical corporation paid Kligman to perform these experiments with the aim of measuring dioxin's effects on the body. Former Holmesburg prisoner and research subject Leodus Jones launched and led Community Assistance for Prisoners, an organization that advocates for current and formerly incarcerated persons in the state of Pennsylvania. He stated, "These tests were unfair; they were barbaric. . . . We were lied to; we were used and were exploited. We were human guinea pigs."[22] Jones and three hundred persons formerly incarcerated at Holmesburg demanded restitution and brought lawsuits against Kligman, Dow Chemical, and the University of Pennsylvania.

The lens of scale allows one to see prison environmental injustices from multiple angles. Consider that some prisons are located on or near former military waste dumps, which offers a sense of how micro- and macroscales of institutional violence converge in one space. Between 2016 and 2019, an immigrant prison known as the Homestead Temporary Shelter for Unaccompanied Alien Children housed several thousands of children who arrived in the United States without a guardian or parent or who were forcibly separated from their families by the government. At that time, this was the largest prison for immigrant children.[23] The news of this imprisonment generated significant protests from human rights and immigrant justice defenders not only because the children were caged but also because the facility is directly adjacent to the Homestead Air Force Base National Priority Superfund Site, where a range of toxic chemicals are present in the soil and groundwater, including arsenic, lead, mercury, polycyclic aromatic hydrocarbons (PAHs), and trichloroethene. These toxins can cause cancer and major damage to the kidneys, liver, and immune system. Furthermore, chronic noise exposure is rampant as a result of the frequent flights of F-16 fighter jets in and out of the Homestead Air Reserve Base. A coalition of human rights, immigrant rights, and environmental organizations is demanding that the government shut down the prison, conduct testing of toxins and noise risks, and stop incarcerating immigrant children altogether.[24] The Homestead Base has served as a training ground for air force pilots since World War II with a focus on "strategic bombardment" and air refueling for planes involved in military conflicts since that time. This story reveals how scale is important for analyzing environmental justice struggles because, in this single space, we can link the health risks posed to the individual bodies of migrant children to the ways in which U.S. empire and militarism have contributed to human migration patterns and extraordinary ecological harm around the world.

Sexual violence is a topic that facilitates a particularly horrifying way to recast environmental injustice. Research has conclusively documented the extreme threats of sexual abuse that women and LGBTQIA people experience in the U.S. carceral system—violence that is often committed and encouraged by prison policies and personnel.[25] Abolitionist Angela Davis writes, "Prison is a space in which the threat of sexualized violence that looms in the larger society is effectively sanctioned as a routine aspect of the landscape of punishment behind prison walls."[26] A number of Indigenous scholars contend that gender and sexual violence constitute a core element of settler colonialism. Sarah Deer argues that rape "can be employed as a metaphor for the entire concept of colonialism," as it is a key element in the broader and continued relations of domination and, as Nick Estes notes, because Indigenous women's bodies "were used to increase white traders' access to new markets through their kin—and by extension, land."[27] If, as Kyle Powys Whyte argues, settler colonialism is a form of environmental injustice (as it undermines the capacity of Indigenous peoples to steward their lands), and if settler colonialism is a form of gender and sexual violence, then gender and sexual violence are intimately linked to environmental injustice.[28] Other scholars have noted that, more specifically, assaults on the bodies of marginalized peoples should be viewed as environmental injustices, since our bodies are akin to "land" and the environment and are inescapably entangled with the ecosystems we rely on.[29]

Environmental Justice and Prison Abolition

One day in the spring of 2016, prisoners across carceral facilities in the state of Alabama sent out text messages (from contraband cell phones) to prison guards and media organizations stating, "We will no longer voluntarily participate in this slave system where economics are placed over our humanity. . . . All [that] is required is for industry workers, kitchen workers, and hall runners to sit down." The announcement declared that on May 1—known around the world as "May Day," a global day of recognition of workers' rights—a labor strike would begin. What became known as the Free Alabama movement had made itself known to prison authorities and the media, intentionally describing prisons as sites of enslavement and refusing to participate in that system for a dramatic moment in time. Incarcerated persons stayed in their cells and refused to show up for work where they would normally be making license plates, preparing and serving food, cleaning, and laboring in recycling centers and on prison farms. Melvin Ray is incarcerated at the state of Alabama's St. Claire Correctional Facility and is the founder of the Free Alabama movement. He told a journalist, "The main reason that we're striking is because there continues to be problems inside of the prison and the state's focus is not on solving the problems—it's on finding new ways to make money. They're not affording us the opportunity to make our concerns known. They're not listening to our complaints. The only way we have to get their attention is to do these shut downs. . . . We're not going to stop fighting back against the system until these walls come down."[30] Ray recorded and shared with supporters a video of mold on the wall, rats and roaches, and contaminated water in his cell. He was able to get the word out by using a contraband phone to take pictures and videos and send them to his family. He also wrote a "manifesto" in which he described deplorable conditions in the prison. The Free Alabama movement's prisoner demands included ending the practice of "prison slavery" as well as reforming harsh sentencing laws and improving educational and rehabilitation programs, among others.

Importantly, many scholars are grappling with the fact that prisons are sites of legal enslavement insofar as incarcerated people are ensnared by the Thirteenth Amendment to the U.S. Constitution, which allows for the enslavement of people "as punishment for a crime." Where I disagree with many scholars, prisoners, and activists is whether "prison slavery" consists entirely of forced, unpaid labor. In fact, the language of the Thirteenth Amendment states that "neither slavery nor involuntary servitude" shall exist in the United States except as punishment for a crime. One of many definitions of *involuntary servitude* includes "slavery," so in many ways, these two terms are indistinguishable. My view is that slavery or enslavement also consists of captivity or the condition of being held against one's will, so regardless of whether one is subjected to forced labor, if one is imprisoned, they are enslaved. That framing of imprisonment and enslavement opens up a much more expansive and radical orientation toward contemporary abolition. Thus prisoner-led movements include actions such as labor strikes but also include a range of tactics and strategies that underscore resistance against *captivity* more broadly. These movements and their constitutive actions reveal how human bodies intersect with broader ecologies through the built environment, water, nonhuman animals, and other actors and subjects conscripted in the construction and maintenance of the U.S. prison system.

As the Free Alabama movement demonstrates, much of that social change work is being done by prisoners themselves, including the hundreds who have sued state governments for excessive heat, water restrictions, water contamination, and other environmental threats (such as the dangers of the fungal infection known as valley fever, which is prevalent in California prisons).

Inequalities, Democracy, and Ecological Health

There is ample evidence of myriad intersections between the prison industrial complex and environmental and climate injustice. I would argue that the larger, more profound reason for this connection is that enslavement, incarceration, and colonization are incompatible with democracy, and that means that those practices are also incompatible with environmental sustainability and justice. In this section of the chapter, I discuss these connections.

Scholars working at the intersection of social justice and environmental quality have produced volumes of research on the problem of environmental racism in particular and environmental injustice more broadly. But there is a larger question that has received less attention than is merited: the relationship between hierarchy/inequality, ecological health, and democracy. This question is, of course, implicit and often assumed in EJ studies scholarship, but it remains underappreciated and undertheorized. Fortunately, a growing number of scholars are exploring these connections, and the conclusion is perhaps not surprising but nonetheless profound: inequality and antidemocratic practices are harmful not only to human beings but to our ecosystems as well. In other words, social inequalities are not only the driving forces behind the phenomenon of environmental injustice; they are also the driving forces behind the broader crises of climate disruption and global ecological decline. Below, I offer specific illustrations of these intersections.

Social scientists have authored studies demonstrating that general measures of social and political inequality are strongly correlated with and contribute to greater levels of ecological harm.[31] For example, James Boyce finds that the level of egalitarianism in a society may be one of the strongest predictors of the general degree of environmental harm in that society. That is, societies exhibiting higher levels of economic and political inequality are characterized by higher overall ecological harm, and the reverse is true for societies with greater egalitarian structures.[32] What might be some of the mechanisms through which this relationship unfolds? Richard Wilkinson and Kate Pickett conclude that rising levels of social inequality in a given society contribute to heightened competitive consumption among its denizens, which, in turn, results in greater levels of industrial-scale activity that contribute to climate change in particular and environmental harm more generally.[33] This body of research is of great importance for linking inequality to ecological harm. Even so, much of it is focused on economic or political measures of inequality that fall short of capturing the complex ways in which inequality also functions across race, gender, sexuality, and species.

Much of the literature on climate justice reveals that—as is the case with environmental injustice—women, communities of color, low-wealth communities, and Indigenous communities face the greatest threats from climate change but contribute the least to the problem.[34] Going further, however, with respect to the drivers of this crisis, we find that the contemporary "wicked problem" of global climate disruption was initiated by the Industrial Revolution—that series of European and Euro-American invasions of Indigenous communities and the enslavement and forced labor of vast swaths of people across the global South, which also ushered in the Anthropocene.[35] Today we find that there are strong correlations between gender and climate-disrupting practices. For example, Christina Ergas and Richard York find that carbon emissions are lower in nations where women have high political status; thus efforts to improve gender equality and gender justice will likely be more effective if they work synergistically with campaigns to address climate change and ecological harm. Ergas and York also find that nations with greater military spending have higher carbon emissions than other nations, supporting the long-standing work of ecofeminist scholars who have argued for an important linkage between masculinist policymaking and ecological harm.[36]

Kevin Bales explores the linkage between contemporary forms of human enslavement and ecocide and finds that many of the present-day practices of enslavement are directly implicated in some of the most ecologically destructive industrial activities.[37] These include but are not limited to the extraction and consumption of shrimp, fish, gold, diamonds, steel, cow products, sugar, cocoa, and sandstone. The reason why enslavement is so ecologically destructive is because it frequently involves brutal, unregulated, industrial-scale extractive activities aimed at some of the most sensitive ecosystems and vulnerable species—producing unimaginable harm to enslaved workers and more-than-human populations and spaces.

Finally, while the environmental justice and climate justice literatures have done an admirable job of demonstrating the strong spatial relationships between marginalized populations and environmental harm, the driving forces behind this violence require more investigation. Voyles's concept of "wastelanding" is immensely useful in that regard because it is a racial and spatial signifier that defines certain human populations and landscapes as pollutable and expendable.[38] The message from this literature is clear: ideologies, policies, and practices that produce and enable human inequities are harmful to the people they target and they are harmful to the planet because they promote climate change and ecological unsustainability.

The U.S. prison industrial complex is a particularly vicious and tangible site of deep inequalities and antidemocratic practices that threaten human and environmental health. This raises the key question motivating this chapter: What might EJ histories and futures look like if we examine them through the lens of incarceration and enslavement? A focus on imprisonment speaks to a number of key concerns that have animated the field of EJ studies from its beginnings: (1) immigrants, low-wealth persons, people of color, LGBTQIA folks, and other vulnerable populations constitute the overwhelming majority of incarcerated persons; (2) prisoners are often overburdened with environmental threats; (3) as people who are confined and disenfranchised, incarcerated persons are excluded from formal decision-making that affects their environments; (4) as juridically enslaved persons facing environmental threats, the prison presents a critical opportunity to explore what environmental racism looks like in the context of contemporary and historical bondage. Dan Berger argues that struggles against the prison system played a major role in shaping the African American civil rights and Black Power movements.[39] I concur and contend that the prison industrial complex is also an important space for environmental justice struggles past, present, and future.

Notes

1. Drucker, *Plague of Prisons.*
2. Ybarra, "Site Fight!"
3. Hall, *Prison in the Woods.*
4. Le, "War, Empire and Incarceration"; Waziyatawin, *What Does Justice Look Like?*
5. Waziyatawin, *What Does Justice Look Like?*; United Nations, "Universal Declaration of Human Rights."
6. Mancini, *One Dies, Get Another.*
7. Baker, Lake, and Wilson, "Rooted in Oppression."
8. Davis, *Political Prisoners.*
9. Estes, *Our History Is the Future,* 67.
10. Nakayama and Jensen, "Professionalism behind Barbed Wire."
11. Nakayama and Jensen, "Professionalism behind Barbed Wire."
12. Jensen, "System Failure."
13. Le, "War, Empire and Incarceration"; McAlpine, "Conditions Inside."
14. National Park Service, "Japanese American Life during Internment."
15. Chiang, *Nature behind Barbed Wire,* 4; see also Tamura, "Gardens below the Watchtower."
16. Julia Rubin, "Alaska's Aleuts—Forgotten Internees of WWII: Captivity: Residents of Strategic Islands Were Rounded Up by U.S. Government in 1942 and Left

to Languish in Old Fish Canneries," *Los Angeles Times*, March 1, 1992, https://www.latimes.com/archives/la-xpm-1992-03-01-mn-5571-story.html.

17. Gaard, *Critical Ecofeminism*; Moraga, "Queer Aztlán"; Stein, *New Perspectives on Environmental Justice*; Sze, *Noxious New York*.

18. Derek Gilna, "Federal Judge Orders Texas Department of Criminal Justice to Provide Safe Water to Prisoners," *Prison Legal News*, November 7, 2016, https://www.prisonlegalnews.org/news/2016/nov/7/federal-judge-orders-texas-department-criminal-justice-provide-safe-water-prisoners/.

19. Gabrielle Banks, "Texas Prisons Take Hit from Harvey, Complaints of Water, Sewage Problems Surface," *Houston Chronicle*, September 4, 2017.

20. Rick Anderson, "California Prisons Struggle with Environmental Threats from Sewage Spills, Contaminated Water, Airborne Disease." *Prison Legal News*, 2017, https://www.earthisland.org/journal/index.php/articles/entry/Texas_Prisoners_Exposure_Floodwaters_Following_Harvey/.

21. Hornblum, *Acres of Skin*.

22. H. Lowe, "Former Inmates Protest They Say They Still Suffer from Experiments Performed on Them in Philadelphia Prisons," *Philadelphia Inquirer*, November 6, 1998.

23. Dan Primack, "America's Only For-Profit Detention Center for Migrant Children," *Axios*, July 27, 2019, https://www.axios.com/2019/06/27/homestead-private-equity-migrant-children-camps.

24. American Friends Service Committee and Earthjustice, "Groups Probe Government over Migrant Children's Possible Exposure to Toxic Chemicals," October 19, 2021, https://earthjustice.org/press/2021/groups-probe-government-over-migrant-children-exposure-to-toxic-chemicals.

25. Amnesty International, "'Shocking Levels' of Sexual Abuse in Prisons Cannot Continue," May 16, 2013, https://www.amnestyusa.org/press-releases/shocking-levels-of-sexual-abuse-in-prisons-cannot-continue/; Coomaraswamy, "Different but Free"; Harris, "Heteropatriarchy Kills."

26. Davis, *Are Prisons Obsolete?*, 78.

27. Deer, *Beginning and End*, xvii; Estes, *Our History Is the Future*, 81.

28. Whyte, "Dakota Access Pipeline."

29. Moraga, "Queer Aztlán."

30. Raven Rakia, "Forget Hunger Strikes: What Prisons Fear Most Are Labor Strikes," *Yes! Magazine*, June 7, 2016, https://www.yesmagazine.org/social-justice/2016/06/07/forget-hunger-strikes-what-prisons-fear-most-is-labor-strikes.

31. Downey and Strife, "Inequality, Democracy, and the Environment."

32. Boyce, "Inequality as a Cause," Boyce, "Is Inequality Bad?"

33. Wilkinson and Pickett, *Spirit Level*.

34. Ciplet, Roberts, and Khan, *Power in a Warming World*.
35. Abram et al., "Early Onset of Industrial-Era Warming"; Dauvergne, *Environmentalism of the Rich*; Du Bois, *Black Reconstruction in America*; Heynen, "Urban Political Ecology II"; McClintock, *Imperial Leather*; Waziyatawin, *What Does Justice Look Like?*; Whyte, "Dakota Access Pipeline."
36. Ergas and York, "Plant by Any Other Name"; Gaard, *Critical Ecofeminism*.
37. Bales, *Blood and Earth*; Bales and Sovacool, "From Forests to Factories."
38. Voyles, *Wastelanding*.
39. Berger, *Struggle Within*.

Bibliography

Abram, Nerilie J., Helen V. McGregor, Jessica E. Tierney, Michael N. Evans, Nicholas P. McKay, and Darrell S. Kaufman. "Early Onset of Industrial-Era Warming across the Oceans and Continents." *Nature* 536, no. 7617 (2016): 411–18.

Baker, Elijah J., Fabiana R. Lake, and Cambria Wilson. "Rooted in Oppression: Why the US Policing and Carceral Systems Are Issues of Systemic Environmental Injustice." *Environmental Justice* 14, no. 6 (2021): 411–17.

Bales, Kevin. *Blood and Earth: Modern Slavery, Ecocide, and the Secret to Saving the World*. New York: Random House, 2016.

Bales, Kevin, and Benjamin K. Sovacool. "From Forests to Factories: How Modern Slavery Deepens the Crisis of Climate Change." *Energy Research & Social Science* 77 (July 2021): 102096.

Berger, Dan. *Struggle Within: Prisons, Political Prisoners, and Mass Movements in the United States*. Binghamton NY: PM Press, 2014.

Boyce, James. *Economics for People and the Planet: Inequality in the Era of Climate Change*. London: Anthem Press, 2019.

———. "Inequality as a Cause of Environmental Degradation." *Ecological Economics* 11, no. 3 (1994): 169–78.

———. "Is Inequality Bad for the Environment?" *Research in Social Problems and Public Policy* 15 (2008): 267–88.

Chiang, Connie Y. *Nature behind Barbed Wire: An Environmental History of the Japanese American Incarceration*. Oxford: Oxford University Press, 2018.

Ciplet, David, J. Timmons Roberts, and Mizan R. Khan. *Power in a Warming World: The New Global Politics of Climate Change and the Remaking of Environmental Inequality*. Cambridge MA: MIT Press, 2015.

Coomaraswamy, Radhika. "Different but Free: Cultural Relativism and Women's Rights as Human Rights." In *Religious Fundamentalisms and the Human Rights of Women*, edited by Courtney W. Howland, 79–90. New York: Palgrave Macmillan US, 1999.

Dauvergne, Peter. *Environmentalism of the Rich*. Cambridge MA: MIT Press, 2016.

Davis, Angela Yvonne. *Are Prisons Obsolete?* New York: Seven Stories, 2003.

———. *Political Prisoners, Prisons, and Black Liberation.* Boston: Anarchist Black Cross, 2005.

Deer, Sarah. *The Beginning and End of Rape: Confronting Sexual Violence in Native America.* Minneapolis: University of Minnesota Press, 2015.

Downey, Liam, and Susan Strife. "Inequality, Democracy, and the Environment." *Organization & Environment* 23, no. 2 (June 2010): 155–88.

Drucker, Ernest. *A Plague of Prisons: The Epidemiology of Mass Incarceration in America.* New York: New Press, 2013.

Du Bois, W. E. B. *Black Reconstruction in America: Toward a History of the Part Which Black Folk Played in the Attempt to Reconstruct Democracy in America, 1860–1880.* 1935. Reprint, New York: Routledge, 2017.

Ergas, Christina, and Richard York. "A Plant by Any Other Name: Foundations for Materialist Sociological Plant Studies." *Journal of Sociology* 59, no. 1 (2023): 3–19.

Estes, Nick. *Our History Is the Future: Standing Rock versus the Dakota Access Pipeline, and the Long Tradition of Indigenous Resistance.* New York: Verso, 2019.

Gaard, Greta. *Critical Ecofeminism.* Lanham MD: Lexington, 2017.

Harris, Angela P. "Heteropatriarchy Kills: Challenging Gender Violence in a Prison Nation." *Washington University Journal of Law & Policy* 37, no. 13 (2011): 13–64.

Hall, Clarence Jefferson. *A Prison in the Woods: Environment and Incarceration in New York's North Country.* Amherst: University of Massachusetts Press, 2020.

Heynen, Nik. "Urban Political Ecology II: The Abolitionist Century." *Progress in Human Geography* 40, no. 6 (2016): 839–45.

Hornblum, Allen M. *Acres of Skin: Human Experiments at Holmesburg Prison.* New York: Routledge, 1998.

Jensen, Gwenn M. "System Failure: Health-Care Deficiencies in the World War II Japanese American Detention Centers." *Bulletin of the History of Medicine* 73, no. 4 (1999): 602–28.

Le, Michelle. "War, Empire and Incarceration across Two Eras: Native American and Japanese American Concentration Camps." In *Exposing Deliberate Indifference: The Struggle for Social and Environmental Justice in America's Prisons, Jails, and Concentration Camps*, edited by David N. Pellow and Yue Shen. Prison Environmental Justice Project. UC Santa Barbara, 2017.

Mancini, Matthew J. *One Dies, Get Another: Convict Leasing in the American South, 1866–1928.* Columbia: University of South Carolina Press, 1996.

McAlpine, Shannon. "Conditions inside Japanese American Concentration Camps." In *Exposing Deliberate Indifference: The Struggle for Social and Environmental Justice in America's Prisons, Jails, and Concentration Camps.* Prison Environmental Justice Project. UC Santa Barbara, 2017.

McClintock, Anne. *Imperial Leather: Race, Gender, and Sexuality in the Colonial Contest*. New York: Routledge, 1995.

Moraga, Cherríe. "Queer Aztlán: The Re-formation of Chicano Tribe." In *The Last Generation: Prose and Poetry*, 145–74. South End, 1993.

Nakayama, Don K., and Gwenn M. Jensen. "Professionalism behind Barbed Wire: Health Care in World War II Japanese-American Concentration Camps." *Journal of the National Medical Association* 103, no. 4 (2011): 358.

National Park Service. "Japanese American Life during Internment." Updated December 13, 2023. https://www.nps.gov/articles/japanese-american-incarceration -archeology.htm.

Stein, Rachel, ed. *New Perspectives on Environmental Justice: Gender, Sexuality, and Activism*. New Brunswick NJ: Rutgers University Press, 2004.

Sze, Julie. *Noxious New York: The Racial Politics of Urban Health and Environmental Justice*. Cambridge MA: MIT Press, 2006.

Tamura, Anna Hosticka. "Gardens below the Watchtower: Gardens and Meaning in World War II Japanese American Incarceration Camps." *Landscape Journal* 23, no. 1 (2004): 1–21.

Torras, Mariano, and James K. Boyce. "Income, Inequality, and Pollution: A Reassessment of the Environmental Kuznets Curve." *Ecological Economics* 25, no. 2 (1998): 147–60.

United Nations. "Universal Declaration of Human Rights." 1948. https://www.un.org/ en/about-us/universal-declaration-of-human-rights.

Voyles, Traci Brynne. *Wastelanding: Legacies of Uranium Mining in Navajo Country*. Minneapolis: University of Minnesota Press, 2015.

Waziyatawin. *What Does Justice Look Like?: The Struggle for Liberation in Dakota Homeland*. Living Justice, 2008.

Whyte, Kyle. "The Dakota Access Pipeline, Environmental Injustice, and US Colonialism." *Red Ink: An International Journal of Indigenous Literature, Arts, & Humanities* 19, no. 1 (2017): 154–69.

Wilkinson, Richard, and Kate Pickett. *The Spirit Level: Why Greater Equality Makes Societies Stronger*. New York: Bloomsbury, 2011.

Ybarra, Megan. "Site Fight! Toward the Abolition of Immigrant Detention on Tacoma's Tar Pits (and Everywhere Else)." *Antipode* 53, no. 1 (2021): 36–55.

PART 2

Almost Green, But Not Quite

NEW PERSPECTIVES ON THE ENVIRONMENTAL
HISTORY OF PARKS AND OTHER GREEN(ISH) PLACES

In these chapters, authors bring a fresh approach to landscapes and topics
that are more familiar to environmental historians: farms, parks, and gardens.
While these sites of analysis might not be unexpected, per se, these chapters
bring an analysis of race and its relationship to environment that has been
missing from traditional environmental histories.

Teona Williams, for example, offers a new reading of the role of environment in the civil rights movement, looking to the struggle to desegregate
Shenandoah and Great Smoky Mountains National Parks—two of the first
national parks below the Mason-Dixon Line. Just as nature was implicated
in segregation, it became a central part of the struggle against Jim Crow
politics in the South. In keeping with this theme of articulating the ways
in which environmental resources and "green" spaces have shaped racial
history, and vice versa, Kathryn Morse and Cecilia Tsu explore the complex
political terrain of government-sponsored gardening programs. Morse argues
that African American home gardens in the New Deal South, which New
Dealers hoped would challenge the inequalities of cotton tenancy, ultimately
revealed long-standing "environmental color lines" both physical—on the

soil—and rhetorical—in coverage of the Farm Security Administration's program. Tsu turns to Hmong refugee community gardens in the 1980s, showing how these gardens were used by U.S. media and policymakers as feel-good, uncontroversial projects requiring relatively little investment and offering the possibility of uplift through self-sufficiency. These gardens thus shored up Reagan-era antagonism to the welfare state, even as they provided, in practice, multifaceted spaces of struggle, adaptation, and hope for the Hmong refugees who they served. In short, the essays in this section together make the case that environmental histories of farms, parks, and gardens can reveal the machinations of race and racial formation in rich and often surprising ways.

6

Islands of Freedom

The Struggle to Desegregate Shenandoah and Great Smoky Mountains National Parks, 1936–41

TEONA WILLIAMS

In the United States the environmental discourses that surround national parks have long centered ideologies on open access, democratic principles, and equity.[1] Past presidents from Franklin Delano Roosevelt to Barack Obama have claimed that national parks represent the very best ideas of this country. In 1934, Franklin Delano Roosevelt gave a presidential address at Glacier National Park, where he proclaimed that "there is nothing so American as our national parks. . . . The fundamental idea behind the parks . . . is that the country belongs to the people."[2] If Roosevelt's proclamations on the democratic principles of national parks seem antiquated, in April 2021, nearly eighty years later, Barack Obama shared similar sentiments in his latest Netflix documentary *Our Great National Parks*.[3] In the opening scenes of the trailer, Obama's voice waxes poetically over stunning visuals of pristine landscapes and rare and endangered species. Obama shared that he wanted to lead this project because "one of the great things about national parks is they belong to everybody."[4] The symbolism felt like a full-circle moment. The United States' first Black president, who symbolized an alleged postracial United States, gave his stamp of approval to national parks, seemingly making their sordid history of Indigenous dispossession a thing of the past.[5] In this way, the conception of national parks as symbolizing both the best form of protecting nature and the best version of democracy continues to endure today.[6] And yet what the national park idea and those who promote it constantly elide are the historical and ongoing ways that parks and other conservation initiatives reify racial exclusion, settler colonialism, and Indigenous and Black land dispossession.[7]

More recently, environmental historians have challenged the idea of national parks as America's purest form of democracy. Historian Mark Spence argues that national parks embody the dispossession of Native land. The creation of Yellowstone National Park and other western national parks was a part of imperial and militaristic campaigns to dislodge Indigenous peoples from their land and reify settler colonialism.[8] The settler colonial logic of land grabbing and enclosures became a standard practice of the National Park Service (NPS) as they established national parks across the United States. Scholar Katrina Powell recounts how, to create Shenandoah National Park, the federal government evicted hundreds of Virginian mountain residents from their land using a combination of eminent domain and state pressure.[9] The federal government partnered with local and state entities to maintain the illusion that wilderness was untouched by humans, and therefore parks had to be people-free.[10] The erasure of Native Americans and even poor whites from the national park landscape represented forms of erasure embedded in the creation of national parks.[11] The modes of racial exclusion and violence encoded in national parks history did not end with Indigenous peoples. National parks also actively excluded African Americans throughout their history.[12]

The history of national parks was also shaped by the history of the Jim Crow era and the legacies of racial discrimination in the United States. Carolyn Finney's and historian William E. O'Brien's work on racial discrimination on public lands attests to the ways in which racial exclusion was embedded into the very landscapes of both national and state parks. Finney argues that African Americans were continually excluded from and discriminated against in national parks. As such, many African Americans feel isolated from national parks and other outdoor recreational spaces. Finney argues that national parks and other recreational areas are constructed as white spaces, undercutting the rhetoric used by Obama and other presidents that national parks are America's playground.[13] O'Brien notes that this discrimination extended to the development of state parks, where Southern state governments resisted establishing state parks for African Americans, thereby denying them access to nature.[14] When nature collides with race, class, and gender, the so-called national park idea becomes indoctrinated with inherent contradictions—for some it becomes a space of open access and democracy, for most it becomes an enduring symbol of racial exclusion and dispossession. This paradox of what national parks should represent is highlighted in African Americans' struggle to desegregate two national parks in the South during the 1930s and early 1940s, which not only led to an early victory in the long battle for civil rights but also revealed the enduring legacy of racial exclusion in America's "best idea."

Earlier scholarship on the intersections of race, class, and national parks provides a useful framework for understanding the inherent contradictions in the national park idea. National parks expose contradictory ideals of both freedom and control, open access and exclusion. They highlight how wilderness functioned as a democratic space for wealthy white Americans, as other marginalized groups were erased from the national park landscape. However, focusing only on the discrimination and exclusion that African Americans faced in wilderness areas often oversimplifies the complex and dynamic relationship that African Americans had with the natural world. African Americans did not allow the discrimination they faced in outdoor recreation to prevent them from engaging in leisure. Instead, they consistently resisted and challenged the discrimination they faced on public lands.[15] Historian Andrew Kahrl and sociologist Dorceta Taylor both highlight how African Americans created and curated their outdoor experiences to escape racial oppression.[16] Thus nature increasingly became the battleground for racial equality during the Jim Crow era.

In this way, a study on the desegregation of Southern national parks weaves together the fields of civil rights and environmental history. Marcia Chatelain argues that the civil rights historiography has well documented the integration of schools and other public spaces but often ignores the "parallel fight to bring recreational activities to children"; in this way Chatelain continues that "camping activism involved many of the same aspects of protest for integrated schools."[17] As such civil rights histories need to extend the battles over camping and nature access as important components of desegregation struggles. Civil rights history therefore is environmental history, and while seldom discussed, the larger struggle for African American equality is embedded in the ideological and physical exclusion of African Americans and Indigenous peoples from outdoor space. Thus, Black activism for equal access reveals the pervasiveness and mutability of white supremacy as well as marks the early formations of the civil rights movement in the South. I extend on the work of Chatelain and other scholars to take a long civil rights movement approach to the desegregation of Shenandoah, Great Smoky Mountains, and by extension, Mammoth Cave National Parks.[18] In this way, I link the enduring modes of Black liberation activism to their ongoing struggles for outdoor recreation access.

As early as 1933, during the initial planning stages of Great Smoky Mountains National Park, African American campers appealed directly to federal officials to ensure that there would be equal opportunities for African Americans in Southern national parks. William Gamble wrote to park superintendent J. Eakin that he and a "delegation of colored men" wanted a meeting to discuss building Negro facilities in Great Smoky Mountains.[19] In response to Gamble, Eakin wrote back that a meeting would be a waste of time, as "plans for the park at this time are so indefinite nothing would come of a conference"—perhaps marking the (at times) ambivalence the NPS had toward Black nature enthusiasts.[20] Yet Black activism persisted as African Americans demanded equal access to national parks. Organizations like the National Association for the Advancement of Colored People (NAACP) and middle-class African Americans would inspire Secretary of the Interior Harold Ickes's advisor of Negro affairs to take up the cause of integrating parks. The NAACP saw national parks as an opportunity in the movement for civil rights and worried that if the federal government set a precedent of endorsing segregation on federal properties, it would slow down the campaign for integration.[21] Middle-class African Americans also enjoyed being out in nature and often saw it as a refuge. Black campers wanted to ensure that quality areas to camp existed and sought to ensure that all people could access nature equally.

The introduction of two national parks below the Mason-Dixon Line redefined how the federal government addressed issues of segregation in the South. After Reconstruction, the federal government agreed to leave the South to its own political makings, which manifested into the subjugation and disenfranchisement of African Americans.[22] The New Deal era was no different, where Franklin Delano Roosevelt's administration often sided with Southern Dixiecrats in order to maintain their power in politics. In this way, from the end of Reconstruction through the collapse of Jim Crow, Southern Democrats successfully demanded that the laws of Jim Crow take precedence over any federal laws or programming.[23] Thus, African Americans sustained activism around park desegregation, which resulted in the federal government ultimately reneging on this tacit compromise with Southern Dixiecrats, creating integrated campgrounds before the start of the modern civil rights movement.

The struggle to desegregate national parks expands the current civil rights movement historiography by centering one of the earlier civil rights victories in nature. Similar to the foundation of other national parks, the creation of Shenandoah and Great Smoky Mountains highlights contradictions inherent in the national park idea. National parks were created in the name of democracy but, in reality, resulted in the violent expulsion of marginalized identities. The desegregation of national parks in the South represented another contradiction. African Americans co-opted the rhetoric of the national park idea to successfully advocate for the desegregation of national park facilities in the South (in 1941). Contrary to the notion that most parks actively excluded African Americans from the recreation landscape, national parks in the South became spaces of freedom in the Jim Crow era, well before the *Brown v. Board of Education* Supreme Court decision. This chapter will explore the creation of Shenandoah and Great Smoky Mountains National Parks and their entanglement in racial politics of the New Deal era. It will highlight the segregation at the very foundation of Southern national parks, the federal government's attempt to localize national parks, and finally, showcase African Americans' use of the national park idea to launch a successful campaign to officially ban segregation in all national parks in 1941.[24]

Creating America's Playground Down South

During the twentieth century, national parks crossed a new frontier in U.S. history: the American South. The NPS wanted to bring nature back to the East, as an attempt to bring the American values of nature closer to the American people. Before 1924, all the major national parks in the United States were located west of the Mississippi, as settlers imagined lands in the West as pristine and reminiscent of preindustrial American landscapes.[25] After 1924, the South appealed to the NPS to designate two national parks in the region. In the nineteenth century, Americans saw national parks as spaces of conservation, cultural heritage, and open access. While these values were seen as foundational to national parks, the twentieth century marked the rise of environmental tourism; thus having national parks located in one's state could also introduce a lucrative tourism industry.[26] The commodification of nature enticed different stakeholders, who opposed conservation due to conservation foreclosing economic development in a park, as an investment in nature.[27]

Two groups emerged out of the campaign to bring national parks to the South. First, conservationists represented by Stephen Mather, director of the fledgling NPS. In 1926, at an NPS conference, Mather argued that it was important "to bring national parks closer to American people," and since most of the population lived in the East or Midwest, "parks there were essential."[28] Mather responded to "purists," or individuals who believed that pristine wilderness did not exist in the East. He saw a unique opportunity to bring wilderness back to the public, in many ways seeking to increase the accessibility of nature to reintroduce American values in the East.

The second group, fledgling tourism businesses, saw a different type of fortune in Southern national parks. They recognized the economic potential of introducing national parks to the South. The NPS's dependence on business groups and private citizens reflected the unique identity of eastern national parks. The federal government claimed and titled land in the West, even though it was forcefully acquired from Native Americans, and placed it under federal jurisdiction. This happened because, at the time, most western lands were still owned by the federal government. The East was different in terms of park development, as most of the lands for national parks were already privately owned. The NPS relied on private citizens, local business groups, and state governments to acquire the necessary acreage of land for national parks.[29] For example, the Tennessee Chamber of Commerce (TCC) wanted to promote tourism in the Smoky Mountains. "It may be admitted," TCC member William C. Gregg claimed, that "they are second to the West in rugged grandeur, but they are first in beauty of woods, in thrilling fairyland glens, and in the warmth of Mother Nature's welcome."[30] The TCC hoped to commodify the natural beauty of the Great Smokies to boost the state's economy. The federal government, the states of Tennessee and North Carolina, and private donors collectively fund-raised to buy parklands and then donate them to the United States.[31] It is under this arrangement that the people of the South felt a particular ownership over national park lands, which shaped the culture that these two parks would then represent.

Segregating America's Playground

While Southern park enthusiasts saw the economic opportunity in national parks and thus agreed to many of the terms set by the federal government, they insisted that the laws that govern Southern parks follow local and state laws, to which the federal government agreed.[32] This meant that both Shenandoah and Great Smoky Mountains National Parks adhered to racial segregation under Jim Crow. On February 28, 1940, Theodore T. Smith, the chief ranger of Shenandoah National Park, wrote a letter to superintendent of Shenandoah James R. Lassiter: "In May of 1939, two [busloads] of Negro school children and their families stopped at the Skyland Coffee Shop and Gift Shop at the height of the noon hour. . . . At this point [the ranger] advised them that they could not make purchase in the Coffee Shop. The leader of the party was courteously informed that separate dining rooms for Negroes were located at the Swift Run Tavern and the Panorama Tea Room. . . . This group was from Powhatan County, Virginia and understood clearly the racial segregation as practiced in the time."[33] Smith sought funding to purchase signs that would clearly delineate the white and Black sections throughout Shenandoah National Park. In that same week, Smith received reports detailing several incidents of African American visitors using the white-only sections of the park. Smith's letter hints at the rising conflicts due to the lack of clear signage. In this case, he notes that conflict did not arise because Southern Blacks were well accustomed to segregation. But he worried that the lack of signage would cause conflict among those not aware of Southern culture. Smith's desire to maintain separation at lunch counters in Shenandoah reflects a broader issue of the discrimination African Americans faced in the national park system.

Although national parks were never explicitly conceived as racially integrated spaces, nowhere was this segregation more institutionalized than in the South. As federally owned properties, national parks were supposed to be open for all citizens, since the federal government did not explicitly uphold discrimination on its own properties, with the exception of Washington DC and the military.[34] Smith's report depicts how the introduction of national parks to Virginia and Tennessee conflicted with the more visible forms of discrimination in the South. The creation of Shenandoah and Great Smoky Mountains shaped the ways in which the federal government addressed integration in federal territories in the South.

When the Department of Interior (DOI) banned segregation in all national parks in 1941, the department's leaders found themselves taking a stance on Jim Crow by creating integrated spaces in the South. This new stance on integration was due to the sustained campaign African Americans launched and not necessarily because the federal government was empathetic to racial issues. In fact, in the initial planning of Shenandoah and Great Smoky Mountains, the DOI did not plan on even providing separate facilities for African Americans, let alone integrated sites. In the past, the DOI resisted building separate facilities for African Americans as one strategy to more tacitly limit or deny African Americans access to national parks.[35] In many cases this relegated African Americans' experiences in national parks to day trips. However, the DOI had to institute more visible forms of segregation in national parks due to pressure from both park officials in the South and even Robert Weaver, the advisor of Negro affairs.

Weaver encouraged Secretary Ickes to "take a definite stand on building Negro facilities."[36] The advisor of Negro affairs was a position under the Department of the Interior as a part of Franklin Delano Roosevelt's effort to improve race relations during his presidency. Weaver's insistence on a definite stand and the very location of Shenandoah and Great Smoky Mountains forced the NPS to abandon its previous use of implicit discrimination in favor of more blatant segregation. In 1938, it built separate camping facilities in Shenandoah, opening itself up to further resistance from African Americans. Eventually, African Americans' efforts to integrate Southern national parks would lay the foundation for how the federal government addressed integration, but initially they also reshaped the strategies the NPS employed to attempt to maintain the oppression inherent in parks.

Before the DOI banned segregation in national parks, it fought vehemently to keep national parks in the South segregated. "There will be some criticism by colored people against segregation," Arno Cammerer, director of the NPS, expressed to Associate Director Arthur Demaray in 1938. "But I think we would be subject to more criticism by the colored people as well as the white people if we put them in with the white people."[37] Cammerer's insistence on maintaining segregation in Shenandoah reveals not only his racism but also the federal government's attempt to maintain the racism inherent in national parks. The Department of the Interior argued against creating "jurisdictional islands," or integrated spaces in the South. They argued against setting a precedent of the federal government endorsing integration. Their attempts to make segregation in parks a jurisdictional issue challenged the alleged national identity of national parks in favor of transforming parks into Southern institutions.

The NPS continued to insist that Southern national parks had to be segregated due to their policy of following local customs and laws. The DOI would repeat the sentiment of jurisdictional islands in its communications surrounding integrating Shenandoah and Great Smoky Mountains. Hilory Tolin, acting director of Great Smoky Mountains National Park, stated, "In general, the National Park Service policy is to follow state rules, regulations, and customs whenever it is not inconsistent with federal law and policy to do so. The history of segregation of many years cannot be changed at once, of course, by order of the Department of the Interior, and to establish conflicting procedures would form incompatible jurisdictional islands within the southern states. There is no segregation in our western park areas."[38] Here, Tolin attempts to make integration a jurisdictional issue by highlighting how parks in the West are free of segregation, seemingly to absolve the federal government of racism. He suggests that the DOI did not have the authority to undo years of segregation with one ruling—thus shifting the blame to Southern states and implying that the DOI was powerless. Tolin's statement implies that politically and socially, the federal government was unwilling to make such a grand statement on racial politics in the South. The issue of whether to integrate quickly changed from an equality issue to one of states' rights. Starting from the end of the Reconstruction era, the federal government turned a blind eye to the South and its racial politics.[39] It would draw on the legacy of "North/South" relations to defend the discrimination and racism embedded in the creation of national parks. Nature and race collided, becoming entangled in the political climate of the 1930s.

The New Deal era is often seen as a racially progressive time in U.S. history, yet the campaign to desegregate Southern national parks challenges that idea. Liberal politicians found themselves placating the South by legitimizing Jim Crow culture. The Roosevelt administration, too, surrendered to the politics of the South. On the one hand, Southern state governments relinquished rights to FDR by accepting the New Deal benefits.[40] On the other hand, these same states resisted any form of race-based intervention. Race became the defining aspect of Southern conservatism, where politicians quickly adopted anti-integration rhetoric in order to garner political support in any given Southern state.[41] The Roosevelt administration did little to strive for integration and social equality in the United States, and in fact many of the New Deal's programs furthered the degradation and exploitation of Black communities across the South.[42] In this way the so-called progressivism of New Deal policies in many cases only institutionalized the power and reach of Jim Crow and racial exclusion.[43] This is reflected in the struggle to desegregate national parks.[44] The NPS utilized similar rhetoric as the FDR administration in handling segregation in the South. NPS officials, too, claimed that creating jurisdictional islands would violate states' rights. The DOI's response to integration highlights how nature became entangled in racial politics and even historical tensions between the "North" and the "South."

The paradox of the national park idea, as highlighted in African Americans' struggle to integrate public accommodations, highlights the contested and political nature of national parks. While national parks were not designed for nonwhite groups, in many ways the discrimination embedded in park development in the West remained opaque, focusing on the erasure of Native Americans from the natural landscape (as opposed to the hypervisible racism that Jim Crow demanded in the South). Unlike in the West, where there were no separate accommodations, when parks headed South, "racism was etched into the geography and design of the region's scenic landscape."[45] That and the fact that the South contained the largest concentration of African Americans meant that the NPS could no longer rely on implicit forms of disenfranchisement or perhaps the rarity of African American visitation.[46] They had to be upfront on their policies of exclusion to maintain the system of white supremacy codified in nature. The DOI would in many ways openly reject the national park idea by redefining national parks as Southern institutions outside of federal control. African Americans sought to revive the vision of the national park idea in order to force the DOI to wrestle with its own legacy of racism and discrimination.

Ending Segregation in Southern National Parks

African Americans sought to co-opt the national park idea to advocate for integration inside of national parks to make nature a refuge during the Jim Crow era. Historically, African Americans who participated in nature-based leisure experienced de facto discrimination while engaging in activities such as swimming, camping, or visiting local parks. The nature they encountered during these activities was color-blind in the sense that there were no signs or markers of segregation. African Americans would employ different strategies to avoid de facto discrimination in nature: traveling in large groups, using certain routes, or even visiting Black-owned establishments.[47] However, this implicit discrimination that African Americans usually faced radically changed once they visited national parks in the South. Both Shenandoah and Great Smoky Mountains National Parks contained explicit signs and markings separating whites from Blacks. What was most appalling to African Americans was the way they were notified about segregation in these national parks. On November 16, 1940, the *Pittsburgh Courier* reported,

> Further proof that the federally approved Jim Crow recreation parks in the Shenandoah National park system are eager to segregate Negroes and keep them as far from the whites as possible is shown in the manner in which maps are presented when auto fees are paid. Colored people receive a map with the jim-crowed [*sic*] section carefully marked out with a red pencil, showing the remote Lewis Mountain section where segregated picnic grounds are located. Signs also indicate the segregated policy of the government in its Shenandoah National park system, throughout the beautiful Blue Ridge mountains in Virginia, and on into the deeper south to the great Smokies.[48]

As evidenced by the signs dictating African Americans' mobility in Southern national parks, white supremacy was legitimized by making inequality visible; thus African Americans challenged the white supremacy that has long plagued national parks by advocating for integration.[49] The *Courier* blamed segregation in Shenandoah on the federal government. During the early civil rights movement, African Americans lobbied federal officials in their efforts to end discrimination, arguing that—as taxpaying citizens of the United States— the federal government could not exclude them from national park facilities through racial segregation policies.[50] Nature was supposed to be a space where African Americans escaped from racial oppression, but in segregated national parks nature became a painful reminder of Jim Crow.[51]

In response to the codified racism African Americans confronted in Shenandoah and Great Smoky Mountains National Parks, the new advisor of Negro affairs, William J. Trent Jr., argued for the immediate desegregation of all national parks. Trent succeeded Robert Weaver in July 1938. Trent first recommended different speaker engagements for Secretary Ickes. He arranged the secretary's travel to national parks and other Department of the Interior sites across the country and coordinated with his counterparts at other agencies in order to advocate for racial equality in national parks.[52] While Trent had never before concerned himself with the great outdoors, he immediately adopted the cause to end discrimination within Southern national parks.

Trent adopted the visionary ideals of national parks and advocated for a "parks-for-all" position to other federal officials from the secretary of the interior to park superintendents, noting that national parks in the South had developed into Southern institutions, contrary to the democratic ideals that were supposed to guide them. He wrote, "As I understand it the National Park has a dual function to perform and the relationship between these two functions is quite complex. . . . It must permit man to come in and enjoy the parks. It is to make the national park and monument system accessible to and comfortable for the visiting public."[53] In his presentation to the national park superintendents on January 5, 1939, Trent recounted the notion that national parks should be accessible and available to all Americans.

In his statement Trent claimed that "the Negro expects the rights and privileges of the citizen and should be allowed and required to assume the responsibilities of citizenship." He continued, "The parks are for the enjoyment of all the citizens of the United States," and that "there has been up to recent years, little concern over the lack of opportunity for Negroes to utilize facilities of the existing parks."[54] Trent challenged the very premise of Jim Crow by asserting that African Americans were full citizens under the Constitution and, as such, were guaranteed full rights. He sought to utilize the national park idea as a tool to advocate for integration in the South. By maintaining that national parks were designed for all Americans, regardless of race, he tried to persuade his fellow federal officials to eliminate federally sanctioned segregation in national parks. In theory, national parks represented places of conservation, cultural heritage, leisure, and open access. Trent made the claim that Shenandoah and Great Smoky Mountains had a duty to follow these principles even for African Americans. While the national park idea was a contradiction, Trent found the vision behind national parks a useful strategy to advocate for civil rights—effectively challenging the NPS to finally live up to the egalitarian principles it promoted when creating the parks.

Trent was not the only individual who utilized the national park idea to advocate for integrated accommodations in Shenandoah and Great Smoky Mountains. A New York attorney, Arthur Ernst, wrote to Secretary Ickes complaining, "It came as a shock to me that in this great National Park separate picnic grounds should be provided for whites and for negroes. . . . It seems entirely out of keeping having the National Government make such discrimination."[55] Ernst too challenged Virginia and Tennessee's position that Southern national parks did not have to adhere to federal policies. Ernst also found the principles behind the park idea a useful tool to advocate for racial equality. He argued that national parks were under federal jurisdiction and therefore not held under the same laws as other spaces in the South.

Discrimination against African Americans in national parks created tension between park officials and visitors. In 1937, a Shenandoah park official observed while in the South River picnic area, "A group of Negroes appropriated a large portion of the area's use. . . . When a seasonal ranger attempted, upon request of white people, to confine them to the area south and east of the driveway, they become highly incensed, and it appeared real violence might develop."[56] After the ranger calmed the group, he remarked, "the contention of the Negro group, repeatedly stated, was that racial segregation was not a policy in the National Parks. The District Ranger pointed out, however, that no precedent had been established in the matter of segregation in National Parks recently created in Southern States where segregation of races was the accepted practice."[57] The location of Shenandoah and Great Smoky Mountains National Parks thus created ambiguity in the national park idea.

National parks represented "open" spaces ideologically, but the racial politics of the Jim Crow South mandated that Shenandoah and Great Smoky Mountains be visibly segregated. The federal government's initial refusal to assert its authority over Shenandoah and the Great Smoky Mountains created contested spaces in the South. Even if the federal government refused to acknowledge its authority over federal jurisdictions in the South, African Americans continued to insist that federal properties ought to be integrated. The park official's observation at the gift shop was the consequence of national parks in the South being ambiguously defined as open spaces for some.

Reacting to the federal government's slow response to discrimination in Southern national parks, Robert Ballou, a frequent visitor of Shenandoah, appealed to Secretary Ickes in hopes of convincing him that segregation on federal properties was illegal, regardless of region. Ballou fired off a letter to Ickes outlining the discrimination he and his son faced:

> I came upon the first picnic ground sign and was inexpressibly shocked and deeply hurt and angered to find that the United States of America, 'conceived in liberty, and dedicated to the proposition that all men are created equal,' is, through the Department of the Interior, sanctioning Jim Crowism . . . For all its magnificence of engineering, for all the indescribably majestic natural beauty which the Sky Line Drive makes available, I regret and resent every cent of my taxes which have gone into its building, so long as a part of that money was spent for painting Jim Crow signs.[58]

Like other African Americans, Ballou was humiliated that in "America's" playground, he was separated from the beauties of nature. The signs controlling his access to park spaces ruined the aesthetic value of national parks. Ballou contended that the federal government and, by extension, national parks represented democracy and equality. The federal government was a representation of all American citizens. Ballou noted he did not want his tax dollars to go toward funding signs that besmirched the symbolism of national parks as being places of open access. He and other African Americans struggled to discredit Shenandoah and Great Smoky Mountains National Parks as Southern institutions governed by Jim Crow in order to legitimize national parks as out of the realm of Southern law.

The history of segregation in Shenandoah and Great Smoky Mountains National Parks and African Americans' struggle to desegregate them complicated the image of national parks in American history. Southern national parks further discredited the vision of national parks first created in the West. National parks now more visibly challenged ideas of open access by sanctioning segregation and discrimination. They were used as another space to control African Americans' access to space in the United States. While national parks are often celebrated in the American imagination as symbols of democracy, parks in the South were cultivated in the land of Jim Crow, embodying its racist values and making visible a more spatial form of racial exclusion and segregation.[59] The creation of Shenandoah and Great Smoky Mountains National Parks, like their state park counterparts, challenged the American imagination by making visible the racial discrimination inherent in the national park idea. However, African Americans would in many ways appropriate the principles of the national park idea by using it to launch a successful campaign to integrate public accommodations in national parks during the height of the Jim Crow era.

African Americans demanded that the federal government rectify the confusion of control over national parks by declaring these national institutions democratic and inclusive spaces. African Americans' appeals to the DOI revealed the federal government's refusal to desegregate public accommodations and campgrounds in Shenandoah and Great Smoky Mountains. Thus African Americans continued to amplify how the DOI continuously rejected the proposals to integrate. The government's refusal reflected the relationship between the South and the national government. While African Americans hoped that the DOI would end discrimination in Southern national parks, instead the DOI sympathized with the plight of African Americans but refused to impose integration in the South.

Even as the federal government was slow to integrate national parks, African Americans continued to make their objections against segregation known. The early 1940s marked the final push for African Americans in their struggle against segregation in Shenandoah and Great Smoky Mountains National Parks. Clyde McDuffie wrote a legal report debunking every response the federal government made against integration:

> The Shenandoah National Park is owned by the government of the United States. Therefore, it has been purchased by income from taxation levied directly or indirectly on all citizens. If the National Park is owned by the federal government, then the laws of the United States are applicable to the conduct and use of the Park. . . . My personal observation in reference to the use of National Parks in the West is that there is no discrimination practiced against any racial group. Southerners who frequent these parks in great numbers accept the federal government's policy there and make no protest.[60]

McDuffie denied the federal government's opportunity to decide on the side of segregation. McDuffie attacked the blatant and seemingly localized racism embedded in Shenandoah by comparing it to his knowledge of national parks out West. While McDuffie was correct that there was no signage that explicitly marked racial exclusion in parks out West, he was incorrect about the existence of racial discrimination in western parks. Terence Young argues that western parks practiced insidious forms of racial exclusion and violence. For example, racism in national parks out west revolved around Indigenous expulsion and exclusion and unpublicized policies discouraging African American visitation. Park officials saw Black campers as impossible to serve inconspicuously. They argued that the hypervisibility of their Blackness resulted in other visitors objecting to their presence. As such, NPS superintendents decided in 1922 that the NPS "cannot openly discriminate against them, [but] they should be told that the parks have no facilities for taking care of them."[61] In this way, whether implicit or explicit, whether in the South or West, racial exclusion was always legible to national park landscapes. However, the power in McDuffie's statement amplified how it should be white Southerners who adjust to integration and Black campers who adjust to segregation. He and other African Americans continued to write letters to Trent and the DOI drawing on the language of the national park idea.

The push to integrate Southern national parks was advocated for across genders. Black women also drew on concepts from the nationalistic identity of parks in pursuit of racial equality. Norma Boyd remarked,

It is shocking to discover that the Department of the Interior endorses discrimination on the basis of color as a policy of the federal government of the United States. The federal government should be more reluctant than any other organization to sanction any policies appearing to discriminate against any of its citizens. No one more than yourself can be aware that such discriminatory practices are fundamentally opposed to the spirit of constitutional democracy. The horror aroused by medieval practices of Nazi Germany is eloquent evidence of American disapproval of governmental distinctions based on race, creed, or color. I understand that Shenandoah National Park is under the jurisdiction of the Department of the Interior and is maintained by federal funds. No particular difficulties to my knowledge occur in any of the other National Parks administered by this Department.[62]

Boyd introduced a global context to segregation, claiming that the United States was on the same plane as the Nazis for practicing discrimination in national parks. She combined the national identity of the park idea with a common example of America's disapproval of discrimination abroad to attack the federal government's response to segregation. A few months after Boyd's letter—perhaps realizing that the "Negro would simply accept its condition," as was the common justification for segregation at the time—the DOI decided to integrate camp facilities slowly and quietly in the South. By August 4, 1941, the federal government ruled that segregation in any national parks was illegal and that all signs indicating such segregation ought to be removed immediately.[63] The violence that politicians feared never occurred. The integration of Shenandoah and Great Smoky Mountains National Parks slipped out of mind as it slipped away from the history books. Despite the hostility from both the federal and state governments, African Americans launched a successful campaign to integrate public accommodations in national parks, a major blow to the Jim Crow politics of the time.

African Americans utilized nature as a space to escape the ills of Jim Crow, making one of the first early civil rights victories in a national park all the more powerful. Before African American students could attend schools with white children, they could camp with them. The ruling to desegregate national parks came before the civil rights movement. It is well established that the creation of national parks across the country represented a tremendous contradiction. The government created parks in the name of democracy, but they represented anything but that. In the South, Shenandoah and Great Smoky Mountains represented another site of contradiction. They became islands of freedom in a sea of discrimination, oppression, and exclusion. African Americans used nature as a safe haven from both the de facto and de jure racism they faced on a daily basis, so it is not surprising that one of the first major civil rights victories occurred in national parks. African Americans fiercely fought to preserve the significance and symbolism of nature in their everyday lives.

Notes

The author thanks Dr. Connie Chiang, associate professor of history at Bowdoin College, for her excellent guidance throughout this project. A special thank you to Mary E. Mendoza and Traci Brynne Voyles for believing in every iteration of this piece. I would also like to thank all my reviewers, including the editors of this volume, for their excellent feedback. While all errors are my own, all the impressive things are credited to them. I also want to thank my family and my partner for always supporting me throughout different academic projects. They are the best sounding boards and always ask questions that push me to complicate the narrative.

1. Nash, *Wilderness and the American Mind.*
2. Roosevelt quoted in National Park Service, "Presidential Quotations about National Parks."
3. Amy O'Rourke, "'Our Great National Parks' Highlights Our Breathtaking Natural World with Narrator Obama," *Daily Campus*, April 25, 2022, https://dailycampus .com/2022/04/25/our-great-national-parks-highlights-our-breathtaking-natural -world-with-narrator-obama/.
4. Obama as quoted in O'Rourke, "'Our Great National Parks.'"
5. Martin-Hardin, "Nature in Black and White," 594–605; Edwards, *Charisma.*
6. Spence, *Dispossessing the Wilderness*, 10; Runte, *National Parks*, 11; Smiles, "Erasing Indigenous History."
7. Sène, "Land Grabs and Conservation Propaganda"; Hernandez, *Fresh Banana Leaves*; Smiles, "Erasing Indigenous History"; Finney, *Black Faces, White Spaces.*
8. Spence, *Dispossessing the Wilderness*, 10.
9. Powell, *Anguish of Displacement.*
10. Smiles, "Erasing Indigenous History."
11. Smiles, "Erasing Indigenous History"; Davies, "Slow Violence and Toxic Geographies," 409–27.
12. Finney, *Black Faces, White Spaces.*
13. Finney, *Black Faces, White Spaces.*
14. O'Brien, *Landscapes of Exclusion.*
15. Kahrl, *Land Was Ours*, 11.
16. Taylor, *Rise.*
17. Chatelain, *South Side Girls*, 145; Martin-Hardin, "Nature in Black and White," 595–97.
18. Hall, "Long Civil Rights Movement," 1233–63.
19. Eakin to Gamble, September 18, 1933, NPS, box 3791; Lambert, *Shenandoah National Park*, 254.
20. Eakin to Gamble, September 18, 1933, NPS, box 3791.
21. Young, "Contradiction in Democratic Government," 656.
22. Peskin, "Was There a Compromise?," 65.
23. Katznelson, *Fear Itself.*

24. Young, *Heading Out*, 177. Also note that in the National Park Service Archives, I found scattered cases of discrimination against Black and Jewish visitors in western national parks. See NARA, Central Classified Files, 1933–49, General Files.

25. Nash, *Wilderness and the American Mind*.

26. Miles, *Wilderness in National Parks*, 3; Taylor, *Rise*, 26

27. Klingle, *Emerald City*, 156.

28. Klingle, *Emerald City*, 54.

29. Simmons, "Conservation, Cooperation, and Controversy," 388.

30. Young, "False, Cheap and Degraded," 173.

31. Young, "False, Cheap and Degraded," 174.

32. Young, *Heading Out*, 178

33. Smith to James R. Lassiter, February 1940, NPS, box 3791.

34. Young, "Contradiction in Democratic Government," 656.

35. Young, "Contradiction in Democratic Government," 656.

36. Weaver to Cammerer, July 1, 1936, NPS-2, box 378.

37. Cammerer to Weaver, July 6, 1936, NPS-2, box 378; Cammerer to Demaray and Wirth, September 30, 1936, NPS-2, box 378; Cammerer to Johnson, May 27, 1937, NPS-2, box 379; Eakin to Cammerer, April 25, 1938, NPS-2, box 1101.

38. Tolen to Ernst, October 23, 1940, NPS-6, box 379.

39. Peskin, "Was There a Compromise?," 65.

40. Badger, *New Deal / New South*, 47.

41. Perman, *Struggle for Mastery*, 22.

42. Cobb, "'Somebody Done Nailed Us,'" 912–36.

43. Woods, *Development Arrested*.

44. Katznelson, *Fear Itself*.

45. O'Brien, *Landscapes of Exclusion*, 2.

46. Bullard, *Dumping in Dixie*.

47. Kahrl, *Land Was Ours*, 11.

48. "Segregated Maps at Recreation Parks," *Pittsburgh Courier*, November 14, 1940.

49. O'Brien, *Landscapes of Exclusion*, 3.

50. Gilmore, *Defying Dixie*; Lear, *Aggressive Progressive*.

51. Fisher, "Frontiers of Leisure."

52. Trent, "A Discussion before Superintendent of the National Parks" W. J. Trent Papers, box 1.

53. Trent, "A Discussion before Superintendent of the National Parks."

54. Trent, "A Discussion before Superintendent of the National Parks."

55. Ernst letter to Ickes, NPS, box 46.

56. Smith to James R. Lassiter, February 1940, NPS, box 3791.

57. Smith to Lassiter, February 1940, NPS, box 3791.

58. Robert Ballou to Harold Ickes, September 23, 1937, NPS, box 46.

59. O'Brien, *Landscapes of Exclusion*, 16.

60. McDuffie, March 15, 1939, NPS-2, box 378.

61. Young, "'Contradiction in Democratic Government,'" 174. The superintendents' statement is quoted in Shaffer, *America First*, 126.

62. Boyd to Trent, April 2, 1941, NPS-2, box 378.

63. Young, "'Contradiction in Democratic Government,'" 681.

Bibliography

ARCHIVE AND MANUSCRIPT COLLECTIONS

NPS. Records of the National Park Service, 1785–2006. Department of the Interior. National Park Service. Southeast Region. National Archives, College Park, Maryland.

NARA. National Archives and Records Administration (II), College Park, Maryland.

W. J. Trent Papers. Moorland Spingarn Research Library. Howard University, Washington DC.

PUBLISHED WORKS

Badger, Anthony. *New Deal / New South*. Lafayette: University of Kentucky Press, 2007.

Bullard, Robert D. "Dumping in Dixie: Race, Class, and Environmental Quality." 1990. Reprint, Boulder: Westview, 2000.

Chatelain, Marcia. *South Side Girls: Growing Up in the Great Migration*. Durham NC: Duke University Press, 2015.

Cobb, James C. "'Somebody Done Nailed Us on the Cross': Federal Farm and Welfare Policy and the Civil Rights Movement in the Mississippi Delta." *Journal of American History* 77, no. 3 (1990): 912–36.

Davies, Thom. "Slow Violence and Toxic Geographies: 'Out of Sight' to Whom?" *Environment and Planning C: Politics and Space* 40, no. 2 (March 1, 2022): 409–27.

Edwards, Erica R. *Charisma and the Fictions of Black Leadership*. Illustrated ed. Minneapolis: University of Minnesota Press, 2012.

Finney, Carolyn. *Black Faces, White Spaces: Reimagining the Relationship of African Americans to the Great Outdoors*. Chapel Hill: University of North Carolina Press, 2014.

Fisher, Colin. *Urban Green: Nature, Recreation, and the Working Class in Industrial Chicago*. Chapel Hill: University of North Carolina Press, 2015.

Fisher, Robert Colin. "Frontiers of Leisure: Nature, Memory, and Nationalism in American Parks, 1850–1930." PhD diss., University of California, Irvine, 1999.

Foster, S. Mark. "In the Face of 'Jim Crow': Prosperous Blacks and Vacations, Travel and Outdoor Leisure, 1890–1945." *Journal of Negro History* 84, no. 2 (1999): 135.

Gilmore, Glenda Elizabeth. *Defying Dixie: The Radical Roots of Civil Rights, 1919–1959.* New York: W.W. Norton, 2008.

Giltner, Scott. *Hunting and Fishing in the New South: Black Labor and White Leisure after the Civil War.* Baltimore: Johns Hopkins University Press, 2008.

Hall, Jacquelyn Dowd. "The Long Civil Rights Movement and the Political Uses of the Past." *Journal of American History* 91, no. 4 (2005): 1233–63.

Hernandez, Jessica. *Fresh Banana Leaves: Healing Indigenous Landscapes through Indigenous Science.* Berkeley: North Atlantic Books, 2022.

Kahrl, W. Andrew. *The Land Was Ours: African American Beaches from Jim Crow to the Sunbelt South.* Cambridge MA: Harvard University Press, 2012.

Katznelson, Ira. *Fear Itself: The New Deal and the Origins of Our Time.* New York: Liveright, 2013.

Klingle, Matthew. *Emerald City: An Environmental History of Seattle.* Illustrated ed. New Haven CT: Yale University Press, 2009.

Lambert, Darwin. *Shenandoah National Park: Administrative History, 1924–1976.* Luray VA: National Parks Service, 1979.

Lear, Linda. *The Aggressive Progressive.* New York: Garland, 1981.

Martin-Hardin, Amanda. "Nature in Black and White: Summer Camps and Racialized Landscapes in the Photography of Gordon Parks." *Environmental History* 23, no. 3 (July 1, 2018): 594–604.

Miles, John C. *Wilderness in National Parks: Playground or Preserve.* Seattle: University of Washington Press, 2009.

Nash, Roderick Frazier. *Wilderness and the American Mind.* New Haven CT: Yale University Press, 2001.

National Park Service. "Presidential Quotations about National Parks." Updated August 19, 2019. https://www.nps.gov/nama/learn/historyculture/presidential -quotations-about-national-parks.htm.

O'Brien, William E. *Landscapes of Exclusion: State Parks and Jim Crow in the American South.* Amherst MA: Library of American Landscape History, 2022.

Perman, Michael. *Struggle for Mastery: Disfranchisement in the South, 1888–1908.* Chapel Hill: University of North Carolina Press, 2001.

Peskin, Allan. "Was There a Compromise of 1877?" *Journal of American History* 60, no. 1 (1973): 63–75.

Powell, Katrina M. *The Anguish of Displacement: The Politics of Literacy in the Letters of Mountain Families in Shenandoah National Park.* 1st ed. Charlottesville: University of Virginia Press, 2007.

Runte, Alfred. *National Parks: The American Experience*. Lincoln: University of Nebraska Press, 1997.

Schmitt, Peter. *Back to Nature: The Arcadian Myth in Urban America*. Baltimore: Johns Hopkins University Press, 1990.

Sène, Aby L. "Land Grabs and Conservation Propaganda." Africa Is a Country, June 17, 2022. https://africasacountry.com/2022/06/the-propaganda-of-biodiversity-conservation.

Shaffer, Marguerite. *See America First: Tourism and National Identity, 1880–1940*. Washington DC: Smithsonian Books, 2001.

Simmons, Dennis. "Conservation, Cooperation, and Controversy: The Establishment of Shenandoah National Park, 1924–1936." *Virginia Historical Society* 89, no. 4 (1981): 387–404.

Smiles, Deondre. "Erasing Indigenous History, Then and Now." Ohio State University, September 2021. https://origins.osu.edu/article/erasing-indigenous-history-then-and-now?language_content_entity=en.

Smith, Kimberly. *African American Environmental Thought: Foundations*. Kansas: University of Kansas Press, 2007.

Spence, David. *Dispossessing the Wilderness: Indian Removal and the Making of the National Parks*. New York: Oxford University Press, 1999.

Taylor, Dorceta E. *The Rise of the American Conservation Movement: Power, Privilege, and Environmental Protection*. Durham: Duke University Press, 2016.

Woods, Clyde. *Development Arrested: The Blues and Plantation Power in the Mississippi Delta*. New York: Verso, 2017.

Young, Terence. "'A Contradiction in Democratic Government': W. J. Trent, Jr., and the Struggle to Desegregate National Park Campgrounds." *Environmental History* 14, no. 4 (2009): 651–82.

———. "False, Cheap and Degraded: When History, Economy and Environment Collided at Cades Cove, Great Smoky Mountains National Park." *Journal of Historical Geography* 32, no. 1 (2006): 169–89.

———. *Heading Out: A History of American Camping*. 1st ed. Ithaca NY: Cornell University Press, 2017.

Conserving Whiteness

The Crisis of Tenancy and New Deal
Rural Rehabilitation in the Cotton South

KATHRYN MORSE

Men and women and children are we, town and
country, white and black, landed and landless.
Tenants of the Almighty, all of us, as time writes
on the face of the earth our care of the land, and in
our own faces our care of each other.

—Arthur Raper, *Tenants of the Almighty*

Central to the meaning of whiteness is a broad,
collective American silence. The denial of white
as a racial identity, the denial that whiteness has a
history, allows the quiet, the blankness, to stand as
the norm. This erasure enables many to fuse their
absence of racial being with the nation, making
whiteness their unspoken but deepest sense of
what it means to be an American.

—Grace Elizabeth Hale, *Making Whiteness*

"'For every field gullied, a man gullied.'" So declared economist Stuart Chase
before the House of Representatives Rivers and Harbors Committee in November 1937.[1] Chase captured the connection New Dealers drew between the
wasting of soil and the wasting of human lives.[2] Waste in both senses linked
two vivid crises in the 1930s: soil erosion and agricultural tenancy—a spike
in the number of farm families living on rented land or as sharecroppers
migrating with every crop or season. President Franklin D. Roosevelt's Special

Committee on Farm Tenancy opened its 1937 report by stating, "Erosion of our soil has its counterpart in the erosion of our society." In the language of soil science, the report went on, "Instability and insecurity of farm families leach the binding elements of rural community life."[3] Sociologist Arthur Raper continued in his 1943 *Tenants of the Almighty*, "In thin soil and gullies the land records its neglect; in weakened bodies and dwarfed hopes, society records its own inhumanities. . . . Man and land are all tied up together."[4] Widespread soil erosion brought together material environments and human lives in newly visible ways.[5]

Perhaps most famously, Farm Security Administration (FSA) photographer Dorothea Lange and her husband, economist Paul S. Taylor, titled their 1939 photo-documentary book on the nation's agricultural crisis *American Exodus: A Record of Human Erosion*. The book portrayed American families across the South, Midwest, Great Plains, and West, uprooted and blown with the wind, like the dust itself—scattered, without roots in the ground, or drifted, piled up together on land that offered neither subsistence nor profit. Taylor wrote of "undernourished families on impoverished land." Woody Guthrie sang in "Pastures of Plenty," "On the edge of the city you'll see us and then / We come with the dust and we go with the wind."[6] Lange's photographs gave visual form to Guthrie's words, capturing families loosed from their ties to land and home by social and environmental storms.

Erosion threatened soil and human rootedness on land in the United States in the 1930s; it also threatened whiteness. As white families lost land and homes, they slid downward, like silt on a treeless hillside, from the socioeconomic tier of landownership and yeoman independence into the gullies and wastelands of tenancy—a "place" historically, socially, and agroecologically reserved for and defined by nonwhites. In response to these dislocations and the stunning poverty they brought, journalists, photographers, filmmakers, sociologists, and public servants produced a body of work and a set of New Deal reforms that defined and then worked to shore up what historian Neil Foley labeled in his 1997 book *White Scourge* "agrarian whiteness." Foley, writing of the Texas cotton fields in the 1930s, defined agrarian whiteness as a "complex social and economic matrix" that connected white identity, land ownership, self-sufficiency, independence, and particular conceptions of manhood and womanhood. Those ideas of whiteness hinged on their opposite—Blackness—defined as dependent labor on land owned by others.

As increasing numbers of white Texans lost their land and "fell" downward into tenancy and wage labor, Foley explains, those families became a white scourge, "culturally and biologically inferior," poor, dependent, and "off-white"—the "racial detritus of whiteness."[7] Social erosion endangered whiteness itself.

Foley's conceptions of agrarian whiteness operated not just in Texas but throughout the nation. New Dealers harnessed growing fears of eroded whiteness to garner political support for federal programs to address tenancy and thus conserve human and natural resources. These programs, overseen after 1937 by the FSA, centered on "rural rehabilitation," a cluster of measures to address the landlessness, poverty, and dependency of tenants and sharecroppers. Though it served clients of all races, FSA rural rehabilitation constituted (rhetorically and on the ground, and most powerfully in the South and Southwest) a program for the conservation of agrarian whiteness.[8] FSA programs sought to rehabilitate poor white families who found themselves out of *place* within a system designed for African American laborers. In seeking to restore white families to security on agricultural land, rural rehabilitation conserved the material, cultural, and social meanings of race defined by particular connections to and uses of the earth's resources. FSA programs *did* also assist Black families through the same programs—but never in proportion to the vast needs of the African American population of the cotton South and never with the goal of widespread social mobility for Blacks. Many Black families *did* succeed in rural rehabilitation programs, achieving far improved standards of living. Yet they remained outside of the bounds of agrarian whiteness.[9]

New Dealers produced a vast body of written and visual work on the problem of tenancy. None of these texts analyzed whiteness as a racial category. Instead, they proclaimed almost without exception that the crisis of social and environmental erosion was *not about race*. Their three main arguments in support of that claim revealed the conservation of whiteness.[10] First, New Dealers documented the growing number of landless families mired in poverty and tenancy, as increasing numbers of white families joined African Americans long relegated to tenant or sharecropper status and thus joined a social category unsuited to whites in the United States. That dangerous loss of status threatened white Americans and the idea of agrarian whiteness—thus the crisis.

Second, in seeking to explain the predicament of rural whites, and in recognizing the losses those families faced, sociologists and policymakers applied social scientific and documentary methods to produce new knowledge and understandings of poverty broadly and of cotton tenancy in particular. Their work revealed cotton tenancy as a complex economic, social, cultural, and environmental system defined by material conditions—class—rather than biological race. Third, New Dealers wrestled with the political firewall of Southern white supremacy in the 1930s. Reformers' focus on the threat to and conservation of whiteness allowed the FSA to garner enough fleeting political support from Southern congressmen and local governments to fund rural rehabilitation programs rhetorically targeting white Americans in crisis. Public reports on FSA goals and programs showed whiteness at work—without naming it—to shape policy and public opinion.

The New Deal commitment to agrarian whiteness thus furthers our understanding of the complexity of Southern reformers' accommodation to and compromise with white supremacy but also reveals the ways in which on-the-ground programs sought to disrupt material inequality at the local level.[11] Finally, government programs to conserve agrarian whiteness revealed the material and environmental construction of whiteness. Americans both inscribed racial difference in and drew racial difference from ideas about soil as well as human relationships to land, plants, animals, and food. In a nation and a region devoted to keeping African Americans in their "place," New Dealers' writings and policies on tenancy constructed that place all too clearly. Whiteness meant independent landownership and self-sufficiency; Blackness meant the impossibility of that specific relationship to land.

Ultimately, while FSA programs in the rural South conserved agrarian whiteness, some researchers and writers confronted and described the ways in which white supremacy worked as a system that they could study and name. Through that work we see the historical reality of tenancy as a system composed of interlocking subsystems: an agroecosystem designed to produce cotton; a tenancy system designed to produce poverty and dependence for workers, nonwhite and white, but not equally; and a racial system designed to conserve agrarian whiteness.

New Deal Narratives

The conservation of agrarian whiteness constructed race and legitimized FSA programs by telling a particular set of stories about the causes of tenancy and about the government's solution: rural rehabilitation, defined as the restoration of (mostly) young white nuclear families to self-sufficiency and independence on small farms. Photographs and stories of men guiding plows on fertilized, terraced fields and of women gardening and canning vegetables exemplified this New Deal vision of white families restored to traditionally gendered work, self-reliance, and financial security. Such stories built on broader New Deal narratives, including the idea of the forgotten man and the long-held concern for a backward and inefficient Southern economy. In 1932 FDR declared "the forgotten man"—the white man "at the bottom of the economic pyramid"—the chief concern and beneficiary of the New Deal.[12] As analyzed by Holly Allen, New Deal narrators portrayed "jobless white breadwinners restored to civic respectability through federal public works" who "invariably affirmed the ideal of white heterosexual masculine authority in the household and the public square."[13] The FSA's image of the deserving tenant farmer/father followed similar patterns.

The New Deal narrative of eroding whiteness also drew from 1930s narratives of soil erosion, based on reports of the highly visible and dramatic gullying of soils in the cotton South. New Deal reformers critiqued that erosion as evidence of a particular "Southern pathology" responsible for the region's woeful state: underdevelopment, cultural backwardness, inefficient production, inadequate education systems, and virulent racism. As Paul Sutter argues, dramatic photographs of eroded gullies and canyons symbolized everything "wrong" with the South in reformers' eyes. Such images used nature to indict a century of careless exploitation and provided evidence for the human failures responsible for leaving the region behind, outside the material and economic mainstream of a modern industrial nation.[14]

New Dealers created scores of still images of eroded fields and gullies, as well as films and paintings, which together narrated the causes and solutions of soil loss and flooding across the nation. Pare Lorentz's films *The Plow That Broke the Plains* (1936) and *The River* (1938) featured *only* white-presenting Americans as agents and victims of ecological profligacy and the floods and dust storms that resulted. *The River* intoned in its final act that "poor land," eroded by plows and floods, meant "poor people," and "poor people" meant "poor land." Every image of rural Americans in the final sequences of the film—which featured the Mississippi Delta—showed only white workers and families. FSA photographer Arthur Rothstein's most famous image of the Dust Bowl, "Farmer and sons walking in the face of a dust storm, Cimarron County, Oklahoma" (Figure 7.1), powerfully evoked the peril of the white farm family: the father and sons separated from the mother, the youngest in danger of being left behind.[15] The image captured the Great Depression as a powerful assault on the white farm family and the land on which it depended.

These New Deal narratives—forgotten men, endangered children, gullied farms, flooding rivers—all bolstered New Deal projects intended to solve the problem, from dams to shelterbelts to chickens and pressure cookers for client families. They also erased other narratives: of nonwhite men and women, of naturally delicate and erodible soils, of Black sharecroppers trapped by design in permanent poverty.[16] As Cara Finnegan argues, New Deal documentary photographs of poor families "operated . . . as circulating images that made some poverty stories more rhetorically available than others."[17] Jack Delano's untitled and never-published photograph of an African American child crossing a gully in Heard County, Georgia (Figure 2), hinted at such less-available stories.

A Crisis of Agrarian Whiteness

The New Deal conservation of whiteness hinged on agrarian ideals constructed as white: upward mobility from renting to owning, small farms, diverse crops, hard work, care for soil and livestock, stability, traditional gender roles, and self-sufficiency in home food production.[18] Government and media attention to the crisis of tenancy peaked in the late 1930s, as magazine and newspaper articles, films, photographs, reports, editorials, and essays featured stories of whites in the United States suffering poverty, degradation, and dependence considered routine and expected for African Americans, Mexicans, and Asians. Neil Foley puts it plainly: "Only when whites were reduced to living like Mexicans and blacks did the nation take notice."[19] An agricultural labor system created to control nonwhite laborers now engulfed millions of white farmers, and shocking photographs and sober accounts of the forgotten white tenants drew public support for FSA programs to rehabilitate the fallen.[20]

FIG. 7.1. Arthur Rothstein, *Farmer and Sons Walking in the Face of a Dust Storm, Cimarron County, Oklahoma*, April 1936, Library of Congress, LC-USF34-004052 LOT 521. Rothstein's famous photograph provided a compelling visual shorthand for the New Deal narrative that soil erosion and the Great Depression were threats to white fathers and the white nuclear family.

Those photographs, reports, articles, and maps constructed tenancy as a problem affecting all poor rural families in similar ways, regardless of race. Because greater numbers of whites in the United States suffered in tenancy—true by the numbers—the crisis remained predominantly white. The whiteness, after all, is what made it a crisis. "The problems of the rural South in general, and of cotton tenancy in particular," began the 1935 report *The Collapse of Cotton Tenancy*, "are those of native white families much more

FIG. 7.2. Jack Delano, untitled photo, possibly related to *Erosion in South Section of Heard County, Georgia*, April 1941, Library of Congress LC-USF34–044012-D. Though FSA photographers captured images of both Black and white Americans facing rural poverty and soil erosion, with few exceptions photos featuring African Americans appeared only in publications for Black audiences.

than of Negroes."[21] The report's authors included Will Alexander—later to head the FSA—and sociologists Edwin Embree and Charles S. Johnson, the future African American president of Fisk University. *Collapse* detailed the post-1910 expansion of cotton tenancy to engulf over eight million in the United States, two-thirds of them white. This "ever-increasing horde of white and black tenants and share-croppers" directly threatened, they noted, "the persistent American ideal" of "a hardy stock of ambitious farm owners." Their language focused on the threat of "physical and moral decadence" and made clear that "this fixed custom of exploitation of the Negro has carried over to the white tenant and cropper," allowing a system based on race to cross boundaries and threaten whiteness.[22]

When Embree took the report to the press in 1936, he declared his concern for Black families but noted, "The fact that this is a white problem more than a colored one makes it more feasible to solve." Calling this "Not a Negro Problem," Embree observed, "Whites have taken on this new kind of slavery."[23] Alexander took the case for whiteness to the *New York Times* two months later under the headline "White Tenant Held Problem of the South": "Far from being essentially or even primarily a Negro question as many people, even of the South, believed it to be, it was one of the absentee ownership affecting even more vitally the white people of the Southern States."[24] In *Survey Graphic* in March, Embree further detailed the "evils" of Southern farm tenancy. "The curse of tenancy," he noted, "is spreading like a dismal infection" and "becoming increasingly a white problem." As white tenancy took over the cotton belt, he noted, "practices which were set up to 'keep the Negro in his place' have been transferred in large part to the whole group of dependent tenants, whether colored or white."[25] "White people have competed," one of Embree's photo captions read, "for the new kind of slavery involved in tenancy," making clear the erosion of white status.[26] Scholar Cara Finnegan analyzed Embree's correspondence with his editors at *Survey Graphic* regarding the choice of images for the article. Her work revealed that Embree specifically suggested two images of white tenants and one of Black migrants in order to emphasize to readers "that cotton tenancy is not a Negro problem."[27]

In 1936, the Works Progress Administration funded T. J. Woofter et al.'s *Landlord and Tenant on the Cotton Plantation*, a study of land tenure systems on six hundred–odd plantations in the eastern cotton belt. While Woofter found some evidence of upward mobility for Black tenants, whites appeared to be literally and figuratively losing ground. "Thus," he wrote, "the present Negro tenants and owners are children and grandchildren of laborers while the white tenants and laborers are children and grandchildren of landowners. For the former, tenancy is a step in advance of the previous generation, for the latter a step backward."[28] Government sociologist Carl Taylor and his coauthors took this argument even further two years later in sketching the downward social trajectory of white landowners, again with nature metaphors. "What was once a rapidly moving stream of farmers making steady progress to ownership has become, in some sections of the Nation, a sluggish stream or pool of congenital tenants." This loss of mobility, Taylor et al. saw, could produce racial tension, as "the frequent intermingling of former renters and owners . . . on the same land with so-called 'poor white trash,' and colored families breeds serious ill feeling."[29]

Arguments about tenancy's threat to whiteness brought support across the political spectrum for legislation to address the crisis: the Bankhead-Jones Tenancy Act. On the liberal end of that political spectrum, the idea of a mounting threat to white as well as nonwhite families fit an argument for fair and equal policy: all tenant lives mattered, if you will. Among Southern conservatives, the white majority in the growing number of tenants demanded aid for those considered racially superior and thus worthy of government support.

The visual representation of the whiteness of tenancy continued across the 1930s. Newspaper and magazine articles featured more images of white men, women, and children than of Black, in keeping with the statistics regarding the total number trapped by tenancy.[30] Most famously, James Agee and Walker Evans's 1941 photo essay *Let Us Now Praise Famous Men* created an intimate portrayal of three tenant families mired in rural poverty: all white.[31] Agee and Evans's work began as an assignment for *Fortune*, but the magazine never published the piece. Published posthumously decades later, Agee's manuscript, *Cotton Tenants*, flatly declared that "one tenant in three is a Negro. But this is not their story."[32] Erskine Caldwell and Margaret Bourke-White's 1937 documentary photo book *You Have Seen Their Faces* and Lange and Taylor's *An American Exodus* presented images of both Black and white families, but both continued the ongoing visual construction of Southern poverty as predominantly white. Taylor wrote in his opening section on the

Old South that "rural poverty in cotton is no longer a problem of race." John Steinbeck's October 1936 reporting for the *San Francisco News* focused on the suffering and hopelessness of white migrant families in California. His 1939 novel *The Grapes of Wrath* made the Joad family's loss of their farm and flight to California the central icon of depression-era tenancy, dispossession, and displacement—again a white family.[33]

Despite this New Deal commitment to color-blindness, tenancy entrapped Blacks and whites unequally, privileging whites even in the depths of rural poverty. However, this "not about race"—or rather "not about black people"—argument did serve limited antiracist purposes.[34] While it conserved agrarian whiteness, it also challenged the belief that tenancy, dependence, and land-lessness resulted from the biological and cultural inferiority of the rural poor. Thus, New Deal reformers countered arguments that blood and descent both caused and explained extreme poverty. Now that whites suffered in tenancy, there must be a cause beyond biology, some argued, and a fair solution. White tenants, logic dictated, deserved aid as members of a superior race. House Speaker William Bankhead—the namesake of the Bankhead-Jones Act—argued that "'some of these poor tenant farmers, by descent, are of the best blood of the Republic, sons of the Cavaliers and the Huguenots.'"[35]

On the other hand, many Southern conservatives argued that white racial superiority had eroded. Perhaps, some suggested, against Bankhead's invocation of "best blood," poor whites had declined genetically—a biological loss that explained their social erosion. For white families to slide down the social and agricultural hierarchy into such dire straits called their whiteness into question, marking them with another racial category: "white trash," or in Neil Foley's words, off-white, eroded, and unequal.[36] Sociologist Rupert Vance explained in 1932 that Southern white supremacists, faced with the growth of white tenancy, developed a new racial theory to explain it, an "unspecified-type of racial degeneracy" exhibited by the "Southern poor white."[37] The *Chicago Defender*, an African American newspaper, reported landlords' attitude that biological and cultural traits caused tenants' bankruptcy and poverty and that all tenants were "either a no-good poor white, or a lazy shiftless Negro."[38]

New Dealers challenged these views with statistical and documentary evidence. Vance's 1932 *Human Geography of the South* had earlier established some of the groundwork for denying specious claims about the racial inferiority of poor farmers. White Southerners, Vance noted, had long argued that the inferiority and laziness of Black workers explained the region's agricultural struggles, its poverty and soil erosion. Vance quoted 1890s Georgia Governor William J. Northen, who explained in 1904, "We have not improved our soil because the Negro is not willing to grow crops to be incorporated into the soil, nor leave his cotton seed to be returned to the fields that he has denuded of humus and all possible traces of fertility. . . . We have accepted his thriftless and destructive methods simply because under our present system we have not been able to do without him."[39] Vance shot back. Cotton cultivation, he argued, was a complex system of plants, weather, labor, economics, and social order that itself "conditioned and perpetuated" the human behaviors Northen defined as biological traits. As proof, Vance offered what had become obvious by the early 1930s: tenancy happened to white people too. "Similar habits and attitudes," he noted, to those ascribed to Blacks, "are held by white croppers, tenants and small farmers." "Whether white or black," he continued, "characteristic traits of cotton culture appear as responses to environment rather than responses to race."[40]

Carl Taylor, Helen Wheeler, and Ellis Fitzpatrick echoed this theme in their 1938 report on rural "disadvantaged classes." Like Vance, they argued that tenancy as a material and economic system, not racial difference, produced poverty and inferior social status over time. Poor land use led to eroded social status rather than the other way around. "More discouraging still," they wrote, "is the gradual development of an inferior status that comes to any segment of a population living for a few generations under persistent economic and social handicaps."[41] Johnson, Embree, and Alexander agreed that the material conditions of impoverished tenants and sharecroppers proved only that "meager and pinched living is not a racial trait but a result of the system of cotton tenancy." Furthermore, they declared, "attempts to justify the existing system of tenure on the score that it is an adaptation to the latent and innate characteristics and capacities of the southern farm population are as baseless as they are vicious." Racial traits did not lead to degradation, they asserted. Rather, a system designed to ensure landlessness and dependence led to ongoing soil erosion as well as the waste of human potential through poverty, malnutrition, disease, and lack of education.[42]

Two 1938 documents further demonstrated this New Deal commitment to both a structural and class-based analysis of tenancy and a profound elision of white supremacy as a factor: the *Report on the Economic Conditions of the South* by the National Emergency Council (NEC) and Taylor et al.'s far less famous *Disadvantaged Classes in American Agriculture*. The final NEC report released in August 1938, with a full version published in the *New York Times*, barely mentioned race or segregation. Instead, in keeping with the party line, the report stated that in tenancy, "whites and Negroes have suffered alike" and "approximately half the sharecroppers are white, living under economic conditions almost identical with those of Negro sharecroppers."[43]

As indicated in their title, Taylor et al. settled on a race-neutral term to explain rural poverty: *disadvantage*. The report listed seven "disadvantaging conditions" affecting rural Americans, with a focus on troubled regions, including the cotton South, the Appalachian-Ozark uplands, and northern New Mexico and Arizona. The New Dealers' commitment to "disadvantage" as the object of study and reform took its most striking form in the maps at the end of the report (Figure 7.3). Layering each of the seven contributing "conditions" on top of one another—low income, low standard of living, high birth rates, tenancy, soil erosion—the authors presented a spatial analysis of, literally, "the black spots" (or "sore spots") in U.S. agriculture, indicated by dark shading on the map.[44] The authors mentioned the nonwhite populations dominating these "sore spots"—including the Pine Ridge Indian Reservation—but avoided all mention of race itself as a major factor in producing "disadvantage."[45] Yet their map directly revealed racialized poverty in obvious ways.

Despite this narrative of race-neutral disadvantage, numerous journalists, scholars, and New Deal agents did at times acknowledge and describe the ways in which race and tenancy worked to produce each other and in which white supremacy shaped the material conditions of tenants' lives. Such sidelong critiques began with the reality that tenancy did not affect Blacks and whites *equally*. Proportionately, a vastly higher percentage of nonwhites suffered in rural poverty and landlessness. Sociologist Charles S. Johnson convinced fellow members of the President's Committee on Farm Tenancy to include his (literal) minority report as an appendix. "While it is true that only one-third of the sharecroppers and tenants in the South are Negroes," he noted in factual language, "four-fifths of all Negro farm operators are tenants or sharecroppers."[46] Woofter's study of the eastern cotton belt agreed flatly that "84 percent of the total tenant households covered in the present

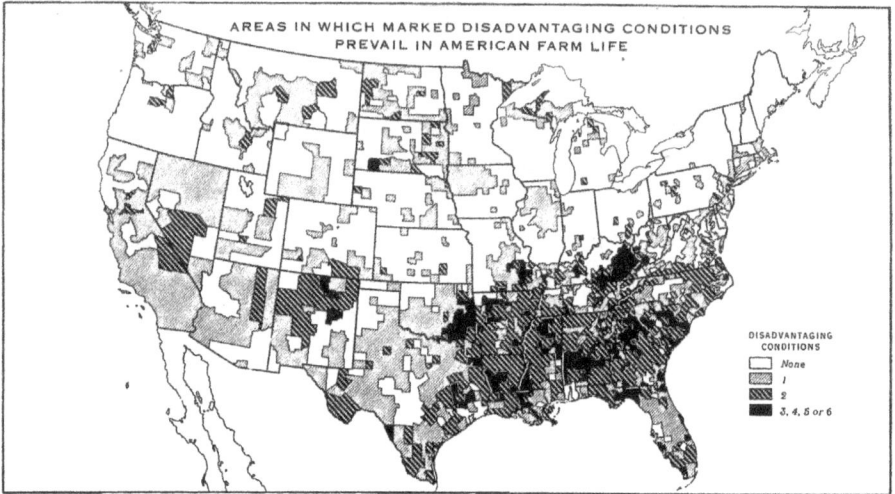

AREAS IN WHICH MARKED DISADVANTAGING CONDITIONS
PREVAIL IN AMERICAN FARM LIFE

DISADVANTAGING
CONDITIONS
None
1
2
3, 4, 5 or 6

FIG. 7.3. *Disadvantaged Classes*, from Taylor, Wheeler, and Kirkpatrick, *Disadvantaged Classes in American Agriculture*, 123. The authors in 1938 presented a map of agricultural "disadvantage" without meaningful commentary on the spatial correlation between those conditions and the conditions for nonwhite populations in the United States.

survey were Negro," which "emphasize[d] forcefully that the Negro is basic to the plantation tenant system and cannot be ignored in the consideration of its problems."[47]

James Agee acknowledged even more fully—though in unpublished work—that Black sharecropper families endured conditions materially worse than those of white sharecroppers. The first appendix to his *Cotton Tenants*, entitled "On Negroes," stated plainly that in the cotton belt communities he saw, "the Negro is a lot worse off, on the land, than the white man." Agee asked his readers to picture the three white families featured in his work—those made famous in 1941 in *Let Us Now Praise Famous Men*—and then, in order to grapple with African American conditions, to imagine their material resources reduced: no garden, no hog, less corn and sorghum, fewer peas. Add to that, he noted "a general tendency, among landlords to enjoy cheating a Negro."[48] Day Monroe's 1940 study agreed: "The Negro families had less than half as much farm-furnished food as the white operators; even though they purchased more food, they did not spend enough to provide meals as good, nutritionally, as those of the white families."[49]

Disrupting Tenancy, Growing Food, Conserving Whiteness

As Agee and Monroe made clear, material inequalities often came down to food, and food sat at the core of rural rehabilitation programs for tenants. Home food production and preservation meant independence and self-sufficiency, central components of agrarian whiteness. Gardens and home canning thus connected ideas of race to the physical realities of soils, plants, and bodies, particularly women's domestic labor in gardens and kitchens. This focus on food grew from sociologists' and reformers' clear understanding that cotton tenancy as an agroecological system required landless families to maximize production of cotton at the expense of gardens, fruit, and livestock for home consumption. Commercial row crops like cotton and tobacco contributed to soil erosion, while tenants' limited salt pork and corn diets contributed to hunger, malnutrition, and disease: human erosion. As Arthur Raper and Ira De A. Reid put it succinctly in their 1941 study *Sharecroppers All*, quoting a Southerner named "Black Jake," "'the way to stop gullies is to fill sharecroppers' stomachs full of food and their souls full of hope!'"[50]

Materially, tenants' and sharecroppers' lack of home food production worsened their entrapment by a crop-lien system of unending debt that ensured hunger and malnutrition. Culturally, it magnified the erosion or absence of a central tenet of agrarian whiteness: the ability of an intact nuclear farm family to live on their own land through home food production. For the descendants of enslaved peoples, none of this was new. W. E. B. Du Bois described crop-lien tenancy with forceful detail in 1903. "There is no use asking the black tenant, then, to diversify his crops," DuBois wrote. "He cannot under this system."[51] By the 1920s, increasing numbers of white tenants had given up home gardening and food production as well.[52] Will Alexander and his coauthors wrote in 1935 that "devotion to a single cash-crop, and the fact that food crops mature during the same season as cotton, make it virtually impossible under the system to raise subsistence crops. . . . As a result the diet is limited to imported foods . . . meat (fat salt pork), meal, and molasses."[53] In keeping with racialized theories of tenants' biological and cultural inferiority, landlords and Southern merchants interpreted tenants' lack of gardens, poor diets and health, and failure to save and preserve food for winter as evidence of laziness, shiftlessness, and racial degeneracy. "The typical tenant, asserts the landlord, will take no interest in a garden," reported Arthur Raper in his 1936 study of Georgia tenancy. "He will not fix a leak over his head . . . repair the garden fence, or build a pig pen; the tenant simply does not see that he would benefit by a good garden."[54] That such stereotypes held for white as well as Black tenants made clear the threat to white racial superiority. Raper further explained that landowners developed these beliefs about tenants "when these tenure groups [tenants and sharecroppers] were still made up almost solely of Negroes."[55]

FSA promotional materials countered such views by explaining the ways in which tenancy as a system used dependency and debt to ensure that few tenants could find ways or reasons to invest labor in gardening and food preservation. Such arguments then presented rural rehabilitation as a set of simple measures—loans, longer leases, equipment, supplies, gardens, livestock, window and door screens, sanitary privies, instruction, supervision—meant to disrupt the system.[56] The tenancy cycle worked by design to ensure that whatever cash a family might clear after the cotton harvest went to resolve outstanding debts and buy food for the winter, given that most tenants produced no food themselves. That in turn meant almost no cash income. With no access to consumer goods beyond flour and meat, no ability to buy nutritious food, and no way to disrupt the cycle, tenants were unable to participate in the national economy as consumers of clothing, appliances, radios, and automobiles.[57] Ideally, for New Deal rural rehabilitation client families, home gardens and food preservation, along with chickens and a cow supplied by the FSA, offered a slight wedge, an opening, by which families might shift their food supply from store-bought flour and pork to home-produced fruits, vegetables, meat, eggs, milk, and butter. This allowed families to produce a higher percentage of their own food (50–90 percent) and thus save cash for other consumer goods. Ideally, they also gained relative independence from the local landlord or furnishing agent, at least with regard to food.[58]

New Deal rural rehabilitation also aimed to shift the tenant's key economic relationship from the landlord to the local FSA office. Literacy and detailed written household records proved central to that goal, just as pressure cookers served home food preservation and storage. Within crop-lien cotton production, landlords held "absolute control," as Woofter stated, over tenants' purchase of food, supplies, and seed, and only landlords (ostensibly) kept records of debts.[59] On "settlement day," when often illiterate tenants delivered their cotton, landlords announced the price for cotton, the tenants' total purchases for the year, and their year-end balance. New Deal field researcher Lorena Hickock reported to FDR's advisor Harry Hopkins from Moultrie, Georgia, in 1934 that "farmers in this section . . . take advantage of the fact that their share-croppers cannot read or write, with the result that in many cases, at the end of the season, the share-cropper doesn't get a thing, and there isn't anything he can do about it."[60] Raper reported as well that "the accepted definition of color precludes the Negro's right to question the landlord's account."[61]

Such was the point, or rather the system, meant to perpetuate the cycle of debt and dependency and thus control a rural labor force. Rural rehabilitation, in response, tried to break that cycle and produce independence, in part by requiring written records of all transactions. Johnson et al. argued in 1935 that for tenants, "to increase independence, is to oppose the system itself."[62] Written leases, negotiated with federal oversight, directly threatened the status quo, as by tradition landlords preferred informal oral agreements.[63] Thus in Lee Alston and Joseph Ferrie's analysis of Southern paternalism, FSA-mediated written leases "opened to negotiation and outside scrutiny what had previously been a process steeped in tradition and unspoken but implicitly understood mutual obligations." Despite the reality that tenants and sharecroppers struggled mightily to keep records as detailed as their supervisors required, landlords resisted. They saw rural rehabilitation, Alston and Ferrie continued, as "a radical, disruptive force."[64] Organized political resistance to FSA programs proved nearly fatal by 1943, when Southern congressmen cut FSA rural rehabilitation funding by 43 percent, and totally fatal by 1946, when the agency became the Farmers Home Administration and for all intents and purposes ceased to exist.[65]

Landowners' resistance could be threatening. Though FSA county agents maintained strict racial segregation, with white supervisors serving white clients and Black *assistant* supervisors serving Black clients, even the presence of Black federal agents associated with rural rehabilitation angered white supremacists in the Deep South. The African American newspaper *Atlanta Daily World* reported on a Ku Klux Klan pamphlet in late 1939 in South Carolina. In the circular, the Klan "uncompromisingly condemned" the presence of an African American FSA employee named William Street in Greenville County, sent to "investigate and advise on the work of Rural Rehabilitation." The Klan further stated, "We vigorously, unflinchingly and uncompromisingly believe in and stand for White Supremacy and are opposed to Negroes acting in connection with government affairs." With copies dispatched to the secretary of agriculture and the entire South Carolina congressional delegation, the point proved clear.[66]

To navigate political opposition and local threats, New Dealers in the late 1930s hewed closely to their narrative of agrarian whiteness, documenting success through stories, articles, photographs, and exhibits for white audiences featuring white client families embodying traditional gender roles—men behind plows or repairing fences, women in kitchens canning garden produce with pressure cookers. Though FSA photographers shot hundreds of images of African American FSA clients (10 percent of the total FSA archive), the FSA publicity section exhibited and published such images only for Black audiences.[67] In *almost* all other cases, the visual and written story of the FSA portrayed white nuclear families with gleaming new FSA homes, rows of canned foods, flocks of chickens, newly fenced pastures, terraced fields, and orderly record books. Such stories of transformation consistently portrayed white families whose good character and visual appearance, in scholar Siobhan Davis's words, "justif[ied] government intervention" through a plucky "individualism" that led them to "reclaim a self-sufficient agrarian lifestyle."[68]

Arthur Raper's use of photographs in his 1943 *Tenants of the Almighty* proved one notable exception, though his private publisher—Macmillan—perhaps gave him greater latitude in racially integrating his story of FSA rural rehabilitation in Greene County, Georgia, where 60 percent of the farmers were African American.[69] In keeping with the race-neutral argument that tenancy as a system affected all sharecroppers equally, the book used photographs, text, and testimony to celebrate the struggle and dignity of the whole community—"white and black, landed and landless."[70] Raper composed the photograph captions in the collective singular voice of Greene County's cotton tenants, using the pronoun *we*. In the photographic sections of the book, Raper and his publishers placed twinned portraits of Black and white FSA clients opposite each other across the book's gutter. Plates 39 and 40 featured Jack Delano's portrait of a white woman in her home in front of shelves of canned garden produce, adjacent to his photograph of an African American woman with dozens of jars arrayed before her on the floor. The caption, using *our* and *we* consistently, read, "In three years those

PLATE 39

PLATE 40

Our canned stuff is like a garden in the house all winter. The whole county is
canning more than ever before. In three years those of us on the FSA have
canned over a half million quarts—almost 500 quarts to the family last year, and
most of us used to have hardly a dozen jars. Last year, eleven families canned
over 900 quarts each. We eat better than before and leave the store-bought
cans for our soldiers.

FIG. 7.4. Plates 39 and 40 from Arthur Raper's *Tenants of the Almighty* (Macmillan, 1943), featuring photographs by Jack Delano, Farm Security Administration Historical Section photographer. In this rare instance Raper published Delano's images of Black and white rural rehabilitation clients together. In doing so he both adhered to and challenged the New Deal narrative of agrarian whiteness. Mrs. Clements and Mrs. Reid appear as equals, working hard to improve their lives with help from an apparently race-neutral federal program. Yet by including photos of African Americans in Georgia throughout the book, intended for a white audience, Raper and Delano pushed beyond the typical limits of New Deal visual storytelling.

of us on the FSA have canned over a half million quarts—almost 500 quarts to the family last year—and most of us used to have hardly a dozen jars."[71]

Beyond Agrarian Whiteness

In placing Delano's photographs of Mrs. Lloyd Clements (left) and Mrs. Edmond Reid (right) alongside each other, Raper both adhered to and challenged the New Deal narrative of agrarian whiteness. The photo pairings presented tenants as equal, fighting their way out of a race-neutral system that impoverished them in similar ways, but merely by showing

African Americans as independent individuals working to improve their homes and farms, Raper pushed beyond convention.[72]

Other social scientists also documented the ways in which the tenancy crisis was, in fact, very much about race. As the FSA and Bureau of Agricultural Economics (BAE) looked beyond rehabilitation and farm security toward ambitious programs in land-use planning and community development, sociologists and FSA administrators named and described white supremacy as a racial system. Their frankness grew from a broadening focus on reform and planning for neighborhoods and communities, as well as individual families. Immersed in fieldwork in the segregated South, social scientists could not describe communities without acknowledging structures of power based on race. At certain moments, some risked funding and government jobs—though both dwindled in the war years—to do so. As James Agee had suggested in his unpublished early version of *Let Us Now Praise Famous Men*, no honest reporter could separate cotton tenancy and white supremacy.

As part of this shift toward community land-use planning after 1938, the BAE's Division of Farm Population and Rural Welfare sponsored detailed county-by-county studies, meant to provide basic demographic and environmental knowledge for conservation planning. A key part of what sociologist Jess Gilbert terms the "Third New Deal" or the "Intended New Deal," these community studies grew out of the recognition that land and soil conservation depended on programs, like rural rehabilitation, that addressed basic human needs for all rural citizens. Rehabilitation and land-use planning had to proceed together and include all citizens to foster community-wide economic development alongside resource conservation. Raper, working in Greene County, saw this clearly. "The likelihood of the soil being conserved and restored," Raper wrote, "turns upon . . . whether the farm people are finding answers to their needs for higher incomes, better houses, good food . . . and participation in the affairs of the local community and the nation."[73]

As BAE researchers and FSA officials worked to make those connections on the ground, they confronted white supremacy as a barrier to all of it— houses, gardens, schools, land-use planning, conservation, and democracy. In Greene County, Georgia, already well documented by Raper and chosen as a pilot county for community land-use planning, teams of rural sociologists set out to execute a first step in the plan to coordinate all government programs related to land use and rural rehabilitation: community delineation maps. These maps captured what researchers called "natural" human communities—the intrinsic ways in which individuals and families clustered in space and on land and organized their economic and social relations. Such spatial knowledge would then allow government agencies like the BAE, the FSA, the Soil Conservation Service, the Forest Service, and the Agricultural Extension Service not only to coordinate their own services but also to form democratic local committees that could engage in coordinated land-use planning with those agencies.[74]

In theory, these local committees represented everyone. The Bureau defined community planning as "the *joint* (democratic) endeavor of farmers, administrators, and technicians to consider the *total soil resources* in relation to the *total farm population*." As a result, "if anyone is left out of the policy-making process, he shall have no will to do what the plan may call for him to do."[75] Yet in mapping human communities in Greene County and elsewhere, BAE researchers ran straight into the spatial realities of white supremacy: not formal segregation but rather complete community separation in shared geographic space. Their interviews with white and Black residents produced two separate maps of neighborhoods and communities, occupying the same territory. In the Greene Country report, one map showed "Negro Neighborhoods" and another "White Communities and Neighborhoods." The accompanying text in the final report added that "the boundaries of Negro and white neighborhoods do not correspond," even though some of those neighborhoods occupied the same space.[76] Another report from Lee County, Alabama, noted "that the negro neighborhood in no way coincided with the white neighborhood, either from the viewpoint of geographical delineation or from the viewpoint of interracial association."[77]

Such realities challenged the BAE's vision that unified, democratic communities might democratically plan their relationships to soil, forests, rivers, and wetlands. New Deal administrator William Hartman stated the fundamental illogic in an internal USDA report. Successful land-use planning had to involve all farmers, Black and white, rich and poor, he argued. "Since . . . a given land area may involve both negro and white families," he wrote, "recommendations concerning its use would necessarily involve both the negro and white neighborhoods within which the land area happens to fall."[78] "It is, in truth," John H. Provinse wrote in the foreword to Waller Wynne's study of Putnam County (southwest of Greene), referencing Black and white residents, "two communities, having little in common except the understanding that keeps them apart and their economic interdependence."[79] Bushrod Allin of the BAE Planning Division wrote to his agents in Georgia that same year asking for photographs of Black farmers "participating" in the land-use planning program in the state. His underling wrote back, "No Negroes Participated as County or Community Committeemen in preparation of Georgia County LUP [land-use planning] Reports." Hence "No pictures available."[80] Raper presented adjacent images of African American and white Georgians in his book (Figure 7.4), but Delano took almost no Greene County photographs with Georgians of both races in the frame.[81]

Raper himself, throughout *Tenants of the Almighty* and despite his carefully integrated photo spreads, detailed the racial disparities in New Deal programs in a majority-Black county (53 percent) with twice as many Black tenants as white. These included twenty-six boys, "all white," granted spots in the Civilian Conservation Corps (though that later included African American boys); five white families for every one Black family given rural rehabilitation loans in 1934; and less than one dollar in twenty for relief projects benefiting schools serving only African Americans.[82] The average white student finished eighth grade, the average Black student third; in the military draft, "one white boy in twenty was turned down because of illiteracy, one colored boy in three."[83] Reporting on rural rehabilitation programs themselves, Raper recorded that in 1937, the number of Black families benefiting from rural rehabilitation had risen to one-third of the total; that number changed dramatically by 1939, however, with a shift to three-fourths Black clients in the expanded or "unified" FSA/rehabilitation program intended to "reach to the last man."[84] In neither case was Greene County typical. Donald Grubbs stated that in some areas of the South, Blacks participated in FSA programs "almost in proportion to their percentage of the population," though of course not in proportion to their percentage of the total number of Southern sharecroppers.[85]

BAE sociologist Frank D. Alexander directly named and described white supremacy in his 1944 cultural reconnaissance survey of Coahoma County, Mississippi. In an early draft of the report, Alexander stated that in addition to cotton plantation agriculture, race relations powerfully determined every aspect of daily life in the county. "Schools, churches, families, law enforcement, earning a living, are all under the domination of the plantation economy," Alexander wrote in his never-published study. "Similarly," he continued, "all of these institutions are carried on within the definitions of white supremacy and racial segregation."[86] As Olaf Larson and Julie Zimmerman relate the story, a Mississippi congressman saw the draft and introduced a bill banning funds for any further cultural studies of communities in the rural South. Congress disbanded the BAE's Division of Farm Population and Rural Life.[87] "Any research that revealed inequalities of class or 'race,'" Larson wrote in 1999, "was seen, apparently, as threatening."[88] Such realities explained further how and why FSA-funded programs and publications stuck to the visual and narrative discourse of agrarian whiteness yet also why academic social scientists stretched toward more complex stories until Congress stopped them in their tracks.[89]

In keeping with the conservation of agrarian whiteness, New Deal reformers and sociologists investigated and documented tenancy as a socioeconomic system that affected human beings regardless of race—a color-blind system of equal inequality. Their work was meant to help, but as David Roediger argued in *The Wages of Whiteness*, "to reduce race to class is damaging."[90] Yet this body of work on the tenancy crisis countered pervasive beliefs that the racial and cultural qualities of the rural poor themselves caused tenancy. It brought widespread national media attention to the crisis of tenancy—though defined as white tenancy—as well as federal aid to poor families. However, on the ground, rural rehabilitation's narrative focus also conserved the racial hierarchy that denied African Americans land and a meaningful purchase on the independent agroecological ideal. Thus the broader literature of tenancy revealed a crisis simultaneously "about" and "not about" race, about conserving whiteness as an agrarian ideal without explicitly naming or confronting white supremacy for public audiences. In their 1941 book *Sharecroppers All*—a book whose title again elided race—Raper and Reid began with the story of two elderly sharecroppers, Seab and Kate Johnson, "old and alone" on an eroded former cotton plantation in Georgia. Only after ten pages of intimate description of the Johnson's dire if not hopeless predicament did the reader learn, through reference to a photograph of a blond child, that the Johnsons were white. As Seab contemplates his family's prospects—his children too are "'caught,'" trapped by the economic system— Raper and Reid continue their portrait: "Slowly it dawns upon Seab that he is a victim of slavery, too," and that he has no means of escape. He and Kate might as well stay in a crumbling plantation house, "here where it has been more important to control the landless masses than to conserve the land they worked."[91] That Blackness remained the most powerful cause of membership in the landless masses brought no mention.

The rhetorical whiteness of tenancy in the 1930s provides just one example of the ways in which Americans have harnessed land and the environment to construct racial difference and to conserve whiteness. So too have Americans used ideas of race—whiteness, Blackness, Brownness—to physically conserve, shape, and reshape their environments. Imagined places in Euro-American thought and history, from wilderness to suburbs and from family farms to border walls, reflected the ongoing and dynamic construction of racial difference. Americans have also deployed racial difference on the ground to build, conserve, transform, and police such places, both imagined and profoundly real.

Notes

The author extends gratitude for research support to the Charles Warren Center for Studies in American History at Harvard University and to Middlebury College, in particular the John C. Elder Chair in Environmental Studies. Many thanks to the readers who helped shape this work over many years, including Holly Allen, Susan Burch, Cathleen Cahill, Finis Dunaway, Neil Foley, Cathy Gudis, Nick Howe, Neil Maher, Mary E. Mendoza, Cindy Ott, Sarah Phillips, Aaron Sachs, Virginia Scharff, Christina Snyder, Rachel St. John, Ellen Stroud, Traci Brynne Voyles, Marsha Weisiger, and Richard White.

1. Stuart Chase, "Says Waste Robs 10,000,000 of Living: Stuart Chase Assails Past Policies of Nation, Asserting Loss of 'Resource Bases,'" *New York Times*, November 24, 1937.
2. Jackson, Markoe, and Markoe, "Chase, Stuart," 145–47; Chase, *Rich Land, Poor Land*. That crucial connection to and focus on human bodies and human lives, as Sarah Phillips, Neil Maher, and others have argued, defined New Deal conservation as far more human centered than Progressive conservation earlier in the century. See Phillips, *This Land, This Nation*, 9, 208–9; Maher, *Nature's New Deal*.
3. U.S. Government et al., *Farm Tenancy*, 7.
4. Raper, *Tenants of the Almighty*, 210, 232.
5. See Phillips, *This Land, This Nation*, 9, 208–9; Maher, *Nature's New Deal*.

6. Lange and Taylor, *American Exodus*, 19; Chase, *Rich Land, Poor Land*, 312; Guthrie, "Pastures of Plenty."

7. Raper defined this opposite of whiteness as referring to those who "can have no place in American life except that of a non-landowning farmer, or casual laborer in the city." See Raper, *Preface to Peasantry*, 170; Foley, *White Scourge*, 6–7, 157, 164, 183, 181.

8. Foley used the term *agrarian whiteness* in 1997, and here I am deeply indebted to and expanding on his work. See Foley, *White Scourge*, 141.

9. By 1938, FSA programs encompassed two distinct but related tracks: rural rehabilitation and tenant purchase. Tenant purchase, a smaller program, provided loans to families deemed qualified to work toward land ownership though long-term mortgages on viable land. See Baldwin, *Politics and Poverty*, 107–8; Roberts, *Farm Security Administration*, xi, 55–56, 72–73, 95–97.

10. New Deal liberals and reformers wrote voluminously about cotton tenancy through the 1930s. This canon included well-known works by Taylor and Lange, James Agee, Erskine Caldwell, and John Steinbeck but also rafts of reports and articles authored by Will Alexander, Edwin Embree, Charles Johnson, Carl Taylor, James Maddox, Paul V. Maris, Arthur Raper, and M. L. Wilson, among others.

11. Ira Katzelson makes clear the widespread racial discrimination in New Deal programs and Roosevelt and Truman's compromise with white supremacy as dictated by Southern Democrats in Congress, the "guardians of racial segregation." See Katzelson, *When Affirmative Action Was White*, x, 19, 21; and *Fear Itself*, 16–17, 21–25. I draw here as well on Gordon, "Dorothea Lange," 698–727, particularly 725.

12. As cited in Allen, *Forgotten Men and Fallen Women*, 11, 13. Supporters of the Southern Tenant Farmers Union used the rhetoric of the forgotten man in reference to tenants facing open repression of union activity in Missouri in 1935. See Conrad, *Forgotten Farmers*, 165–66.

13. Allen, *Forgotten Men and Fallen Women*, 3–4.

14. Sutter, *Let Us Now Praise*, 167–70.

15. Finis Dunaway notes the remarkable whiteness of Lorentz's *The River* in *Natural Visions*, 63. The voice-over in the film at minute 22:25 says, "And poor land makes poor people. Poor people make poor land," while panning over white workers picking cotton. *The River* (directed by Pare Lorentz, 1938), Farm Security Administration, https://archive.org/details/TheRiverReformatted. Artist Alexandre Hogue drew from FSA photographs in paintings that gave eroded hillsides the contours of a woman's naked body, a mother nature. He literally projected soil erosion onto the female body, symbolizing the nation's future. See

Alexandre Hogue, "Erosion No. 2, Mother Earth Laid Bare," 1936, in Whitney, "Making of 'Modern America.'" Most of the scholarship on Rothstein's father-and-sons image focuses on his elaborate staging as he directed his subjects to appear impoverished and to emphasize the wind and dust on a calm, sunny day. See Curtis, *Mind's Eye, Mind's Truth*, 83.

16. Paul Sutter also notes that Arthur Raper, among a wide range of New Deal reformers and scholars, powerfully linked soil erosion with white supremacy and Jim Crow segregation. See Sutter, *Let Us Now Praise*, 155–56; Raper, "Gullies and What They Mean," 202–3.

17. Finnegan, *Picturing Poverty*, xi. Gordon's work on Dorothea Lange argues, on the other hand, that Lange's photographs made counternarratives visible, including those of race and racism. See Gordon, "Dorothea Lange," 698–727.

18. As Foley puts it, "The complete economic independence of the white yeoman farmer lay at the heart of this rural creed." Foley, *White Scourge*, 141–42.

19. Foley, *White Scourge*, 161, 179–80, 200.

20. On this peak focus on tenancy, see Conrad, *Forgotten Farmers*, 8; Grubbs, *Cry from the Cotton*, 145–46; Roberts, *Farm Security Administration*, 65–66; and Mertz, *New Deal Policy*, 98–100.

21. Johnson, Embree, and Alexander, *Collapse of Cotton Tenancy*, 5.

22. Johnson, Embree, and Alexander, *Collapse of Cotton Tenancy*, 4, 1, 23, 10.

23. "Tenant Farmers of South Seek Relief in Washington; Share Croppers State Case," *Christian Science Monitor*, April 7, 1936. As Roediger notes, antebellum white workers feared the specter of slavery defining their own working lives and defined whiteness partly in terms of the mobility Black slaves did not possess. See Roediger, *Wages of Whiteness*, 46.

24. Winifred Mallon, "White Tenant Held Problem of the South, Negro an Exaggerated Factor, Dr. Alexander Tells Chapel Hill Conference," *New York Times*, June 24, 1936, 25.

25. Embree, "Southern Farm Tenancy," 150–51. *Migrant Mother* first appeared in the *San Francisco News* (March 11, 1936) and six months later in *Survey Graphic* 25 no. 9 (September 1936): 524.

26. Embree, "Southern Farm Tenancy," 149–51.

27. Finnegan, "What Is This?," 121.

28. Woofter, *Landlord and Tenant*, 13.

29. Taylor, Wheeler, and Kirkpatrick, *Disadvantaged Classes*, 30, 39. For a helpful discussion of the "agricultural ladder" of white agrarian mobility, see Foley, *White Scourge*, 10.

30. Some examples include L. P. Davis, "Relief and the Sharecropper," 20–22, with two images of white sharecroppers; "Tenant Farmers of South," 1, 4, with all

photographs of white tenants; Felix Belair Jr., "Portrait of the Tenant: Farming's Stepchild," *New York Times*, April 18, 1937, with five images dominated by portraits of white tenants; and *Atlanta Constitution*, February 12, 1938, 10, with a feature on the first white tenant to receive a tenant purchase loan under the Bankhead-Jones program.

31. Further evidence is in U.S. Department of Agriculture, Farm Security Administration, *Nation's Soil and Human Resources*, 12. Trent wrote, "The problem of tenancy is a problem of general disadvantage, distress and poverty and malnutrition and despair among both whites and blacks and its solution is in no sense through a racial approach." See also Agee and Evans, *Let Us Now Praise*.

32. Agee, Evans, and Haslett, *Cotton Tenants*, 31.

33. Lange and Taylor, *American Exodus*, 19; Steinbeck and Wollenberg, *Harvest Gypsies*; Steinbeck, *Grapes of Wrath*.

34. David Roediger's work on the antebellum white working class established the privileges or "wages" of whiteness, even among poor and working-class whites. He argues that for white workers—and in the South in the 1930s for white tenants—"race could be used to make up for alienating and exploitative class relationships." See Roediger, *Wages of Whiteness*, 13.

35. As quoted in Grubbs, *Cry from the Cotton*, 129–30. On race and tenant purchase, see also Foley, *White Scourge*, 180.

36. Foley, *White Scourge*, 7, 10, 183.

37. Vance, *Human Geography of the South*, 463.

38. *Chicago Defender*, October 20, 1934, 12. On literary and other popular depictions of poor whites as inferior and less white, see Foley, *White Scourge*, 6; and Brinkmeyer, "Marginalization and Mobility," 227–30.

39. Vance, *Human Geography of the South*, 192.

40. Vance, *Human Geography of the South*, 193, 200.

41. Taylor, Wheeler, and Kirkpatrick, *Disadvantaged Classes*, 38–39. Taylor headed the Division of Farm Population and Rural Life within the Bureau of Agricultural Economics. See Larson and Zimmerman, "USDA's Bureau of Agricultural Economics," 227–40.

42. Johnson, Embree, and Alexander, *Collapse of Cotton Tenancy*, 14, 22–23.

43. Carlton and Coclanis, *Confronting Southern Poverty*, 25; "Child Labor, Farm Tenancy and Single Crops Called Handicaps of the South," *New York Times*, August 13, 1938, 5. On the rhetoric and details of the NEC report in the summer of 1938, see also Katznelson, *Fear Itself*, 1691–72. The report, Katznelson writes on page 172, "made no mention whatsoever of segregation. Its powerful catalog of regional economic ailments reads as if the race issue did not exist."

44. Taylor, Wheeler, and Kirkpatrick, *Disadvantaged Classes*, 122.

45. Taylor, Wheeler, and Kirkpatrick, *Disadvantaged Classes*, 121, 124.

46. U.S. Government et al., *Farm Tenancy*, 28. On the report, see Roberts, *Farm Security Administration*, 66.

47. Woofter, *Landlord and Tenant*, 126.

48. Agee, Evans, and Haslett, *Cotton Tenants*, 209–10.

49. Monroe, "Patterns of Living," 860. The same held for income. However low the average cash income of white tenants, the average for African Americans fell lower, as FSA head Will Alexander acknowledged. See Mertz, *New Deal Policy*, 195.

50. Raper and Reid, *Sharecroppers All*, 16.

51. Du Bois, *Souls of Black Folk*, 122.

52. Roberts, *Farm Security Administration*, 141; Raper, *Tenants of the Almighty*. Foley notes that in Texas, fewer African American women could afford pressure cookers, and African American women "relied more heavily on commercially canned food than white farm women." Similar limits affected Mexican women. Foley, *White Scourge*, 155.

53. Johnson, Embree, and Alexander, *Collapse of Cotton Tenancy*, 16–17; Roberts, *Farm Security Administration*, xxviii–xxix. Historian Grace Elizabeth Hale explains that white storekeepers and furnishing agents even further controlled the quality of store-bought foods that tenants and sharecroppers could purchase, particularly with African American consumers. Hale, *Making Whiteness*, 173.

54. Raper, *Preface to Peasantry*, 158, 165, and on tenant-landlord attitudes and relations broadly, 157–80.

55. Raper, *Preface to Peasantry*, 163–64.

56. Mertz, likewise, termed rural rehabilitation the "most effective New Deal effort in behalf of impoverished southerners." Mertz, *New Deal Policy*, 260, and on rural rehabilitation broadly, 63–66.

57. Mary B. Settle, "Abstract of Improving the Social and Economic Life of the South through the Production of Subsistence," 2–3, folder 85–161, box 1, entry 93, FHA/FSA-OD.

58. Roberts, *Farm Security Administration*, 140–41; Kuhn, "'It Was a Long Way,'" 68–90.

59. Woofter, *Landlord and Tenant*, 11.

60. Hickock, Lowitt, Beasley, *One Third of a Nation*, 158. See also Conrad, *Forgotten Farmers*, 11–12; Schultz, *Rural Face of White Supremacy*, 35–36; Kirby, *Rural Worlds Lost*, 145. The same oral practices and traditions governed sharecroppers' purchases, sales, and debts at southern village stores controlled by white merchants. See Raper, *Tenants of the Almighty*, 280.

61. Raper, *Preface to Peasantry*, 162.

62. Johnson, Embree, and Alexander, *Collapse of Cotton Tenancy*, 22.

63. Many sources reveal this information. See Woofter, *Landlord and Tenant*, 82; Raper, *Preface to Peasantry*, 165. For more examples, see Roberts, *Farm Security Administration*, xxvi.

64. Ferrie and Alston, *Southern Paternalism*, 85; Alston and Ferrie, "Resisting the Welfare State," 103.

65. Baldwin, *Politics and Poverty*, 394. On political opposition, see also Mertz, *New Deal Policy*, 218–20; Schultz, *Rural Face of White Supremacy*, 208–9; and Brown, "Benign Public Policies, Malignant Consequences," 141.

66. "Circular Issued by S.C. Klan: Oppose Race Man Holding FSA Position," *Atlanta Daily World*, December 13, 1939, 1, 6.

67. Nicholas Natanson's meticulous research reveals that 10.1 percent of the FSA Historical Section archive featured Black figures or their dwellings, with a higher percentage for those images from rural America. See Natanson, *Black Image*, 66.

68. Davis, *Reading Southern Poverty*, 57.

69. Two years later, in January 1942, a key report noted, "The various committees are charged with planning for all the farm people of the county, of whom perhaps two-thirds are Negroes, but Negroes have no voice in this planning." Coleman, "Community Organization and Agricultural Planning, Greene County, GA," January 1942, 32, box 9, folder "Greene County, GA: Unified County," BAE-DSLP. The same maps were reproduced in U.S. Department of Agriculture, Bureau of Agricultural Economics, *Communities and Administrative Areas*.

70. Raper, *Tenants of the Almighty*, 364.

71. Raper, *Tenants of the Almighty*, plates 39–40.

72. Though Delano and Raper did not name the women in these photographs in the book, Delano's originals in the Library of Congress identify them by their married names. See Jack Delano, "Mrs. Lloyd Clements, FSA Borrower Living on the Jackson Place, near Mosquito Crossing, Greene County, Georgia," November 1941, LC-USF34-046461-D; "[Mrs. Edmond Reid], FSA (Farm Security Administration) Client, with Her Canned Goods. Oakland Community, Greene County, Georgia," November 1941, LC-USF34-046448-D.

73. Raper, *Tenants of the Almighty*, 232.

74. Carl Taylor headed the BAE's Division of Farm Population and Rural Welfare. His team of forty sociologists, along with geographers, anthropologists, and psychologists, conducted this research. By the middle of 1941, they had completed community delineation studies for 1,800 communities and 11,000 neighborhoods in thirty-two states. See Gilbert, *Planning Democracy*, 180.

75. John M. Brewster to O.V. Wells, "Report on Trip in Southeast Region, Feb. 12-March 2, 1940," 3, box 1, BAE-WA.

76. U.S. Department of Agriculture, Bureau of Agricultural Economics, *Community and Administrative Areas*, 24, 4.

77. "The wider community ties of Greene County rural Negroes are very weak," the written report on delineation noted; "the neighborhood is still their most meaningful local group . . . and there are few ties with the towns and villages." Lee Coleman, "Community Organization and Agricultural Planning, Greene County, GA," 4, box 9, folder "Greene County, GA: Unified County, Southeast Area, January 1942," BAE-DSLP.

78. Memo from William Hartman to Mr. P. O. Davis, director, Agricultural Extension Service, February 16, 1940, 2–3, folder "Mr. Hartman, Regional," BAE-WA.

79. Provinse, foreword, inside front cover.

80. Memo, James C. Council to Bushrod Allin, May 14, 1940, 1–2, Bureau of Agricultural Economics, Records Relating to Studies, Projects, and Surveys, Correspondence 1939–46, box 141, folder "Southeast Region," BAE-SPSC.

81. Delano and other FSA photographers did of course photograph white New Deal supervisors and bureaucrats with Black clients.

82. Raper, *Tenants of the Almighty*, 194, 313, 195, 365, 371, 340.

83. Raper, *Tenants of the Almighty*, 308–9.

84. Raper, *Tenants of the Almighty*, 234, 197, 311; see also Mazzari, *Southern Modernist*, 129–30.

85. Grubbs, *Cry from the Cotton*, 158. The numbers and proportions of Black clients benefited by rural rehabilitation varied across time and geography. Paul Mertz notes that in the earlier version of rural rehabilitation under the Federal Emergency Relief Act (FERA), before the creation of the FSA, Black participation by state varied from 30 percent in Alabama to 8 percent in Arkansas, where 26.5 percent of the population was Black. See Mertz, *New Deal Policy*, 89. Within the overarching rural rehabilitation programs of the FSA, Black clients constituted 22 percent, according to Mertz, 194. In his recent monograph, Charles Kenneth Roberts agrees that African American FSA clients constituted 13 percent of the total nationally (proportional to a 12 percent national Black population), with 22 percent African American clients in the south, where Blacks constituted 23 percent of all farm workers of all types. See Roberts, *Farm Security Administration*, 96. However, like all New Deal programs, FSA rehabilitation discriminated directly against Black clients and structurally in favor of white candidates more likely to qualify due to their farming experience, relative prosperity, and race. Donald Holley put the total number of rural rehabilitation loans to Black clients at fifty thousand total—a very small number in relation to the need across the nation. See Holley, "Negro in the New Deal," 192.

86. As quoted in Larson, Zimmerman, and Moe, *Sociology in Government*, 52.

87. Larson, Zimmerman, and Moe, *Sociology in Government*, 52–53.

88. Larson, Williams, and Wimberley, "Dismissal of a Sociologist," 549–50.

89. Larson and Zimmerman note this clearly in *Sociology in Government*, 195.

90. Roediger, *Wages of Whiteness*, 8.

91. Raper and Reid, *Sharecroppers All*, 3–17, quotations 15–17.

Bibliography

ARCHIVES AND MANUSCRIPT MATERIALS

FHA/FSA-OD: Records of the Farmers Home Administration (formerly Farm Security Administration), Office of the Director, General Correspondence 1934–42, record group 96, National Archives and Records Administration, College Park, MD.

BAE-DSLP: Records of the Bureau of Agricultural Economics, Division of State and Local Planning, Reports 1938–42, record group 83, National Archive and Records Administration, College Park, MD.

BAE-SPSC: Records of the Bureau of Agricultural Economics, Division of State and Local Planning, Records Relating to Studies, Projects, and Surveys, Correspondence 1939–46, National Archive and Records Administration, College Park, MD.

BAE-WA: Records of the Bureau of Agricultural Economics, Records of Wilhelm Anderson, National Archive and Records Administration, College Park, MD.

PUBLISHED WORKS

Agee, James, and Walker Evans. *Let Us Now Praise Famous Men*. Illustrated ed. Boston: Mariner Books, 2001.

Agee, James, Walker Evans, and Adam Haslett. *Cotton Tenants: Three Families*. Edited by John Summers. 1st ed. Brooklyn NY: Melville House, 2013.

Allen, Holly. *Forgotten Men and Fallen Women: The Cultural Politics of New Deal Narratives*. 1st ed. Ithaca NY: Cornell University Press, 2015.

Alston, Lee J., and Joseph P. Ferrie. "Resisting the Welfare State: Southern Opposition to the Farm Security Administration." *Research in Economic History*, supplement 4 (1985): 83–120.

Baldwin, Sidney. *Politics and Poverty: The Rise and Decline of the Farm Security Administration*. Chapel Hill: University of North Carolina Press, 1968.

Brinkmeyer, Robert H., Jr., "Marginalization and Mobility: Segregation and the Representation of Southern Poor Whites." In *Reading Southern Poverty between the Wars, 1918–1939*, edited by Richard Godden and Martin Crawford, 223–37. 1st ed. Athens: University of Georgia Press, 2006.

Brown, William P. "Benign Public Policies, Malignant Consequences, and the Demise of African American Agriculture." In *African American Life in the Rural South*,

1900–1950, edited by R. Douglas Hurt, 129–51. 1st ed. Columbia: University of Missouri, 2011.

Carlton, David L., and Peter A. Coclanis. *Confronting Southern Poverty in the Great Depression: The Report on the Economic Conditions of the South with Related Documents*. Boston: Bedford / St. Martin's, 1996.

Chase, Stuart. *Rich Land, Poor Land: A Study of Waste in the Natural Resources of America*. New York: McGraw Hill, 1936.

Conrad, David E. *The Forgotten Farmers: The Story of Sharecroppers in the New Deal*. New ed. Westport CT: Praeger, 1982.

Curtis, James. *Mind's Eye, Mind's Truth: FSA Photography Reconsidered*. Philadelphia: Temple University Press, 1991.

Davis, Lillian Perrine. "Relief and the Sharecropper." *Survey Graphic* 25, no. 1 (January 1936): 20–22.

Davis, Siobhan. "Not Readily Visualized by Industrial Workers and Urban Dwellers: Published Images of Rural Women from the FSA Collection, 1935-37." In *Reading Southern Poverty between the Wars, 1918–1939*, edited by Richard Godden and Martin Crawford, 48–74. 1st ed. Athens: University of Georgia Press, 2006.

Du Bois, W. E. B. *The Souls of Black Folk*. New York: Viking Penguin, 1989.

Dunaway, Finis. *Natural Visions: The Power of Images in American Environmental Reform*. Illustrated ed. Chicago: University of Chicago Press, 2005.

Embree, Edwin. "Southern Farm Tenancy: The Way Out of Its Evils." *Survey Graphic* 25, no. 3 (March 1936): 149–53, 190.

Ferrie, Joseph P., and Lee J. Alston. *Southern Paternalism and the American Welfare State: Economics, Politics, and Institutions in the South, 1865–1965*. Cambridge: Cambridge University Press, 1999.

Finnegan, Cara A. *Picturing Poverty: Print Culture and FSA Photographs*. Washington DC: Smithsonian Institution Scholarly Press, 2003.

———. "What Is This a Picture Of? Some Thoughts on Images and Archives." In "Forum: The Politics of Archival Research." *Rhetoric and Public Affairs* 9, no. 1 (Spring 2006): 116–23.

Foley, Neil. *The White Scourge: Mexicans, Blacks, and Poor Whites in Texas Cotton Culture*. Berkeley: University of California Press, 1997.

Gilbert, Jess. *Planning Democracy: Agrarian Intellectuals and the Intended New Deal*. Reprint, New Haven CT: Yale University Press, 2016.

Gordon, Linda. "Dorothea Lange: The Photographer as Agricultural Sociologist." *Journal of American History* 93, no. 3 (December 2006): 698–727.

Grubbs, Donald. *Cry from the Cotton: The Southern Tenant Farmers' Union and the New Deal*. Fayetteville: University of Arkansas Press, 2000.

Guthrie, Woody. "Pastures of Plenty." Woody Guthrie Publications, Inc., & TRO Music, Inc., BMI, 1963. https://www.woodyguthrie.org/Lyrics/Pastures_Of_Plenty.htm.

Hale, Grace Elizabeth. *Making Whiteness: The Culture of Segregation in the South, 1890–1940*. New York: Vintage, 1999.

Hickock, Lorena, Richard Lowitt, and Maurine H. Beasley. *One Third of a Nation: Lorena Hickock Reports on the Great Depression*. Reprint, Urbana: University of Illinois Press, 1983.

Holley, Donald. "The Negro in the New Deal Resettlement Program." *Agricultural History* 45, no. 3 (July 1971): 179–93.

Jackson, Kenneth T., Karen Markoe, and Arnold Markoe, eds. "Chase, Stuart." In *The Scribner Encyclopedia of American Lives, Vol. 1: 1981–1985*, 145–47. New York: Charles Scriber's Sons, 1998.

Johnson, Charles Spurgeon, Edwin Embree, and W. W. Alexander. *The Collapse of Cotton Tenancy: Summary of Field Studies & Statistical Surveys, 1933–35*. Chapel Hill: University of North Carolina Press, 1935.

Katznelson, Ira. *Fear Itself: The New Deal and the Origins of Our Time*. Liveright, 2013.

———. *When Affirmative Action Was White: An Untold History of Racial Inequality in Twentieth-Century America*. New York: W. W. Norton, 2005.

Kirby, Jack Temple. *Rural Worlds Lost: The American South, 1920–1960*. 5th ed. Baton Rouge: LSU Press, 1986.

Kuhn, Clifford M. "It Was a Long Way from Perfect, but It Was Working': The Canning and Home Production Initiatives in Greene County, Georgia, 1940–1942." *Agricultural History* 82, no. 2 (Spring 2012): 68–90.

Lange, Dorothea, and Paul Taylor. *An American Exodus: A Record of Human Erosion*. Paris: Editions Jean-Michel Place, 1999.

Larson, Olaf F., and Julie N. Zimmerman. "The USDA's Bureau of Agricultural Economics and Sociological Studies of Rural Life and Agricultural Issues, 1919–1953." *Agricultural History* 74, no. 2 (Spring 2000): 227–40.

Larson, Olaf F., Julie N. Zimmerman, and Edward O. Moe. *Sociology in Government: The Galpin-Taylor Years in the U.S. Department of Agriculture, 1919–1953*. 1st ed. Penn State University Press, 2003.

Larson, Olaf F., Robin Williams, and Ronald Wimberly. "Dismissal of a Sociologist: The AAUP Report on Carl C. Taylor." *Rural Sociology* 64, no. 4 (1999): 549–50.

Maher, Neil M. *Nature's New Deal: The Civilian Conservation Corps and the Roots of the American Environmental Movement*. Illustrated ed. Oxford University Press, 2009.

Mazzari, Louis. *Southern Modernist: Arthur Raper from the New Deal to the Cold War*. Baton Rouge: LSU Press, 2006.

Mertz, Paul E. *New Deal Policy and Southern Rural Poverty*. Baton Rouge: LSU Press, 1978.

Monroe, Day. "Patterns of Living of Farm Families." In *Farmers in a Changing World: The Yearbook of Agriculture 1940*, edited by Gove Hambidge and Marion Julia Drown, 848–69. Washington DC: GPO, 1940.

Natanson, Nicholas. *The Black Image in the New Deal: The Politics of FSA Photography.* 1st ed. Knoxville: University of Tennessee Press, 1992.

O'Connor, Alice. *Poverty Knowledge: Social Science, Social Policy, and the Poor in Twentieth-Century U.S. History.* Princeton NJ: Princeton University Press, 2002.

Phillips, Sarah T. *This Land, This Nation: Conservation, Rural America, and the New Deal.* Illustrated ed. New York: Cambridge University Press, 2007.

Provinse, John H. Foreword to *Culture of a Contemporary Rural Community: Harmony, Georgia*, by Waller Wynne. Rural Life Studies no. 6. Washington DC: U.S. Bureau of Agricultural Economics, 1942.

Raper, Arthur F. "Gullies and What They Mean." *Social Forces* 16, no. 2 (1937): 202–3.

———. Preface to *Peasantry: A Tale of Two Black Belt Counties.* Chapel Hill: University of North Carolina Press, 1968.

———. *Tenants of the Almighty.* New York: Macmillan, 1943.

Raper, Arthur F., and Ira De A. Reid. *Sharecroppers All.* New ed. University of North Carolina Press Enduring Editions, 2009.

Roberts, Charles Kenneth. *The Farm Security Administration and Rural Rehabilitation in the South.* Knoxville: University of Tennessee Press, 2015.

Roediger, David R. *The Wages of Whiteness: Race and the Making of the American Working Class.* New ed. London: Verso, 2007.

Schultz, Mark Roman. *The Rural Face of White Supremacy: Beyond Jim Crow.* New ed. Urbana: University of Illinois Press, 2006.

Steinbeck, John. *The Grapes of Wrath.* New York: Viking, 1939.

Steinbeck, John, and Charles Wollenberg. *The Harvest Gypsies: On the Road to the Grapes of Wrath.* New ed. Berkeley, California: Heyday, 2011.

Sutter, Paul S. *Let Us Now Praise Famous Gullies: Providence Canyon and the Soils of the South.* 1st ed. Athens: University of Georgia Press, 2015.

Taylor, Carl Cleveland, Helen Wheeler, and Ellis Lore Kirkpatrick. *Disadvantaged Classes in American Agriculture.* Washington DC: United States Department of Agriculture, Farm Security Administration, and Bureau of Agricultural Economics Cooperating, 1938.

U.S. Department of Agriculture, Bureau of Agricultural Economics. *Communities and Administrative Areas of Greene County, Georgia.* Washington DC: GPO, 1941.

U.S. Department of Agriculture, Farm Security Administration. *The Nation's Soil and Human Resources: Soil Impoverishment and Human Impoverishment*, by Dover P. Trent. Washington DC: GPO, 1938.

U.S. Government, Special Committee on Farm Tenancy, Franklin Delano Roosevelt, Lewis Cecil Gray, and Henry Agard Wallace. *Farm Tenancy: Message from the President of the United States Transmitting the Report of the Special Committee on Farm Tenancy.* Washington DC: GPO, 1937.

Vance, Rupert B. *Human Geography of the South: A Study in Regional Resources and Human Adequacy.* Chapel Hill: University of North Carolina Press, 1932.

Whitney, Catherine. "The Making of 'Modern America.'" Philbrook. Accessed August 2, 2024. https://philbrook.org/the-making-of-making-modern-america/.

Woofter, T. J., Jr. *Landlord and Tenant on the Cotton Plantation.* Research Monograph V, Division of Social Research, Works Progress Administration. Washington DC: GPO, 1936.

8

Harvest of Self-Help

The Politics and Paradoxes of
Southeast Asian Refugee Community Gardens

CECILIA M. TSU

On August 22, 1982, NBC *Nightly News* broadcast a segment on Hmong refugees in Providence, Rhode Island, featuring scenes of the Indochinese Gardening Project, a community garden established on seven acres of an undeveloped state park. Over three hundred refugee families eventually gardened at the site. The favorable publicity from national television and other media outlets prompted other individuals and organizations to offer more land and free plowing services for the garden program.[1] Nearly halfway across the country in Minnesota, Pillsbury-Waite Neighborhood Services—a charitable organization affiliated with the Minneapolis-based Pillsbury Company, of refrigerated baked goods fame—sponsored the Hmong Community Garden Cooperative in May 1983. A private donor later offered over one hundred acres of land in the Minneapolis suburb of Eagan, and Pillsbury-Waite provided bus transportation for Hmong families to travel to their garden plots. By the mid-1980s, the garden cooperative had one hundred participating families and a long waiting list for prospective members.[2] In Portland, Oregon, scores of volunteers contributed to the establishment of the city's refugee gardens. Church-initiated community gardens for Southeast Asian refugees in Memphis, Tennessee, received donations of seed, fertilizer, and equipment from the University of Tennessee and the local Kiwanis club.[3]

During the 1980s, from coast to coast and practically everywhere in between, thousands of refugees from Vietnam, Cambodia, and Laos cultivated community gardens across the United States. Though the gardens varied in size, location, resources, and administration, they were all universally popular projects that relied on a pastiche of public funding, private donations, local government sponsorship, and volunteer initiative. A 1985 Office of Refugee Resettlement report commented on the impressive breadth of philanthropic support for community gardens in diverse locales, giving examples of "the donated tractor in Salt Lake City, gardening hoes, seeds and fertilizer in Kansas City; technical assistance from the agricultural extension service in several places; educational services at a college in North Carolina; time on public radio stations and church funds for newsletters in Wisconsin."[4] Aware that refugees faced a host of intractable problems in their new home, from poverty and unemployment to posttraumatic stress and mental illness, advocates and backers of community gardens believed these were places where refugees could regain a sense of pride and purpose through growing food for home consumption, easing their transition into American society.

This chapter recounts the history of refugee community gardens in the United States and the interplay of their stakeholders. It examines how giving refugees derelict, marginal land on which to grow their own food generated enormous enthusiasm as a resettlement initiative in the 1980s while at the same time centering Southeast Asian refugees' material experiences of gardening and the meanings they ascribed to these new spaces. Whereas sociologists and geographers have viewed refugee gardens as "visible representations of a transplanted culture" and "conspicuous evidence of the persistence of rural traditions," my research shows that they were far more contested and complicated spaces.[5] Southeast Asian refugees welcomed the chance to take part in familiar agrarian pursuits, but they also recognized the economic necessity of small-scale gardening as one of numerous strategies they had to adopt in order to survive in their new homes, to enter the ranks of the American working poor who pieced together disparate sources of income for subsistence.

Examining the origins and expansion of refugee community gardens in the United States from the 1980s into the 1990s, this chapter draws on historical research that has analyzed the environmental practices of Asian Americans. For the most part, this literature has centered on the agricultural experiences of Chinese and Japanese Americans as farmers and farm laborers and Filipino Americans' participation in the farmworkers movement.[6] The notable work of historian Connie Chiang highlights the interactions of Japanese American detainees with the natural world, arguing that their World War II incarceration must be understood as an environmental process.

Japanese Americans engaged in agricultural production and gardening within the camps, leveraging their prior knowledge of farming to reap harvests on desolate, submarginal lands.[7] Foreshadowing the emphasis on self-help through community gardening as a means to offset the cost of supporting newly resettled refugees in the 1980s, government officials implemented an agricultural program at the camps so that incarcerated Japanese Americans could produce their own food and thus "pay their own way."[8] Even though many refugees from Vietnam, Cambodia, and Laos hailed from rural backgrounds, few historians have considered the relationship between Southeast Asian Americans and the environment, how their attitudes toward the natural world and cultivation practices shifted with migration, or the environmental implications of refugee resettlement.[9]

On a broader level, a critical analysis of Southeast Asian refugee gardens offers an alternative narrative about the relationship between communities of color to the environment. Research has focused on environmental racism, injustice, and the exploitation of natural resources that harm people of color as well as their mobilization against multinational corporations responsible for ecological disasters.[10] Sociologists, anthropologists, and food studies scholars have linked local food access inequities to systemic racism, calling attention to the exploitative and environmentally destructive nature of the modern industrialized food system. Within this literature, scholars have noted that for nonwhite communities, gardening represented and continues to serve as an act of self-determination and political agency. They have pointed to agriculture as a long-standing site of Black resistance to a food system shaped by racial, economic, and environmental discrimination. In community gardens and through engagement in the contemporary food justice movement, African Americans have navigated what anthropologist Ashanté Reese calls "geographies of self-reliance" to challenge structures of oppression.[11] Likewise, through their involvement in urban agriculture, refugees from Southeast Asia confronted inequities in power and used their intimate knowledge of nature and the environment to sustain and bolster their communities. These acts became an integral part of what leading Critical Refugee Studies scholar Yến Lê Espiritu calls "refugees' rich and complicated lived worlds."[12]

Refugee gardeners' lived experiences of community gardening and their articulation of what these interactions with the natural world meant to them point to a new conceptualization of the relationship between Asian Americans and the environment. As gardeners, they were neither agricultural wage laborers nor farmers like the many Asian immigrants who preceded them since the nineteenth century. Yet resettled refugees from the American war in Southeast Asia capitalized on popular sentiment and philanthropic endeavors that linked community gardening to larger debates about how government and society should address poverty and economic inequality and what obligations a developed nation has to support refugee populations. Southeast Asian refugees embraced opportunities to garden within the confines of well-intentioned but limited, sometimes hastily conceived policies and philanthropic endeavors. Demonstrating adept horticultural skill and knowledge, I argue that refugees used the gardens to empower themselves and to secure a dignified standard of living at the same time as they identified a vast disjuncture between their previous rural existence and the functions of vegetable growing in the United States. Beyond their rosy depiction as inspirational collaborations between citizens and newcomers, community gardens became multifaceted sites of struggle and adaptation to new physical and social environments.

Community Gardening in Historical Context

The association of community gardens with self-help ideology for the poor predated the arrival of Southeast Asian refugees by nearly a century. In the United States, community garden programs originated in the economic recession of 1893–97 when city officials provided unemployed laborers and their families with plots of land on vacant lots, seeds, and instructions for growing food. Piloted in Detroit by mayor Hazen Pingree as an alternative to charitable relief and a temporary measure to help the poor, vacant lot gardening spread to twenty other cities including New York, Chicago, and Boston by 1895. For garden promoters, giving the unemployed land to cultivate food was a way to encourage people to help themselves, keeping them free from the idleness that business interests feared would result in union unrest.[13] Community gardening again emerged on a national level in the form of work-relief projects and subsistence garden programs to counter unemployment and economic distress during the Great Depression. A 1934 report estimated that more than 2.3 million families across the country were involved in public gardens, which produced food valued at $36 million.

Industrial employers also granted garden sites to workers as compensation for reduced hours and layoffs. Some individuals who applied for public assistance during the 1930s through relief agencies received a plot in a community garden along with fuel vouchers, food, and work relief. Concerns about individuals profiting from free land and seed drove prohibitions against the sale of surplus produce grown in these gardens. As scholar of urban agriculture Laura Lawson observes, the "double-edged sword of 'self-help'" at the core of community gardening programs discouraged any possibility of personal gain from participation in these ventures.[14] Public support and funding to help impoverished individuals were acceptable, provided that they worked for their own subsistence and nothing more.

Gardening captured the interest of activists in the 1970s as a grassroots solution to urban decline. Nonprofit organizations like the Green Guerillas in New York City, Milwaukee Shoots 'N' Roots, and the San Francisco League of Urban Gardeners (SLUG) founded gardens to serve residents who did not have access to property of their own as well as homeless populations, low-income youth, and the formerly incarcerated. The movement gained momentum and a huge boost from the federal government when the U.S. Department of Agriculture announced the creation of the Urban Gardening Program in 1976 to fund education, demonstration gardens, and technical support in twenty-three cities.[15] Composed of volunteers and professionals, the American Community Gardening Association (ACGA) was formed in 1980 as a nonprofit organization designed to support community gardening. In 1996, an ACGA survey estimated there were over six thousand community gardens in thirty-eight cities.[16]

Community garden programs for refugees developed in this context. Between 1975 and 1997, approximately 1.1 million Southeast Asian refugees entered the United States, the vast majority requiring some form of public assistance. Despite the bipartisan consensus that the United States had a moral obligation to assist the Southeast Asian refugees its interventionist foreign policies helped produce, pouring millions of dollars into refugee resettlement was not high on the agendas of U.S. policymakers and taxpayers.[17] As uncontroversial, feel-good projects requiring relatively little investment and offering uplift through self-help, refugee community gardens matched the ethos of the 1980s, when a recognition of the need for therapeutic measures to address mental health concerns emerged alongside a growing wariness of government spending on social programs and entitlements. The idea that the poverty-stricken should engage in proactive measures to improve their own plight resonated with many U.S. citizens who resented seeing their tax dollars diverted to "hand outs."[18]

The refugee community gardens that flourished around the country during the 1980s fall under the broader category of urban garden programs, comprising various cooperative endeavors that provide space for city dwellers to grow fresh produce. Unlike home gardens privately managed by families, community gardens are public, open spaces that allow members to engage in urban agriculture.[19] Although the term *community garden* tends to be associated with a neighborhood garden managed by individuals who also garden there, county and municipal entities operate many of these spaces. For the most part, community gardeners produce limited quantities of vegetables for household consumption and exchange among families, not for large-scale marketing, though in a few cases, the refugee gardeners discussed here sold surplus produce in informal enclave marketplaces and local farmers' markets.[20]

Tabulating exactly how many of these gardens existed, however, is difficult. For example, the Parks Bureau of Portland, Oregon, ran twenty community gardens in the 1980s but did not track how many were primarily for refugees.[21] Scattered records from municipal and county agencies, surveys, news reports, and anecdotal accounts indicate there were at minimum hundreds of these geographically dispersed community gardens aimed at refugee populations. Some gardens were short-lived and did not last more than one or two seasons. Gardens formed on private property and through informal arrangements are even more challenging to document. The most detailed data comes from a survey of gardens in the Central Valley, which showed twenty-four active community garden sites on a total of twenty-eight acres in four counties (Fresno, Tulare, Merced, San Joaquin) with 850 participating Southeast Asian families.[22]

In addition to community gardens, refugee resettlement agencies sponsored other farming projects aimed at producing substantial supplementary income and complete self-sufficiency for refugee families. During the early 1980s, resettlement officials viewed these commercially oriented projects as an effective way to combine refugees' affinity for agriculture with income-generating potential that would ultimately curtail welfare dependence. Always far fewer in number than the refugee community gardens and much more difficult to execute, these more ambitious, larger-scale projects declined during the decade while seasonal vegetable gardening continued to draw widespread support.[23]

Garden founders who worked for voluntary and government agencies articulated a twofold purpose for organizing community gardens on behalf of Southeast Asian refugees: the gardens provided cultural continuity and psychological healing for rural refugees disoriented by resettlement to urban centers while simultaneously serving the pragmatic function of lowering their food expenses. Consultants evaluating garden programs for the Office of Refugee Resettlement in 1985 commended the gardens for allowing refugees to "reap not only food for their families' tables, thus supplementing meager incomes, but also satisfaction from exercising familiar skills and contributing to the well-being of their families."[24] Similarly, staff from the city of Merced's Social Services Department in California summed up two objectives for establishing a 2.2-acre community garden in 1983 that served over two hundred Hmong, Mien, and Lao refugee families: "It was considered important for the mental health of the refugees to be able to do something constructive to 'heal the wounded spirit.' The other objective was simply a desire to help the refugees save money."[25] Resettlement officials, social service staff, and volunteers in the 1980s concurred that these enterprises were tremendously worthwhile. Joe Peterson, who maintained community gardens for Ramsey County in Minnesota, home of the largest urban Hmong refugee population in the country, told reporters in 1980 that he believed the gardens were the best program the county offered "to help them help themselves."[26]

Founders of community gardens had their specific agendas for providing refugees with urban agriculture opportunities, but the gardens proliferated due to refugees' initiative and desire for space to grow food. Refugees approached property owners with requests to use vacant land in the 1980s and took responsibility for preparing overgrown, abandoned lots and assigning parcels among themselves.[27] They also eagerly conveyed their wishes for land to nonprofit and social services groups. When word of garden plots opening spread to the Hmong community of St. Paul in 1980, fifty refugees showed up within thirty minutes to meet the county official in charge of making assignments. Hmong who were able to speak English helped others fill out applications to obtain garden plots, and by the end of the day, no available spaces remained. In the Central Valley during the mid-1980s, over four hundred families from four counties were on waiting lists for garden plots. More than three-quarters of Southeast Asian refugees who had plots in community gardens there said that they knew other refugees in their city who did not garden but would if they had access to land.[28] Southeast Asian community gardens thus materialized in U.S. urban centers when the social and economic goals of garden advocates merged with refugees' own expressed desires.

Community Gardening and Rural (Dis)continuity

Garden coordinators promoted the programs as a means of recreating the sense of rural community refugees had been accustomed to in their home-lands. Karen Gensmer, a board member with an organization that estab-lished a community garden on Hiawatha Avenue, a main thoroughfare in Minneapolis, noted that many of the refugees had a "cultural heritage of agriculture," and the community gardens were "one way to allow these people to continue that life style." Describing the 1982 summertime scene at a 1.5-acre YMCA garden site outside of Minneapolis where Laotian, Hmong, and Cambodian refugee families tended plots, project coordinator Steve Sutton estimated there were often more than sixty adults working in the fields at a time. Dozens of children helped their parents or played in the nearby woods and pastures. "At least one day a week, they get a sense of village working here together," he said of the refugee participants. "For a little while they get that feeling."[29] Garden supporters observed the intergenerational gathering of families at the garden plots during the evenings before dinner. Mothers hoed, weeded, and caught up with family and friends; many instructed older offspring to water plants and mind younger children.[30]

Southeast Asian refugees experienced the gardens as communal spaces in urban enclaves where they could socialize and engage in familiar activ-ities. One Hmong gardener in Eureka, California, recalled the cooperative rhythms of agricultural work in Laos: "In my country sometime[s] all the people can work together for one day, like today all the people go to my field, tomorrow all the people go to another field because they want to meet each other and talk together—they work like that." The community gardens in the United States functioned similarly, though she noted that rather than comprising the bulk of the day, refugees had to tack on gardening tasks to the end of their work days or weekends. According to another Hmong refugee gardener, the social aspect of community gardening helped ease feelings of isolation, commenting, "A lot of people can plant a garden and they can mix over there and talk and get more friends."[31] Resettled and scattered in urban neighborhoods, Southeast Asian refugees utilized gardens as spaces to congregate and connect with one another.

The gardeners' planting choices reflected their desire for continuity, as many cultivated fresh produce from their traditional diets and medicinal plants unavailable in U.S. supermarkets. In California, Hmong community gardeners grew a combination of vegetables and herbs: mustard greens, squash, cucumbers, eggplants, long beans, lemongrass, bitter melon, chili peppers, and coriander. Some planted sweet sorghum around the perimeter of their plots as a snack food for children, who enjoyed extracting its sweet sap by chewing on ripe stalks.[32] Even though crops like wax and winter melons could only be harvested once a year in New England as opposed to three or four times annually in Cambodia, the refugees affiliated with the Khmer Growers community garden in Massachusetts still planted them on their four-acre site, supporting the vines and heavy fruit on intricate trellises they wove of sticks and branches.[33] Vietnamese growers in New Orleans found the similarity in climate between the physical environments of southern Louisiana and lowland Vietnam conducive to the cultivation of their familiar agricultural repertoire, which included taro, bitter melon, lemongrass, water spinach, Malabar nightshade, and ginger.[34]

Older gardeners steeped in folk medicine traditions propagated a greater variety of medicinal plants than their younger counterparts. The Vietnamese in New Orleans used the skin of garden-grown bitter cucumber to reduce hypertension, a common affliction among elderly refugees. They also prized tuberous turmeric and ginger for medicinal purposes, harvesting the plants in late summer.[35] Older Hmong women reserved a portion of their community garden plots exclusively for medicinal herbs to treat their own ailments as well as those of family members. They used Ceylon spinach as a tonic for back pain and arthritis and cultivated sweet flag, an herbaceous perennial, for postpartum dietary use, making various preparations for daughters and female family members.[36]

Offering a connection to the past and a sense of purpose, community gardens served an important function for older refugees, according to garden organizers. Lacking English skills and employment, refugees over the age of sixty faced a host of acculturation challenges, from depression and isolation to excessive dependence on children and feelings of worthlessness. In the enclave of Versailles, home of the largest concentration of Vietnamese refugees in New Orleans, the average age of Vietnamese gardeners surveyed in the early 1990s was sixty-six. Geographers Christopher Airriess and David Clawson concluded that gardening had the therapeutic effect of heightening self-esteem for the elderly refugees, since the cultivation of plants required "daily attention, a sense of responsibility, commitment, and accomplishment." Through gardening, the homebound older refugees supplied their families with an abundance of vegetables and herbs essential to the traditional Vietnamese diet, engendering "emotional well-being and economic empowerment."[37]

Gardening allowed elderly refugees to regain the respected status in their communities that they had lost upon arrival in the United States. Translator and community organizer Sokehn Mao, whose father and brother had been executed by the Khmer Rouge, arrived in Amherst, Massachusetts, in 1982 with the rest of his family, former rice farmers. He spoke of how the opportunity to garden fostered a new identity among Cambodian elders:

> The skills that they have learned from their parents, the things that they used to do, is no longer exist in America. And nothing else for them to do in America. In Cambodia they would be venerated for their wisdom. What they give up in Cambodia, it's a tragedy. Because now they have to give up even their own identity. They want to do something, to be creative or to be useful, maybe not to Americans but to themselves, while they have a few life left in America. So they start to grow their garden. . . . These are the skills that they came with—their hands, their knees, their legs, this knowledge. So as soon as they put the seed on the ground and it grow, they feel special. Maybe they're not good at raising their children in America, but this is thing they wanted to show American[s] and their children—this is the thing that they're good at.[38]

Mao recognized that for elderly Cambodian refugees facing the disruption of family relations and community hierarchy, the chance to "start to grow their gardens" brimmed with significance. The act of putting "the seed on the ground" and tending what grew from it would not bring back the world they had lost, but it did restore some measure of dignity.

Though they took their gardening activities seriously as labor that helped feed their families, many refugee gardeners believed it paled in comparison to what they were accustomed to in Asia. Despite the immense significance American garden promoters attached to these enterprises, some refugees downplayed the work entailed in community gardening. "This plot is very small," a Hmong woman in Sacramento said. "I am just playing."[39] In Madison, Wisconsin, an older Hmong gardener compared her agricultural undertakings in Asia and America by waving her hand across the entire span of the community garden, saying, "In Laos I could farm this whole area of land by myself. These little pieces [the plots] are nothing to what I am used to doing."[40] When a graduate student researcher commented on the large size of the Hmong Community Farm, which fifty families cultivated in Scituate, Rhode Island, grower Phillip Yang laughed and said that the amount of land was insignificant compared to what families habitually operated in Laos. In the Central Valley, 60 percent of the Southeast Asian community garden participants surveyed stated that they would like a bigger garden than the one they currently had. "A piece of land like the palm of my hand isn't enough," a Hmong gardener declared.[41]

Advocates of urban gardens assumed that providing gardening space for refugees would foster continuity between their experiences at home and in the United States, but the gardeners often took a different view. Practitioners of slash-and-burn or swidden agriculture, the Hmong in Laos were accustomed to a seminomadic agrarian existence, farming rice, corn, and vegetables for subsistence and occasionally opium as a cash crop. They cleared forest land to grow their crops and moved to new areas after the land had been depleted. Family members spanning several generations walked substantial distances each day to tend large plots outside of their villages or at times camped out in the fields.[42] Mai Moua described the rhythms of cultivation prior to the arrival of Communist soldiers in Laos:

We started by cutting down trees. A few weeks later, we burned them. Two or three days after the burning, we planted rice and corn. We did not stay home at all. We did not even come home to sleep sometimes; we slept in little shacks in the fields. We had a few *rai* of rice, a few *rai* of corn, and a few *rai* of opium. We went back and forth among the different fields that grew these crops. We always had to make sure each was growing properly. We had good harvests in some years but in other years we did not. In bad years, we did not have enough rice to eat.

Following the rice harvest each season, Moua and her children proceeded to work in the opium fields. To extract the opium latex, they made careful incisions in the plants' mature pods. With her skill, she was able to collect several bowls of raw opium each day during harvest time. When the soil was exhausted, they migrated to a new plot of fertile land.[43]

For Hmong refugees, small, intensively planted gardens were not exactly a relic from their homeland. Community gardening in the United States more closely resembled the cultivation practices they developed during long sojourns at refugee camps in Thailand. In camps like Ban Vinai, they worked small plots outside of family living quarters, farming them intensively to produce vegetables, fruit, and spices that supplemented their paltry camp rations. Refugees sold and traded surpluses among each other and in local Thai markets.[44] Conversely, in Vietnam and other parts of Southeast Asia, small dooryard or kitchen gardens adjacent to homes were common, so cultivating plots in U.S. community gardens bore at least some resemblance to the gardening practices of Vietnamese refugees. The commercially oriented market gardens that elderly Vietnamese cultivated in New Orleans to meet the demands of enclave residents, however, were much larger than the village ones grown almost exclusively for home consumption and more akin to the "market garden landscape traditionally common to the edges of Southeast Asian cities."[45] Contrary to white American assumptions, intensive gardening in small spaces did not represent an authentic direct transfer of culture for most refugees.

Ironically but perhaps not surprisingly, refugees expressed feelings of loss and displacement when they gardened. Their interactions with the natural world in the United States made them long for the environments they left behind. "The mountains, trees, flowers, and animals here are all so different. There is nothing here to remind me of my country, and that makes me sad," Xang Mao Xiong said of his Santa Barbara County surroundings in the early 1990s, lamenting, "I am sad not knowing whether I will ever see the flowers and bamboo groves in Laos again."[46] While appreciative of opportunities to garden, some expressed how the activity also elicited melancholy. As one Hmong gardener remarked, "When the vegetables or things that we grow sprout and come out, the vegetables just remind us of our country so [we] feel sad and miss our country." Similarly, another woman said, "When we have a garden, we feel homesick for our country."[47] Community garden projects received unremitting support because of the presumption that the spaces would provoke joy and delight for refugees longing to grow food. What refugee gardeners expressed instead was a multilayered mix of emotions that included recurrent admissions of sorrow and dislocation.

The frequency of theft, vandalism, and harassment in the gardens also underscored the chasm between the refugees' agricultural experiences in Asia and America. In southern Sacramento, Hmong gardeners reported that local teenage boys rode their bicycles over plants and broke water pipes. Occasionally vegetables were stolen, but smashed or purposely damaged produce was more common. An eighty-five-year-old Hmong woman recounted, "One of my neighbors had a big cabbage, someone just chopped it up and left it." Teens intimidated the women while they were gardening and made obscene gestures. When some gardeners brandished their garden knives in self-defense, the boys recoiled and left them alone.[48] In San Joaquin County, children shot BB gun pellets at community gardeners and trampled the gardens on their bikes after school. At night, unknown individuals pulled out crops ("some people who live around here just come by and help themselves") and destroyed property ("several American kids came to the field and broke the water pipes"). One coordinator in the county erected a six-foot wire fence around the garden he operated and gave each gardener a key. According to a 1986 report, he felt that "all of the gardens in his county should have fences because there is just too much vandalism."[49]

The gardeners encountered other forms of hostility from white neighbors with racial overtones. Some nearby residents grumbled about the unsightliness and messy appearance of the Southeast Asian gardens, though, as geographer Jan Corlett notes, "whether a growing garden was more or less unsightly than a vacant lot filled with weeds, was of course, a matter of opinion." At the Khmer Growers community garden near Amherst, Massachusetts, birdwatchers complained about the noise from the gardeners' water pump, claiming it frightened away all the birds. Angry residents unleashed their dogs to crush the growers' newly planted crops, resulting in so much damage that the Cambodian gardeners had to replant their plots three times in one season. On another occasion, they found that someone had cut the irrigation hoses, and their water pump was stolen twice.[50] A white St. Paul resident who rented a county garden plot in the 1980 season scorned the influx of Hmong refugee gardeners in her neighborhood. She grumbled that they used too much water from the pump and "didn't follow the same rules." Even more pointedly, as a citizen and taxpayer, she felt threatened and taken advantage of by the refugees: "They're the aliens, living off my tax dollar, that's what fries me. We're now in the minority out here. It's reverse discrimination. We're paying their way, and we're paying through the nose."[51] For refugees, racial animosity reflected the incongruous and at times deeply troubling aspects of urban gardening and were intense reminders of their forced displacement.

Poverty, Abundance, and the Economics of Community Gardening

Despite these tensions, community garden advocates frequently pointed to the economic benefits of their programs as much as they did the cultural and psychological impacts. Local government officials and social services staff viewed refugee community gardens as cost-effective and economical. In 1984, Merced County staff surmised that a planned new garden for Southeast Asian refugees required just a small loan from the Merced City Council, which could be paid back within three years from the nominal fees charged to the participating gardeners. Organizers believed that community gardens were "easy and inexpensive to do," with fairly trivial start-up costs. Within a short time frame, they would "pay for themselves."[52]

Gardens usually occupied neglected, underutilized, or abandoned land that public entities and private property owners readily relinquished. The nonprofit Self-Reliance Center of Minneapolis established a community garden on Minnesota Department of Transportation property in 1982. The group offered twenty-by-twenty-foot spaces for gardening on land that had served previously as a dumping site for salt-filled snow. Nearly two-thirds of those who cultivated the plots were Southeast Asian refugees.[53] When refugees or social services staff approached church leaders and other private owners about starting a community garden on their property, the response was usually affirmative. Allowing refugees to garden at these sites posed no loss to property owners, who were keen to "keep the weeds down" while helping hardworking newcomers. A farm advisor with the University of California Cooperative Extension in Humboldt County arranged to start a large garden for Hmong refugees on the property of a retired schoolteacher in Eureka in 1986; the owner expressed gratitude that the gardeners had cleared a massive overgrown bramble of wild blackberries. As Minnesota garden coordinator Joe Peterson declared, refugees accepted "land no one would take" and transformed it into flourishing vegetable gardens, a proposition few could refuse.[54]

Even more importantly, the gardens produced savings for refugee households in the form of lower grocery bills. As Portland garden coordinator Jeff Strang remarked, "Last growing season, they didn't have to buy any vegetables. They still harvested crops as winter came on." He estimated that one hundred families tilling one thousand square feet each at one Portland garden site produced food for about six hundred people.[55] Garden organizers celebrated the financial benefits of the gardens and how they increased the "purchasing power of a given amount of money income," whether from wages or welfare payments.[56]

Many coordinators computed precise dollar amounts of the harvests, though it was an inexact science, and numbers varied considerably. A Portland-area volunteer who coordinated refugee gardens for the Multnomah County Community Action Agency calculated that gardening yielded approximately thirty cents worth of vegetables for each square foot tilled, or $13,000 an acre. The National Gardening Survey estimated the value of produce grown in community gardens during the 1984–85 season to be $9,230 per acre. Using that dollar figure, University of California, Davis Small Farm Center director Claudia Myers surmised the value of produce Southeast Asian refugees grew in Fresno, Tulare, Merced, and San Joaquin Counties in the mid-1980s totaled over $258,000. This was a low figure, she added, considering that Hmong refugees in California typically gardened year-round.[57] Across the country, for the contemporaneous Indochinese Gardening Project in Providence, the dollar-amount-per-acre calculation was much lower, just $4,470 per acre based on retail prices. Nevertheless, given that the project investment was $715 per acre, federal resettlement evaluators praised the results, noting that the 313 participating families consumed an average of $10 a week in produce for ten weeks, "a saving of $100 per family for the season, or $31,000 for the community as a whole." The Providence branch of the Hmong-Lao Unity Association noted that many families from the IGP also took a canning and preservation course, which helped them to stretch the dollar amount of their harvest even further.[58]

Like garden proponents envisioned, refugee growers demonstrated pride and satisfaction with the money they were able to save by cultivating produce. A sixty-five-year-old Hmong woman in Sacramento appreciated not having to purchase vegetables: "If you buy it from the store, you only get a little bit, and you have to go buy more. But if I grow it, I can re-pick it." In Portland, Viraphone Cha shared the fall harvest from her twenty-by-twenty-foot plot in St. Johns Community Garden with six immediate family members and five in-laws. "The garden does pretty good," she said in 1984. "It saves us money." For Hmong women, gardens were like bank accounts used to supplement the family's meager monetary resources. The time and labor they invested in their gardens paid off in the form of grocery savings for the entire household. Refugee families residing in cold climates took special satisfaction in having stockpiles of preserved vegetables and hard squash, pumpkins, and gourds from their summer and fall harvests to feed themselves through the winter when they could not garden.[59]

To maximize production in the community gardens, refugees engaged in a host of strategic farming practices. Because plots were much smaller than they were used to in their homeland, gardeners planted their crops intensively to guarantee that every square inch was productive, intercropping and making use of vertical space to trellis climbing vines above other plants. Gardeners in every locale took care to select crops with varied maturation cycles. For the elderly Vietnamese in New Orleans who faced more physical limitations, this helped stagger labor requirements over much of the last half of the growing season. It also ensured a continuous harvest of fresh produce. Hmong gardeners often planted faster-growing vegetables like mustard greens, onions, and peas several times in the season as they waited for tomatoes, cabbage, pumpkins, and squash to reach maturity. Particularly in locations where cold weather lingered into the spring months, refugee families started seeds indoors as early as February so they could transfer the plants to their community garden plots as soon as conditions permitted. This sometimes involved moving and rearranging furniture in their homes to "make room for seedlings on tables and sills in every sunny window."[60] A white American gardener who had a plot at a Minneapolis community garden that served many refugees said, "The Hmong can grow anything and everything," marveling that they seemed to have uncanny knowledge of "how to make use of a small plot and get the most out of it."[61]

Seed saving and sharing took on important economic dimensions within the gardening communities, reflecting how refugee growers strategized to stretch and maximize output from limited resources. Few refugee growers bought prepackaged seeds but collected and dried seeds from the previous year's harvest for spring planting. "Seed saving multiplies the amount we are able to grow each year, and it's free," said Phillip Yang of the Hmong Community Farm in Scituate, Rhode Island. Refugee growers identified the strongest plants among their crops and left them to go to seed, often loosely braiding or knotting tall stems so they would not be harvested prematurely.[62] Gardeners freely traded seeds and cuttings with relatives and friends. A Northern California Hmong gardener said, "My seeds, I just get them from my friends. . . . I save my seeds and I can share with whoever."[63] It was second nature for refugee gardeners to help each other grow productive gardens to feed their families.

There were key differences in how Southeast Asian refugees couched the monetary gains they obtained from community gardening that contrasted with the rhetoric of white garden advocates. Refugees tended to see garden produce as a supplement to welfare entitlements, not replacements for food stamps or cash payments. As such, they feared the loss of benefits under welfare rules, which lowered or eliminated payment amounts if household gross income increased during the 1980s.[64] In Sacramento, some Hmong gardeners thought that the value of the food they grew could be subtracted from their welfare checks and were suspicious of white American researchers who inquired about their crops. Wary that an "American woman" accompanied by a young Hmong American translator hailed from the local welfare office, the gardeners refused to answer questions concerning the produce.[65]

Such concerns on the part of refugee gardeners revealed the reality of their poverty in the United States and their efforts to scrape together various sources of income to make ends meet. In her study of Vietnamese refugees in Philadelphia during the 1980s, Nazli Kibria describes "patchworking," the sharing of resources within households, as a central economic practice Vietnamese Americans used to survive in their new home. Patchworking was characterized by an "uneven and unplanned quality of members' contributions to the household economy."[66] But economic practices were also calculated and deliberate. Refugee households pooled together myriad wage and nonwage economic resources—wages from entry-level factory jobs, food stamp allotments, Social Security and AFDC benefits, piecework (usually electronic assembly or sewing work that could be done at home), and seasonal farm labor. Mee Moua, the first Hmong American elected to a state legislature, recalled how she and her family harvested earthworms for fishermen in Appleton, Wisconsin, when she was a girl: "It was hard and pretty yucky, but we were always looking for ways to make a little cash." Such strategies are akin to what Eric Tang observes as refugees constantly "hustling to find alternative sources of income and in-kind donations."[67]

Refugees were acutely aware that community gardening helped them make ends meet but did not free them from dependence on low-wage work or government assistance. The fundamental difference between subsistence agriculture in Asia and the small-scale gardening endeavors in the United States was that the former led to self-sufficiency and independence. As an older Hmong man declared, "But even though it [Laos] is a poor country I could take care of myself there. . . . Everything is money here. Over there even if you don't have a job, there is still a lot of land and you can grow potatoes and corn and rice and raise chickens and you are free yourself."[68] The irony that one felt *more* impoverished in a wealthy, economically developed country was not lost on refugees.

Articulating an alternate definition, refugees conceived of "freedom" as providing for themselves and their families by harnessing the earth's bounty through astute agricultural and animal husbandry practices, a way of life that was implausible in the United States. Sokehn Mao recalled the abundance of food that surrounded him growing up in central Cambodia before the country's civil war and the genocidal reign of the Khmer Rouge: "In the countryside, there's plenty to eat. You don't need to go to the market. You feed yourself. Lots of edible herbs and fruits and spices all over the forest. . . . And each house has mango trees all around the house, and jackfruit, at least five kinds, and papaya trees, banana trees, everywhere. . . . So that's why there was no starving in Cambodia before the wars." Likewise, Hmong refugee Khou Her described farming rice, corn, bananas, pineapples, and other vegetables near the mountain Phu Kho on the border between Laos and Thailand. Her family was not dependent on the crops they grew, however, because "everywhere you looked there were trees, there was water running a lot from all the rain we had. There were a lot of fruit trees, so even if our farm turned out bad we still had this forest of fruit to eat."[69] Resettled refugees found safe haven from war and persecution, but for some, their existence in the United States was a poor shadow of what they had at home prior to wartime displacement.

As the older generation of refugees passed away and the American-raised children of Southeast Asian refugees came of age, the prevalence of community gardening declined, but new forms of commercial agricultural production emerged. A few refugees leveraged gardening into profitable side businesses. In the 1990s, the Khmer Growers began selling produce at farmers' markets in Lowell, Massachusetts. In recent years, commercial agriculture has provided significant income for some Southeast Asian American farmers. By 2005, few of the Versailles community gardens cultivated by Vietnamese refugees in the 1980s remained, but Vietnamese entrepreneurs in Southern California and Houston came to operate large-scale produce farms and greenhouses to supply the Asian vegetable needs of ethnic communities.[70] The renewed interest in local food, the proliferation of farmers' markets, and the "farm-to-table" movement have created a demand for produce that Southeast Asian farmers are poised to meet. In California's Central Valley, Hmong and other highland Lao cultivate thousands of acres of peas, strawberries, cherry tomatoes, and eggplant for mostly Anglo-American consumers and, to a lesser extent, crops like long beans, lemongrass, mustard greens, and bitter melon for the ethnic Asian community. In the Twin Cities, Atlanta, northern Virginia, and other locales, Southeast Asian farmers engage in high-value commercial farming on a modest scale, usually as a secondary or supplementary source of income.[71] Since 2015, more than one thousand Hmong Americans have moved to remote rural parts of Northern California to cultivate another profitable crop: marijuana. Raids, racial intimidation, wildfires, and most recently, restrictive water ordinances not so subtly aimed at Hmong farmers in Siskiyou County have called into question the long-term viability of cannabis growing.[72] These contemporary agricultural operations bear little resemblance to the refugee community gardens that saw their heyday in the 1980s.

Although garden advocates, policymakers, the press, and the public wanted to believe otherwise, community gardening was never a practicable pathway for refugees to attain economic security and independence nor a viable substitute for effective government-sponsored programs. The powerful consensus that community gardens were win-win endeavors—good for refugees, good for blighted neighborhoods, and good for U.S. taxpayers—had the effect of glossing over the nuances in refugees' experiences of the gardens and indirectly absolving the state of the responsibility to adequately assist refugees. During the 1980s, transferring the burden of turning new refugees into taxpaying, employed members of society from the federal government to private organizations and the refugees themselves was enormously appealing to policymakers, and the popularity of community gardens must be seen in this neoliberal context.[73]

Ultimately, refugees from Vietnam, Cambodia, and Laos attached their own meanings and functions to gardening that countered advocates' expectations. They experienced the gardens as spaces of productivity, community, and physical nourishment but also as dissonant environments inherently tinged with sadness and loss for their homes and lives in Southeast Asia, calling to task those who would erase or minimize the trauma embodied in their presence in the United States. Refugee gardeners reconstituted homeland practices to suit changing environments and circumstances, creating spaces where new agrarian dreams could flourish.

Notes

The author thanks the editors and anonymous reviewers for their insightful feedback. Corrie Decker, Charlotte Glennie, the editors of the *Amerasia Journal* Critical Refugee Studies Special Issue, Yến Lê Espiritu and Lila Sharif, and the participants of the Yale Agrarian Studies Colloquium also provided valuable comments on earlier versions of this chapter.

1. *Hmong Resettlement Study*, 3:36–38; "Hmong Refugees from Laos Try to Settle in Rhode Island," NBC *Nightly News*, August 22, 1982.
2. *Hmong Resettlement Study*, 3:39–43.
3. "Exotic Vegetables to Sprout at Two Sites," *Oregonian*, May 3, 1983; "Refugees Cultivate Hope," *Times Picayune*, May 29, 1984.
4. Yeang et al., *Highland Lao Initiative*, 116.
5. Corlett et al., "Hmong Gardens," 377–78; Airriess and Clawson, "Vietnamese Market Gardens," 16; Helzer, "Continuity and Change," 58.
6. Chan, *This Bittersweet Soil*; Chiang, *Shaping the Shoreline*; Chung, *Chinese in the Woods*; Mabalon, *Little Manila*; Matsumoto, *Farming the Home Place*; Tsu, *Garden of the World*.

7. Chiang, *Nature behind Barbed Wire*; Lillquist, "Farming the Desert"; Tamura, "Gardens below the Watchtower"; Wilson, "Landscapes of Promise and Betrayal."

8. Chiang, *Nature behind Barbed Wire*, 97.

9. Exceptions include Tsu, "'Plow Your Field'"; Vang, *Hmong in Minnesota*, 21–29.

10. See, for example, Pellow and Park, *Silicon Valley of Dreams*; Sze, *Noxious New York*; Taylor, *Toxic Communities*; Voyles, *Wastelanding*.

11. Alkon and Agyeman, *Cultivating Food Justice*; Broad, *More Than Just Food*; Reynolds and Cohen, *Beyond the Kale*; Reese, *Black Food Geographies*; White, "Sisters of the Soil"; White, *Freedom Farmers*.

12. Espiritu, *Body Counts*, 13. On Vietnamese refugee protest and agency, see Lipman, *In Camps*, 23–49, 172–77; and Vong, "'Compassion,'" 108–37.

13. Lawson, "Planner in the Garden," 154–55.

14. Lawson, "Planner in the Garden," 161–62, 165.

15. Lawson, *City Bountiful*, 213–26; Lawson, "Planner in the Garden," 163.

16. ACGA, "Coalition."

17. For an overview of the Southeast Asian refugee experience and the historical circumstances that produced their forced migration, see Lee, *Making of Asian America*, 314–33. For more on political debates over refugee resettlement in the late 1970s to 1980s, see Bon Tempo, *At America's Gates*, 168–71.

18. Nadasen, Mittelstadt, and Chappell, *Welfare*, 63–72; Rodgers, *Age of Fracture*, 200–209; Schaller, *Right Turn*, 41–43.

19. Lawson, *City Bountiful*, 3; Guitart, Pickering, and Byrne, "Past Results and Future Directions," 364.

20. Fass and Bui, *Hmong Resettlement Study*, 2:43–45.

21. "Ethnic 'Veggies' Lend a Worldly Flavor to Community Gardens," *Oregonian*, October 1, 1984.

22. Myers, *Highland Lao Agricultural Activities*, 7–9.

23. Fass and Bui, *Hmong Resettlement Study*, 2:43, 47. On agricultural projects aimed at refugee self-sufficiency, see Tsu, "'Plow Your Field,'" 38–73.

24. *Hmong Resettlement Study*, 3:35.

25. Myers, *Highland Lao Agricultural Activities*, 15.

26. "Crop of Resentment Growing," *St. Paul Dispatch*, October 20, 1980.

27. Myers, *Highland Lao Agricultural Activities*, 21–22.

28. "Crop of Resentment Growing"; Myers, *Highland Lao Agricultural Activities*, 29.

29. "YMCA Farm Project Helps Asian Refugees to Make Transition in Minnesota," *Minneapolis Star and Tribune*, August 3, 1986; "East and West Meet in Gardens on Hiawatha Avenue," *Minneapolis Star and Tribune*, October 21, 1982.

30. Ross, "Hmong Farmers of Providence," 109–10.

31. Giraud, "Shared Backyard Gardening," in Francis and Hester Jr., *Meaning of Gardens*, 168.

32. Myers, *Highland Lao Agricultural Activities*, 22–23; Corlett, "Landscapes and Lifescapes," 206, 222; Helzer, "Continuity and Change," 58.

33. Klindienst, *Earth Knows My Name*, 111.

34. Airriess and Clawson, "Vietnamese Market Gardens," 21.

35. Airriess and Clawson, "Vietnamese Market Gardens," 20, 27–28.

36. Corlett, Dean, and Grivetti, "Hmong Gardens," 376; Ross, "Hmong Farmers of Providence," 101–2.

37. Airriess and Clawson, "Vietnamese Market Gardens," 19–20. Recent research has shown evidence of the benefits of gardening on stress, especially for the elderly. See, for example, Van Den Berg and Custers, "Gardening," 3–11; Rodiek, "Influence of an Outdoor Garden," 13–21.

38. Klindienst, *Earth Knows My Name*, 126–27.

39. Corlett, "Landscapes and Lifescapes," 211.

40. Koltyk, *New Pioneers in the Heartland*, 108.

41. Ross, "Hmong Farmers of Providence," 124; Myers, *Highland Lao Agricultural Activities*, 29.

42. On Hmong agricultural practices in Laos, see Lee, "Shaping of Traditions," 14–16; Hillmer, *People's History of the Hmong*, 27–29; Chan, *Hmong Means Free*, 12–16, 30–31.

43. Chan, *Hmong Means Free*, 133. One *rai* is equivalent to 1,600 square meters or 0.3954 acre.

44. Miyares, "Changing Perceptions," 217, 219.

45. Airriess, "Creating Vietnamese Landscapes," in Berry and Henderson, *Geographical Identities of Ethnic America*, 242–43.

46. Chan, *Hmong Means Free*, 102.

47. Giraud, "Shared Backyard Gardening," 170.

48. Corlett, "Landscapes and Lifescapes," 214.

49. Myers, *Highland Lao Agricultural Activities*, 37–38.

50. Corlett, "Landscapes and Lifescapes," 238; Klindienst, *Earth Knows My Name*, 111–12.

51. "Crop of Resentment Growing."

52. Myers, *Highland Lao Agricultural Activities*, 15. In 1985, the YMCA spent five hundred dollars on its garden project; for expanded operations the following year, the cost was one thousand dollars. "YMCA Farm Project."

53. "East and West Meet."

54. Myers, *Highland Lao Agricultural Activities*, 21; Giraud, "Shared Backyard Gardening," 166–71; "Crop of Resentment Growing."

55. "Exotic Vegetables."

56. *Hmong Resettlement Study*, 2:49.

57. Myers, *Highland Lao Agricultural Activities*, 9.

58. *Hmong Resettlement Study*, 2:49; *Hmong Resettlement Study*, 3:36–38.

59. Corlett, "Landscapes and Lifescapes," 236; "Ethnic 'Veggies'"; Koltyk, *New Pioneers in the Heartland*, 111.

60. Airriess and Clawson, "Vietnamese Market Gardens," 27; Koltyk, *New Pioneers in the Heartland*, 108–9.

61. "East and West Meet."

62. Corlett, "Landscapes and Lifescapes," 215; Airriess and Clawson, "Vietnamese Market Gardens," 20; Ross, "Hmong Farmers of Providence," 111–12.

63. Koltyk, *New Pioneers in the Heartland*, 108; Giraud, "Shared Backyard Gardening," 171.

64. On welfare reform in this period, see Chappell, *War on Welfare*; Nadasen, Mittelstadt, and Chappell, *Welfare*, 63–84.

65. Corlett, "Landscapes and Lifescapes," 236.

66. Kibria, *Family Tightrope*, 77.

67. "American Odyssey," *Smithsonian Magazine*, September 2004; Tang, *Unsettled*, 92–93.

68. Hein, *From Vietnam, Laos, and Cambodia*, 140.

69. Klindienst, *Earth Knows My Name*, 105; Faderman with Xiong, *I Begin My Life*, 37–38.

70. Airriess, "Creating Vietnamese Landscapes," 173–74; "Transcript of Interview," 26–27; Airriess and Clawson, "Mainland Southeast Asian Refugees," 338–39.

71. Bittman, "The Changing Face of California Agriculture," *New York Times*, September 30, 2015; Parsons, "Exotic, Redefined," *Los Angeles Times*, August 25, 2004; Airriess and Clawson, "Mainland Southeast Asian Refugees," 338.

72. "Hills like Home in Laos. And Now a Crop Too," *New York Times*, June 4, 2017; "'It Is an Open Decret': Hmong Pot Farmers Seeking Identity, Profit—or Both," *Los Angeles Times*, September 17, 2017; "In Cannabis Country, They Hope the Pot Doesn't Burn," *Los Angeles Times*, September 25, 2020; "Northern California Water Restrictions Prompt Accusations of Racial Profiling of Hmong Farmers," *NBC News*, August 10, 2021, https://www.nbcnews.com/news/asian-america/northern-california-water-restrictions-prompt-accusations-racial-profiling-hmong-farmers-n1276375.

73. On contemporary incarnations of refugee community gardens, see "Ohio City Farm Hopes to Keep Its Mission of Aiding Refugees, Residents," *Plain Dealer* (Cleveland OH), March 14, 2018; "When the Uprooted Put Down Roots," *New York Times*, October 9, 2011.

Bibliography

Airriess, Christopher A. "Creating Vietnamese Landscapes and Place in New Orleans." In *Geographical Identities of Ethnic America: Race, Space, and Place*, edited by Kate A. Berry and Martha L. Henderson. Reno: University of Nevada Press, 2002.

Airriess, Christopher, and David Clawson. "Vietnamese Market Gardens in New Orleans." *Geographical Review* 84, no. 1 (January 1994): 16–31.

———. "Mainland Southeast Asian Refugees: Migration, Settlement, and Adaptation." In *Ethnicity in Contemporary America: A Geographical Appraisal*, edited by Jesse O. McKee, 311–46. Lanham MD: Rowman & Littlefield, 2000.

Alkon, Alison Hope, and Julian Agyeman, eds. *Cultivating Food Justice: Race, Class, and Sustainability*. Cambridge MA: MIT Press, 2011.

American Community Gardening Association (ACGA). "The Beginning of the ACGA Coalition." *National Community Gardening Survey*. Philadelphia, June 1998.

Bon Tempo, Carl. *At America's Gates: The United States and Refugees during the Cold War*. Princeton NJ: Princeton University Press, 2008.

Broad, Garrett. *More Than Just Food: Food Justice and Community Change*. Oakland: University of California Press, 2016.

Chan, Sucheng. *Hmong Means Free: Life in Laos and America*. Philadelphia: Temple University Press, 1994.

———. *This Bittersweet Soil: The Chinese in California Agriculture*. Berkeley: University of California Press, 1986.

Chappell, Marisa. *The War on Welfare: Family, Poverty, and Politics in Modern America*. Philadelphia: University of Pennsylvania Press, 2010.

Chiang, Connie Y. *Nature behind Barbed Wire: An Environmental History of the Japanese American Incarceration*. New York: Oxford University Press, 2018.

———. *Shaping the Shoreline: Fisheries and Tourism on the Monterey Coast*. Seattle: University of Washington Press, 2008.

Chung, Sue Fawn. *Chinese in the Woods: Logging and Lumbering in the American West*. Urbana: University of Illinois Press, 2015.

Corlett, Jan. "Landscapes and Lifescapes: Three Generations of Hmong Women and Their Gardens." PhD diss., University of California, Davis, 1999.

Corlett, Jan L., Ellen A. Dean, and Louis E. Grivetti. "Hmong Gardens: Botanical Diversity in an Urban Setting." *Economic Botany* 57, no. 3 (Autumn 2003): 365–79.

Espiritu, Yến Lê. *Body Counts: The Vietnam War and Militarized Refuge(es)*. Berkeley: University of California Press, 2014.

Faderman, Lillian, with Ghia Xiong. *I Begin My Life All Over: The Hmong and the American Immigrant Experience*. Boston: Beacon, 1998.

Fass, Simon M., and Diana D. Bui. *The Hmong Resettlement Study*. Vol. 2, *Economic Development and Employment Projects, March 1984*. Washington DC: Office of Refugee Resettlement, 1984.

Giraud, Deborah D. "Shared Backyard Gardening." In *The Meaning of Gardens: Ideas, Place, and Action*, edited by Mark Francis and Randolph T. Hester Jr. Cambridge MA: MIT Press, 1990.

Guitart, Daniela, Catherine Pickering, and Jason Byrne. "Past Results and Future Directions in Urban Community Gardens Research." *Urban Forestry and Urban Greening* 11, no. 4 (2012): 364–73.

Hein, Jeremy. *From Vietnam, Laos, and Cambodia: The Refugee Experience in the United States*. New York: Twayne, 1995.

Helzer, Jennifer J. "Continuity and Change: Hmong Settlement in California's Sacramento Valley." *Journal of Cultural Geography* 14, no. 2 (1994): 51–64.

Hillmer, Paul. *A People's History of the Hmong*. St. Paul: Minnesota Historical Society Press, 2010.

The Hmong Resettlement Study. Vol. 3, *Exemplary Projects and Projects with Unique Features of Programmatic Interest*. Washington DC: Office of Refugee Resettlement, 1985.

Kibria, Nazli. *Family Tightrope: The Changing Lives of Vietnamese Americans*. Princeton NJ: Princeton University Press, 1993.

Klindienst, Patricia. *The Earth Knows My Name: Food, Culture, and Sustainability in the Gardens of Ethnic Americans*. Boston: Beacon, 2006.

Koltyk, Jo Ann. *New Pioneers in the Heartland: Hmong Life in Wisconsin*. Boston: Allyn & Bacon, 1998.

Lawson, Laura J. *City Bountiful: A Century of Community Gardening in America*. Berkeley: University of California Press, 2005.

———. "The Planner in the Garden: A Historical View into the Relationship between Planning and Community Gardens." *Journal of Planning History* 3 (May 2004): 151–76.

Lee, Erika. *The Making of Asian America: A History*. New York: Simon & Schuster, 2015.

Lee, Gary Yia. "The Shaping of Traditions: Agriculture and Hmong Society." *Hmong Studies Journal* 6 (2005). https://www.hmongstudiesjournal.org/uploads/4/5/8/7/4587788/leehsj6.pdf.

Lillquist, Karl. "Farming the Desert: Agriculture in the World War II–Era Japanese-American Relocation Centers." *Agricultural History* 84 (Winter 2010): 74–104.

Lipman, Jana K. *In Camps: Vietnamese Refugees, Asylum Seekers, and Repatriates*. Oakland CA: University of California Press, 2020.

Mabalon, Dawn Bohulano. *Little Manila Is in the Heart: The Making of the Filipina/o American Community in Stockton, California*. Durham NC: Duke University Press, 2013.

Matsumoto, Valerie J. *Farming the Home Place: A Japanese American Community in California.* Ithaca NY: Cornell University Press, 1993.

Miyares, Ines M. "Changing Perceptions of Place and Space as Measures of Hmong Acculturation." *Professional Geographer* 49, no. 2 (1997): 214–24.

Myers, Claudia. *Highland Lao Agricultural Activities in California: Small Farms and Community Gardens.* Davis CA: University of California, Davis Small Farm Center, 1986: 7–9. Gayle Morrison Files on Southeast Asian Refugees, box 3, folder 17. Special Collections and Archives, UC Irvine Libraries, Irvine CA.

Nadasen, Premilla, Jennifer Mittelstadt, and Marisa Chappell. *Welfare in the United States: A History with Documents, 1935–1996.* New York: Routledge, 2009.

Pellow, David N., and Lisa Sun-Hee Park. *The Silicon Valley of Dreams: Environmental Injustice, Immigrant Workers, and the High-Tech Global Economy.* New York: NYU Press, 2002.

Reese, Ashanté M. *Black Food Geographies: Race, Self-Reliance, and Food Access in Washington, D.C.* Chapel Hill: University of North Carolina Press, 2019.

Reynolds, Kristin, and Nevin Cohen. *Beyond the Kale: Urban Agriculture and Social Justice Activism in New York City.* Athens: University of Georgia Press, 2016.

Rodgers, Daniel T. *Age of Fracture.* Cambridge MA: Belknap Press, 2011.

Rodiek, S. D. "Influence of an Outdoor Garden on Mood and Stress in Older Persons." *Journal of Therapeutic Horticulture* 13 (2002): 13–21.

Ross, Hannah. "The Hmong Farmers of Providence, Rhode Island: Roles of Agricultural Adaptation and Persistence in Hmong American Life." Master's thesis, Brown University, 2013.

Schaller, Michael. *Right Turn: American Life in the Reagan-Bush Era, 1980–1992.* New York: Oxford University Press, 2007.

Sze, Julie. *Noxious New York: The Racial Politics of Urban Health and Environmental Justice.* Cambridge MA: MIT Press, 2006.

Tamura, Anna Hosticka. "Gardens below the Watchtower: Gardens and Meaning in World War II Japanese American Incarceration Camps." *Landscape Journal* 23, no. 1 (January 2004): 1–21.

Tang, Eric. *Unsettled: Cambodian Refugees in the NYC Hyperghetto.* Philadelphia: Temple University Press, 2015.

Taylor, Dorceta E. *Toxic Communities: Environmental Racism, Industrial Pollution, and Residential Mobility.* New York: NYU Press, 2014.

"Transcript of Interview with Mao Chhoun Danh." Folk Arts and Heritage Collection, 1982–2016, 26–27. Massachusetts Archive Digital Repository, Boston MA. http://digitalarchives.sec.state.ma.us/uncategorised/digitalFile_e9aa1faf-6d54-4f8f-8889-5db11d5739bb/.

Tsu, Cecilia M. *Garden of the World: Asian Immigrants and the Making of Agriculture in California's Santa Clara Valley*. New York: Oxford University Press, 2013.

——. "'If You Want to Plow Your Field, Don't Kill Your Buffalo to Eat': Hmong Farm Cooperatives and Refugee Resettlement in 1980s Minnesota." *Journal of American Ethnic History* 36, no. 3 (2017): 38–73.

Van Den Berg, Agnes E., and Mariette H. G. Custers. "Gardening Promotes Neuroendocrine and Affective Restoration from Stress." *Journal of Health Psychology* 16, no. 1 (2011): 3–11.

Vang, Chia Youyee. *Hmong in Minnesota*. St. Paul: Minnesota Historical Society Press, 2008.

Vong, Samuel. "'Compassion Gave Us a Special Superpower': Vietnamese Women Leaders, Reeducation Camps, and the Politics of Family Reunification, 1977–1991." *Journal of Women's History* 3, no. 30 (Fall 2018): 108–37.

Voyles, Traci Brynne. *Wastelanding: Legacies of Uranium Mining in Navajo Country*. Minneapolis: University of Minnesota Press, 2015.

White, Monica M. *Freedom Farmers: Agricultural Resistance and the Black Freedom Movement*. Chapel Hill: University of North Carolina Press, 2018.

——. "Sisters of the Soil: Urban Gardening as Resistance in Detroit." *Race/Ethnicity: Multidisciplinary Global Contexts* 5, no. 1 (Autumn 2011): 18–22.

Wilson, Robert M. "Landscapes of Promise and Betrayal: Reclamation, Homesteading, and Japanese American Incarceration." *Annals of the Association of American Geographers* 101, no. 2 (March 2011): 422–44.

Yeang, Teng, Shoua Vang, Paoze Thao, David North, John Finck, and Bruce Downing. *An Evaluation of the Highland Lao Initiative, October 1985*. Washington DC: Office of Refugee Resettlement, 1985.

PART 3

Not Just White

DIVERSE ENVIRONMENTALISMS AND
ENVIRONMENTAL NARRATIVES IN
HISTORICAL PERSPECTIVE

One of the central critiques of mainstream environmentalism is how deeply and persistently *white* it has been. There is a perniciously normative cultural understanding that people of color have simply never been interested in environmental politics, in part because environmental politics have been so closely associated with white middle- and upper-class recreation and leisure. Closer examination, however, reveals that communities and people of color have long been invested in environmental concerns and protection of the natural world, developing rich and complex environmentalisms that have too frequently been overlooked by environmental historians, in part because the people involved do not always "look" like environmentalists. These chapters seek to correct the record, looking at various ways in which people of color have engaged with environmentalism and in so doing brought diverse standpoints and epistemologies to bear on what environmental politics can be.

In his chapter, Bryon Williams looks to the nineteenth-century roots of the association between whiteness, class status, and environmentalism: the "eco-author," a hyperliterate nature hero who wrote highly influential environmental prose and thus shaped American understandings of nature and human relationships to it. Williams explores first-person narratives of Black refugees who fled the United States to settle in the wilds of Ontario, arguing that these texts, quite apart from hegemonic white nature writers, stake out the principles of communitarianism and integrationism in counterpoint to the individualism and separatism propagated by dominant ideologies of nature retreat. In their chapters, Erika Bsumek and Miles Powell turn to the political and economic purchase of Indigenous environmentalisms, looking to the complex negotiations Indigenous nations have had to make in order to protect their sovereignty and promote their self-interest. Bsumek explores how Diné (Navajo) made legal claims to sites as a way of seeking to protect areas of religious and environmental importance to Diné life. Her case alerts us to the tension surrounding the ways in which Indigenous people have attempted to preserve their sacred sites and manage the growth in southwestern economy in the face of rapid and highly destructive development of natural resources. Powell turns to Native Hawaiian opposition to shark finning and in so doing adds a promising layer of analysis, ultimately questioning the presumption that mainstream environmentalism has always been exclusively defined by whites. Finally, Carolyn Finney invites us to consider deviating from the master narrative (read—the white one) and consider what it might mean to embrace Black environmentalisms and ways of being as what she refers to as a "radical presence."

Amputated from the Land

Black Refugees from America and the Racialized Roots of the Environmentalism–Environmental Justice Divide

BRYON WILLIAMS

In 1992, when local residents organized to protest large-scale hog factories in North Carolina, the activist group included numbers of both white members and Black members. Subsequent researchers found that while the whites characterized the group's role as "saving the environment," the Black protesters saw their aim as mitigating the ways in which the hog facilities "negatively affect people."[1] George Garrison, one of the Black activists interviewed for the study, had this to say: "Most of the whites are concerned about the surface waters because *it is recreation for them*. And most of us who live in rural communities [and have old and shallow wells] are more concerned about the ground water because *it is life for us* and the potential contamination of that from the chloroform that comes out of lagoons."[2]

In this episode, the tensions described—between leisure and necessity, between concern for the environment and concern for people, and between surface pleasures and deep survival—exemplify key aspects of larger ideological divides between mainstream environmentalism and the environmental justice movement, especially as those divisions affect Black Americans. In what follows, my central argument is that the roots of these modern conflicts are very old and are surface manifestations of some of the deepest racial fault lines in American environmental history. Starting in the mid-nineteenth century, influential white writers (Ralph Waldo Emerson, Henry David Thoreau, Frederick Jackson Turner) laid down the most enduring template for mainstream environmental identity, presenting as universal an entire range of privileges that were, in practice, racially exclusionary in the extreme. According to this template, the pastoral nature hero voluntarily retreats alone into an idealized environment, and by entering a putatively race-free natural world and inhabiting a purportedly race-free body, the figure presents nature as universally accessible and his own voluntary separatism as a redemptive embodiment of mythic American independence and as a universally emulatable model for environmental identity. These authors and their works established a set of what I call *retreat* values: leisure, solitude, voluntary separatism, and universalism. Retreat values function to institutionalize normative links between whiteness and mainstream environmentalism, and they are central to contemporary divides.

During the same era when these white authors were writing, however, Black environmental agents were also engaged in a form of separatism, one pursued out of desperation rather than privilege. While Thoreau and others were inscribing an overdeterminative retreat template, a largely ignored group of Black pioneers was exemplifying a set of *refuge* values, emphasizing cohesion with family and community in narratives that admit embodied experience, lived realities, and practical relationship with the natural world. Unlike the retreat writers whose idealized separatism served to deploy America-as-idea, Black refugees who fled *from* the United States were in effect amputated from their homelands. Their struggles—for legal rights, political power, education, property, and agency—are of a piece with concerns at the heart of today's environmental justice movement. I contend that fundamental seeds of modern, racially aligned divisions between environmentalism and environmental justice lie in the much older tensions between retreat and refuge.

Scholarship has begun to establish the vast and deep environmental experience of African Americans during the late pre–Civil War period, but the rub is this: the era during which the American nature writing genre emerged as a definitive fusion of experience and writing is the same era in which American historical realities drove a wedge between eco-experience and writing for African Americans, resulting in a significant blank at the heart of Black environmental expression from the nineteenth century, compelling modern writers and scholars to "re-create" Black experience from the era (in fictional forms such as neoslave narratives or in historiographical re-creations such as Sylviane Diouf's study of American maroons and Cheryl LaRoche's work on the Underground Railroad).[3] But in a largely overlooked chapter in ecological history, Black environmental agents from the nineteenth century express in their own voices the refuge values that counter the retreat values at the heart of American environmental orthodoxy.

Before turning to these narratives, I will first illustrate in overview form some of the key ways in which dominant retreat values serve to under-represent Black experience and overrepresent white identity in contemporary environmentalist discourse. I will then demonstrate the ways in which the connection of whiteness to (and the exclusion of Blackness from) mainstream environmentalist concerns was institutionalized in the mid-nineteenth century.

Black, White, and Green

Critics have described again and again the persistent invisibility of African Americans in mainstream environmental discourse. Black Liberation Theology founder James Cone asserts that it "is a well-founded belief in the African American community" that "white people care more about the endangered whale and the spotted owl than they do about the survival of young blacks in our nation's cities."[4] For Theodore Walker, "too often what passes for a wider concern inclusive of the environment is in fact a white racially gerrymandered concern which reaches out to include plants and animals while continuing to exclude black and colored peoples."[5] Willis Jenkins cites the ubiquitous Sierra Club calendar, with its "sublime, people-less landscapes," as being emblematic of a "fantastic hegemonic imagination" that "erases past and present traumas" and carries on the "cultural production of white power."[6]

Indeed, while environmental activism includes the preservation of scenic wilderness and protection of endangered species, environmentalism connotes as well a penumbra of related phenomena that constitute the most visible cultural faces of eco-dispositions: Earth Day, camping, hiking, green living, organic farming, as well as the national organizations (Sierra Club, Audubon Society) and consumer retailers (REI, L.L.Bean) whose glossy calendars, magazines, and catalogs propagate "the cultural activities that mediate environmental sensibilities . . . including birding, hiking, and back-packing."[7] And mainstream eco-identity often aligns with whiteness. In a 2016 study of "Race and Self-Presentation in the Labor Market," researchers found that applicants of color who "whitened" their résumés frequently did so by adding experiences they thought sounded "white," with the main activities added being "outdoorsy stuff such as hiking, kayaking. . . . Those were the kinds of things that people thought were tied to more mainstream white American culture."[8]

A key moment in the launching of the environmental justice movement came in 1990, when local advocacy groups sent two letters to a collection of national environmental organizations called the "Group of Ten."[9] Together, the letters "called for the environmentalist movement to review comprehensively and address its own culpability in patterns of environmental racism and undemocratic processes."[10] Subsequent promises of inclusivity were so dramatic that many die-hard environmentalists feared an "appeasement" by environmentalist groups to environmental justice demands.[11] Decades later, whatever results orthodox environmentalists feared from said appeasement are not apparent in empirical data on the demographics of mainstream environmental groups. An exhaustive 2014 study of "The State of Diversity in Environmental Organizations" concluded that there is "an overwhelmingly white 'Green Insiders' Club.'"[12] Voices from within largely white mainstream green groups have often expressed overtly inhospitable dispositions toward the social implications of environmental issues. Kevin DeLuca, for instance, argues that "despite the logical inanity of the environmental justice positions and the blatant use of the race and class cards, many environmental movement groups have acquiesced to environmental justice demands."[13] DeLuca further contends that mainstream environmental groups should continue catering to the tastes of the white donor classes who make up their core constituencies.[14] Subtler forms of de facto demographic segregation emerge from other sites of mainstream eco-sensibilities such as neohomesteader movements. Numerous book-length studies of contemporary back-to-the-land movements present homesteaders who are almost exclusively white, financially secure, and educated; who equate their voluntarily chosen "right ways of living" with mainstream environmental identities and with American cultural myths; and who explicitly invoke Thoreau in terms such as *guide, mentor, model, touchstone,* and *savior*.[15]

The contention that these class- and race-inflected eco-sensibilities are universally worthy of emulation exemplifies the most troublesome assumptions underlying an environmentalist retreat-to-nature ethos. In fact, the "choosing" aspect of the back-to-the-land impulse marks a sharp point of divergence along lines of race and class. The very old leisure/necessity divide continues to form a wedge in racially aligned attitudes into the modern environmentalist era, leading many environmental justice activists to hesitate to embrace identities or purposes labeled as "environmental." Lois Gibbs, Dollie Burwell, and George Garrison all relate their resistance to being labeled "environmentalists," with Gibbs saying, "Calling our movement an environmental movement would inhibit our organizing and undercut our claim that we are protecting people, not birds and bees."[16] The modern gulf between freely chosen retreat and desperate refuge necessary for survival is a phenomenon with deep and racialized roots in the nineteenth century.

The practically unknown chapter of Black environmental history that I lay out comes from a set of 114 dictated narratives from the 1840s and '50s, accounts delivered by Black people who fled the United States to settle in the wilds of Ontario and collected by white amanuensis Benjamin Drew in an 1856 volume called *The Refugee* (and I will, for clarity, refer to the speakers/protagonists as "the Refugees"). Considered only briefly for their ethnographic relevance in a few studies (even though they present the first published mention of Harriet Tubman), the *Refugee* accounts have not been read closely as narratives for their environmental significance. Hiding within a volume credited solely to a white author, the first-person accounts of environmental encounters and expertise are unrivaled in depth, breadth, and detail among Black writing of the era. Many of the Refugees easily qualify as nature heroes by the standards of American environmental orthodoxy, relating pioneer homesteading accounts as daring and exemplary as any on record. Such surface convergences aside, however, the *Refugee* narratives serve a more important function in diverging from the retreat values at the heart of mainstream environmental orthodoxy and thus speaking to modern fissures on race, environment, and justice.

The relevance of these nineteenth-century accounts to twenty-first-century concerns is striking. *The Refugee* is subtitled *Narratives of Fugitive Slaves in Canada*, but this is misleading to the point of falsehood. Of the 114 speakers in the volume, 31 of them were free or had moved to Canada from a free state; that is, more than a quarter of the Refugees were seeking refuge not from slavery but from the injustice and intolerable conditions in so-called free states. Then as now, slavery was far from the only racial evil faced by Black people in America. The reason most frequently given by the non-enslaved for crossing to Ontario was the desire for legal rights and protections.

Many Refugees cited Black Laws designed to discourage Black residency, and others described laws denying or limiting rights to own property, to bequeath or inherit land and possessions, or to seek redress in court. Other motivations for leaving a free state included personal safety, especially the fear of being kidnapped into slavery; the opportunity for children to go to school and receive a decent education; and acts of racial discrimination and prejudice. Though a handful of speakers mentioned general abstract benefits such as "true liberty," "respect," or "opportunity," the overwhelming number of motivations were for specific, concrete rights and benefits at the heart of environmental justice goals today: legal standing, adequate schooling, property rights, economic self-determination, political agency, enfranchisement, and bodily security.

Canonical white environmental heroes such as Thoreau tended to seek liberty in moving away from civilization and toward greater freedom in the natural world. But their redemptive relinquishment was predicated upon unspoken legal-political belonging, and their accounts perpetuated the myth that human concerns can be segregated from strictly environmental concerns. In their accounts, the Refugees dispelled such myths. They encountered nature, yes, in the wilds of Ontario, but they at the same time sought *more* civilization— the legal protections and civil liberties they were denied in the United States.

Retreat and Refuge

Thoreau's centrality to environmentalist hegemony lies in his perfecting two distinctively American fantasies: what I am labeling a "blank nature" (definitive of American exceptionalism, and usually located in the West) and the "blank body." The blankness here signifies an erasure of the concrete realities and inequalities of America-as-practiced and the positing instead of the universal and ideologically neutral abstraction of America-as-theorized. These abstract domains become the sites in which the pastoral experience of voluntary and solitary retreat to nature becomes universalized as definitive of American environmental identity. And these blank regions are the myths challenged most emphatically in the *Refugee* narratives.

BLANK NATURE

Starting in the 1830s, Ralph Waldo Emerson asserted that American cultural energy depends on a severance from European influence, proclaiming, "We have listened too long to the courtly muses of Europe" and proceeding to define America's culture and character—its individualism, independence, and boldness—by the extent to which it rejected European timidity, tameness, and decorousness.[17] Thoreau took Emerson's cultural separatism and cast the figurative "distance" from Europe in spatial-environmental terms, identifying a terrain (nature) and a direction (West) into which the individual may retreat to enact a definitively American independence. In "Walking," arguably the most influential nature essay ever written (one published posthumously in 1862 but composed in the 1840s and '50s, contemporaneous with the discourse of Manifest Destiny), Thoreau devoted an entire middle section to the West. The West he presented here is an idealized realm of freedom, wildness, and possibility, and he universalized the westward pull by presenting it in the language of myth and of biological science (with westward movement being a form of migratory instinct seen in wild animals).

"Walking" has a companion piece in *Walden*, in which Thoreau dramatized his own experience as an American Adam, offering in his own example proof that the freedom-in-nature he championed is indeed universal and available to all, his own homesteading project a literally emulatable template for any who choose to follow his example. In his retreat to Walden Pond, Thoreau perfected a perennially relevant form of American separatism: *Walden* inaugurated the "founding" strain of nature writing, in which the acts of homesteading and settling are declarations of independence by which American ideologies of separatism and self-identity are deployed. It is not enough to leave the old order behind; the retreating hero must then found a more perfect order that bears out the utopian promise definitive of America.[18]

Thoreau's portrait of an idealized West in "Walking" culminated in the essay's most famous words: "The West of which I speak is but another name for the Wild; and what I have been preparing to say is, that in Wildness is the preservation of the world."[19] The syllogism inherent here implies a question: If West equals wildness, then what happens when we run out of West, therefore exhausting the store of wild nature that perpetually regenerates and preserves American character? This anxiety animated Frederick Jackson Turner's Frontier Thesis (first presented in 1893), in which Turner institutionalized pastoral retreat elements of individualism, wildness, foundings-in-nature, and rejection of Europe by placing them at the heart of his recapitulation of American history: "The advance of the frontier has meant a steady movement away from the influence of Europe, a steady growth of independence on American lines."[20] Turner presented the archetypal retreater-founder as the central agent of American history, and "the demand for land and the love of wilderness freedom drew the frontier ever onward."[21] Land and freedom work together to form one of the most definitive of American ideals: opportunity.

In Turner's conception, key parts of the past that the frontier allowed escape from are the national, ethnic, and racial distinctions among various immigrant groups. Turner saw America's natural environment as the grounds for a miraculous process of unification: "In the crucible of the frontier the immigrants were Americanized, liberated, and fused into a mixed race, English in neither nationality nor characteristics," with even formerly indentured servants (of European descent) able to transcend class limitations and at the frontier become equal Americans.[22] Of course, this "field of opportunity" has its unspoken limits, with Turner's silence deafening on the issue of those for whom racial markers may not disappear so readily. While the idealized western frontier is a place where people can escape a past of racial difference and even discord to become an American "mixed race," the actual West entailed a more exclusionary utopia. While African Americans after the Civil War began to form a more visible part of the West's history as Exodusters and Buffalo Soldiers, before the war many white pioneers headed west not just to escape the past but to escape Black people; as John Dippel argues, "One of the factors pushing pioneers westward was race. . . . For them, a major attraction of the West lay in its racial exclusivity."[23] While subsequent scholars have presented theories that challenge Turner's too-tidy story of the frontier (with Mary Louise Pratt's "contact zones" and Annette Kolodny's "borderlands" most prominent among them), Turner's myth of a blissfully race-free and universally accessible natural world into which any may voluntarily retreat has maintained a tenacious hold on American self-conceptions, such as the myth of "the voluntary society" that political journalist Jamelle Bouie cites in his discussion of Michelle Obama's speech at the 2016 Democratic National Convention.[24] The West (and the wild nature it signifies) of Thoreau and Turner was the ground for just such a voluntary society, an ideal space where race is elided—Indigenous peoples removed or eradicated, ethnic distinctions among European immigrants erased to achieve a "composite nationality" otherwise known as "whiteness," and non-European peoples ignored altogether.[25]

The classic American nature retreat usually functions as a separation redemptive of both the self and the nation, one seen not as a severance from America but a distillation of the utopian American project. The narratives in the Black-authored *Refugee* accounts disrupted American spatial and ideological vectors by not only being oriented by a northern, and not western, frontier (and one that entails another nation-state's boundary and not just so-called open territory) but also by quite intentionally and emphatically leaving America behind. Unlike the retreats deemed redemptive of America, the flights in *The Refugee* were amputations from America in favor of Europe and the opportunities and legal protections offered in the imagined communities to which Ontario belonged, with settlers even boasting triumphantly of their rejection of America's oppressive republic and their escape to the liberties of England's much freer monarchy. Thus attention to the *Refugee* narratives means not only recognizing neglected versions of the retreat to nature but also questioning the myths of America embedded in and propagated by traditional nature writing.

In contrast to pioneers in America seeking freedom in moving away from England and Europe, Black settlers expressed again and again a preference for Canada and its British legal-political system, believing it to be explicitly superior to the American system they fled. Refugee Alexander Hamilton stated plainly, "I am naturalized here, and have all the rights and privileges of a British subject."[26] Ephraim Waterford, who was born free but bound in Virginia until age twenty-one, settled in Indiana and established a prosperous life for his family without the benefit of education: "I left on account of oppression in Indiana. I had a farm of forty acres paid for, and I had the deed. A law was passed that a colored man could not devise real estate to his wife and children, and there were equally unjust laws enacted. I told them 'if that was a republican government, I would try a monarchical one.'"[27] Waterford's flight from oppression in Indiana illustrates the linguistic (and thus conceptual) deception performed by the very term *free state* and further undercuts myths equating America with liberty and the English monarchy with tyranny, with Waterford finding greater legal and property rights (not to mention opportunity for his children to receive an education) in the freer English system.

Another of the Refugees Drew interviewed was the Reverend Alexander Hemsley, who recounted his feelings on at last crossing over to Toronto: "When I finally reached English territory, I had a comfort in the law—that my shackles were struck off, and that a man was a man by law. I had been in comfortable circumstances, but all my little property had been *lawed* away. I was among strangers, poverty-stricken, and in a cold country."[28] The relief of reaching a land of law and liberty in English territory is especially telling from a man who had actually *won* the most important fugitive slave legal case to date in the United States but felt still the shackles that deprived him of liberty and full humanity.[29]

Reverend Hemsley eventually gained a foothold in the countryside near St. Catharines, and though "enfeebled in health," he cleared five acres of pines to establish a farm. Nonetheless, his sense of exile plagued him still.[30] After years of such limbo, Hemsley reached a final realization. Despite never having the material comfort and prosperity he had once had in New Jersey, he made an emphatic judgment: "I then made up my mind that salt and potatoes in Canada were better than pound-cake and chickens in the United States. Now I am a regular Britisher. My American blood has been scourged out of me; I have lost my American tastes; I am an enemy to tyranny."[31] Thus in contrast to pervasive American pastoral narratives in which freely chosen westward retreat is a further distillation of American liberty—with retreat being the reenactment of a national story rooted in escape from British tyranny—the northern vector of Hemsley's flight told a different story altogether. In his telling, bolstered by lived experience and well-documented historical events, the United States is the land of tyranny and British Canada a land of refuge— colder, and for him lonelier and less comfortable, but above all free.

In contrast to the lack of standing and security for Black people in American courts of law, the experience of Refugee Alfred T. Jones pointed to a British legal system fully inclusive of immigrants from the United States. Jones, enslaved in Kentucky before escaping by writing himself a pass that he admitted "was not spelled correctly," became part of a prospering community in Canada, and he matter-of-factly described his plans for appearing in person before Parliament, empowered by the English rights he rightly saw as superior to the treatment he had endured in America.[32] Despite such emphatic statements of preference for British legal-political rights, numerous *Refugee* speakers disclosed the unbearable tension of exile, the tragedy of loving the laws of England while loving the land (and often the people) of the United States, a land many still referred to as home. No fewer than fifteen Refugees stated explicitly that they liked the United States and would, despite many having secure and prosperous lives in Canada, return to the States if slavery were abolished and legal equality were upheld.

In America's deepest pastoral myths, the ideal freedom universally bequeathed to every individual by America's land—expressed in the notion of a blank and idealized West, a catchword for wild nature itself—is predicated upon unspoken legal-political belonging. The ideal homesteader-founder—the Thoreauvian retreater or Turner's frontier pioneer—sought this West to escape constricting civilization, to declare independence anew in further execution of the American utopian project, moving diametrically away from British tyranny. But this West indeed turned out to be a utopia—etymologically, a no-place. Black Refugees from America presented powerful counternarratives. The *Refugee* actors disclosed the innumerable transatlantic realities that dispelled such myths, fleeing northward (or even sailing eastward to the House of Lords) to find liberty and equality in the British monarchy. Their homesteading experiences, while displaying the familiar rugged independence of the nature retreat, also encompassed the precarity of exile. The Refugees' environmental engagement in and even affinity for creating homesteads and livelihoods in Canada nonetheless came at a heavy price: amputation from what they called their native land in America. Severed from yet another home, the Refugees inhabited a compound exile, a diaspora-beyond-diaspora that refuted the ideal America-as-theorized in the pastoral nature retreat and exposed the tragic realities of America-as-practiced.

THE BLANK BODY

To this idealized blank West, Thoreau married the notion of the "blank body" as a second idealized, unmarked site of the universality central to nature writing's retreat pastoralism. Emerson, once again, was foundational. In *Nature*'s famous "transparent eyeball" passage, Emerson posited a radical unity of soul and nature and God, a union awaiting the ordinary individual as he walked across a common: "I become a transparent eyeball; I am nothing; I see all; the currents of the Universal Being circulate through me; I am part or parcel of God."[33] The erasure of the boundaries between the individual and the universe presented such experience as a universal birthright available to all. The spiritual and abstract nature of this union, in which the individual is all subject and no body, lends to its universal accessibility. Emerson's nominally benign affirmation of this Platonic dualism as the foundation of his transcendentalist philosophy, articulated in the universalist language of metaphysics, in reality disguised an exclusionary freedom reserved for the select: the freedom to *not* be identified with one's body, to relegate one's body to the realm of the "not me," to treat one's own body as a voluntary aspect of the self. Emerson's abstract disembodiment is universal only when untethered from concrete American historical and political realities; then as now, bodies matter, and only some bodies are so normative as to become transparent. Other bodies (the nonmale, the nonwhite) have been persistently marked for difference and exclusion, not so easily cast off or theorized out of view.

The higher laws of Emerson's transcendentalist metaphysics, by which one's body must disappear in the interest of spiritual union with the collective oversoul, had their secular counterparts in the American Revolution's higher laws of political inclusion, by which particular bodies are effaced in the interest of extending universal rights to the abstract "persons" of the founders' rhetoric. Disembodiment as a central factor in American political inclusion is a trend well documented in scholarship on the relations between the individual body and the body politic. Michael Warner argues that "the principle of self-abstraction . . . is a ground rule of argument in a public discourse that defines its norms as abstract and universal, but it is also a political resource available only . . . to those participants whose social role allows such self-negation (that is, by persons defined by whiteness, maleness, and capital)."[34] Bruce Burgett notes that print gave citizens the means by which to "imagine forms of political authority that were rational and noncoercive to the degree that they were abstract and disembodied. Citizens, in other words, gained political power only insofar as they were able to represent their local and embodied experience as universal and disinterested through the medium of print."[35] As is the case with Thoreauvian nature writing, print is the vehicle of abstraction by which particular bodies disappear and universal rights extend to all "persons."

Feminist scholars have advanced the argument that within this discourse of universal rights, this abstract equality exists in inverse proportion to the corporeal visibility of actual bodies, especially when it comes to gender and race. Karen Sánchez-Eppler focuses on the rhetorical sleight of hand that allows the "fleshy specificity of embodied identities" to be "masked behind the constitutional language of abstracted and implicitly bodiless 'persons.'"[36] She cites the feminist theorists who challenge the inherent privilege of bodily invisibility: "Their arguments suggest not only that this juridical 'person' has always implicitly occupied a white male body, but, more important, that success in masking this fact has secured and legitimized the power that accrues to that body."[37] Sánchez-Eppler zeros in on the *voluntary* nature of embodiment for those who occupy the "right" kinds of bodies: "All the 'men' who, Thomas Jefferson declared 'are created equal' shed their gender and their race; in obtaining the right to freedom and equality they discard bodily specificity. The problem, as feminists and abolitionists surely suspected, was that women and blacks could never shed their bodies and become incorporeal 'men.'"[38] In other words, disappearing one's body is not a voluntary option for those with bodies marked by difference, and thus exclusion, from the norms disguised within universalist rhetoric.

Along with the blank West, the blank body is the second site into which Thoreau retreated from fraught ideological realities and into an idealized refuge of displaced and disembodied universality, as his erasure of actual bodies performed for abstract environmental inclusion what the Declaration of Independence had done for abstract political inclusion. In his conception of the body, Thoreau built upon the Emersonian dualism that cast the body as "not-me," with Thoreau's founding-in-nature project treating the body as—along with his house, his bean field, his book—yet another site of utopian self-determination, another domain over which he assumed full creative agency.

But while Thoreau in some sense *objectified* his own body by asserting a spiritual mastery over it, he tempered any potential corporeality by rarely, if ever, *particularizing* his body. When he did refer to constitutive individual body parts, he spoke of them simply as the representative instances at hand of *a* body, unmarked by anything distinguishing them from another human body. Thoreau's act in this regard was nature writing's founding instance of what Donna Haraway in her work on discourses of science characterizes as the "leap out of the marked body and into a conquering gaze from nowhere": "This is the gaze that mythically inscribes all the marked bodies, that makes the unmarked category claim the power to see and not be seen, to represent while escaping representation. This gaze signifies the unmarked positions of Man and White."[39] This unmarked position is a cornerstone of the proclaimed universality that made Thoreau as exemplar influential and emulated into the present.

Such universality deployed the stratagem of disembodiment into new domains, aligning with other culturally embedded attempts to purify political and philosophical discourses of bodily presences and thus masking the concrete inequalities of an America inclusive in theory but exclusive in practice. As Jefferson and other founders employed the disembodied "person" to present inalienable democratic rights as universal, and as Emerson presented the disembodied metaphysical subject as heir to a universally accessible communion with God in a spiritual democracy, Thoreau likewise elided his own unmarked body so as to universalize his example of redemptive, solitary retreat to nature. And as with the theorists before him, the power to make bodies disappear resided primarily in the power of writing. With this power, Thoreau inscribed fictions at the heart of nature writing's hegemony; he inhabited a quite particular site (squatting on his wealthy friend Emerson's land a mile from a cultural hub) while appearing universally representative of being at home anywhere in nature, and he inhabited a particular body (white and male) while appearing to inhabit a representative body free from any contingencies of particularity.

In this marriage of the blank West and the blank body, nature writing establishes forms of environmental identity that are predicated on retreat from political-corporeal particularities and realities. In turning to the *Refugee* accounts, we face those realities. Where the paradigmatic narratives of *retreat* center on volitionality and universality, narratives of *refuge* center on oppression and particularity, especially with respect to the body. As exemplified in Thoreau, the retreat hero enjoys agency over his body and his labor; future Refugees, especially those enslaved, usually enjoyed neither. The retreat hero treats his body as erasable and revisable; for Refugees, however, racial markers, scars, and disfigurements were indelible. The retreat hero may hide his body from view, while his Black counterparts relayed being subjected to dehumanizing public inspection and violation of their bodies. And the retreat hero through writing maintains control over his own representation, while Refugees deprived of literacy depend on a white amanuensis for a lasting printed record of their lives and narratives. Yet the

Refugees performed a corrective act of reappropriation, seizing conditions once oppressive—the visibility of one's body, the presence of wounds and scars—and transmuting these signs of trauma into vehicles of expression, memory, and agency.

Numerous Refugees punctuated their narratives by indicating wounds incurred during their flight and escape; in addition to bite scars from pursuit hounds, many (John Little, Henry Banks, William Street, and John Holmes among them) carried lead in their bodies still from gunshots years before. Such wounds (and the resulting chronic disabilities) suffered during their flights underscored both the lethal risk of attempting escape and the belated (and hard-earned) agency over their own bodies that eventually justified those risks. Along with the psychic wages of exile, the lead within their bodies was a cruel reminder of brutality's cost into the present. But in using their scars as the texts of their liberation narratives, Refugees authored their own accounts of the journey from objectification to agency, their bodies bearing witness as no written text could.

Still other *Refugee* speakers attested that human violence is far from the only bodily danger entailed by a long northward escape into the unknown, citing the marks left by perilous environmental encounters. William Johnson lost two toes to frostbite and could not work, but he proclaimed his disfigurement a sacrifice preferable to the alternative of enslavement: "My feet were frostbitten on my way north, but I would have rather died on the way than to go back."[40] Henry Morehead was driven to attempt a desperate escape from Kentucky with his family when his wife and children were ordered to be sold down South. Morehead paid a bodily price for the journey: "I was on the road longer than I should have been without my burden: one child was nine months old, one two years old, and one four. The weather was cold, and my feet were frostbitten, as I gave my wife my socks to pull on over her shoes."[41] Despite such hardship, Morehead put these costs into perspective: "With all the sufferings of the frost and the fatigues of travel, it was not so bad as the effects of slavery."[42] Not only does Morehead's desperate search for refuge read as a powerful counterpoint to the freely chosen retreat of the solitary pastoral hero, but the family's communal flight challenges the individualism and separatism central to the retreat narrative. The nature writing tradition lionizes the unencumbered bachelor and his homesteading self-reliance, but such heroism seems cheaply bought in contrast to the fortitude and mutual reliance of husband and wife, father and mother, as they bear the awful responsibility of keeping their family of dependents intact at all costs. Solitude and separation may be the hallmarks of the retreat hero, but these refuge heroes risked death and disfigurement to avoid separation and to pursue the more difficult route of seeking liberation *together*.

Along with the men who recounted the bodily sacrifices of seeking refuge beyond the United States, women in *The Refugee* offer some of the most compelling testimonies of former brutality and assert authority over their life stories by disclosing their scars as evidence. A Mrs. Ellis of St. Catharines recalled her former life while enslaved in Delaware: "I have been whipped with a wagon whip and with hickories—have been kicked and hit with fists. I have a bunch on my head from a blow my master gave me, and I shall carry it to my grave."[43] Like Mrs. Ellis, Nancy Howard bore an indelible mark of violence, and incorporated her scars into her narrative. Howard recounted once forgetting a fork while setting the table, resulting in her master's "hitting [her] on the head with the carving-knife."[44] She continued, "The blood spurted out—you can see," and here her scar entered directly into the printed text.[45] In one of the only instances in the entire volume in which he editorializes in the course of another's narrative, Benjamin Drew inserted a bracketed statement: "[Here the woman removed her turban and showed a circular cicatrice denuded of hair, about an inch in diameter, on the top of her head]."[46] Yet not all marks are tamed as such. After relating the numerous ways in which she had been beaten with all manner of weaponized objects, Mrs. Howard said, "It seemed to me I could not bear another lick. I can't forget it. I sometimes dream that I am pursued, and when I wake, I am scared almost to death."[47] The enduring psychic scar of past brutality was not a mark to be wrapped beneath a turban and disclosed at her discretion but a trauma that erupted beyond the bounds of her will. In the Refugees' testimonies, bodily experience and psychic experience were of a piece with mental and emotional trauma, as permanent and debilitating as the most extreme physical abuse. Not only do scars serve as a form of memory, but memory is indeed itself a scar.

Legacies of Invisibility

We should conclude by returning to the ultimate relevance of these instances for our purposes. While seminal nature writers were carefully erasing the particulars of their own embodiment, making their own bodies invisible so as to universalize their redemptive pastoral experiences, Black homesteaders *filled* their accounts with the particular and exploited bodies that testify to the costs of struggling toward liberation and agency. Lest we think such issues are relics of a bygone era, irrelevant to current attitudes related to environmentalism or environmental justice, modern testimonials often tell a regrettably familiar story. In "Black Women and the Wilderness," Evelyn C. White resists invitations to go on hikes and swims (experiences considered universally pleasurable and redemptive by her white colleagues) during a writing retreat in the Cascades, and she locates her fear in a deep collective history: "My genetic memory of ancestors hunted down and preyed upon in rural settings counters my fervent hopes of finding peace in the wilderness. Instead of the solace and comfort I seek, I imagine myself in the country as my forebears were—exposed, vulnerable, and unprotected—a target of cruelty and hate."[48] Such objectification is woven into everyday lived experience for many communities of color, in less graphic but nonetheless devastating forms of violence and neglect; ethnographic environmental studies report that Black people experience "not having the political position to affect decisions that profoundly affect their lives [and] being treated like objects by doctors and many other professionals who minister to their needs."[49] Finally, harrowing accounts of Black refugees fleeing the United States for Canada in the year 2017, when multiple Ghanaian refugees suffered frostbite and subsequent amputation as they fled to Canada from the United States out of fear of Trump administration policies, tragically recapitulate the links between the environmental and the political conditions expressed in *The Refugee.*[50]

Affirmative Black nature narratives such as those in *The Refugee* have often languished in obscurity or neglect, but new environmental histories need stories of beauty and agency that augment the necessary, powerful documentation of trauma and burden. Eco-actors in *The Refugee* navigated the doubleness of what Kimberly K. Ruffin calls the "ecological beauty-and-burden paradox."[51] Torn by exile, Refugees carried in their minds and bodies the bullets, scars, and memories of past traumas into their new lives. Yet in their resistance and their struggle for their fundamental human rights, and in their narratives' challenge to America's foundational environmental myths, the Refugees serve as exemplars in transmuting trauma into beauty and agency. As enduring cultural touchstones for environmentalist identity,

Thoreau and other nature writers extolled the pastoral retreat ideals of separation, solitude, self-reliance, universality, and leisure amid a paradisiacal nature, a utopia in which retreat is "not a hardship but a pastime."[52] For the Refugees, the environment offered a sober beauty rooted in a different set of realities: the mutual reliance among friends, family, and community; the contingencies of lived experience; the need for political and economic standing; the freedom to worship, sing, learn, or enjoy the fruits of one's labor. In their clear-eyed assessments of the world's injustices and in their determined optimism to exercise agency over their own lives, the Refugees stand as a touchstone for environmental justice. The retreat to utopia is, literally and etymologically, a journey to no-place. The Refugees remind us all that any paradise must start with the actual places where we live, play, work, and worship.

Notes

1. Allen, Daro, and Holland, "Becoming an Environmental Justice Activist," 121.
2. Allen, Daro, and Holland, "Becoming an Environmental Justice Activist," 121.
3. See Ashraf Rushdy, *Neo-Slave Narratives: Studies in the Social Logic of a Literary Form* (Oxford: Oxford University Press, 1999); Sylviane Diouf, *Slavery's Exiles: The Story of the American Maroons* (New York: New York University Press, 2014); and Cheryl Janifer LaRoche, *Free Black Communities and the Underground Railroad: The Geography of Resistance* (Urbana: University of Illinois Press, 2014).
4. Cone, "Whose Earth Is It Anyway?," 138.
5. Walker, "African-American Resources," 279.
6. Jenkins, *Future of Ethics*, 204.
7. Allen, Daro, and Holland, "Becoming an Environmental Justice Activist," 127.
8. Bouree Lam, "When Resumes Are Made 'Whiter' to Please Potential Employers," *Atlantic*, March 23, 2016, https://www.theatlantic.com/business/archive/2016/03/white-resume-diversity/475032/.
9. The Group of Ten included the Audubon Society, Environmental Defense Fund, Friends of the Earth, Izaak Walton League, National Parks and Conservation Association, National Wildlife Federation, Natural Resources Defense Council, Sierra Club, Sierra Club Legal Defense Fund, and the Wilderness Society. See Sandler and Pezzullo, *Environmental Justice and Environmentalism*, 19n4.
10. Sandler and Pezzullo, *Environmental Justice and Environmentalism*, 4.
11. DeLuca, "Wilderness Environmentalism Manifesto," 28.
12. Taylor, "State of Diversity."

13. DeLuca, "Wilderness Environmentalism Manifesto," 32.

14. DeLuca, "Wilderness Environmentalism Manifesto," 37.

15. Gould, *At Home in Nature*, 25.

16. In Gottlieb, *Forcing the Spring*, 401.

17. In Gottlieb, *Forcing the Spring*, 401.

18. The nature retreat enacts in microcosm the ties between separatism and founding that are central to the macroscopic American political project; as Gordon S. Wood notes, the founding of a republic "meant more for Americans than the simple elimination of a king and the institution of an elective system. It added a moral dimension, a utopian depth, to the political separation from England—a depth that involved the very character of their society." *Creation of the American Republic*, 47.

19. Thoreau, "Walking," 239.

20. Turner, *Rereading Frederick Jackson Turner*, 34.

21. Turner, *Rereading Frederick Jackson Turner*, 47.

22. Turner, *Rereading Frederick Jackson Turner*, 47.

23. Dippel, *Race to the Frontier*, 2–3.

24. Pratt, "Arts of the Contact Zone," and Kolodny, "Letting Go Our Grand Obsessions." Bouie recounts the first lady's casting of the nation's history— she said, "The story [of America is] of generations of people who felt the lash of bondage, the shame of servitude, the sting of segregation, but who kept on striving and hoping and doing what needed to be done so that today I wake up every morning in a house that was built by slaves"—and deems it a "radical message" in contrast to what Bouie calls the nation's default myth of "the voluntary society": "Overwhelmingly, when telling the story of America, our presidents lean on the idea of a voluntary society—a nation of frontiersmen and immigrants who came willingly to these shores to find freedom and opportunity. . . . [The Obamas'] America is a nation [including] immigrants . . . who were brought here as chattel and forced to work under the lash, but who kept their belief in better days and salvation." Jamelle Bouie, "The Radical Message of Michelle Obama's Speech," Slate, July 26, 2016, http://www.slate.com/articles/news_and_politics/politics/2016/07/the_radical_message_of_michelle_obama_s_speech.html.

25. Turner, *Rereading Frederick Jackson Turner*, 51.

26. Drew, *Refugee*, 173.

27. Drew, *Refugee*, 335.

28. Drew, *Refugee*, 58.

29. Reverend Hemsley had been released from slavery in 1836 in a case decided by Chief Justice John Hornblower of New Jersey. The case challenged the constitutionality of the Federal Fugitive Slave Law of 1793, and the decision was widely

revived by abolitionists for its potential applicability to the new Fugitive Slave Law of 1850.

30. Drew, *Refugee*, 59.
31. Drew, *Refugee*, 60.
32. Drew, *Refugee*, 151–52.
33. Emerson, "Nature," 6.
34. Warner, *Letters of the Republic*, 52.
35. Burgett, *Sentimental Bodies*, 13.
36. Sánchez-Eppler, *Touching Liberty*, 1.
37. Sánchez-Eppler, *Touching Liberty*, 3.
38. Sánchez-Eppler, *Touching Liberty*, 3.
39. Haraway, "Persistence of Vision," 283.
40. Drew, *Refugee*, 51.
41. Drew, *Refugee*, 175.
42. Drew, *Refugee*, 175.
43. Drew, *Refugee*, 63.
44. Drew, *Refugee*, 69.
45. Drew, *Refugee*, 69.
46. Drew, *Refugee*, 69.
47. Drew, *Refugee*, 69.
48. White, "Black Women and the Wilderness," 378.
49. Allen, Daro, and Holland. "Becoming an Environmental Justice Activist," 122.
50. Catherine Porter, "After a Harrowing Flight from U.S., Refugees Find Asylum in Canada," *New York Times*, July 16, 2017, https://www.nytimes.com/2017/07/16/world/canada/refugees-in-canada.html.
51. Ruffin, *Black on Earth*, 2–3.
52. Thoreau, *Walden*, 70.

Bibliography

Allen, Kim, Vinci Daro, and Dorothy C. Holland. "Becoming an Environmental Justice Activist." In *Environmental Justice and Environmentalism: The Social Justice Challenge to the Environmental Movement*, edited by Kim Allen, Vinci Daro, and Dorothy C. Holland, 105–34. Cambridge MA: MIT Press, 2007.

Burgett, Bruce. *Sentimental Bodies: Sex, Gender, and Citizenship in the Early Republic*. Princeton NJ: Princeton University Press, 1998.

Cone, James. "Whose Earth Is It Anyway?" *Sojourners Magazine*, July 2007. https://sojo.net/magazine/july-2007/whose-earth-it-anyway.

DeLuca, Kevin Michael. "A Wilderness Environmentalism Manifesto: Contesting the Infinite Self-Absorption of Humans." In *Environmental Justice and*

Environmentalism: The Social Justice Challenge to the Environmental Movement, edited by Kim Allen, Vinci Daro, and Dorothy C. Holland, 27–56. Cambridge MA: MIT Press, 2007.

Dippel, John. *Race to the Frontier: "White Flight" and Westward Expansion*. New York: Algora, 2007.

Drew, Benjamin. *The Refugee: Narratives of Fugitive Slaves in Canada*. Toronto: Dundern, 2008. Originally *A North-Side View of Slavery. The Refugee: Or the Narratives of Fugitive Slaves in Canada. Related by Themselves, with an Account of the History and Condition of the Colored Population of Upper Canada*. Boston: J. P. Jewett, 1856.

Emerson, Ralph Waldo. "The American Scholar." In *The Essential Writings of Ralph Waldo Emerson*, edited by Brooks Atkinson. New York: Modern Library, 2000.

———. "Nature." In *The Essential Writings of Ralph Waldo Emerson*, edited by Brooks Atkinson. New York: Modern Library, 2000.

Gottlieb, Robert. *Forcing the Spring: The Transformation of the American Environmental Movement*. Washington DC: Island Press, 1993.

Gould, Rebecca Kneale. *At Home in Nature: Modern Homesteading and Spiritual Practice in America*. Berkeley: University of California Press, 2005.

Haraway, Donna. "The Persistence of Vision." In *Writing on the Body: Female Embodiment and Feminist Theory*, edited by Katie Conroy, Nadia Medina, and Sarah Stanbury. New York: Columbia University Press, 1993.

Jenkins, Willis. *The Future of Ethics: Sustainability, Social Justice, and Religious Creativity*. Washington DC: Georgetown University Press, 2013.

Kolodny, Annette. "Letting Go Our Grand Obsessions: Notes Toward a New Literary History of the American Frontiers." *American Literature* 64, no. 1 (1992): 1–18.

Pratt, Mary Louise. "Arts of the Contact Zone." *Profession* (1991): 33–40.

Ruffin, Kimberly N. *Black on Earth: African American Ecoliterary Traditions*. Athens: University of Georgia Press, 2010.

Sánchez-Eppler, Karen. *Touching Liberty: Abolition, Feminism, and the Politics of the Body*. Berkeley: University of California Press, 1993.

Sandler, Ronald, and Phaedra C. Pezzullo, eds. *Environmental Justice and Environmentalism: The Social Justice Challenge to the Environmental Movement*. Cambridge MA: MIT Press, 2007.

Taylor, Dorceta E. "The State of Diversity in Environmental Organizations: Mainstream NGOS, Foundations, and Government Agencies." Green 2.0, July 2014. https://diversegreen.org/wp-content/uploads/2021/01/FullReport_Green2.0_FINAL.pdf.

Thoreau, Henry David. *Walden*. Princeton NJ: Princeton University Press, 2004.

———. "Walking." In *The Essays of Henry David Thoreau*, edited by Lewis Hyde. New York: North Point, 2002.

Turner, Frederick Jackson. *Rereading Frederick Jackson Turner: "The Significance of the Frontier in American History" and Other Essays.* New York: Holt, 1994.

Walker, Theodore, Jr. "African-American Resources for a More Inclusive Liberation Theology." In *This Sacred Earth: Religion, Nature, Environment,* edited by Roger S. Gottlieb. New York: Routledge, 2004.

Warner, Michael. *The Letters of the Republic: Publication and the Public Sphere in Eighteenth-Century America.* Cambridge MA: Harvard University Press, 1990.

White, Evelyn. "Black Women and the Wilderness." In *The Stories That Shape Us: Contemporary Women Write about the West,* edited by Teresa Jordan and James R. Hepworth. New York: W. W. Norton, 1995.

Wood, Gordon S. *The Creation of the American Republic, 1776–1787.* Chapel Hill: University of North Carolina Press, 1998.

10

Glen Canyon Dam, Rainbow Bridge, and Hole-in-the-Rock

Diversifying Environmentalisms and the Struggle over "Sacred" Landmarks in the American West

ERIKA MARIE BSUMEK

Glen Canyon Dam and the waters of Lake Powell have been ongoing sites of controversy between states, federal agencies, and environmental activists. In 1956, Congress passed legislation approving the Bureau of Reclamation's proposal to construct a massive dam on the Utah/Arizona border.[1] Eventually, environmentalists like the Sierra Club's most visible leaders, who had initially agreed to support the dam in a bid to kill the construction of a dam in Dinosaur National Monument, came to oppose the construction of a dam at Glen Canyon and argued it marred the area's natural beauty, eroded alluvial and riverbank ecosystems, and endangered one of the world's largest known natural bridges, Rainbow Bridge.[2] While much has been written on the debate surrounding Glen Canyon Dam, the role of the Sierra Club, and the environmental impact of the Colorado River Storage Project Act, little attention has been paid to the crucial role that members of the Navajo Tribal Council and Indigenous residents from the Navajo Mountain area played in later controversies surrounding the completion of the dam and the ultimate effect that the waters of Lake Powell would have on culturally significant, spiritual landmarks.

In the 1950s, Navajo (Diné) politicians were instrumental in helping politicians from Utah, Colorado, New Mexico, and Wyoming win the congressional support they would need to get the dam built. More than twenty years later, however, Navajo residents from the Navajo Mountain area fought to get a key provision of that legislation upheld—that provision stipulated that "as part of the Glen Canyon unit, the Secretary of the Interior shall take adequate protective measures to preclude the impairment of the Rainbow Bridge National Monument [RBNM]."[3] Years earlier, the Bureau of Reclamation (BOR) had, in part, gained the Navajo Tribal Council's support for the dam's construction with such assurances. In the 1970s, when it became clear that Lake Powell's waters would reach not just the edges of RBNM but Rainbow Bridge itself, Navajos Lamar Badoni, Betty Holiday, Jessie Yazzi Black, and Begay Bitsinnie—along with the Shonto, Navajo Mountain, and Inscription House Chapters of the Navajo Nation—entered into an alliance with environmentalists and turned to the courts to protect Rainbow Bridge and their gods from the waters of Glen Canyon Dam's reservoir, Lake Powell, and the tourists it brought to the arch.[4]

This chapter examines how different groups claimed cultural authority over Rainbow Bridge through settlement, proximity, recreational activities, heritage tourism, and their use of the natural sandstone arch as a sacred space in order to maintain or gain economic and political control of the landscape. Known as Tsé Naní' áhígíí (rock span) to Navajos, the majestic rock arch had long been sacred space for the region's Indigenous populations, including Navajos, Utes, Hopis, and Paiutes who not only used the site to perform specific ceremonies but also considered the arch itself culturally significant and sacred.[5] By the 1950s, Mormon recreationists laid claim to the arch by linking it to 1881 Mormon colonization efforts that occurred near the arch—at a location called "Hole-in-the-Rock." Thus, Tsé Naní' áhígíí / Rainbow Bridge became part of Latter-day Saints' ancestral heritage. When traveling to the region, Latter-day Saint (LDS) tourists not only celebrated their own cultural ties to it; they co-opted and appropriated Indigenous spirituality for their own purposes in the process. They were not alone in doing so. By the 1970s, environmental activists decided that the best way to stop Glen Canyon Dam from filling to capacity was to recognize the arch's cultural importance as a religious site. Woven throughout this chapter is a discussion of how different groups—LDS river runners, Navajo Nation leaders, Diné religious leaders (hatáli), environmental activists, BOR officials, and eventually, the Tenth Circuit Court leveraged, invoked, or contested the idea of sacred space as a geographical category and a cultural symbol that warranted protection. The limits of such invocations illustrate how the category of "sacred space" became a crucial tool in the struggle over the meaning and future use of regional water and landscapes—as well as who would get to control access to them, use them, and ultimately define them.

Glen Canyon Dam and Lake Powell, the reservoir it created, are two of the more remarkable man-made features of the arid landscape spanning the Utah-Arizona border. The 750-foot-high dam, approved by Congress in early 1956 and constructed in the late 1950s through the mid-1960s, irrevocably altered the flow of the powerful Colorado River. Among environmentalists, Glen Canyon is often cast as a kind of ecological sacrifice zone by activists like David Brower who claimed, "Glen Canyon died in 1963, and I was partly responsible for its death." In 1963, the Sierra Club memorialized the canyon in an award-winning book titled *The Place No One Knew: Glen Canyon on the Colorado*.[6]

Yet people did know Glen Canyon. Local Indigenous populations had used and revered the canyon along with other notable landscape features for generations prior to the Sierra Club's assertion that the Glen Canyon region was unknown. Navajos, Utes, Paiutes, and Hopis knew it well, and some of their most sacred sites are in, or are in close proximity to, the canyon and the dam bisecting it.[7] Knowledge and reverence of place, however, did not mean that all the region's Indigenous peoples were unwilling to embrace the technology that would alter the face of the familiar red-sandstone walls of the canyon. In fact, Navajo Tribal Council leaders initially supported the idea of the dam. Tribal leaders anticipated that it would bring much-needed economic development and water to the reservation as the dam's power generation helped electrify and irrigate the region and stimulated an infusion of tourist dollars through Navajo-run concessions.

A failure to recognize this history contributes to a pervasive erasure of Native American engagement with technology, infrastructure, and politics and their roles in constructing both the "natural" and the built environment. It also reifies a narrative where Indigenous peoples were estranged from either modernity or obstructions to it (or even oblivious of it).[8] Indigenous residents of the Colorado Plateau were neither. Until recently little has been published about Native Americans and their relationship to Glen Canyon before, during, and after the dam's construction. Much of what has been written usually focuses on the "Indian ruins" flooded by the dam rather than how contemporary Native Americans engaged with the controversies surrounding the dam from the time it was initially proposed in the 1920s through its construction in the 1950s and early 1960s to the radical aftermath of the region's hydrological transformation in 1970s and beyond.[9] Navajos in particular have an ongoing historical relationship—that is both spiritually and economically minded—with the rivers, canyons, natural bridges, and irrigation schemes that formed and reformed the contours of the larger Colorado Plateau.

The complexities of Navajos' relationship with Tsé Naní' áhígíí were, in part, outlined in a contentious court case, *Badoni v. Higginson* (1977, 1980), that sought to balance the rights of non-Native boaters whose rowdy visits to the bridge were at odds with the wishes and rights of Navajo spiritual leaders who wished to practice site-specific religious ceremonies away from the prying eyes and raucous noise of those tourists. This fairly straightforward plea encompassed a larger set of entangled issues. For many Navajos, concepts of nature, religion, self-determination, and indigeneity could not be neatly separated.[10] Arguments over the use and perceived desecration of Tsé Naní' áhígíí have been viewed through what legal scholar Marcia Yablon and others call the "issue of control" when sacred environments become tourist attractions.[11] Beyond that, the case sought to cap the rising waters of Lake Powell, pitting the Bureau of Reclamation against a hastily formed coalition of Navajos and environmentalists arguing to protect the practice of Indigenous religion on lands controlled by the federal government.

Sacred Sites, Prayers, and Cultural Misunderstanding

Tsé Naní' áhígíí, or Rainbow Bridge, is one of many geological formations that Navajos view as sacred—and it is also part of a federal monument. The Rainbow Bridge National Monument, founded in 1910, encompasses a 160-acre tract in Southern Utah and is entirely surrounded by the Navajo Nation's reservation. Often promoted as the "world's largest known natural bridge," Rainbow Bridge is frequently called one of the seven wonders of the world. The arch itself stands 290 feet high and spans 277 feet across the river.[12] Given its size, it has been an object of fascination for non-Indigenous peoples since Byron Cummings and William Boone Douglass raced to document its "discovery" in 1909.[13] Because of its fairly remote location on the Colorado Plateau, only committed explorers, hikers, and boaters made the arduous 17.5-mile trek that was required to reach the bridge up until the 1960s. Once Glen Canyon Dam was finished and Lake Powell made the natural arch accessible by boat, countless non-Indigenous visitors made the trip and sometimes engaged in offensive behavior such as swimming naked under the arch, partying, and littering in the adjacent area.

While archaeologist Byron Cummings and surveyor William B. Douglass argued over who officially "discovered" Rainbow Bridge in 1909, oral histories and archaeological studies demonstrate that the region's Indigenous peoples utilized, visited, and practiced religious ceremonies there for centuries before the supposed discovery date. For Navajos, Tsé Naní' áhígí along with some other rock formations are "actual incarnate forms of Navajo gods." Given the bridge's cultural significance, hatáli have long performed ceremonies on or around the bridge.[14] Such ceremonies are rooted in the fact that Tsé Naní' áhígíí is linked to Navajo origin stories and is an integral part of the story of the Hero Twins, the sons of White Shell Woman and the Sun. According to Navajo creation stories, the Hero Twins are said to have traveled across the western oceans, using a magic rainbow to bridge great distances in order to visit their mother. Later, a different set of Navajo Holy Beings placed the magic rainbow in the safest place they could imagine: Bridge Canyon, below Naatsis'áán, or Navajo Mountain. Once in place, the rainbow turned to stone, creating Tsé Naní' áhígíí.[15] Comparing non-Native and Native understanding of the bridge provides an example of a deeper cultural chasm separating the two groups. Non-Natives have tended to see the arch as a "natural" formation, and much scientific study has gone into explaining how the arch was formed. Navajos, on the other hand, see the arch as intentionally placed in its specific location by Navajo Holy Beings. Hopi religion also connects the bridge to creation stories.[16] In short, we can see diverse "environmentalisms" or ways of engaging with, and thinking about, nature by contrasting Native and non-Native understandings of this specific place.

According to oral interviews with residents from the Navajo Mountain community, the rock span was an "instrument of spiritual and religious significance" for Navajos. For instance, the Navajo gods Monster Slayer and Born for Water were raised in the cradle of Bridge Creek, with the stone rainbow forming the handle of their cradle-board.[17] There is obviously much more to the oral histories than can be related here, but these brief hints demonstrate how the bridge is connected to Navajo religion and provide a glimpse of the importance of the site in Navajo cosmology.[18] Navajos from the Navajo Mountain area, for example, also told interviewers that the lessons referenced in the origin story are meant to serve as teachings for the community and to link generations to each other. David Sproul, who wrote an administrative history of the Rainbow Bridge National Monument, learned that "the specifics of worship, including what specific substances were offered to which gods or the details of various ceremonies are told from Navajo parents and grandparents to Navajo youth," not to non-Navajos.[19] Community members felt, and feel, that Tsé Naní' áhígíí is of particular importance to them. The existence of the bridge helps them maintain their culture and sustains their community—in the same way the Sistine Chapel might help Catholics perpetuate and pass down their history, culture, and traditions to their children.[20]

Recognition of the Navajo origin stories does not mean that Navajos' relationships to the bridge are limited to the distant past. The bridge figures into more recent Navajo history as well. It is, for instance, one of the places where many of the Navajos who escaped Kit Carson's violent campaign to destroy Navajo homelands and force Navajos to their imprisonment at Bosque Redondo fled.[21] Since the bridge provided fugitive Navajos with a hiding place, many saw it as a sign that Navajo gods were, in the words of one Navajo elder, "watching over them." Given the horrors of that particular episode in Navajo history, it is not surprising that the Protectionway ceremony is one of the most commonly held ceremonies at Tsé Naní' áhígíí.[22] Cummings and Douglass, the scholars who sprinted to document their "discovery" of the massive natural arch, found evidence that Indigenous peoples used the bridge when they observed a shrine on the north side of the bridge in 1909. Navajo Mountain residents reported that such practices date back long before the 160-acre monument was established, without consultation with Navajos or other Indigenous peoples, by President Taft in 1910. Other ceremonies, such as the Blessingway and rain-requesting ceremonies, were (and are) also held there. In 1977, RBNM staff reported that local Navajos continued to leave "prayer offerings" for the Holy People at Tsé Naní' áhígíí and surrounding areas.[23]

Indigenous peoples were not the only ones who revered Rainbow Bridge. Latter-day Saint recreationists also traveled to the bridge prior to the dam's construction and imbued it with spiritual significance. However, the overall purpose and behavior of such groups were both dramatically different and culturally distinct from that of Navajos and other Indigenous people who worshipped there. Even though LDS visitors did not venerate the bridge as inherently sacred, they did link the structure to the progenitors of their religion. Between 1948 and 1963, for instance, a sizable number of Mormon tourists made an annual trip to Rainbow Bridge, traveling sections of the Colorado and San Juan Rivers by boats to get there.[24] The purpose of these trips was both spiritual and recreational. Members from a Mormon ward located in South Salt Lake formed a recreational club called SOCOTWA, named after their home church, the South Cottonwood Ward. By the 1950s, over a thousand people had joined the group and the organization owned thirty inflatable rafts. According to historian and river runner Roy Webb, this meant they could "have half a dozen trips on the water at one time." Glen Canyon was an especially popular destination for group members seeking adventure. "If you could get there," notes Webb, "you were home free. No rangers, no rules, no regulations, almost nothing save for scenery."[25] Such trips were centered around Latter-day Saint history, values, and faith.

Latter-day Saint Recreationists, Hole-in-the-Rock, and Rainbow Bridge

Members of the SOCOTWA were self-proclaimed "river rats" who went on the trips in order to retrace the routes of early Latter-day Saint missionaries who settled areas surrounding the Colorado and Escalante rivers and sought to convert local Indigenous peoples, whom they called Lamanites.[26] For instance, during a 1958 trip, one SOCOTWA group stopped at a location below a culturally significant landmark named Hole-in-the-Rock, which had been named by members of the late nineteenth-century LDS San Juan Missionary Expedition. After steering their boats to a campsite, SOCOTWA members sang a variety of songs while they watched their "crew" perform various stunts as young people flirted with each other. The evening culminated with a retelling of how, years earlier, LDS settlers reckoned with the region's harsh terrain in order to settle it. One of the guides who also served as an LDS bishop, Merlin Shaw, told the group how the "Mormon Pioneers of the San Juan Valley crossed the river at Hole-in-the-Rock on January 26, 1881." This SOCOTWA tour group, and many others like it, learned that it was at Hole-in-the-Rock that early missionaries had lowered "twenty six wagons . . . over the cliff on the first day" and that it took 250 Mormon pioneers "to build a road down a steep canyon, face to the edge of the river" in order travel

2,000 feet down to the Escalante River and cross to the opposite riverbank. During the lecture, the religious recreationists reported gazing up at the cliffs and imagining what a harrowing ordeal it must have been for their theological ancestors to get down to the river.[27] The following year, in 1959, another SOCOTWA group also stopped on the river below the Hole-in-the-Rock and "retraced the trail" of the "Mormon pioneers" by making the steep climb up to the opening in the canyon wall. In doing so, they "marveled at how they [their LDS ancestors] had blasted out the crevice which is in the hole in the rock down which to lower with ropes their wagons and animals." The route, which had taken expedition members three months to carve out of the sandstone, could now be traversed by SOCOTWA members in an hour. Mormon tourists on such trips noted that their "respect for the courage and faith of those Mormon pioneers" only increased along the way.[28]

Guided SOCOTWA river trips tended to be quite large and devoted to worshipping God while enjoying nature and its links to Mormon history. The June 1959 "Glen Canyon-Colorado River Expedition" included thirty-four people. Mornings and evenings on the river started with a prayer of thanks, a blessing of the food, and a prayer for each traveler's safety on the river. As the group made its way down the river, they made periodic stops in order to marvel at the "towering heights of the beautiful tapestry" of the sandstone walls. At key moments, they would stop the boats in order to hike to natural pools to swim and "be refreshed" or photograph "Indian hieroglyphics at the bottom of a smooth vertical canyon walls."[29] Sometimes the group did more than leave footprints and take photos.

As SOCOTWA members noted, the "highlight of the trip . . . was the hike to Rainbow Bridge."[30] In the middle of their week-long journey down the river, a June 1950 group, for instance, prepared to make the fourteen-mile trek to Rainbow Bridge through the "spectacular Aztec Canyon," which the group also colloquially called "the Canyon of the Gods." Such terminology indicates that SOCOTWA members may have been appropriating Native American culture in some way, but they were also layering nonphysical meaning onto the landscape. Describing the hike itself, the group's official diarist reported that the trekkers were awed by the canyon's "sheer walls, fantastic formations, bath tubs, tributary canyons and fun spots" as well as a feature that the group dubbed the "Dairy Queen Rock" about halfway up the canyon. Heartier members of the group used fixed ropes "to climb a buttress on one side of the bridge."[31] In order to make it to the top of Rainbow Bridge itself, the group's leader directed his followers through a series of foot and finger holds that had been chiseled by a previous expedition, but he had positioned himself thirty feet above the group. Using steel rings that had been set in the sandstone, "those who wished" could then lower "themselves to one end of the top of the bridge and then [hike] to the top of its great arch." Once there, they signed their names in the stone and then returned to those waiting below.[32] When they inscribed their names into the landscape, they did so to memorialize their trip and validate their claim to Rainbow Bridge. They had not only seen it; they had climbed it and gotten closer to other members of their church in the process. Such strenuous activities indicated that this mixed-age group of travelers was devoted to fully experiencing and embracing nature.

Besides swimming and hiking, worship was a regular feature of SOCOTWA expeditions. On a Sunday night in 1959, a member of the tour group named Oman "conducted a sacrament meeting in a grotto a few steps from camp." Making do with what they had, the group improvised and turned a canteen into the sacred vessel from which they drank the water taken as part of their sacrament. As per Mormon religious practice, the devoted boaters then bore their own testimony, relating their conversion stories and missionary experiences to the wider group. Recording such events, the official diarist noted, "Under the stars in this narrow canyon and with perfect attending and order, the meeting was very impressive and inspirational."[33] When the group experienced the misfortune of losing a few of their boats that were towing the food and other supplies the group needed, they turned to prayer, realizing that "without those three boats we had problems."[34] If prayer marked unfortunate occurrences during the middle of the trip, it was followed by a kind of playful ceremonialism as the end of their time on the river grew closer.

By melding religious practice with recreation, the Mormons who went on these trips sought to reaffirm their faith communally. While most of the prayers SOCOTWA "rats" offered were sincere, the group was not above engaging in rituals of a less-than-serious nature. As the end of the trip neared, one of the group's leaders "conducted the final river ceremony," which consisted of "offering to the river god Yogi an article of clothing." When finished with "this appeasement ritual" to their imagined river deity, the group packed up their rafts, loaded their trucks, and proceeded to the Glen Canyon damsite, where they met their bus and spent a little bit of time observing the construction of the structure before continuing onto Page, Arizona. There, they not only saw the new dam being constructed; they also purchased "ice cold soda pop and ice cream." The unnamed diarist who recounted the groups' activities concluded, "Our expedition was a marvelous experience," and they subsequently complemented the leadership, food, and congeniality of the group, noting that the "river was fascinating; the side trips were varied, amazing, and beautiful."[35] Other SOCOTWA groups reported holding Sunday school in a beautiful rock grotto "called 'the Tabernacle,'" noting that a "sincere spiritual service was enjoyed by all."[36] SOCOTWA "rats" considered the reassertion of their faith in the landscape an important part of these trips. In short, while being out in nature visiting important ancestral landmarks and celebrating both their own God and the land meant that the SOCOTWA trips enabled boaters to create and celebrate sacred spaces, they also provided those who went on them with a form of spiritual renewal.

Part of that assertion of faith meant trying to reckon with the region's pre-LDS past. In so doing, the "rats" frequently ruminated on Native American "superstitions," evoked their own mythologized river spirits, and hypothesized about the region's Indigenous population. During a 1958 trip, one SOCOTWA rafter demonstrated a tacit if simplistic understanding of Navajo cosmology by noting that "the Indians worshipped it as a God and refused to go under" Rainbow Bridge.[37] Meanwhile, SOCOTWA guides created Yogi, the "mock" river god who seemingly required sacrifices. Deween Canning and Barbara Cook, the "official historians" of the 1959 May 30–June 6 trip declared that "Yogi had another victim" when the group's official flag "flew the coop." Flags were not the only thing that faced risk on the river. John C. Josephson, from Salt Lake City, learned that lighthearted play could easily turn dangerous. After he broke his leg in an attempt to test a river swing, he suffered for four days until the trip came to an end. In addition to his physical pain, he lamented that he "couldn't carry out his idle threats of throwing the girls over the cliff as a Moqui [Hopi] sacrifice." Once the group reached Lake Canyon, those who were able-bodied hiked up to an "old out-moded dwelling that existed hundreds of years before [it] was found against the mountain wall." The "explorers" speculated about who built it, investigated the structure itself, and then collected nearby pottery shards and flint pieces. A few of the more curious "rats" crawled through a small opening to explore the interior of the "Moqui dwelling." The trip's official historians concluded, "Not much history is known of this strange Indian tribe. Some say they were of a giant stature, others believe they must have been midgets."[38] Clearly, the fact that Hopi residents of the region were still very much alive and well and living nearby did not seem to register with the boaters. Nor did the fact that Hopi history existed in a number of different accessible forms. Ultimately, asides about the original inhabitants of the region were meant to demonstrate humor—but they also reveal the less-than-serious nature with which they viewed Indigenous peoples and their religious beliefs.

In this case, LDS tourists understood "the sacred" through their own cultural lens. This limited perspective made it difficult for them to fully respect Navajo or Hopi religious beliefs. The belittling of Indigenous cultures, ceremonies, and respectful treatment of Rainbow Bridge occurred alongside SOCOTWA's reenactment of key LDS historical events. Although SOCOTWA represents a small subgroup of some of the first non-Indigenous tourists to use the river as a tourist destination, the flippant way in which they contemplated and treated Indigenous sacred spaces would become all too common among the rising number of recreationists who followed them. SOCOTWA trips demonstrate how Mormons interacted with the riparian environment and layered their own meaning onto the canyon and river through their actions. But it also exposes them as members of the racially dominant society who peeled away and dismissed the layers of meaning Indigenous peoples had attached to the landscape. In so doing, they cast the region's Indigenous peoples as members of "strange" unknown "tribes" of days gone by.

This kind of environmental engagement and Indigenous estrangement reflected the ways spaces, landmarks, and landscapes were racialized through a celebration, and continuation, of settler colonialism. In short, some LDS recreationists claimed the rivers, canyons, and natural bridges as their own sacred spaces because of the actions of their ancestors, the members of the San Juan Missionary Expedition. Likewise, they dismissed Indigenous claims—both contemporary and ancestral—to those same spaces through their unwillingness to acknowledge the presence or claims of contemporary Indigenous peoples. Though packaged in playful rhetoric, such actions reflect one way that Indigenous ties to the environment could be dismissed. The kinds of attitudes we see expressed by participants in SOCOTWA trips would eventually be expressed in more serious formats, particularly in the formal proceedings of the Tenth Circuit Court.

Navajos, Tourism, and Protection of Sacred Lands

While SOCOTWA tourists certainly made their mark on the area with their river trips, they were not the only ones who supported tourism to the area. The fact that some Navajo leaders supported Glen Canyon Dam, and related development, hinged on the fact that they believed that visitors to the dam would bring additional revenue into Navajo coffers. By 1969, Chairman Nakai spoke in support of a proposal to expand federal control in the area through the establishment of a "Glen Canyon National Recreation Area," stating, "We are excited with the prospect of building up our tourist trade through these prospective recreational areas. This too will bring employment to Navajo people." Since the opening of the dam, he noted that "our roads are becoming choked with campers and trailers seeking a hideout far from the noise . . . of our crowded cities."[39] The fact that Navajo leaders embraced the creation of an official recreation area reflected their ongoing hope of engagement with the tourist industry. It was a relationship they wished to expand on their own terms. In particular, they did not want to lose access and control of their sacred sites.[40]

In 1969 many Navajos still believed it possible that Tsé Naní' áhígíí could be protected by the construction of a diversion dam *and* that Navajo jobs would be created through the establishment of Navajo-run concessions on the shores of Lake Powell and in surrounding recreation areas. In the 1950s, the Navajo Tribal Council had taken the lead in efforts to support Navajo citizens who wanted to run their own tourist venues. They not only saw the development of Navajo businesses as moneymaking endeavors but also viewed the establishment of them as a matter of self-determination and subsistence.[41] Their efforts were based on careful study of the shifting travel patterns linked to the dam and its reservoir. By the 1960s, both Navajo and non-Navajo experts anticipated a dramatic rise in the number of tourists in the area. Dr. Angus Woodbury—a retired zoology and ecology professor at the University of Utah, an expert on the region's fauna, and an eventual opponent of the proposed Rainbow Bridge diversion dam—was commissioned to write a prospectus on Navajo National Monument for the Department of the Interior. In it, he anticipated that the number of tourists to the area in proximity to the region and to Navajo National Monument in particular "will increase travel from 4,600 visitors in 1962 to an anticipated 115,000 in 1972."[42] Leaders of the Tribal Council were well aware of such figures, studied them, and pushed for additional Navajo-controlled economic development—as well as partnerships with non-Navajo business owners—in the region.[43]

Yet even as leaders of the Navajo Nation continually extolled the possibility of "economic opportunities" from tourism and related endeavors, it was clear that they did not speak for all Navajos. A subset of Navajos who lived in the vicinity of Navajo Mountain and Tsé Naní' áhígíí, for instance, began to express dismay at the jump in regional tourism and the resulting land and water use practices. As the canyon beneath the bridge filled with water, many local residents feared that the environments linked to their sacred sites would be destroyed. Their anxieties were justified when high water levels brought motorboats filled with tourists to Rainbow Bridge in dramatically increasing numbers. By the early 1970s, hundreds of tourists visited the bridge every day.[44] These tourists either ignored or remained ignorant of the fact that the Navajos considered the bridge a sacred space—in much the same way SOCOTWA visitors had. One touring company ran fifty-six-foot luxury boats accommodating up to eighty-eight people from Wahweap Marina to Rainbow Bridge on a regular basis. By 1980, one hundred thousand people per year were making the trip.[45] These groups did not just hike to the bridge and mock Indigenous religion as superstition as had SOCOTWA members; they also played loud music, drank copious amounts of beer and alcohol under the arch, and swam naked in the waters below the bridge. Despite the National Park Service's (NPS) efforts to prohibit swimming under the bridge and to inform tourists that such behavior was offensive to local Navajos, tourists continued to come and disregard the information provided by the NPS.[46]

Such activities increasingly antagonized Navajo spiritual leaders—a fact that did not go unnoted by the Sierra Club and Friends of the Earth (FOE). Both environmental organizations hoped that Navajo concerns could be manipulated to force the BOR to keep the water level of Glen Canyon Dam from filling to capacity and inundating RBNM. After losing an initial case in 1973 to protect Rainbow Bridge on secular and scientific grounds, the Sierra Club and FOE refiled their case and supported a new court case in cooperation with Navajo elders from the Navajo Mountain area who wished to limit the water level and thus curtail the actions of boaters at the stone rainbow on religious grounds. In a February 1974 memo sent to David Brower, the founder of Friends of the Earth, a legal strategist, noted that the

> FOE et. al. will ask for a petition for Rehearing from the Supreme Court using as 'new evidence' the fact that the Indians' interest(s) have not been properly presented in our previous appeal. One day after our petition is filed the Navajos (a tribe plus seven individual Navajos including a number of medicine men) will file an appeal of their own. They will 'scold' us for ignoring them previously but will ask the court for the same ruling we do. (Owen [Olpin, our lawyer] thinks this scolding is all to the good and will appeal to some judges who are more sensitive to Indian than environmental problems.)[47]

Not coincidentally, in September of 1974, eight Navajos, three of whom were recognized hatáli (spiritual leaders), sued the BOR, the NPS, and the Department of the Interior over the protection of Tsé Naní' áhígíí. This case came to be known as *Badoni v. Higginson* (1977, 1980) and the stated goal of the plaintiffs was to get people to stop "acting in such a matter as to destroy and desecrate the Navajo gods and sacred sites threatened by the rising waters of Lake Powell and by the influx of tourists."[48] They based their claim on First Amendment guarantees of the freedom of religion and did not separate religious claims from environmental ones.

Two court rulings on this case reveal some of the ways in which religion and sacred practices were used in the struggle over control of this space. In 1977, the Utah State District Court ruled that the Navajo plaintiffs had no property interest in RBNM because it was federally managed land. Thus, "the court feels that the lack of a property interest is determinative of the First Amendment question and agrees with defendants (the BOR) that that plaintiffs have no cognizable claim under the circumstances presented." The phrase "of a property interest" is an interesting one, since Navajos clearly had an ongoing interest in the "property" or environment in question: Rainbow Bridge. Moreover, the land surrounding Rainbow Bridge had been removed from Paiutes and Navajo control, with no tribal consultation, in order to create the monument. Then the court endorsed "as a persuasive hypothetical situation" an example that the defendants had offered of a hypothetical "plaintiff who petitioned a federal court to restrict public access to the Lincoln Memorial because he had had a[n] intense religious experience there."[49] Legal scholar Howard Stambor has concluded that "the facile acceptance of the defendant's hypothetical situation . . . ignores the difference between Indians seeking to protect their religion and the situation described in the hypothetical."[50] Clearly, the court failed to recognize that the land itself could be sacred and that the interest Navajos might have in it would extend beyond the notion of "ownership."

The defendants in the Badoni case, the NPS, the Bureau of Reclamation, and the Department of Interior did more in the case than fight to fill the dam to capacity. They sought to establish *cultural authority* over the site. To do so, the government diminished Navajo spiritual claims to the landscape and what it represented—Navajo gods and Navajo religion. Ultimately the Tenth Circuit Court of Appeals recognized the core issue for Navajos when they noted "with respect to the government action of impounding water in Lake Powell" that the plaintiffs objected to the "drowning of the Navajo gods, the increased tourist presence attributable to the level at which the lake is kept, and the denial of access to the prayer spot now under water." The court later "agree[d] with the trial court that the government's interest in maintaining the capacity for Lake Powell at a level that intrudes into the Monument outweighs the plaintiffs' religious interest."[51] In sum, the court ruled that the interests of the energy and tourist industries—along with the recreational pursuits of boaters—outweighed the interest of the Navajo spiritual leaders and the environmentalists who sought to prevent the flooding of a site that was sacred to Indigenous people.

The Sierra Club had anticipated a line of argument that evoked sacred spaces almost fifteen years earlier. In 1966 in response to the publication of a glossy magazine printed by the Bureau of Reclamation to celebrate Glen Canyon Dam and promote the construction of a proposed new dam in the Grand Canyon (see fig. 10.1), the organization took out a full-page ad in a number of major American newspapers, asking, "Should we also flood the Sistine Chapel so tourists can get nearer the ceiling?" As we can see, the ad does not reference Indigenous sacred spaces—only an iconic European space. Strangely enough, in their 1966 publication responding to the Sierra Club's ad, the BOR referenced a revered Indigenous symbol and used a "mock" totem pole to extol the beauty and accessibility of Glen Canyon. The back cover of the *Jewel of the Colorado* showed a photograph of the "Lake Powell 'Totem Pole'" (see fig. 10.2). This "totem," however, presumably showed that Glen Canyon's Lake Powell could be seen as a modern space made "primitive" by a simple rotation of the page. Once turned, the blue sky and the blue water of Lake Powell seemed to bring out the primitive character of the sandstone shoreline. Totem poles are artistic carvings made by Indigenous peoples in the Pacific Northwest that were used to document significant stories and histories of specific places, peoples, families, or communities. They are (and were) "physical manifestations of tribal stories" and a way to transmit oral stories and histories.[52] By rotating the photograph, the BOR was creating a "fake totem" pole to convey its own story and message: the dams supposedly made the region better, and there should be more of them. It also had the effect of obscuring the stories and wants of the real Indigenous people of the region.

In both the Sierra Club ad and the BOR booklet, each organization seemed to be saying that perspective matters. Were canyons and arches sacred spaces akin to the Sistine Chapel? Should they be afforded the same respect? Were they primitive, symbolic places awaiting use by the dominant society to transform them into something of value? Should the places worn away by an ancient ocean, and revered by Indigenous people, be put to use in order to generate jobs and energy and provide leisure experiences for whites? While such questions matter, both groups ignored a key group: the region's Navajo, Ute, Paiute, Puebloan, Havasupai, Hualapai, and other Indigenous peoples.

Landmarks and Layered Histories

It is interesting to note, finally, that all the different players in this particular legal environmental drama invoked tourism first to launch their various appeals to either the judicial system or the court of public opinion in order to achieve their goals. The fact that Glen Canyon Dam generated valuable hydroelectric power, at first glance, almost seems a secondary concern in the *Badoni* ruling. That both environmental groups like FOE and government agencies like BOR and NPS—the groups that managed Glen Canyon Dam and RBNM—invoked an iconic religious and tourist site, the Sistine Chapel, and an iconic Indigenous symbol, a totem pole, that held meaning for different groups (the Sistine Chapel for Catholics and totem poles for Indigenous peoples of the Pacific Northwest, Alaska, and Canada) to make Americans think about the appropriate intersection between technology and nature should not come as a surprise. A wide swath of white Americans—including many who hiked or took boats to see the magnificent Rainbow Bridge—saw nothing wrong with the fact, as Lady Bird Johnson noted at the dam's dedication, that "feats of

SHOULD WE ALSO FLOOD THE SISTINE CHAPEL SO TOURISTS CAN GET NEARER THE CEILING?

EARTH began four billion years ago and Man two million. The Age of Technology, on the other hand, is hardly a hundred years old, and on our time chart we have been generous to give it even the little line we have.

It seems to us hasty, therefore, during this blip of time, for Man to think of directing his fascinating new tools toward altering irrevocably the forces which made him. Nonetheless, in these few brief years among four billion, wilderness has all but disappeared. And now these:

1) There are proposals *still* before Congress to "improve" Grand Canyon. If they succeed, two dams could back up artificial lakes into 93 miles of canyon gorge. This would benefit tourists in power boats, it is argued, who would enjoy viewing the canyon wall more closely. (See headline.) Submerged underneath the tourists would be part of the most revealing single page of earth's history. The lakes would be as deep as 600 feet (deeper for example, than all but a handful of New York buildings are high) but in a century, silting would have replaced the water with that much mud, wall to wall.

There is no part of the wild Colorado River, the Grand Canyon's sculptor, that would not be maimed.

Tourist recreation, as a reason for the dams, is in fact an afterthought. The Bureau of Reclamation, which has backed them, calls the dams "cash registers." It expects they'll make money by sale of commercial power.

They will not provide anyone with water.

2) In Northern California, during only the last 115 years, nearly *all* the private virgin redwood forests have been cut down.

Where nature's tallest living things have stood silently since the age of the dinosaurs, there is, incredibly, argument against a proposed park at Redwood Creek which would save a mere 2% of the virgin growth that was once there. For, having cut so much and taken the rest for granted, the lumber companies are eager to get on with business. They see little reason why they should not.

The companies have said tourists want only enough roadside trees for the snapping of photos. They offered to spare trees for this purpose, and not much more. The result would remind you of the places on your face you missed while you were shaving.

3) And up the Hudson, there are plans for a power complex —a plant, transmission lines, and a reservoir near and on Storm King Mountain—effectively destroying one of the last wild and high and beautiful spots near New York City.

4) A proposal to flood a region in Alaska as large as Lake Erie would eliminate at once the breeding grounds of more wildlife than conservationists have preserved in history.

5) In San Francisco, real estate interests have for years been filling a bay that made the city famous, putting tract houses over the fill; and now there's a new idea — still more fill, enough for an air cargo terminal as big as Manhattan.

There exists today a mentality which can conceive such destruction, giving commerce as ample reason. For 74 years, the Sierra Club (now with 48,000 members) has opposed that mentality. But now, when even Grand Canyon is endangered, we are at a critical moment in time.

This generation will decide if something untrammelled and free remains, as testimony we had love for those who follow.

We have been taking ads, therefore, asking people to write their Congressmen and Senators; Secretary of the Interior Stewart Udall; The President; and to send us funds to continue the battle. Thousands *have* written, but meanwhile, Grand Canyon legislation *still* stands a chance of passage. More letters are needed and much more money, to help fight the notion that Man no longer needs nature.*

David Brower, Executive Director
Sierra Club
Mills Tower, San Francisco

☐ Please send me more details on how I may help.
☐ Here is a donation of $_____ to continue your effort to keep the public informed.
☐ Send me "Time and the River Flowing," famous four color book which tells the complete story of Grand Canyon, and why T. Roosevelt said, "leave it as it is." ($25.00)
☐ Send me "The Last Redwoods" which tells the complete story of the opportunity as well as the destruction in the redwoods. ($17.50)
☐ I would like to be a member of the Sierra Club. Enclosed is $14.00 for entrance and first year's dues.

Name_____
Address_____
City_____ State_____ Zip_____

---

*The Sierra Club, founded in 1892 by John Muir, is nonprofit, supported by people who, like Thoreau, believe "In wildness is the preservation of the world." The club's program is nationwide, includes wilderness trips, books and films—as well as such efforts as this to protect the remnant of wilderness in the Americas. There are now twenty chapters, branch offices in New York (Biltmore Hotel), Washington (Dupont Circle Building), Los Angeles (Auditorium Building), Albuquerque, Seattle, and main office in San Francisco.

(Our previous ads, urging that readers exercise a constitutional right of petition to save Grand Canyon from two dams which would have flooded it, produced an unprecedented reaction by the Internal Revenue Service threatening our tax deductible status. IRS called the ads a "substantial" effort to "influence legislation." Undefined, these terms leave organizations like ours at the mercy of administrative whim. [The question has not been raised with organizations that favor Grand Canyon dams.] So we cannot now promise that contributions you send us are deductible — pending result of what may be a long legal battle.)

FIG. 10.1. An ad that appeared in the *New York Times*. Courtesy of the Sierra Club (William E. Colby Memorial Library, 1966).

FIG. 10.2. Bureau of Reclamation, "Totem Pole," on the back cover of *Lake Powell: Jewel of the Colorado* (Government Printing Office, 1965).

technology" (like the dam) might provide Americans with access to "untouched" corners of the Earth where people could encounter nature as a "spiritual touchstone and a recreation asset."[53] SOCOTWA rafters, for instance, greatly valued Rainbow Bridge and their experiences on the river—and their recreation became a way to express their faith in their religion through nature.

While we do not know how SOCOTWA members who floated the river in the late 1950s felt about the key issues in the *Badoni* case, we do know that they came to view Hole-in-the-Rock as worthy of spiritual pilgrimage. Along the way, Rainbow Bridge became a notable tourist destination where they worshipped, prayed, and played. In doing so, they appreciated it as a stunning natural bridge, yet they did not fully view it as a sacred space. They could worship out in nature, but the landscapes themselves were not worthy of worship. We do, however, know that they stopped and viewed the dam as it was being constructed. While there, they ate ice cream and drank soda pop. The diarist who recorded that stop offered no thoughts about the dam, perhaps indicating that they viewed it as a normal extension of their pioneer ancestors' vision of the West.

Navajos, Mormon tourists, and government agencies had all, in one way or another, embraced the concept of progress at Glen Canyon Dam—yet all saw the sacred nature of the surrounding landscape through a different cultural lens and embraced different forms of environmentalism along the way. Navajos saw the advent of the dam, initially, as compatible with their religious practices and fought to keep it that way. The Navajos who pressed their case in *Badoni*, such as Lamar Badoni, saw Tsé Naní' áhígíí as natural and sacred and wanted it to be protected, as Congress had promised. In the 1880s, Mormon pioneers, fought to settle the landscape, and later generations casually venerated those endeavors by marking Hole-in-the-Rock as a pilgrimage site and, eventually, a registered historic landmark. SOCOTWA river runners found faith and fun through such environmental pilgrimages. Many still do. Today, the National Park Service notes that Hole-in-the-Rock "remains a silent monument to the faith and tenacity of those first Mormon pioneers."[54] The Mormon Historic Sites Foundation goes a step further and contends that the story of the Mormons who ventured through the hole "is one of the great stories, not only in LDS Church history, but also in the history of the West."[55] As contests over spaces such as Rainbow Bridge demonstrate, however, the history of the West and its sacred environments is one of competition, dispossession, and ultimately, reconfiguration; it is one where competing expressions of the sacred were imbued on the landscape, manipulated by environmentalists, and ignored in court. Tsé Naní' áhígíí is still sacred to many Navajos, and whether the non-Indigenous tourists who visit it recognize it as such—be they recreationists, environmentalists, or both—will not diminish the significance of the place. As a landmark, it represents the layered and contested history of the region, spanning eras of continued Indigenous habitation through the period of Mormon colonization. Debates about the arch also provide a window into the environmental controversies surrounding Glen Canyon Dam, especially those that attempted to legally define and regulate Native American spiritual practices.

Notes

Portions of this chapter previously appeared as "Legal Paradigms and Dispossession: Navajos, Environmentalists, and the Law, 1969–1980" in *The Foundations of Glen Canyon Dam* by Erika Marie Bsumek (Austin: University of Texas Press, 2023).

1. Congress passed the Colorado River Storage Project Act in 1956. Public Law 485, 84th Congress (April 11, 1956).
2. The fight over Glen Canyon has been well documented in numerous books, among them Martin, *Story That Stands*; Worster, *Rivers of Empire*; and Harvey, *Symbol of Wilderness*. On the debates surrounding the potential threat to Rainbow Bridge, see Halliday and Woodbury, "Protection of Rainbow Bridge."
3. Halliday and Woodbury, "Protection of Rainbow Bridge."
4. *Badoni*, 455 F. Supp. 641.
5. While there are numerous names for Rainbow Bridge, I use the name utilized by Long Salt in an interview with Karl W. Luckert and published in Luckert, *Navajo Mountain*, 1:40. As per Navajo linguist and scholar Anthony Webster, the translation of Tsé Naníʼ áhígíí is as follows: Tsé = "rock," Naníʼ á = "reaching (stretches) across," hí ʼ = "the one," gí = "at." So while it is also translated as "rock arch," it's closer to "rock span," than "rock arch." Private email correspondence with Dr. Anthony Webster, August 16, 2017. Regarding the sacred nature of the arch, "Rainbow Bridge and a nearby spring, prayer spot and cave have held positions of central importance in the religion of some Navajo people living in that area for at least 100 years. These shrines are regarded as the incarnate forms of Navajo gods, which provide protection and rain-giving functions." *Badoni*, 638 F.2d 172.
6. Brower, "Let the River Run." Brower also made the same claim in the introduction to Porter, *Place No One Knew*.
7. Sproul, *Bridge between Cultures*.
8. On narratives that pit American Indians and modernity against each other, see Deloria, *Indians in Unexpected Places*; Bsumek, *Indian-Made*; and Raibmon, *Authentic Indians*.
9. Fowler, *Glen Canyon Country*; Jennings and Fowler, *Glen Canyon*; Martin, *Story That Stands*; Harvey, *Symbol of Wilderness*.

10. By 1968, for instance, only two years after completion of the dam, Lake Powell attracted four hundred thousand visitors annually. See "Glen Canyon National Recreation Area."

11. Yablon, "Property Rights and Sacred Sites," 1625.

12. Numerous websites promote Rainbow Bridge as the largest natural bridge in the world. The Xianren Bridge in China has the world's longest span at 396 feet.

13. Jett, "Great 'Race'"; Weber and deBuys, "Rainbow Bridge."

14. Stambor, "Manifest Destiny."

15. Sproul, *Bridge between Cultures*, 49. Other Holy Men followed in their tracks in order to visit White Shell Woman, in part to counter disharmony. Eventually, those who sought out White Shell Woman, returned to the Navajo mountain area (another sacred geographic marker).

16. Sproul, *Bridge between Cultures*, 29; On scientific and geological studies of Rainbow Bridge, see National Resource Report, "Rainbow Bridge," 19–27.

17. Sproul, *Bridge between Cultures*, 49.

18. Kelley and Francis, *Navajo Sacred Places*.

19. Sproul, *Bridge between Cultures*, 50.

20. Luckert, *Navajo Mountain*. All the Navajo residents of the Navajo mountain community interviewed for a National Park Service administrative history in the 1970s detailed the importance of the bridge to their origin story.

21. Denetdale, *Long Walk*; Trafzer, *Kit Carson Campaign*.

22. Luckert, *Navajo Mountain*.

23. "Expedition of 1909," August 10, 1909, fieldnotes of Dr. Byron Cummings, University of Utah Anthropological Archives; Jett, "Testimony"; Douglass, "Discovery," 8–9.

24. Wards are administrative and organization units within the Mormon Church. See Roy Webb, "Set My Spirit Free: A History of SOCOTWA," SOCOTWA, box 4, folder 2, 13–16, accessed December 24, 2021, http://www.riverguides.org/ Confluence/27/27SocotwaWebb.pdf. Merly Shaw was killed along with eleven others in a terrible automobile accident while on a SOCOTWA expedition in 1963. Webb reports that two events, Shaw's death and the closing of the gates at Glen Canyon Dam that same year, meant that "the heart went out of the SOCOTWA river program."

25. Webb, "Set My Spirit Free," box 4, folder 2, 12–13.

26. SOCOTWA eventually incorporated into a full-fledged river running group. See SOCOTWA Collection, accessed August 19, 2024, https://archiveswest .orbiscascade.org/ark:80444/xv80462. Brigham Young sent early missionaries to meet with, and potentially convert, Native Americans—whom Mormons cast as "Lamanites." They also wished to establish a stronghold in the region

through settlement in order to protect Mormons in the northern reaches of the Utah Territory. The Arizona Strip, as it is now called, was part of the larger "Mormon corridor" that reached from southern Utah to northern Idaho. See Flake, "Mormon Corridor," in Shipps and Silk, *Religion and Public Life*, 91–114.

27. Author unknown, "SOCOTWA Colorado River Trip," 1958 diary entry, SOCOTWA, box 12, folder 12, 5. Mormon Pioneers actually crossed the Escalante River (which runs into the Colorado River) in 1880. See National Park Service, "Hole-in-the-Rock," accessed August 24, 2017, https://www.nps.gov/glca/learn/historyculture/holeintherock.htm.

28. "SOCOTWA Glen Canyon-Colorado River Expidition [*sic*]," June 20–27, 1959, SOCOTWA, box 3, folder 1, 3.

29. "SOCOTWA Glen Canyon-Colorado River," box 3, folder 1, 1.

30. Webb, "Set My Spirit Free," box 4, folder 2, 14.

31. Webb, "Set My Spirit Free," box 4, folder 2, 14.

32. "SOCOTWA Glen Canyon-Colorado River," box 3, folder 1, 5. I am unsure if they signed their names in an RBMN guest book or carved them into the wall.

33. "SOCOTWA Glen Canyon-Colorado River," box 3, folder 1, 2.

34. "SOCOTWA Glen Canyon-Colorado River," box 3, folder 1, 5.

35. "SOCOTWA Glen Canyon-Colorado River," box 3, folder 1, 8.

36. "SOCOTWA Glen Canyon-Colorado River," box 3, folder 1, 3–8. Tabernacle quote from May 30, 1959, trip is found on page 3.

37. Unknown, "SOCOTWA Colorado River Trip," box 12, folder 12, 5.

38. SOCOTWA History, "Glen Canyon Trip," May 30, 1959, SOCOTWA, box 12, folder 12, 1–6. The Josephson story is found on pages 5–6. This folder contains additional diaries of the expedition and accounts of Mormon settlement and its reenactment.

39. Raymond Nakai, "Glen Canyon Speech, 1969," June 19, 1969, CPDC, item no. 79146. Speech given to support the formation of Glen Canyon Recreational Area.

40. Bsumek, *Indian-Made*.

41. "Authorizing 25 Year Leases," November 14, 1963, Bureau of Indian Affairs, Office of Reservation Programs, Industrial and Tourism Development Programs, Navajo Area Office, National Archives and Records Administration, box 12, 52–54.

42. "'Interpretive Prospectus: Navajo National Monument' for the Department of the Interior," Angus Woodbury Collection, University of Utah, Marriott Library, special collections, box 32, folder 13, 2.

43. On Navajo seeking outside partnerships, see "Indian Industrial Conference Speech," April 24, 1968, Los Angeles, CA, CPDC, item no. 78568.

44. Farmer, *Glen Canyon Dammed*, 166.

45. Farmer, *Glen Canyon Dammed*, 166.

46. Farmer, *Glen Canyon Dammed*, 168.
47. N.R. to David Brower and Tom Turner, memo, February 20, 1974, David Ross Brower Papers, Bancroft Library, University of California Berkeley, MSS 79/9c, carton 42, folder 25.
48. *Badoni*, 638 F.2d 172.
49. *Badoni*, 638 F.2d 172.
50. Stambor, "Manifest Destiny."
51. *Badoni*, 638 F.2d 172 at 180.
52. Hillaire, *Totem Pole History*, 63.
53. Lady Bird Johnson, "Glen Canyon Dam Dedication Ceremony," September 22, 1966, CPDC, item no. 75982.
54. National Park Service, "Hole-in-the-Rock."
55. Ensign Peak Foundation. "Hole in the Rock Expedition," accessed August 24, 2017, http://mormonhistoricsites.org/hole-in-the-rock-expedition/.

Bibliography

ARCHIVES/MANUSCRIPT MATERIALS

Angus Woodbury Collection. University of Utah, Marriott Library, Special Collections. "'Interpretive Prospectus: Navajo National Monument' for the Department of the Interior."

Colorado Plateau Digital Collections (CPDC). Northern Arizona University Libraries, Cline Library, Flagstaff.

South Cottonwood Ward Collection (SOCOTWA). University of Utah Libraries Special Collections, J. Willard Marriott Library, Salt Lake City. 1948–2003.

PUBLISHED WORKS

Badoni v. Higginson. 455 F. Supp. 641 (U.S. District Court for the District of Utah 1977).
———. 638 F.2d 172 (10th Circuit 1980).

Brower, David. "Let the River Run through It." *Sierra Magazine*, March/April 1997. https://vault.sierraclub.org/sierra/199703/brower.asp.

Bsumek, Erika. *Indian-Made: Navajo Culture in the Marketplace, 1868–1940.* Lawrence: University Press of Kansas, 2008.

Deloria, Philip J. *Indians in Unexpected Places.* Lawrence: University Press of Kansas, 2004.

Denetdale, Jennifer. *The Long Walk: The Forced Navajo Exile.* New York: Chelsea House, 2007.

Douglass, William B. "The Discovery of Rainbow Natural Bridge." *Our Public Lands* 5, no. 2 (1955): 8–9.

Farmer, Jared. *Glen Canyon Dammed: Inventing Lake Powell and the Canyon Country.* Tucson: University of Arizona Press, 1999.

Flake, Kathleen. "The Mormon Corridor: Utah and Idaho." In *Religion and Public Life in the Mountain West: Sacred Landscapes in Transition*, edited by Jan Shipps and Mark Silk, 91–114. Walnut Creek CA: AltaMira, 2004.

Fowler, Don D. *The Glen Canyon Country: A Personal Memoir.* Salt Lake City: University of Utah Press, 2011.

"Glen Canyon National Recreation Area." Washington DC: Government Printing Office, July 24, 1968.

Halliday, William R., and Angus M. Woodbury. "Protection of Rainbow Bridge National Monument." *Science* 133, no. 3464 (May 19, 1961): 1572–79. https://doi .org/10.1126/science.133.3464.1572.

Harvey, Mark. *A Symbol of Wilderness: Echo Park and the American Conservation Movement.* Seattle: University of Washington Press, 2001.

Hillaire, Pauline R. *A Totem Pole History: The Work of Lummi Carver Joe Hillaire.* Edited by Gregory P. Fields. Lincoln: University of Nebraska Press, 2013.

Jennings, Jesse D., and Don D. Fowler. *Glen Canyon: An Archaeological Summary.* Salt Lake City: University of Utah Press, 1998.

Jett, Stephen C. "The Great 'Race' to 'Discover' Rainbow Natural Bridge in 1909." *Kiva* 58, no. 1 (1992): 3–66.

———. "Testimony of the Sacredness of Rainbow Natural Bridge to Puebloan, Navajos, and Paiutes." *Plateau* 5 (Spring 1973): 133–42.

Kelley, Klara Bonsack, and Harris Francis. *Navajo Sacred Places.* Bloomington: Indiana University Press, 1994.

Luckert, Karl W. *Navajo Mountain and Rainbow Bridge Religion.* Vol. 1, *American Tribal Religions.* Flagstaff: Museum of Northern Arizona, 1977.

Martin, Russell. *A Story That Stands like a Dam: Glen Canyon and the Struggle for the Soul of the West.* New York: Henry Holt, 1989.

National Resource Report. "Rainbow Bridge National Monument Geologic Resources Inventory Report." Denver: Geologic Resources Division, National Resources Program Center, 2009.

Porter, Eliot, and David Brower. *The Place No One Knew: Glen Canyon on the Colorado.* San Francisco: Sierra Club, 1968.

Raibmon, Paige. *Authentic Indians: Episodes of Encounter from the Late-Nineteenth-Century Northwest Coast.* Durham NC: Duke University Press, 2005.

Sproul, David Kent. *A Bridge between Cultures: An Administrative History of Rainbow Bridge National Monument.* Denver: National Park Service, Intermountain Region, 2001. http://www.npshistory.com/publications/rabr/adhi.pdf.

Stambor, Howard. "Manifest Destiny and American Indian Religious Freedom: Sequoya, Bandoni, and Drowned Gods." *American Indian Law Review* 10, no. 1 (1982): 59–89.

Trafzer, Clifford E. *The Kit Carson Campaign: The Last Great Navajo War*. 1st ed. Norman: University of Oklahoma Press, 1982.

Weber, David J., and William deBuys. "Rainbow Bridge." In *First Impressions: A Reader's Journey to Iconic Places of the American Southwest*, 176–93. New Haven CT: Yale University Press, 2017.

Woodbury, Angus M. "Protecting Rainbow Bridge." *Science* 132, no. 3426 (August 26, 1960): 519–28. https://doi.org/10.1126/science.132.3426.519.

Worster, Donald. *Rivers of Empire: Water, Aridity, and the Growth of the American West*. Oxford: Oxford University Press, 1992.

Yablon, Marcia. "Property Rights and Sacred Sites: Federal Regulatory Responses to American Indian Religious Claims on Public Land." *Yale Law Journal* 113, no. 7 (May 2004): 1623–62. https://doi.org/10.2307/4135775.

How Would You Feel If Someone Were Allowed to Kill One of Your Grandparents?

Native Hawaiian Opposition to the Pacific Shark Fin Trade

MILES A. POWELL

On April 13, 2000, in Washington DC, a tanned, silver-haired kanaka maoli (Native Hawaiian) man, William Aila, stood before a congressional sub-committee.[1] He had traveled nearly five thousand miles from his home near Honolulu to speak in support of a bill to ban shark finning in U.S. waters. In its language and content, this legislation closely resembled an act Hawaiian policymakers had passed days earlier. By emphasizing Native Hawaiian reverence for sharks, Aila and other kanaka maoli activists had played a key role in passing this act—the first such law enacted by a U.S. state. In this manner, Native Hawaiians had mobilized Indigenous beliefs to shape the direction and objectives of mainstream environmentalism in important ways. Now Aila hoped to extend this influence over the rest of the United States' ocean domain.[2]

A prominent kanaka maoli spokesman and politician who would go on to become chairman of the Hawai'i Board of Land and Natural Resources, Aila denounced shark finning. He condemned the U.S. Western Pacific Regional Fisheries Management Council (WESPAC) for having just authorized an annual harvest of fifty thousand blue sharks within their area of jurisdiction, which included Hawaiian waters. As a member of this organization's advisory panel, Aila had opposed this policy on behalf of kānaka maoli. He informed the subcommittee that this harvest would result in "wasting over 95% of the resource." He added that the council had calculated this level of exploitation based on incomplete data regarding stock size and fishing pressure. Moreover, because the Hawaiian shark fin trade generally took place in an unregulated, cash-only black market—for "beer money," as one WESPAC official put it—it was difficult to assess the economic benefits the practice brought to the state. Finally, Aila described how finning violated kanaka beliefs regarding sharks: "Individual sharks of the many species known to Hawaiians, including blue sharks, served and continue to serve as family guardians. My grandfathers and great-grandfathers cared for certain sharks, our family Aumakua. Kamohoali'l is the name of the shark that I malama, or care for. The relationship is that of grandchild to grandparent . . . How would you feel if someone were allowed to kill one of your grandparents, just for 'beer money'"? Later that year, a slightly amended version of this bill received nearly unanimous congressional approval before President Bill Clinton signed it into law as the Shark Finning Prohibition Act.[3]

A variety of factors accounted for the passage of this legislation. But its primary sponsor, Representative Randy "Duke" Cunningham of California, repeatedly cited Hawaiian and specifically kanaka maoli opposition to finning as important considerations. The story of how past and present Native Hawaiian beliefs concerning sharks entered into first state and then national debates over finning is complex and revealing. Kanaka maoli activists influenced mainstream environmentalism, but they also used this movement to achieve outcomes in line with Native Hawaiian objectives. At the same time, non-Indigenous environmentalists frequently spoke of the need to honor Native Hawaiian mores surrounding sharks. While some of these individuals seemed to genuinely respect kanaka maoli customs, others likely seized on one aspect of a culture for which they otherwise held little appreciation. These dynamics speak to the complex exchanges that arise when Indigenous peoples and mainstream environmentalists work side by side in pursuit of shared goals.[4]

In recent years, growing numbers of environmental historians have asserted that the field must deal more seriously with issues of race and ethnicity.[5] One result has been an uptick in research exploring the ways that U.S. wilderness preservation became entangled with the nation's white racial identity.[6] While this work is useful, it risks creating the impression that concern for the environment has historically been the exclusive prerogative of affluent whites, who could afford to set aside economic opportunity for the benefit of plants, animals, waterways, and soils.[7] Although some excellent scholarship has emerged exploring the environmental perspectives of nonwhite Americans and how they translated their concerns into actions, much work remains on this front.[8]

FIG. 11.1. William Aila (*center*) helps oversee an environmental
rehabilitation project in Hawai'i, December 21, 2011. U.S.
Fish and Wildlife Service, Wikimedia Commons.

This chapter examines the recent struggles of kānaka maoli to restrict the
shark fin industry in and around their islands by articulating beliefs dating
back centuries. It highlights how they were able to draw on cultural values
surrounding sharks to advocate for their protection. As Aila's testimony
reveals, Native Hawaiians consider some sharks ʻaum-ākua (family gods
consisting of deified ancestors in natural form)[9]. Many Native Hawaiians
have therefore opposed the fin industry, which they perceive as not only
cruel and wasteful but also as an affront to customary Hawaiian attitudes
of respect and reverence for the ocean.

Of course, Hawai'i's original peoples did not act alone to ban this practice.
Hawai'i is a diverse state, with recent census estimates placing the population

at 38.6 percent Asian, 24.7 percent white, 10 percent kānaka maoli and other Pacific Islanders, 26.2 percent part kānaka maoli and other Pacific Islanders, and 0.5 percent other races. This ethnic heterogeneity has deep roots and was already a defining characteristic of the islands when Hawaiʻi achieved statehood in 1959. In light of this diversity, and considering the association of shark fin consumption with people of East Asian and especially Chinese ancestry, the eventual passage of state finning legislation required kānaka maoli and other Hawaiians to negotiate complex racial politics.[10]

In relating the story of Native Hawaiian opposition to the shark fin industry, this study engages with numerous themes that warrant further consideration in U.S. environmental history. Despite some excellent recent work on Hawaiʻi and other overseas possessions, the overarching narrative of U.S. environmental history tends to focus predominantly on the continental United States.[11] But the nation's environmental influence has extended into the Pacific, and Pacific peoples have shaped U.S. environmental beliefs and policies in important ways. Likewise, marine environmental history remains underexplored among Americanists and scholars of other regions.[12] Yet oceans have their own histories, which are as intertwined with humans as those of forests, fields, lakes, and rivers. Perhaps most significant—and representing the central claim of this chapter—this episode reveals that, in spite of the elitist roots and often-exclusionary rhetoric of mainstream U.S. environmentalism, nonwhite Americans have persistently pursued their own conservation agendas, sometimes significantly influencing the broader movement in the process.

One of the challenges confronted in the writing of this chapter is that I am approaching the topic as an outsider. I conducted this research as part of a broader project addressing the global environmental history of human interactions with sharks in the twentieth century. As leading world environmental historian J. R. McNeill notes, the field often presents its practitioners with research subjects that are too rich to overlook but for which we lack the specialized training—in terms of language comprehension or scientific expertise—we would preferably possess to analyze the material. In the case of environmental histories of Hawaiʻi, this is particularly problematic. Historians Noenoe K. Silva and David A. Chang stress that kānaka maoli recorded their histories and knowledge of the natural world in their own language. These accounts were often at odds with the English-language sources that have formed the basis for mainstream interpretations of Hawaiian history and ecology. Moreover, as Noelani Arista notes, Native Hawaiian texts—oral or written—often contained hidden references, or "kaona," easily lost when non-kānaka maoli drew on these sources to create historical narratives privileging the agency of missionaries and other settlers. Finally, as demonstrated in the work of social justice scholar Linda Tuhiwai Smith, Indigenous peoples are generally distrustful of academic studies conducted by outsiders. These groups recognize that such scholarship has played a role in "othering," colonizing, and dispossessing them. Hence, to write Hawaiian environmental history based solely on English-language materials is in a sense to uphold and reinforce a hegemonic knowledge system that has operated to justify Anglo-American conquest of the islands.[13]

While recognizing these concerns, I have done my best to respect and foreground kanaka perspectives in this study, both in terms of my selection of primary sources and with regard to my interpretive and analytic framework. My account of the colonial period draws largely on the writings of Native Hawaiian chroniclers—although, as Arista has demonstrated, it is possible that some meaning has been lost in translation. Moving nearer the present, the legislative battles surrounding Hawai'i's shark fin industry required concerned kānaka to provide testimony in English. Thus, government records provide useful and accessible insights into the attitudes of numerous Native Hawaiians toward this issue. While examining these sources, I have constantly borne in mind admonishments from Silva, Chang, and other kanaka maoli scholars that Native Hawaiians were not passive victims of colonization. On the contrary, Native Hawaiians have actively engaged with new arrivals to their island home in a manner that shaped their shared destiny. This process has continued in debates over finning. Following Chang's lead, I have opted not to italicize Native Hawaiian terms in this chapter, since the kanaka language is the Indigenous dialect of Hawai'i.[14]

This story centers on the kānaka maoli's unique relationship to Hawai'i's lands and waters, a connection rooted in history, culture, and spirituality. This exchange began approximately 1,700 to 1,250 years ago when the kānaka's Polynesian ancestors arrived in Hawai'i via long-distance canoe voyages from Tahiti and other islands far to the south. These settlers maintained contact with those southerly islands for centuries, but such exchanges ceased around 1400 CE, perhaps owing to shifting ocean currents. For nearly four centuries, until Captain James Cook encountered Hawai'i in 1778, kānaka maoli remained isolated from other human groups. They developed a distinctive understanding of their island home and of nature more generally. But contrary to Cook's assertion that kānaka were unaware of a realm outside Hawai'i, their cosmology—entrenched in songs and stories—included knowledge of their distant origins and of a much broader world.[15]

Kānaka maoli intimately knew their surrounding terrestrial and marine environments and felt a profound connection to them. They considered themselves and the 'āina (land) to be kin, linked by a relationship of mo'oku'aukau (genealogy). For Native Hawaiians, the god Wākea not only helped create the islands but also engendered the first kānaka, Hāloa. Kānaka described this connection to the land in mele (songs), mo'olelo (stories), and narratives surrounding wahi pana (storied places). Among the most significant of these texts was the Kumulipo, a chant recounting Hawai'i's creation story and the genealogy of its royalty.[16]

Kānaka created an elaborate religious system that structured their interactions with the land and sea. It included an immense number of deities, the stories of whom recorded elements of the group's history, and provided lessons for how the people should interact with the environment and each other. Today, Pele, the volcano deity, is Hawai'i's most famous god. But she was and still is only one figure in an immensely rich pantheon of spirits. Besides the four main akua (gods) of Kū, Kāne, Lono, and Kanaloa, kānaka peoples also worshipped many additional gods and a series of lesser spirits. The latter included 'unihipili (spirits that did the bidding of their sorcerer masters) as well as 'aum-ākua. Attesting to sharks' spiritual and material significance to kānaka, these fish figured prominently among all these entities.[17]

The nineteenth-century kanaka historian and scholar Samuel Kamakau recorded that Native Hawaiians revered many shark gods, collectively referred to as kumupa'a. The most celebrated of these gods was Kamohoali'i. Pele's favorite brother, he had traveled with her from Tahiti to Hawai'i. Also significant was Ka'ahupāhau. She was the most powerful of the shark deities of Pu'uloa (Pearl Harbor). They guarded O'ahu against attacks from more malevolent sharks. As revealed by Ka'ahupāhau's connection to Pu'uloa, many shark gods were associated with particular bodies of water, often serving as protectors to the region's human inhabitants. Native Hawaiian mythology also referenced a great shark war in which benevolent gods had driven many of the human-eating sharks from their ranks.[18]

Kamakau noted that shark spirits could also be ʻunihipili. Magically inclined kānaka created these often-evil spirits from the remains of deceased relatives. This process involved stripping the flesh from the bones of the departed and wrapping them in a mat or woven case that took the shape of the cadaver. The individual's spirit would then enter into the body of a living shark. When properly worshipped, a ʻunihipili was duty-bound to obey the wishes of its master.[19]

ʻAum-ākua were the final form of shark spirits identified by Kamakau. Like ʻunihipili, ʻaum-ākua emerged from the ceremonial reincarnation of a departed ancestor. But unlike ʻunihipili, which broadly carried out the good or evil wishes of their sorcerer masters, ʻaum-ākua were specifically devoted to the protection of their relatives. ʻAum-ākua could take the form of a wide array of natural entities, including animals, plants, stones, and even volcanoes, but sharks were especially common. A family's ʻaum-ākua did not include all representatives of a type of natural entity, such as a species of shark. Rather, a family recognized an individual being as their ʻaum-ākua. It often possessed some distinctive markings demonstrating a connection with the deceased relative. Families passed down knowledge of these guardian deities from one generation to the next. Frequently, the group assigned one from their ranks as a kahu (caretaker) who "fed" or propitiated the ʻaum-ākua through prayers and offerings.[20]

Demonstrating the cultural significance of shark ʻaum-ākua, Kamakau describes them at length in his writings. According to Kamakau, "Because sharks save men in times of peril, protect them when other sharks try to devour them, and are useful in other ways in saving lives at sea . . . some people were made into shark ʻaumakua." Shark ʻaum-ākua served as protectors to family members in the water. When properly worshipped, they "became beloved friends . . . defenders and guides . . . quieting the stormy ocean and bringing their people back to land."[21]

Upon visiting Hawaiʻi in the early twentieth century, pioneering U.S. folklorist and ethnographer Martha Warren Beckwith published a paper entitled "Hawaiian Shark Aumakua" for *American Anthropologist*. Her kanaka informant, Kaiwi, described a pair of brothers named Puhi (eel) who possessed a shark ʻaum-ākua. According to Kaiwi, this ʻaum-ākua aided the

Puhi in fishing. "[N]ame the kind of fish you want and it will bring it," he assured Beckwith. Like other shark 'aum-ākua, this spirit also protected the Puhi from drowning. As with Kamakau, Kaiwi provided an account of shark 'aum-ākua that presented the fish as kind and helpful, and integral to the spiritual and socioecological systems of the region.[22]

Until 1819, when the paramount chief Kamehameha II overthrew the practice, an elaborate set of taboos, the kapu system, also governed kānaka interactions with the land, sea, and each other. Once again, sharks figured prominently. When it came to dining, it was kapu (forbidden) for women to eat in the presence of men or to consume bananas, coconuts, pork, turtle, shark, and a number of other foods. Sharks were associated with ali'i (royalty), and so additional kapu governed the consumption of these fish. Not only were women forbidden from eating sharks, but certain species were also off limits to all but the highest-ranking men.[23]

Despite kānaka attributing immense spiritual power to sharks, or perhaps because of this, the people did kill and make use of them in a number of ways. Kānaka distinguished between manō (regular sharks) and niuhi (large dangerous sharks, like great whites and tiger sharks). Depending on the desired quarry, kānaka used three primary methods to catch sharks: kiholo (large wooden hooks), ho'omoemoe (set nets), and kumano (nooses). Historical kanaka shark harvests involved a high degree of reverence and ceremony, and participants would certainly have taken care to avoid killing individual sharks recognized as 'aum-ākua. Hence many Native Hawaiians have come to oppose the shark fin industry on cultural grounds, even if their ancestors once hunted the fish.[24]

Because it required the most skill, targeted niuhi, and was the preferred technique of the ali'i and those who fished on their behalf, the kumano method figures most prominently in the primary sources. Kamakau describes it at length, as does Minister Stephen L. Desha in his writings from the early twentieth century. The fishers boarded a large double-hulled canoe and paddled far from shore, dangling a sack of putrid chum in the water from a plank running between the two hulls. While paddling, the crew chanted and tapped the side of the canoe to attract a shark. When a dorsal fin began to trail the canoe, the harvesters prepared the pahele (noose). Eventually, the shark would swim between the two hulls, and a skilled fisher would slip the noose over its head. When the shark was safely secured, the crew either immediately killed it by stabbing it or guided it into shallower water where they could more easily dispatch it.[25]

Kānaka maoli utilized sharks in a variety of ways. Some Native Hawaiians consumed shark flesh, although they generally only considered manō kihikihi (hammerhead sharks) and manō lalakea (whitetip reef sharks) edible. Owing to the reverence owed to niuhi, just the ali'i ate them, but they did so infrequently. Kānaka also made use of shark skins. They used niuhi skins as covering for the pahu (temple drum) and ka'eke (hula drums). Prior to the arrival of Europeans, kānaka also used shark teeth as their primary cutting utensil.[26]

All told, historical kanaka interactions with sharks reveal a high degree of respect and reverence, which helps explain twenty-first-century Native Hawaiian opposition to the fin industry. Native Hawaiian communities expressed the importance of sharks through culturally specific stories, myths, and songs. This constituted a form of Indigenous knowledge, also sometimes referred to as local ecological knowledge (LEK), that portended much later Western scientific studies demonstrating the ecological value of sharks. As recent scholarship has revealed, LEK is based on centuries of place-based interactions with nature and is not so much an alternative to scientific knowledge as a broader epistemological framework that combines scientific insights with other forms of environmental knowledge. Like all predator species, sharks can help maintain the health of prey populations by removing weak and sickly individuals. Moreover, as apex predators, large sharks play a pivotal role in maintaining relative balance and stability in an ecosystem. Researchers have shown that the removal of such species frequently results in a process labeled "trophic cascading." This involves shifts in population ratios and feeding patterns as the organisms within each level of a food web adjust to new opportunities and perils. Observance of such processes has convinced ecologists that at least some sharks represent "keystone" species, the elimination of which might disrupt an entire ecosystem.[27]

The arrival of Europeans brought profound changes to Hawai'i. But despite the efforts of Anglo-American colonizers to erase kanaka language, history, culture, and sovereignty, the beliefs described above have persisted in many ways through the present. The colonization of Hawai'i occurred over a period of nearly two centuries, and many kānaka would be quick to point out that this process never ended. From Cook's arrival in 1778 through the first two decades of the nineteenth century, the archipelago became an important Pacific stopover for American and European trade vessels. Benefiting from European allies and weaponry, and hoping to secure foreign recognition of kānaka sovereignty, the warrior chief Kamehameha unified the majority of the islands in 1795 to form the Kingdom of Hawai'i. From 1819, whaling ships joined the trade vessels, and in the 1820s and 1830s, a permanent merchant community arose to serve these visitors. By the 1860s, with whale stocks dwindling, Hawai'i's economy shifted to plantation agriculture, especially sugarcane production. From this point forward, U.S. landholdings and economic concerns in Hawai'i continued to grow, often through the violent dispossession of Native Hawaiians.[28]

Coveting control over the islands, this expanding Anglo-American settler community strove to erase kanaka culture and sovereignty. In 1887, Anglo-Americans and other white settlers forced the Hawaiian monarchy to sign the so-called Bayonet Constitution, curtailing the ali'i's authority. When Queen Lili'uokalani sought to restore some of these powers, a group of Anglo-American sugar planters, backed by U.S. troops, ousted the kanaka ruler in 1893. The colonizers established a republic and called on the United States to annex the islands. They also quickly banned Hawaiian-language schools and decreed that English would be Hawai'i's official language. In 1898, after five years of heated political disputes, the U.S. government annexed Hawai'i. This action violated the wishes of kānaka maoli. In 1897, they produced an antiannexation petition with signatures from more than half of the Native Hawaiian population. In 1900 Hawai'i became a U.S. territory, and in 1959 it voted for statehood, officially ending its colonial status. Yet for the kānaka, who made up a minority of the population by the time of this plebiscite, statehood merely intensified an ongoing process of political marginalization, economic impoverishment, and cultural dispossession.[29]

Through all of this, Native Hawaiians retained their unique attachment to the archipelago and its natural environment. In the 1960s and 1970s, an Indigenous sovereignty movement emerged in Hawai'i—as in many other parts of the United States—that desired to overthrow Anglo-American control, partly on the grounds that the colonizers had failed to serve as stewards and protectors of the environment. An early focal point for this movement was Kaho'olawe, the smallest of the state's eight major islands. Overgrazed by introduced livestock, and used as a military bombing range since the

1930s, Kahoʻolawe was in a state of severe environmental degradation by the 1960s. Concerned kānaka allied with non-Indigenous environmentalists to demand the island's restoration. Linking environmental and cultural renewal, some kanaka leaders envisioned the island as the future site of a restored autonomous Native Hawaiian nation.[30]

This historical and political context is essential for understanding kanaka maoli efforts to assert greater control over the management of local shark stocks. In the 1990s, a debate emerged over how best to respond to recent fatal shark attacks in the state's waters. In some respects, this mirrored earlier conversations surrounding a fatal shark attack on a Native Hawaiian teenager, Billy Weaver, in 1959, which resulted in the state waging an outright war on large sharks in the Oʻahu area. But times had changed over the ensuing decades, and not only owing to a greater appreciation for the ecological value of sharks. By this point, many kānaka recognized that assertions of environmental stewardship could reinforce, and be reinforced by, demands for cultural renewal and Indigenous sovereignty. This insight owed partly to Native Hawaiian experiences in the ongoing battle over Kahoʻolawe. Such claims had gained legislative clout in 1978 when Hawaiian policymakers modified the state constitution to guarantee kānaka maoli "all rights, customarily and traditionally exercised for subsistence, cultural and religious purposes." Native Hawaiians could also draw inspiration from the successes of other American Indigenous peoples. Most notably, in the 1970s and 1980s Washington state tribes had won a series of pathbreaking and well-publicized court decisions. These granted the groups a greater share of the state's salmon harvest plus a say in managing the resource. Kānaka maoli could look to this as an example of how they might expand their control over their historical lands, waters, and resources.[31]

In November of 1991, tiger sharks killed Martha Morell near Olowalu on Maui. The state responded by hiring an experienced shark hunter, James Stegmueller, to seek out and kill large tiger sharks in the vicinity of the attack. Stegmueller quit when a group of kanaka youths warned him that he would be "bodily harmed" if he brought any sharks to shore. According to a reporter for the *Honolulu Advertiser*, the young men opposed the expedition on the grounds that "sharks were *aumakua*—personal or family gods—to ancient Hawaiians."[32]

With public interest mounting, a contentious debate erupted over the merits of the cull. Charles K. Maxwell, a kanaka radio personality and the vice

FIG. 11.2. Tiger shark killed in Hawaiian waters in 1966, during a
period of intense culls stretching from 1959 through 1976. U.S. National
Oceanic and Atmospheric Administration, Wikimedia Commons.

chairman of the State Advisory Committee to the U.S. Civil Rights Commission, came out strongly against the practice. He conceded that not all sharks were 'aum-ākua. Yet he maintained that many were, and since some families could no longer identify their guardian spirits, the cull's "indiscriminate killing" imperiled these sacred beings. Bill Paty, director of the State Department of Land and Natural Resources (DLNR), countered in an oversimplified reading of kanaka history that "ancient Hawaiian *alii* (royalty) actively hunted sharks, and for pure sport, not food." Maxwell retorted that when Native Hawaiians hunted sharks historically, "there was ritual to it."[33]

As the conflict intensified, Martha Morrell's husband, David, stated that he did not want to see the dispute "develop into a racial conflict." Yet opinions on this issue did not break neatly along ethnic lines. Foreshadowing the loose alliance that would emerge between Native Hawaiian activists and non-Indigenous environmentalists in opposition to the shark fin industry, many members of the dominant culture opposed the hunt. At the same time, not all Native Hawaiians supported Maxwell's position of zero tolerance for culls.[34]

In early December, the DLNR and concerned kānaka attempted to bring an end to their dispute. The agency temporarily discontinued the cull, and Native Hawaiians performed a healing ritual for Martha's family. A year later, officials created a Hawai'i Shark Task Force with Paty chairing and Maxwell representing kanaka interests. After another confirmed fatal attack and three disappearances that were attributed to sharks, the DLNR resumed the hunts. This action prompted Maxwell to quit the task force in protest.[35]

Considering the enduring reverence many kānaka felt for sharks, and the group's rising association of environmental stewardship, cultural renewal, and Indigenous sovereignty, it is little surprise that numerous Native Hawaiian activists became staunch opponents of the fin trade. Multiple factors contributed to the explosion of the fin industry beginning in the 1990s, but demand from ethnic Chinese consumers was the primary driver. Between 1987 and 2004, the global fin trade expanded from 4,907 to 13,614 metric tons of product. With fins typically making up approximately 5 percent of a shark's body weight, the latter figure amounts to over 270,000 metric tons of sharks being killed. A 2004 study by the United Nations Food and Agriculture Organization (FAO) found that over 90 percent of shark fin imports reported to the agency went to either Hong Kong (58 percent) or China (36 percent).[36]

Chinese demand for shark fins stemmed overwhelmingly from their use in a soup prized as a luxury item. Contrary to popular perceptions, this soup rarely featured anything recognizable as a shark's fin. Rather, the soup included gelatinous collagen and elastin fibers, often termed "fin needles" or "fin rays," extracted from between the fin's cartilaginous skeletal features. These fibers contributed little flavor, but they offered a distinctive texture somewhat similar to rice noodles. In Chinese medicine, shark was a *bu* food, meaning it could serve as a health tonic. More significant to the contemporary fin trade, many ethnic Chinese placed immense importance on maintaining their "face" or respect in the eyes of others. At weddings and other feasts, hosts strove to demonstrate "face" by providing luxury food items, among which shark fin soup became a favorite dish.[37]

Occupying a strategic location in the central North Pacific, Hawaiʻi emerged as a major hub in the fin trade. Not only did its ports serve as transfer points for fins harvested outside Hawaiian waters, but the state's longline fishing fleet also began finning sharks caught alive as bycatch instead of releasing them. These fishers expanded their landings of sharks from 200,000 pounds in 1991 to 4.5 million pounds just five years later.[38]

Because this harvest only utilized the fins, which made up a small percentage of body mass, the fin industry involved considerable waste. This meant a larger biomass had to be removed from the ocean to meet market demands. Unfortunately, shark populations generally do not hold up well to exploitation. Nearly all sharks are among the species ecologists dub "K-selected" organisms. As opposed to "R-selected species," which reproduce prolifically and thus rebound quickly from harvests, most sharks engender few young and mature slowly. This allows them to thrive in undisturbed conditions but renders them ill-suited to recover from population declines. For this reason, researchers have warned that many species will face dramatic collapses in the next few decades.[39]

A variety of factors have contributed to global declines in shark populations, but experts agree that finning is a chief component. Like any at-risk species, shark populations wax and wane within a dynamic environment. Relevant variables include fluctuating oceanic temperatures, variations in prey species abundance, and accumulations of marine pollution. Yet on a worldwide scale, human consumption remains the primary cause of plummeting shark numbers. Researchers estimate that over the second half of the twentieth century, shark catches rose by 400 percent to approximately eight-hundred-thousand metric tons annually. The development of new technologies allowing for the exploitation of deep seas and other once-inaccessible spaces has contributed to rising harvests. So too has the depletion of customary food species, forcing fishers to turn to lower-grade fish, including sharks. Yet investigators attribute a large proportion of this increase to the shark fin trade, and it is easy to understand why. Nonfin shark meat has a low market value (fetching approximately 2 percent of the price of fins). Hence for many fishers, sharks would not be worth landing if not for the exorbitant prices some buyers pay for their fins.[40]

Multiple international efforts have emerged to address the threat facing global shark populations. But poor compliance among the nations involved and a lack of enforcement mechanisms have generally rendered this legislation ineffective. The best known of these efforts emerged in 1999, when the FAO Committee on Fisheries created an International Plan for the Conservation and Management of Sharks. It requests that member nations voluntarily form National Plans of Action. These were to involve population assessments, improved catch reporting, and regulations where necessary. In 2011, the Pew Environment Group reported that the twenty most significant shark-fishing countries, which accounted for 80 percent of shark harvests, had failed to fulfill these expectations. Such failures have convinced many that effective shark protection will have to begin at local and national levels.[41]

In the late 1990s, a movement arose in Hawai'i to curtail the local shark fin industry by making it illegal to land fins without the carcasses attached. After intense debate, this legislation passed in 2000 as Act 277. Kānaka played a key role in securing this legislation. As the bill made its way through the state legislature, Native Hawaiians provided testimony emphasizing the cultural significance they attributed to sharks, and highlighting kanaka values of environmental stewardship. Nonkānaka environmentalists also began weaving Native Hawaiian arguments into their testimony. In effect, kānaka maoli beliefs had found their way to the center of a statewide debate over finning. This represented an important example of nonwhite Americans shaping the mainstream environmental movement through the pursuit of distinct environmental objectives.[42]

Numerous kānaka maoli lent their support to the bill. Charles Maxwell called on policymakers to consider "Hawaiian spirituality towards the oceans and the animals within." Deeming shark finning "wasteful and very inhumane," he asserted that the practice "is very upsetting to us as native people." William Aila also wrote several letters endorsing the bill. He warned that if policymakers failed to pass the legislation, they might as well acknowledge that "mālama kai" (customary Hawaiian stewardship of the ocean for future generations) was a "lie" and did not exist. Many other kānaka also stressed that finning violated Native Hawaiian beliefs surrounding shark ʻaum-ākua.[43]

Influential kanaka organizations also supported the bill. Devoted to the advancement of Native Hawaiian interests, the Office of Hawaiian Affairs (OHA) endorsed the legislation through testimony from its vice chair, Colette Machado. She stressed that finning violated key kanaka values of environmental "stewardship" and reverence for "aumakua." Hence finning was "for many [kanaka] families, the equivalent of desecrating one's own ancestors." Noa Emmett Aluli, the chairperson of the Kahoʻolawe Island Reserve Commission (KIRC), also endorsed the bill. The KIRC had assumed the task of managing the island's reserve until it could become a sovereign Native Hawaiian entity. Aluli asserted that "shark finning is a shameful act that painfully attacks the cultural and spiritual belief that sharks are our ʻaumakua.'" Revealing how the debate over the shark fin industry intersected with questions of Native Hawaiian sovereignty, Aluli added that the legislation "would give us one more opportunity to charge those violating our Reserve rules. That's one more option we can use to protect our ocean resources." Such themes would become even more pertinent with the establishment of the Papahānaumokuākea Marine National Monument in Hawaiian waters in 2006. Among the largest marine protected areas in the world, it benefits from significant Native Hawaiian stewardship, with William Aila chairing its advisory council.[44]

The bill also enjoyed support from several non-kanaka environmentalists. Representatives from organizations including Earthtrust, the Green Peace Foundation, the Hawaiʻi Green Party, the Hawaiʻi Audubon Society, the Marine Conservation Biology Institute, the Ocean Wildlife Campaign, and local chapters of the Sierra Club testified in favor of the legislation. They stressed the wastefulness of finning, the limited capacity of shark populations to endure harvests, and the potential unforeseen consequences of removing apex predators. Some non-kanaka environmentalists also highlighted how shark finning violated Native Hawaiian beliefs. Paul H. Achitoff of Earthjustice asserted that "shark finning is not only leading to a disastrous depletion . . . of one of the top predators in the marine food chain, but is particularly inappropriate culturally in Hawai'i, where the shark is the 'aumakua . . . of many Native Hawaiians."[45]

Some Chinese Hawaiians opposed the bill on economic and cultural grounds—although debates over subsequent legislation revealed the diversity of Chinese opinions on the issue. Zheng Qirong, president of the Chinese Culinary Arts Society of Hawai'i, objected to the bill for unfairly targeting the islands' Chinese community. He noted that no similar backlash had emerged against wasteful and environmentally damaging Western delicacies, such as caviar. Observing that Chinese people had lived in Hawai'i since 1789 and contributed much to its culinary traditions, he found criticism from "insensitive newcomers" offensive. Seafood company owner Calvin Wong also opposed the bill. Maintaining that "shark fin is an Asian delicacy," he warned that restricting this trade would put his company out of business and devastate Chinese tourism to Hawai'i.[46]

Besides overcoming Chinese resistance, proponents of the bill also faced predictable opposition from some longline fishers as well as hostility from proexploitation WESPAC officials, who felt the legislation violated their jurisdiction. Captain Stephen W. Gates criticized the bill for placing restrictions on a fishery before sufficient data existed. Other harvesters made similar arguments. WESPAC chair James Cook strongly opposed the bill. Noting that WESPAC was responsible for developing management plans in the two-hundred-mile exclusive economic zone around Hawai'i, he suggested that this legislation infringed on the council's jurisdiction. He further asserted that "there is no evidence at this time that blue sharks are being harvested in the Council's area of jurisdiction beyond sustainable limits." While this was technically true, the Hawai'i-based longline fishery at this time harvested sixty-thousand sharks annually, and some argued that policymakers should err on the side of caution when operating with limited information. Dismissing Native Hawaiian concerns, and hoping to capitalize on Chinese opposition to the bill, Cook added, "One wonders if this argument is really based on culture or ethnicity," rather than sound fisheries policy. Some fishers, however, supported the legislation on the grounds that robust shark populations helped maintain overall ecosystem health.[47]

Cook's suggestion that anti-Chinese sentiments fueled opposition to the shark fin industry is difficult to assess. White Americans have historically demonstrated racial animosity toward Chinese people. In the mid-nineteenth century, when the California gold rush brought large numbers of Chinese laborers to the United States for the first time, they faced distrust, hostility, and violent aggression. White Americans alleged that Chinese immigrants undercut wages and were barbaric, devious, and diseased. In 1882 U.S. policymakers passed the Chinese Exclusion Act, the first federal legislation to specifically restrict the entry of a particular ethnic group to the United States. Such hostility persisted throughout much of the twentieth century. U.S. citizens briefly celebrated the Chinese as allies against Japan during World War II, but China's subsequent turn to communism erased much of this goodwill. In recent years, Chinese Americans have carved out a reputation as "model minorities" for their educational and commercial achievements. Yet racial intolerance persists, albeit now often expressed in cultural terms. With its long history of Chinese settlement and its ethnically diverse population, Hawai'i did not possess identical race politics to those of the mainland, but it was not free of anti-Asian sentiment.[48]

Such animosity is not evident, however, in testimony presented in support of Hawaiian shark finning legislation, either by Native Hawaiians or the general public. This does not negate the possibility that tacit hostility to Chinese people may have motivated some individuals. Lending support to this interpretation, shark finning has generated a disproportionate amount of negative publicity when compared to other equally wasteful and destructive industries such as sturgeon caviar or the Atlantic bluefin tuna industry. Yet there are other explanations for heightened attention to shark finning. These include sharks' increasing popularity as charismatic megafauna, rising awareness of their ecological importance, and opportunities for gruesome photos presented by finning sharks on deck.

Despite intense industry opposition, a coalition of Native Hawaiian activists and environmentalists—some of whom also cited kanaka beliefs—secured passage of this act. In turn, the state of Hawai'i became a key proponent of the similarly worded U.S. Shark Finning Prohibition Act. As Aila's testimony at the beginning of this chapter demonstrates, kānaka maoli also lent support to this federal legislation. The passage of this law represented an important counterpoint to the prevailing narrative that, since colonization, influence has extended overwhelmingly from the continental U.S. core outward to the nation's Pacific periphery.[49]

By the late 2000s, some Hawaiians had become concerned that Act 277 did not go far enough. It still left open the possibility of harvesters landing a whole shark carcass, finning it on shore, and then discarding the body. Critics also believed the act was not sufficient to address an enduring black market for fins in Hawai'i. Demands emerged for a law that would make it illegal to sell, distribute, or even possess shark fins in the state. Such legislation was passed in 2010 as Act 148. Native Hawaiians were central to this movement.[50]

Clayton Hee, a Democratic member of the Hawai'i Senate, championed the bill. A half-Chinese kānaka maoli, Hee stated that "sharks have a very unique and distinguished presence in Hawaiian culture as . . . our 'aumakua.'" Other Native Hawaiians also testified in support of the legislation. Julie A. K. Leialoha wrote that shark finning "is culturally insensitive to Native Hawaiians and the practice must be banned outright." As in the case of Act 277, the OHA also endorsed this legislation. Beyond helping "hold the entire ocean ecosystem in balance," wrote a representative of the office, "some manō also are . . . aumakua for various families." Relating the ban to the question of kanaka Indigenous rights, the writer cited the state constitution's mandate to uphold historical Native Hawaiian practices, whether engaged for "subsistence, cultural," or "religious purposes."[51]

Non-kanaka environmentalists also supported the new legislation, in some cases incorporating Native Hawaiian beliefs into their arguments. Members of the Coalition to Protect Ocean Diversity, the Conservation Council for Hawai'i, Dorsal Fins, the Hawai'i Audubon Society, Oceanic Defense, and the Shark Safe Network endorsed the bill. They stressed sharks' ecological significance and the risks of trophic cascading. Some of them also highlighted kanaka values. For instance, Mary O'Malley of the Shark Safe Network contended that banning shark fins in Hawai'i would show "respect to this important aumakua." With the landing of shark fins already illegal in Hawai'i, this new bill encountered relatively limited opposition from fishers.[52]

The Chinese response to this bill was complex, revealing a growing sentiment among many Chinese Hawaiians that shark fin soup was not a vital cultural practice. City councillor Rod Tam opposed the legislation on historical grounds. Avowing that he "strived to preserve the cultural values and traditions of my ancestors," he condemned a ban on shark fins, which had "long been revered in Chinese cuisine." Yet many other ethnically Chinese Hawaiians rejected this line of reasoning. Ginny Tiu asserted that "Shark Fins Soup is as much a part of our culture as the practice of binding women's feet was. It was ignorance that allowed such practices, but now we know better."[53]

Further complicating the Chinese response to this legislation, many inhabitants of Hawaiʻi were of mixed Chinese and kanaka ancestry, including the bill's champion, Senator Hee. While we might expect this to become a source of personal or family conflict, virtually all the self-identifying mixed-ethnicity individuals who provided testimony endorsed the bill. For his part, Hee asserted that the legislation did not place Chinese and Native Hawaiian cultures at odds, because shark fin soup was not a meaningful Chinese tradition. Brandi-Leigh Adams wrote that as someone who was "both native Hawaiian and Chinese," she supported the bill "because it is not only about culture, it is about being a global citizen." Other mixed Chinese-Native Hawaiian people made similar arguments.[54]

Even more so than the preceding legislation, Hawaiʻi's bill to ban shark fins generated immense interest in the continental United States and around the world. Hee stated that in his twenty-six years as an elected official, he never encountered an issue that was "so deeply cared about by both local and international communities." Mary O'Malley of Shark Savers observed that "people from around the world have been following this Hawaiʻi bill every step of the way." Indeed, government records reveal that environmental advocates from across the globe wrote to express their support for the legislation. Following the act's passage, California, Illinois, Maryland, Oregon, and Washington as well as all three U.S. Pacific territories of Guam, American Samoa, and the Northern Mariana Islands passed similar legislation. Environmentalists in Canada, Hong Kong, Ireland, and Malaysia were also inspired by Hawaiʻi's example to pursue bans on fins.[55]

The story of kanaka maoli opposition to the Hawaiian shark fin industry reminds us that, despite the disproportionately white and affluent makeup of the mainstream environmental movement, nonwhite Americans possess their own histories of environmental concern and activism. For Indigenous peoples, like kānaka maoli, these environmental issues have become entwined with questions of cultural autonomy and sovereignty. This chapter contends that people of color have shaped the environmental thinking of America's dominant culture, leading to legislative changes at both local and national levels. In the case explored here, this influence represented an important instance of Pacific peoples affecting the broader course of U.S. environmental history. Perhaps most significant, the coalition of kanaka and non-kanaka individuals (including many Chinese Hawaiians) who came together to restrict shark finning in the state hints at possibilities for a more diverse and inclusive U.S. environmental movement moving forward.

Notes

1. When used as an adjective, *kanaka maoli* lacks the macron above the first "a"; when referencing the people themselves, it is spelled *kānaka maoli*. In both instances, the current standard is to avoid capitalization.

2. William Aila, "Testimony: WESPAC Pelagic Advisory Panel House, Resources, Fisheries, Wildlife and Oceans Shark Finning," Federal Document Clearing House Congressional Testimony, April 13, 2000 (this and all other Federal Document Clearing House materials accessed online via Lexis Nexis Academic, August 15–20, 2016).

3. Aila, "Testimony."

4. Randy "Duke" Cunningham, representative, "Testimony: House Resources Fisheries, Wildlife and Oceans Shark Finning and Coral Reef Preservation," Federal Document Clearing House Congressional Testimony, October 21, 1999; Randy "Duke" Cunningham, "Prepared Testimony before the House Committee on Resources Subcommittee on Fisheries Conservation, Wildlife and Oceans, Subject—H.R. 3535, The Shark Finning Prohibition Act," Federal News Service, April 13, 2000.

5. See, for instance, Merchant, "Shades of Darkness," 380–94; Mendoza, "Unnatural Border."

6. See, for instance, Brechin, "Conserving the Race," 229–45; Isenberg, *Destruction of the Bison*, 170; Lowenthal, *George Perkin Marsh*, 59; Stern, *Eugenic Nation*, 115–55; Kosek, *Understories*, 144–61; Spiro, *Defending the Master Race*; Allen, "Culling the Herd," 31–72; Powell, *Vanishing America*.

7. For the diverse roots of the contemporary environmental movement, see Gottlieb, *Forcing the Spring*.

8. See, for instance, Glave and Stoll, *To Love the Wind*.

9. This definition and all other definitions of Hawaiian terms in this essay paraphrased from Ulukau, accessed August 16, 2022, https://wehewehe.org/.

10. Dell'Apa, Smith, and Kaneshiro-Pineiro, "Influence of Culture," 154. For a useful discussion of race relations in Hawai'i, see Bailey and Farber, "'Double-V Campaign,'" 817–43.

11. For examples of work on Hawaiʻi, see Fischer, *Cattle Colonialism*; McNeill, "Of Rats and Men," 299–349. For an overarching narrative of American environmental history, see Fiege, *Republic of Nature*.

12. Bolster calls marine environmental history a new research "frontier"; see Bolster, "Opportunities."

13. McNeill, "Perils of Writing," 15–17; Silva, *Aloha Betrayed*, 1–3; Chang, *World*, ix; Arista, "Navigating Uncharted Oceans," 663–69; Arista, "'Moʻolelo and Mana,'" 415–43; Smith, *Decolonizing Methodologies*, 3, 44.

14. Silva has identified some errors in these translations; see Silva, *Aloha Betrayed*, 22. Also see Silva, *Aloha Betrayed*, 2; Chang, *World*, vii, ix.

15. Chang, *World*, viii, 4, 6, 9, 15; Joesting, *Hawaii*, 14–15; Kirch, *Shark Going Inland*, 19.

16. Chang, *World*, 8; Osorio, *Remembering Our Intimacies*.

17. Kamakau, *Ka Poʻe Kahiko*, 73; Beckwith, "Hawaiian Shark Aumakua," 503; DellʼApa, Smith, and Kaneshiro-Pineiro, "Influence of Culture," 153; Chang, *World*, 1, 9; Chun, *No Na Mamo*, 179; Taylor, *Sharks of Hawaiʻi*, 19.

18. Kamakau, *Ka Poʻe Kahiko*, 73, 76; Beckwith, "Hawaiian Shark Aumakua," 510–11; Nunes, *Investigation*, 3, 14; Taylor, *Sharks of Hawaiʻi*, 19, 26–27.

19. Beckwith, "Hawaiian Shark Aumakua," 513–15; Nunes, *Investigation*, 14; Taylor, *Sharks of Hawaiʻi*, 19.

20. For accounts of this reincarnation process, see Kamakau, *Ka Poʻe Kahiko*, 77; Malo, *Hawaiian Antiquities*, 82; Beckwith, "Hawaiian Shark Aumakua," 505–6; Pukui, Haertig, and Lee, *Nānā I Ke Kumu*, 116; McGregor, *Na Kuaʻaina*, 75. Also see Nunes, *Investigation*, 14, 15; DellʼApa, Smith, and Kaneshiro-Pineiro, "Influence of Culture," 153; Goldberg-Hiller and Silva, "Sharks and Pigs," 429.

21. Kamakau, *Ka Poʻe Kahiko*, 73–76.

22. Beckwith, "Hawaiian Shark Aumakua," 503, 504.

23. Chun, *No Na Mamo*, 169; Joesting, *Hawaii*, 15; Taylor, *Sharks of Hawaiʻi*, 19; Kirch and OʼDay, "New Archaeological Insights," 487–90; DellʼApa, Smith, and Kaneshiro-Pineiro, "Influence of Culture," 153; Kirch, *Shark Going Inland*, 65.

24. Desha, *Kamehameha*, 12; Taylor, *Sharks of Hawaiʻi*, 25; Nunes, *Investigation*, 3.

25. Kamakau, *Na Hana*, 87; Desha, *Kamehameha*, 11–12; Nunes, *Investigation*, 7.

26. Nunes, *Investigation*, 3, 8–12; Taylor, *Sharks of Hawaiʻi*, 19.

27. Osseweijer, "Toothy Tale," 114; Heupel and Simpfendorfer, "Shark Biology," 519; Klimley, *Biology of Sharks*, 443; Bornatowski et al. "Ecological Importance," 1586–92. For useful discussions of traditional ecological knowledge and its relationship to science, see Reo and Whyte, "Hunting and Morality," 15–27; Whyte, "Traditional Ecological Knowledge," 1–12.

28. Merry, *Colonizing Hawaiʻi*, 22.

29. Merry, *Colonizing Hawai'i*, 23; Silva, *Aloha Betrayed*, 3, 16; Dougherty, *To Steal a Kingdom*, 160–76; Chang, *World*, viii; Kamahele, "'Īlio'ulaokalani," 76.

30. Blackford, "Environmental Justice," 544. Also see Kamahele, "'Īlio'ulaokalani," 77–80.

31. Boxberger, *To Fish in Common*, 154–72; Newell, *Tangled Webs of History*, 171; Goldberg-Hiller and Silva, "Sharks and Pigs," 429.

32. Lila Fujimoto, "Shark Hunter Quits Search after Threat," *Honolulu Star Bulletin*, November 28, 1991, A1, A8; Jon Yoshishige, "Threats End Shark Hunt," *Honolulu Advertiser*, November 29, 1991, A1, A4.

33. Yoshishige, "Threats End Shark Hunt," A1, A4. Also see "Editorial: Sharks: Let's Decide When to Hunt," *Honolulu Advertiser*, November 30, 1991, A8.

34. Edwin Tanji, "Maui Shark-Hunt Dispute Reportedly Resolved," *Honolulu Advertiser*, November 30, 1991, A1. Also see Becky Ashizawa, "Shark's Guardian Role Valued by Hawaiians," *Honolulu Star Bulletin*, November 30, 1991, A1.

35. Lila Fujimoto, "Shark Hunt Put on Hold over Cultural Issues," *Honolulu Star Bulletin*, November 30, 1991, A3; Christopher Neil, "Hawaiian Rite Planned to Help Ease Rift on Shark Hunt," *Honolulu Advertiser*, December 1, 1991, A3; Lila Fujimoto, "Shark Yielded Lone Lobster: But the State Says the Predator Could Have Been the Olowalu Killer," *Honolulu Star Bulletin*, December 12, 1991, A3; Thomas Kaser, "Shark Task Force Called Offensive," *Honolulu Advertiser*, January 1, 1993, A1; Tino Ramirez, "Shark," *Honolulu Advertiser*, September 19, 1993, A1, A2; Jan TenBruggencate, "Biting Back: Some on Kauai Urge State to Take Action and Fish for Sharks," *Honolulu Advertiser*, November 18, 1993, A3; Taylor, *Sharks of Hawai'i*, 28; Chun, *No Na Mamo*, 184; Dell'Apa, Smith, and Kaneshiro-Pineiro, "Influence of Culture," 153–54.

36. Dell'Apa, Smith, and Kaneshiro-Pineiro, "Influence of Culture," 151–54; Verlecar et al., "Shark Hunting," 1078; Klimley, *Biology of Sharks*, 450.

37. Dell'Apa, Smith, and Kaneshiro-Pineiro, "Influence of Culture," 152–53; Klimley, *Biology of Sharks* 451.

38. National Coalition for Marine Conservation to Mr. Jim Cook, November 24, 1998, HSA, box 304-1999-10; Tony Costa to Committee on Ocean Recreation and Marine Resources, February 6, 1999, HSA, box 305-1999-11; Jefferies, "Think Globally, Act Locally," 157.

39. Compagno, "Shark Exploitation and Conservation," 412; Verlecar et al., "Shark Hunting," 1078; Heupel and Simpfendorfer, "Shark Biology," 517; Harry et al., "Evaluating Catch," 710–11; Carlson et al., "Relative Abundance," 1749–64; Klimley, *Biology of Sharks*, 443, 452–54.

40. Klimley, *Biology of Sharks*, 438, 450–451; Barausse et al., "role of Fisheries," 1593–1603; Verlecar et al., "Shark Hunting," 1078–82; Baum et al., "Collapse and Conservation," 389–92.

41. Jefferies, "Think Globally, Act Locally," 127, 133, 135; Dell'Apa, Smith, and Kaneshiro-Pineiro, "Influence of Culture," 157.

42. "Session Laws of Hawaii: Regular Session, 2000," HSA, call number KFH 25.A28, 2000.

43. Kahu Charles Kauluwehl Maxwell Sr., "Testimony," February 25, 1999, HSA, box 305-1999-5, 1; William J. Aila Jr. to Honorable Chairperson Colleen Hanabusa, April 5, 1999, HSA, box 305-1999-5, 1. Also see William J. Aila to Committee on Ocean Recreation and Marine Resources, February 5, 1999, HSA, box 305-1999-11; William J. Aila Jr. to Honorable Chairperson Colleen Hanabusa, April 2, 2000, HSA, box 304-2000-9; Bernard Keliikoa to Senator Colleen Hanabusa, April 3, 1999, HAS, box 305-1999-5; Bonnie Bator to Senator Colleen Hanabusa, April 1, 1999, HAS, box 305-1999-5; Duane C., "Relating to HB 1706," March 28, 1999, HSA, box 305-1999-5, 1.

44. Colette Machado to Senate Committee on Water, Land, and Hawaiian Affairs (hereinafter SCWLHA), March 30, 2000, HSA, box 304-2000-9, 1; Noa Emmett Aluli, "Testimony On HB No. 1947 HD 2 SD 1—Relating to Fisheries. Before the SCWLHA," April 3, 2000, HSA, box 304-2000-9, 1. Also see Governmental Affairs and Sovereignty Committee (GAS) of the Office of Hawaiian Affairs (OHA) to Senator Colleen Hanabusa, April 5, 1999, HSA, box 305-1999-5; "Reserve Advisory Council Members," Papahānaumokuākea Marine National Monument, accessed September 8, 2022, https://www.papahanaumokuakea.gov/new-about/council/members/.

45. Paul H. Achitoff, "Testimony Relating to House Bill 1706," February 25, 1999, HSA, box 305-1999-5, 2; Linda Paul to CWLHA, April 3, 2000, HSA, box 304-2000-9; Sue White, to SCWLHA "Testimony in Support of House Bill No. 1947 HD 2 SD1," April 3, 2000, HSA, box 304-2000-9; Judy Dalton, "HB1947 WLH Senate Committee—Monday April 3, 1pm," April 3, 2000, HSA, box 304-2000-9; Eric Gilman to Members of the SCWLHA, 30 March 2000, HSA, box 304-2000-9; Ira Rohter, "Related to Fisheries," April 6, 1999, HSA, box 305-1999-5; Caroline F. Gibson to Bob Endreson, April 1, 1999, HSA, box 305-1999-5; Jeffrey Mikulina to SCWLHA, April 5, 1999, HSA, box 305-1999-5; Don White to SCWLHA, April 3, 1999, HSA, box 305-1999-5; David Wilmot and Russell Dunn to the Honorable Colleen Hanabusa, March 18, 1999, HSA, box 305-1999-5; Jeffrey Mikulina to House Committee on Ocean Recreation and Marine Resources (hereinafter HCORMR), February 6, 1999, HSA, box 304-1999-10; Carroll Cox, "Testimony in Support of House Bill #1706," n.d., HSA, box 304-1999-10; Linda M. Paul to HCORMR, February 6, 1999, HSA, box 305-1999-11.

46. Zheng Qirong to Senator Hanabusa, April 3, 2000, HSA, box 304-2000-9, 1; Calvin Wong to Committee on Water, Land, and Hawaiian Affairs (hereinafter

CWLHA), n.d., HSA, box 305-1999-5. Also see Norman L. Cheu to SCWLHA, April 4, 1999, HSA, box 305-1999-5; Michael E. Lau to CWLHA, April 4, 1999, HSA, box 305-1999-5.

47. James Cook, "Testimony Submitted to the [CORMR] in Opposition to House Bill 1706," February 6, 1999, HSA, box 305-1999-11, 1; "Testimony October 21, 1999 James D. Cook House Resources Fisheries, Wildlife and Oceans Shark Finning and Coral Reef Preservation," Federal Document Clearing House Congressional Testimony, October 21, 1999, accessed November 18, 2016 via Lexis Nexis Academic. Also see James Cook, "Testimony Submitted to the [CWLHA] Regarding HB 1706, HD3, SD1," April 5, 1999, HSA, box 305-1999-5, 1, 7; James Cook, "Testimony Regarding HB 1947 SD 1," April 3, 2000, HSA, box 304-2000-9, 1; Captain Stephen W. Gates to CWLHA, April 4, 1999, HSA, box 305-1999-5, 1; Edwin "Junior" Cross to the Committee Concerning Fishing Regulations, February 5, 1999, HSA, box 305-1999-11; Bob Endreson, "Testimony Relating to HB 1706 HD 3," n.d., HSA, box 305-1999-5; Captain Rick Gaffney, "Testimony in Favor of HB 1706," March 25, 1999, HSA, box 305-1999-5.

48. Hu-Dehart, "Writing and Rewriting," 224–33; Ngai, *Impossible Subjects*, 7, 18; Lee, "'Yellow Peril,'" 537–62.

49. "Testimony April 13, 2000, William Aila, Fisherman, WESPAC Pelagic Advisory Panel House, Resources, Fisheries, Wildlife and Oceans Shark Finning," Federal Document Clearing House Congressional Testimony, April 13, 2000, accessed November 18, 2016 via Lexis Nexis Academic. Also see Dell'Apa, Smith, and Kaneshiro-Pineiro, "Influence of Culture," 152, 154; Jefferies, "Think Globally, Act Locally," 147.

50. Session Laws of Hawaii, Regular Session of 2010, Act 148, box 2169, 243; Jefferies, "Think Globally, Act Locally," 148.

51. "The HSUS, Hawaii Environmental Groups Urge House to Pass Bill to Protect Sharks," *Targeted News Service*, April 5 2010, 1; Julie A. K. Leialoha to House Committee on Judiciary, March 30, 2010, HSA, box 305-2010-17; Office of Hawaiian Affairs, "Legislative Testimony: SB 2169 SD 2, HD 2, Relating to Shark Fins, House Committee on Judiciary," March 30, 2010, HSA, box 305-2010-17. Also see Kathy Valier, "Testimony on SB 2169," March 28, 2010, HSA, box 305-2010-17; Jefferies, "Think Globally, Act Locally," 150.

52. Mary O'Malley to Committee on Judiciary, March 30, 2010, HSA, box 305-2010-17, 1. Also see George Massengale to Committee on Judiciary, March 28, 2010, HSA, box 305-2010-1, 1; Paula Walker to Committee on Economic Revitalization, Business and Military Affairs, March 6, 2010, HSA, box 305-2010-17; Erika Marchino, "Testimony for: COMMITTEE ON JUDICIARY. Re: Measure SB2169, SD2, HD2, Relating to Shark Fins," March 30, 2010, HSA, box 305-2010-17; Marjorie Ziegler,

"Testimony Submitted to the House Committee on Judiciary, SB 2169 SD 2 HD 2 Relating to Shark Fins," March 30, 2010, HSA, box 305-2010-17; Jeff Shaw, "Re: Measure SB2169, SD2, HD2 Relating to Shark Fins," March 26, 2010, HSA, box 305-2010-17; Bob Endreson, "Testimony Relating to: HB 1706," n.d., HSA, box 305-1999-11, 1.

53. Rod Tam to Representative Jon Karamatsu, March 30, 2010, HSA, box 305-2010-17, 1; Ginny Tiu to the Honorable Chair Karamatsu, March 29, 2010, HSA, box 305-2010-17. Also see Jefferies, "Think Globally, Act Locally," 156.

54. John Windrow, "Senator Pushing to Get Vote on Shark Fin Ban," *Honolulu Advertiser*, April 19, 2010, B1; Brandi-Leigh Adams, "Testimony for JUD," March 27, 2010, HSA, box 305-2010-17; Brandon Adams, "Testimony for SB2169," March 27, 2010, HSA, box 305-2010-17.

55. Jefferies, "Think Globally, Act Locally," 149, 151. For examples of international support, see Aline Pizani Zunino to Committee on Judiciary, n.d., HSA, box 305-2010-1; Katrien Vandevelde to Committee on Judiciary, n.d., HSA, box 305-2010-17; Andreas Keppeler, "Measure SB2169, SD, HD 2 Relating to Shark Fins," March 30, 2010, HSA, box 305-2010-17.

Bibliography

ARCHIVES AND MANUSCRIPT MATERIALS

HSA. Hawai'i State Archives, Honolulu, Hawai'i.

PUBLISHED WORKS

Allen, Garland E. "'Culling the Herd': Eugenics and the Conservation Movement in the United States, 1900–1940." *Journal of the History of Biology* 46 (2013): 31–72.

Arista, Noelani. "'Mo'olelo and Mana: The Transmission of Hawaiian History from Hawai'i to the United States, 1836–43." *Journal of the Early Republic* 38, no. 3 (Fall 2018): 415–43.

———. "Navigating Uncharted Oceans of Meaning: Kaona as Historical and Interpretive Method." *PMLA* 125, no. 3 (May 2010): 663–69.

Bailey, Beth, and David Farber, "The 'Double-V Campaign' in World War II Hawaii: African-Americans, Racial Ideology, and Federal Power." *Journal of Social History* 26, no. 4 (Summer 1993): 817–43.

Barausse, Alberto, et al. "The Role of Fisheries and the Environment in Driving the Decline of Elasmobranchs in the Northern Adriatic Sea." *ICES Journal of Marine Science* 71, no. 7 (2014): 1593–1603.

Baum, Julia K., et al. "Collapse and Conservation of Shark Populations in the Northwest Atlantic." *Science* 299, no. 5605 (January 17, 2003): 389–92.

Beckwith, Martha Warren. "Hawaiian Shark Aumakua." *American Anthropologist* 19, no. 4 (October–December 1917): 503–17.

Blackford, Mansel G. "Environmental Justice, Native Rights, Tourism, and Opposition to Military Control: The Case of Kahoʻolawe." *Journal of American History* 91, no. 2 (September 2004): 544–71.

Bolster, W. Jeffrey. "Opportunities in Marine Environmental History." *Environmental History* 11 (July 2006): 567–97.

Bornatowski, Hugo, et al. "Ecological Importance of Sharks and Rays in a Structural Foodweb Analysis in Southern Brazil." ICES *Journal of Marine Science* 71, no. 7 (2014): 1586–92.

Boxberger, Daniel L., *To Fish in Common: The Ethnohistory of Lummi Indian Salmon Fishing*. Lincoln: University of Nebraska Press, 1989.

Brechin, Gray. "Conserving the Race: Natural Aristocracies, Eugenics, and the U.S. Conservation Movement." *Antipode* 28, no. 3 (1996): 229–45.

Carlson, J. K., et al. "Relative Abundance and Size of Coastal Sharks Derived from Commercial Shark Longline Catch and Effort Data." *Journal of Fish Biology* 80 (2012): 1749–64.

Chang, David A. *The World and All the Things upon It: Native Hawaiian Geographies of Exploration*. Minneapolis: University of Minnesota Press, 2016.

Chun, Malcolm Naea. *No Na Mamo: Traditional and Contemporary Hawaiian Beliefs and Practices*. Honolulu: University of Hawaiʻi Press, 2011.

Compagno, L. J. V. "Shark Exploitation and Conservation." In *Elasmobranchs as Living Resources: Advances in the Biology, Ecology, Systematics, and the Status of the Fisheries*, NOAA Technical Report NMFS 90, edited by Harold L. Pratt Jr. et al., 391–414. Springfield VA: U.S. Department of Commerce, August 1990.

Dell'Apa, Andrea M., Chad Smith, Mahealani Y. Kaneshiro-Pineiro. "The Influence of Culture on the International Management of Shark Finning." *Environmental Management* 54 (2014): 154.

Desha, Stephen L. *Kamehameha and His Warrior Kekuhaupioʻo*. Translated by Frances N. Frazier. Honolulu: Kamehameha Schools Press, 2000.

Dougherty, Michael. *To Steal a Kingdom: Probing Hawaiian History*. Waimanalo HI: Island Style, 1994.

Fiege, Mark. *The Republic of Nature: An Environmental History of the United States*. Seattle: University of Washington Press, 2013.

Fischer, John Ryan. *Cattle Colonialism: An Environmental History of the Conquest of California and Hawaii*. Chapel Hill: University of North Carolina Press, 2015.

Glave, Dianne D., and Mark Stoll, eds. *To Love the Wind and the Rain: African Americans and Environmental History*. Pittsburgh PA: University of Pittsburgh Press, 2006.

Goldberg-Hiller, Jonathan, and Noenoe K. Silva. "Sharks and Pigs: Animating Hawaiian Sovereignty against the Anthropological Machine." *South Atlantic Quarterly* 110, no. 2 (Spring 2011): 429.

Gottlieb, Robert. *Forcing the Spring: The Transformation of the American Environmental Movement*. Washington DC: Island, 2005.

Harry, Alastair V., et al. "Evaluating Catch and Mitigating Risk in a Multispecies, Tropical, Inshore Shark Fishery within the Great Barrier Reef World Heritage Area." *Marine and Freshwater Research* 62, no. 6 (June 24, 2011): 710–21.

Heupel, Michelle R., and Colin A. Simpfendorfer. "Shark Biology, Ecology and Management: Introduction." *Marine and Freshwater Research* 62, no. 6 (June 24, 2011): 517.

Hu-Dehart, Evelyn. "Writing and Rewriting Women of Color." *Journal of Women's History* 13, no. 3 (Autumn 2001): 224–33.

Isenberg, Andrew C. *The Destruction of the Bison*. New York: Cambridge University Press, 2000.

Jefferies, Cameron S. G. "Think Globally, Act Locally: How Innovative Domestic American Efforts to Reduce Shark Finning May Accomplish What the International Community Has Not." *University of Hawai'i Law Review* 34, no. 202 (2012): 125–57.

Joesting, Edward. *Hawaii: An Uncommon History*. New York: W. W. Norton, 1972.

Kamahele, Momiala. "'Īlio'ulaokalani: Defending Native Hawaiian Culture." In *Asian Settler Colonialism: From Local Governance to the Habits of Everyday Life in Hawai'i*, edited by Candace Fujikane, 76–92. Honolulu: University of Hawai'i Press, 2008.

Kamakau, Samuel M. *Ka Po'e Kahiko: The People of Old*. Honolulu: Bishop Museum Press, 1964.

———. *Na Hana a ka Po'e Kahiko*. Honolulu: Bishop Museum Press, 1976.

Kirch, Patrick Vinton. *A Shark Going Inland Is My Chief: The Island Civilization of Ancient Hawai'i*. Berkeley: University of California Press, 2012.

Kirch, Patrick Vinton, and Sharyn Jones O'Day. "New Archaeological Insights into Food and Status: A Case Study from Pre-contact Hawaii." *World Archaeology* 34, no. 3 (February 2003): 487–90.

Klimley, A. Peter. *Biology of Sharks and Rays*. Chicago: University of Chicago Press, 2013.

Kosek, Jake. *Understories: The Political Life of Forests in Northern New Mexico*. Durham NC: Duke University Press, 2006.

Lee, Erika. "The 'Yellow Peril' and Asian Exclusion in the Americas." *Pacific Historical Review* 76, no. 4 (November 2007): 537–62.

Lowenthal, David. *George Perkin Marsh: Prophet of Conservation*. Seattle: University of Washington Press, 2003.

Malo, Davida. *Hawaiian Antiquities (Moolelo Hawaii)*. Translated by Nathaniel B. Emerson. Honolulu: Bishop Museum Press, 1951.

McGregor, Davianna Pomaikaʻi. *Na Kua ʻaina: Living Hawaiian Culture*. Honolulu: University of Hawaiʻi Press, 2007.

McNeill, J. R. "Of Rats and Men: A Synoptic Environmental History of the Island Pacific." *Journal of World History* 5, no. 2 (Fall 1994): 299–349.

———. "Perils of Writing Global Environmental History." *World History Bulletin* 29, no. 2 (Fall 2013): 15–17.

Mendoza, Mary E. "Unnatural Border: Race and Environment at the U.S.-Mexico Divide." PhD diss., University of California, Davis, 2015.

Merchant, Carolyn. "Shades of Darkness: Race and Environmental History." *Environmental History* 8, no. 3 (July 2003): 380–94.

Merry, Sally Engle. *Colonizing Hawaiʻi: The Cultural Power of Law*. Princeton NJ: Princeton University Press, 2000.

Newell, Dianne. *Tangled Webs of History: Indians and the Law in Canada's Pacific Coast Fisheries*. Toronto: University of Toronto Press, 1993.

Ngai, Mae M. *Impossible Subjects: Illegal Aliens and the Making of Modern America*. Princeton NJ: Princeton University Press, 2004.

Nunes, Keone. *Investigation of the Cultural Importance of Sharks to the Indigenous People of the U.S. Flag Areas in the Central and Western Pacific*. Hawaiʻi State Library: RH799.173 Nu. Honolulu: Hawaiʻi Audubon Society, 2003.

Osorio, Jamaica. *Remembering Our Intimacies: Moʻolelo, Aloha ʻĀina, and Ea*. St. Paul: University of Minnesota Press, 2021.

Osseweijer, Manon. "A Toothy Tale: A Short History of Shark Fisheries and Trade in Shark Products in Twentieth-Century Indonesia." In *A World of Water: Rain, Rivers, and Seas in Southeast Asian Histories*, edited by Peter Boomgaard, 103–21. Leiden: KITLV, 2007.

Powell, Miles A. *Vanishing America: Species Extinction, Racial Peril, and the Origins of Conservation*. Cambridge MA: Harvard University Press, 2016.

Pukui, Mary Kawena, E. W. Haertig, and Catherine A. Lee. *Nānā I Ke Kumu: Look to the Source* Vol. 1. Honolulu: Hui Hānai, 1972.

Reo, Nicholas James, and Kyle Powys Whyte. "Hunting and Morality as Elements of Traditional Ecological Knowledge." *Human Ecology* 40 (2012): 15–27.

Silva, Noenoe K. *Aloha Betrayed: Native Hawaiian Resistance to American Colonialism*. Durham NC: Duke University Press, 2004.

Smith, Linda Tuhiwai. *Decolonizing Methodologies: Research and Indigenous Peoples*. 2nd ed. London: Zed, 2012.

Spiro, Jonathan Peter. *Defending the Master Race: Conservation, Eugenics, and the Legacy of Madison Grant*. Lebanon NH: University Press of New England, 2009.

Stern, Alexandra Minna. *Eugenic Nation: Faults and Frontiers of Better Breeding in Modern America*. Berkeley: University of California Press, 2005.

Taylor, Leighton. *Sharks of Hawaiʻi: Their Biology and Cultural Significance*. Honolulu: University of Hawaiʻi Press, 1993.

Verlecar, X. N., Snigdha, S. R. Desai, and V. K. Dhargalkar. "Shark Hunting—an Indiscriminate Trade Endangering Elasmobranchs to Extinction." *Current Science* 92, no. 8 (April 25, 2007): 1078–82.

Whyte, Kyle Powys. "On the Role of Traditional Ecological Knowledge as a Collaborative Concept: A Philosophical Study." *Ecological Processes* 2, no. 7 (2013): 1–12.

Radical Presence—the Shadows Take Shape

African Americans (Re)making a Green World

CAROLYN FINNEY

And I could tell you about things we been through,
some awful ones, some wonderful, but I know that
the things that make us more than that, our lives
are more than the days in them, our lives are our
line and we go on.

—Lucille Clifton, *Good Woman: Poems and a Memoir*
1969–1980

We story, therefore we be.

—Kevin Young, *The Grey Album: On the Blackness of*
Blackness

In 2013 a *New York Times* article entitled "Urban Gardening: An Appleseed with an Attitude" profiled Ron Finley as a guerrilla gardener who believes that "you ain't gangsta" unless you're planting something.[1] Linking the image of a "gangsta" with gardens, Finley challenges predominant narratives of urban blight and Blackness by tapping into a radical imagining of space, place, and self in order. His words, in effect, sought to redefine perceptions of urban Blackness and resurrect a sense of connection to a hopeful future.

He's not alone.

In the United States, there are historical and contemporary spaces (including slavery, Jim Crow segregation, economic disenfranchisement, and racial profiling) in which African Americans have survived and thrived, revealing a geographical intelligence that defies ongoing attempts to bind Black life through cultural mores and norms, policy, and law. By becoming adept at "making [a] way out of no way," African Americans like Finley engage in the "critical labor of the positive" to construct the landscape in their own image; one that reflects a radical repositioning of who African Americans are (and what we are capable of) from our own perspective.[2] It's not so much about the form that labor takes—it can be gardening, starting a green business, creating art on the streets, or telling a story. Instead, our potential is revealed through a claiming of our own creativity and potential for "becoming" in relationship to a set of systems and a dominant narrative that has historically limited our possibilities.

What does the word *radical* mean? How does it manifest itself on the ground, in real time? How might we theorize Blackness as a radical presence, and why does it matter? Definitions of the word *radical* speak to new origins or roots. It is defined as "of or going to the root or origin" or as something "very new and different from what is traditional or ordinary."[3] I like both of these definitions because going to the root of something can be revelatory and expansive while also keeping us grounded by remaining connected to who we've always been. For African Americans in particular, this can be both life-affirming and empowering, especially when your presence has been diminished, erased, and dismissed. African American poet Nikky Finney's (no relation) definition of *radical*—"grabbing it by the root"—however, highlights an agency and undeniable tenacity that makes the idea of "radical" sexy, bold, boisterous, and even a little outrageous.[4] Cab Calloway in a zoot suit struttin' and singin' in Harlem on a Saturday night is an excellent depiction of this, or Zora Neale Hurston driving her jalopy through the South collecting stories while Jim Crow watched from the sidelines. Angela Davis flashing her brilliance in defiance of the mediocrity of limited thinking that whiteness tried to impose on Others is yet another fabulous example, as well as Muhammad Ali, like poetry in motion, signaling his right to fight a different battle than the war imposed on the rest of us. These historical actors flashing their radical brilliance are points on a compass, a way of orienteering oneself over a topography of lived Blackness that cannot necessarily be captured by "traditional" or "ordinary" measurements and articulations. These elements have no shape, no tactility, and yet, without them, we miss what is and has been truly radical about their presence.

Everything that we do in life is spatial. Our social worlds, our domestic, private lives, and even our imagined worlds, all unfold in space. Our lives take shape temporally through a number of diverse interactions across space and time.[5] So our geographies—the why we do what we do where we do it—are exposed in our relationships, in our everyday practices, and in our dreams. And how those different elements come together can reveal the character of radical presence, with no one element necessarily more important than the other. Within the constellation of Black experience real and imagined each strand brings with it the possibility of something different, something fresh, something radical.

Consider the Guild in Boston, founded by community activist and Harvard-trained scholar Jhana Senxian.[6] She believes there is a different way to do sustainable urban development and all things green, particularly in Black communities. By taking a holistic approach to the project, Ms. Senxian recognizes it is more than making sure that their buildings are LEED certified (they are) or engaging inner city youth (they do) as central to their plan.[7] Creating the Guild was and is also about the practice of being a "community-driven social enterprise" that considers all aspects of our lives and is not afraid to define what being green looks like in more expansive ways, including the creation of medicinal gardens and birthing stations, developing the Washington Street Food Forest, and inviting artists to do year-long residencies that consider the city as a hub of sustainability and innovation. In a sense, "sustainability work" here is an artistic act that embodies an African American tradition of responding to challenging issues with imagination and creativity. By intentionally tapping into the diverse elements of Black life and dreams, Senxian and her community "grab the root" of what is possible in order to honor and express Black identity.

The title of this chapter is borrowed from an art show on display at the Studio Museum in Harlem in 2013. The exhibition, *The Shadows Took Shape: Radical Presence, Black Performance in Contemporary Art*, spotlighted the work of various Black artists from the 1960s to the present who employ multiple methods of artistic expression to mark their radical presence. The Studio Museum highlighted the work of several artists, including Theaster Gates, Carrie Mae Weems, David Hammons, and Girl (Chitra Ganesh and Simone Leigh). The show, organized by Valerie Cassel Oliver, "chronicle[d] the emergence and development of black performance art over three generations."[8] Analyzed through the lens of cultural geography, the artists revealed how they showed up, in all their Blackness, on the street, in their homes, in their art studios, in crowds, and in both real and imagined ways of everyday living. This chapter builds upon these ideas to push the field to consider the meaning of *radical* in Black life and, in particular, what that looks like when Black folks engage in all things "green."

In the broadest sense, being "green" is embracing an understanding and a set of practices about the environment that reflect an awareness of the need to consume, protect, and engage nonhuman nature with an eye toward the future. By encouraging certain behaviors and practices that respect the limitations of what "nature" has to offer (and understand the consequences if we don't), we make it possible for our children and our children's children to thrive. But embedded within this idea of being green is a set of assumptions that elevates a Eurocentric experience of the environment as universal while obscuring the day-to-day realities of being nonwhite in a country that, among other things, was built on the backs of enslaved Africans who were forced to work the land but were denied any benefits from the fruits of that labor. For African Americans like Ron Finley, "being green" is also about transforming that forced relationship to land through slavery into a relationship where we can see and be ourselves beyond the definitions and inherent limitations imposed on our lives by the dominant culture.[9]

What does that look like? How do we understand, what Rebecca Walker calls, the "audacious aesthetic choices" that are an expression of lived Blackness in a green and white world?[10] First, to understand "radical presence" means to take stories seriously. For African Americans, seeing the world from some universally accepted theoretical framework—a metanarrative, a single story (read: whiteness)—obscures what is both unique and specific to the Black experience.[11] Tapping into that "intelligence of the soul," that "sophisticated frequency" of understanding that African Americans have collectively developed over time in response to social and economic sanctions on our lives means inviting in the radical presence of those experiences on their own terms, narrated as a kaleidoscope of stories.[12] Allowing stories to infiltrate our geographical conversations about the Black experience as insights into alternative epistemological starting points offers us a way to see "black folks embodying a spirit of abundance and plenty" with "unsuppressed elegance and grace."[13] This is not to deny the systemic modes of oppression that diminish the material existence of Black people. Instead, it can paint a fuller picture of Blackness that is radical in interpretation and embodiment. As geographers Katherine McKittrick and Clyde Woods have put it, "Within and against the grain of dominant modes of power, knowledge, and space, these black geographic narratives and lived experiences need to be taken seriously because they reconfigure classificatory spatial practices."[14]

Mere linear narrative and words on a page make it difficult to paint a picture of Black possibility on the landscape that continues to pay no attention to the rules but instead taps into something W. E. B. Du Bois called "spiritual striving."[15] The roots of that striving manifest as resilience. With that in mind, this chapter will do three things: First, it will explore some of the ways African Americans are living Black in a green world. Second, it will "mix and blur" creative and academic writing as a way to "challenge conventional perceptions created by our attachment to fixed ways of looking that lead to blindspots."[16] Finally, it will use "storying" as Kevin Young calls it, to get at the nonlinear forms of expression and embodiment of radical presence that can be difficult to see and articulate through traditional analysis.

Despite the limitation of words, this chapter aims to capture the "space between the words" and prove its value for those within intellectual and academic circles.[17] It is time to disrupt the relationship from the margin to the center and consider the possibilities of a different configuration. It is time to consider Black histories that incorporate mystery, superstition, religion, family lore, and passed-down knowledge—it's time to consider different stories. When we do that, we can see the ways in which Black radical presence is and always has been green in one way or another, and this chapter can only explore but a few of those examples.

This "reconfiguring" not only changes how we engage in our empirical work but redistributes the power of knowledge construction and impacts the flow of ideas. For the purposes of this piece, we should consider the creative as a mode of everyday practice that becomes legible as a form of place-making and self-definition integral to creating a sense of home and belonging. We see the stories, like the gardens, not simply as anecdotes to our analysis but as a "form of rescue," revelation, and possibility.[18]

Cultural geographer Edward Soja states that "we make our geographies just as it has been said that we make our histories, not under conditions of our own choosing but in the material and imagined worlds we collectively have already created—or that have been created for us."[19] In the environmental movement, Black people are often seen as marginalized, on the edges, in the shadows of the conceptual and material manifestations of mainstream environmentalism. But the margins can be a place of "radical openness," in the sense described by bell hooks, where spatial appropriation is an act of creative rebellion.[20] By "connecting black self-recovery and ecology," the shadows take shape in the form of creative and innovative responses to environmental challenges that reflect a historical trajectory of using ingenuity as a tool for survival and expression of presence that will not be denied. The following stories are prescriptions that provide what Dianne Rocheleau calls a "relational ontology from the good dirt."[21]

Once Upon a Time . . .

Gee's Bend is the name of the predominately African American community located on the bend of the Alabama River in Wilcox County, Alabama. Founded in the 1800s, the town was originally named for the first white settler in the area, John Gee, who, along with purchasing six thousand acres of land, brought with him eighteen enslaved people. In 1949, the town was officially renamed Boykin after Frank Boykin, a white congressman from Mobile. The reservoir was named after white judge William Dannelly. In each of these instances, despite the presence of a majority African American community in the area, official place names honored white rather than Black people. In the context of Jim Crow, where African Americans were denied access to spaces and opportunities that might enhance their lives (receiving loans, being able to choose the neighborhoods they could live in, participating freely in the political arena, etc.), naming and claiming the land through traditional means was not an open avenue for the Black community.[22]

And yet, this community found ways to express and validate its presence in this geographically isolated settlement, a place often "regarded as a throwback: an antebellum artifact, even an Alabama Africa."[23] Geographic isolation; the imposition of cultural, social, and economic interventions (such as federal farm cooperative initiatives and the civil rights movement); and the "contributions" of outsiders all lent themselves to the construction of a mythology of Gee's Bend—a place made unique by its location and its tenacity in holding onto its past in the present. Historical accounts of living in this place are filled with tales of people being impoverished as children, working hard in the fields instead of going to school, receiving minimal help from the government, and being offered limited employment opportunities. "Piecing, cooking, working in the fields. Had to," says Annie Bell Pettway, a descendant of the enslaved Africans belonging to one of the area's original slaveholding families.[24] These day-to-day tasks of providing for one's self and family were further complicated by the legacy of slavery, segregation, and poverty that permeate the history of Gee's Bend.

The "piecing" that Mrs. Pettway speaks about has drawn national and even international attention to Gee's Bend. Since the 1920s, the women in this small town of approximately seven hundred have been producing extraordinary quilts as a practical response to livelihood needs and as an act of self-definition. Using whatever scraps of material they could find, the women of Gee's Bend created these quilts as family heirlooms that symbolized self-reliance, "stoic resilience," socialization, a sense of the sacred, and survival.[25] And unlike fieldwork, child-raising, and keeping house, quilt-making as a form of self-expression made space for creating more complex self-portraits of these women and, by extension, creating a portrait of Gee's Bend as a home place. Piecing a quilt was "a genuine and culturally sanctioned occurrence of artmaking as an emancipatory act."[26]

There are many African American communities around the United States that have a history of quilt-making. What is particularly unusual about the quilts of Gee's Bend is the context from which they sprang and their abstract quality. Their quilts "embody a free adaptation of form that appears to be both accidental and transgressive."[27] So inspired by their beauty, which was sharpened by the contrast to the economic and social challenges facing the inhabitants of Gee's Bend, art collector Will Arnett began a project (over a ten-year period) to document the quilts and the voices of the women of Gee's Bend. Together with curators, researchers, and photographers, Arnett set out to "detail the community of women who created some of the most incredible works of art of the twentieth century."[28] To date, there have been many national exhibitions and numerous books published about the quilts of Gee's Bend.[29] Art critic Michael Kimmerman has compared these quilts to the work of Matisse and Klee.[30] After the first exhibit of their quilts in 2002 in Houston, Texas, the women of Gee's Bend founded the Gee's Bend Quilters Collective. Quilts range from $1,000 to $20,000, prices that reflect their popularity and their beauty. Quilt-making, in short, has transformed the lives of those who make them.

Gee's Bend as a place is also undergoing a transformation. The Department of Architecture, Design, and Construction at nearby Auburn College is working with local inhabitants to design a plan that makes Gee's Bend a sustainable tourist destination.[31] Ideas include a community and education center, focus on agriculture and food production, sustainable housing, and a rainwater collection system. Both environmental and economic sustainability are central to current ideas being considered by the college and the community.

How do we interpret these quilts as a representation of radical presence on the landscape? While the quilts were seen as a "cushion" against real world elements, they were also an expression of the complexity of their lives where improvisation meant the difference between survival and death. In the same way that singers such as Mahalia Jackson infused their hands with wild thinking (some of the quilt-makers listened to gospel singing for inspiration, and Jackson is considered by many to have been the "Queen of Gospel"), an examination of the quilts reminds us that "such improvisation in the black community is . . . expected . . . the striving towards ingenuity is represented in everything: in playing an instrument or singing, in plowing or planting, in hair styling and personal adornment, in cooking and . . . in quilting."[32] And as it was historically across the United States, "ingenuity in Gee's Bend was not exceptional; as in black culture at large, it was expected."[33] The making of the quilts by these Black women also tells a story about the making of Gee's Bend. The quilts reflect an imaginary landscape uninhibited by "slave owners and landlords alike, convulsed by government intervention, fortified by fervent Christianity, and now eddied in the flood of globalization."[34] Instead, that existence is sewn into the complexity of the quilts themselves and becomes part and parcel of the everyday practices, material possibilities, and radical imaginings of the women of Gee's Bend. The quilts represent stories, both real and imagined, experienced by the women who make them.

While Gee's Bend is not an "environmental" story in the traditional sense, it is a story about place-making and radical thinking expressed in forms that shatter misconceptions about who these people are and what might be possible in the place that they live. Their actions and practices extend from "a centered and anchored self" that is not solely contingent on material externalities that define their existence.[35] On its surface, we might understand Gee's Bend as a place severely lacking in opportunity; its inhabitants' ability to construct a life imbued with meaning and vision is inhibited by history, economic and social constraints, and social and cultural geography. The overwhelming nature of religious, capitalist, and government interventions—all things that have clearly affected those who live in Gee's Bend over the past several decades—can cloud our ability to recognize other, equally important transformative influences that shape everyday practices.

Imagine looking at an object—say a quilt, garden, or a place—from one angle only; you get a sense of and an idea about it that captures only one aspect of that object. If we take only that one experience and we codify it in a particular way, it obfuscates greater understandings of what that quilt, garden, or place truly represents. If we instead broaden our view to account for the various viewpoints, experiences, policies, and other factors that have helped to shape Gee's Bend (and in turn, the quilts made there), we see the quilt, garden, or place differently, which in turn impacts your original assumptions about that object—its use, its nature, its value, and its meaning.

Just looking at the story of Gee's Bend from the perspective of the Black majority who lives there rather than from the white men it was named for exposes new worlds of possibility and changes from what we historically privilege as being important in the lives of the people who live there. This, in turn, opens up the possibility of recognizing radical presence on its own terms—at once both jarring and surprising—as something that defies intellectual boundaries, challenges conventional thinking, and requires us to settle into the tension of not fully understanding what it is that we're seeing and what it all means.

The story of Gee's Bend sets the tone for how we might understand radical presence as a state of being where "the rules"—those accepted understandings, definitions, and expectations of what it means to be poor and Black in the United States—do not necessarily apply. Gee's Bend can be a kind of legend, a way to read other stories of Black and green, to understand a topography of lived experience that sings and even sews with defiance, rhythms, contradictions, and joy, where the geographies we live in are "not just dead background or a neutral physical stage for the human drama but are filled with material and imagined forces that affect events and experiences."[36] Those imagined forces are literally interwoven with our material realities thrusting us into a state of radical openness and possibility. Using the story of Gee's Bend as a kind of conceptual kaleidoscope, we begin to see the many complex patterns that continue to change with each turn of our hand.

The Beach Lady

When she was a little girl, MaVynee Betsch loved digging and making mud pies on her beloved American Beach. Bought by her great-grandfather A. L. Lewis, American Beach was one of the few places in the South where African

Americans could own a home on the beach during the Jim Crow era. The beach was designated as *the* premier Black beach resort in the 1940s and was frequented by the rich as well as the working class. It was known as a place where Black society could find respite from the stress of living in the Jim Crow South. For MaVynee, it was simply home.

MaVynee enjoyed a life of economic privilege. She attended the conservatory of music at Oberlin College in 1955 and soon after went to Germany, where she pursued a career in opera. For many years, she achieved success and was undeterred by the societal limitations placed on those with Black skin during the 1950s and '60s in the United States. But in the 1970s MaVynee decided to return home to American Beach after years of living in Europe.

She was motivated to do so because of her extensive involvement with environmental causes. When she first returned home, she set her sights on international concerns. She became the patron for Dr. Robert Pyle, who studied the monarch butterfly and contributed money to organizations that supported indigenous pygmy communities in Central Africa. (When I asked her why she was motivated to give to efforts supporting the pygmies, she replied, "To know that they're here.")[37] But it was her environmental work in the United States that began to bring her national attention. In the end, she gave away all her wealth to environmental causes—over $750,000, including her great-grandfather's house that she had inherited.[38] MaVynee talked about how, for a period of time, she slept on a chaise lounge on the beach. Kids would come along and try to give her a hard time, but she managed to scare them off.[39] Eventually, her sister, well-known scholar Johnetta Cole, provided Betsch with a trailer home, which she promptly turned into a local archive where she would share the history of American Beach. Known as the "Beach Lady," Betsch became the person visitors wanted to meet because of the wealth of knowledge she possessed about American Beach and her radical life choices concerning the protection and care of the place where she had grown up. Betsch was passionate and motivated because she was worried that both the natural environment and the cultural history of American Beach would be swept away like so many grains of sand.

By the 1970s, developers were salivating at the possibilities that American Beach presented with its maritime forests and its white sand beaches and dunes, which MaVynee lovingly called NaNa. But Betsch refused to accept their desires to transform her community beach. Striking a formidable presence with her floor-length dreadlocks adorned with shells and buttons, Betsch would stand in the back of community meetings reciting the Pledge of Allegiance along with other concerned community members. Her voice was just one of the many until she reached the last line, "with liberty and justice for all," and instead would shout out "for all white folks who got money!" Betsch knew that she raised more than just a few eyebrows, but she was adamant about the ways in which money seduced people into making decisions that would negatively impact American Beach.

"I am the freest person you will ever meet," Betsch once said to me with a smile.[40] She believed that giving away all her money allowed her to be free from an economic system that locked her into traditional thinking and the risk of insecurity, which would ultimately lead to the detriment of her work. While she admits to experiencing challenges, Betsch also said that she always had what she needed. Her everyday practices of living, eating, and working were adjusted, revealing a whole set of radical possibilities that Betsch leaned into with courage and conviction. She was on a mission to be heard, and while many considered her approach to be somewhat unusual, it worked for her. Almost single-handedly, Betsch brought attention to the importance of recognizing the beach as a wellspring of African American history—a place where Black families were making history by living and playing on beachfront property at a time where having Black skin limited one's mobility and possibility of building a legacy for their children. She enlisted numerous community members, local, state, and national organizations to her cause. Along with the American Beach Historical District being listed as a national historic site in 2002 (the periods of significance listed are 1925–49 and 1950–74), the National Park Service has put 8.5 acres of the sand dunes under their protection.[41]

While the story of the "Beach Lady" has appeared in numerous magazine and newspaper articles (and journalist Russ Rymer wrote a book with MaVynee at the center, and there are two films about MaVynee's life), the mainstream environmental movement has been slow to adopt Betsch's story of radical presence in an environmental movement that appears to want to engage a more diverse constituency.[42] Betsch's story does not fit within mainstream narratives of environmentalism—race, class, and gender come together in her story in a way that does not compute with traditional frameworks about individuals who make innovative, bold, and radical environmental choices like giving up luxury as a means of preservation. MaVynee's life trajectory was not solely determined by the social and economic mores of the time (she was born in 1935, under the specter of Jim Crow, and died in 2005). Instead, like the quilt-makers of Gee's Bend, who lived and worked in challenging circumstances, Betsch radically repositioned herself to the norms and expectations of the times, and the expression of that repositioning was both revealing and emancipatory. What she was able to imagine was so much more than the limitations on and assumptions about what Black people could offer. In a way, Betsch challenged the idea that we have to play in a sandbox that was created for us, but not by us; she believed we could and should play on the beach. Her sense of self was her own definition fueled by dreams, faith, and old-fashioned chutzpah.

In 2005, MaVynee Betsch passed away after a long battle with cancer. But her legacy lives on as Black and white Floridians continue to protect and preserve American Beach. To add to that, before she died, MaVynee told me that "even in death I will haunt those developers." In that vein, radical presence takes on a whole new meaning.

The Irresistible Ones

They arrive knocking at Osborne's great garnet door. They want to study
mathematics, join the debate team, and sing in the choir. They are
    three in a sea of
six thousand. With each step, they pole-vault shards of doubt, sticks
    of dynamite, and
stubborn hate mail. With them arrives the bright peppermint of
    change. The new
laws of the new day can no longer resist these three irresistible ones,
    in a sea of six
thousand, stepping through a door now garnet and black.
  —Nikky Finney, 2013

There is one final story that I would like to share. On September 11, 1963, three African Americans defied the laws of segregation and walked through the doors of the University of South Carolina to register for classes. To commemorate that particular moment of radical presence, the university asked the poet Nikky Finney, a homegrown South Carolinian, and topiary artist

Pearl Fryar to create poetry through words and greenery that lay witness to this moment.

I met Pearl Fryar in the fall of 2014 in Bishopville, South Carolina, a largely rural, white, impoverished area where Pearl (as he is commonly known) and his wife, Metra, made their home more than thirty years ago. Now in his seventies, he was still bustling about his famed topiary garden like a man twenty years his junior. As the son of a sharecropper, Pearl was no stranger to living an agriculturally dependent life. But while internationally known for his topiary and gardening skills today, he had never engaged in any kind of horticultural work until he settled in Bishopville. "I couldn't afford my talent until I turned forty," he confided.[43] He was determined to challenge the prevailing idea in that community that "Black people don't keep their yards looking nice" by turning his yard into a topiary masterpiece. Pearl had a vision, and with an electric saw in hand, he took discarded plants and trees to help make that vision a reality. "When he's in the garden, it's man relating to nature," says his wife, Metra.[44] Indeed, thousands of people come from all over the world to experience his masterful rendition of "nature" as *he* sees it.

It should come as no surprise that he was asked to help create a garden (along with poet Nikky Finney) that commemorates the lives of Henri Monteith Treadwell, Robert Anderson, and James Solomon, three African Americans who defied the "rules" of Jim Crow and became the first African Americans students to attend the University of South Carolina. For his part, Pearl contributed three juniper trees that he cultivated and turned into "living sculptures." Reflecting on the experience, he remembered standing on picket lines and taking an active role in the civil rights movement. "If you had told me 50 years ago that one day, I would be asked to do this sculpture, I would have thought I'd lost my mind. This is huge—shows how far we've come."[45]

These stories are but snapshots of experiences, stories, and possibilities of Black radical presence on landscapes that have been dominated by white power and privilege. While differentiated by location, time, and individual proclivities, there is a common thread of improvisation, ingenuity, and attention to self-definition that continues to shape lived experiences of possibility and radical practice for Black people engaged in place-making and environmental issues. The use of storying as a way of pointing to shared themes also affirms the "depth and range of experience to testify about reality" and the many ways that Black people make meaning in the world.[46] "We story, therefore we be," as Kevin Young states. This is a reminder that we make and remake ourselves through the very act of telling—and living—stories on our terms.

Despite the interventions designed to restrict, subvert, and deny Black life on the U.S. landscape, African Americans utilize agency, identity, and civic engagement as a means to expand this narrative of disenfranchisement. Adaptiveness, resilience, fearlessness, and courage aren't the anomaly; they are the reality. While marginalization as a by-product of white supremacy and oppression was and is certainly part of lived reality for many African Americans, focusing primarily on their/our subjugation denies the malleability of the Black imagination to create and construct a rich reality that is not grounded primarily in victimhood but in human ingenuity and the rhythms and flows of life.[47] According to Soja, whether "efforts to make changes in our existing spatial configurations involve redecorating our homes, fighting against racial segregation in our cities, creating policies to reduce income inequalities between the developed and developing countries, or combating global warming do not express innocent or universally held objectives," they "are the target and source of conflicting purposes, competing forces, and contentious political actions for and against the status quo. Space is not an empty void. It is always filled with politics, ideology, and other forces shaping our lives and challenging us to engage in struggles over geography."[48] Creating radical presence is also an act of embodying the everyday in a way that acknowledges and respects the diverse contours of Black life that is often depicted as limited and wanting. It is about self-definition on one's own terms on a cultural, social, and economic landscape that does not recognize or privilege an ability to see the world that is not reflective of or in service to the dominant culture in a way that is legible. It's about the *extraordinary* being *ordinary*—as ingenuity is understood as being expected in African American culture.

Finally, radical presence is about creating home in places that historically have tried to deny us our right to be here and be seen and belong in a way that honors our full humanity. U.S. poet laureate Sonia Sanchez, in a conversation about Black people with critical theorist and activist Angela Davis, said, "We have a right to be here. We have to reimagine ourselves on this American landscape."[49] That reimagining is revealed over and over again by how African Americans grab the root of who we are, past and present, and create and re-create ourselves again and again on the U.S. landscape. Ron Finley, MaVynee Betsch, Pearl Fryar, and the women of Gee's Bend are but a few Black expressions of green in a world that denies, erases, and forgets the complexity of lived experience as it relates to place and belonging in a world that centers whiteness as universal.

The shadow of what we might become continues to take shape in the world around us.

Notes

1. David Hochman, "Urban Gardening: An Appleseed with an Attitude," *New York Times*, May 3, 2013, https://www.nytimes.com/2013/05/05/fashion/urban -gardening-an-appleseed-with-attitude.html.

2. Williams-Forson, *Building Houses*; hooks, *Art on My Mind*, 67.

3. "Why We Are Radical," The Body Is Not An Apology, accessed April 18, 2023, https://thebodyisnotanapology.com/about-tbinaa/why-we-are-radical/; "Radical," in *The Britannica Dictionary*, accessed April 18, 2023, https://www.britannica .com/dictionary/radical.

4. Finney has published numerous books of poetry on Black life. But perhaps she is best known for her 2011 National Book Award–winning publication, *Head Off & Split*. She is currently the John H. Bennett Jr. Chair in Southern Letters and Literature at the University of South Carolina. Nikky Finney, *Head Off & Split: Poems* (Evanston IL: TriQuarterly, 2011).

5. These ideas are taken from cultural geographer Edward Soja. According to Edward Soja, "Human life is consequently and consequentially spatial, temporal, and social, simultaneously and interactively real and imagined. Our geographies, like our histories, take on material form as social relations become spatial but are also creatively represented in images, ideas, and imaginings." Soja, *Seeking Spatial Justice*, 18.

6. Formerly called the Sustainability Guild.

7. LEED certification is the globally recognized symbol of sustainability (creating carbon and cost-saving green buildings) and stands for Leadership in Energy and Environmental Design.

8. "Home," The Studio Museum in Harlem, accessed April 18, 2023, https://www .studiomuseum.org/.

9. White, "Sisters of the Soil"; Penniman, *Farming While Black*; Penniman, "To Free Ourselves," 521–22.

10. Walker, introduction to *Black Cool*, xxi.

11. Chimamanda Ngozi Adichie, "The Danger of a Single Story," TED Talk, accessed August 1, 2022, https://www.ted.com/talks/chimamanda_ngozi_adichie_the _danger_of_a_single_story.

12. Davis, "Resistance," in Walker, *Black Cool*, 64.

13. Lewis and Garnier, *Carrie Mae Weems*, 17.

14. McKittrick and Woods, *Black Geographies*, 5.

15. Du Bois, *Souls of Black Folk*.

16. Lewis and Garnier, *Carrie Mae Weems*, 19.

17. Carolyn Finney, "The Space between Words," *Harvard Design Magazine*, no. 45, S/S 2018, https://www.harvarddesignmagazine.org/issues/45/the-space-between -the-words.

18. Young, *Grey Album*, 58.

19. Soja, *Seeking Spatial Justice*, 103.

20. hooks, "Choosing the Margin," 15–23.

21. Dianne Rocheleau. "Plenary Panel: Engaging Difference: Displacing the Subject in Political Ecology." panel discussion at the Dimensions of Political Ecology conference, University of Kentucky, February 2014.

22. The limitations on naming were not only confined to land; there are a number of Black families bearing the names of the white men who owned their enslaved ancestors.

23. Beardsley, *Quilts of Gee's Bend*, 22.

24. Quoted in Beardsley, *Quilts of Gee's Bend*, 316.

25. Beardsley, *Quilts of Gee's Bend*, 41.

26. Beardsley, *Quilts of Gee's Bend*, 41.

27. Beardsley, *Quilts of Gee's Bend*, 215.

28. Wardlaw, *Gees Bend*, 11.

29. I had the good fortune to attend the Quilts of Gees Bend exhibit at the High Museum of Art in Atlanta, Georgia, in 2005.

30. Amel Wallach, "Fabric of Their Lives," *Smithsonian Magazine*, October 2006, https://www.smithsonianmag.com/arts-culture/fabric-of-their-lives-132757004/.

31. Shermika Dunner and Erin Z. Bass, "The Future of Gee's Bend," *Deep South Magazine*, April 17, 2012, http://deepsouthmag.com/2012/04/the-future-of-gees-bend/.

32. Born in 1911 in New Orleans, Mahalia Jackson was an African American gospel singer considered by many to be the "Queen of Gospel." She was also influential as a civil rights activist, and according to Harry Belafonte, she was considered to be the "most powerful black woman in the United States." "Mahalia Jackson, Gospel Singer and Civil Rights Symbol, Dies," *New York Times*, January 28, 1972, 1. She passed away in 1972.

33. Wardlaw, *Gees Bend*, 17.

34. Beardsley, *Quilts of Gee's Bend*, 35.

35. Beardsley, *Quilts of Gee's Bend*, 17.

36. Soja, *Seeking Spatial Justice*, 19.

37. I had the privilege of interviewing MaVynee Betsch on October 31, 2004, on American Beach, Amelia Island.

38. Rymer, *American Beach*.

39. Author interview with Betsch.

40. Author interview with Betsch.

41. "Florida—Nassau County," National Register of Historic Places, accessed April 18, 2023, https://nationalregisterofhistoricplaces.com/fl/nassau/state.html.

42. Rymer, *American Beach*; Russ Rymer, "Beach Lady," *Smithsonian Magazine*, June 2003, https://www.smithsonianmag.com/history/beach-lady-84237022/.

43. Pearl Fryar, in conversation with author at his home in South Carolina, November 13, 2014.

44. *A Man Named Pearl*, directed by Scott Galloway and Brian Pierson (Waterville, Maine: Shadow Distribution, 2008), DVD.

45. Glenn Hare, "Topiary Artist Honors Past, Shapes Future," University of South Carolina Online, April 8, 2014, https://sc.edu/uofsc/posts/2014/04_desegregation _commemoration_topiary_garden.php.

46. Jenoure, *Navigators*, 198.

47. Finney, *Black Faces, White Spaces*.

48. Soja, *Seeking Spatial Justice*, 38.

49. I attended the event, "WURD Speaks: Embracing Our Culture Coast to Coast with Angela Davis and Sonia Sanchez," on May 24, 2014, at the Oakland Marriott hotel.

Bibliography

Beardsley, John, and Museum of Fine Arts Houston. *The Quilts of Gee's Bend*. Atlanta: Tinwood, 2002.

Clifton, Lucille. *Good Woman: Poems and a Memoir 1969–1980*. BOA Editions, 1987.

Davis, Michaela Angela. "Resistance." In *Black Cool: One Thousand Streams of Blackness*, edited by Rebecca Walker, 59–80. Berkeley CA: Soft Skull, 2012.

Du Bois, W. E. B. *The Souls of Black Folk*. Chicago: AG McClurg, 1903.

Finney, Carolyn. *Black Faces, White Spaces: Reimagining the Relationship of African Americans to the Great Outdoors*. Chapel Hill: University of North Carolina Press, 2014.

hooks, bell. *Art on My Mind: Visual Politics*. New York: New Press, 1995.

———. *Belonging: A Culture of Place*. New York: Routledge, 2009.

———. "Choosing the Margin as a Space of Radical Openness." *Framework: The Journal of Cinema and Media* 36 (1989): 15–23.

Jenoure, Theresa. *Navigators: African American Musicians, Dancers, and Visual Artists in Academe*. Albany: State University of New York Press, 2000.

Lewis, Sarah Elizabeth, and Christine Garnier. *Carrie Mae Weems*. Cambridge MA: MIT Press, 2021.

McKittrick, Katherine, and Clyde Woods, eds. *Black Geographies and the Politics of Place*. Boston: South End, 2007.

Penniman, Leah. *Farming While Black: Soul Fire Farm's Practical Guide to Liberation on the Land*. White River Junction VT: Chelsea Green, 2018.

———. "To Free Ourselves We Must Feed Ourselves." *Agriculture and Human Values* 37, no. 3 (September 1, 2020): 521–22. https://doi.org/10.1007/s10460-020-10055-3.

Rymer, Russ. *American Beach: A Saga of Race, Wealth, and Memory*. 1st ed. New York: HarperCollins, 1998.

Soja, Edward. *Seeking Spatial Justice*. Minneapolis: University of Minnesota Press, 2010.

Wardlaw, Alvia. *Gees Bend: The Women and Their Quilts*. Atlanta: Tinwood Books, 2002.

White, Monica M. "Sisters of the Soil: Urban Gardening as Resistance in Detroit." *Race/Ethnicity: Multidisciplinary Global Contexts* 5, no. 1 (2011): 13–28.

Williams-Forson, Psyche. *Building Houses Out of Chicken Legs: Black Women, Food, and Power*. Chapel Hill: University of North Carolina Press, 2006.

Young, Kevin. *The Grey Album: On the Blackness of Blackness*. Minneapolis: Graywolf, 2012.

PART 4

Reimagining Justice

STRUGGLES OVER MEANING, POWER, AND PRIVILEGE

What do we mean when we talk about "justice" in environmental justice studies? Too often, the field of environmental justice has focused on more legal measures of justice or incremental distributional changes, often overlooking the evidence that communities on the ground view and seek justice in considerably more creative and structural ways than the "system" often offers.

In these chapters, authors explore historical sites of contestation over environment and justice, together giving us a richer understanding of what we mean when we say "environmental justice." Mary E. Mendoza explores the ways in which migrants of color have been excluded from the most central story about the role of nature in making Americans *American*: Frederick Jackson Turner's Frontier Thesis, which posited that American identity was forged in the experience of migrants (moving from east to west) wrestling with the wild lands of unknown places. Mendoza's chapter points to the deeply racialized nature of the Turner thesis, exploring how a politics of justice in environmental history must contend with these deeply rooted stories of race and nature in the (white) American experience. Traci Brynne Voyles argues for an intersectional and decolonized approach to environmental politics, using environmental history of colonialism in California to explore the ways in which environmental degradation and colonization were coproduced. In his chapter, Kent Blansett examines the origins of the Idle No More movement, situating it in the histories of Red Power and Native Nationalist movements of the 1960s. Blansett considers how resource extraction for settler colonialism has shaped Native activist movements in the late twentieth and early twenty-first centuries, from Idle No More to Standing Rock. Ari Kelman then looks to questions of environment and justice in the struggle to save the "witness trees" at the site of the Sand Creek massacre. Here, Kelman helps us think about environmental justice as encompassing a community's right to define their own environmental world and ultimately identify and lay claim to their own narratives about history and land. In each of these chapters, the meaning of "environmental justice" is expanded to include diverse struggles over power and privilege between and among human communities and the natural world.

13

¡Turnerian, Sí! ¡Americano, No!

Disentangling Wilderness, Whiteness, and the American Immigration Story

MARY E. MENDOZA

In 1986 U.S. president Ronald Reagan signed the Immigration Reform and Control Act (IRCA), which, for the first time, allowed undocumented immigrants to emerge from the shadows and apply for legal permanent status. The law came with conditions, though, and provisions to curb future unauthorized migration, especially across the U.S.-Mexico border. To receive amnesty, immigrants had to prove that they have been living and working consistently in the United States since 1982, and any applicant with a significant criminal record would be automatically denied. The act also outlined new rules for employers in the United States, mandating that all jobs should first be offered to U.S. citizens before any employer could hire a foreigner. This new statute ensured that any person who slipped across the international boundary would struggle to find work without proper documentation. Finally, the law provided funding to secure the border, ensuring that future covert crossing would be even more arduous.

Although Reagan's law allowed over two million undocumented immigrants to become U.S. citizens, it also created both concrete and systemic barriers for Latin Americans who wanted to be incorporated into the United States. From 1986 onward, any new immigrant would have a harder time getting into the country, whether through bureaucratic methods or furtively. If they did enter surreptitiously, they would face obstacles finding work, leading to a cascading series of problems that might force them to return home. Without income, finding and paying for housing, food, and other necessities could be nearly impossible.

In addition to these hurdles, the 1986 amnesty act excluded countless people already in the United States who had hoped to apply because of its criminal record stipulation. The law denied eligibility to any person convicted of one or more felonies or three misdemeanors. Many Americans argued that this provision was important, because it prevented the most dangerous immigrants from becoming U.S. citizens. But conviction rates for people of color have always been much higher than their white counterparts for the same or similar crimes. Statistics suggest that people of color are often pursued by police and convicted for crimes through a discriminatory, racially targeted justice system. This raises questions about how many immigrants of color with criminal records might have been charged with felonies in the 1980s if they were white. In other words, for many immigrants, their perceived racial classification may have excluded them from benefiting from the amnesty law because of an inequitable criminal justice system.[1] In an interview about his border-crossing experiences and his time in the United States, Porfirio, a migrant who crossed the border several times in the 1980s and 1990s, recounted that some of his own arrests stemmed from nonviolent domestic disagreements between him and his spouse: "[In the United States] the neighbors call the police and they arrest you for yelling."[2] He compared that to Mexico, where that had not been his experience. For Porfirio, arguing with his spouse—something that any partnered person would likely confirm that they too have done—resulted in his arrest. Given all the statistics of the criminal justice system, even not knowing all the facts of Porfirio's arrest, had he been white, we cannot be *sure* that he would have been detained in the exact same context.

Many U.S. politicians have celebrated the diverse heritage of the United States, claiming proudly that their nation is a nation of immigrants. But Mexicans and other Latin Americans who have traveled north across the U.S.-Mexico border have rarely, if ever, been included in this celebratory rhetoric. This can be partially explained because of the ways the U.S. national narrative rests on a myth of "Manifest Destiny," in which European immigrants moved westward across the continent, purportedly conquering nature and the Indigenous peoples who lived in it as they persevered and laid the foundation for American democracy.[3] Historian Frederick Jackson Turner famously outlined this trajectory in his scholarly work, which continues to not only influence how many Americans see themselves and their history but also whose stories are worthy of telling and remembering. As several scholars collectively known as the "New Western Historians" have argued, Turner's story leaves out the massive dispossession, genocide, and targeted violence that those European immigrants wrought on Indigenous peoples across the continent and later upon other marginalized groups in American history.[4] In short, Turner championed American whiteness, leaving little room for anyone else. Despite these criticisms, Turner's ideas continue to infiltrate our minds and shape our historical narratives, particularly in the field of environmental history.

The United States is and always has been a nation of race-based, systematic exclusion. Even in moments when it seems to be welcoming some, such as the amnesty policy of Reagan's IRCA, it is still actively and systemically barring most from both entry into the country and freedom of movement within it. Over the course of the past seventy-plus years, the United States has increasingly targeted Mexican and Latin American immigrants with mounting efforts to bar their entry and criminalize their migrations. Fences and walls have erupted from the ground, and swelling border patrol forces police the boundary to halt any person who dares to step over the line. Should anyone breach this stronghold, a network of jails and detention centers that have been growing since the 1950s await them. Once they are here, immigrants like Porfirio worry about racial profiling from an increasingly violent police force. These methodical forms of criminalization have produced not a nation of immigrants but a nation of immigrant inmates.[5]

As a result, notwithstanding their hard labor to build this nation, people at the margins—Indigenous peoples, Asians, Asian Americans, Africans, African Americans, Latinos, and Latin Americans—have remained largely ignored for their positive contributions and/or actively targeted by the police state.

Mexican and Latin American immigrants in particular reveal just how strong Turner's influence remains, because migrants traveling south to north have done everything that Europeans who traveled from east to west did, yet they get none of the glory. Turner exalted the ways in which European immigrants traveled across some of the harshest landscapes to work land and build new lives. Latin American migrants traverse treacherous terrain to settle in the United States to work the land and make new lives just the same, in arguably worse conditions. In addition to facing harsh landscapes, these migrants also fight smart technologies like drones, lasers, motion detectors, and night-vision binoculars attached to a human police force tasked with stopping them alongside big walls and fences. Continued efforts to curb migrations from south to north reflect American disdain for those who immigrate, rather than respect.

The Bonds of Wilderness and Whiteness

In 1993, President Bill Clinton delivered a proposal to the Department of State to fortify the U.S.-Mexico border to stop Mexican and Latin American immigrants from entering the United States. His plan involved a massive buildup of the border to block migration in Texas, Arizona, and California. Each state would have its own operation: Operation Hold the Line in Texas, Operation Blockade in Arizona, and Operation Gatekeeper in California. "The simple fact is that we must not, and we will not, surrender our borders to those who wish to exploit our history of compassion and justice," Clinton proclaimed.[6] He announced his request for $172.5 million to put his plan into action, and he received the funding.

In the coming year, new fences made of old military landing strips would mark the borderline; new, bright lights would illuminate the landscape; and hundreds of newly assigned border patrol agents would join an already massive force charged with policing the entire region to stop people from entering the United States. Southern California would see the largest transformation, in part because its dense population made the San Diego/Tijuana area a prime spot for migrants to stealthily cross. If they could manage to sneak by, they would almost immediately blend in with a relatively diverse population.

By 1993, building fences in urban areas to divert migrant traffic into the wilds of the borderlands was not new. Fence construction to curb human migration from Mexico had been going on in earnest since the 1940s.[7] These three operations existed among many iterations of border fortification that targeted Mexicans and Latin Americans over the course of the twentieth century. By the time Bill Clinton proposed to construct new border infrastructure, immigrants from Mexico had been forced to undergo medical examinations, ride in cattle cars, climb or burrow under fences, trek through deserts, cross roaring rivers, evade border patrol agents, avoid deportation raids, and risk apprehension, arrest, and detention just to arrive and remain within the boundaries of the United States.[8]

FIG. 13.1. Operation Gatekeeper fence at San Diego–
Tijuana border. Courtesy of the author.

Now rewind one hundred years. In January of 1893, a full century before
Clinton pushed his anti-immigrant policy, historian Frederick Jackson Turner
delivered his now infamous Frontier Thesis at the annual meeting of the
American Historical Association. Turner famously argued that, by 1890,

the frontier had closed. A line on a map of North America that had once divided settled and unsettled "empty" land was no longer distinguishable. According to Turner's analysis of U.S. history, it was the process of migration across the continent and interaction with the harsh environment that explained American development and, perhaps more importantly, made European immigrants into Americans. "In the Crucible of the frontier," he argued in 1893, "immigrants were Americanized."[9] As he delivered his talk, Turner explained that as immigrants moved westward into the American frontier, nature beyond civilization's edge forced them back into primitive societal ways. Then they slowly turned the wilderness they encountered into a new and vibrant civilization *even as the wilderness turned them into strong Americans*. It was an environmentally grounded, reciprocal relationship, from people to nature and back again. At the frontier, the meeting point between so-called savagery and society, the wilderness plunged "pioneers" into primitive life where they garnered the skills to eventually transform wilderness into urban centers. As these intrepid immigrants settled the U.S. West, they went from hunter to trader, then settled farms or ranches, and finally, developed factories. In that process, they encountered several harsh environmental conditions and the "common danger" of Indians.[10] As Turner's thesis explains it, that experience built a unique American character and laid the foundation for American democracy.

The purported closing of the frontier presented quite a conundrum. As Miles Powell has noted, for Turner, "America posed a paradox: its territorial and industrial expansion was awe inspiring, yet this progress also threatened to destroy the wilderness that had been the font of American virtue."[11] It should come as no surprise, then, that in the same period that Turner exalted American wilderness as a critical feature to the making of the modern United States, new studies of ecological management, the rise of the national park, and a nascent conservation movement were born.[12] Wilderness became precious and seemingly rare, and to preserve the American immigrant story, the nation had to preserve its remaining wild lands. In many ways, Turner's thesis reflected the national rhetoric of his time. As Powell also suggests, by making his claims, Turner "lent academic credibility to an origin myth already in circulation among many influential Americans."[13] Turner simply officiated the marriage between wilderness and whiteness—two concepts that had been associated with one another for decades before his thesis solidified their bond.

But as many New Western Historians argued, there was never any distinct closing of the frontier, and the West was never entirely uninhabited wilderness.[14] Despite the supposed closing of the frontier in 1890, opportunities for migration, work, and settlement in the North American West abounded across the twentieth century and, to some extent, they remain. As such, immigrants continue to cross the U.S.-Mexico borderlands, pouring into the North American West, many hoping to find work, and sometimes to settle, hoping to make better lives for themselves. Many of these non-European immigrants have done the same thing that Turner argued "turned immigrants into Americans." They have crossed the continent, faced common and diverse enemies (although in this case, that enemy is not considered to be Native peoples; it's the American police state), and they have indeed transformed much of the U.S. West with their labor.[15]

"A Nation of (White) Immigrants"

William John French was a classic frontiersman. A European immigrant who traveled to the United States, he embodied Frederick Jackson Turner's Frontier Thesis in nearly every respect. French was born in Ireland in 1854, and at age twenty-two, he joined the Royal Irish Regiment. He traveled with his comrades to their assigned posts until 1883, when he decided to leave for the United States. On his transatlantic journey, he met three men who owned a ranch in New Mexico, and before he knew it, he agreed to join them there if he did not find what he wanted in his original destination, California. Shortly after he reached the coastal state, he decided he would try his luck in New Mexico after all. Not knowing what he would find, he hopped on a train to Deming. From there, he booked a stagecoach to Silver City.

No longer a young man, French, who was nearly thirty years old on that stagecoach ride, realized that despite his age and being set in his ways, he would need to be a quick study if he was going to make it in the American West. Luckily, French's propensity for finding fast friends when he traveled once again served him well. He met some men on the ride who gave him a few lessons on what he called "Western etiquette."[16] They taught him that, even though he did not like to indulge before dinner, if he refused a drink when offered, he would offend, unless he instead asked for a cigar. Recounting this conundrum not long after learning this lesson, he moaned, "My pockets were soon bulging with these substitutes."[17] From Silver City to

Alma, he learned more about transportation in the West and the Mormons, the Apache people, and the others who lived in the region. Once he arrived at Alma, he met two men who provided him a horse. His memoir makes the American West sound replete with some of the most generous people on the planet, as he never makes mention of purchasing a thing. When he sat on his first western saddle, he found it "awkward, but comfortable."[18] From there, he rode to the ranch where he would reconnect with the men from his journey across the ocean. Once settled, he rode about the region, taking in the beautiful western landscape but also struggling to adjust to the arid climate at times.

He suffered, but he also persevered. With time, his persistence transformed him from a plucky young Irishman setting out for adventure to a genuine American cowboy. The conversion from Irishman to cowboy seemed quick. Just days after his arrival in New Mexico, he said, "The only thing foreign about me was a pair of hunting spurs which I happened to have in my kit."[19] From that day forward, he began a new phase of his life herding stock as a rancher in the cattle industry. He had become a completely different person.

After his arrival in New Mexico, French did not just acquire a cowboy's clothes and western saddle—he eventually also acquired an American cowboy's legal status. By 1895, French became a naturalized U.S. citizen and a well-known cattleman. He had made a career running and selling cattle across the American West. After years of ranching, he returned to California to retire in Los Angeles. Like many, French spent his life working with other frontiersmen, fighting the natural elements. He drove cattle across rivers and through canyons, hunted for food, and traipsed through Indian Country.

Men like French loom large in the American imagination. They are the men in iconic books and films like *Lonesome Dove* or *Far and Away*, driving cattle or taking Indigenous land to build their lives. In *Lonesome Dove*, two Irishmen join with several other mostly white settlers, an African American, and a Mexican cook to drive cattle north. One of them dies as he crosses a river and encounters water moccasins; the other triumphantly makes it to Montana. In *Far and Away*, Irish immigrants face hardship until they ultimately succeed in grabbing Native land in Oklahoma's land rush of 1893. These are the stories we privilege. These are the stories of U.S. history and settlement. These and the British settlers fleeing religious persecution who founded this nation are America's immigrants. When we hear claims that the United States is a nation of immigrants, these are the (white) immigrant heroes we imagine.

Access Denied and Criminalized

In the 1980s, a Mexican migrant named Porfirio traveled from his hometown in Puebla to the thriving capital of Mexico City and then to the border boomtown of Tijuana. Originally from a tiny village, Porfirio had left at age twelve to live with his godfather in the Federal District. His godfather already had four daughters, and living with only women did not suit Porfirio. Reflecting on his time in the capital city, where he had moved to from his hometown, he lamented his lack of freedom because he was constantly surveilled by his female housemates. As much as he wanted to, he was never allowed to go out on his own. So when, on a short visit to his home village, he heard someone say "you could sweep money up with a broom" in the United States, he, like so many of his countrymen, decided to head north, where he hoped he would find more independence as well as prosperity. He left for the United States at age seventeen. Shortly after his arrival in Tijuana, he crossed the border to Escondido, California. He never felt fully safe or free there either. Police targeted and arrested Mexicans regularly. Neighbors watched your every move. He was surveilled in the United States too, albeit differently.[20]

Between 1986 and the early 2000s, Porfirio married, then divorced, and he crossed back and forth between Mexico and the United States several times. When scholars Laura Velasco Ortiz and Oscar F. Contreras met Porfirio to interview him in the early 2000s, they found Porfirio in a small *colonia* in Tijuana at the *Casa del Migrante*, a refuge for recently deported migrants and for soon-to-be-emigrants hoping to rest up before attempting to cross the U.S.-Mexico border. The *Casa* had a revolving door. Ortiz and Contreras described the air as "heavy with the stress of waiting." The *Casa* was filled with mostly men. Porfirio was there as a recent deportee. He seemed discouraged and felt as though he experienced abuse no matter what he did. In Mexico, he suffered. In the United States, he not only suffered, but he also constantly faced the threat of removal. Recalling his experience, he said, "Living in the United States is good in some ways. A man earns good money, but everything can change in an instant. Suddenly, everything falls apart, everything collapses, and you end up here [in the *Casa del Migrante*], like me, and it feels awful."[21]

As he told his life story, he explained what it had been like to cross the border. It was difficult, but he had had decent luck. His favorite way to get in was to jump the fence near the San Diego trolley system. According to Porfirio, few people crossed there, making it less patrolled and easier. When he crossed with other people though, which he occasionally did, he recalled wanting to avoid the mountains and talked about the dangers of making one's way across the landscape. He recounted the risks of running into other people who might stop and rob you in the wilderness on the journey. Once while crossing, he and the people he was with were robbed at gunpoint. The unknown assailants stole their food and all their clothes. They walked on, totally naked, fighting just to keep warm.

He suffered, but he also persevered. For Porfirio and many others who made the same journey, crisscrossing the U.S.-Mexico borderlands presented several challenges. Immigrants faced hazards of the harsh, natural environment of the region. Some risked drowning in the mighty Rio Grande while others risked total dehydration or hypothermia in the arid western deserts. Snakes, jaguars, scorpions, and other creatures threatened to creep from around a corner at any moment. Spiny cacti and poisonous plants lay in wait with every step, threatening to pierce flesh or release an irritant onto skin. Human actors, ranging from other desperate migrants to drug traffickers to state-sponsored border patrol agents, also presented risks of violence and deportation.

The same year of Porfirio's interview in 1986, Congress passed IRCA, which famously granted amnesty to undocumented immigrants who had continuously lived in the United States since January of 1982 and had not committed any crimes. Since Porfirio had not lived in the country consistently and because he had been arrested, he did not qualify. The new law also cracked down on employers and undocumented immigrants going forward, making life even harder for Porfirio. From then on, employers would be required to prove they were not hiring undocumented workers. Although amnesty did relieve some pressure for those who qualified for the program, it did not stop the gross discrimination that Mexicans and Mexican Americans alike faced in the United States.

Not all stories of Mexican and Latin American migration are identical. Some include one person leaving their family to make a better life—to work in the north and send money back. Others are stories of entire families

FIG. 13.2. The treacherous West Texas border landscape. Courtesy of the author.

traversing the international boundary together, hoping to settle some-where. Other times, people like Porfirio hope to go back and forth, and they know the difficulties of crossing multiple times. Most though, if not all, recognize the dangers of not only the natural environment when they make this trek; they understand that on the journey and even when they arrive, Americans will not see them the same way they saw European immigrants in the nineteenth century. Instead, many Americans will consider them to be dangerous criminals.

When Latin American immigrants successfully enter the United States, they are never fully incorporated into it. Instead, they enter a massive carceral state—one where their mobility is severely limited and their own identities are all but erased because they are forced to live in the shad-ows.[22] As soon as they reach the U.S.-Mexico border, they are greeted by a massive border control apparatus aimed at caging them out of the United States. Border patrol agents block their entry, sometimes using brutal force to do so. If they are fortunate enough to get in, they then must deal with the constant threat of deportation or detention.[23] In a compilation of interviews with migrants living in northern Vermont in the early 2000s, one migrant woman, known as "Z," wrote about her experience, and lamented that in crossing the border, she essentially lost herself. "I have lost my name," she said. She went on to proclaim that she was not a criminal, implying that being in the United States made her feel like one. She explained how, while in the United States, she simply wanted to work and "achieve something better."[24] Z's words powerfully reveal not only the pain of crossing the border, but also the agony of having to live a life in hiding as an outcast who feels devalued, dehumanized, and excluded.

Another migrant, A.B., explained that he felt trapped and linked that feeling to the lingering trauma of his crossing experience: "Because of my migratory situation I can't go out and travel around freely—I am afraid of being deported."[25] A.B. felt stuck at home because if he was deported, he would have to endure the migration journey all over again. As a result, he chose to live in isolation, with limited mobility. Another migrant noted that the desert they crossed had "diverse dangers that confront all people who walk through the desert in an attempt to cross."[26] Another recounted that the dangers of crossing sometimes claim the lives of those who try: "Some of our companions have lost their lives there. While crossing, you can see skeletons in some places, human remains maybe, of those who did not achieve their dreams; some end up lost."[27] Like those who traveled from Europe and crossed the American continent from east to west, migrants who traveled from south to north also faced harsh environs that altered their lives.

They suffered, but they also persevered. Once they arrived at their destinations, they too transformed the American landscape by plowing fields, planting crops, tilling land, and building cities. These migrants, however, were rarely praised for their contributions. Instead, they were forced into the shadows, called names, threatened, discriminated against, exploited, policed, and sometimes caged. Their offspring often continued to face discrimination, whether through limited access to education, social services, targeted policing in neighborhoods, or everyday racial biases through personal interactions. Relegated to the margins, Latinos in the United States continue to fight for their place in the American fabric.

FIG. 13.3. "Close Immigrant Prisons" sign painted on the Operation Gatekeeper fence in Tijuana, Mexico. Courtesy of the author.

Disentangling Whiteness

For decades, millions of migrants have replicated a *version of the Turnerian story* as they crossed the U.S.-Mexico border. In the early twentieth century, Mexican migrants began crossing into the United States in growing numbers and, over time, became targeted for exclusion at the border and beyond. By the middle of the twentieth century, the U.S. Border Patrol began to single out Mexican migrants and remove those who managed to penetrate U.S. boundaries.[28] The buildup of the border continued apace into the twenty-first century. During the twentieth century, as increasing numbers of Latin Americans crossed the U.S.-Mexico divide, trekking across vast and harsh landscapes, facing hardships, and then toiling on U.S. soil, they found fewer and fewer opportunities for incorporation into American society. For them, the act of crossing treacherous terrain to secure new opportunity in the United States has prompted American officials to deploy a massive arsenal of resources and energy to halt migration from south to north—a stark contrast to official policies from a century before, when migration from east to west was heralded as the providence of a young nation and the critical transformative process for immigrants to become Americans.[29]

In the larger American narrative, Latino immigrants and their descendants have followed a Turnerian process, but they have never been able to achieve equal status as Americans. Why? Because as other scholars have pointed out, in Turner's thesis whiteness was overdetermined. Turner assumed that Indigenous peoples and people of color on the so-called frontier were simply *part* of an untamed wilderness. As such, they could not *experience* wilderness in the ways that white settlers could. They could not tame it, and thus they could not be changed by it. Turner not only passed over American Indians, Asians, and Mexicans already living on the edges who resisted westward movement, but he also crafted a master narrative that, in privileging whiteness, drew lines around the meaning of *American* that continue to justify the exclusion and elimination of non-European stories. In other words, Turner not only refused to acknowledge the diverse histories of the frontier when he wrote in the 1890s, but his framework also profoundly influenced who could be fully included in the national master narratives. His legacy persists.

Turner's privileging of whiteness and his associations of that whiteness with wilderness pose an even deeper-seated problem for the field of environmental history, and that problem has kept us from critically and productively engaging with diverse histories—narratives that have run parallel to and have intersected with the Turnerian progression. In short, the argument that the "frontier" environment forged a unique American character still shackles the field of U.S. environmental history to white American identity. Turner was arguably the first historian to explicitly analyze the reciprocal and changing relationship between humans and nature, with a focus on how one shapes the other.[30] His work, though, problematically equated whiteness with a ubiquitous "American" identity; and that identity as he defined it has been unequivocally tied to the idea of wilderness as nature. Generations of environmental historians have followed his lead and in doing so left out many diverse environmental histories.

We have yet to explicitly deconstruct the presumption of whiteness implicit in this mode of historical thought. In Turner's framing, whiteness was made normative. It has remained so. As such, the conceptualization of wilderness has been inextricably bound to white American identity, and the practice of environmental history has remained embedded (and festering) within that snare. Thinking through the parallels of Latin American migration to European migration and asking ourselves why one gets treated differently from the other is but one example of how we can break free from that trap.

Notes

1. See Hernández, "Amnesty or Abolition?"; and Hernández, *City of Inmates*, 131–57.
2. Ortiz et al., *Mexican Voices*.
3. Turner, *Frontier in American History*.
4. Historians such as Richard White, Patricia Limerick, William Cronon, and Donald Worster took on Turner's work in the 1980s and 1990s with a massive body of work collectively referred to as "The New Western History." These works have had a profound influence on the field, reshaping how historians conceive of and think of the American West. "The New Western History" is now just "Western History." Some of these works include but are not limited to White, *Roots of Dependency*; White, *Middle Ground*; Limerick, *Legacy of Conquest*; Worster, *Rivers of Empire*; and Cronon, *Nature's Metropolis*.
5. Mendoza, "Caging Out, Caging In."
6. Clinton, *Public Papers*.
7. Mendoza, "Caging Out, Caging In"; and Hernández, *City of Inmates*.
8. Mendoza "Tierra Pica," 474; and Mendoza, "Treacherous Terrain," 117–19.
9. Turner, *Frontier in American History*, 1.
10. Turner, *Frontier in American History*, 1.
11. Powell, *Vanishing America*, 48.
12. Warren, *Hunter's Game*; Spence, *Dispossessing the Wilderness*; Fiege, *Republic of Nature*; Powell, *Vanishing America*.
13. Powell, *Vanishing America*, 48.
14. Worster, *Under Western Skies*; White, *It's Your Misfortune*, 1; Limerick, *Legacy of Conquest*; Montoya, "Onward," 3.
15. Shah, *Contagious Divides*; Ngai, *Impossible Subjects*; Lee, *Making of Asian America*; Lim, *Porous Borders*.
16. French, *Some Recollections*, 16.
17. French, *Some Recollections*, 16.
18. French, *Some Recollections*, 17.
19. French, *Some Recollections*, 19.

20. Hernández, *Migra!*; Kang, *INS on the Line*; Escobar, *Captivity beyond Prisons*; Hernández, *City of Inmates*; Lim, *Porous Borders*; Mendoza, "Caging Out, Caging In."
21. Ortiz et al., *Mexican Voices*, 124.
22. Mendoza, "Caging Out, Caging In."
23. Mendoza, "Caging Out, Caging In."
24. "Z.," in Amore, *Invisible Odysseys*, 28.
25. "A.B.," in Amore, *Invisible Odysseys*, 33.
26. "A Mexican Immigrant," in Amore, *Invisible Odysseys*, 41.
27. "Ismael," in Amore, *Invisible Odysseys*, 23.
28. In the 1880s, before Turner had even proclaimed that the frontier had closed, Chinese immigrants found themselves barred from entry. By 1917, U.S. Congress had passed an immigration law excluding immigrants from Asia writ large. To enter the United States, Chinese, Japanese, and other Asian immigrants sometimes entered through Mexico and migrated across the land boundary to enter the United States. Established in 1924, the U.S. Border Patrol policed the U.S.-Mexico boundary to stop Asian migrants from entering the United States.
29. The U.S. government encouraged and sponsored these migrations through various Homestead Acts from the 1860s to the 1910s.
30. Although wilderness writers such as William Byrd III (mentioned in the introduction of this book), Henry David Thoreau, and Ralph Waldo Emerson wrote essays on nature and ecology, historians later did this kind of work and did so in ways that explicitly considered how nature shaped culture and vice versa.

Bibliography

Amore, B. *Invisible Odysseys: Art by Mexican Farmworkers in Vermont*. Benson VT: Kokoro Press, 2011.

Clinton, William J. *Public Papers of the Presidents of the United States, 1993*, bk 1, January 20–July 31, 1993. Washington DC: Government Printing Office, 1994.

Cronon, William. *Nature's Metropolis: Chicago and the Great West, 1848–1893*. New York: W. W. Norton, 1991.

Escobar, Martha D. *Captivity beyond Prisons: Criminalization Experiences of Latina (Im)migrants*. Austin: University of Texas Press, 2016.

Fiege, Mark. *The Republic of Nature: An Environmental History of the United States*. Seattle: University of Washington Press, 2012.

French, William. *Some Recollections of a Western Ranchman; New Mexico, 1883–1889*. New York: Frederick A. Stokes, 1928.

Hernández, Kelly Lytle. "Amnesty or Abolition?" *Boom* 1, no. 4 (2011): 54–68.

———. *City of Inmates: Conquest, Rebellion, and the Rise of Human Caging in Los Angeles, 1771–1965*. Chapel Hill: University of North Carolina Press, 2017.

———. *Migra! A History of the U.S. Border Patrol*. Vol. 29. Berkeley: University of California Press, 2010.

Kang, S. Deborah. *The INS on the Line: Making Immigration Law on the U.S.-Mexico Border, 1917–1954*. New York: Oxford University Press, 2016.

Lee, Erika. *The Making of Asian America: A History*. New York: Simon and Schuster, 2015.

Lim, Julian. *Porous Borders: Multiracial Migrations and the Law in the U.S.-Mexico Borderlands*. Chapel Hill: University of North Carolina Press, 2017.

Limerick, Patricia. *Legacy of Conquest: The Unbroken Past of the American West*. New York: W. W. Norton, 1987.

Mendoza, Mary E. "Caging Out, Caging In: Building a Carceral State at the U.S.-Mexico Divide." *Pacific Historical Review* 88, no. 1 (February 1, 2019): 86–109. https://doi.org/10.1525/phr.2019.88.1.86.

———. "La Tierra Pica / The Soil Bites. Hazardous Environments and the Degeneration of Bracero Health, 1942–1964." In *Disability Studies and the Environmental Humanities: Toward an Eco-Crip Theory*, edited by Sarah Jaquette Ray and J. C. Sibara, 201–41. Lincoln: University of Nebraska Press, 2017.

———. "Treacherous Terrain: Racial Exclusion and Environmental Control at the U.S.-Mexico Border." *Environmental History* 23, no. 1 (2018): 117–26.

Montoya, María E. "Onward to the Next Western History." *Western Historical Quarterly* 43, no. 3 (2012): 271–73.

Ngai, Mae M. *Impossible Subjects: Illegal Aliens and the Making of Modern America*. Princeton NJ: Princeton University Press, 2014.

Ortiz, M. Laura Velasco, and Oscar F. Contreras Montellano, eds. *Mexican Voices of the Border Region*. Translations by Sandra del Castillo. Philadelphia: Temple University Press, 2011.

Powell, Miles A. *Vanishing America: Species Extinction, Racial Peril, and the Origins of Conservation*. Cambridge MA: Harvard University Press, 2016.

Shah, Nayan. *Contagious Divides: Epidemics and Race in San Francisco's Chinatown*. Vol. 7. Berkeley: University of California Press, 2001.

Spence, Mark David. *Dispossessing the Wilderness: Indian Removal and the Making of the National Parks*. New York: Oxford University Press, 1999.

Turner, Frederick Jackson. *The Significance of the Frontier in American History*. 1893. Reprint, Tucson: University of Arizona Press, 1986.

Warren, Louis S. *The Hunter's Game: Poachers and Conservationists in Twentieth-Century America*. New Haven CT: Yale University Press, 1997.

White, Richard. *It's Your Misfortune and None of My Own: A New History of the American West*. Norman: University of Oklahoma Press, 2015.

———. *The Middle Ground: Indians, Empires, and Republics in the Great Lakes Region, 1650–1815.* Cambridge: Cambridge University Press, 1991.

———. *The Roots of Dependency: Subsistence, Environment, and Social Change among the Choctaws, Pawnees, and Navajos.* Lincoln: University of Nebraska Press, 1988.

Worster, Donald. *Rivers of Empire: Water, Aridity, and the Growth of the American West.* New York: Oxford University Press, 1992.

———. *Under Western Skies: Nature and History in the American West.* New York: Oxford University Press, 1992.

14

Pushed into the Margins

New Approaches to Environmental History
in Settler California

TRACI BRYNNE VOYLES

Sometime around 1912, a girl named Delfina Cuero crossed the international border line from Southern California into Mexico.[1] She did so after a childhood spent being kicked off one piece of land after another, engaging in unpaid or barely paid labor, while also living to quite a large extent off the land. In her childhood, she and her family members harvested wild fruits, nuts, and roots; caught fish; dried meat; and carried entire seasons' worth of provisions on their backs as they traveled back and forth across what is currently San Diego County. She would not return to the U.S. side of the border until much later in life and would only do so with the support and advocacy of other Kumeyaay community members as well as that of non-Native anthropologists who had taken a keen interest in her life and story.

In her lifetime Cuero witnessed extraordinary changes to Southern California's environment and resources as well as its human population and land status. When she crossed into Mexico, she was unaware that she was crossing an international boundary line that would become increasingly policed, fenced, and infused with geopolitical and racial power structures.[2] She was unaware, moreover, that she might never be able to return to the northern part of her peoples' homeland, cleaved as it was from the Kumeyaays' land south of the Mexican border. She knew only that there was a community on the Mexican side that spoke her language and lived relatively unmolested on their land, two conditions that were no longer true in San Diego. She knew that since she was a young child her grandparents had gone "farther and farther looking for food and a place where they would be left alone to live," finally finding it in Ha-a, a place in Baja California where other Kumeyaays had made their homes.[3]

Despite finding a sense of home and belonging in Ha-a, the experience of being cut off from the environment and resources north of the border dramatically impacted Cuero's life and ability to care for herself and her family. When her husband died and she was left to care for five young children, Cuero struggled to "keep [her] children together and fed."[4] She was forced, by circumstance and poverty, to sell her children into servitude or marry them into abusive relationships to keep the rest alive. Her motherhood, in short, was impacted in dramatic ways by larger settler colonial conditions and the impacts of those conditions on her access to natural resources.

This chapter offers a close reading of Delfina Cuero's autobiography, as told to anthropologist Florence Shipek. In Cuero's telling of her life story, key themes rise to the surface: her own and her family's relationships to the nonhuman world and cultivation of natural resources; their experiences with non-Native settlers in early twentieth-century San Diego; and Kumeyaay gender relations and gendered life experiences. Read as a primary source of the environmental and Indigenous history of Southern California, Cuero's autobiography provides rich knowledge about how settler colonialism impacted the nonhuman environment and thus Kumeyaay lifeways. This chapter uses environmental, Indigenous, and women's and gender history to understand how changes to the environment in settler California have manifested in Indigenous women's lives. Cuero experienced settler colonialism as labor exploitation, dispossession, gender-based violence, and the increasing buildup of the international border. However, perhaps the most profound and overarching manifestations of settler colonial power in her life showed up as changes to the land, which then shaped her life and experiences in intimate ways, particularly in ways that touched on gender roles.

This argument presupposes that settler colonialism is a primary organizing framework for understanding U.S. environmental history. This means that environmental historians should grapple with not only the environmental impacts of colonization and the role of environmental change in settler colonialism but also how settler colonialism has functioned as a system that orders the conditions of life for humans and nonhumans alike. Viewing settler colonialism as "a structure, not an event," as most Indigenous studies scholars do, means understanding it as a structure with material as well as ideological consequences that have implications for trees, wolves, shellfish, deserts, fungi, and rodents, as well as human communities. Myriad environmental problems that trouble U.S. environmental historians—climate change, pollution, mining, resource exploitation, species extinction and decline, and so on—can be understood as effects of the settler colonial structure. That is to say, they can be understood as part of a structure and a logic that requires Native elimination and dispossession for the purpose of practicing settler homemaking and home-claiming. Environmental violence, unsustainable resource exploitation, rampant pollution—all these manifestations of environmental degradation can be understood as central to the settler colonial logic of Native "elimination for the service of establishing, defending, and reproducing a settler society."[5] Thus, settler colonialism shapes not only historical phenomena and processes like wars, expansionism, race relations, politics, and property (all subjects that historians address as key to the story of the U.S. past) but also *environmental* history, *environmental* politics, and cultural understandings of "nature" itself.

This chapter also presupposes the crucial importance of gender to any analysis of environmental change over time, but particularly with regard to settler colonialism. Indigenous feminists have pointed out that "settler colonialism has been and continues to be a gendered process."[6] Moreover, these scholars assert that the lived experiences of Indigenous peoples speak to how settler colonialism's impacts are intersectional, deploying a framework ("intersectionality," as coined by legal scholar Kimberlé Crenshaw) that draws from long traditions of Black feminist theory to describe how formations of social power—such as racism, patriarchy, dispossession, capitalism, and ableism—work together to compound individual and group experiences of oppression and privilege. Intersectionality is a theory of both power and identity and a way of understanding how, for women of color and Indigenous women in particular, "the synthesis of these oppressions creates the conditions of our lives."[7] Using intersectionality as a keystone framework for their analysis, Indigenous feminists unpack how the lived experiences of Native peoples have reflected the "synthesis of oppressions" within settler colonialism.[8]

Delfina Cuero's life story makes it clear that gender deeply shaped how she experienced the environmental change that came along with the non-Native colonization of Southern California. Changes to the land, her story reveals, have been experienced through both settler and patriarchal power relations, as exemplified in California's environmental history. This history illustrates the need for intersectional approaches to environmental storytelling because the historical forces of settler racism, dispossession, patriarchy, and environmental destruction are and have been enmeshed here, as elsewhere. Cuero's story is complex and multifaceted, but taken as a whole, the salient details reveal the gender and environmental politics of settler colonialism and the interweaving of patriarchy with settlement, dispossession, and environmental degradation.

Cuero's California

Delfina Cuero was a Kumeyaay woman born in Southern California at a time in which the Kumeyaay—the "Diegueño," San Diego's "Mission Indians"—had no U.S.- or state-granted rights, no property, and no formal citizenship status. Her family's story as well as her own illustrate the lived conditions of Native people in California from the beginning of statehood through the turn of the twentieth century.[9]

At the close of the U.S.-Mexico War, California rushed from being a U.S. territory to a new state. News of gold at Sutter's Mill in 1848, not long after the United States seized this rich land from Mexico, brought in a deluge of humanity to this new western edge of the nation. As in other parts of the Southwest taken over by the Americans in 1848, Mexicans and Native peoples who occupied these lands at the onset of the U.S. period experienced swift and often devastating consequences. White settlers and land speculators, as well as the federal government itself, winnowed away Mexican land grants acre by acre or took them over wholesale. Native peoples in California endured intensely violent decades of attempted genocide at the hands of new settlers, tacitly endorsed by state and federal officials.

The new arrivals represented a highly diverse polyglot of people who had often crossed immense geographies to gather in the new state. The gold rush brought white, Black, and Native Americans as well as immigrants from China, Ireland, Scotland, England, Germany, Italy, and so on.[10] Highly diverse communities of people in burgeoning California cities and towns created complex social relations that were often mercurial and sometimes explosive. Historian Nayan Shah has described these kinds of diverse milieus in the nineteenth-century West in terms that would seamlessly apply to California in these poststatehood decades: it was truly an "immense plurality of human mobility."[11] This plurality was organized according to complex racial and gender power relations. In a nation in which whiteness was "overdetermined" as a prerequisite to full citizenship, white Californians sought to develop a "'white' political democracy and forg[e] racial apartheid by subordinating, segregating, and exploiting nonwhite 'races.'"[12]

Cuero's own family bore witness to these immense changes on and around Kumeyaay land in the nineteenth century. Cuero's great-grandparents were born at a time when Mexico's influence in present-day California had waned considerably in the aftermath of the Spanish mission system that had devastated previous generations of Kumeyaays (as well as other coastal nations).[13] They would have witnessed firsthand the bloody wave of genocidal violence that accompanied the initial decades of U.S. settler colonialism in the new state (1848–60), bearing their children, Cuero's grandparents, when nearly 70 percent of California-based Natives had died of murder, starvation, or infectious diseases in the space of little more than two decades.

In their own homeland, the San Diego-based Native population went from about 10,000 people in 1850 to 1,500 in 1900 when Delfina was born. During these decades, local newspapers fomented violent white aggression against the Kumeyaay, and Kumeyaay land was persistently "invaded . . . their pastures consumed by the stock of white settlers; the water turned away from their ditches."[14] During this same period, Kumeyaay land, which the Kumeyaay people had occupied, traversed, and cultivated for centuries, was rapidly dispossessed of nonwhite—Native and Mexican—occupancy and ownership. While some land tenure was secured for Mexicans (now Mexican Americans), who were afforded citizenship rights by the Treaty of Guadalupe Hidalgo, Natives were considered noncitizen "savage tribes" that needed to be "forcibly restrain[ed]."[15]

Cuero herself came of age at a time when U.S. settler hegemony was being cemented in San Diego in the form of rabid land privatization, infrastructural development, and non-Native population growth. Between 1900 and 1930, San Diego's non-Native population shot from 17,700 to nearly 148,000. The built infrastructure of the new city strained to keep pace with this astronomical influx of people. Thousands of acres were privatized, and thousands more were brought under federal control as "public" domain—"public," of course, being clearly limited to non-Mexican whites.[16] During that time, non-Native settlers squeezed the Kumeyaay out of the already marginal places they had come to occupy in the wake of the genocidal wave of white encroachment after the U.S.-Mexico War. As anthropologist Florence Shipek notes, "Until 1900 and 1910 many Diegueño [Kumeyaay] Indians had lived in Mission Valley [northeast of present-day downtown San Diego and southeast of the Spanish mission of San Diego] and in various places around San Diego. . . . Other Indian living areas were: on the bay at the foot of Fifth Street, along the Silver Strand, at the foot of Rose Canyon, along Ocean Beach, around the edge of Mission Bay . . . , and all up and down Mission Valley."[17]

Cuero, in fact, explained how her parents were born in current-day Mission Valley, instead of at the San Diego Mission, and lived there until "a lot of Chinese and Americans came into the Valley and told them that they had to leave."[18] They had to leave, she lamented, because "they did not own the land that their families and ancestors had always lived upon."[19] Her parents and grandparents "were all born in Mission Valley," and her maternal grandmother is still buried there underneath the strip malls, hotels, and freeways that abound in current-day Mission Valley.[20] By about 1910, white and Asian farmers had largely taken over Mission Valley, shunting out Cuero and her relatives. Elsewhere in San Diego, white housing developments filled the urbanizing areas of the growing city and the coastal areas. Wherever they went, the Kumeyaay were told, again and again, to leave—after all, as Shipek reiterated, they "were technically 'squatting' and did not own the land they occupied."[21]

It took a particularly hardened settler logic to regard Indigenous peoples as squatters on their own ancestral homeland. This counterintuitive outcome—regarding Indigenous people as squatters on their own ancestral land—was the result of significant settler exertions undertaken to dispossess the Kumeyaay, as with other California Native nations. These exertions include the refusal of the U.S. Senate to ratify the Treaty of Santa Ysabel, negotiated between the Kumeyaay and Indian agent Oliver Wozencraft in January of 1852, along with a set of seventeen other California treaties. The Senate, egged on by the vehement protestations of California settlers who worried that rich agricultural and mineral land would be lost to those treaty rights, then took the extraordinary step of having the treaties sealed for more than fifty years—evidence of the threat *any* recognition of Indigenous sovereignty and Indigenous need for land posed to the state.[22] This was compounded by an orchestrated silence of California and federal officials to inform the Kumeyaay (or any other California tribes) of an 1852 deadline to file any land claims before unclaimed land passed into the federal public domain.[23]

The settler drive toward Native elimination in California, in other words, was overdetermined. It was superlative in terms of genocidal physical violence and in terms of extreme dispossession of land and resources. When it comes to Southern California coastal tribes—the Kumeyaay, the Tongva, the Chumash, and so on—historians tend to emphasize the aftereffects of the Spanish mission system, which left the coastal peoples landless and suffering population decline due to violence and disease. The genocidal nature of the U.S. colonization of California from 1848 to 1900 has also been well documented by scholars. As a number of contemporary accounts put it, non-Native settlers explicitly pursued "extermination" of California Natives.[24]

Cuero's own account speaks to the fact that Kumeyaay land uses, relationships to resources, cultural and medicinal practices, gender relations, and religiosity all endured Spanish and Mexican colonization (although by no means emerging unscathed). Her grandmother, as an example of this, "was only at the Mission under a priest for a little while," and, away from the mission, had gotten traditional facial tattoos (which guided Kumeyaays "on the straight road" when they died) and underwent the Kumeyaay puberty ceremony for young women. By the time Cuero was an adolescent, these practices were no longer common. She herself never underwent the ceremony to transition to womanhood and lamented her lack of facial tattoos. It was the American period, and particularly the American *settler* form of colonization, which emphasized permanence and homemaking that transformed the natural and human environment in ways that foreclosed Native presence and the viability of Kumeyaay lifeways. The California experience of U.S. settler colonialism, in other words, was one of excessive violence in an already violent structure.

Environmental Degradation as Intersectional Experience

Cuero's autobiography vividly recounts her memories of her childhood in Kumeyaay land. The Kumeyaays' relationships to their natural environment—relationships characterized by what anthropologist Kat Anderson calls the labor of "tending the wild"—required both mobility across a broad swath of land, from foothills and mountains to tidepools and sea, *and* regular access to planted areas of cultivated crops.[25] In Cuero's account, this work of tending the wild was both laborious and rewarding. She reflects on memories of how her family would travel to the coast and spend their days gathering and preparing shellfish, preserving it with salt gathered from the San Diego Bay. They would "pound the meat of abalone soft with a rock" and use its shells as spoons; dig holes big enough for ollas to harvest clams; and trap and clean fish, sometimes with nets woven from agave fiber and sometimes with the aid of boats woven so tightly of reeds that water would not seep through.[26] The Kumeyaay in Cuero's lifetime, relegated to migratory and inconsistent wage labor (and, too often, unwaged labor) were restricted from both forms of environmental management for their own sustenance. "We had to move too much to plant anything," Cuero notes, "always being told to leave, it was no use."[27]

By the time her story was recorded, these landscapes were very nearly unrecognizable. San Diego's rapid development after 1848 transformed the land as well as land claims, privatizing property in ways that reflected the economic, political, racial, and familial priorities of the dominant white settler community. When she returned to San Diego later in her life to attend her father's funeral or visit family members, Cuero found most of the places from her childhood utterly transformed. Plants she had cultivated with her family and harvested no longer existed, replaced with housing subdivisions, farms, and busy roads. There had been "water in places that are dry now." Ocean Beach, by that time partially filled in, was so full of houses that Cuero complained, "I can't find my way any more." In fact, in many Kumeyaay places, housing developments posed a primary barrier to Kumeyaay land uses: "If there weren't so many houses," she notes, "maybe I could find my way to all the places again."[28]

The implications of settler colonialism on both the environment and Kumeyaay life are revealed through the distinct contrast between settler and Kumeyaay uses of natural resources. As Cuero mused upon her return to San Diego, "There are too many people all through the mountains now for Indians to live by hunting and gathering the wild food the way we could when . . . I was young."[29] These impacts on the natural environment also impacted Kumeyaay family life and gender roles; if white settler Californians relied on particular kinds of familial arrangements and environmental management—individual families to tend settled plots of land—Kumeyaay family models required extended intergenerational networks with broad knowledge of diverse ecosystems.[30]

In this and other ways, Cuero's story illustrates how patriarchy, settler colonialism, and environmental degradation worked hand in hand to compound her experiences of being a Kumeyaay woman and mother in a settler colonial context. For Kumeyaay women like Cuero, experiences of settler colonialism and its attendant changes to the environment and Kumeyaay access to natural resources were felt most deeply in their reproductive lives and in their roles as mothers. Reading Cuero's accounts of her life through a lens of reproduction, reproductive health, and motherhood reveals that women and mothers experienced environmental degradation and Kumeyaay dispossession from their homeland in deeply gendered ways. Her story reveals, in short, the ways in which settler colonialism in California has always been simultaneously racial, sexual, and environmentally disastrous. All these threads come together—intersect—in Cuero's reflections on her life.

In her detailed account of childbirth, postpartum care, and parenting, Cuero explained the multiple ways in which Kumeyaay women cared for their babies and for their own reproductive health. Natural resources, often Indigenous and unique to the ecosystem of the Kumeyaay homeland, played key roles in Kumeyaay reproductive life. Knowledge about how to use those natural resources, in turn, was cultivated by generations of women. In labor, Cuero recounted, "I did what I had been taught [by my grandmother]": she bathed in a decoction of Parish's bluecurls and laurel sumac, both plants that are particular to the Kumeyaay homeland.[31] She brewed and sipped laurel sumac tea.[32] For particularly difficult labors, Cuero noted that Kumeyaay mothers prepared tea from the yellow petals of rock rose flowers.[33] Right after birth, Cuero's infants were bathed in elderberry blossom or willow bark tea, and their faces were cleaned with burned honey. After waiting an appropriate amount of time after delivery, she broke her fast with simple atole and then "[ate] lots of vegetables and [drank] lots of herbs or mint teas," such as tea made of istap (crown daisy), which was gathered near current-day Mission Bay, or the bark of huusill or huutat (lemonade sumac).[34]

Kumeyaay women also had resources to "keep from having babies," an essential component of reproductive health for women the world over, and particularly for California Indigenous nations, who maintained community health in their arid homelands in part by limiting reproduction.[35] Drinking "lots and lots" of Parish's bluecurls was effective for birth control. But even more so, Cuero noted, "is another herb," which she declined to name, "even better, that the Indians used to use to keep from having babies every year." For menstrual cramps, women would gather michkal (western blue-eyed grass) from near current-day Torrey Pines State Park, and "boil the whole plant as tea" or seek out chap (sharp-toothed snakeroot) and boil the leaves.[36] The roots of millykupish (Chinese parsley) would make a tea that regulated menstruation.[37] Some ailments Shipek described as "venereal diseases" could be treated with 'ektii (laurel sumac).[38]

During the course of Cuero's life, however, the realities of territorial encroachment by settlers and the impacts of San Diego's rapid growth on the environment manifested themselves in Kumeyaay reproductive life. The herb that Cuero credited for being "even better" for helping women keep from having babies was more or less lost to her generation of Kumeyaay; this unnamed herb, Cuero lamented, is "hard to find now because we can't go everywhere to look for [it]."[39] Several of the herbs and plants Cuero listed as being essential to Kumeyaay women's reproductive health—including laurel sumac for help during labor and for the treatment of sexually transmitted diseases, Parish's bluecurls for labor and for birth control, lemonade sumac for recovery after childbirth, and blue-eyed grass for the treatment of menstrual cramps—are native plant species to California and are not found far outside the traditional Kumeyaay homeland. The incursions of housing developments, deforestation, and invasive species on this land are thus significantly impactful for these plants in particular, just a handful of the "6,300 native plant species [that] are endemics" to California "and grow nowhere else on earth."[40]

The impact of settler colonialism, felt largely through environmental degradation and poverty, manifested in other parts of Cuero's experiences of being a Kumeyaay woman. In order to promote strength and health, Kumeyaay women of Cuero's grandmother's generation underwent a ceremony for "girls as they were about to become women." Cuero explained, "Grandma told me they dug a hole, filled it with warm sand and kept the girl in there. They tattooed her all around her mouth and chin. They would sing about food and see if she would get hungry. . . . A week, I think they kept her there, I'm not sure. They didn't want the girls to get wrinkled early or to get grey, but to have good health and good babies. This helped them." By the time Cuero achieved the right age for the ceremony, "They had already stopped doing it. . . . I would have gone through with it if they had asked me," she noted;

"I believe in it, but they didn't ask me."[41] Her husband, Sebastian Osun, on the other hand, had undergone the "boys' ceremony" in part because he was from "the mountains," somewhat removed from the onslaught of settlers in Cuero's coastal home. "The people who stayed always in the mountains," Cuero reports, "did these things longer than the people who lived closer to the coast." The ceremony for boys endured longer than the ceremony for girls regardless of geography, but in the end, "they used things" to initiate boys into the community as Kumeyaay men "that we don't know now."[42]

Her narrative makes clear that something significant fell away with the loss of these ceremonies, in large part because of the role of grandmothers. Grandmothers during the puberty ceremony, in Cuero's account, served as the conduit for knowledge about "the special things women had to know"—in short, "all that a girl needed to know to be a good wife, and how to have babies and to take care of them was learned in the ceremony, at the time when a girl became a woman." The ceremony was "the proper time to teach" this knowledge. "In the real old days," she explains, "grandmothers taught these things about life."

The loss of knowledge imparted from her grandmother, which would have ideally occurred during the puberty ceremony, manifested in Cuero's life in devastating ways. "Some of the other girls had the same trouble I did after I was married," she asserted. The rest of Cuero's explanation for the implications of not having a puberty ceremony linked environmental degradation, labor exploitation, and these changes to Kumeyaay gender roles:

> No one told me anything. I knew something was wrong with me but I didn't know what. Food was becoming hard to find then and we had to go a long way to find enough greens. My husband was away hunting meat. . . . One day I was a long way from Ha-a looking for greens. I had a terrible pain. I started walking back home but I had to stop and rest when the pain was too much. Then the baby came, I couldn't walk any more, and I didn't know what to do. . . . My grandmother had not realized my time was so close or she would not have let me go so far alone. They carried me back but I lost the baby.[43]

For the future deliveries of her children, Cuero "knew what to do," having learned from her grandmother. She used plants and herbs to ease labor pains, "dug a little place and built a hot fire," and used the ashes, covered with bark, to keep the baby warm.[44] She bathed her newborns in elderberry blossom or willow bark tea. She abstained from food other than atole. "I did this all myself," she says.[45]

In addition to the effects of hunger and lack of access to natural resources and intergenerational knowledge on puberty ceremonies and childbirth, the encroachment of non-Native settlers and the impact of settlement on environmental resources and the Kumeyaays' access to those resources also altered the ways in which young children were parented, named, and welcomed into the community. Cuero described how when her first child, Aurelio, was old enough, "everybody got together and they built a big ramada for me and they brought their food together" in a grand welcoming party for the child, in which he was given his name. There was a "big fire" and singing and dancing, including a fire dance led by her uncle. There were presents for the child in celebration of the fact that the family "would have more Indians, another baby added to the group."[46] By the time her second child, Lupe, was old enough for a similar celebration, "we didn't have parties for the new children any more," perhaps because "it was too hard to get enough to eat."[47] Cuero's narrative makes clear that the loss of the welcoming celebration was a significant blow to the community, for mothers and children alike: "The fire dance was religious," she explains. "The songs that go with it have to be sung in the right order, from early evening until dawn. . . . The dance for a child brings good luck and blessing to the child and to all the people who dance. That is what they did for me and my first child to live."[48] What is implied here is the fact that this ceremony honored the mother as well as the child, acknowledging her role in the community and her transformation into parenthood. "They might have done more before," but due to hunger and larger changes to community life, "they don't even do this now."[49]

Hunger from lack of access to money and the traditional Kumeyaay homeland figures prominently in Cuero's experiences of motherhood, in ways that transcend the lack of ceremonies for womanhood or new births. In Ha-a, cut off from the coastal San Diego landscape of her childhood, Cuero struggled for enough food to feed her family, particularly after her husband died during her youngest child's infancy.[50] After his death, she reports, "I went hungry and my children went hungry." She finally resorted to allowing her oldest, twelve-year-old Aurelio, to live with another family. That family promised to treat Aurelio like a son but instead abused him for free labor. He spent the rest of his life running from them, as did, to a significant extent, Cuero and her other children. Her youngest child, Santos, experienced similar near-enslavement.[51] In general, Cuero's strongest lamentations in the autobiography are reserved for the restrictions that hunger placed on her motherhood: "The terrible things I went through trying to keep my children together and fed, I can't begin to tell. Then, I didn't succeed after all. I feel like crying when I think of that time. My children were hungry and cold so many times." Cuero tried to protect her children by entering into new marriages—but "if I didn't do enough to suit him, he would beat me. I have been black and blue all over so many times because there was still more work to do. Even with all that, each man would get mad about feeding my children and beat me for that."

In Cuero's telling, these experiences together reflect the complex outcomes of the twinned forces of the Kumeyaays' displacement by settlers and the buildup of the U.S.-Mexico border. These forces manifested in Native women's lives in ways that reveal the interplay between the nonhuman environment, settler colonialism, and heteropatriarchy. To understand Cuero's life story from the point of view of environmental history, one has to take seriously the dynamic intersectionality of Native women's experiences of environmental degradation and settler power.

Environmental Histories of Settler California

This evidence from Cuero's life gives us a window into how U.S. environmental historians can set about centering settler colonialism in their work. But how does a focus on settler colonialism change the way we approach and understand environmental history as a whole? Here, looking at California and California's environmental history is instructive. Such a perspective on California's environmental history would posit that fundamental technologies of settler colonialism—including Native elimination, dispossession, and settler homemaking—suffuse the history of human relationships to the environment in California. Native elimination, the most fundamental component of settler colonialism, is foundational to environmental interactions in settler California, whether it's a foreclosure of Native existence and sovereignty in the land grabs that made the state a state, or representations of "Indianness" that serve settler ends as savage and/or romantic Others, or removal of Natives to reservations that then open up territory or other environmental resources for settlers, or, most nakedly, outright violence against Native peoples toward the end of genocidal elimination and dispossession for settler hegemony over new territory.

The centrality of settler colonialism to California's environmental history is hinted at in its classic texts. For example, in *Green versus Gold: Sources in California's Environmental History*, the editors open the book with accounts of

> Euro-American men and women who experienced the sierras, deserts, central valley, coasts, and lakes recorded their impressions of the terrain, its dangers, and beauties. They engage us in their anxieties, joy, awe, and excitement over a *new land* and its impressive array of plants and animals. They involve us in their concerns over travel and *settlement* in the landscape that became famous as the state of California. The words of geologists, ecologists, and historians help us appreciate the massive natural forces that created the terrain, the animals that once inhabited it, and *the kinds of changes that European settlement would bring to it.*[52]

Here, the notion of California as *terra nullius*, "new [and presumably empty] land" awaiting "the kinds of changes that European settlement would bring to it," functions as the starting point, the first chapter in the state's environmental history. This origin story for California's environmental history reiterates long-standing notions that Indigenous California nations did not cultivate the landscape and that "'traditional Indian use of land' left the land in its 'natural wild state' without any effect on, or human manipulation of, the land and its plant or animal biota."[53] Quite to the contrary, in fact, Native nations in Southern California extensively "tended" to their home ecosystems, using fire, agriculture, animal husbandry, and water resources to significantly shape and impact their environment and its resources. As noted by anthropologist Florence Shipek, the high population density of Indigenous Southern California prior to Spanish colonization meant that the Kumeyaay and other Native nations "must have utilized each type of land at its highest potential."[54] Thus, the history of human-environment relationships in California does not begin with the kinds of changes white settlers brought to a "new land." Nor, for that matter, did Indigenous environmental cultivation and Indigenous relationships to the environment end with the arrival of white settlers. Rather, there is a contiguous Indigenous environmental history of what is currently California that has been pushed to the margins of our studies of the environmental past.

Placing settler colonialism at the center of our study of California's environmental history would dramatically shift our understandings of how we understand this state—and this is not just true, as the passage above suggests, of seeing *environmental destruction* as a settler project (although, of course, it is) but also *settlement* itself, *population changes*, *urbanization*, and even *conservation movements* in this now-famously "green" state. In fact, we could examine the standard topics in California environmental history, inquiring of each how they relate to settler and white supremacist power structures. *Green versus Gold* summarizes key topics in California environmental history in this way: "In California, the kinds of organizations people formed, such as *nature and hiking groups, conservation organizations, and citizens' action groups*, have been instrumental in *using and setting aside land* or halting perceived forms of pollution or degradation. Similarly the political process and various government bureaus and departments have produced laws and bond measures that transform the landscape in the form of *freeways, bridges, dams, and water projects*. Powerful bureaucracies in tension with an active citizenry can open up major *environmental conflicts over issues such as redwoods, wild rivers, incinerators, and nuclear power plants*."[55]

Taking each of these key topics in turn and examining each with settler colonialism and Native elimination at the center of our study, new kinds of stories emerge. Nature and hiking groups, conservation organizations, and citizens' action groups, for example, are often predicated on protecting an "empty" wilderness or derive discursive currency from stereotypes of "ecological Indians." Most famously, the formation of the Sierra Club around John Muir's preservationist politics in places like Yosemite Valley turned on both the U.S. wilderness ethic and its assumption of a sublime landscape empty of human (read: Native) life and on the actual removal of Native people from those same wilderness areas. Transformations of landscapes in the form of freeways, bridges, dams, and water projects have displaced communities of color and Indigenous nations in notoriously violent ways: from water projects like the dam at Hetch Hetchy and the diversion of Lake Owens to provide water for Los Angeles to the use of the freeway system to deepen racial segregation in cities and disrupt and displace urban communities of color. This is to say nothing of the government bureaus and departments that have systematically denied representation to communities of color so that they might have a say in the environmental conditions that affect their lives. In short, each of these key topics in California's environmental history can be seen through the lens of settler colonial white supremacy. Each is predicated in one way or another on a particular iteration of white settler supremacy—Native elimination, anti-Blackness, or nationalist enclosure—to produce white sovereignty over land and resources.[56]

As this might suggest, I do not mean to imply that Native dispossession functions apart from, or is more important than, other forces of white supremacy in California or in the United States as a whole. Cuero's experiences, in fact, speak to the ways in which settler colonialism is linked to other white settler supremacist forces in the United States historically. Her inability to reenter San Diego is the result of the deeply nativist and exclusionary anxieties of white settlers who found (and find) themselves in constant defense against the mere presence of nonwhite people, signified in this case by the militarization of the border line between the United States and Mexico, the dispossession of Mexican American land grantees, the dispossession of Asian immigrant land owners via the Alien Land Laws, and systematic racial violence against immigrants of all nonwhite backgrounds. Cuero's great-grandparents lived during a time of widespread systems of enslavement that borrowed, structurally and culturally, from the chattel enslavement of Blacks elsewhere in the United States—what one historian calls "California's own 'peculiar institution.'"[57] They and other Natives in California, as well as Asians and Mexicans, experienced tactics of racial terrorism such as lynching, segregation, incarceration, and state-sanctioned violence that emerged from and characterized the politics and culture of anti-Blackness.[58] This kind of complex theorization of the intersectional formations of settler colonialism is in line with the thinking of Indigenous feminist scholars who have made related analyses.[59]

Delfina Cuero's story reveals how these complex machinations played out in people's everyday lives in early twentieth-century San Diego and Baja California. As she sought to harvest plants for traditional remedies, raise her children, keep her grandmother's memory alive, return to San Diego, and tell her story for posterity, Cuero spoke to the ways in which gender and environmental resource use shaped her experiences of colonization. Seen one way, her story is one of longing to return home and asserting Kumeyaay lifeways in the face of intense colonization. Seen another, through the lens of environmental history and Indigenous feminisms, it lays bare how what might seem on the surface to be *changes in the land* in fact made for diverse, nuanced, and intersectional changes in women's lives.

Notes

1. Cuero describes herself as being "big but not a woman yet when we went down there." Cuero and Shipek, *Delfina Cuero*, 26. Her crossing occurred sometime before her marriage and subsequent first pregnancy, which occurred when she was about fourteen.
2. Hernández, *Migra!*; Kang, *The INS on the Line*; Lim, *Porous Borders*; Mendoza, "Caging Out, Caging In," 86–109; Mendoza, "Treacherous Terrain," 1–10; St. John, *Line in the Sand*.
3. Cuero reports that when her grandparents crossed the border, "we didn't know it was a [border] line, only that nobody chased them away"; "they found a place where no one told them to move on, so they just stayed there. Some Indians were already at [Ha-a] who spoke the same [Kumeyaay] language, just as we did." Cuero and Shipek, *Delfina Cuero*, 26.
4. Cuero and Shipek, *Delfina Cuero*, 62.
5. Hernández, *City of Inmates*.
6. Arvin, Tuck, and Morrill, "Decolonizing Feminism," 9.
7. Quoted from Combahee River Collective, "The Combahee River Collective Statement," BlackPast.org, 1977, https://www.blackpast.org/african-american -history/combahee-river-collective-statement-1977/. For more on this concept, its origins, and its uses, see Crenshaw, "Mapping the Margins"; Keeanga-Yamahtta, *How We Get Free*; Collins, *Intersectionality*.
8. Denetdale, "Chairmen, Presidents, and Princesses"; Green, *Making Space*; Hall, "'Sea of Islands'"; Million, "Felt Theory"; Arvin, Tuck, and Morrill, "Decolonizing Feminism"; Aikau et al., "Indigenous Feminisms Roundtable," 84; Deer, *Beginning and End*; Barker, *Critically Sovereign*; Risling Baldy, *We Are Dancing*; Nickel and Fehr, *In Good Relation*.
9. Few Indigenous nations have been so variously named as the Kumeyaays. In different geographies and time periods, they have been known by non-Natives as the Cumia, the Kamia, the Diegueño, and the Ipai and Tipai Nation. The diversity of these names reflects the wide swath of the Kumeyaays' homeland and their expertise in cultivating a livelihood out of a plethora of ecosystems, stretching from the coast, across the foothills and mountains, to the deserts. Hedges, "Notes on the Kumeyaay"; May, "Brief Survey"; Shipek, "Kumeyaay

Socio-political Structure,"; Shipek, "Myth and Reality"; Shipek, *Pushed into the Rocks*; Shackley et al., *Early Ethnography*; Miskwish, *Kumeyaay*.

10. Johnson, *Roaring Camp*; Stremlau, "Witnessing the West."

11. Shah, *Stranger Intimacy*, 3.

12. Jacobson, *Whiteness*, 23; Shah, *Stranger Intimacy*, 3.

13. The mission system was brought to a close by the Mexican Secularization Act of 1833, which formally converted the missions to parish churches and conferred Mexican citizenship and some individual land plots to Natives but informally constituted "an excuse for the settlers and retired soldiers and their families to strip the missions of livestock, supplies, and lands, and to turn the Indians into peon villagers on the ranchos." Shipek, *Pushed into the Rocks*, 21.

14. DA Dryden, quoted by Edward P. Smith, "Annual Report of the Commissioner of Indian Affairs for the Year 1875," U.S. Department of the Interior, Office of Indian Affairs, 10. Native peoples present in San Diego county during this time were primarily Kumeyaay, but they were also Payómkawichum (Luiseño), Cahuilla, and Cupeño. Richard L. Carrico and Florence C. Shipek, "Indian Labor in San Diego County, California, 1850–1900," Kumeyaay.com, accessed December 3, 2020, https://www.kumeyaay.com/indian-labor-in-san-diego-county,-california, -1850-1900.html.

15. Treaty of Guadalupe Hidalgo, February 2, 1848, Perfected Treaties, 1778–1945, General Records of the United States Government, record group 11, National Archives Building, Washington DC, article XI. These citizenship rights, while guaranteed on paper, were never respected at the local, state, or federal levels. If Mexican Americans were "white by law," they were never afforded the full privileges of legal or cultural citizenship.

16. Citizenship in California at this time was explicitly racialized as white, often via the mechanism of who could access and use purportedly "public" spaces. The 1853 Greaser Act, for example, was a vagrancy law that sought to police Mexican Americans, whites by law and full citizens of the state and country, as trespassers in "public" (read: white) spaces.

17. Cuero and Shipek, *Delfina Cuero*, 9.

18. Cuero and Shipek, *Delfina Cuero*, 23.

19. Cuero and Shipek, *Delfina Cuero*, 23.

20. Cuero doesn't know exactly where in Mission Valley her grandmother is buried. Cuero and Shipek, *Delfina Cuero*, 23.

21. Cuero and Shipek, *Delfina Cuero*, 10.

22. Shipek, *Pushed into the Rocks*, 30–31.

23. Executive Summary, "Advisory Council on California Indian Policy: Final Reports and Recommendations to the Congress of the United States Pursuant

to Public Law 102–416," September 1997, 3–4. The U.S. Senate not only refused to ratify the Treaty of Santa Ysabel along with a set of seventeen other California treaties (which have collectively come to be known as the "18 Lost Treaties" and together would have set aside 8.5 million acres in a series of reservations running down the spine of the state) but also took the extraordinary step of having them sealed for more than fifty years. These treaties, negotiated across the length and breadth of California (not always with appropriate tribal representatives) would have secured a significant land base for California tribes but ran aground in the Senate due to the protestations of California settlers who worried that rich agricultural and mineral land would be lost.

24. Rawls, *Indians of California*, 162, 170, 179, 180, 183, 206, 240. For full accounts of the attempted genocide, see Norton, *When Our Worlds Cried*; Carranco and Beard, *Genocide and Vendetta*; Norton, Costo, and Costo, "Path of Genocide," 111–30; Heizer, *Destruction of California Indians*; Costo and Costo, *Natives*; Lindsay, *Murder State*; Madley, *American Genocide*.

25. Gamble and Wilken-Robertson, "Kumeyaay Cultural Landscapes"; Miskwish, *Kumeyaay*; Shipek, "Intensive Plant Husbandry," 163; Wilken-Robertson, *Kumeyaay Ethnobotany*.

26. Cuero and Shipek, *Delfina Cuero*, 29.

27. By Cuero's memory, despite the long hours of difficult labor she and her family undertook for settlers, clearing land, cutting trees, tending crops, "they never gave the Indians money. We didn't know what money was in those days." Cuero and Shipek, *Delfina Cuero*, 25.

28. Cuero and Shipek, *Delfina Cuero*, 27.

29. Cuero and Shipek, *Delfina Cuero*, 32, 64.

30. For example, in Ha-a, "the agave gathering and roasting was men's work. Hunting game for meat and hunting for bees and honey were men's jobs also. The women hunted for wild greens, seeds, and fruit. The whole family helped with gathering acorns and pine nuts," Cuero and Shipek, *Delfina Cuero*, 57.

31. Parish's bluecurls is also called Trichostema parishii Vasey, of the mint family. Laurel sumac is also called Rhus laurina Nutt.

32. Cuero and Shipek, *Delfina Cuero*, 44.

33. Helianthemum scoparium. Cuero and Shipek, *Delfina Cuero*, 91.

34. Crown daisy is also called *Chrysanthemum coronarium*, and lemonade sumac is also called Rhus integrifolia. Cuero and Shipek, *Delfina Cuero*, 45, 87, 95.

35. Cuero and Shipek, *Delfina Cuero*, 45; Sowards, *United States West Coast*, 74.

36. Western blue-eyed grass is also called Sisyrinchium bellum, and sharp-toothed snakeroot is also called Sanicula arguta. Cuero and Shipek, *Delfina Cuero*, 97.

37. Heliotropium curassavicum. Cuero and Shipek, *Delfina Cuero*, 91.

38. Cuero and Shipek, *Delfina Cuero*, 95.

39. Cuero and Shipek, *Delfina Cuero*, 45.

40. Anderson, *Tending the Wild*, 13.

41. Cuero and Shipek, *Delfina Cuero*, 39.

42. Cuero and Shipek, *Delfina Cuero*, 40.

43. Cuero and Shipek, *Delfina Cuero*, 43.

44. Cuero and Shipek, *Delfina Cuero*, 44.

45. Cuero and Shipek, *Delfina Cuero*, 45.

46. Cuero and Shipek, *Delfina Cuero*, 45–46.

47. Cuero and Shipek, *Delfina Cuero*, 46.

48. Cuero and Shipek, *Delfina Cuero*, 45–46.

49. Cuero and Shipek, *Delfina Cuero*, 47.

50. Cuero and Sebastian Osun had five children who survived their infancy: Aurelio, Guadalupe ("Lupe"), Lola, Eugenia, and Santos. Cuero and Shipek, *Delfina Cuero*, 66.

51. Cuero and Shipek, *Delfina Cuero*, 74–75.

52. Merchant, *Green versus Gold*, xix. Emphasis added.

53. Shipek, *Pushed into the Rocks*, xi.

54. Anderson, *Tending the Wild*.

55. Merchant, *Green versus Gold*, xviii. Emphasis added.

56. Hernández, *City of Inmates*.

57. Benjamin Madley delineates the various iterations of Native slavery practiced in California after 1848, ranging from "*de jure* apprenticeship, convict leasing, indenture, and custodianship of minors, as well as *de facto* debt peonage, chattel slavery, and . . . disposable unfree labor." Madley, "'Unholy Traffic,'" 628. Almaguer, *Racial Fault Lines*, 49–50, notes that the "paternalism" that characterized Native enslavement in California was "similar to that which bound black slaves to white masters." Magliari, "Free Soil, Unfree Labor," 351.

58. Pfeifer, *Rough Justice*, 32, 85, 87. See also Rodriguez, "Noose"; Hernández, *City of Inmates*.

59. For example, Indigenous feminist scholars Maile Arvin, Eve Tuck, and Angela Morrill have defined settler colonialism as "a persistent social and political formation in which newcomers/colonizers/settlers come to a place, claim it as their own, and do whatever it takes to disappear the Indigenous peoples that are there. Within settler colonialism, it is exploitation of land that yields supreme value. . . . Extracting value from the land also often requires systems of slavery and other forms of labor exploitation." Arvin, Tuck, and Morrill, "Decolonizing Feminism," 12. For other useful definitions that reflect this complex theorization, see Snelgrove et al., "Unsettling Settler Colonialism," 2; Tuck and Yang,

"Decolonization Is Not a Metaphor," 5; J. Kehaulani Kauanui, "'Structure, Not an Event,'" 2; Hernandez, *City of Inmates*, 8.

Bibliography

Aikau, Hokulani K., Maile Arvin, Mishuana Goeman, and Scott Morgensen. "Indigenous Feminisms Roundtable." *Frontiers: A Journal of Women Studies* 36, no. 3 (2015): 84.

Almaguer, Tomas. *Racial Fault Lines: The Historical Origins of White Supremacy in California*. Berkeley: University of California Press, 2008.

Anderson, Kat. *Tending the Wild: Native American Knowledge and the Management of California's Natural Resources*. Berkeley: University of California Press, 2013.

Arvin, Maile, Eve Tuck, and Angie Morrill. "Decolonizing Feminism: Challenging Connections between Settler Colonialism and Heteropatriarchy." *Feminist Formations* 25, no. 1 (2013): 8–34. https://doi.org/10.1353/ff.2013.0006.

Barker, Joanne, ed. *Critically Sovereign: Indigenous Gender, Sexuality, and Feminist Studies*. Durham NC: Duke University Press, 2017.

Carranco, Lynwood, and Estle Beard. *Genocide and Vendetta: The Round Valley Wars in Northern California*. 1st ed. Norman: University of Oklahoma Press, 1981.

Collins, Patricia Hill. *Intersectionality as Critical Social Theory*. Durham NC: Duke University Press, 2019.

Costo, Jeannette Henry, and Rupert Costo. *Natives of the Golden State: The California Indians*. San Francisco: Indian Historian Press, 1995.

Crenshaw, Kimberlé. "Mapping the Margins: Identity Politics, Intersectionality, and Violence against Women." *Stanford Law Review* 43, no. 6 (1991): 1241–99.

Cuero, Delfina, and Florence Connolly Shipek. *Delfina Cuero: Her Autobiography, an Account of Her Last Years, and Her Ethnobotanic Contributions*. Menlo Park CA: Ballena, 1991.

Deer, Sarah. *The Beginning and End of Rape: Confronting Sexual Violence in Native America*. Minneapolis: University of Minnesota Press, 2015.

Denetdale, Jennifer. "Chairmen, Presidents, and Princesses: The Navajo Nation, Gender, and the Politics of Tradition." *Wicazo Sa Review* 21, no. 1 (2006): 9–28. https://doi.org/10.1353/wic.2006.0004.

Gamble, Lynn H., and Michael Wilken-Robertson. "Kumeyaay Cultural Landscapes of Baja California's Tijuana River Watershed." *Journal of California and Great Basin Anthropology* 28, no. 2 (2008): 127–51.

Green, Joyce. *Making Space for Indigenous Feminism*. New York: Zed, 2007.

Hall, Lisa Kahaleole. "Navigating Our Own 'Sea of Islands': Remapping a Theoretical Space for Hawaiian Women and Indigenous Feminism." *Wicazo Sa Review* 24, no. 2 (2009): 15–38.

Hedges, Ken. "Notes on the Kumeyaay: A Problem of Identification." *Journal of California Anthropology* 2, no. 1 (1975): 71–83.

Heizer, Robert F., ed. *The Destruction of California Indians*. Reprint. ed. Lincoln: Bison, 1993.

Hernández, Kelly Lytle. *City of Inmates: Conquest, Rebellion, and the Rise of Human Caging in Los Angeles, 1771–1965*. Justice, Power, and Politics. Chapel Hill: University of North Carolina Press, 2017.

———. *Migra! A History of the U.S. Border Patrol*. Berkeley: University of California Press, 2010.

Hokulani, K. Aikau, Maile Arvin, Mishuana Goeman, and Scott Morgensen. "Indigenous Feminisms Roundtable." *Frontiers: A Journal of Women Studies* 36, no. 3 (2015): 84. https://doi.org/10.5250/fronjwomestud.36.3.0084.

Jacobson, Matthew Frye. *Whiteness of a Different Color: European Immigrants and the Alchemy of Race*. Cambridge MA: Harvard University Press, 2002.

Johnson, Susan Lee. *Roaring Camp: The Social World of the California Gold Rush*. 1st ed. New York: Norton, 2000.

Kang, S. Deborah. *The INS on the Line: Making Immigration Law on the US-Mexico Border, 1917–1954*. 1st edition. New York, NY: Oxford University Press, 2017.

Kauanui, J. Kehaulani. "'A Structure, Not an Event': Settler Colonialism and Enduring Indigeneity." *Lateral* 5, no. 1 (May 2016).

Taylor, Keeanga-Yamahtta, ed. *How We Get Free: Black Feminism and the Combahee River Collective*. Chicago: Haymarket Books, 2017.

Lim, Julian. *Porous Borders: Multiracial Migrations and the Law in the U.S.-Mexico Borderlands*. David J. Weber Series in the New Borderlands History. Chapel Hill: University of North Carolina Press, 2017.

Lindsay, Brendan C. *Murder State: California's Native American Genocide, 1846–1873*. Lincoln: University of Nebraska Press, 2012.

Madley, Benjamin. *An American Genocide: The United States and the California Indian Catastrophe, 1846–1873*. New Haven: Yale University Press, 2017.

———. "'Unholy Traffic in Human Blood and Souls': Systems of California Indian Servitude under U.S. Rule." *Pacific Historical Review* 83, no. 4 (2014): 626–67.

Magliari, Michael. "Free Soil, Unfree Labor: Cave Johnson Couts and the Binding of Indian Workers in California, 1850–1867." *Pacific Historical Review* 73, no. 3 (August 2004): 349–90.

May, Ronald V. "A Brief Survey of Kumeyaay Ethnography: Correlations between Environmental Land-Use Patterns, Material Culture, and Social Organization." *Pacific Coast Archaeological Society Quarterly* 11, no. 4 (October 1975): 1–25.

Mendoza, Mary E. "Caging Out, Caging In." *Pacific Historical Review* 88, no. 1 (February 1, 2019): 86–109.

———. "Treacherous Terrain: Racial Exclusion and Environmental Control at the U.S.-Mexico Border." *Environmental History* 23, no. 1 (January 2018): 1–10.

Merchant, Carolyn, ed. *Green versus Gold: Sources in California's Environmental History*. Washington DC: Island, 1998.

Million, Dian. "Felt Theory: An Indigenous Feminist Approach to Affect and History." *Wicazo Sa Review* 24, no. 2 (2009): 53–76. https://doi.org/10.1353/wic.0.0043.

Miskwish, Michael Connolly. *Kumeyaay: A History Book*. El Cajon CA: Sycuan, 2007.

Nickel, Sarah, and Amanda Fehr. *In Good Relation: History, Gender, and Kinship in Indigenous Feminisms*. Winnipeg: University of Manitoba Press, 2020.

Norton, Jack. *When Our Worlds Cried: Genocide in Northwestern California*. San Francisco: Indian Historian Press, 1979.

Norton, Jack, Rupert Costo, and Jeannette Henry Costo. "The Path of Genocide: From El Camino Real to the Gold Mines of the North." In *The Missions of California: A Legacy of Genocide*, edited by Rupert Costo and Jeanette Henry Costo. 111–30. San Francisco: Indian Historian Press, 1987.

Pfeifer, Michael James. *Rough Justice: Lynching and American Society, 1874–1947*. Urbana: University of Illinois Press, 2004.

Rawls, James J. *Indians of California: The Changing Image*. Norman: University of Oklahoma Press, 1984.

Risling Baldy, Cutcha. *We Are Dancing for You: Native Feminisms and the Revitalization of Women's Coming-of-Age Ceremonies*. 1st ed. Indigenous Confluences. Seattle: University of Washington Press, 2018.

Rodriguez, Annette M. "The Noose That Builds the Nation: Mexican Lynching in the Southwest." PhD diss., University of New Mexico, 2008.

Shackley, M. Steven, T. T. Waterman, Leslie Spier, and Edward Winslow Gifford, eds. *The Early Ethnography of the Kumeyaay*. Classics in California Anthropology. Berkeley: Phoebe Hearst Museum of Anthropology, University of California, 2004.

Shah, Nayan. *Stranger Intimacy: Contesting Race, Sexuality, and the Law in the North American West*. American Crossroads 31. Berkeley: University of California Press, 2011.

Shipek, Florence C. "An Example of Intensive Plant Husbandry: The Kumeyaay of Southern California." In *Foraging and Farming: The Evolution of Plant Exploitation*, edited by David R. Harris and Gordon C. Hillman, 163. Routledge, 2014.

———. "Kumeyaay Socio-political Structure." *Journal of California and Great Basin Anthropology* 4, no. 2 (1982): 296–303.

———. "Myth and Reality: The Antiquity of the Kumeyaay." In *Proceedings of the 1983, 1984 and 1985 Hokan-Penutian Languages Workshop*, edited by James E. Redden, 4–11. Occasional Papers on Linguistics 13. Carbondale: Southern Illinois University, 1986.

———. *Pushed into the Rocks: Southern California Indian Land Tenure, 1769–1986.* Lincoln: University of Nebraska Press, 1988.

Snelgrove, Corey, Rita Dhamoon, and Jeff Corntassel. "Unsettling Settler Colonialism: The Discourse and Politics of Settlers, and Solidarity with Indigenous Nations." *Decolonization: Indigeneity, Education & Society* 3, no. 2 (2014).

Sowards, Adam M. *United States West Coast: An Environmental History.* Nature and Human Societies. Santa Barbara CA: ABC-CLIO, 2007.

St. John, Rachel. *Line in the Sand: A History of the Western U.S.-Mexico Border.* America in the World. Oxford: Princeton University Press, 2011.

Stremlau, Rose. "Witnessing the West: Barbara Longknife and the California Gold Rush." In *The Native South: New Histories and Enduring Legacies*, edited by Tim Alan Garrison and Greg O'Brien, 162–80. Lincoln: University of Nebraska Press, 2017.

Taylor, Keeanga-Yamahtta, ed. *How We Get Free: Black Feminism and the Combahee River Collective.* Chicago: Haymarket, 2017.

Tuck, Eve, and K. Wang Yang. "Decolonization Is Not a Metaphor." *Decolonization: Indigeneity, Education & Society* 1, no. 1 (2012): 1–40.

Wilken-Robertson, Michael. *Kumeyaay Ethnobotany: Native People and Native Plants of Baja California's Borderlands.* 1st ed. San Diego: Sunbelt, 2017.

From Idle No More to Standing Rock

The Fight for Indigenous Environmental Justice

KENT BLANSETT

On October 17, 2013, in Rexton, a small eastern Canadian town on the Elsipog-tog First Nation Reserve, over one hundred Royal Canadian Mounted Police (RCMP) wielding riot gear, side arms, tasers, tear gas, attack dogs, pepper spray, rubber bullets, nightsticks, and a variety of other weapons marched against a peaceful encampment of Mi'kmaq First Nation citizens and outside supporters. Among the chaos that ensued, RCMP Emergency Response teams armed with assault weapons and dressed in military fatigues took aim upon the men, women, and children within the encampment along Route 134. Armed only with the power of song and eagle feathers, Native women formed a protective line against the ominous and threatening march of the armed police force. On this lone highway, First Nations women stood up against the combined assault of the RCMP and Southwestern Energy Company to defend their families, community, and ultimately their future. The RCMP had been requested by Southwestern Energy to service an injunction against protesters who formed a peaceful blockade around exploratory equipment to search for shale gas deposits. The Houston, Texas-based company never consulted with the Mi'kmaq to gain their consent for exploratory testing or drilling on the reserve. Yet on Southwestern Energy's public website in 2013, they claimed to be fulfilling the necessary steps toward drilling their first wells.[1]

As the RCMP marched against the blockade, much of the media who arrived late on the scene were forced to remain behind police barricades for "their own safety." This media barrier was conveniently positioned at a considerable distance away from any observable view of the RCMP's assault on the encampment of tribal leaders, lawyers, and other supporters. As reporters frantically huddled behind police lines, the only hint of danger emerged from the loud disapproval of protesters and a billowing cloud of dark smoke that soared above the tree lines.

Not long after the smoke had cleared, the only photo images and video that broke through police lines had been captured by the protesters themselves who carried smartphones and other digital devices. Social media sites soon exploded with activity as citizens on both sides of the border grew in support and outrage. Hundreds of images from the Elsipogtog First Nation Reserve infiltrated blog and social media sites. Every photo and video released had documented another part of the story about RCMP abuses. Social media had informed the world about the arrest of over forty protesters. For example, on that day, a quick search on Google Trends for Canada revealed nearly a 100 percent spike in search information for Rexton, New Brunswick. Making national headlines in Canada, the Rexton story failed to be picked up by mainstream American media channels.[2]

As a "modern" society, every Canadian and American should ask themselves how far have we really advanced on the issue of Indigenous rights? Why are colonial governments throughout the Western Hemisphere so threatened by Indigenous nations asserting their sovereign rights? As much as Americans point the finger at Canada, we also have three more fingers pointing back at ourselves. After the assault by RCMP officers, it stands to reason that Indigenous sovereignty is a threat to large corporate interests. This ominous financial threat as perceived by corporations, like Southwestern Energy, has lent probusiness politicians the ammunition to attack Indigenous sovereignty and rights. While entire libraries, congressional inquiries, and special investigations should be devoted to these larger questions, the main purpose of this chapter is to uncover the historic roots and philosophies that influenced the modern Idle No More movement and its lead up to the Water Protector encampment at Standing Rock. This chapter draws a clear link between how major corporations on both sides of the North American border have lobbied political interests for a new Manifest Destiny, a campaign to accelerate the exploitation of Indigenous lands, resources, and peoples.

The history of the Idle No More movement began in the early 1960s at the juncture of Native nationalism and Red Power politics. Indigenous peoples on both sides of the border started to embrace a new brand of intertribalism and coalition politics. This was a progressive populism that strove to unite

FIG. 15.1. Painting based on Ossie Michelin photograph of Amanda Polshies, a Lakota-Mi'kmaq woman who stood up to the RCMP with an eagle feather at the October 17, 2013, Elsipogtog First Nations standoff over fracking. Courtesy of Fanny Aishaa, http://www.fannyaishaa.com.

First Nations, American Indian peoples, and allies into an intertribal coalition. Such a coalition held both the real and imagined potential to actively support grassroots Native nationalist causes (fishing rights, land rights, mineral and water rights—just to name a few). Several major organizations (Metis Society, Federation of Saskatchewan Indians, National Indian Brotherhood, National Congress of American Indians, National Indian Youth Council, and United Native Americans are only some examples) championed Native rights well before the intellectual foundations of the Red Power movement appeared in literature.[3]

Two of the most influential manifestos made their way onto bookshelves toward the end of the 1960s; First Nations Cree author Harold Cardinal's *Unjust Society* and Dakota scholar Vine Deloria Jr.'s famed *Custer Died for Your Sins* equally supplied clarity and definition to this international Indigenous rights movement, widely known as Red Power. Cardinal's work lent scholastic and popular support toward overturning Prime Minister Pierre Trudeau's White Paper, a policy that strove to limit and eradicate First Nation sovereignty. Similarly, Deloria's book provided an ideological anchor for a repeal of termination legislation and supported self-determination (from 1953–70s over 109 Native nations in the United States had their federal trust status terminated through individual acts of Congress).[4]

Throughout the 1960s to 1970s, various Red Power movements clashed with corporations, police, and military forces on both sides of the border, from the fish-ins in the American Northwest to the Indians of All Tribes takeover of Alcatraz (1969) to the Kanora Protest (1965) and the 1967 Expo to Wounded Knee (1973) and the march on Ottawa in 1974. Thousands of Indigenous peoples crossed the U.S.-Canadian border in solidarity and support of Red Power. The end results are complicated, but overall the Red Power movement aided in the defeat of Trudeau's White Paper and repeal of termination legislation. These coalition politics gathered lawyers, activists, writers, artists, and scholars together that jumpstarted the era of self-determination. Red Power struggled for legislative and governmental reform and land and treaty rights, but one of the movement's most imposing obstacles dealt with the continued corporate and industrial abuse of Native lands and peoples.

Previous scholars have argued that the military industrial complex that emerged following the end of World War II transformed the national economy and shaped the modern West—yet this complex also had a devastating effect on Indian Country in the form of extractive colonization.⁵ The September of 1969 issue of *Nation's Business*, a once popular U.S. business magazine, published an interesting piece entitled "Indian Country Is a Frontier Again." On page 77, the article highlighted a growing trend, the use of Indian lands for corporate investment: "The Bureau of Indian Affairs provides what it calls a 'one-stop service' to industries seeking new locations and to Indian tribes seeking industrial development through private investment. . . . In return . . . what do Indians offer Industry? Manpower, space and a choice of sites, and the opportunity to become part of the growth plans of areas newly emerging from rural isolation."⁶ As the keywords in the *Nation's Business* article testified, Native lands were isolated and contained an exploitable source of cheap labor—all backed by the federal government. Of course, it would have been great if Ford or Chevy had attempted to open an auto factory on any reservation, but this was never the type of industrial development supported by the federal government. Ultimately, the military industrial complex focused on exploiting mineral-rich Native lands. To date this one-stop chop shop has never worked out well for Indian Country. A future corporate history of Native North America might reveal that TransCanada, Platinex, Suncor, Syncrude, Hydro-Quebec, Eagle-Picher Corporation, Anaconda, Kerr McGee, St. Regis Paper Company, Hearst, Kimberly Clark, PG&E Corporation, AMAX, Alcoa or Reynolds, General Electric, Monsanto, Barrick Gold, and Peabody Coal, just to name a few, evaded environmental restrictions and responsibilities, exploited mineral and natural resources, and aided in promoting the toxic destruction of Indigenous lands and peoples. For example, in the United States over six hundred hazardous waste sites exist in Indian Country, which is at least one hazardous site for every federally recognized tribe; approximately 34 percent of all Superfund sites are located on Indigenous lands. In Canada there are close to 4,486 contaminated sites on First Nation reserves, and that represents 20 percent of Canada's total toxic sites.⁷

Perhaps a modern divestment movement might aid in the current fight against corporate abuses occurring all across Turtle Island. American Indian history often reads like the miner's canary, an eerie harbinger of our global future—it is only a matter of time before the effects of overzealous natural resource extraction begin to impact every individual around the world. It is this historical base, rooted in Red Power, which informs the political foundations of the Idle No More and all subsequent movements. In other words, the Idle No More movement didn't just spring up overnight (some have tried falsely to liken it to the former occupy movements).[8] While Idle No More is founded in Canada, it is not separate from Red Power; rather, it is an extension and progression of this same movement.[9]

Throughout the 1990s and into the recent present, several key protests and standoffs have occurred between the Canadian government and First Nation peoples. The following list briefly highlights some of these key movements:

- July 11 to September 26, 1990, the seventy-eight day occupation at Oka, located on the Kanesatake Mohawk Reserve, squared off Canadian military against the local community eager to protect their sacred lands from a proposed golf course expansion.[10]
- July to November 1990, Lil'wat People Movement's blockade against logging roads on the Reserve led to the arrest of sixty-seven First Nations peoples. The Lil'wat blockade also led to the ongoing protest over the proposed development of Cayoosh Ski Resort in British Columbia.[11]
- September 6, 1995, Anishinaabeg citizens at Stoney Point Reserve were attacked by Ontario Provincial Police (OPP) for the return of Ipperwash Provincial Park, which had been loaned to Canada temporarily for the war effort in World War II. In the police raid on the peaceful encampment, Dudley George, a Stoney Point citizen, was gunned down by the OPP.[12]
- 1995, at the Gustafsen Lake standoff, over four hundred Royal Canadian Mounted Police marched against the Shuswap First Nation peoples and Ts'Peten Defenders in British Columbia. The month-long standoff had resulted from non-Native ranchers threatening their religious freedom and the Shuswap Sun Dance.[13]
- 1999, Mi'kmaq on the Burnt Church Reserve of New Brunswick were engaged in a fishing rights struggle and outright naval war that led to two groundbreaking Canadian Supreme Court Decisions. Known as the Marshall Decisions, these Supreme Court decisions defended both treaty and fishing rights.[14]
- 2003 to 2006, on the Six Nations Reserve, Mohawk activists fought against OPP forces to protect their treaty lands at Caledonia from a suburban development sponsored by Henco Corporation.[15]

Each of these peaceful movements ultimately led to violent clashes over human, treaty, land, and harvesting rights with Canadian police. From this long and at times violent history emerged Idle No More, a nonviolent movement that began with the TransCanada (a company founded in 1951) or Keystone XL pipeline. The pipeline has been in operation since 2010 and acts to convert some former natural gas lines into crude oil pumps from Saskatchewan and Manitoba. The pipeline stretches across the Medicine Line for over one thousand miles running through the states of North Dakota, South Dakota, Nebraska, Kansas, Missouri, and Illinois. The second phase of the Keystone pipeline included an extension line from Steele City, Nebraska, to Cushing, Oklahoma. Over eleven new pump stations would have delivered close to six hundred thousand barrels of crude oil every day. Two more phases of the Keystone pipeline are still on the table that would add another estimated five hundred thousand barrels of crude oil to the lines. Projections estimate that these additional lines might potentially net over one million barrels of black gold per day (for comparison, the United States alone consumes approximately twenty million barrels of oil a day).[16]

As of May of 2013, the Northern Gateway Line proposed by Enbridge has been blocked by provincial officials in British Columbia. This legislative action by British Columbia effectively cutoff access to Pacific oil markets and accelerated a renewed corporate campaign to approve the expansion of the Keystone XL pipeline in the United States. At an Idle No More rally in Toronto, First Nations people joined with labor unions to lobby enough support to block the proposed Enbridge Line 9 that was slated to run east from Sarnia to Montreal along a thirty-seven-year-old pipeline structure. On the "closed" Red Lake Anishinaabeg Reservation (closed meaning it is one of the few Native nations that avoided allotment) in northern Minnesota, Red Lake tribal citizens also launched a concerted campaign to prevent Enbridge from extending its pipeline through Red Lake lands.[17]

Ample evidence and examples abound that highlight the vulnerability and numerous leaks that have increased in frequency over the last few years (like the 2013 Mayflower Oil spill in Arkansas). Some of the blame centers squarely on the number of pump stations; when the number of pump stations are increased on any line it automatically raises the pressure/flow within the pipeline itself, and this action can jeopardize the overall integrity of the pipe. Pipelines are not guaranteed by some supernatural force from ever rupturing. It is not a

FIG. 15.2. Map of Alberta showing the extent of oil sand occurrences (*left*) and an annotated satellite image of the same area in 2011, showing oil sand open-cast mines and in situ production sites along the Athabasca River north of Fort McMurray (*right*). As of 2015, the photographed area was the only place in Alberta where oil sands were mined in open pits. All other oil sand bitumen production sites are used (mainly steam-based) in situ methods. SAGD, CCS, May 31, 2015, by Gretarsson/Wikimedia Commons.

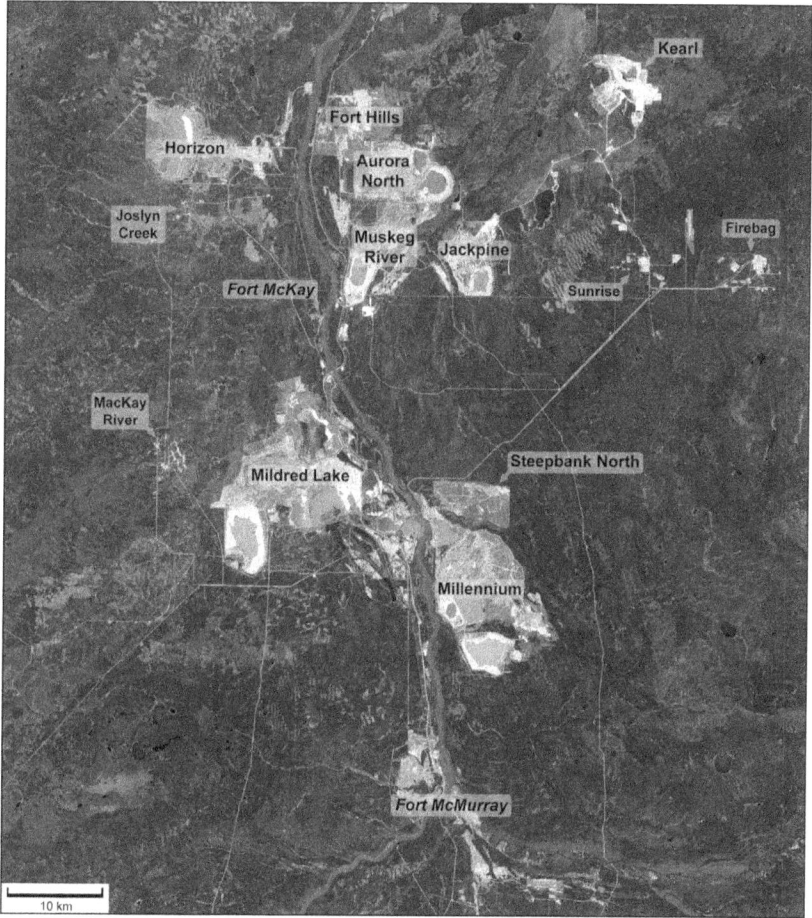

question of if but only a matter of when—despite constant satellite inspection at central command centers, a spill or break is inevitable. In 2013, Greenpeace Canada estimated that over 1.5 million barrels of tar sands have leaked and are continuing to leak at four different sites in Alberta.[18]

If leaks are inevitable, then the former Keystone XL pipeline that was slated to run dangerously close to the great Ogallala Aquifer remains a national threat. Any spill could endanger this precious freshwater resource that is being recharged less and less every year despite chronic dependence on the aquifer by area farmers. A 2013 *Kansas City Star* article cited a Kansas State University study that calculated that the Ogallala Aquifer has just enough water to last until 2110 (a single lifespan). A major pipeline spill would drastically reduce this estimate. Considering that the Great Plains are still America's bread basket, we could also face a major food shortage without access to adequate freshwater supplies. Is it possible that America's access to freshwater resources are growing scarcer than natural gas or oil, which deserves our protection? Our national security is not only threatened by our dependence on foreign oil; this threat is multiplied tenfold if we lack access to fresh water. More importantly, this issue moves beyond a conservative or liberal agenda . . . at stake is the trust of preserving a better world for future generations.[19]

Presently, the Canadian branch of the Keystone pipeline has been constructed not less than fifty miles from over 150 First Nation communities and twelve reserves. In the United States over one hundred miles of pipeline are located on Native lands. In September of 2011, Indigenous leaders from both Canada and the United States were arrested outside of the White House when they protested against the expansion of the Keystone pipeline. In a mass public relations campaign in Canada, TransCanada made sizable financial contributions to the University of Toronto to support Aboriginal studies. Despite mass arrests and corporate buy-ins to major universities, both First Nations and American Indian communities are struggling to ward off the negative effects imposed by large multinational corporate interests promoting tar sands oil production and hydraulic fracking.[20]

To combat against the rise of a corporate police state in Canada, First Nations and non-Indigenous leaders Nina Wilson, Sheelah Mclean, Sylvia McAdam, and Jessica Gordon sponsored a new political platform and coalition to peacefully unite both Indigenous nations and supporters around a central Indigenous Environmental Justice campaign. Together these four leaders founded the Idle No More movement, which sought to actively block the former conservative administration of Prime Minister Stephen Harper, who without parliamentary debate passed anti-Indigenous legislation that favored multinational corporate interests. For instance, Harper's administration sponsored Bill c-45, which changed over forty-four laws that once protected fish habitat and threatened First Nation fisheries; it removed the environmental assessment requirement in the Navigation Protection Act which left only 1 percent of Canada's waterways protected. Secondly, Bill c-38 ignored more than seventy laws to protect game, fish, and water. Finally,

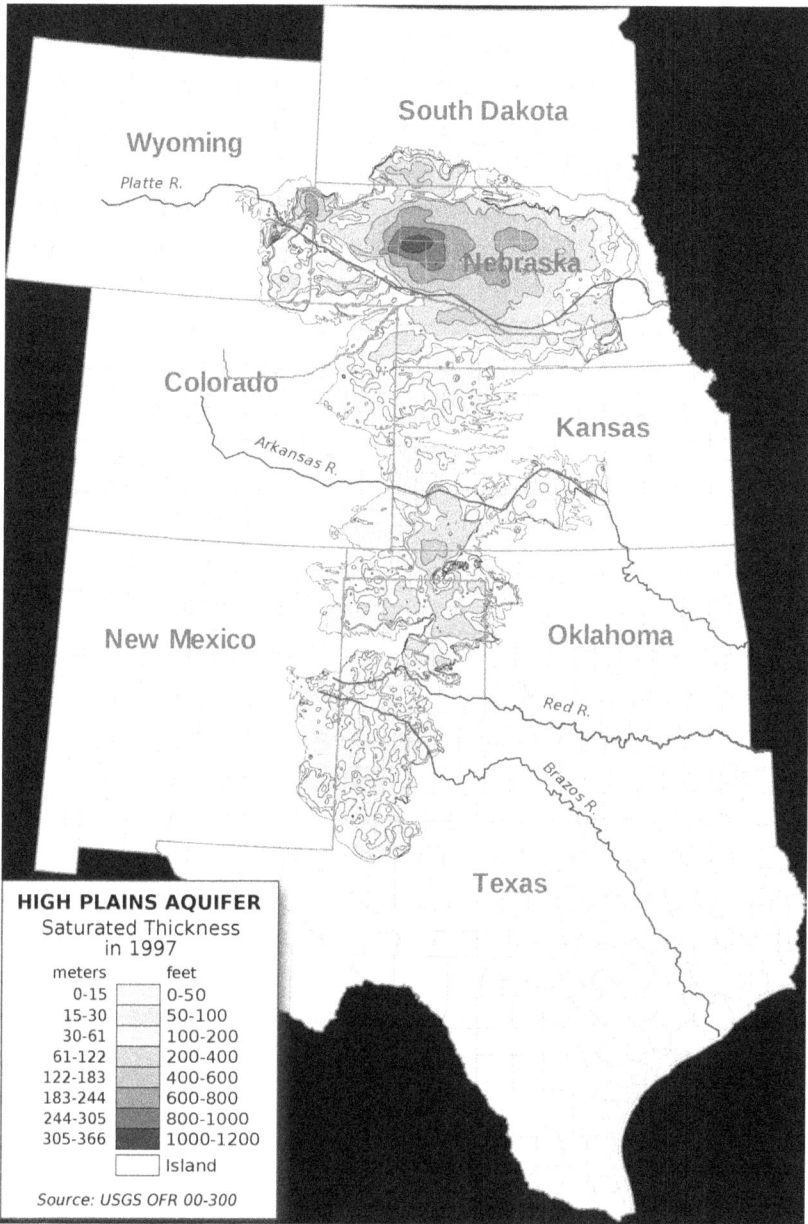

FIG. 15.3. Map showing the proposed route of the Keystone XL pipeline and its proximity to the Ogallala Aquifer. Wikimedia Commons.

Bill c-27, required for the first time that First Nation–owned businesses publicly report all their earnings and expenses—an act that undermined the economic competitiveness and integrity of First Nation–owned businesses.

Canadian prime minister Stephen Harper's "reforms" called for the outright surrender of thousands of acres of First Nation Reserve lands for selective development by oil and gas industries. These lands were specifically targeted by TransCanada and other corporations for the exclusive right to expand oil, nuclear, and gas industries. Already witnessing the permanent effects of environmental degradation on their First Nation lands from the tar sands industry, the four women Idle No More leaders organized a National Day of Solidarity and Resurgence. On December 21, 2012, hundreds gathered in major cities and Indigenous communities throughout the world to call for an end to Harper's destructive anti–First Nations policies and legislation. One month later, on January 28, 2013, First Nations peoples and supporters marched on thirty Canadian cities to protest against the illegal seizure and ruin of First Nations lands. Elders like Attawapiskat First Nation chief Theresa Spence and Pimicikamak Cree elder Raymond Robinson, who had each witnessed the tar sand apocalypse occurring in First Nations communities in Alberta, issued an immediate call for a meeting with Prime Minister Stephen Harper. Their pleas were ignored and went unheard by Harper's administration. In opposition, Spence and Robinson sponsored a hunger strike to draw Harper to the negotiation table. While the hunger strikes failed to produce fruitful results, it did draw international support and criticism of Harper's policies.[21]

The raid on the peaceful antifracking demonstration on Mi'kmaq lands sparked an international outcry over the development of a corporate police state in Canada. Proof is in the hundreds of photos that streamed across the internet. Photos that revealed First Nations women who willingly placed their unarmed bodies before the marching armies of the RCMP—it looks like the same old cavalry. Replacing gold with oil, bluecoats with camouflage, rifles with pepper spray, forests with wastelands, and streams with flammable water—all under the name of progress. Such events have sponsored a revival of Manifest Destiny and frontier politics. Idle No More embraced nonviolent strategies that sought to expose the corporate and governmental exploitation of Indigenous rights and lands. This movement also supported amendments to the 1994 Violence against Women Act to include American

Indian women and violations of the Indian Child Welfare Act, to seek justice for the thousands of missing and murdered First Nations women and children, and to issue a review of deaths and abuses that took place within Canadian Residential Schools.[22] As a modern Indigenous movement, its leadership extended far beyond the four original founders, for this became a coalition of Indigenous peoples and allies who collectively advocate for the protection of western and Native lands from a threat of environmental degradation.[23]

In solidarity with Idle No More, two key events changed the course of the movement to block the Keystone XL pipeline in America. On March 5, 2012, several Lakota grandmothers—Debra White Plume, Marie Randall (who was ninety-two years-old), and Renabelle Bad Cob Standing Bear (in her wheelchair)—lined up alongside Alex White Plume Sr., Sam Long Black Cat, Andrew Iron Shell, and Tyrel Iron Shell and over seventy supporters who together maintained a human blockade backed by twenty parked cars along Highway 44 located on the Pine Ridge Reservation near Wanblee, South Dakota. The blockade stopped and rerouted two massive northbound semitrucks as well as their police escorts that hauled two key sections of "Treater Vessels" for the TransCanada pipeline. In a moment that could best be likened to an Indigenous Tiananmen Square, these enormous trucks served as symbols of state-sponsored violence against Indigenous peoples. Six hours into the standoff, tribal police arrested five of the leaders for disorderly conduct. The peaceful blockade captured national headlines, and subsequent arrests lit up various social media networks as the blockade rallied further national disdain for the Keystone XL pipeline.[24]

The second major event occurred in March of 2014 with the establishment of the Sicangu Wicoti Iyuksa Spirit Camp near Ideal, South Dakota, on the Rosebud Reservation. This encampment set the stage for strategies and tactics that helped inspire the leadership for the Water Protector fight at Standing Rock. The Rosebud Sioux tribal government feared TransCanada would utilize the power of eminent domain to establish the Keystone XL pipeline on its treaty lands. The Spirit Camp became a part of the "Shielding the People" and "Moccasins on the Ground" campaigns to train Indigenous peoples in strategies for how to organize in opposition to the pipeline. It served as the central organizing headquarters for a campaign that linked the Rosebud Tribe with several key allied organizations like Dakota Rural Action and

Bold Nebraska. By November of 2015, these actions along with many other events provided President Obama with enough support to officially reject TransCanada's application to construct the Keystone xl pipeline. These two major events to halt the pipeline were indicative of a larger campaign that set in motion the next major environmental war.[25]

Since the early 2000s, over thirty different oil companies have staked their financial futures on the Bakken oil fields of North Dakota utilizing hydraulic fracking to extract the oil from deep below the northern plains surface; Energy Transfer Partners (a Texas-based company) sought to construct a new pipeline that would transport over 450,000 barrels of oil a day through a 1,200-mile pipeline from North Dakota to Illinois refinement facilities. Geographically, the Bakken oil fields stretch from Montana and North Dakota and into Saskatchewan and Manitoba. The U.S. development of these fields is primarily located on Mandan, Hidatsa, and Arikara or Three Affiliated Tribes homelands. After frequent negotiations between 2008 and 2009, Three Affiliated Tribes granted tribal consent for oil companies to mine their lands. Four years later, in 2013, the plans to mine this region received final approval from the Environmental Protection Agency.[26]

The Army Corps of Engineers originally granted authorization to Energy Transfer Partners to construct the Dakota Access pipeline (DAPL) without tribal consultation or consent, which started within one month after having received mining approval. While originally slated to be built near the more populous Bismarck, North Dakota, it was soon rerouted to cross Lakota treaty lands near Lake Oahe (the only freshwater resource for the entire Standing Rock Sioux Tribe), only five hundred feet away from official Standing Rock Reservation lands. Several Indigenous organizations immediately filed for a delay until an environmental impact statement could be completed to halt construction and failed to receive any action or response. Since 2014, the Standing Rock Sioux Tribe continues to stand in opposition to DAPL's construction.[27]

In April 2016, the Sacred Stone Camp was founded as one of three main camps (the 1851 Treaty camp and Oceti Sakowin "Seven Council Fires" camp and dozens of other encampments were later established to challenge DAPL's construction under the Mni Sose or Missouri River). The original idea for establishing the first camp came from Lakota historian LaDonna Brave Bull Allard, who established one of the first and main camps on her own lands

FIG. 15.4. The People's Climate march represented the largest activist event sponsored by the People's Climate movement to advocate for political reform and thwart the devastating effects of climate change. The march took place in New York City on September 21, 2014. *02 idle no more (23)a, September 21, 2014*, by Guano/Flickr.

located near the Cannonball River (this area is traversed by three rivers: Cannonball, Grand, and Missouri Rivers). In July, a prayer run founded by Standing Rock citizen Bobbi Jean Three Legs and other Indigenous students called "Rezpect Our Water," a sponsored run from Omaha to Washington DC to deliver antipipeline petitions against the pipeline to politicians.[28] Simultaneously in Minnesota Indigenous activists and allies successfully blocked the Enbridge Sandpiper pipeline from being constructed.[29]

By August Standing Rock tribal chairman Dave Archambault II and council member Dana Yellowfat were arrested after they tried to protect an ancestor's remains that had been dug up and left exposed by the construction company. Quickly, Standing Rock tried to block construction, asserting that close to 380 archaeological sites and associated graves were located along the proposed route of the pipeline.[30]

By September, activists attempted to halt the construction of the pipeline and were attacked by security dogs, stirring images reminiscent of civil

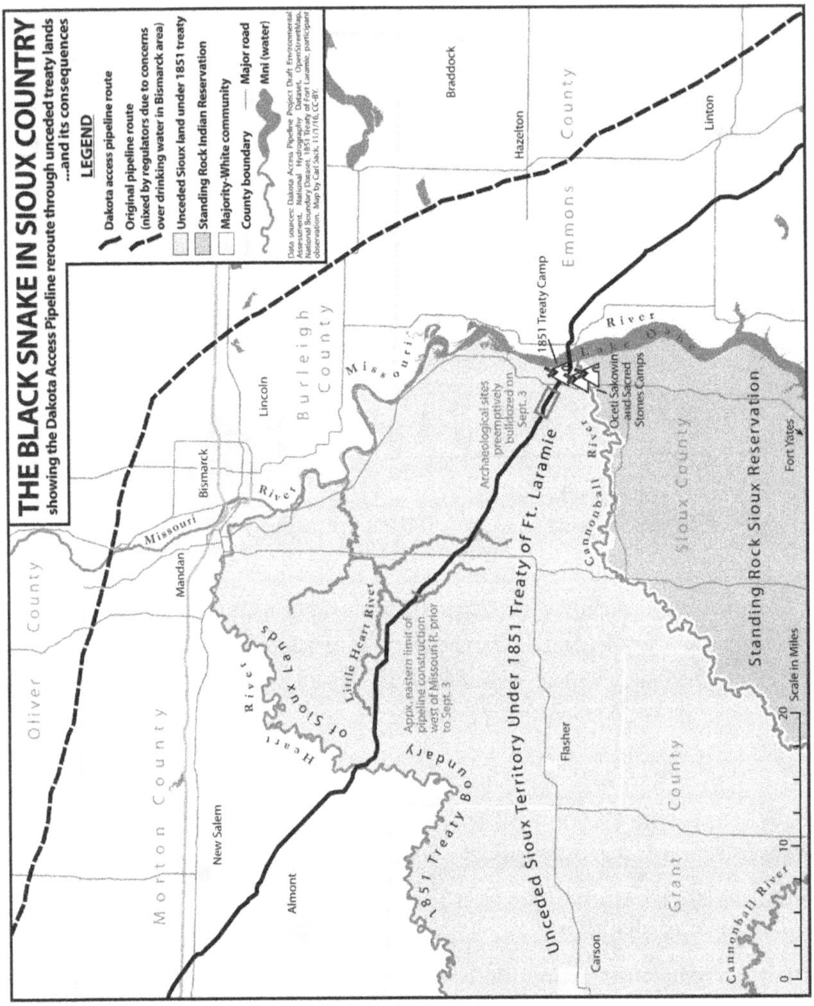

FIG. 15.5. Between the Heart River and Lake Oahe, the Dakota Access pipeline passes through 1851 Sioux territory. *Dakota Access pipeline reroute, November 1, 2016*, map by Carl Sack/Wikimedia Commons.

rights demonstrators some fifty years earlier being mauled by police dogs in the American South—such scenes question just how far the United States has come on issues of civil and human rights? Later that same month, U.S. district judge James Boasberg issued an order to suspend construction on the pipeline crossing the Missouri River under Lake Oahe. A few days later

FIG. 15.6. Panoramic view of Oceti Sakowin camp. Photo courtesy of Beth Castle.

the governor of North Dakota Jack Dalrymple ordered 500 National Guard troops to join a coalition of police officers recruited from seventy-five law enforcement agencies across America to curb protests (altogether a military force that numbered close to 1,300) at the construction site, and Judge Boasberg soon reversed his position. Throughout October and November, after multiple arrests at the construction site, Chairman Archambault filed a civil rights violation against Energy Transfer Partners and requested an investigation into police abuses with the U.S. attorney general's office. Soon checkpoints appeared along the highways between Bismarck and Standing Rock to monitor and regulate the increased traffic of supplies and supporters. In a show of solidarity and to draw attention to the checkpoints, tribes in the Northwest sponsored a canoe journey that sent eighteen canoes down the Missouri River to the Sacred Stone camp.

Early in November, protests increased in number and size partly inspired by a call for a national day of action that ignited a mass of support demonstrations for Standing Rock in over three hundred cities around the world. As both national and international sentiment swelled in support of blocking the pipeline, law enforcement soon thereafter engaged in more violent tactics as a part of their crowd dispersal strategy. Drones and all types of aircraft surveillance became a daily occurrence in the skies above Water Protectors, in direct violation of a no-fly zone over the area.

FIG. 15.7. *Top left*: Photo from Water Protector action that occurred on August 14, 2016, in Cannonball, North Dakota, taken around 2:00 p.m. The names of the participants are unknown but symbolize a day that ancestral remains were disturbed by the construction of the pipeline. The men offered prayers, believing that nothing else could be done, but the women grew anxious and elected to put prayer into action. Soon they had cut the fence guarding the construction site and began to jump over the barrier. Lee Ann Eastman remembers that all you could see were skirts running across the prairie to stop the bulldozers. "We stopped them. We then got chased to the water and a couple of young guys followed to keep us safe. I ran from the helicopter and when we got to the river they all stopped and asked, what do we do now? Without hesitation, I jumped into the river and swam across, making it back to Sacred Stone. We changed our clothes and went back to the front lines. It was a beautiful day that I will never forget." Lee Ann Eastman, email message to Kent Blansett, November 23, 2023. *Top right*: Near St. Anthony, North Dakota, September 6, 2016, around 2:00 p.m. Many of these riders were regulars on horse rides, including the Dakota 38, a modern ride to honor the Dakota warriors who died in 1862 at the

November 20, 2016, represented one of the most violent days of the resistance. On the heavily barricaded Backwater Bridge, which looms over the Missouri River, law enforcement utilized tear gas, rubber bullets, grenades, and water cannons in freezing temperatures that severely injured and wounded over three hundred Water Protectors. One individual in particular, a twenty-one-year-old ally, Sophia Wilansky, nearly lost her arm after a concussion grenade exploded near her, sending shrapnel into her arm. In the final days of the 2016 presidential election between Hillary Clinton and Donald Trump (an Energy Transfer Partners investor), President Barack Obama remained quiet about the heightened violence that targeted Water Protectors at Standing Rock. Before the end of his presidency, Obama halted the pipeline's construction until after the completion of an environmental impact statement.[31]

At the start of the new year, Standing Rock's Tribal Council voted to close all the camps and facilitated the eviction of Water Protectors from the encampments. Four days after his inauguration, President Trump issued an executive order to expedite the review process and force the U.S. Army Corps of Engineers to approve the impact statements and resume construction of the pipeline. In opposition to the executive order, Cheyenne River and Standing Rock Sioux Tribes each filed their own restraining order to block the

largest mass execution in American history. The riders are riding the pipeline's path, a strip of land where all signs of life have been bulldozed and erased. *Bottom Left*: On September 6, 2016, near St. Anthony, North Dakota, a young Anishinaabe woman kneeled in a red dress and painted a rising sun and "Protect Our Water" on the bulldozer's front-end shovel while others stand guard over the enormous machine. For safety reasons the woman preferred to remain anonymous and unidentified. *Bottom Right*: Around 8:30 a.m. on the morning of September 1, 2016, in Cannonball, North Dakota, an unidentified Indigenous woman is being arrested who served as a medic for the movement. While being arrested by law enforcement, she twisted her ankle. Another Water Protector has attached themselves to the front end of the giant shovel, hoping to delay construction at the site. Shortly after Lee Ann Eastman took this picture to document and offer protection to fellow Water Protectors, she was arrested. All photos courtesy of Lee Ann Eastman, Sisseton Wahpeton Oyate citizen and Water Protector who lived at the encampment from August 2, 2016, to the last day on February 23, 2017.

FIGS. 15.8 AND 15.9. No ThanksTaking (Police Standoff) as Morton County police stand over a gravesite located at the top of Turtle Island near the Water Protector camps. Photo stills from *Warrior Women*, courtesy of Beth Castle.

pipeline's construction. Federal district court judge James Boasberg denied both restraining order requests against Energy Transfer Partners.[32]

By January of 2017, major investors in the Dakota Access pipeline began to divest from DAPL like BNP Paribas, DNB bank in Norway, and ING bank in the Netherlands—each having cited their disapproval over the project

FIG. 15.10. People protesting in the Dakota Access pipeline march, moving past San Francisco City Hall, November 15, 2016. Photo by Pax Ahimsa Gethen/ Funcrunch Photo, info@funcrunchphoto.com /Wikimedia Commons.

and its treatment of Indigenous peoples as their primary reasons for having pulled their capital out of the project. It is estimated that Energy Transfer Partners and their financial backers lost nearly $9 billion in costs due to the delays in construction.[33]

After a February tour of the Oceti Sakowin camp and having witnessed protests around the construction site, Victoria Tauli-Corpuz, the United Nations (UN) special rapporteur on the rights of Indigenous peoples, alongside UN official Edward John condemned Energy Transfer Partners, TigerSwan, and federal/state law enforcement for human rights violations and abuses. The UN report highlighted a shocking 2017 global issue when it cited the deaths of over 312 Indigenous activists from twenty-seven countries around the world, all killed in defense of their Indigenous rights and standing against extractive colonialism within their respective homelands.[34]

By February 2017, after the last Water Protector had been removed from the camps, fires consumed what remained of the former housing structures. Altogether over ten thousand Indigenous peoples and allies, representing

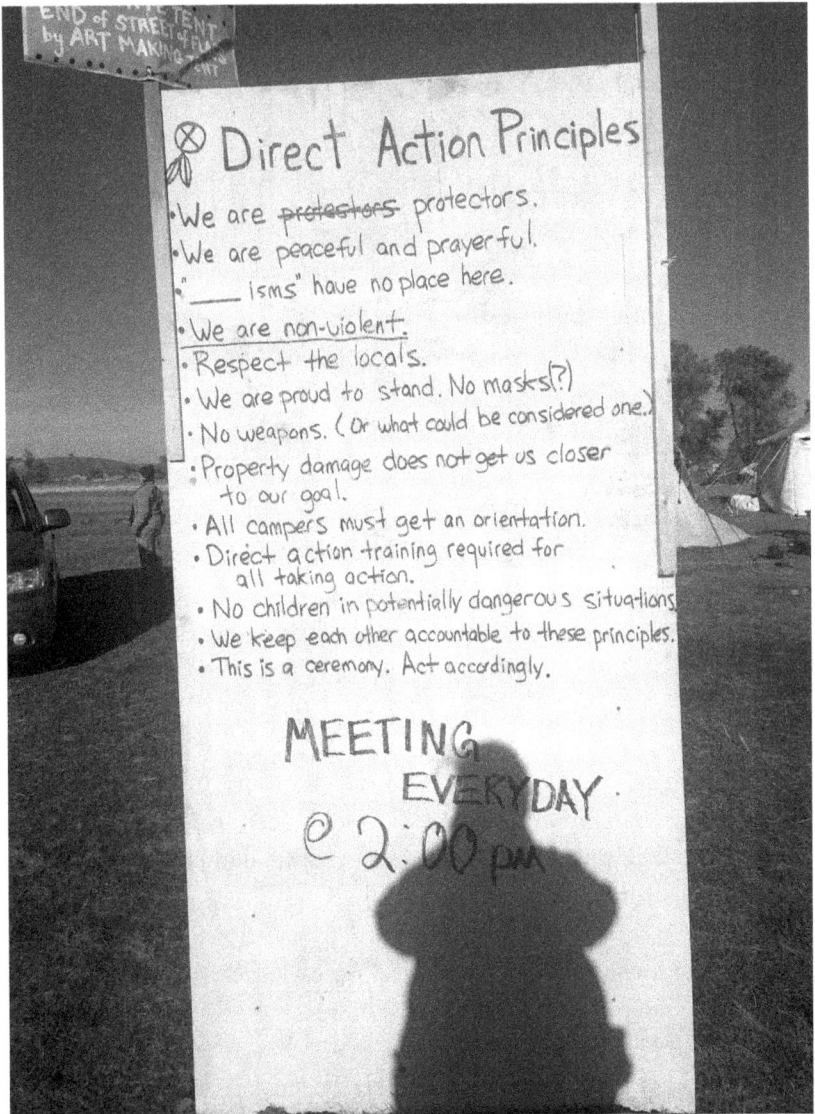

FIG. 15.11. Direct Action Principles sign at Oceti Sakowin,
October 9, 2016. Photograph by Beth Castle, courtesy Beth Castle.

over three hundred Indigenous nations, resided at the camps (representing the tenth most populated town in North Dakota).[35] White Earth citizen and activist Winona LaDuke fondly remembered life in the camps:

> We remembered what it feels like to be free. We remembered what it was like to create a village of thousands of people, a powerful Indigenous space that welcomed people of all different colors and nations. And we remembered what it feels like to create the infrastructure we need to care for ourselves entirely outside the colonized money economy—to feed and clothe our people, to have stable housing and quality medical care for everyone, to have control of our children's upbringing, to practice our spirituality freely and share our stories unafraid. . . . I was so proud to be a part of that moment.[36]

While the direct confrontations against DAPL's construction ended, the fight to stop the pipeline was far from over. At this point, close to eight hundred people had been arrested, and Oglala Lakota activist Red Fawn Fallis had received a fifty-seven month federal prison sentence; many other Water Protectors also received extralong prison sentences for trumped up charges.[37] In 2019, Louisiana, Oklahoma, North Dakota, South Dakota, and Iowa enacted new "critical infrastructure" laws that included stiffer penalties for trespassing and increased the charge from a misdemeanor to a class 4 felony with sentences that included a decade in prison as well as $100,000.00 in fines.[38] These tough new crime or antiprotest laws were solely meant to prevent any further public actions or protests against the oil, fracking, and pipeline industries.

Several years later and long after the Standing Rock camps sat empty, Judge Boasberg in 2020 declared that the effects of the pipeline qualified as "highly controversial," and he ordered that the U.S. Army Corp of Engineers must finally sponsor a detailed environmental impact statement. The decision was appealed by Energy Transfer Partners, and after two years their appeal of the decision made its way up to the U.S. Supreme Court, where justices refused to overturn lower federal courts decision. It was a major legal victory, and yet, still to this day, the pipeline at Standing Rock is transporting oil to Illinois. In 2023, Standing Rock tribal chairwoman Janet Alkire called upon the U.S. Army Corps of Engineers to order DAPL's shut down after Energy Transfer Partners formally admitted to twenty-three crimes in 2021

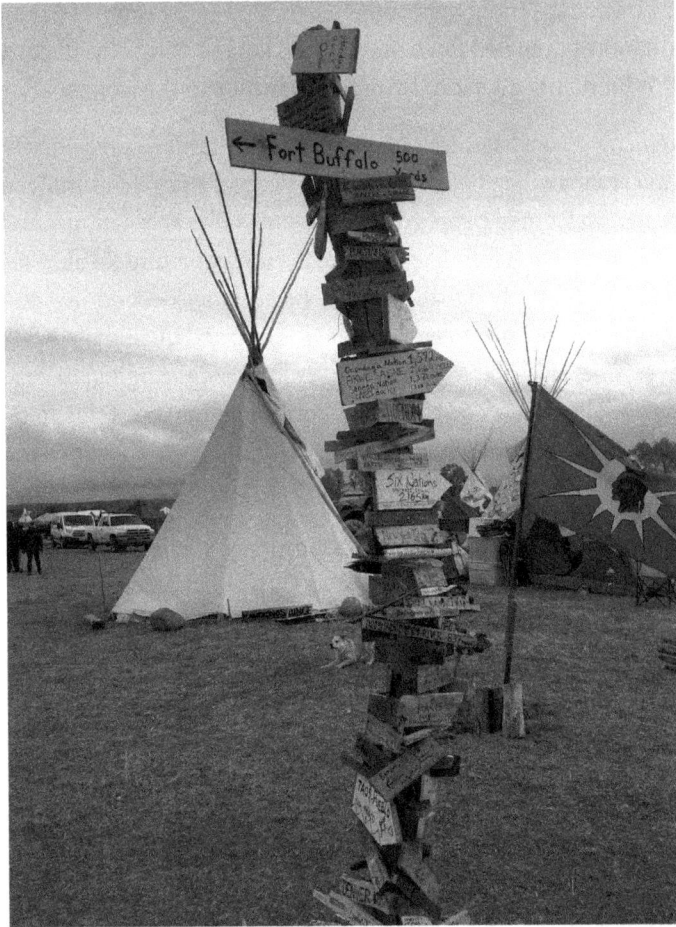

FIG. 15.12. Directional pole at Oceti Sakowin, Standing Rock Sioux Nation. "From nearby Fort Buffalo, distant Six Nations, Denver, and Flagstaff, or transoceanic cities like Paris, Tokyo, and Edinburgh, people converged in rural North Dakota to ally with citizens of the Standing Rock Sioux Tribe. . . . Materially, it is a work of art in its own right . . . Water Protectors secured the pole's safe passage to Washington DC, where it remains an artifact of twenty-first-century Indigenous reorientation and resistance in the Smithsonian's National Museum of the American Indian." From Dana E. Powell, "NODAPL Encampments: Twenty-First-Century Indian City," in *Indian Cities: Histories of Indigenous Urbanization*, edited by Kent Blansett, Cathleen D. Cahill, and Andrew Needham (Norman: University of Oklahoma Press), 267–70. Photo by Dana E. Powell, November 2016, courtesy of Dana E. Powell.

that stemmed from charges of Clean Water Act violations connected to the Mariner East pipeline spills in Pennsylvania.[39]

The struggle continues on at Standing Rock as well as Line 3 in Minnesota and many other sites, from Oak Flat to the recent 2023 defeat of Pebble Mine in Alaska. In Nebraska, the Cowboy and Indian Alliance helped sponsor a massive "No Pipelines" campaign; they were able to shut down the Keystone pipeline that threatened the Ogallala Aquifer.[40] In a joint report issued by the Indigenous Environmental Network and Oil Change International, together they estimated that in seventeen cases of Indigenous resistance to extractive colonialism, these movements eradicated "12 percent of annual U.S. and Canadian pollution, or 779 million metric tons of CO_2e [CO_2 Equivalent]. If these struggles prove successful, this would mean Indigenous resistance will have stopped greenhouse gas pollution equivalent to nearly one-quarter (24 percent) of annual total U.S. and Canadian emissions."[41] In multiple efforts from Idle No More to Standing Rock, Indigenous peoples have made tremendous strides to protect future generations from the dangers of extractive colonialism and climate change.

Now is the time for the United States and Canada to atone for its sins against Indigenous peoples and embrace a true call to action centered upon Indigenous Environmental Justice. Such a foundational shift might be a step toward reconciliation and a path toward a realignment of the core values that sit at the heart of democratic nations. It is important to understand a key distinction: Indigenous Environmental Justice is unique from environmental justice as it expands the discussion beyond environmental racism or natural resource exploitation to exposing a clear link between racism and colonialism.[42] As a movement it recognizes the unique legal and political status of Indigenous sovereignty and stands in direct opposition to colonial occupation, repression, erasure, and exploitation. The ideological and philosophical roots for Indigenous Environmental Justice stems from Traditional Ecological Knowledge systems and practices that acknowledge and maintain sovereign lands and spaces—a relational ontology of plants, animals, earth, sea, ocean, rivers, sky, and universe as living, animate beings that each contain a spirit. A central value of Indigenous Environmental Justice involves restorative healing to *rematriate* lands, wildlife, resources, and waterways as cultural identities—in other words, a community of sovereign beings/bodies who each possess their own distinct legal rights as well as all the accompanying entitlements of personhood. It

FIG. 15.13. Idle No More protest in support of Standing Rock at the state capitol in Bismarck, North Dakota, on September 9, 2016. Photograph by Beth Castle, courtesy of Beth Castle.

is a political, economic, social, and cultural movement deeply rooted in the protection of Indigenous sacred sites, food and medicinal sovereignty, energy sovereignty, biodiversity/habitat protection, reclamation of toxic sites, bio-power and renewable energy development, and direct opposition to extractive colonialism. Indigenous Environmental Justice acknowledges land and water personhood through a process of decolonization that holds the potential to dismantle oppressive structures and systems of gender/sexuality suppression, white supremacy, and settler colonialism. As a crucial component of the larger Indigenous Land Back movement, Indigenous Environmental Justice advocates for Free, Prior, and Informed Consent (right to grant or deny consent) as well as instills tribal direct and/or comanagement of public lands (such as national parks) and natural resources. Finally, as an environmental movement, its strategies and tactics honor the restorative power and healing prospects of place to amplify human closeness to nature—that ultimately, at its core, argues that land rights are human rights.[43]

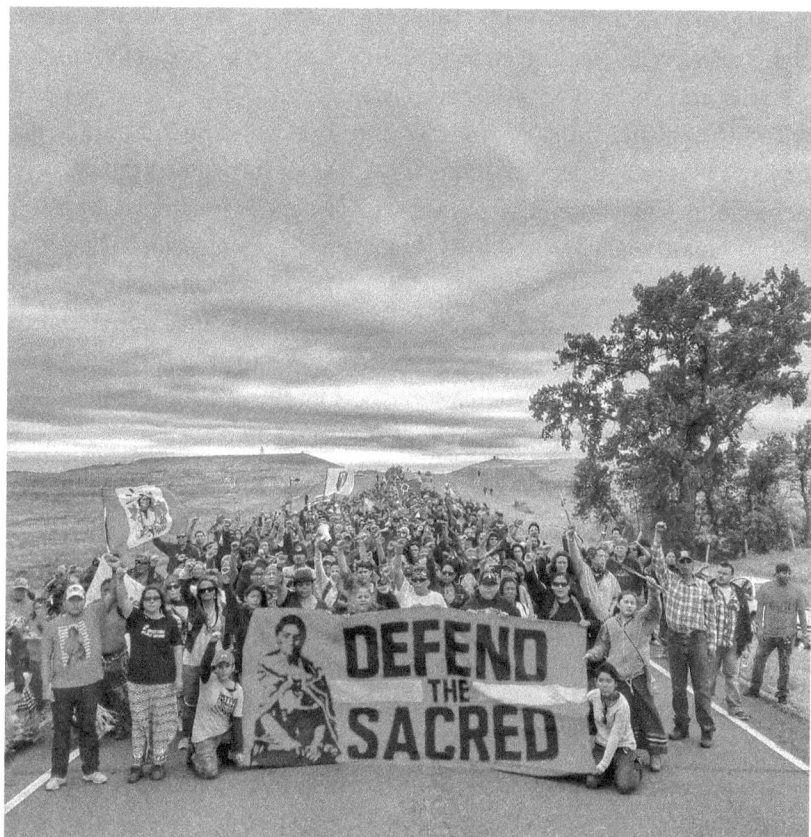

FIG. 15.14. Over five hundred Water Protectors peacefully marched to a sacred site where the Dakota Access pipeline company had bulldozed grave markers on Saturday, September 3, 2016. Photo by Dallas Goldtooth, courtesy of Indigenous Environmental Network.

In 2016, the corporate- and state-sponsored violence unleashed against Water Protectors at Standing Rock serves as the coal miner's canary. America's natural resources cannot be owned by any one individual or corporation. Natural resource extraction and its exploitation negatively impacts every citizen and is worthy of a national referendum, reform, and oversight through the lens of Indigenous Environmental Justice. The mere granting of personhood rights to crucial resources can help turn the tide against ecocide and minimize the long-term environmental risk to future generations. The world is watching, and the stakes have never been higher; American and Canadian sovereignty as well as their international integrity, respect, and resolve is fast eroding.

The nonviolent actions of Water Protectors at Standing Rock are indicative of the larger struggle of Indigenous peoples throughout the Western Hemisphere who continue to pay the ultimate price for colonization's sins against nature.[44] The history of the Water Protectors' struggle at Standing Rock has deep roots in the Indians of All Tribes occupation of Alcatraz Island (1969–71). Almost fifty years apart, each occupation rested upon a central organizing principle, a great collective idea to protect future generations. At Standing Rock, Alcatraz veterans locked arms with a new generation of Indigenous freedom fighters in their call for progressive change as they marched together in pursuit of Indigenous Environmental Justice.[45] Throughout the NoDAPL camps, Indigenous activists and their allies risked everything, as they each placed their dreams, hearts, spirits, and bodies on the front lines of this resource war. Years from now, like with Alcatraz Island, these encampments and places of action around Standing Rock will emerge as sacred spaces, an environmental Selma—a place that forever changed the course of American history. This site shall forever serve as an international site of reckoning where Indigenous peoples unified their voices in a call to action for every nation around the world to not just acknowledge but to honor Indigenous lands and waterways.

While a series of environmental reforms and laws were passed in the 1970s to protect Indigenous human rights, such laws only masked the greater exploitation of tribal lands, natural resources, and mineral rights. The nonviolent Water Protectors confronted attack dogs, Tasers, riot sticks and shields, tear gas, pepper spray, water cannons, and even false imprisonment; some unarmed protectors lost eyes to rubber bullets while others dodged real bullets fired from DAPL's military enforcers. Responsibility for this violent state and history resides squarely at the feet of Energy Transfer Partners and runs completely counter to America's democratic ideals. The violence perpetrated against the Water Protectors injured hundreds and targeted hundreds more for expensive and lengthy legal fights to stay out of prison.[46] After their arrest, many protectors faced cruel and indecent punishment; some individuals were locked inside dog cages brought to the frontlines of the war to carry out a psychological strategy to further dehumanize Indigenous peoples as law enforcement went even further to actively suppress journalists from reporting about the many injustices leveled upon Water Protectors.[47] The extreme tactics employed by corporations backed by colonial governments created a police state in North Dakota to severely restrict the civil liberties of the very American citizens they had sworn to protect; the duality of these competing definitions of protection is not lost on the irony of these circumstances. Many of these abuses remain unreconciled and only add to the long and violent historical legacy of colonization. Thankfully, in all this violence, no one lost their physical life. Why did American political leaders stand idly by as violence escalated in North Dakota? Does action or public outrage over an injustice require the actual taking of an Indigenous life? Are Native lives worth less than other Americans? Where is the national and worldwide outrage over the treatment of this continent's first peoples? How blind or complacent has the world grown in relation to Indigenous colonization, oppression, and genocide? Every day throughout the struggle from Idle No More to Standing Rock, Indigenous peoples and allies placed themselves before an uncertain and indefinite environmental future.

If asked, most Indigenous peoples throughout the Western Hemisphere can point out hypocrisy in colonial legal systems that enforce a carceral state that benefits from a dual sense of justice, one system for settlers and another for Native peoples. Alarming statistics point to flaws and failures in colonial justice systems that are punctuated by the highest percentage of Indigenous incarceration, suicide, and murder rates (among many others). In a colonized state it is of little surprise to settlers that Native homelands contain the largest percentage of Superfund sites accompanied by some of the highest statistics of systemic and generational poverty. Contemporary Indigenous peoples continue to fight the longest war in American history, a war that for centuries has targeted the total eradication of distinct sovereign Native nations, lifeways, families, lands, languages, and our future. In the face of ongoing American and Canadian colonization and oppression, Indigenous peoples continue to overcome insurmountable odds. We do more than survive; we persevere and thrive. Indigenous nations and lifeways represent this planet's future. A more exhaustive history of the twenty-first-century Red Power movement is needed, but this brief overview provides a glimpse into this complex and dynamic period in Indigenous environmental history.

Notes

Portions of this chapter originally appeared as "The New Manifest Destiny: A Brief Political History of the Idle No More Movement," *Blog West*, October 28, 2013; another version, titled, "Idle No More Lives on: Rifles vs. Songs," appeared in *Indian Country Today*, January 16, 2014, https://ictnews.org/archive/idle-no -more-lives-on-rifles-vs-songs.

1. Melanie Patten, "Rexton Protest in N.B. Sparks Renewal of Idle No More," *Huffpost*, October 18, 2013, http://www.huffingtonpost.ca/2013/10/18/rexton -protest-nb-photos_n_4121035.html; CBC *News*, "RCMP, Protesters Withdraw after Shale Gas Clash in Rexton," October 17, 2013; Howe, "Prelude to the Raid"; Martha Troian, "Mi'kmaq Anti-fracking Protest Brings Women to Front Lines to Fight for Water," *Indian Country Today*, November 10, 2013, https://newsmaven .io/indiancountrytoday/archive/mi-kmaq-anti-fracking-protest-brings-women -to-the-front-lines-to-fight-for-water-alK1jV5GEOSa-gXWtatWwQ; Jorge Barrera, "Mi'kmaq Claim Another Highway Victory in Ongoing Battle against Shale Gas Exploration," APTN *National News*, November 18, 2013, https://www .sacredfirenb.wordpress.com/2013/11/18/aptn-mikmaq-claim-another-highway -victory-in-ongoing-battle-against-shale-gas-exploration/. For Southwestern Energy corporate information, see also https://www.swn.com/.

2. Michael MacDonald, "Shale Gas Conflict in New Brunswick Underscores Historic Grievances, Rights of First Nations," *Toronto Star*, December 25, 2013, https:// www.thestar.com/news/canada/shale-gas-conflict-grievances-rights-of-first -nations/article_e851ba65-eac0-54ad-8419-b420eb96e2fc.html; Chelsea Vowel, "The Often-Ignored Facts about Elsipogtog," *Toronto Star*, November 14, 2013, https://www.thestar.com/opinion/contributors/the-often-ignored-facts-about -elsipogtog/article_e687a65b-6d06-5e9f-b1bb-2851adc22fa2.html; *Toronto Star*, "Police Arrest 40 at New Brunswick Fracking Protest," October 17, 2013, https:// www.thestar.com/news/canada/police-arrest-40-at-new-brunswick-fracking -protest/article_bd91db76-7306-5570-bd98-5335b4229c56.html; Sean Craig, "RCMP Tracked 89 Indigenous Activists Considered 'Threats' for Participating in Protests," *National Post*, November 13, 2016, https://nationalpost.com/ news/canada/rcmp-tracked-89-indigenous-activists-considered-threats-for -participating-in-protests; Gloria Galloway and Jane Taber, "N.B. Protesters Plan More Protests after Violent Clash with RCMP over Shale-Gas Project," *Globe and Mail*, October 17, 2013, https://www.theglobeandmail.com/news/ national/rcmp-move-in-on-first-nation-protesting-shale-gas-development/ article14904344/; Melanie Patten, "Violente Manif Contre Le Gaz De Schiste Au

N.-B: 40 Arrestations," *La Presse*, October 17, 2013, https://www.lapresse.ca/actualites/national/201310/17/01-4700671-violente-manif-contre-le-gaz-de-schiste-au-n-b-40-arrestations.php. On Google Trends the month of October 2013 reveals a 91 percent spike in online media coverage of Rexton, New Brunswick, Canada (https://trends.google.com/trends/explore?q=%2fm%2f06pn2j&date=all&geo=US).

3. For more on the history of Red Power, consult Maracle, *Bobbi Lee*; Warrior and Smith, *Like a Hurricane*; Bruyneel, *Third Space*; Cobb, *Native American Activism*; Blansett, *Journey to Freedom*.

4. Cardinal, *Unjust Society*; Deloria, *Custer Died*. For more on the history of the White Paper, see McFarlane, *Brotherhood to Nationhood*; Manuel and Posluns, *Fourth World*, originally published in 1974; Fixico, *Termination and Relocation*.

5. Fixico, *Invasion of Indian Country*, 1st ed.; Hosmer and O'Neill, *Native Pathways*; Smith and Frehner, *Indians and Energy*; Needham, *Power Lines*.

6. Mooney, "Indian Country."

7. Gedicks, *New Resource Wars*, 41; Fixico, *Invasion of Indian Country*. See also Voyles, *Wastelanding*; LaDuke, *All Our Relations*; and Grinde and Johansen, *Ecocide of Native America*. See also Terri Hansen, "Kill the Land, Kill the People: There Are 532 Superfund Sites in Indian Country!," *Indian Country Today*, June 17, 2014; Chong and Basu, "Contaminated Sites"; and Government of Canada, "Inventory of Federal Contaminated Sites."

8. The occupy movement, also known as Occupy Wall Street, was a nonviolent protest founded by a Canadian anticonsumerist publication called *Adbusters* on September 17, 2011. Following the Arab Spring, it lasted a total of fifty-nine days in the United States to protest economic inequality and corporate corruption. Protesters occupied and created an encampment at Zuccotti Park located near Wall Street in New York City. The Occupy Wall Street movement captured worldwide headlines and led to subsequent occupations in major cities around the world, especially after the NYPD raided the encampment and forcibly removed the protesters. This movement was important for two primary reasons: (1) it revealed the significant power wielded by the top 1 percent of financial earners under the slogan "We are the 99%" after the global financial crisis of 2008; and (2) the movement successfully used the tool of social media to control and spread its message. For more on the Occupy Wall Street movement, see Andrew Anthony, "'We Showed It Was Possible to Create a Movement from Almost Nothing,'" *Guardian*, September 12, 2021.

9. For more on the history of Idle No More, see the movement's website, http://www.idlenomore.ca; Tristin Hopper, "How the Idle No More Movement Started and Where It Might Go from Here," *National Post*, December 26, 2012, https://

nationalpost.com/news/canada/idle-no-more-first-nations-protest-movement
-theresa-spence; Sommerstein, "Canada's Indigenous People"; Makuch, "Idle
No More"; and Coulthard, *Red Skin, White Masks*.

10. Obamsawin, *Kanesatake*; York and Pindera, *People of the Pines*. See also Simpson,
Mohawk Interruptus; and Miller, *Skyscrapers Hide the Heavens*.

11. Blomley, "'Shut the Province Down.'"

12. Jane Sims, "Ipperwash 25 Years Later: Dudley George's Brother Won't, and Can't
Forget," *London Free Press*, September 6, 2020, https://lfpress.com/news/local
-news/ipperwash-25-years-later-dudley-georges-brother-wont-and-cant-forget.

13. Lambertus, *Wartime Images, Peacetime Wounds*.

14. Peters, "Settler Forgetting in Saulnierville."

15. McCarthy, *In Divided Unity*.

16. Sierra Club, "Keystone XL Pipeline."

17. Gloria Galloway and Oliver Moore, "Idle No More Protests, Blockades Spread
across Country," *Globe and Mail*, January 16, 2013, https://www.theglobeandmail
.com/news/politics/idle-no-more-protests-blockades-spread-across-country/
article7406990/; Lynne Peeples, "Keystone XL and Native Americans: South
Dakota Tribes Fight the 'Black Snake,'" *Huffington Post*, April 17, 2013, https://
www.huffpost.com/entry/keystone-xl-native-americans-tribes_n_3102454; CBC,
"Line 9 Protests See Hundreds Converge in Downtown Toronto," October 19,
2013, https://www.cbc.ca/news/canada/toronto/line-9-protests-see-hundreds
-converge-in-downtown-toronto-1.2126943; Robert Desjarlait, "Enbridge and
the Takeover of Red Lake Land," *Intercontinental Cry*, December 29, 2015,
http://www.intercontinentalcry.org/enbridge-and-the-takeover-of-red-lake
-land/; Robert Desjarlait, "Idle No More and the Implications on Anishinaabe
Treaty Lands in Minnesota," *Intercontinental Cry*, January 6, 2013, http://www
.intercontinentalcry.org/idle-no-more-and-the-implications-on-anishinaabe
-treaty-lands-in-minnesota/.

18. Caplan-Bricker, "This Is What Happens"; CBC News, "2nd Largest Pipeline Spill
in Alberta History Leads to Charges," April 26, 2013; and Greenpeace, "Four
Proposed Tar Sands."

19. Karen Dillon, "The Ogallala Aquifer, an Important Water Resource, Is in Trouble," *Kansas City Star*, September 1, 2013, http://www.kansascity.com/news/
local/article326510/The-Ogallala-Aquifer-an-important-water-resource-is-in
-trouble.html.

20. Indigenous Environmental Network, "Leaders Arrested"; Tidwell and Zellen,
Land, 84.

21. Martin Lukacs, "Canada's First Nations Protest Heralds a New Alliance," *Guardian*, December 20, 2012, https://www.theguardian.com/commentisfree/2012/

dec/20/canada-first-nations-new-alliance; Brenna Bhandar, "The First Nations of Canada Are Still Waiting for the Colonial Era to End," *Guardian*, October 21, 2013, https://www.theguardian.com/commentisfree/2013/oct/21/canada-colonial-mentality-first-nations; Isabeau Doucet, "Rising Anger of Canada's First Nations over Living Conditions," *Guardian*, December 21, 2012, https://www.theguardian.com/world/2012/dec/21/candas-first-nations-people-protest; and Kristin Moe, "Idle No More: Indigenous Uprising Sweeps North America," *Yes! Magazine*, January 9, 2013, https://www.yesmagazine.org/people-power/idle-no-more-indigenous-uprising-sweeps-north-america.

22. For more on missing and murdered Indigenous women, see Deer, *Beginning and End*; and also the Truth & Reconciliation Final Report (Government of Canada, 2007–15, https://www.rcaanc-cirnac.gc.ca/eng/1450124405592/1529106060525), which exposed injustices in Canada's war upon First Nation families through the Residential School System.

23. "The continued existence of Native nationhood today undermines the claims of settler-colonial states to the land. Unlikely alliances can help chip away at the legitimacy of these colonial structures, *even among the settlers themselves*. To act in solidarity with Indigenous nations is not just to 'support Native rights' but to strike at the very underpinnings of the Western social order and begin to free both Native and non-Native peoples." Grossman, *Unlikely Alliances*.

24. Chase Iron Eyes, "Oglala Nationals Roadblock Oil Pipeline Trucks on Pine Ridge Rez," *Intercontinental Cry*, March 7, 2012, https://intercontinentalcry.org/oglala-nationals-roadblock-oil-pipeline-trucks-on-pine-ridge-rez/; Debra White Plume, "Oglala Lakota Arrested at Blockade," *Censored News*, March 6, 2012, https://bsnorrell.blogspot.com/2012/03/debra-white-plume-oglala-lakota.html; *Environmental News Service*, "Native Americans Arrested Blockading Keystone XL Pipeline Trucks," March 7, 2012. In September of 2011, Debra White Plume had also been arrested protesting against Keystone outside of the White House. Other noteworthy events included a September 27, 2014, benefit concert by Willie Nelson and Neil Young called "Harvest the Hope" that raised money and educated the general public about the dangers of the Keystone XL pipeline (Hefflinger, "Harvest the Hope") and the march of over four hundred Indigenous peoples and allies to Pierre, South Dakota, to protest the Keystone XL pipeline (Stephen Lee, "400 Cross Missouri against Keystone XL," *Capital Journal*, July 26, 2015, http://www.capjournal.com/news/400-cross-missouri-against-keystone-xl/article_ff7307aa-33de-11e5-a86c-bfb1f201ff94.html). On June 10, 2018, Ponca Nation leaders and activists Casey Camp-Horinek from Oklahoma and Larry Wright Jr. from Nebraska, accompanied by one hundred activists gathered for the fifth annual planting of sacred Ponca corn in the proposed pathway

of Keystone XL pipeline (Justin Perkins, "A New Native-Led Strategy for Fighting Keystone XL," *In These Times*, July 18, 2018, http://inthesetimes.com/article/a -new-native-led-strategy-for-fighting-keystone-xl).

25. Barnett and Angel, "Standing Rock"; Jorge Barrera, "Keystone XL 'Black Snake' Pipeline to Face 'Epic' Opposition from Native American Alliance," *APTN News*, January 31, 2014, https://www.aptnnews.ca/national-news/keystone-xl-black -snake-pipeline-face-epic-opposition-native-american-alliance.

26. Deaton, "Tribal Nation"; *Federal Register*, "Approval and Promulgation of Federal Implementation Plan for Oil and Natural Gas Well Production Facilities: Fort Berthold Indian Reservation (Mandan, Hidatsa, and Arikara Nation), North Dakota," March 22, 2013, https://www.federalregister.gov/documents/2013/03/ 22/2013-05666/approval-and-promulgation-of-federal-implementation-plan -for-oil-and-natural-gas-well-production. For more on the history of Fracking, consult Maddow, *Blowout*.

27. David Archambault II, "Taking a Stand at Standing Rock," *New York Times*, August 24, 2016, http://www.nytimes.com/2016/08/25/opinion/taking-a-stand -at-standing-rock.html. For more information on the history of Oahe Dam and the fight against the Pick Sloan Project that flooded Standing Rock, see Lawson, *Dammed Indians Revisited*.

28. Julian Brave Noisecat, "The Standing Rock Generation Is Changing the World: A Young Man from Standing Rock Reflects on the Dakota Access Pipeline Court Decision," *Rolling Stone*, July 9, 2020, http://www.rollingstone.com/politics/ politics-features/dakota-access-pipeline-decision-standing-rock-1026122/.

29. LaDuke, *Water Protector*, 88–89.

30. LaDuke, *Water Protector*, 90–91; Hersher, "Key Moments." On August 4, 2016, the Standing Rock Sioux Tribe sued the U.S. Army Corps of Engineers. The tribe alleged that the Corps had failed to adequately consult tribe members before approving the pipeline and had violated the National Historic Preservation Act when it "effectively authorized construction of the vast majority of the pipeline in and around federally regulated waters without any provision to ensure against destruction to culturally important sites" (Hersher, "Key Moments"). For more on the federal protection of Indigenous ancestral remains, consult the American Indian Religious Freedom Act (1978) and Native American Graves Protection and Repatriation Act (1990).

31. LaDuke, *Water Protector*, 121–23. "Police deny that they used concussion grenades that night. . . . The FBI seized key evidence in the days after the injury. Agents took both the shrapnel removed from Wilansky's arm and the clothes she was wearing when she was injured. Wayne Wilansky said he plans to sue

for their return." See Nathan-Kazis, "Can't Use Her Hand," https://forward.com/news/387898/a-year-after-a-grenade-blew-up-her-arm-at-standing-rock-sophia-wilansky-is/?amp=1.

32. Hersher, "Key Moments."
33. "They cite a 2018 analysis by First Peoples Worldwide . . . dedicated to increasing corporate accountability to Indigenous peoples, which found that, despite the initial cost estimate of $3.8 billion, the pipeline cost more than $12 billion by the time it was operational in June 2017." Mark Trahant, "Indigenous People on the 'Front Lines' of Climate Solutions," *Indian Country Today*, January 21, 2023, http://ictnews.org/indigenous-people-on-the-front-lines-of-climate-solutions; Sarah Sax, "Free, Prior and Informed Consent 'Is More than Just a Checklist,'" *High Country News*, April 21, 2023, http://www.hcn.org/articles/indigenous-affairs-politics-free-prior-and-informed-consent-is-more-than-just-a-checklist.
34. United Nations, "End of Mission Statement"; Goldtooth, Saldamando, and Gracey, *Indigenous Resistance*, 5.
35. For more on the infrastructure of the camps, see Powell, "NODAPL Encampments," in Blansett, Cahill, and Needham, *Indian Cities*, 267–89.
36. LaDuke, *Water Protector*, 96–101.
37. Levi Rickert, "Water Protector Red Fawn Fallis Released from Federal Prison," *Native News Online*, September 11, 2020, https://nativenewsonline.net/currents/standing-rock-water-protector-red-fawn-fallis-released-from-federal-prison; LaDuke, *Water Protector*, 118–20.
38. Sadasivam, "After Standing Rock."
39. *Indian Country Today*, "Standing Rock Sioux Tribal Chairperson Janet Alkire Decries DAPL Criminal Convictions and Government Secrecy," February 3, 2023, https://ictnews.org/the-press-pool/standing-rock-sioux-tribal-chairperson-janet-alkire-decries-dapl-criminal-convictions-and-government-secrecy.
40. Nina Lakhani, "U.S. Supreme Court Rejects Dakota Access Pipeline Appeal," *Guardian*, February 22, 2022; Sutherland, "Standing Rock Withdraws"; Lisa Friedman, "Standing Rock Sioux Tribe Wins a Victory in Dakota Access Pipeline Case," *New York Times*, March 25, 2020, http://www.nytimes.com/2020/03/25/clmate/dakota-access-pipeline-sioux.html.
41. Goldtooth, Saldamando, and Gracey, *Indigenous Resistance*, 12.
42. For more on the Indigenous Environmental movement, see Rosier, "'Modern America,'" 711–35; and Warren, "Nature of Conquest," in Deloria and Salisbury, *Companion*.

43. My definition of Indigenous Environmental Justice was compiled from the following sources: Tom, Adams, and Goode, "Solastalgia to Soliphilia," 3–8; Kimmerer, *Braiding Sweetgrass*, 322, 328, 330–38; Gilio-Whitaker, *As Long as Grass Grows*, 19, 25–26, 147; Chiang, "Race and Ethnicity," in Isenberg, *Oxford Handbook*, 589–90; Jarratt-Snider and Nielson, *Indigenous Environmental Justice*, 9–10; Wildcat, *Red Alert*, 73–74; Carroll, *Roots of Our Renewal*, 173, 192; Dawson, Longo, and Survival International, *Decolonize Conservation*, 227; and Case, *Everything Ancient*, 23–24; Powell, "Technologies of Existence," 125–32; Goldtooth, Saldamando, and Gracey, *Indigenous Resistance*, 1–17; and David Treuer, "Return the National Parks Back to the Tribes," *Atlantic*, May 2021, https://www.theatlantic.com/magazine/archive/2021/05/return-the-national-parks-to-the-tribes/618395/.

44. I've always thought that if the geopolitical borders were removed throughout the Western Hemisphere, Indigenous peoples might represent a majority of the population. How can such a statistic reinforce Indigenous Environmental Justice and the decolonization of settler states? Ultimately, power is not in the state but in the people. If these numbers are combined with allies in a global intertribal movement, then we might experience radical environmental change and sustainable reform. Zoltán Grossman posits four strategies of alliance: (1) alliances are more successful if they focus on building from the grass roots instead of institutional relationships; (2) alliances can work if the goal is centered upon a local place identity and not a state citizenship; (3) alliances must define place in inclusive and not exclusionary terms; and (4) true alliances must respect diversity and identity differences among their organizational membership in order to avoid universalist messages. Grossman, *Unlikely Alliances*, 287–90.

45. Powell, "NoDAPL Encampments," in Blansett, Cahill, and Needham, *Indian Cities*, 273.

46. "Well over 800 were charged at Standing Rock. Some of those people are sitting in federal prisons, and the state's actions are becoming more punitive." LaDuke, *Water Protector*, 104–9, 118–25, 177.

47. Erin McCann, "Judge Rejects Riot Charge against Amy Goodman of 'Democracy Now' over Pipeline Protest," *New York Times*, October 17, 2016, https://www.nytimes.com/2016/10/18/us/judge-rejects-riot-charge-against-amy-goodman-of-democracy-now-over-pipeline-protest.html.

Bibliography

Barnett, Tracy L., and Cheryl Angel. "Standing Rock: Three Years and Still Fighting." *Esperanza Project*, April 27, 2019. https://www.esperanzaproject.com/2019/native-american-culture/many-standing-rocks/.

Blansett, Kent. *A Journey to Freedom: Richard Oakes, Alcatraz, and the Red Power Movement*. New Haven CT: Yale University Press, 2018.

Blomley, Nicholas. "'Shut the Province Down': First Nations Blockades in British Columbia, 1984–1995." *BC Studies* 111 (Autumn 1996): 9.

Bruyneel, Kevin. *The Third Space of Sovereignty: The Postcolonial Politics of U.S.-Indigenous Relations*. Minneapolis: University of Minnesota Press, 2007.

Caplan-Bricker, Nora. "This Is What Happens When a Pipeline Bursts in Your Town." *New Republic*, November 18, 2013. https://newrepublic.com/article/115624/exxon-oil-sill-arkansas-2013-how-pipeline-burst-mayflower.

Cardinal, Harold. *The Unjust Society*. Seattle: University of Washington Press, 1999.

Carroll, Clint. *Roots of Our Renewal: Ethnobotany and Cherokee Environmental Governance*. Minneapolis: University of Minnesota Press, 2015.

Case, Emalani. *Everything Ancient Was Once New: Indigenous Persistence from Hawai'i to Kahiki*. Honolulu: University of Hawai'i Press, 2021.

Chiang, Connie. "Race and Ethnicity in Environmental History." In *The Oxford Handbook of Environmental History*, edited by Andrew C. Isenberg, 589–90. New York: Oxford University Press, 2017.

Chong, Katherine, and Nilardri Basu. "Contaminated Sites and Indigenous Peoples in Canada and the United States: A Scoping Review." medRxiv, August 10, 2022. https://www.medrxiv.org/content/10.1101/2022.08.08.22278551v1.

Cobb, Daniel M. *Native American Activism in Cold War America: The Struggle for Sovereignty*. Lawrence: University Press of Kansas, 2008.

Coulthard, Glen Sean. *Red Skin, White Masks: Rejecting the Colonial Politics of Recognition*. Minneapolis: University of Minnesota Press, 2014.

Dawson, Ashley, Fiore Longo, and Survival International, eds. *Decolonize Conservation: Global Voices for Indigenous Self-Determination, Land, and a World in Common*. Brooklyn: Common Notions, 2023.

Deaton, Jeremy. "A Tribal Nation Dependent on Fossil Fuels was Left in the Cold When the Pandemic Hit." The Hill, April 22, 2021. https://thehill.com/changing-america/sustainability/environment/549731-a-tribal-nation-dependent-on-fossil-fuels-was/.

Deer, Sarah. *The Beginning and End of Rape: Confronting Sexual Violence in Native America*. Minneapolis: University of Minnesota Press, 2015.

Deloria, Vine, Jr. *Custer Died for Your Sins: An Indian Manifesto*. Norman: University of Oklahoma Press, 1988.

Fixico, Donald L. *The Invasion of Indian Country in the Twentieth Century: American Capitalism and Tribal Natural Resources*. 1st ed. Niwot: University Press of Colorado, 1998.

———. *The Invasion of Indian Country in the Twentieth Century: American Capitalism and Tribal Natural Resources.* 2nd ed. Denver: University Press of Colorado, 2011.

———. *Termination and Relocation: Federal Indian Policy, 1945–1960.* Albuquerque: University of New Mexico Press, 1986.

Gedicks, Al. *The New Resource Wars: Native and Environmental Struggles against Multinational Corporations.* Boston: South End, 1993.

Gilio-Whitaker, Dina. *As Long as Grass Grows: The Indigenous Fight for Environmental Justice, from Colonization to Standing Rock.* Boston: Beacon, 2019.

Goldtooth, Dallas, Alberto Saldamando, and Kyle Gracey. *Indigenous Resistance against Carbon.* Washington DC: Oil Change International, 2021.

Government of Canada. "Inventory of Federal Contaminated Sites." Accessed June 1, 2023. http://www.canada.ca/en/environment-climate-change/services/federal-contaminated-sites/inventory.html.

Greenpeace. "Four Proposed Tar Sands Oil Pipelines Pose a Threat to Water Resources." Accessed December 1, 2023.

Grinde, Donald A., and Bruce E. Johansen. *Ecocide of Native America: Environmental Destruction of Indian Lands and Peoples.* Santa Fe: Clear Light, 1994.

Grossman, Zoltán. *Unlikely Alliances: Native Nations and White Communities Join to Defend Rural Lands.* Seattle: University of Washington Press, 2017.

Hefflinger, Mark. "Harvest the Hope: Neil Young and Willie Nelson in Concert." Bold Nebraska, August 18, 2014. https://boldnebraska.org/concert/.

Hersher, Rebecca. "Key Moments in the Dakota Access Pipeline Fight." National Public Radio, February 22, 2017. https://www.npr.org/sections/thetwo-way/2017/02/22/514988040/key-moments-in-the-dakota-access-pipeline-fight.

Hosmer, Brian, and Colleen O'Neill, eds. *Native Pathways: American Indian Culture and Economic Development in the Twentieth Century.* Denver: University Press of Colorado, 2004.

Howe, Miles. "Prelude to the Raid." Halifax Media Co-op, November 5, 2013.

Indigenous Environmental Network. "First Nations and American Indian Leaders Arrested in Front of White House To Protest Keystone XL Pipeline." PR Newswire, September 2, 2011. https://www.prnewswire.com/news-releases/first-nations-and-american-indian-leaders-arrested-in-front-of-white-house-to-protest-keystone-xl-pipeline-129088003.html.

Jarratt-Snider, Karen, and Marianne O. Nielsen, eds. *Indigenous Environmental Justice.* Tucson: University of Arizona Press, 2020.

Kimmerer, Robin Wall. *Braiding Sweetgrass: Indigenous Wisdom, Scientific Knowledge, and the Teachings of Plants.* Minneapolis: Milkweed, 2013.

LaDuke, Winona. *All Our Relations: Native Struggles for Land and Life.* Boston: South End, 1999.

———. *To Be a Water Protector: The Rise of the Wiindigoo Slayers*. Manitoba: Fernwood & Spotted Horse, 2020.

Lambertus, Sandra. *Wartime Images, Peacetime Wounds: The Media and the Gustafsen Lake Standoff*. Toronto: University of Toronto Press, 2004.

Lawson, Michael L. *Dammed Indians Revisited: The Continuing History of the Pick-Sloan Plan and the Missouri River Sioux*. Pierre: South Dakota Historical Society Press, 2009.

Maddow, Rachel. *Blowout: Corrupted Democracy, Rogue State Russia, and the Richest, Most Destructive Industry on Earth*. New York: Crown, 2019.

Makuch, Ben. "What Exactly Is Idle No More?" Vice, January 10, 2013. http://www .vice.com/en_us/article/xd43yd/what-exactly-is-idle-no-more.

Manuel, George, and Michael Posluns. *The Fourth World: An Indian Reality*. Minneapolis: University of Minnesota Press, 2019.

Maracle, Lee. *Bobbi Lee: Indian Rebel*. Toronto: Women's Press, 1990.

McCarthy, Theresa. *In Divided Unity: Haudenosaunee Reclamation at Grand River*. Tucson: University of Arizona Press, 2016.

McFarlane, Peter. *Brotherhood to Nationhood: George Manuel and the Making of the Modern Indian Movement*. Toronto: Between the Lines, 1993.

Miller, J. R. *Skyscrapers Hide the Heavens: A History of Indian-White Relations in Canada*. Toronto: University of Toronto Press, 2017.

Mooney, Prentice. "Indian Country Is a Frontier Again," *Nation's Business*, September 1969.

Nathan-Kazis, Josh. "She Still Can't Use Her Hand, a Year after a Grenade Injury at Standing Rock." Forward, November 17, 2017. https://forward.com/news/387898/ a-year-after-a-grenade-blew-up-her-arm-at-standing-rock-sophia-wilansky-is/ ?amp=1.

Needham, Andrew. *Power Lines: Phoenix and the Making of the Modern Southwest*. Princeton NJ: Princeton University Press, 2014.

Obamsawin, Alanis, dir. *Kanesatake: 270 Years of Resistance*. National Film Board of Canada, 1994.

Peters, Mercedes. "Settler Forgetting in Saulnierville: The Sipekne'katik Mi'kmaw Fishery as Reminder." *Niche* (Network in Canadian History & Environment), October 19, 2020. https://niche-canada.org/2020/10/19/settler-forgetting-in -saulnierville-the-sipeknekatik-mikmaw-fishery-as-reminder/.

Powell, Dana E. "NoDAPL Encampments: Twenty-First-Century Indian City." In *Indian Cities: Histories of Indigenous Urbanization*, edited by Kent Blansett, Cathleen D. Cahill, and Andrew Needham, 267–89. Norman: University of Oklahoma Press, 2022.

———. "Technologies of Existence: The Indigenous Environmental Justice Movement." *Development* 49, no. 3 (2006): 125–32.

Rosier, Paul C. "'Modern America Desperately Needs to Listen': The Emerging Indian in an Age of Environmental Crisis." *Journal of American History* 100, no. 3 (December 2013): 711–35.

Sadasivam, Naveena. "After Standing Rock, Protesting Pipelines Can Get You a Decade in Prison and $100K in Fines." Grist, May 14, 2019. https://grist.org/article/after-standing-rock-protesting-pipelines-can-get-you-a-decade-in-prison-and-100k-in-fines/.

Sierra Club. "Keystone XL Pipeline." 2013.

Simpson, Audra. *Mohawk Interruptus: Political Life across the Borders of Settler States.* Durham NC: Duke University Press, 2014.

Smith, Sherry L., and Brian Frehner, eds. *Indians and Energy: Exploitation and Opportunity in the American Southwest.* Santa Fe: School for Advanced Research Press, 2010.

Sommerstein, David. "Canada's Indigenous People Rally for Rights around 'Idle No More' Initiative." National Public Radio, January 9, 2013. https://www.npr.org/2013/01/09/168983530/canadas-indigenous-people-rally-for-rights-around-idle-no-more-initiative.

Sutherland, Laurel. "Standing Rock Withdraws from Ongoing Environmental Assessment of Dakota Access Pipeline." Mongabay, February 2, 2022. https://news.mongabay.com/2022/02/standing-rock-withdraws-from-ongoing-environmental-assessment-of-dakota-access-pipeline/#:~:text=The%20Standing%20Rock%20Sioux%20Tribe,the%20pipeline%20operators%2C%20Energy%20Transfer.

Tidwell, Alan C., and Barry Scott Zellen, eds. *Land, Indigenous Peoples and Conflict.* New York: Routledge, 2016.

Tom, Erica, Melinda M. Adams, and Ron W. Goode. "Solastalgia to Soliphilia: Cultural Fire, Climate Change, and Indigenous Healing." *Ecopsychology* 20, no. 20 (May 2023): 3–8.

United Nations. "End of Mission Statement by the United Nations Special Rapporteur on the Rights of Indigenous Peoples, Victoria Tauli-Corpuz of Her Visit to the United States of America," UN *Statements/Special Procedures the Office of High Commission of Human Rights*, March 3, 2017. http://www.ohchr.org/en/statements/2017/03/end-mission-statement-united-nations-special-rapporteur-rights-indigenous.

Voyles, Traci Brynne. *Wastelanding: Legacies of Uranium Mining in Navajo Country.* Minneapolis: University of Minnesota Press, 2015.

Warren, Louis S. "The Nature of Conquest: Indians, Americans, and Environmental History." In *A Companion to American Indian History*, edited by Philip J. Deloria and Neal Salisbury, 287–306. Malden MA: Blackwell, 2004.

Warrior, Robert, and Paul Chaat Smith. *Like a Hurricane: The Indian Movement from Alcatraz to Wounded Knee*. New York: New Press, 1997.

Wildcat, Daniel R. *Red Alert! Saving the Planet with Indigenous Knowledge*. Golden CO: Fulcrum, 2009.

York, Geoffrey, and Loreen Pindera. *People of the Pines: The Warriors and the Legacy of Oka*. New York: Little Brown, 1992.

Seeing the Trees

The Fight for Cultural Sovereignty
along the Banks of Sand Creek

ARI KELMAN

When Norma Gorneau speaks in public about her family's relationship to the Sand Creek massacre, she always begins by stressing the matrilineal origins of her narrative: "My grandmother told this story to my mother. My mother told it to me." Gorneau goes on to recount how, early in the morning on November 29, 1864, U.S. troops commanded by Colonel John Chivington struck a peaceful Arapaho and Cheyenne village. The Native people there, she says, were not expecting the attack: "Most of the men were out hunting. The soldiers started murdering women, children, and elders. Nearly two hundred of them died, and all they wanted in those bands was peace." She drives the point home by noting that one of her forebears, Cheyenne chief Black Kettle, flew an American flag and a white flag over his lodge, signaling that the bands with him were friendly and under federal protection. The semiotics had no impact; the assault continued. The killing lasted the better part of the day and featured episodes of terrible cruelty: soldiers disemboweling pregnant women; taking trophies, including scalps, fingers, and genitalia, from their victims; and burning what remained of the camp before riding back to Denver, where they were greeted as heroes. Gorneau always concludes with a final detail, emphasizing how her ancestors struggled to survive the ordeal. "Some of the people tried to hide in the cottonwoods down by the creek," she recalls. "The women put children inside the stumps of dead trees. They kept them safe that way. A few of those trees are still there, still at the massacre site." She concludes, "We [referring here to the Cheyenne descendants of Sand Creek's victims] call them witness trees."[1]

Gorneau's engagement with Sand Creek is part of a project, dating back to the immediate aftermath of the massacre, aimed at preserving histories of the violence. The descendants have memorialized Sand Creek despite institutionalized pressures to forget, part of a settler colonial society's strategy of assimilating Indigenous peoples within a sanitized narrative of American innocence. Gorneau explains that although federal authorities meted out punishment to Native Americans who dared speak of Sand Creek, her ancestors continued to recount details of their collective trauma. They passed lore from one generation to the next, in the process constructing a foundation for individual, family, and group identity. That these tales were protected and shared, passed from grandparent to parent to grandchild, regardless of the risk, bespeaks their significance. Descendants' Sand Creek memories document efforts at ethnic cleansing and also cultural persistence, of traditions imperiled and of those saved. Tribal protocols suggest that the stories have to be repeated verbatim. Changing details, even unwittingly, risks bastardizing the meaning of sacred texts and dishonoring ancestors. Stories of the massacre, then, lay bare ligatures connecting past and present for the Cheyenne descendants of Sand Creek. They are, in aggregate, a vast, informal archive constructed by those who survived and then maintained by their heirs.[2]

Recollections of Sand Creek often focus on elements of environmental history, especially features of the local environs: bone-chilling cold the morning of November 29, 1864, and then the night after the bloodletting, when freezing Arapahos and Cheyennes looked for scattered family members wandering the surrounding countryside; the dry creek bed, up which many Native people fled during the slaughter; the shortage of game animals in the area, a dearth that frustrated hungry hunters before the carnage; the sandy soil, which provided shelter for panicked women and men who dug makeshift trenches to protect themselves from rifle and artillery fire; clumps of grass scattered here and there, scarce feed for the tribes' livestock; and groves of cottonwoods that offered sanctuary for some nursing mothers and their infant children. As one of the descendants notes, "A lot of our Sand Creek stories talk about that place. That place sustained our people. Our people camped there in the years before the massacre. They found water, wood, food there. When Chivington came, we knew that place. We knew where to find shelter. That knowledge helped us survive." A recurring emphasis on the landscape of violence, in other words, suggests a tight connection between material conditions, between how the Arapahos and Cheyennes at Sand Creek experienced their environment and how the massacre has been recalled since.[3]

Over the past two decades, Native ethnographies and oral histories have played a central, though often contested, role in an initiative that culminated in 2007 with the opening of the Sand Creek Massacre National Historic Site (SCMNHS) in southeastern Colorado. The SCMNHS is the first unit within the national park system to question the logic and rectitude of settler colonialism, as well as that process's complex relationship to the U.S. Civil War. Labeling some citizen soldiers and Union officials as neither heroes nor victims but rather perpetrators, the SCMNHS grew out of a series of struggles over how the massacre should be remembered—not just its gruesome fine points but also the methods used for understanding its history and geography. Time and again, the Park Service, though typically well-intentioned, failed to make room for the Sand Creek descendants' relationship to the historical, commemorative, and physical landscape, either ignoring or rejecting the veracity of Indigenous recollections of the violence and thereby undermining important elements of tribal sovereignty. Those disputes pivoted on struggles over narratives and collective memories of place, space, and the built and natural environment, underscoring how the Sand Creek descendants' desire to control and deploy their history emerged from and then buttressed broader struggles for Native persistence.[4]

The Sand Creek massacre has an environmental history: a history of extraction, expropriation, dispossession, and privation. The roots of the violence run deep in Colorado's soil, at least back to 1858 and 1859. Prospectors found gold in the mountains west of Denver in those years. A rush of argonauts arrived, competing with local Indigenous people for control of territory. These settlers, who believed their migration enjoyed a special providence, a Manifest Destiny to civilize the region, viewed tribal property claims as an impediment to progress and an affront to the will of the Almighty. The Cheyennes and Arapahos discovered that parchment barriers, including the Treaty of Fort Laramie (1851), which ostensibly guaranteed the Arapahos and Cheyennes unfettered access to an enormous parcel of territory, stretching from the North Platte River to the Arkansas River and from the foothills of the Rocky Mountains to the western edge of Kansas, would not stem the tide of new arrivals. A flood of self-styled pioneers washed away the enumerated rights of Native nations, destroying crops and forage growing on fragile prairies and leaving destruction in their wake. By the dawn of the new decade, with Southern secessionists threatening to sunder the Union, peace chiefs, including Black Kettle, looked for ways to navigate these deadly currents, to chart a course to safe harbor for their people. In 1861, they agreed to sign onto the Treaty of Fort Wise, a document that constrained the tribes' mobility, confining them to a new, much smaller reservation in southeastern Colorado. Seizing Native land had once again served as an engine for American imperialism and capitalism.[5]

The environmental impact of the Treaty of Fort Wise, especially the way it restricted the mobility of Indigenous people, threw the political economy of the affected tribes into disarray. Only a small group of peace chiefs, a fraction of the Arapahos' and Cheyennes' civilian leadership, had signed onto the compact, suggesting that their followers would be bound by its details. Meanwhile, members of several tribal military societies, especially the Cheyenne Dog Soldiers, insisted that the signatories had betrayed their constituencies and the broader community. The new reservation, slightly less than a tenth of the size of the holdings laid out in the Fort Laramie Treaty, seemed dangerously confining. Many Dog Soldiers understood resource scarcities not just as a threat to their bands' subsistence but also to the gendered power that men derived from the ability to provide for their families as they had traditionally, hunting as far away as Wyoming and Kansas, where vast herds of bison still roamed lands that the tribes had traversed for generations. Some militants refused to be bound by a new geography of power that seemed to them far too parsimonious to sustain their people and culture over time. White settlers, by contrast, insisted that the Treaty of Fort Wise applied to every Arapaho and Cheyenne. Territorial governor John Evans stood with them. He warned that flouting the new treaty meant war.[6]

The Civil War, already underway, soon acted as an accelerant, exacerbating injustices embedded in the Treaty of Fort Wise and hastening the onset of the conflict between U.S. troops and tribal peoples. When the cost of fighting Confederates depleted federal coffers, the federal government could not deliver annuities guaranteed to the Arapahos and Cheyennes (among others). Denied those subsidies and confined to a smaller parcel of land than ever before, some Native people starved on the plains. In the spring of 1863,

Governor Evans, panicked by unverified reports of an alliance among the region's Indigenous nations and haunted by the specter of violence between Dakota peoples and settlers in Minnesota, warned that Union soldiers might join a war of extermination prosecuted against local tribes if they entered into such a confederation. Conditions worsened throughout that summer and fall. The Dog Soldiers, increasingly willing to upend tribal politics, scuttled plans for a parley between peace chiefs and Colonel Chivington. Evans became more convinced that Colorado stood poised at the brink of an all-out war with Indigenous peoples on the plains. He corresponded with officials in the Departments of the Interior and War, apprising them of what he saw as an existential threat to settlers in the West. The following spring, he lobbied officials in Washington for permission to raise a regiment of volunteers to fight Indians.[7]

Many Arapahos and Cheyennes rejected the boundaries of their new reservation. They refused to be constrained by a settler colonial society's vision of an imperial landscape, and violence escalated throughout the spring and summer of 1864. A series of bloody skirmishes between soldiers and warriors and several incidents of depredations against settlers led Colonel Chivington to tell subordinates that trying to sort hostile and friendly tribes was a waste of time. Writing to the commander of Fort Lyon, a federal installation in southeastern Colorado, he employed eliminationist rhetoric: "The Cheyennes will have to be soundly whipped before they will be quiet. If any of them are caught in your vicinity, kill them, as that is the only way." The region's Native peoples, whether Dog Soldiers or peace chiefs, were for Chivington as monolithic as they were inscrutable. Then on June 11, neighbors found the Hungate family, including two young children, scalped on the plains east of Denver. Word spread: "hostile savages," likely still roaming the countryside, had killed noble ranchers. Friends brought the bodies into the city and displayed them as a combined memorial and prompt for retribution. For days, the Hungates' ruined corpses became the center of a community gripped by collective panic. Tales of more Indian attacks pushed the crisis past the breaking point. On June 15, false reports circulated of an Indigenous army, thousands strong, just outside the capital. This force would attack without mercy, people said, wiping out white settlers along the Front Range of the Rocky Mountains. But what onlookers initially took for an enemy column turned out to be cattle on their way to market.[8]

Governor Evans responded to the crisis by trying to curtail Native movement still further. On June 27, he issued a statement intended for "the friendly Indians of the plains." He directed those people to "go to places of safety," bulwarks of federal authority like Fort Lyon, Fort Larned, and Fort Laramie. "The object," Evans insisted, "was to prevent friendly Indians from being killed through mistake." As for "hostile Indians," a "war" had already begun, and that conflict "would continue until they [were] all effectually subdued." For a time, the plan seemed to work. But in mid-July, federal soldiers shot and killed Left Hand, a leading peace chief. Tribal warriors retaliated; settlers locked doors and tried to stay out of harm's way. On August 11, Evans issued a second proclamation, authorizing Coloradans to "go in pursuit of all hostile Indians on the plains" and "to kill and destroy, as enemies of the country, wherever they may be found, all such hostile Indians." The governor offered members of these state-sanctioned militias an incentive: their victims' property, yet another way a settler colonial society sought to dispossess Native peoples on the plains. The next day, Evans received word that the War Department had authorized him to raise a volunteer regiment to fight Indians: the Third Colorado.[9]

Black Kettle still believed that he and his allies could forge a truce with white authorities. Late in August, he worked with George Bent, son of William Bent, a borderlands trade tycoon, and Owl Woman, Bent's Cheyenne wife, and sent delegates to seek an audience with military authorities at Fort Lyon. Major Edward Wynkoop and Captain Silas Soule greeted those emissaries and returned with them to the Indian camp. The officers recovered white captives taken earlier that spring and then met with Black Kettle, agreeing to bring a peace party to Denver for a discussion with Evans. On September 28, Evans and Chivington rode out to Camp Weld, on the outskirts of the capital city. They talked with a group of chiefs, including Black Kettle, as well as Wynkoop and Soule. Soule later recalled that Evans claimed, because of the ongoing conflict with the tribes and also the Civil War context, that he could not "make peace." The Arapahos and Cheyennes must, the governor insisted, "look to military power for protection." Chivington, too, refused to discuss specifics. "He left the matter with Major Wynkoop," who told the Native leaders that they should gather their followers, return to Fort Lyon, subject themselves to martial law, and prepare to wait nearby. The chiefs, Soule understood, were under the impression that if they followed

Wynkoop's instructions, they would place themselves under the protection of the army and the U.S. flag. By mid-October, the peaceful bands had made their way back to Fort Lyon and camped nearby at a spot familiar to them on the banks of Sand Creek.[10]

Having agreed to linger at a specific location, tying themselves to a pre-determined place, the chiefs found themselves trapped in political riptides swirling around settler colonialism and the construction of an American empire in the West. Evans and Chivington faced scrutiny after the Camp Weld meeting. The men of the Third Colorado had enlisted for a period of just one hundred days. By mid-October, that term was more than half over, and observers began questioning the unit's purpose. Critics hurled insults at the "Bloodless Third." Angry observers charged that the unit's troops were cowards and wastrels, that Evans and Chivington had devised a corrupt scheme to enrich themselves with federal funds, and that the two politicians were more focused on advancing Colorado's quest for state-hood, potentially advancing their careers, than they were with protecting settlers, the shock troops of white civilization advancing into the West. On November 16, aware that peaceful Arapahos and Cheyennes could be found near Fort Lyon, Chivington and his men began heading southeast from Denver. The chiefs waited with their bands along the banks of Sand Creek. Black Kettle, following instructions from Fort Lyon's commander, had run up Old Glory and a flag of surrender over his lodge. There could be no mistaking his peaceful intentions, but ironically, the Cheyenne leader had rendered his people more vulnerable than ever before.[11]

The moment the massacre ended, struggles over how it would be remem-bered began. The production, circulation, and consumption of competing narratives, and the effort to embed them in the cultural and physical land-scape, marked that conflict. Stories included John Chivington's depiction of Sand Creek as a heroic battle, a key to saving the Union and constructing an American empire in the West; Silas Soule's rebuttal of Chivington, including letters Soule wrote that led to federal inquiries into the violence; reformer Helen Hunt Jackson's publication, in 1881, of *Century of Dishonor*, an exposé of "the United States Government's repeated violations of faith with the Indians," in which Sand Creek figured prominently; George Bent's fight, around the turn of the twentieth century, to preserve Cheyenne histories of the massacre and to map its location; the work of heritage organizations that, in 1909, erected a statue on the steps of the Colorado capital building, casting Chivington's memories in bronze by listing the bloodbath among an honor roll of engagements in which the state's citizens had fought during the Civil War; the unveiling, in 1950, of a memorial near the massacre site, an obelisk whose text—"Sand Creek: Battle or Massacre"—hinted that ambiguities increasingly surrounded the episode; the success of Dee Brown's *Bury My Heart at Wounded Knee* (1970), which features a chapter about the massacre; and the Park Service's opening, in 2007, of a national historic site devoted to Sand Creek.[12]

The modern memorialization effort hinged on several moments in which the descendants asserted their cultural authority and sovereignty by drawing upon their ancestors' stories, laying claim to the historical and physical landscape. When Senator Ben Nighthorse Campbell decided, in 1998, to sponsor legislation to create the SCMNHS, he learned that nobody knew the precise location of the killing field. When Campbell held hearings in Washington on March 24, Kate Stevenson, a Park Service witness, suggested that absent "solid physical, archaeological, scientific, historically documented evidence," a site might "commemorate the event on the wrong spot." The Park Service would "dishonor the victims, distort the history, and deceive the visitor." As a result, she warned, "Nothing about your consideration of this legislation could be more important than to make certain that we have the correct location." Steve Brady and Laird Cometsevah, leaders among the Cheyenne descendants, were frustrated that the Park Service relied on the language of scientific inquiry, undercutting the validity of the "traditional tribal methods," oral histories, and archival sources upon which they based their understanding of the site's location. Nevertheless, Brady and Cometsevah stood by the Park Service. They agreed to help with a site search that would last eighteen months. Congress passed Campbell's bill in September of 1998. The next month, President Clinton signed the "Sand Creek Massacre Study Act" into law.[13]

The search that ensued became contentious when epistemological disagreements over how to interpret the past divided the people looking for the site. The descendants typically based their understanding of Sand Creek's history and geography on tribal methods, oral histories, and the documentary record, including maps and essays that George Bent had penned in the early 1900s. For decades, the Arapahos and Cheyennes had used Bent's maps and writings as a guide, making pilgrimages to a spot overlooking a bend in the creek, where they had performed ceremonies. But that connection to the landscape did not satisfy the Park Service, which relied on what it called an "interdisciplinary, comprehensive, and scientific" approach. Historians would scour document collections. Anthropologists would conduct ethnographies. Aerial photographers would take to the skies to look for historic trails. Geomorphologists would study Sand Creek, trying to determine if the streambed had remained constant through the years. Finally, battlefield archaeologists would dig for possible sites. Some of the descendants questioned the need for "such an enormous fuss," noting that they "never had any doubt whatsoever about the massacre's location." But the Park Service forged ahead, sending its site searchers into the field.[14]

As the work progressed, the Park Service's emphasis on a "scientific approach" privileged stories of the massacre generated by agents of settler colonialism rather than oral histories provided by Native people. The historians working on the project preferred written documents composed by individuals with direct experience of the horrors at Sand Creek rather than by people who had second- or third-hand knowledge of the violence. This predisposition meant that the Park Service's researchers emphasized accounts produced by the volunteer soldiers under Chivington. Even as the site searchers tried "to locate and consider Cheyenne and Arapaho participant accounts of the Sand Creek massacre," the thousands of pages of transcribed testimony from Chivington and his men overwhelmed the relatively few sources with Indigenous provenance. As one of the descendants involved in the search explained, even if his ancestors had been asked in late 1864 or early 1865 to recount their experiences, they almost certainly would have distrusted whites too much in the wake of the carnage to comply with such a request. After all, "Black Kettle's people had been killed because they had listened to the white government. Why would they have cooperated again?" The result was that the historians, who counted written records as more reliable than other kinds of sources, had few Native perspectives on Sand Creek available to them during the search. In short, the Park Service mostly bound itself to a settler colonial archive produced as part of the project of empire building in the American West during the era of the Civil War.[15]

Had the project historians been more committed to incorporating Native voices into their study, they could have turned to the work of George Bent.

Late in the nineteenth century, with the West at the center of debates about the future of the United States, Bent worried that Native Americans typically had no voice in those conversations. He began working with a historian named George Hyde, together publishing articles and books about Cheyenne history based on stories that Bent had collected from tribal elders. Approximately a century later, several maps that Bent produced with Hyde offered the Park Service a Native perspective on the massacre. But the historians worried that Bent had drawn those maps decades after the massacre and also that the documents were composite sketches, visual representations of the memories of many Cheyenne people rather than of a single survivor of the violence at Sand Creek. As the searchers studied the documents further, their misgivings ossified into skepticism. They realized that Hyde had traced a flawed U.S. Geological Survey map of southeastern Colorado and then sent the sketch along to Bent. Hyde had reproduced a misleading original, leaving "poor George Bent looking at this inaccurate map." It appeared that the massacre site had been misplaced on Bent's maps.[16]

The Park Service team relied on a different source that seemed to them more likely to point to the killing field's location. In 1868, Lieutenant Samuel Bonsall escorted General William Sherman on a tour of western battlefields. Bonsall prepared a diagram of their journey, including annotating landmarks. The Sand Creek site, labeled "Chivington's Massacre," was one of them. Sherman wanted to bring trophies from the wars of imperialism that the United States was still fighting with Native nations back to Washington DC. He ordered his subordinates to comb the Sand Creek site for "relics": crania, arrowheads, and "other things too numerous to mention." Troops filled a wagonload. Some of those artifacts, especially the human remains, eventually made their way to the Army Medical Museum, where researchers used parts of shattered Native bodies to study the impact of gunshots on anatomy. Regardless, the Park Service historians took to calling Bonsall's map their "Rosetta Stone." The document led them directly to a hypothesis: they had pinpointed not just the massacre's location but the precise spot where Black Kettle's people had camped on the eve of Chivington's attack. "The village site," as it came to be known to many of the searchers, stood a bit less than a mile north of the area typically associated with the violence: a big bend in the creek that the descendants called "the traditional site."[17]

The Park Service team believed that the descendants would be thrilled by the news that archaeological findings—fragments from an artillery piece fired only once in the area, during the massacre—seemed to confirm the historians' conjecture. But instead, the Cheyennes were outraged, insisting that the claim about Black Kettle's village amounted to a "cultural genocide" and "bureaucratic imperialism." Laird Cometsevah suggested that "the federal government shouldn't be so quick to tell Indian people that they don't understand their own history and the land where it happened." The descendants rejected "mute testimony" offered by artifacts from the site, suggesting that their oral histories were every bit as reliable and, in terms of tribal sovereignty, far more relevant. They also pointed out that they were not relying exclusively on memory to inform their understanding of the site's location. They had consulted archival materials, including maps produced by George Bent and George Hyde. Regardless, what most galled the descendants was not that the historians preferred to work with written records but that the Park Service, drawing from an imperial rather than an Indigenous archive, had elevated one primary source over another primary source. The Park Service was relying on evidence produced by Sand Creek's perpetrators instead of its victims. Bent had survived Sand Creek. Bonsall had served as an agent of settler colonialism. Bent had been a respected Cheyenne. Bonsall had been white. Bent's maps were graphic expressions of tribal memory. Bonsall had produced his map only after desecrating corpses of Arapahos and Cheyennes at the presumptive massacre site.[18]

As the fight over competing cartographies intensified, the descendants refused to capitulate. They explained that they preferred no memorial at all to one at which their ancestors' voices would be silenced. The "village controversy," as some of the searchers began calling the dispute, suggested that the Park Service would not let tribal Sand Creek stories shape how the massacre would be memorialized. Historical narratives connected the Cheyennes to the land, they explained, and could not be cast aside without doing violence to the past. "The feds promised that they would listen to us, listen to what we know about our history and about that place," Laird Cometsevah fumed, "but they never did. They were so sure of their science, so sure that their soldier's map was more reliable than George Bent's map, that they kept ignoring us. They ignored how our stories of Sand Creek have taught us about the past and how we never lost the site. They might have lost the site. But we never did." The Bonsall map, Cometsevah feared, would be the cornerstone of the massacre's interpretation at the historic site. But in the end, the Park Service, faced with the descendants abandoning the project, floated a compromise: a site boasting boundaries capacious enough to encompass many different interpretations. After several additional twists and turns, including a casino corporation purchasing a key piece of property for the site, the Park Service finally, in 2007, opened the SCMNHS to the public.[19]

Seven years after that, on November 29, 2014, Arapaho and Cheyenne people gathered at the historic site to mark the sesquicentennial anniversary of Sand Creek. The ceremony began with invocations. Then drum groups performed veterans' songs and flag songs before concluding with White Antelope's death song. In the months leading to the massacre, White Antelope had reassured his followers that Colorado's settlers and government could be trusted, "that peace was going to be made." He "induced many people to come to this camp," promising them they would be "under the protection of Fort Lyon and that no harm would come to them." When Chivington's men arrived, White Antelope, ashamed of his complicity in the unfolding destruction, "made up his mind not to live any longer." He "stood in front of his lodge with his arms folded across his breast, singing the death song: 'Nothing lives long, Only the earth and the mountains.'" The soldiers "shot him and he fell dead in front of his lodge." When the song concluded 150 years later, Norma Gorneau, with tears in her eyes, gestured toward the creek bed. "Our people were slaughtered there," she said. "Chivington tried to kill them all. But," she continued, "some of them hid and survived." Pointing to a copse of cottonwoods, she asked "if those trees were there, I wonder if they were at the massacre? I wonder if those are the witness trees?"[20]

Two years before the SCMNHS opened, Park Service officials posed that question to dendrochronologists. The answer they offered suggested that the descendants' commitment to pushing back against agents of a settler colonial society, against federal officials who tried to police the boundaries of how the past would be interpreted at the historic site, had shaped how the massacre would be remembered. In late 2005, soil scientists and foresters from the University of Colorado Boulder, accompanied by a group of Arapahos and Cheyennes who monitored their work and spoke with them about tribal methods of understanding history, surveyed Sand Creek's floodplain. Their goal "was to locate the oldest trees within the study area and determine their ages." They took samples from especially venerable cottonwoods. Their analysis suggested that none of those trees was extant at the time of the massacre: "We found no conclusive proof (i.e., cores containing the 1864 growth ring) that any of the trees were alive in 1864." But rather than finding definitively that no trees standing at the SCMNHS in the early twentieth century could possibly have provided shelter during Sand Creek, the scientists took seriously Native stories, allowing that it was plausible that several had germinated around that time. "While no trees were definitively dated to 1864, the collective evidence suggests that multiple trees were alive at that time, probably as seedlings or saplings," they concluded. The "collective evidence" included material drawn from Indigenous as well as imperial archives, a measure of how the descendants' focus on preserving their cultural and political sovereignty throughout the site location study had shifted the epistemological dynamics of future investigations at the historic site.[21]

Because tribal stories of Sand Creek were inscribed in the memorial landscape, they became one of the facts on the ground, one of the data points, informing the dendrochronologists' study. At the 150th anniversary of the massacre, Otto Braided Hair, director of the Northern Cheyenne Sand Creek Office, considered the case of the witness trees and the fight to create the SCMNHS: "It was hard sometimes. But we kept working with the Park Service. We kept talking even when they didn't want to listen. We eventually taught them to respect our history. If you look at this place [the historic site], it's right where George Bent mapped it." Norma Gorneau nodded her head. The descendants had helped to create a memorial where their ancestors' stories would always be heard, she said. She gestured to a tribal cemetery, where repatriated remains of Sand Creek's victims "could rest peacefully, instead of sitting in private collections and the vaults of museums." She noted that scant interpretative apparatus littered the prairie, reflecting the wishes of Laird Cometsevah and Steve Brady, who believed that "the place should mostly speak for itself." The creek bed, tribal representatives had decided, should remain off limits to the public "because that's where our people were killed. We don't want tourists stepping on hallowed ground." Gorneau noted that she "was satisfied" with the fruits of her labor. "My grandmother wouldn't believe that this could happen. But she made it possible," Gorneau said.[22]

Notes

1. All quotes from Norma Gorneau, member, Northern Cheyenne Tribe Sand Creek Massacre Descendants' Committee, interview by author, July 1, 2004, Lame Deer, Montana, tape recording in author's possession, transcription in uncataloged Files of the Sand Creek Massacre National Historic Site (FSCMNHS), National Park Service, Western Archeological and Conservation Center (NPS-WACC), Tucson, Arizona.

2. Gorneau interview, July 1, 2004; National Park Service, *Site Location Study*, 1:158–60, 186–89, 275–81; Alexa Roberts, site superintendent, Sand Creek Massacre National Historic Site, interview by author, April 29, 2003, Eads, Colorado, tape recording in author's possession, transcription in uncataloged FSCMNHS at NPS-WACC. See also Norma Gorneau, "Sand Creek Massacre: 150 Years Remembrance," National Museum of the American Indian, Washington DC, October 9, 2014, notes in author's possession; Norma Gorneau, "Perspectives on the Sand Creek Massacre," Eiteljorg Museum of American Indians and Western Art, Indianapolis IN, September 15, 2015, notes in author's possession; and Norma Gorneau, "Remembering Sand Creek," Annual Meeting of the American Studies Association, Denver CO, November 19, 2016, notes in author's possession.

3. Quote from Conrad Fischer, director, Northern Cheyenne Cultural Center, interview by author, July 1, 2004, Lame Deer MT, tape recording in author's possession, transcription in uncataloged FSCMNHS at NPS-WACC. See also National Park Service, *Site Location Study*, 1:186–89, 275–81; Mildred Red Cherries, member, Northern Cheyenne Sand Creek Massacre Descendants' Committee, interview by author, August 13, 2003, Lame Deer MT, tape recording in author's possession, transcription in uncataloged FSCMNHS at NPS-WACC; Joe Big Medicine, Sand Creek representative, Southern Cheyenne tribe, interview by author, July 8, 2003, Lame Deer MT, tape recording in author's possession, transcription in uncataloged FSCMNHS at NPS-WACC.

4. Kelman, *Misplaced Massacre*, 3–19, 27–42, 263–79.

5. West, *Contested Plains*, 99–113, 148–70, 280–85; Roberts, "Sand Creek," 62–69, 76–80, 94–102; Hoig, *Sand Creek Massacre*, 4–18, 35, 220.

6. A. B. Greenwood, Commissioner of Indian Affairs, to J. Thompson, Secretary of the Interior, October 25, 1860, *Report of the Commissioner of Indian Affairs Accompanying the Annual Report*, 228–30; Berthrong, *Southern Cheyennes*, 147–50; West, *Contested Plains*, 196–97; Roberts, "Sand Creek," 201–19; Hoig, *Sand Creek Massacre*, 31–33.

7. John Evans to Secretary of War Edwin Stanton, December 14, 1863, in *Report of the Commissioner of Indian Affairs for the Year 1864*, 225–26; Governor John

Evans to Colonel John Chivington, November 7, 1863, in Letters Received, Office of Indians Affairs, Colorado Superintendency, National Archives, record group 75; West, *Contested Plains*, 198–200; Roberts, "Sand Creek," 236–40; Hoig, *Sand Creek Massacre*, 75–102.

8. Colonel John Chivington to Major Edward Wynkoop, May 31, 1864, *Official Records of the War of the Rebellion* (hereafter OR), series 1, 34, pt. 4, 151. See also Major General Samuel Curtis to Colonel John Chivington, June 20, 1864, OR, series 1, 34, pt. 4, 595; Governor John Evans to Colonel John Chivington, March 16, 1864, OR, series 1, 34, pt. 2, 633–34; Major General Samuel Curtis to Colonel John Chivington, April 8, 1864, OR, series 1, 34, pt. 2, 85; Lieutenant George Eayre to Colonel John Chivington, April 18, 1864, OR, series 1, 34, pt. 1, 880–81; Governor John Evans to Major General Samuel Curtis, April 25, 1864, Indian Letter Book, Colorado State Archives, Denver CO; Senate Executive Doc. 26, 39th Cong., 2nd Sess., *Report of the Secretary of War*, 226; Governor John Evans to Commissioner of Indian Affairs William Dole, June 15, 1864, Indian Letter Book, Colorado State Archives, Denver CO; *Annual Report of the Commissioner of Indian Affairs*, 1863, 240; Governor John Evans to Secretary of War Edwin P. Stanton, OR, series 1, 34, pt. 4, 381; Burkey, "Site of the Murder," 135–42; Hill, *Tales of Colorado Pioneers*, 79–80; West, *Contested Plains*, 289–94; Roberts, "Sand Creek," 241–47; Hoig, *Sand Creek Massacre*, 58–64.

9. Quotes from Governor Evans's first proclamation can be found in *Condition of the Indian Tribes*, 55. Quotes from Governor Evans's second proclamation can be found in "Proclamation of Governor Evans of Colorado Territory" in "Massacre of Cheyenne Indians" in *Report of the Joint Committee*, 101–2. See also Governor John Evans to Secretary of War Edwin M. Stanton, August 10, 1864, OR, series 1, 41, pt. 2, 644; Colonel John Chivington to Major General Samuel Curtis, August 8, 1864, OR, series 1, 41, pt. 2, 614; Governor John Evans to Major General Samuel Curtis, July 18, 1864, OR, series 1, 41, pt. 1, 73; "Massacre of Cheyenne Indians" in *Report of the Joint Committee*, 31; West, *Contested Plains*, 290–94; Roberts, "Sand Creek," 155–64; and Hoig, *Sand Creek Massacre*, 62–80.

10. All quotes from Silas Soule testimony, "Report of the Secretary of War" 39th Cong., 2nd Sess., S. Ex. Doc. 26, 8–9. See also Silas Soule to Mother, December 18, 1864, Carey Collection, box 5, folder 13, University of Denver Special Collections, Penrose Library, Denver CO; Samuel Forster Tappan diary, MSS 617, Colorado Historical Society, Denver CO; Roberts and Halaas, "Written in Blood," 25; Seay, "Pioneers of Freedom," 107–15; West, *Contested Plains*, 300–308; Roberts, "Sand Creek," 262–66, 272–95; and Hoig, *Sand Creek Massacre*, 170–72.

11. Report of Lieutenant Colonel Leavitt L. Bowen, Third Colorado Cavalry, November 30, 1864, OR, series 1, 41, pt. 1, 957; Breakenridge, *Helldorado*, 32. See also

Colonel John Chivington to Major General Samuel Curtis, December 16, 1864, OR, series 1, 41, pt. 1, 948–50; "Report of the Secretary of War" 39th Cong., 2nd Sess., S. Ex. Doc. 26, 10–11; West, *Contested Plains*, 301–6; Roberts, "Sand Creek," 313–30; and Hoig, *Sand Creek Massacre*, 129–33.

12. Jackson, *Century of Dishonor*, 29. "Sand Creek: Battle or Massacre" from an image of the obelisk found in file 287, "Sand Creek Massacre," in Colorado Historical Society, Denver CO. See also Kelman, *Misplaced Massacre*, 9–18, 22–29, 33–42, 51–55, 73–79, 208–18.

13. Laird Cometsevah, chief, Southern Cheyenne Tribe, interview by author, May 12, 2003, Denver CO, tape recording in author's possession, transcription in uncataloged FSCMNHS at NPS-WACC; Cathy Spude, National Park Service, interview by author, June 21, 2003, Denver CO, tape recording in author's possession, transcription in uncataloged FSCMNHS at NPS-WACC; "Statement by Katherine H. Stevenson, Associate Director, Cultural Resource Stewardship and Partnerships, National Park Service, United States Department of the Interior, before the Subcommittee on National Parks, Historic Preservation and Recreation, Senate Energy and Natural Resources Committee, concerning S. 1695, the Sand Creek Massacre National Historic Site Preservation Act of 1998" in uncataloged FSCMNHS at NPS-WACC. See also Steve Brady, headsman, Crazy Dogs Society, Northern Cheyenne Tribe, interview by author, August 29, 2004, Lame Deer MT, tape recording in author's possession, transcription in uncataloged FSCMNHS at NPS-WACC; "Senator Ben Nighthorse Campbell Statement in Support of S. 1695," unpublished manuscript in uncataloged FSCMNHS at NPS-WACC; Public Law 105–243, "An Act to Authorize the Secretary of the Interior to Study the Suitability and Feasibility of Designating the Sand Creek Massacre National Historic Site in the State of Colorado as a Unit of the National Park System, and for Other Purposes"; Deborah Frazier, "Massacre Mystery," *Denver Post*, September 21, 1998, B-6; Michael Romano, "Massacre Remembered," *Rocky Mountain News*, October 7, 1998, 7-A; Michael Romano, "Save Site of Massacre, Indians Say," *Rocky Mountain News*, March 25, 1998, 8-A; Elliot Zaret, "House OKS Bill for Massacre Site," *Denver Post*, September 19, 1998, 6-B.

14. Christine Whitacre, historian, Intermountain Region, National Park Service, interview by author, May 27, 2003, Denver CO, tape recording in author's possession, transcription in uncataloged FSCMNHS at NPS-WACC; Otto Braided Hair, director, Northern Cheyenne Sand Creek Office, interview by the author, May 11, 2007, telephone, tape recording in author's possession, transcription in uncataloged FSCMNHS at NPS-WACC. See also National Park Service, *Site Location Study*, 1:287; and National Park Service, *Special Resource Study*, 2:2–14.

15. Douglas Scott, chief archaeologist, National Parks Service Midwest Archeological Center, interview by author, October 3, 2003, telephone, tape recording
in author's possession, transcription in uncataloged FSCMNHS at NPS-WACC;
National Park Service, *Site Location Study*, 1:34; Cometsevah interview, May 12,
2003. See also Greene and Scott, *Finding Sand Creek*, xvii–xxiv, 25–31; Scott,
"Site Significance," 53; and Scott, "Oral Tradition and Archaeology," 57–62.

16. Lysa Wegman-French, historian, Intermountain Region, National Park Service,
interview by author, June 9, 2003, Denver CO, tape recording, in author's possession, transcription in uncataloged FSCMNHS at NPS-WACC. See also George Bent
map, folder 1, Bent-Hyde Collection, Western History Collections, University
of Colorado Library, Boulder; George Bent map, Oklahoma Historical Society;
Lysa Wegman-French to Cathy Spude, email, August 26, 1998, in uncataloged
FSCMNHS at NPS-WACC; Bent, "Forty Years," 5; Hyde, *Life of George Bent*, 144–
53; and Halaas and Masich, *Halfbreed*, 337–39.

17. Jerry Greene, research historian, National Park Service, interview by author,
May 27, 2003, Denver CO, tape recording, in author's possession, transcription
in uncataloged FSCMNHS at NPS-WACC; Samuel W. Bonsall map, in National
Archives, Great Lakes Region, Chicago; Luke Cahill, "Recollections of a Plains-
man," unpublished manuscript, ca. 1915, MSS 99 in Manuscripts Division, Colo-
rado Historical Society, Denver CO; Gary L. Roberts, "The Sand Creek Massacre
Site: A Report on Washington Sources," 11, in uncataloged FSCMNHS at NPS-
WACC; Rick Frost, associate regional director for Communications and External
Relations, Intermountain Region, National Park Service, interview by author,
June 11, 2003, Denver CO, tape recording in author's possession, transcription
in uncataloged FSCMNHS at NPS-WACC.

18. Brady interview, August 29, 2004; Cometsevah interview, May 12, 2003; National
Park Service, *Site Location Study*, 1:132.

19. Cometsevah interview, May 12, 2003. See also "National Park Service News
Release: National Park Service Announces 391st Unit, Sand Creek Massacre
National Historic Site," in uncataloged FSCMNHS at NPS-WACC; and Kelman,
Misplaced Massacre, 197.

20. Hyde, *Life of George Bent*, 149–55; Norma Gorneau, Bureau of Indian Affairs
Superintendent, Wind River Reservation, interview by author, November 30,
2014, Eads CO, tape recording in author's possession, transcription in uncataloged FSCMNHS at NPS-WACC. See also Eric Gorski, "The Sand Creek Massacre:
Searching for Culpability 150 Years Later," *Denver Post*, November 29, 2014, A-1.

21. All quotes from Jeff Lukas and Connie Woodhouse, "Riparian Forest Age Structure and Past Hydroclimatic Variability, Sand Creek Massacre National Historic
Site," final report, October 2006, in uncataloged FSCMNHS at NPS-WACC. See also

Otto Braided Hair, director, Northern Cheyenne Sand Creek Office, interview by author, November 30, 2014, Eads CO, tape recording in author's possession, transcription in uncataloged FSCMNHS at NPS-WACC.

22. Braided Hair interview, November 30, 2014; Gorneau interview, November 30, 2014.

Bibliography

Bent, George. "Forty Years with the Cheyennes." Edited by George Hyde. *The Frontier: A Magazine of the West* IV (January 1906).

Berthrong, Donald J. *The Southern Cheyennes.* Norman: University of Oklahoma Press, 1975.

Breakenridge, William. *Helldorado: Bringing Law to the Mesquite.* Boston: Houghton Mifflin, 1928.

Burkey, Elmer R. "The Site of the Murder of the Hungate Family by Indians in 1864." *Colorado Magazine* 12 (1935).

Condition of the Indian Tribes: Report of the Special Joint Committee, Appointed under Joint Resolution of March 3, 1865. With an Appendix. Washington DC: Government Printing Office, 1867.

Greene, Jerome A., and Douglas D. Scott. *Finding Sand Creek: History, Archeology, and the 1864 Massacre Site.* Norman: University of Oklahoma Press, 2004.

Halaas, David Fridtjof, and Andrew E. Masich. *Halfbreed: The Remarkable True Story of George Bent, Caught between the Worlds of the Indian and the White Man.* New York: De Capo, 2004.

Hill, Alice Polk. *Tales of Colorado Pioneers.* Denver: Pierson & Gardner, 1884.

Hoig, Stan. *The Sand Creek Massacre.* Norman: University of Oklahoma Press, 1961.

Hyde, George E. *Life of George Bent: Written from His Letters.* Edited by Savoie Lottinville. Norman: University of Oklahoma Press, 1968.

Jackson, Helen Hunt. *Century of Dishonor: A Sketch of the United States Government's Dealings with Some of the Indian Tribes.* New York: Harper & Brothers, 1881.

Kelman, Ari. *A Misplaced Massacre: Struggling over the Memory of Sand Creek.* Cambridge: Harvard University Press, 2013.

National Park Service. *Site Location Study.* Vol. 1, *Sand Creek Massacre Project.* Denver: National Park Service, Intermountain Region, 2000.

———. *Special Resource Study.* Vol. 2, *Sand Creek Massacre Project.* Denver: National Park Service, Intermountain Region, 2000.

Report of the Commissioner of Indian Affairs Accompanying the Annual Report of the Secretary of the Interior, for the Year 1860. Washington DC: George W. Bowman, 1860.

Report of the Commissioner of Indian Affairs for the Year 1864. Washington DC: Government Printing Office, 1865.

Report of the Joint Committee on the Conduct of the War, at the Second Session, Thirty-Eighth Congress. Washington DC: Government Printing Office, 1865.

Report of the Secretary of War, Communicating, in Compliance with a Resolution of the Senate of February 4, 1867, a Copy of the Evidence Taken at Denver and Fort Lyon, Colorado Territory, by a Military Commission Ordered to Inquire into the Sand Creek Massacre, November, 1864. Washington DC: Government Printing Office, 1867.

Roberts, Gary Leland. "Sand Creek: Tragedy and Symbol." PhD diss., University of Oklahoma, 1984.

Roberts, Gary Leland, and David Fridtjof Halaas. "Written in Blood: The Soule-Cramer Sand Creek Letters." *Colorado Heritage* (Winter 2001).

Scott, Douglas D. "Site Significance and Historical Archaeology—a Scenario and Commentary." *Historical Archaeology* 24 (1990).

———. "Oral Tradition and Archaeology: Conflict and Concordance Examples from Two Indian War Sites." *Historical Archaeology* 37 (2003).

Seay, Virginia Claire. "Pioneers of Freedom: The Story of the Soule Family in Kansas." *Kansas Magazine* (1943).

West, Elliott. *The Contested Plains: Indians, Goldseekers, and the Rush to Colorado.* Lawrence: University of Kansas Press, 1998.

Conclusion

Transforming the Field, Transforming the Future

MARY E. MENDOZA AND TRACI BRYNNE VOYLES

The chapters in this volume collectively highlight the varied, complex, and significant ways that environment shapes power relations across diverse communities. Together, these chapters analyze the relationships between environment, race, and justice through a historical lens, exploring how environmental injustices are produced in different historical contexts in ways that profoundly shaped, and still shape, power relations between and among us all. More broadly, the authors in this volume ask how power relations have been articulated through resources and resource exploitation; how the environment has been a literal and figurative terrain of struggle over rights, inclusion, or differentiation; and how nature has come to signify and symbolize race in ways that produce unequal or unjust power relations. Ultimately, the collection underscores the reality, long apparent to communities of color and Indigenous peoples but too rarely articulated in scholarship on environmental history, that racial injustice and environmental degradation (and sometimes environmental preservation) are coconstituted.

Not Just Green, Not Just White demonstrates that it is not enough to say that marginalized people engage in environmental work, or enjoy being in national parks, or that they should be included in those parks, though those stories are vital. Classic environmental histories have focused on wilderness, whiteness, and white ideals of pure nature, leaving unexamined the different ways in which peoples of color and Indigenous peoples experience the nonhuman world and engage in environmental politics. This tendency in environmental history reflects dominant American narratives that focus on white individuals and how they have changed landscapes, ignoring how expansion, settler colonialism, economic and agricultural development, resource extraction, and urban planning have dramatically influenced relationships between people of color and their own natural and built environments. This, in short, is a totalizing, universalizing framework that flattens the diversity of human relationships to the nonhuman world and does not account for the myriad ways that all people think about and act on nature and the environment. Together, the chapters in this collection bring together a number of historians thinking about a range of environmentalisms and environmental histories, with an eye toward building a more environmentally just future—as well as piecing together a more complete picture of our diverse environmental pasts.

There is not a lack of diverse voices to draw from in the field of history or in primary sources (though those sources might require new approaches to our archival methods). Incorporating diverse stories yields fruitful and more holistic conversations about our many histories—our many pasts. The field needs more environmental histories that critically engage race and gender, as well as other intersecting social locations, as tools of analysis. As these chapters collectively confirm, when we abandon the classic parameters of environmental history, which has largely been green and white, we move beyond the study of changing relationships between people and nature to more complex analyses of race, racism, and the environment. Rather than a wide-ranging notion of what "environment" means, we trap ourselves in what we might—glibly, but we think correctly—call the "white wilderness box."

Environments, like the people who inhabit them, are diverse—not just pristine places or landscapes that some think should have been left pristine rather than exploited. They are jail cells filled with people of color. They are border landscapes that are increasingly racialized and exclusionary. They are Native lands where sheep graze and cacti are sacred. They are workscapes where people harvest fruit. They are construction sites where laborers take pride in the work that they have done. These diverse environments shape people's identities and lives, and to truly account for those experiences, environmental historians must step outside of our own comfort zone. The field can no longer afford to normalize whiteness and its settler colonial relationships to environment in our studies of the past.

In short, the perspectives and frames of analysis in these chapters unlock powerful new approaches to environmental history. The field, it is clear, can no longer be solely about the changing relations between humans and nature because humans are not a monolith. Nor are environments. There are multiple power dynamics that dictate how those relationships unfold on land, in water, and through space. In the end, we find that land and resources are indeed crucial to better understandings of the past. Taking an additional step toward seeing that land and those resources as being at the center of shaping power relations between and among peoples leaves us with better understandings of the past and clearer engagements with the present. Perhaps most important of all, it leaves us more prepared for the future.

CONTRIBUTORS

Kent Blansett is a Cherokee, Creek, Choctaw, Shawnee, and Potawatomi descendant from the Blanket, Panther, and Smith family lines. He is the Langston Hughes Associate Professor of Indigenous Studies and History at the University of Kansas. He is the author of *A Journey to Freedom: Richard Oakes, Alcatraz, and the Red Power Movement* (2018) and coeditor of *Indian Cities: Histories of Indigenous Urbanization* (2022). Blansett is the founder and executive director of the American Indian Digital History Project (www .aidhp.com), a digital history cooperative that strives to expand both free and open access to critical Indigenous research and archival materials. His scholarship explores the links between Native nationalism and Red Power, urban Indigenous history, intertribalism, pop culture, and global Indigenous history.

Elizabeth Grennan Browning is an assistant professor of history at the University of Oklahoma and a former faculty fellow at Indiana University's Environmental Resilience Institute. She is the author of *Nature's Laboratory: Environmental Thought and Labor Radicalism in Chicago, 1886–1937* (2022). Her research and teaching interests focus on U.S. urban environmental history, the history of capitalism, and histories of environmental health and environmental justice since the late nineteenth century. Her current research examines intersecting histories of environmental inequality and carceral labor in the federal prison system and American criminology studies during the long twentieth century.

Erika Marie Bsumek holds the Ellen Clark Temple Chair of American history at the University of Texas at Austin. She has written on Native American history, environmental history/studies, the history of the built environment, and the history of the U.S. West. She is the author of *Indian-Made: Navajo*

Culture in the Marketplace, 1848–1940 (2008) and the coeditor of a collection of essays on global environmental history titled *Nation States and the Global Environment: New Approaches to International Environmental History* (2013). Her book *The Foundations of Glen Canyon Dam: Infrastructures of Dispossession on the Colorado Plateau* (2023), explores the social and environmental history of the area surrounding Glen Canyon on the Utah-Arizona border from the 1840s to the present.

Carolyn Finney is a storyteller, an author, and a cultural geographer who is deeply interested in issues related to identity, difference, creativity, and resilience. Grounded in both artistic and intellectual ways of knowing (pursuing an acting career for eleven years and backpacking around the world before returning to school to complete three degrees), she is passionate about interrogating our past and dreaming a future that is liberatory, just, and green. Along with public speaking, writing, media engagements, and consulting, she served on the National Parks Advisory Board and is the author of numerous publications, most notably her first book, *Black Faces, White Spaces: Reimagining the Relationship of African Americans to the Great Outdoors* (2014). She was a Fulbright Scholar and a Canon National Parks Science Scholar and has received two Mellon Fellowships, including a residency at the New York Botanical Gardens. She is currently working on her second book and is a scholar/artist in residence at the Franklin Environmental Center at Middlebury College.

Colin Fisher is a professor of history at the University of San Diego, where he teaches environmental history, history of food, and historical documentary film production. His research centers on urban parks as well as subaltern environmentalisms and cultures of nature. He is the author of *Urban Green: Nature, Recreation, and the Working Class in Industrial Chicago* (2015). He has also written on the climate science of antebellum Black abolitionists, the environmental vision of Gilded Age anarchists, the intersection of migration history and environmental history, and the appropriation of wilderness parks by marginalized communities.

Katherine Johnston is an assistant professor of history at Montana State University. She is the author of *The Nature of Slavery: Environment and Plantation Labor in the Anglo-Atlantic World* (2022). Her research, which has also been published in *Early American Studies* and *Atlantic Studies*, focuses on slavery, race, the environment, and the history of the body across the Atlantic world.

Ari Kelman is the Chancellor's Leadership Professor of History at the University of California, Davis. He is the author of *Battle Lines: A Graphic History of the Civil War* (2015), *A Misplaced Massacre: Struggling over the Memory of Sand Creek* (2013), and *A River and Its City: The Nature of Landscape in New Orleans* (2003). Kelman has received numerous grants and fellowships, including from the Guggenheim Foundation and the National Endowment for the Humanities. He is currently writing a book titled *For Liberty and Empire: How the Civil War Bled into the Indian Wars* and editing the journal *Reviews in American History*.

Patty Limerick is a professor of history, the director of the Applied History Initiative, and the campus partner for academic affairs for the Veteran and Military Affairs office at the University of Colorado at Boulder. She is the author of *Desert Passages* (1985), *The Legacy of Conquest* (1987), *Something in the Soil* (2000), and *A Ditch in Time* (2012). She has served as president of the American Studies Association, the Western History Association, the Organization of American Historians, and the Society of American Historians; as vice president of the Teaching Division of the American Historical Association; and as a member of the National Council on the Humanities. She received a MacArthur Fellowship in 1995 and was elected to the American Academy of Arts and Sciences in 2021. Limerick has dedicated her career to bridging the gap between academics and the general public and to demonstrating the benefits of applying a historical perspective to contemporary dilemmas and conflicts.

Mary E. Mendoza is an assistant professor of history and Latino/a studies at Penn State University. She writes about the intersections between race and environment in the U.S.-Mexico borderlands and is interested in how the environment mediates human relationships more broadly. Her scholarly works have appeared in *Environmental History*, *Pacific Historical Review*, and *Journal of the West*, among other publications. Her scholarly endeavors have been funded by the U.S. National Science Foundation, the Smithsonian Institution, the Ford Foundation, the National Endowment for the Humanities, the Woodrow Wilson Foundation, and the Huntington Library, among other funding sources.

Kathryn Morse is a professor of history and the John C. Elder Professor in Environmental Studies at Middlebury College. She is the author of *The Nature of Gold: An Environmental History of the Klondike Gold Rush* (2003) as well as essays including "There Will Be Birds: Images of Oil Disasters in the Nineteenth and Twentieth Centuries" (*Journal of American History*) and "Dad (and Mom) vs. Nature, 1975: *Jaws* and *The Adventures of the Wilderness Family*" (*Environmental History*). Her essay "Conserving Whiteness" is part of a larger project on race, gender, poverty, visual images, and land in Farm Security Administration rural rehabilitation programs of the 1930s and early 1940s.

David Naguib Pellow is the Dehlsen Chair and Distinguished Professor of Environmental Studies and director of the Global Environmental Justice Project at the University of California, Santa Barbara, where he teaches courses on social change movements, environmental justice, human-animal conflicts, sustainability, and social inequality. Pellow has published a number of works on environmental justice issues in communities of color in the United States and globally. Some of his books include *What Is Critical Environmental Justice?* (2017), *Garbage Wars: The Struggle for Environmental Justice in Chicago* (2002), and *Power, Justice, and the Environment: A Critical Appraisal of the Environmental Justice Movement* (edited with Robert J. Brulle, 2005).

Miles A. Powell is an affiliate researcher at the Rachel Carson Center for Environment and Society in Munich, Germany. He was previously an associate professor of history at Nanyang Technological University, Singapore, where he headed the university's Green Humanities Research Cluster, and a research affiliate of the Rachel Carson Center for Environment and Society in Munich, Germany. He researches and teaches marine and global environmental history. His first book, *Vanishing America: Species Extinction, Racial Peril, and the Origins of Conservation* (2016), uses discourses of extinction to explore connections between racial attitudes and environmental thought in late nineteenth- and early twentieth-century America. His current research projects include a global environmental history of human interactions with sharks and a grant-funded study of Singapore's marine environmental history. His research has been published in *Environment & History, Environmental History, International Review of Environmental History, Springs, Pacific*

Historical Review, Western Historical Quarterly, and edited anthologies. He currently serves on the editorial board of *Environment and History.*

Cecilia M. Tsu is an associate professor of history at the University of California, Davis. She is the author of *Garden of the World: Asian Immigrants and the Making of Agriculture in California's Santa Clara Valley* (2013) and coauthor of *The Elusive Eden: A New History of California,* 5th ed. (2019). Her current book project is titled *Starting Over: Hmong Refugees and the Politics of Resettlement in Modern America.* Tsu's articles have appeared in *Amerasia Journal, Journal of American Ethnic History, Pacific Historical Review,* and *Western Historical Quarterly,* among other publications.

Traci Brynne Voyles is a professor of history and a department head at North Carolina State University. She is the author of *The Settler Sea: California's Salton Sea and the Consequences of Colonialism* (2021) and *Wastelanding: Legacies of Uranium Mining in Navajo Country* (2015).

Bryon Williams is a scholar and educator whose research and teaching focus on the environmental humanities. He earned his master's from Stanford University and his PhD from Duquesne University after studying environmental philosophy at the University of North Texas. His scholarship has previously appeared in *Romantic Ecocriticism: Origins and Legacies* (2017), *Critical Insights: Macbeth* (2017), and *The Wild That Attracts Us: New Critical Essays on Robinson Jeffers* (2015). He has presented his work on race and the environment at the Environmental History Seminar Series of the Massachusetts Historical Society and other conferences. Bryon teaches at Northfield Mount Hermon in Massachusetts.

Teona Williams is a Presidential Postdoctoral Fellow in the Department of Geography at Rutgers University. She studies Black geographies, twentieth-century African American and environmental history, and Black feminist theory. Her current work explores the role of disaster and hunger in shaping Black feminist ecologies from the 1930 to the 1990s. She follows a cadre of rural Black feminists who articulated visions of food sovereignty, overhauled anti-Black disaster relief, and vigorously fought for universal basic income, radical land reform, and food and clean water access as a human right.

Carl A. Zimring is a professor of sustainability studies and the director of the Center for Critical Discard Research at Pratt Institute. He is an environmental historian interested in how attitudes concerning waste shape society, culture, institutions, and inequalities. His books include *Cash for Your Trash: Scrap Recycling in America*; *Clean and White: A History of Environmental Racism in the United States*; *Aluminum Upcycled: Sustainable Design in Historical Perspective*; and *Technology and the Environment in History* (with Sara B. Pritchard). His edited volumes include *Coastal Metropolis: Environmental Histories of New York City* (with Steven H. Corey) and *Encyclopedia of Consumption and Waste: The Social Science of Garbage* (with William L. Rathje).

INDEX

Page numbers in *italics* refer to illustrations.

agriculture (*continued*)
refugees and, 241–42, 248; subsistence, 253; swidden, 246; urban, 238
Aila, William, 312, 313, *314*, 327
Airriess, Christopher, 245
Alabama Africa, 347
Alabama River, 347
Alberta, map of, *412*
Alcatraz Island, 408, 432
Alcoa, 409
Aleutian Islands, 163
Alexander, Frank D., 222
Alexander, Will, 209, 212, 215, 225n10, 228n49
Ali, Muhammad, 343
Alien Land Laws, 396
ali'i, 319, 320, 324
Alkire, Janet, 427
Allard, LaDonna Brave Bull, 418–19
Allen, Holly, 205
Allin, Bushrod, 222
Alston, Lee, 217
Aluli, Noa Emmett, 327
AMAX, 409
American Anthropologist, 318
American Beach, 350–51, 352, 353
American Beach Historical District, 352
American Community Gardening Association (ACGA), 240
An American Dilemma (Myrdal), 123
An American Exodus (Lange and Taylor), 202, 210
American Federation of Labor, 87
American Federation of State, County, and Municipal Employees (AFSCME), 88
American Historical Association, 367
American Indian Religious Freedom Act, 438n30

American Natural History Museum, 146
American Negro Exposition, 122
American Revolution, political inclusion and, 276
American River, 165
American Samoa, 331
American Society for Environmental History (ASEH), xiv, xv, 71
American Sociological Society, 108
Anaconda, 409
Anderson, Benedict, 33n50
Anderson, Kat, 387
Anderson, Robert, 354
Anderson, Virginia DeJohn, 33n52
Anderson, Warwick, 89
Andrews, Thomas, 71
animals, weaponization of, 19
Anishinaabegs, 410
Anthropocene, 170
anti-Asian sentiment, 329
anti-Blackness, 75, 396
anticolonial movement, 8
antidemocratic practices, 170–71
antiracism, 8, 211
Appalachian Mountains, 4, 5, 213
Arab Spring, 435n8
Arapahos, 447, 449, 450, 451, 452, 453, 457; massacre of, 446, 448, 454
Archambault, Dave, II, 319, 421
Arista, Noelani, 316
Arizona Strip, 307n26
Arkansas River, 448
Army Corps of Engineers, 418
Army Medical Museum, 455
Arnett, Will, 348
Arvin, Maile, 400n59
ASEH. *See* American Society for Environmental History (ASEH)

Asian American and Pacific Islanders (AAPI), 79, 315
Asian Americans, xvi, 84, 365; coercive labor and, 20; environment and, 237, 238, 239
assimilation, 34n70, 90, 108, 110, 143, 144, 148, 447
Athabasca River, 412
athletic clubs, 107
Atlanta Anti-Tuberculosis Association, 86
Atlanta Constitution, 227n30
Atlanta Daily World, 217
Atlantic bluefin tuna, 329
Attawapiskat First Nation, 416
Audubon Society, 32n32, 267, 282n9
ʻaum-ākua, 313, 314, 317, 318–19, 322, 324, 327, 328, 330
Aztec Canyon, 294
Aztlán, 146

Back of the Yards, 119, 136
Backwater Bridge, 423
Badoni, Lamar, 288, 305
Badoni v. Higginson (1977, 1980), 290, 300, 301, 302, 305
BAE. *See* Bureau of Agricultural Economics (BAE)
Baja California, 381, 396
Bakken oil fields, 418
Bales, Kevin, 170
Ballou, Robert, 192
Bankhead, William, 211
Bankhead-Jones Tenancy Act, 210, 211, 227n30
Banks, Henry, 279
Ban Vinai, 247
Barrick Gold, 409
Bayonet Constitution, 321

Beckwith, Martha Warren, 318–19
Belafonte, Harry, 357n32
The Bell Curve (Herrnstein and Murray), 103
beneficial ideas, roots of, xvii–xviii
Bent, George, 451, 452, 458; maps by, 453–54, 455, 456
Bent, William, 451
Berger, Dan, 171
Berkeley, Busby, 142
Betsch, MaVynee, 350–53, 356
Biden, Joe, 95–96n50
Bill C-27, 416
Bill C-38, 414
Bill C-45, 414
Billiken, Bud, 149
Bitsinnie, Begay, 288
Black, Jessie Yazzi, 288
Black Belt, 105, 113, 136, *137*
Black bodies, 50, 51, 63
Black Boy (Wright), 110
Black Chicago, 134, 138–39, 144, 145, 148, 149; African American identity and, 143; history of, 135. *See also* South Side
Black Codes, 162
Black communities, 86, 126–27n52; cultural cohesion in, 109; imagined, 145; marginalized, 114
Black Cross Nurses, 144
Black elites, 119, 143, 145
Blackfeet Reservation, 17
Black Forest, 146
Black Ghetto, 122
Black Jake, 215
Black Kettle, 446, 449, 451, 454, 455, 456
Black Laws, refugees and, 270
Black Liberation Theology, 267

Burgett, Bruce, 276
Burnt Church Reserve, 410
Burwell, Dollie, 269
Bury My Heart at Wounded Knee (Brown), 453
"Bye and Bye," 141
Byrd, William, II, 4, 5, 378n30

Caldwell, Erskine, 210, 225n10
Caledonia, 410
California Men's Colony, 165
California Natives, 386, 389; attempted extermination of, 387; removal of, 393–94
Calloway, Cab, 343
Camarillo, Luis, 92
Cambodians, gardening by, 243, 245–46, 249
Cammerer, Arno, 186
Campaign to Fight Toxic Prisons, 160
Campbell, Ben Nighthorse, 453
Camp-Horinek, Casey, 437n24
Camp Weld, 451, 452
Canadian Residential Schools, 417
Canadian Supreme Court, 410
Canning, Deween, 296
Cannonball River, 419, 422
Canyon of the Gods, 294
capitalism, 383; American, 449; exploitation and, 26; industrial, 26, 102, 118; racial, 26, 33n44, 160
Cardinal, Harold, 408
Carnegie Corporation, 123
Carson, Kit, 292
Carson, Rachel, 6, 8
Cartwright, Samuel, 105
Casa del Migrante, 371
Castle, Beth, 421

CAUSE. *See* Center for Africanamerican Urban Studies and the Economy (CAUSE)
Cayoosh Ski Resort, 410
Cayton, Horace R., 85, 87, 101, 103–4, 110, *111*, 114, 117, 119, 122, 123; ecological process and, 118; on women's work, 86
CCC. *See* Civilian Conservation Corps (CCC)
Center for Africanamerican Urban Studies and the Economy (CAUSE), 93n3
Central Valley, 9, 243, 246; gardening in, 241, 254
Century of Dishonor (Jackson), 452
Century of Progress Exposition, 139, 145
ceremonialism, 295, 297, 318
Chang, David A., 315, 316
Changes in the Land (Cronon), 30n9
Chase, Stuart, 201
Chatelain, Marcia, 181
Chavez, Cesar, 133
Chavis, Benjamin, 93n6
Cheyenne River Sioux Tribe, 423
Cheyennes, 447, 449, 450, 451, 452, 453, 455, 456, 457; massacre of, 446, 448, 454
Chiang, Connie, 8, 15, 16, 237–38
Chicago: laundry work in, 87; as model city, 101; racial violence in, 107; remembering African motherland in, 138–39, *140*, 141–42; waste work in, 83. *See also* South Side
Chicago Black Renaissance, 122
Chicago Coliseum, 122
Chicago Commission on Race Relations, 107

Chicago Commons, 107

Chicago Defender, 105, 121, 122, 139, 149, 211

Chicago school, 102, 103, 110, 114, 117, 123; human ecology and, 124n3

Chicago School of Civics and Philanthropy, 107

Chinese: enslavement of, 20; health issues for, 23; immigration of, 23; racial animosity toward, 329; shark finning and, 328, 332; shark fin soup and, 330

Chinese Americans: agricultural experiences of, 237; as model minority, 329

Chinese Culinary Arts Society of Hawai'i, 328

Chinese Exclusion Act, 23, 329

Chivington, John, 450, 451, 457; memories of, 453; Sand Creek and, 446, 447, 452, 454, 455

Chorro Creek, 165

Chumash, 387

citizenship, 145, 384, 398n16, 440n44; American, 144; cultural, 398n15; legal, 398n15; Mexican, 398n13; privileges of, 26, 27; responsibilities of, 190; second-class, 143

"City of Destruction" (Frazier), 122

Civilian Conservation Corps (CCC), 222

civilization, 12, 22, 108, 270, 275, 368, 452; wilderness and, 5

civil rights, 83, 138, 182–83, 195, 420, 433; advocating for, 181, 190–91; African American, 171

civil rights movement, xx, 8, 75, 181–83, 189, 195, 347, 354

Civil War, 73, 76, 79, 86, 272, 448, 449, 454

class: analysis by, 134; anxieties, 146; justice, 9; race and, 181, 268; status, 263

Clawson, David, 245

Clean Water Act, 429

Clements, Mrs. Lloyd, 219, *219*

Clifton, Lucille, 342

climate change, 1, 19, 49, 164, 169, 383, 429; promoting, 170

Clinton, Bill, 313, 366; anti-immigrant policy and, 367; Sand Creek Massacre Study Act and, 453

Clinton, Hillary, 92, 423

Coalition to Protect Ocean Diversity, 330

Cobb, Charles, 8

Cole, Johnetta, 351

The Collapse of Cotton Tenancy, 207, 209

colonialism, xiii, 3, 10, 361; extractive, 30n10, 409, 429; focus on, 31n25; rape and, 166. *See also* settler colonialism

colonization, 12, 168, 320, 329, 396, 397; environmental impacts of, 382; Indigenous, 433; Mexican, 387; Mormon, 288, 306; Spanish, 387

Colorado Plateau, 289, 290

Colorado River, 208n27, 289, 293

Colorado River Storage Project Act, 287, 306n1

color-blindness, 211, 223

Columbia Broadcasting System, 139

Cometsevah, Laird, 453, 456, 458

Commission on Wartime Relocation and Internment of Civilians, 163

Committee on Fisheries (FAO), 326

communities of color, 2, 83, 396, 465; environmental injustice and, 169

Community Assistance for Prisoners, 165

community gardens, 237; collaboration over, 239; dispersal of, 241; economics of, 249–55; founding, 242, 249, 250; function of, 243–44; impact of, 246, 250; poverty and, 249–55; production in, 251; purpose of, 244–45; resettlement and, 241–42; rural (dis)continuity, 243–49; YMCA, 243. *See also* gardening

concentration camps, 162, 163

concentric zone model, 109, 113, 114, 118

Cone, James, 267

conservation, 330; as colonizing force, 10; movement, 102, 395; spaces of, 183

Conservation Council for Hawaiʻi, 330

Contreras, Oscar F., 371

Cook, Barbara, 296

Cook, James, 317, 328, 329, 330–32

Cook County Democratic Party, 139

Cook County Forest Preserves, 148

Corbould, Clare, 144

Corlett, Jan, 248

cotton cultivation, 162, 212, 216; race relations and, 222

cotton tenancy, 177, 204, 207, 209, 212, 215, 218, 220, 225n10

Cotton Tenants (Agee, Evans, and Haslett), 210, 214

Coulten, Charles Edward, 82

Coulthard, Glen, 32n41

Cowboy and Indian Alliance, 429

Crang, Mike, 89, 90

Crees, 408

Crenshaw, Kimberlé, 383

Critical Refugee Studies, 238

Critical Resistance, 160

Cronon, William, 30n9, 30n18, 377n4

crown daisy (*Chrysanthemum coronarium*), 399n34

Cubic Air Acts, 23

Cuero, Aurelio, 392

Cuero, Delfina, xxii, 382, 388, 389, 396, 397n3, 398n20, 399n27, 400n50; border crossing by, 381, 397n11; California of, 384–87; life story of, 383, 387, 390; parenthood for, 392; puberty ceremony and, 391

Cuero, Lupe, 392

Cuero, Santos, 393

cultural misunderstanding, 290–93

culture, 102, 183, 184, 187, 223, 243, 396; African, 109–10; African American, 123, 355; American, 104, 107, 123, 268; Black, 104, 143; Chinese, 331; colonial, 54; dominant, 345; Hawaiian, 331; Indigenous, 17, 297; kanaka, 321; nature and, 48, 145–50, 378n30; transplanted, 237, 247; urban, 48, 105; Western, 110

Cummings, Byron, 290, 291, 292

Curonian Spit, 146

Custer Died for Your Sins (Deloria), 408

Dairy Queen Rock, 294

Dakota Access pipeline (DAPL), 424, 431, 432; map of, *420*; opposition to, 418, *425*, 427

Dakota Rural Action, 417

Dalrymple, Jack, 421

Dannelly, William, 347

DAPL. *See* Dakota Access pipeline (DAPL)

Davis, Angela, 166, 343, 355

Davis, Siobhan, 218

Dawson, Charles Clarence: poster art by, *140*

Death Valley, 1

Drake, St. Clair, 85, 87, 101, 103, 114, 117, 119, 122, 123; ecological process and, 118; on women's work, 86

Drew, Benjamin, 269, 274, 280

Du Bois, W. E. B., 1, 8, 102, 133, 215; spiritual striving and, 346; on whiteness/ownership, 13

Dumping in Dixie (Bullard), 75

Dunaway, Finis, 225n15

Dust Bowl, 206

Eagle-Picher Corporation, 409

Eakin, J., 182

Earth Day, 267

Earthjustice, 327

Earthtrust, 327

Eastman, Lee Ann, 422, 423

ecocide, 170, 431

ecological health, 162, 168–71

ecology, 170; self-recovery and, 346; urban, 114. *See also* human ecology

economic development, 90, 106, 184, 298

economic recession (1893–97), 239

economic security, refugees and, 254–55

ecosystems, 26, 160, 163, 167, 287, 394; contamination of, 164–65; Indigenous-stewarded, 14; stress on, 162

education, 167, 205, 237, 266, 270; access to, 374; lack of, 212

1851 Treaty camp, 418

"18 Lost Treaties," 399n23

elimination, 4, 13, 162; Indigenous, 18, 383, 387, 396; settler colonialism and, 16–18

Ellis, Mrs., 280

Elsipogtog First Nation Reserve, 405, 406, 407, 416

Emancipation Proclamation, 141, 162

Embree, Edwin, 209, 212, 225n10

Emergency Response teams (RCMP), 406

Emerson, Ralph Waldo, 265, 270, 276, 378n30

Enbridge Line 9, 411

Enbridge Sandpiper pipeline, 411, 419

Enclosure Act, 147

Energy Transfer Partners, 418, 421, 423, 424, 425, 427, 432

engaging in green, 344–45, 350

enslavement, 3, 4, 13, 18–21, 55, 161, 162, 279, 345; African, 52; de facto / de jure, 20; ecocide and, 170; environment and, 19; framing, 168; incarceration and, 171; nature of, 21; as punishment for crime, 168; uncompensated, 26; white settler supremacy and, 19. *See also* slavery

environment, 4, 15, 16, 26, 80, 123, 239, 373, 381, 387, 448, 465; African, 149; analysis of, 466; dissonant, 255; enslavement and, 19; establishing/policing of, 75; Eurocentric experience of, 345; exclusion and, 25; hazardous, 55; identity/behavior, 104; marginalized peoples and, 167; metropolitan, 124; nature and, 466; power relations and, 465; race and, xviii, 2, 26, 28, 47; refugees and, 282; saving, 265; social, 239; spatial, 271; tropical, 149

environmental causes, 9, 315, 351

environmental conditions, 15, 18, 51, 396

Environmental Defense Fund, 282n9

environmental degradation, 7, 169, 206, 322, 362, 384, 390, 393, 395, 417, 465; as intersectional experience, 387–88; stories of, 3

extermination, 15, 161, 387, 450

extraction, 10, 27–29; systemic structural changes and, 27; white settler supremacy and, 28

ExxonMobil, 164

Fallis, Red Fawn, 427

family organization, natural history of, 108–9

FAO. *See* United Nations Food and Agriculture Organization (FAO)

Far and Away, 370

Farmer and Sons Walking in the Face of a Dust Storm, Cimarron County, Oklahoma (Rothstein), 207

Farmers Home Administration, 217

Farm Security Administration (FSA), xx, 110, *116*, 178, 202, 203, 204, 205, 206, 209, 219, 220, 221, 223; Blacks and, 218; rehabilitation and, 230n85; rehabilitation programs and, 222; segregation and, 217; tenancy and, 216

"farm-to-table" movement, 255

FBI, 438n31

Federal District, 371

Federal Emergency Relief Act (FERA), 230n85

Federation of Saskatchewan Indians, 408

feminists, 164, 276–77; Black, 383; Indigenous, 383, 396, 400n59

FERA. *See* Federal Emergency Relief Act (FERA)

Ferrie, Joseph, 217

field: evaluation of, 3; future of, 10–13; state of, 4–10; thinking about, xxiii–xxiv

Finley, Ron, 342–43, 345, 356

Finnegan, Cara, 206, 209

Finney, Carolyn, xxii, 180, 264

Finney, Nikky, 343, 353, 354

finning. *See* shark finning

First Amendment, 300

First National POC Environmental Leadership Summit, 9

First Nations, 406, 408, 409, 411, 417, 437n22; businesses of, 416; fisheries of, 414; protests by, 410

First Peoples Worldwide, 439n33

Fisher, Colin, xix, 48

fishing rights, 408, 410

Fitzhugh, George, 105

Fitzpatrick, Ellis, 212

Flint, MI: case of, 160

FOE. *See* Friends of the Earth (FOE)

Foley, Neil, 203, 206, 211, 228n52; on agrarian whiteness, 202; on economic independence, 226n18

folk medicine, refugees and, 244

Folsom State Prison, 165

food, growing, 215–19

foreign interventionism, refugees and, 240

Forest Service, 221

Fort Buffalo, 428

Fort Laramie, 451

Fort Larned, 451

Fort Lyon, 450, 451, 452, 457

Fort Marion, 161

Fort McMurray, 412

Fort Snelling, 161

Fortune, 210

fracking, 414, 416, 427

Frazier, E. Franklin, 108, 109, 110, 114, 122, 123

Free, Prior, and Informed Consent, 430

Free Alabama movement, 167, 168

history: analysis of, xiv, 368; cultural, 145; field of, xxiii, xxiv; gender, 134, 150; Indigenous, 17, 150, 382; intellectual, xv; layered, 302, 304–6; migrant, 150; oral, 448; queer, 150; social, 134, 150

History of the Dividing Line (Byrd), 5

Hmong, xx, 178, 250; agricultural practices of, 257n42; gardening by, 236, 242–44, 247–49, 251–54; harassment of, 248

Hmong Community Farm, 246, 252

Hmong Community Garden Cooperative, 236

Hmong-Lao Unity Association, 251

Hole-in-the-Rock, 288, 293–98, 305

Holiday, Betty, 288

Holiday, Billie, 143

Holley, Donald, 230n85

Holmes, John, 279

Holmesburg Prison, 165

Homestead Acts, 25, 378n29

Homestead Air Force Base National Priority Superfund Site, 166

Homestead Air Reserve Base, 166

Homestead Temporary Shelter for Unaccompanied Alien Children, 165

Honey, Michael K., 88

Honolulu Advertiser, 322

hooks, bell, 73, 346

Höpfl, Heather, 78

Hopis, 288, 289, 296; religion of, 291, 297

Hopkins, Harry, 217

Hornblower, John, 283n29

horse rides, 422

housing, 107, 112, 363, 427; government-built, 15; policies, 114

Howard, Nancy, 280

Hualapais, 302

Huizenga, Harm, 91

Huizenga, Wayne, 91

human behavior, 11, 104; differences in, 103; racial/biological theories of, 102

human ecology, 101–2, 103, 108, 117, 124, 124n3, 125n22

Human Geography of the South (Vance), 211–12

human relationships, 2, 11, 394, 466

human rights, 281, 411, 420, 425; Indigenous, 432; land rights and, 430

humans, 11, 382; nature and, 376

Hungate family, murder of, 450

Hunter, Tera, 72, 86, 93n3, 95n42

Hurley, Andrew, 74, 133

Hurricane Harvey, 164

Hurston, Zora Neale, 343

Hyde, George, 455, 456

Hydro-Quebec, 409

hygiene, 74, 79, 95n50, 119

Ickes, Harold, 190, 192

identity, 104, 355; American, 376, 377; Black, 142–45, 344; cultural, 109, 142, 429; environmental, 265, 266, 268, 270, 278; formation of, 150; national, 187, 194; national park, 195; nature and, 146; racial, 73, 201, 313; white, 73, 267, 377

Idle No More, 362, 410, 411, 414, 416, 417, 429, 433, 435n9; history of, 406; protest, 430

Illinois Black Codes, 135

imagined community, 14, 33n50

immigrants, 78, 79, 164, 364, 371, 396; Americanization of, 272, 368; Asian, 146; environmental justice and, 171; European, 145, 146, 364, 369;

German, 147; Irish, 147; Latin American, 373, 376; marginalized, 84; Mexican, 146; status of, 77; undocumented, 372

immigration: European, 147; nation of, 369–71

Immigration Reform and Control Act (IRCA), 363, 365, 372

imperialism, 31n25, 449, 455, 456

imprisonment, 20, 162, 166, 168, 171

incarceration, xx, 15, 20, 21, 168; enslavement and, 171; environmental threats and, 171; hardships of, 163; history of, 161–64; immigrant, 160, 166; Indigenous, 433; Japanese-American, 14, 16, 162, 163, 237–38; mass, 21, 160; racial domination and, 18; riskscapes of, 164–67; women and, 160

Indiana Dunes, 148, 149

Indian Child Welfare Act, 417

Indian Country, 370; extractive colonization of, 409

"Indian Country Is a Frontier Again" (*Nation's Business*), 409

Indians of All Tribes, 408, 432

Indigenous communities, 3, 414; enslavement/forced labor and, 170; environmental injustice and, 7, 169

Indigenous Environmental Justice, 429, 430, 431, 432, 440n44

Indigenous Environmental Network, 429

Indigenous Land Back movement, 430

Indigenous peoples, 2, 3, 11, 14, 20, 31, 55, 164, 166, 180, 264, 272, 287, 288, 289, 292, 293, 296, 297; assimilation of, 447; conquest of, 161; dehumanization of, 432–33; environmentalism

and, 1, 313; industrial abuse of, 408; mobility of, 449; nature and, 9, 17, 22, 28; removal of, 13, 16, 17, 162, 395; slavery and, 65n8, 65n10; war on, 161. *See also* Native Americans

Indigenous rights, 330, 406, 416, 425

Indigenous sovereignty, 322, 386, 406

individualism, 107, 218, 264, 279

Indochinese Gardening Project, 236, 250

industrialization, 76, 79, 118, 169, 368, 409

industrial labor, 118, 119, 148, 167; brutal logic of, 113; women and, 135

Industrial Revolution, 169

inequalities, 11, 75, 90, 92, 168–71, 177; antidemocratic practices and, 169; color-blindness and, 223; economic, 169, 239, 435n8; environmental, 2, 71, 74, 78, 81, 87–88, 92, 104, 125n21, 133, 134, 135–36, 138, 149; hierarchies and, 169; political, 169; racial, 29n3, 74, 90; social, 169, 188; structural, 107, 108, 123; systemic, 117; urban, 123, 150n2

ING, 424

injustice: environmental, xx, 2, 3, 10, 134, 146, 151n4, 161, 162, 166, 168, 169; racial, 465; social, xx, 2; women and, 169

Inscription House Chapters, 288

Integrated Public Use Microdata Series (IPUMS), 77, 88

integration, 188, 189, 264; national park, 186, 191, 193, 195; public space, 181, 195

International Plan for the Conservation and Management of Sharks, 326

"In the City of Rebirth" (Frazier), 123

invisibility, legacies of, 280–82
Inyo National Forest, 1
Ipperwash Provincial Park, 410
IPUMS. *See* Integrated Public Use
    Microdata Series (IPUMS)
IRCA. *See* Immigration Reform and
    Control Act (IRCA)
Iron Shell, Andrew, 417
Iron Shell, Tyrel, 417
Isenberg, Andrew, 30n7
Izaak Walton League, 282n9

Jackson, Andrew, 35n93
Jackson, Helen Hunt, 452
Jackson, Mahalia, 349, 357n32
Jacobs, Margaret, 30n10
Jacobson, Matthew Frye, 33n50, 73
jails, 21, 160, 365
James, Henry, 73
janitorial work, 79, 82, 83, 88
Japanese Americans, 15; agricultural
    experiences of, 237–38; compensa-
    tion for, 164; incarceration of, 14, 16,
    162, 163, 237–38
Jefferson, Thomas, 25, 277
Jenkins, Willis, 267
Jews, 35n94, 77, 88
Jim Crow, 110, 138, 181, 185, 186, 187, 188,
    189, 190, 191, 192, 193, 195, 347, 351,
    353, 354; history of, 180; Southern
    Democrats and, 182
John, Edward, 425
Johnson, Charles S., 209, 212, 213, 217,
    225n10
Johnson, Lady Bird, 302–3
Johnson, Robert, 65n9
Johnson, Seab, 223–24
Johnston, Katherine, xix, 47, 223
Jones, Alfred T., 274

Jones, Leodus, 165
Josephson, John C., 296
Journal of American History, xv, xvi
Julius Rosenwald Fund, 139
Jung, Moon-Ho, 20
The Jungle (Sinclair), 136
junk workers, 77, 87
justice: climate, 169, 170; racial, 8, 9;
    social, 4, 161, 168. *See also* environ-
    mental justice; environmental justice
    movement
juvenile delinquency, 102, 106

Kaʻahupāhau, 317
Kahoʻolawe, 321–22
Kahoʻolawe Island Reserve Commis-
    sion (KIRC), 327
Kahrl, Andrew, 181
Kaiwi, 318–19
Kamakau, Samuel, 317, 318–19
Kamehameha II, 319, 321
Kamohoaliʻl, 313, 317
kanaka, 313, 317, 318, 319, 321, 322, 326,
    329, 332; ancestry, 330; history of,
    324; language, 316, 320; organiza-
    tions, 327; sharks and, 320; values
    of, 330
kānaka maoli, 312, 313, 314, 315, 317, 320,
    321, 322, 329, 330; beliefs, 326; shark
    fin industry and, 331; term, 332n1
Kanaloa, 317
Kanesatake Mohawk Reserve, 410
Kanora Protest, 408
Kansas City Star, 413
Kansas State University, study by,
    413–14
Katznelson, Ira, 225n11
Kelley, Robin D. G., 73, 95n42
Kelly, Edward Joseph, 139